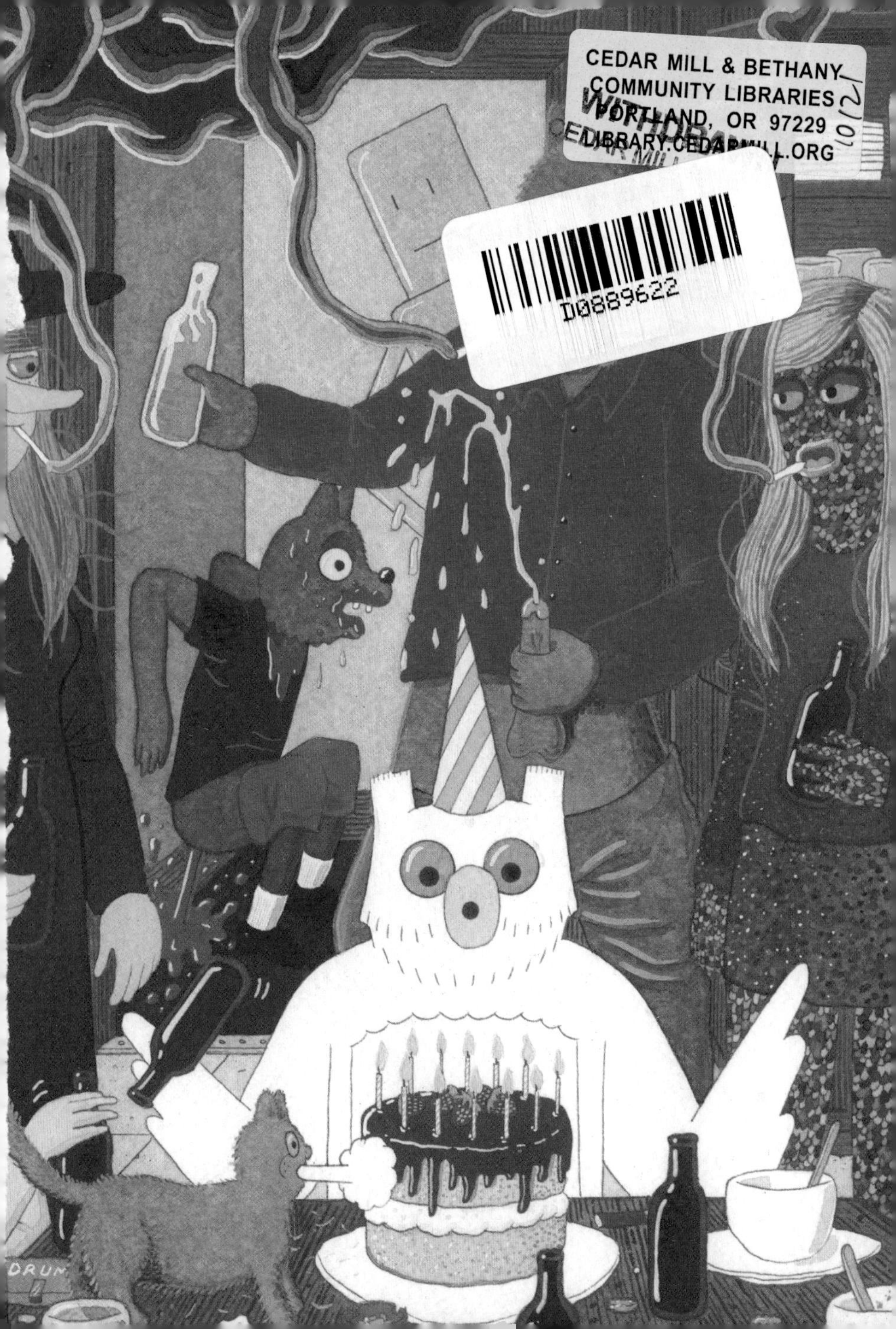

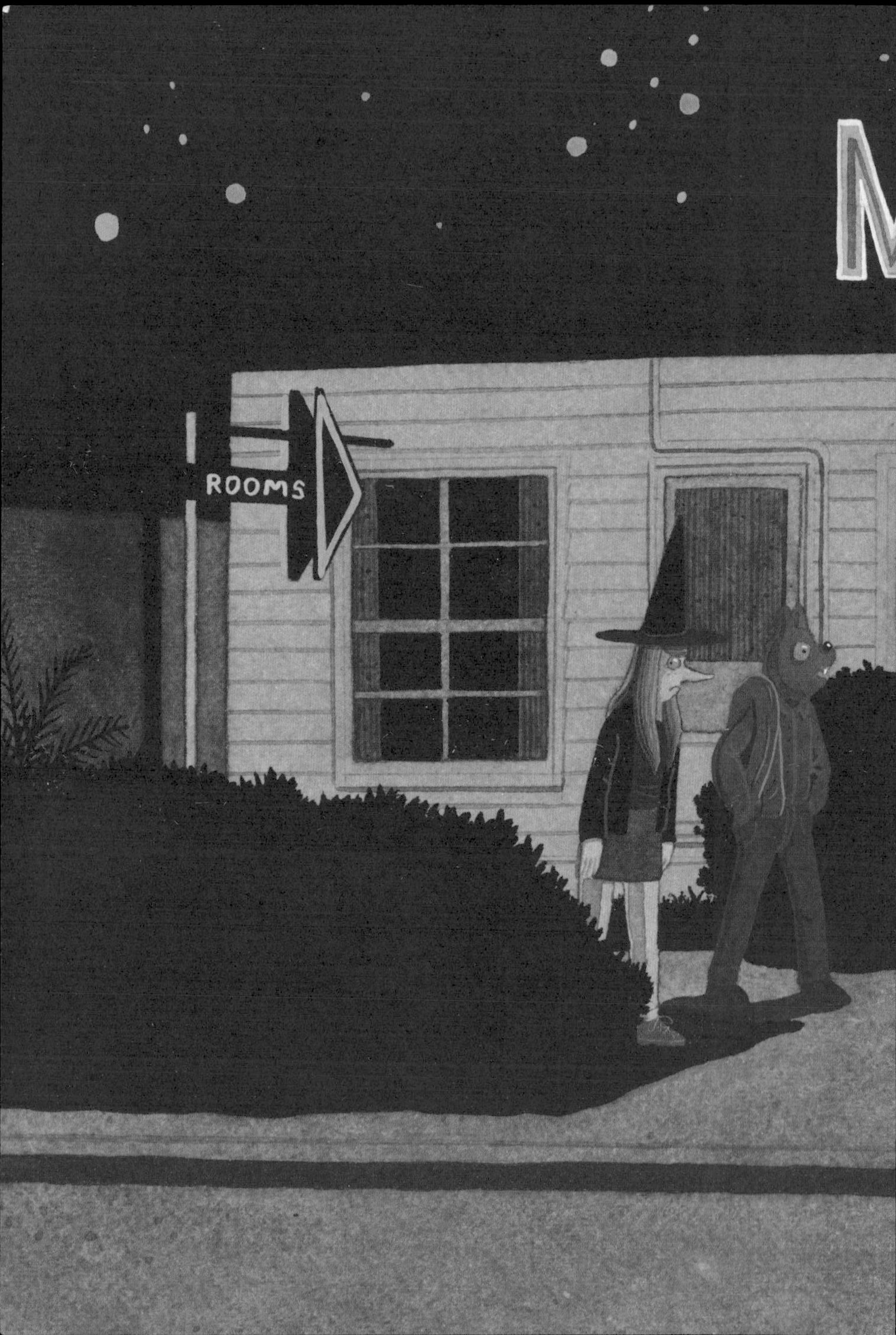
ROOMS

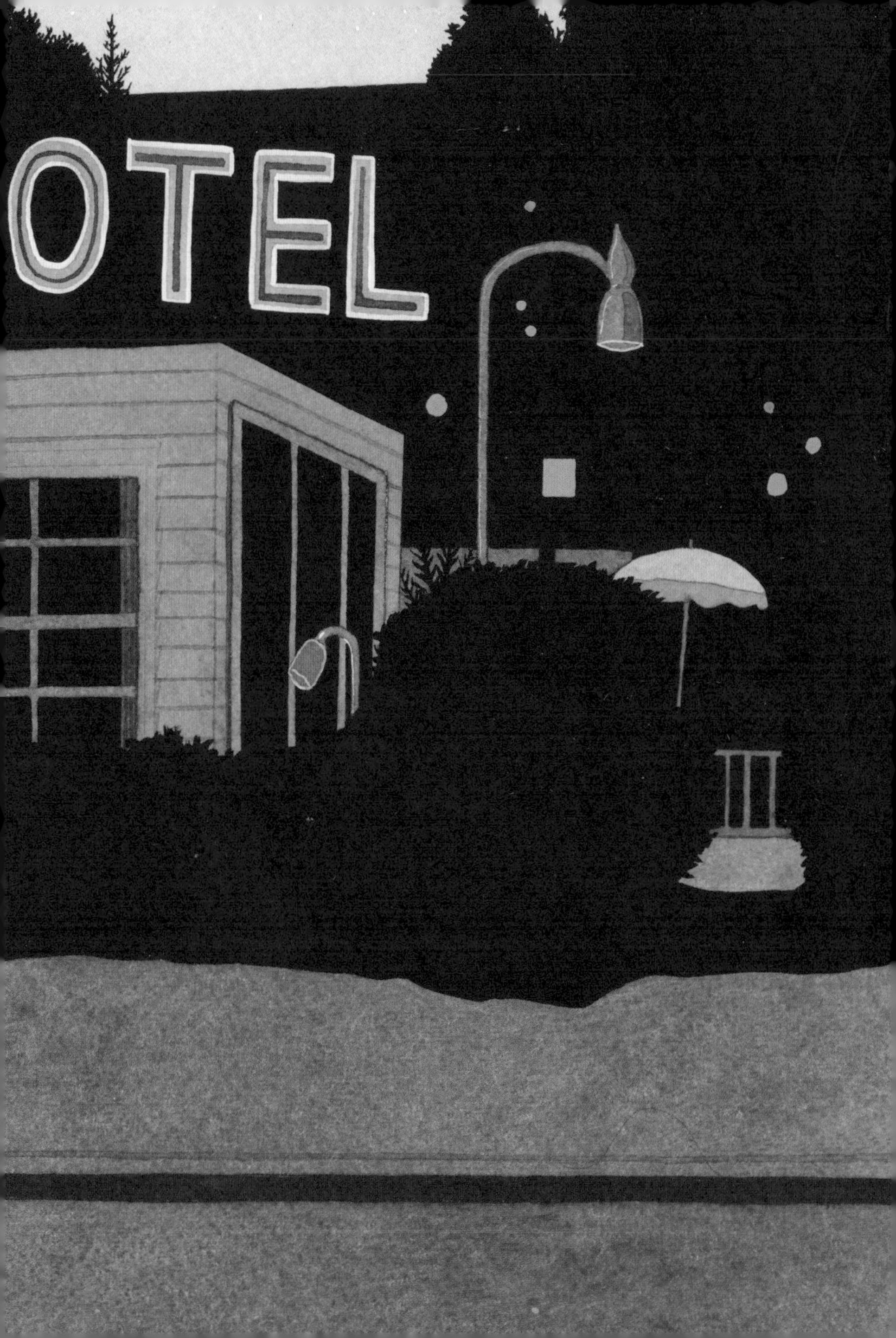
OTEL

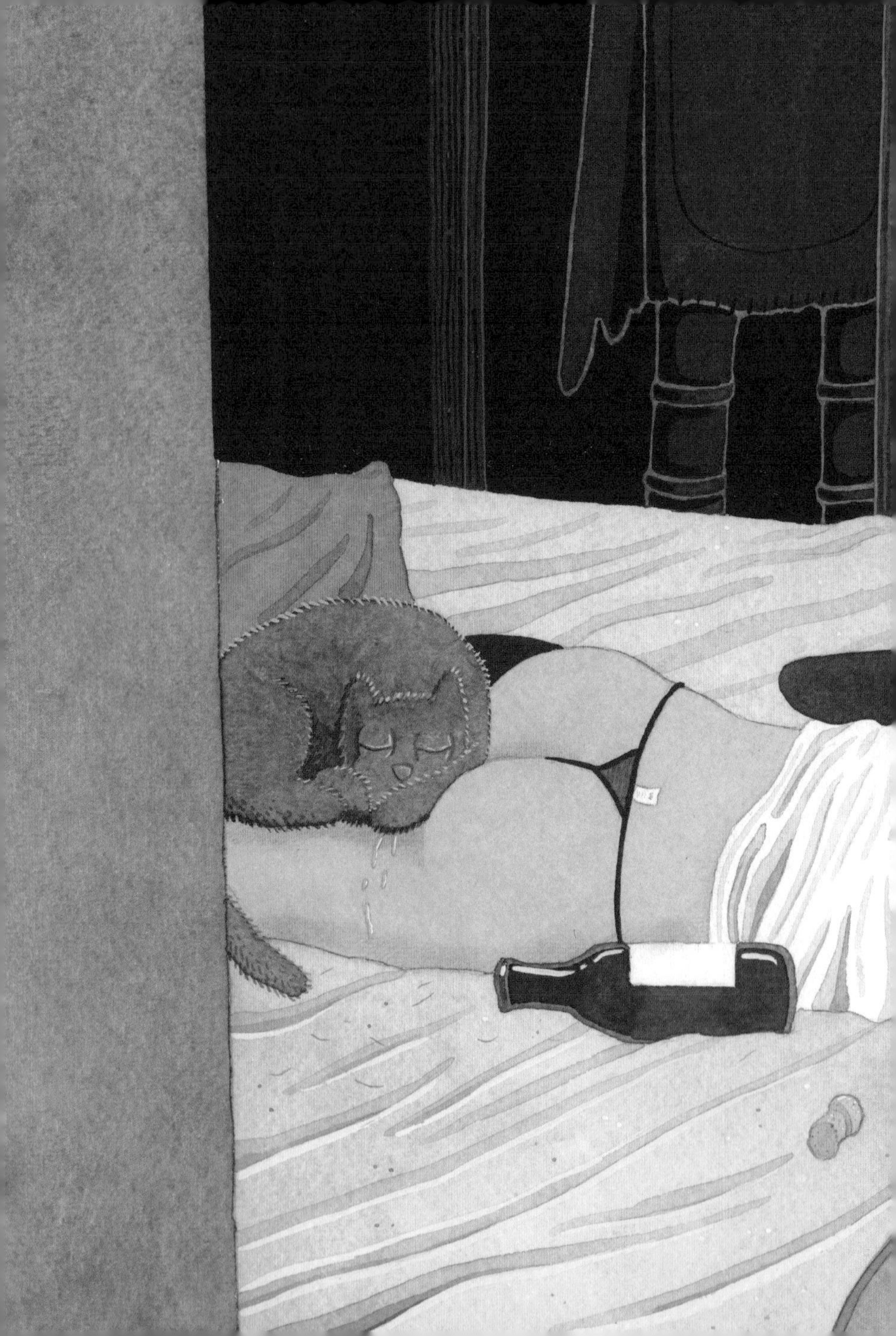

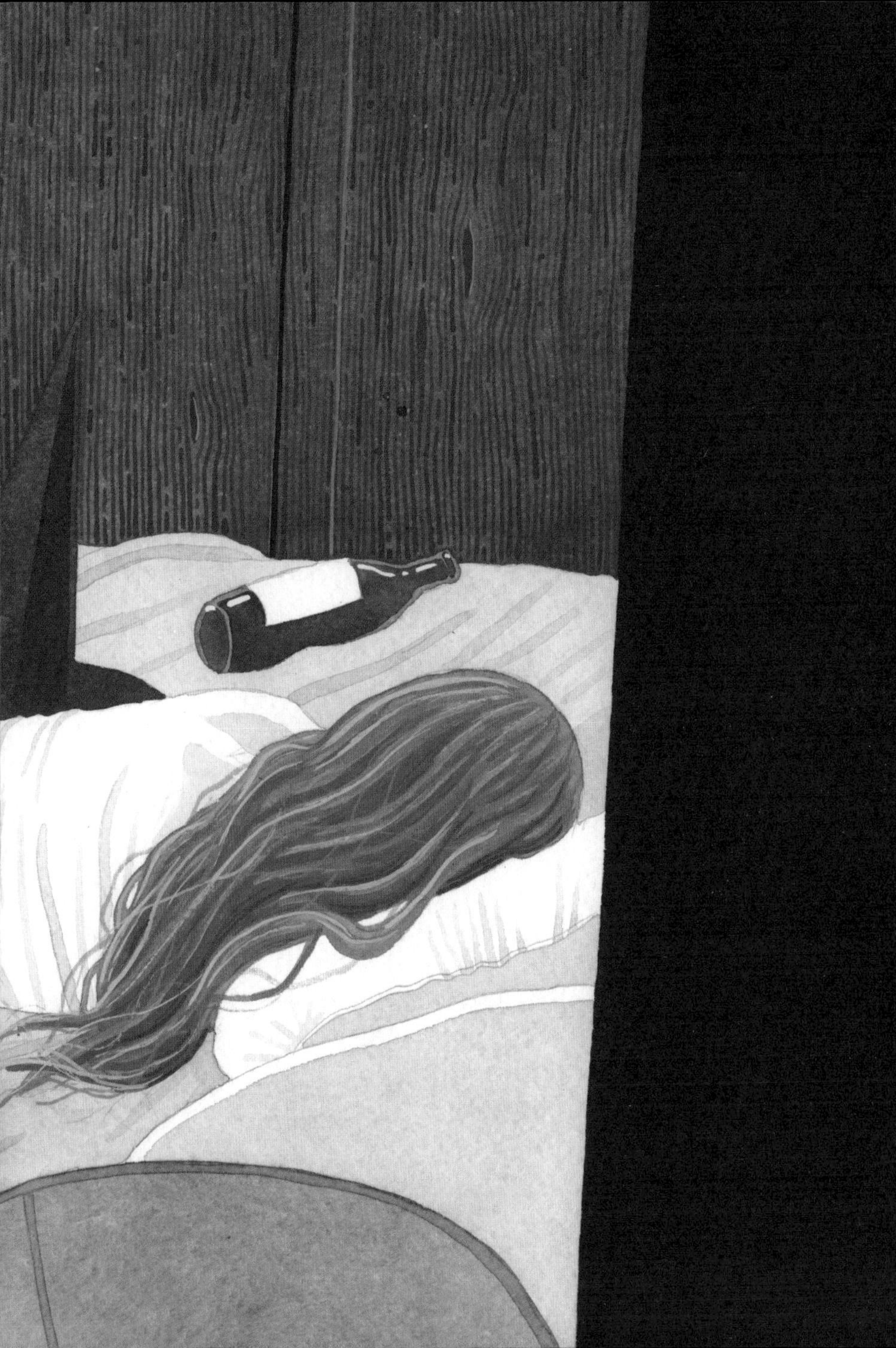

SEEDS AND STEMS

STORAGE NOTICE:

THIS BOOK HAS BEEN DESIGNED PRIMARILY FOR TOILET-BASED READING. PLEASE SHELVE TOILET ADJACENT. (PLASTIC PISS-GUARD INCLUDED)

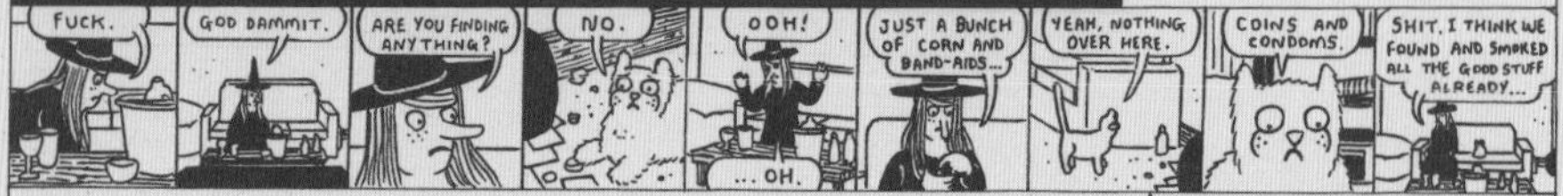
FUCK.
GOD DAMMIT.
ARE YOU FINDING ANYTHING?
NO.
OOH!
... OH.
JUST A BUNCH OF CORN AND BAND-AIDS...
YEAH, NOTHING OVER HERE.
COINS AND CONDOMS.
SHIT, I THINK WE FOUND AND SMOKED ALL THE GOOD STUFF ALREADY...

FANTAGRAPHICS BOOKS INC.
7563 LAKE CITY WAY, NE
SEATTLE, WASHINGTON, 98115
WWW.FANTAGRAPHICS.COM
ISBN 978-1-68396-309-7
LIBRARY OF CONGRESS CONTROL NUMBER 2019954473

EDITOR AND ASSOCIATE PUBLISHER: ERIC REYNOLDS
BOOK DESIGN: SIMON HANSELMANN
PRODUCTION: PAUL BARESH
STICKER DESIGN: JACOB COVEY
PUBLISHER: GARY GROTH
SECOND PRINTING: NOVEMBER 2020
PRINTED IN THAILAND

126	OWL'S GUTS	RELEASED AS ONE-SHEET ZINE, 2013 AT MELBOURNE ART SHOW W/ HTMLFLOWERS.
128	HEAVY DUDES	SAME AS ABOVE.
130	XMP-165	"HALO CHAMBER" PORTION APPEARED IN LAGON REVUE #3. REPRINTED WITH BOOKENDS AS "XMP-165", ZINE, JULY 2017.
155	JONES ALONE	BACK COVER TO "XMP-165".
156	ROYALTY	FROM "MEGAHEX 2020 WINTER TRAUMA ANNUAL", ZINE, 2019.
163	ROYAL BLOOD	FROM RANDOM ART SHOW. MELBOURNE, 2013.
164	WEREWOLF JONES LOW INCOME SINGLE FATHER / HOT TEA	BACK-UP FEATURE IN "KNIFE CRIME", ZINE, 2019. APPEARED IN "SUPER TOWERS", ZINE BY VINCENT FRITZ, 2017.
165	DENTAL DAMS / BAND PRACTICE	FROM "THE BELIEVER". 2014.
166	TOO STONED TO EAT A SANDWICH	APPEARED IN "COLD CUBE 2", SEATTLE RISOGRAPH ANTHOLOGY BY COLD CUBE PRESS, 2017.
167	HEALTH KICK	SAME AS ABOVE.
170	HALLOWEEN	FROM "MEGAHEX 2020 WINTER TRAUMA ANNUAL" ZINE. 2019.
189	FALLING	LARGE PAINTING FROM GALERIE MARTEL EXHIBITION. 2017.
190	MEGG, MOGG AND MICHAEL SNOW	ONE OF THE EARLIEST MEGG & MOGG STRIPS, 2008. APPEARED IN FIRST "MEGAHEX" ZINE, EARLY 2009.
193	SUGAR SACK	SAME AS ABOVE.
194	BUILDERS	SAME AS ABOVE.
196	DELETED SCENE	FROM "CLEAR COOKIES", PROMOTIONAL PREMIUM ZINE PUBLISHED BY FANTAGRAPHICS, 2019.
199	WEREWOLF JONES DELETED FISTING SCENES	SAME AS ABOVE.
202	JONES GANG	BACK COVER TO FRENCH EDITION OF "MEGG & MOGG IN AMSTERDAM", MISMA EDITIONS, 2017.
203	MIKE AND HIS MOTHER	FROM "MEGAHEX 2020 WINTER TRAUMA ANNUAL" ZINE, 2019.
204	ENTERTAINMENT	ZINE. JULY 2018.
224	SHARK JUMP	FROM "CLEAR COOKIES" ZINE, 2019.
225	SELF-HATING WOMAN	FROM "LANDSCAPE", ZINE, 2016.
226	HEALTH CLUB	SAME AS ABOVE.
227	SELF CARE TIPS / FUCK YOU	FROM "PORTRAIT", ZINE, MARCH 2017.
228	NO BRAINS	FROM "CASTLES IN THE SKY" ZINE, PUBLISHED BY MERV HEERS, MELBOURNE, 2017.
230	A JONES BOYS MYSTERY: SECRET OF THE DOGFINGERER	FROM "WEREWOLF JONES AND SONS" ISSUE TWO. STORY WRITTEN W/ HTMLFLOWERS. SCRIPT & ART: HANSELMANN.
243	MOGG'S TRAY	FROM "CLEAR COOKIES" ZINE. 2019.
244	TWILIGHT ZONE	FROM KUŠ ANTHOLOGY, LATVIA, DECEMBER 2019. ANTHOLOGY THEME WAS AUSTRALIAN ARTISTS.
253	WAR OF THE WORLDS / DIY	ORIGINALLY PUBLISHED AS ZINE IN 2012 BY SPACE FACE BOOKS, VERMONT. REPUBLISHED AS "WOTW" IN 2017 W/ BONUS DIY PAGE.
267	FOUNTAIN	SEE ENDPAPER NOTES.
268	BEAUTY PAGEANT	FROM "WEREWOLF JONES & SONS" ISSUE 3, NOVEMBER 2019. STORY: HTMLFLOWERS & HANSELMANN SCRIPT & ART: FLOWERS.
276	HOLE MEGG	BADGE ART FOR SPX AWARDS SHOW. 2019.

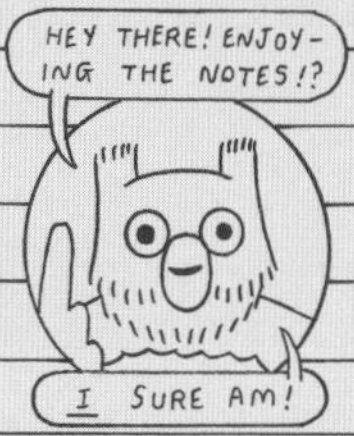
HEY THERE! ENJOYING THE NOTES!?
I SURE AM!

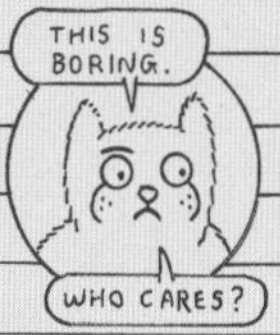
THIS IS BORING.
WHO CARES?

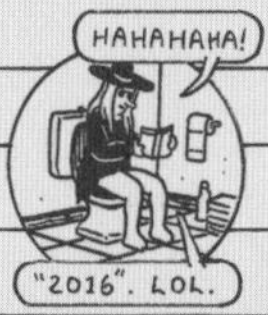
HAHAHAHA!
"2016". LOL.

THANKS: JACQ, FLOWERS, ERIC, TAN, ALE, RINA & AMELIE, COLD CUBE, SADLER, MISMA, COCONINO, LAGON, ALVIN, NICK, FEUK, FULGENCIO, MERV, FIKARIS, LEAH, CAT, MA AND ALL MY OLD ZINE HAUNTS: LAUNCESTON XEROX, DUNCAN KERR'S OFFICES, STICKY INSTITUTE, RYMAN'S UPON THAMES.

OTHER MEGG AND MOGG BOOKS AVAILABLE FROM FANTAGRAPHICS BOOKS:
(IN SUGGESTED READING ORDER)
- ONE MORE YEAR
- MEGG & MOGG IN AMSTERDAM
- MEGAHEX
- BAD GATEWAY

CHECK OUT MEGGANDMOGG.BIGCARTEL.COM FOR ZINES, MERCHANDISE ETC. THANKS!

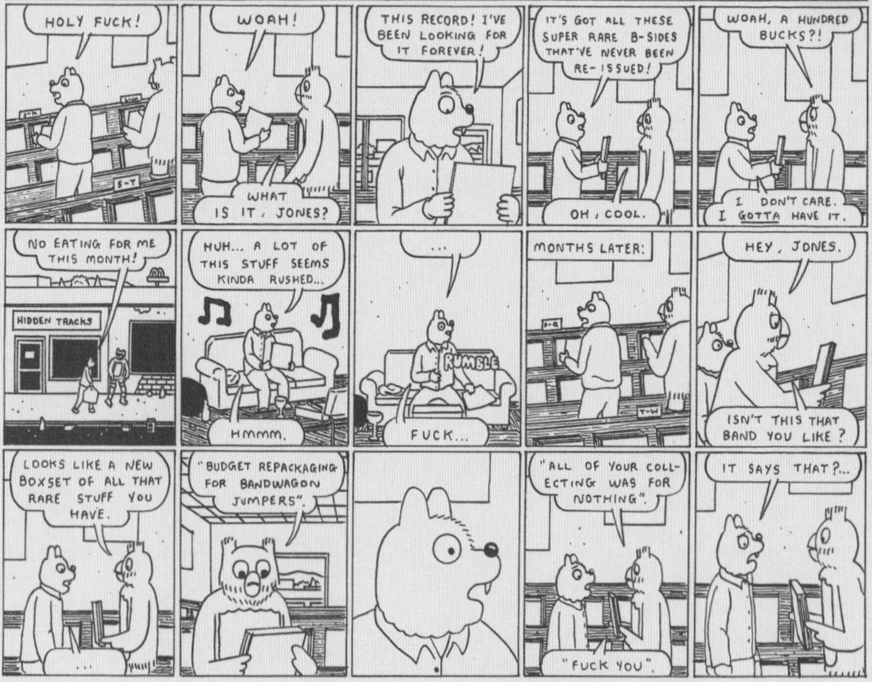
HOLY FUCK!
WOAH!
WHAT IS IT, JONES?
THIS RECORD! I'VE BEEN LOOKING FOR IT FOREVER!
IT'S GOT ALL THESE SUPER RARE B-SIDES THAT'VE NEVER BEEN RE-ISSUED!
OH, COOL.
WOAH, A HUNDRED BUCKS?!
I DON'T CARE. I GOTTA HAVE IT.
NO EATING FOR ME THIS MONTH!
HIDDEN TRACKS
HUH... A LOT OF THIS STUFF SEEMS KINDA RUSHED...
HMMM.
...
RUMBLE
FUCK...
MONTHS LATER:
HEY, JONES.
ISN'T THIS THAT BAND YOU LIKE?
LOOKS LIKE A NEW BOXSET OF ALL THAT RARE STUFF YOU HAVE.
...
"BUDGET REPACKAGING FOR BANDWAGON JUMPERS".
"ALL OF YOUR COLLECTING WAS FOR NOTHING".
"FUCK YOU".
IT SAYS THAT?...

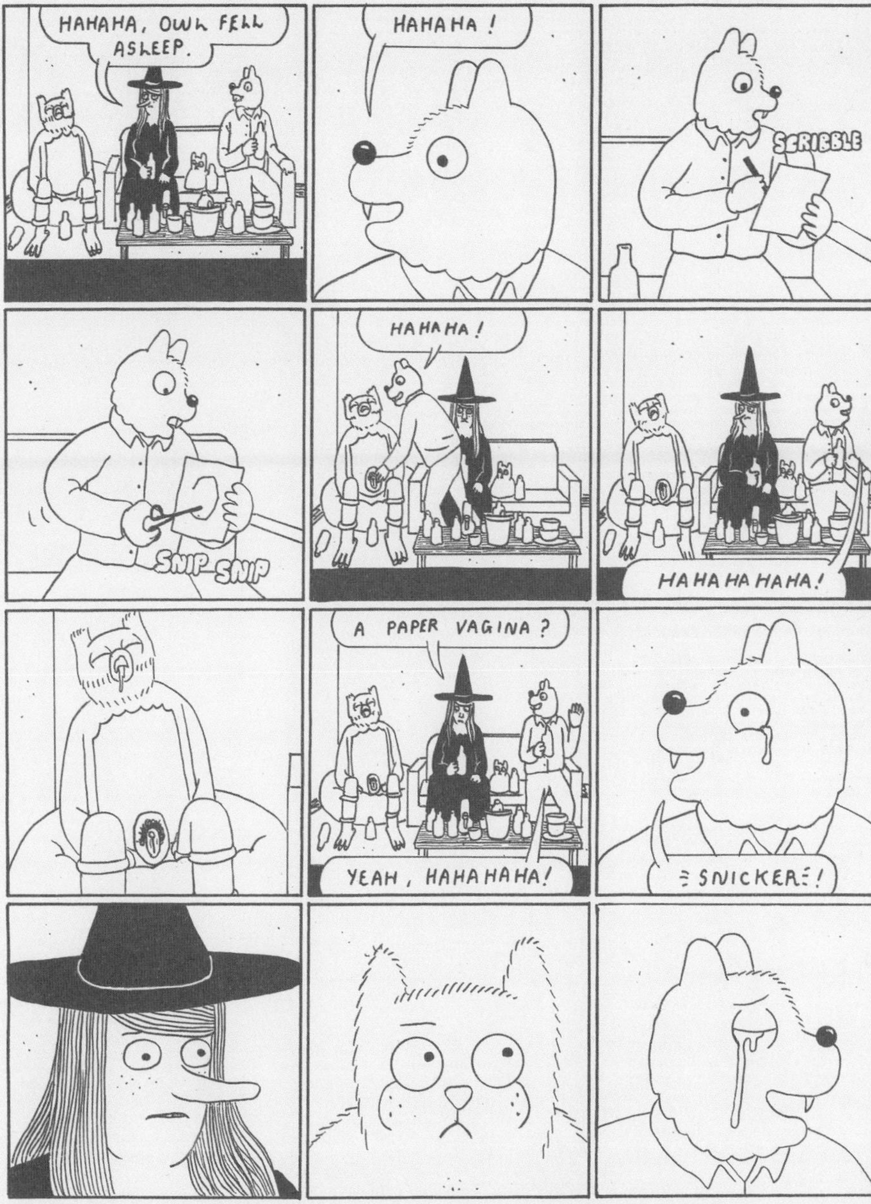
HAHAHA, OWL FELL ASLEEP.
HAHAHA!
SCRIBBLE
SNIP SNIP
HAHAHA!
HAHAHAHAHA!
A PAPER VAGINA?
YEAH, HAHAHAHA!
SNICKER!

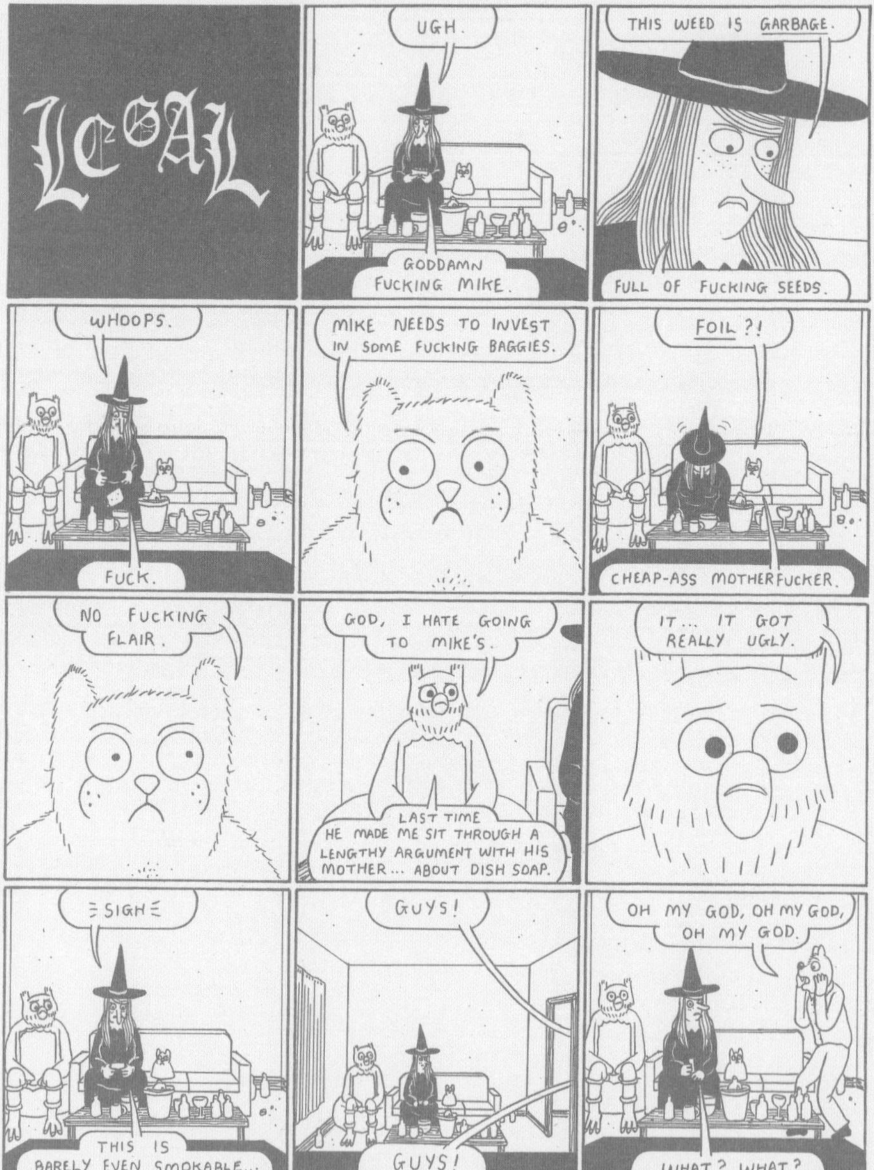
LEGAL
UGH.
GODDAMN FUCKING MIKE.
THIS WEED IS GARBAGE.
FULL OF FUCKING SEEDS.
WHOOPS.
FUCK.
MIKE NEEDS TO INVEST IN SOME FUCKING BAGGIES.
FOIL?!
CHEAP-ASS MOTHERFUCKER.
NO FUCKING FLAIR.
GOD, I HATE GOING TO MIKE'S.
LAST TIME HE MADE ME SIT THROUGH A LENGTHY ARGUMENT WITH HIS MOTHER... ABOUT DISH SOAP.
IT... IT GOT REALLY UGLY.
≡SIGH≡
THIS IS BARELY EVEN SMOKABLE...
GUYS!
GUYS!
OH MY GOD, OH MY GOD, OH MY GOD.
WHAT? WHAT?

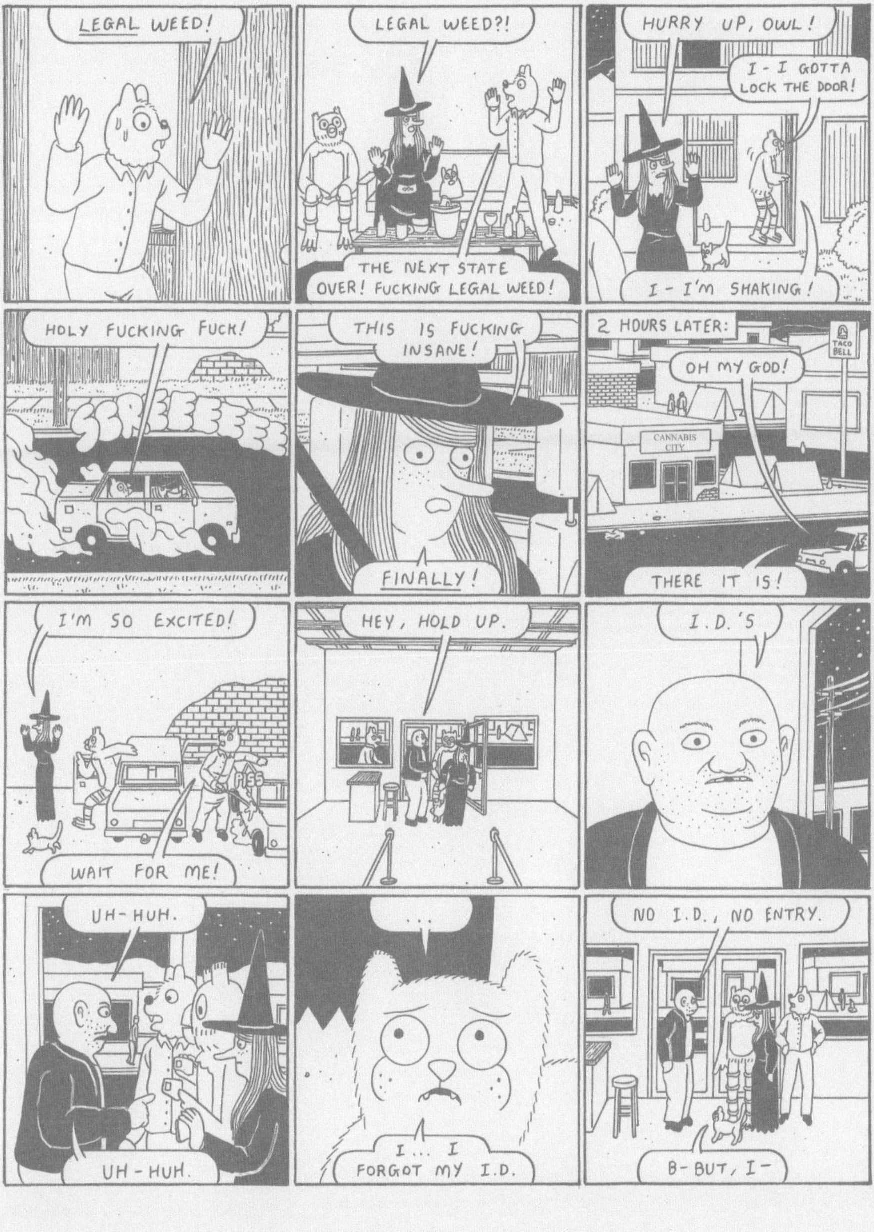
LEGAL WEED!
LEGAL WEED?!
THE NEXT STATE OVER! FUCKING LEGAL WEED!
HURRY UP, OWL!
I - I GOTTA LOCK THE DOOR!
I - I'M SHAKING!
HOLY FUCKING FUCK!
SCREEEEEEE
THIS IS FUCKING INSANE!
FINALLY!
2 HOURS LATER:
TACO BELL
OH MY GOD!
CANNABIS CITY
THERE IT IS!
I'M SO EXCITED!
PISS
WAIT FOR ME!
HEY, HOLD UP.
I.D.'S
UH-HUH.
UH-HUH.
...
I... I FORGOT MY I.D.
NO I.D., NO ENTRY.
B-BUT, I-

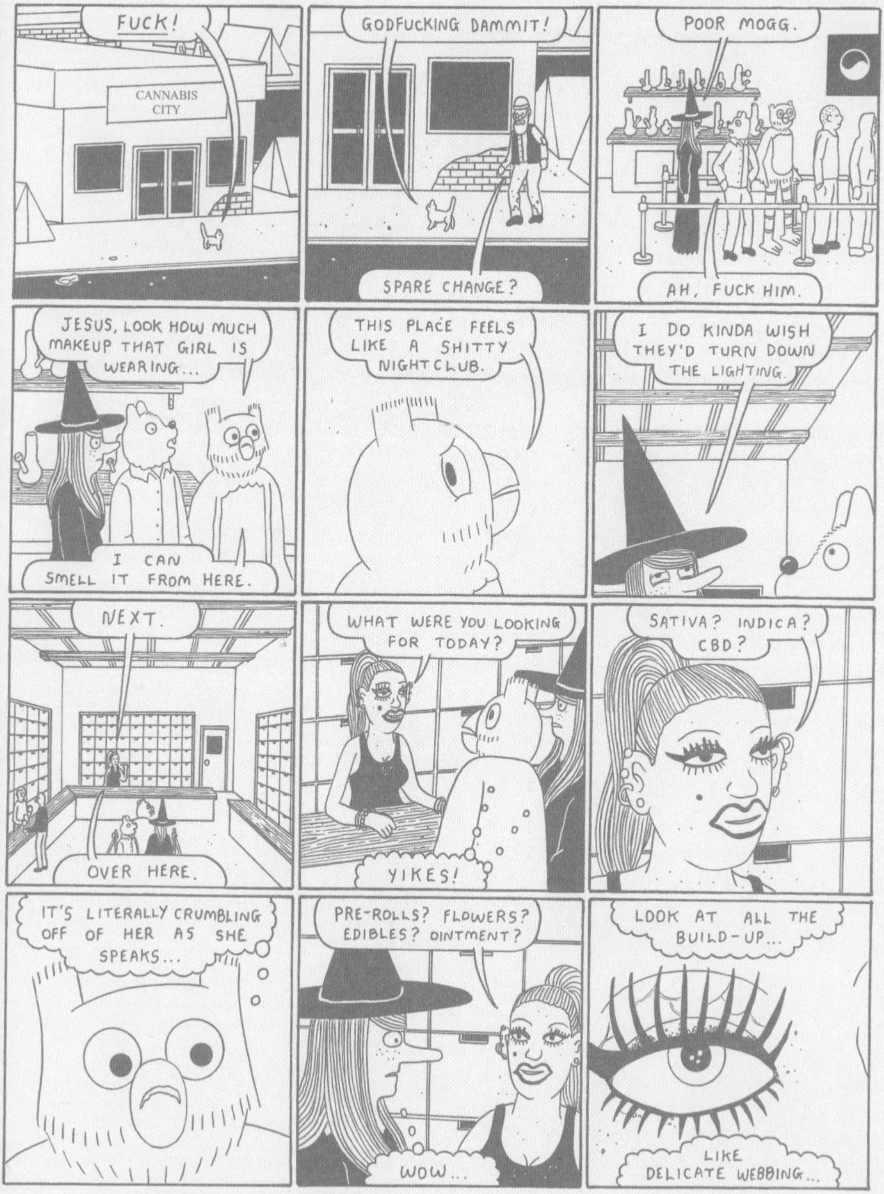
FUCK!
CANNABIS CITY
GODFUCKING DAMMIT!
SPARE CHANGE?
POOR MOGG.
AH, FUCK HIM.
JESUS, LOOK HOW MUCH MAKEUP THAT GIRL IS WEARING...
I CAN SMELL IT FROM HERE.
THIS PLACE FEELS LIKE A SHITTY NIGHTCLUB.
I DO KINDA WISH THEY'D TURN DOWN THE LIGHTING.
NEXT.
OVER HERE.
WHAT WERE YOU LOOKING FOR TODAY?
YIKES!
SATIVA? INDICA? CBD?
IT'S LITERALLY CRUMBLING OFF OF HER AS SHE SPEAKS...
PRE-ROLLS? FLOWERS? EDIBLES? OINTMENT?
WOW...
LOOK AT ALL THE BUILD-UP...
LIKE DELICATE WEBBING...

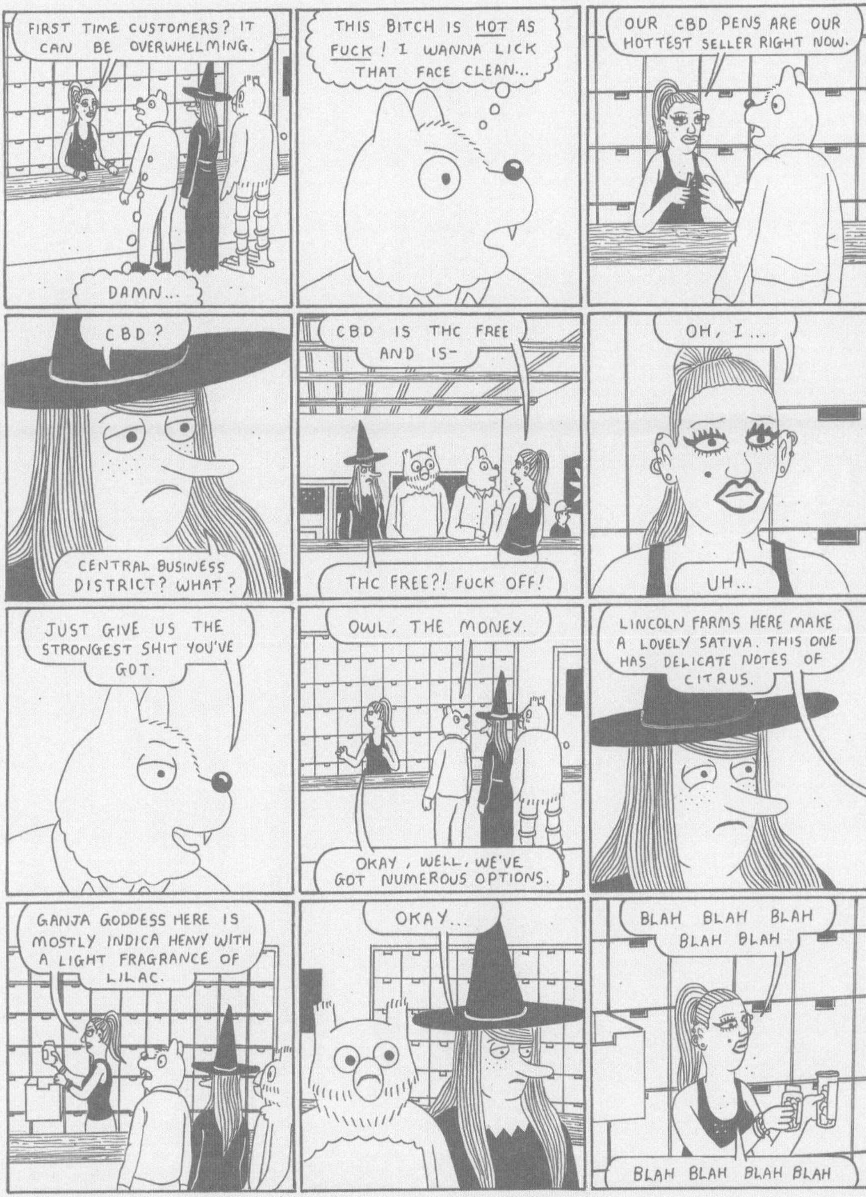
FIRST TIME CUSTOMERS? IT CAN BE OVERWHELMING.
DAMN...
THIS BITCH IS HOT AS FUCK! I WANNA LICK THAT FACE CLEAN...
OUR CBD PENS ARE OUR HOTTEST SELLER RIGHT NOW.
CBD?
CENTRAL BUSINESS DISTRICT? WHAT?
CBD IS THC FREE AND IS-
THC FREE?! FUCK OFF!
OH, I...
UH...
JUST GIVE US THE STRONGEST SHIT YOU'VE GOT.
OWL, THE MONEY.
OKAY, WELL, WE'VE GOT NUMEROUS OPTIONS.
LINCOLN FARMS HERE MAKE A LOVELY SATIVA. THIS ONE HAS DELICATE NOTES OF CITRUS.
GANJA GODDESS HERE IS MOSTLY INDICA HEAVY WITH A LIGHT FRAGRANCE OF LILAC.
OKAY...
BLAH BLAH BLAH BLAH BLAH
BLAH BLAH BLAH BLAH

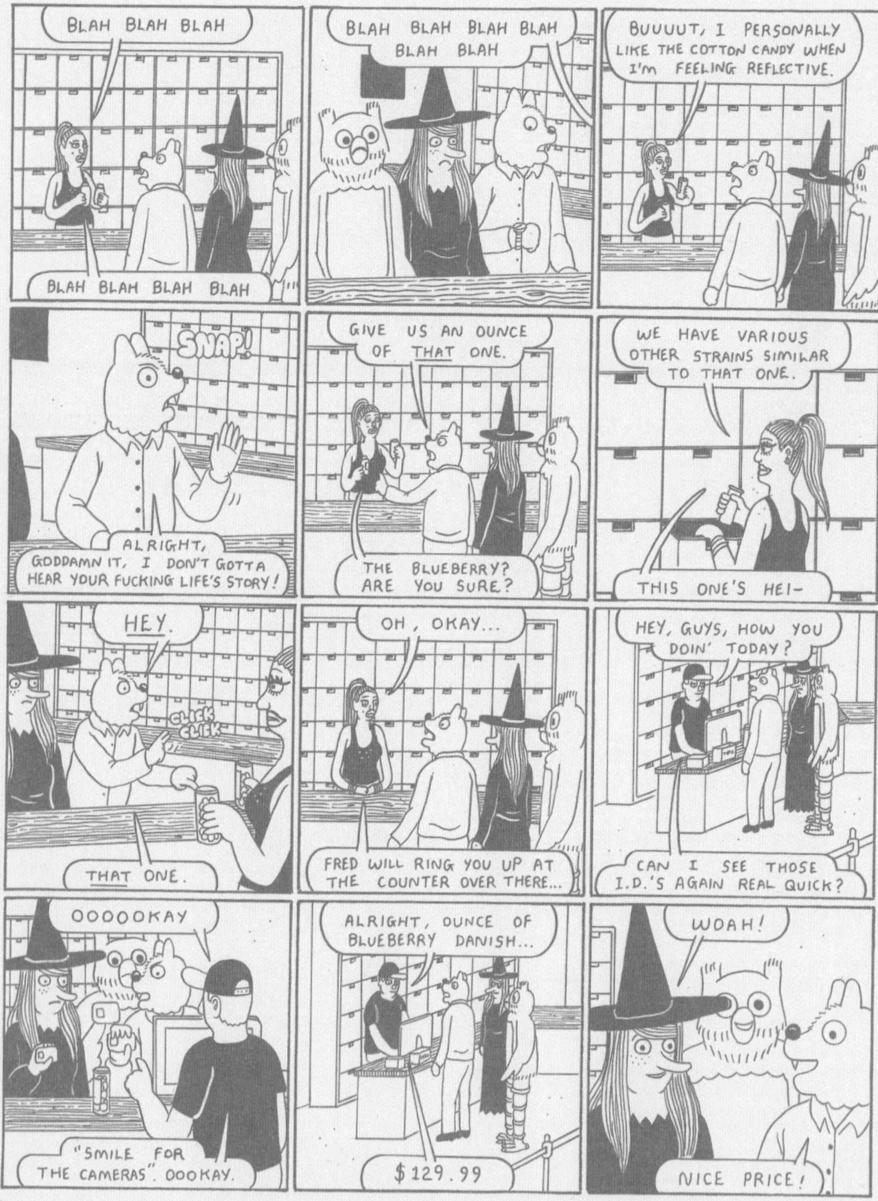
BLAH BLAH BLAH
BLAH BLAH BLAH BLAH
BLAH BLAH BLAH BLAH
BLAH BLAH
BUUUUT, I PERSONALLY LIKE THE COTTON CANDY WHEN I'M FEELING REFLECTIVE.
SNAP!
ALRIGHT, GODDAMN IT, I DON'T GOTTA HEAR YOUR FUCKING LIFE'S STORY!
GIVE US AN OUNCE OF THAT ONE.
THE BLUEBERRY? ARE YOU SURE?
WE HAVE VARIOUS OTHER STRAINS SIMILAR TO THAT ONE.
THIS ONE'S HEI-
HEY.
CLICK CLICK
THAT ONE.
OH, OKAY...
FRED WILL RING YOU UP AT THE COUNTER OVER THERE...
HEY, GUYS, HOW YOU DOIN' TODAY?
CAN I SEE THOSE I.D.'S AGAIN REAL QUICK?
OOOOOKAY
"SMILE FOR THE CAMERAS". OOOKAY.
ALRIGHT, OUNCE OF BLUEBERRY DANISH...
$129.99
WOAH!
NICE PRICE!

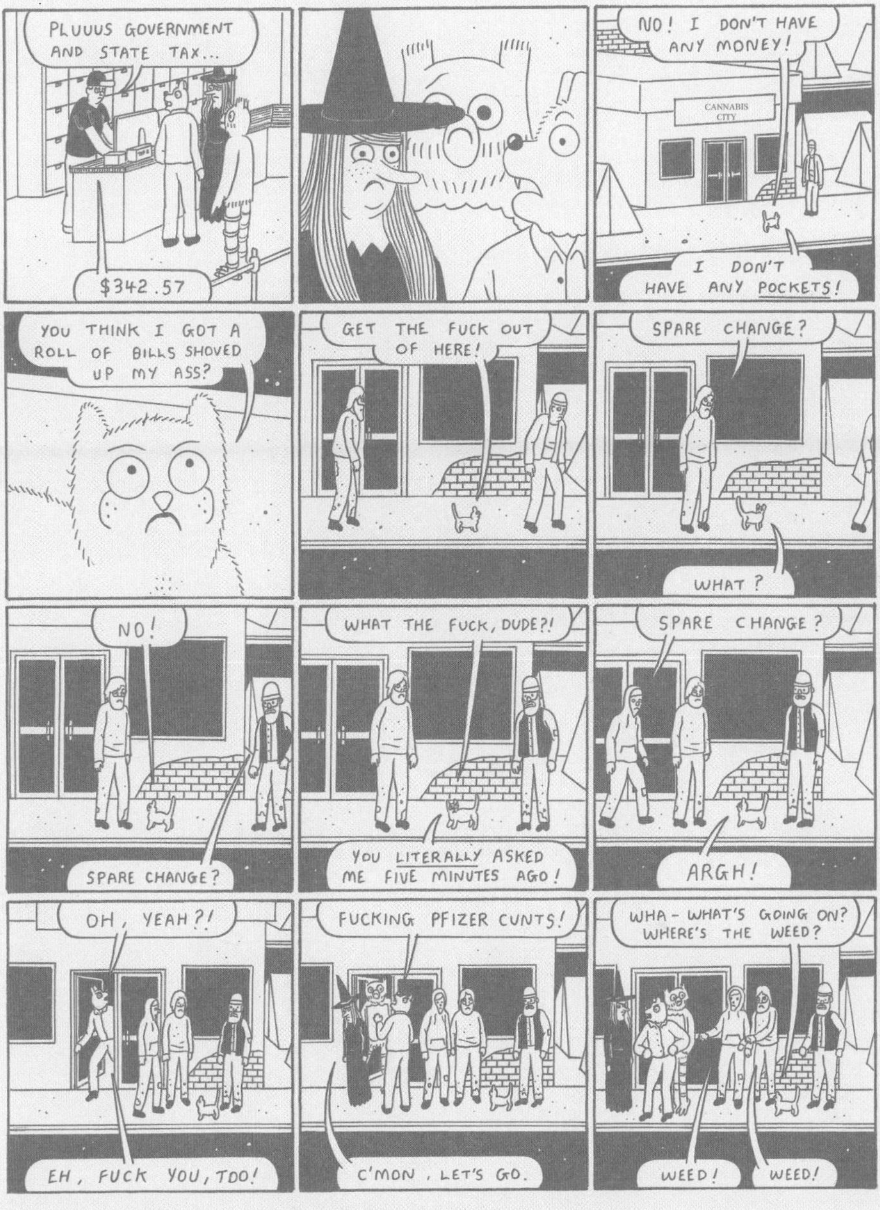
PLUUUS GOVERNMENT AND STATE TAX...
$342.57
NO! I DON'T HAVE ANY MONEY!
CANNABIS CITY
I DON'T HAVE ANY POCKETS!
YOU THINK I GOT A ROLL OF BILLS SHOVED UP MY ASS?
GET THE FUCK OUT OF HERE!
SPARE CHANGE?
WHAT?
NO!
SPARE CHANGE?
WHAT THE FUCK, DUDE?!
YOU LITERALLY ASKED ME FIVE MINUTES AGO!
SPARE CHANGE?
ARGH!
OH, YEAH?!
EH, FUCK YOU, TOO!
FUCKING PFIZER CUNTS!
C'MON, LET'S GO.
WHA-WHAT'S GOING ON? WHERE'S THE WEED?
WEED!
WEED!

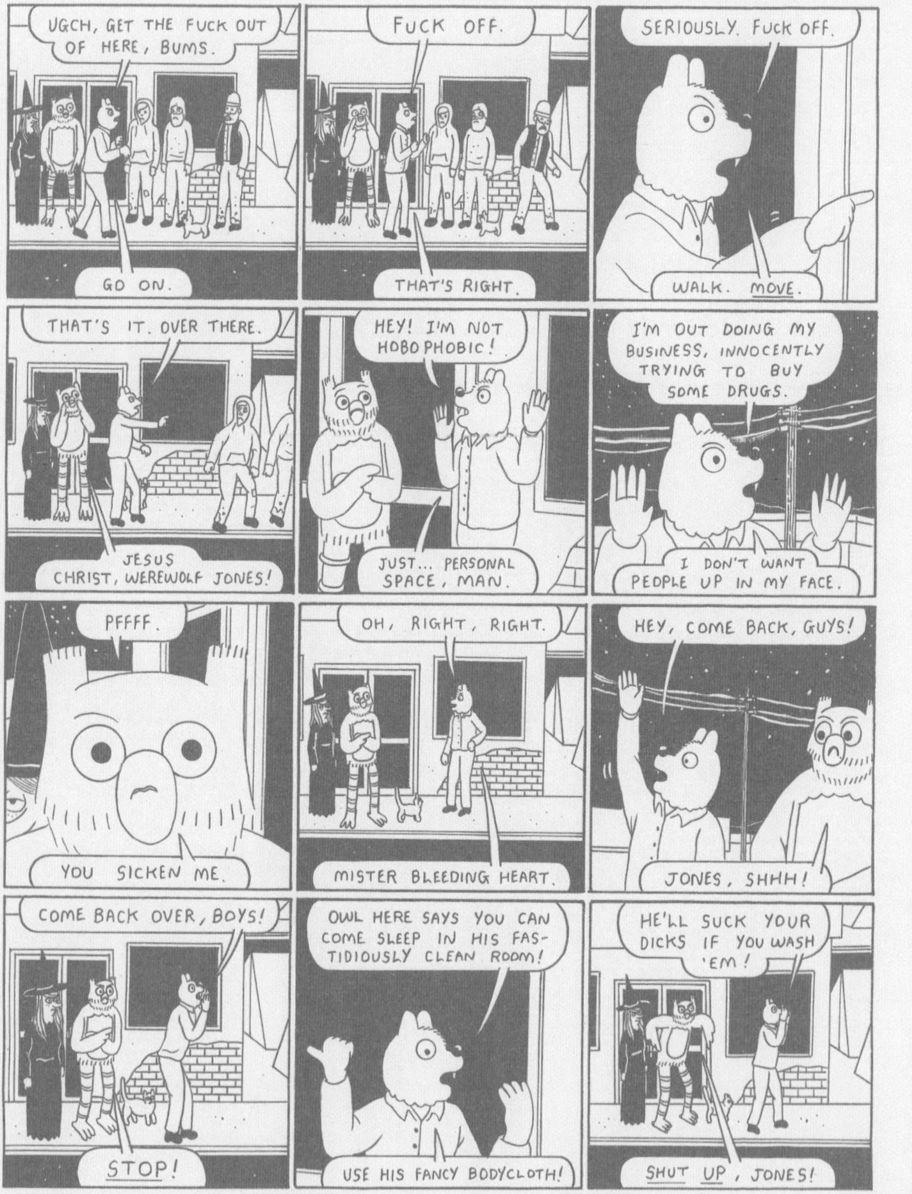
UGCH, GET THE FUCK OUT OF HERE, BUMS.
GO ON.
FUCK OFF.
THAT'S RIGHT.
SERIOUSLY. FUCK OFF.
WALK. MOVE.
THAT'S IT. OVER THERE.
JESUS CHRIST, WEREWOLF JONES!
HEY! I'M NOT HOBOPHOBIC!
JUST... PERSONAL SPACE, MAN.
I'M OUT DOING MY BUSINESS, INNOCENTLY TRYING TO BUY SOME DRUGS.
I DON'T WANT PEOPLE UP IN MY FACE.
PFFFF.
YOU SICKEN ME.
OH, RIGHT, RIGHT.
MISTER BLEEDING HEART.
HEY, COME BACK, GUYS!
JONES, SHHH!
COME BACK OVER, BOYS!
STOP!
OWL HERE SAYS YOU CAN COME SLEEP IN HIS FASTIDIOUSLY CLEAN ROOM!
USE HIS FANCY BODYCLOTH!
HE'LL SUCK YOUR DICKS IF YOU WASH 'EM!
SHUT UP, JONES!

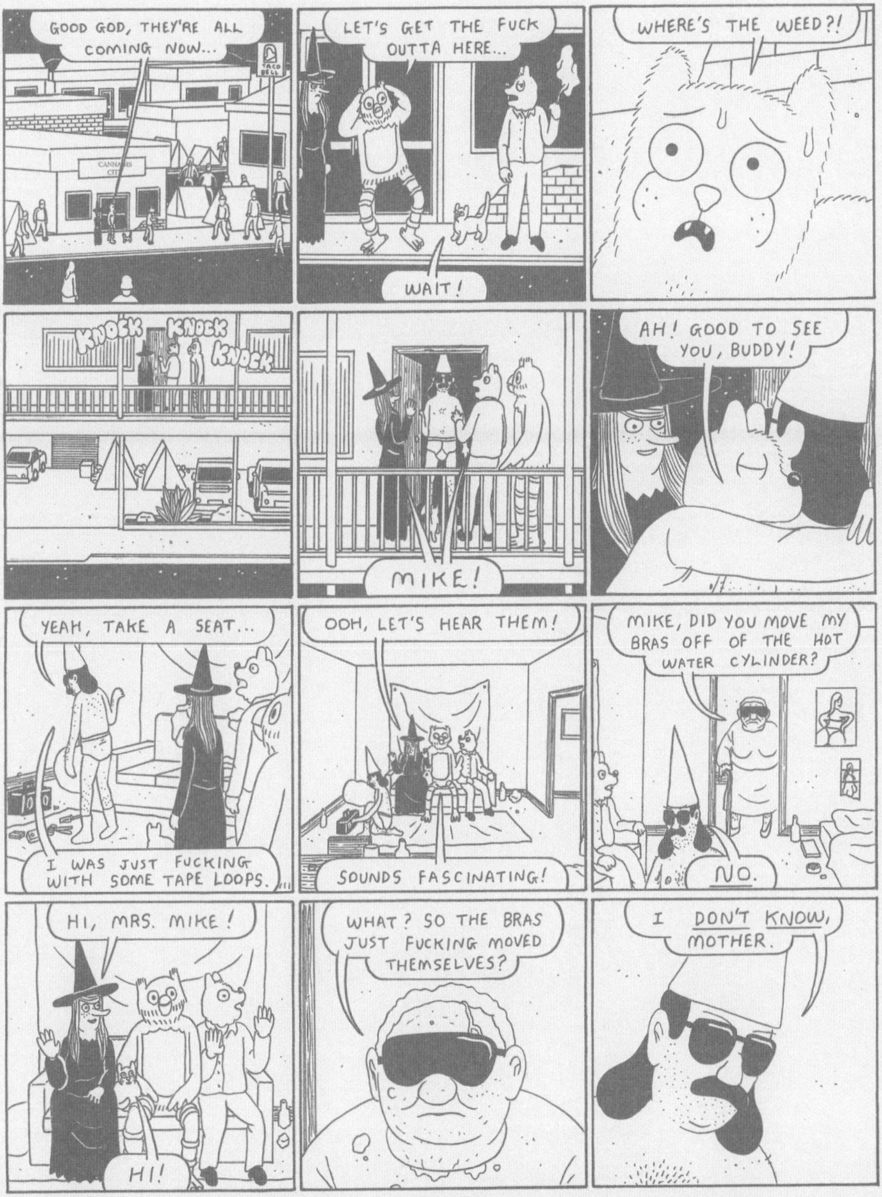
GOOD GOD, THEY'RE ALL COMING NOW...
TACO BELL
CANNABIS CITY
LET'S GET THE FUCK OUTTA HERE...
WAIT!
WHERE'S THE WEED?!
KNOCK KNOCK KNOCK
MIKE!
AH! GOOD TO SEE YOU, BUDDY!
YEAH, TAKE A SEAT...
I WAS JUST FUCKING WITH SOME TAPE LOOPS.
OOH, LET'S HEAR THEM!
SOUNDS FASCINATING!
MIKE, DID YOU MOVE MY BRAS OFF OF THE HOT WATER CYLINDER?
NO.
HI, MRS. MIKE!
HI!
WHAT? SO THE BRAS JUST FUCKING MOVED THEMSELVES?
I DON'T KNOW, MOTHER.

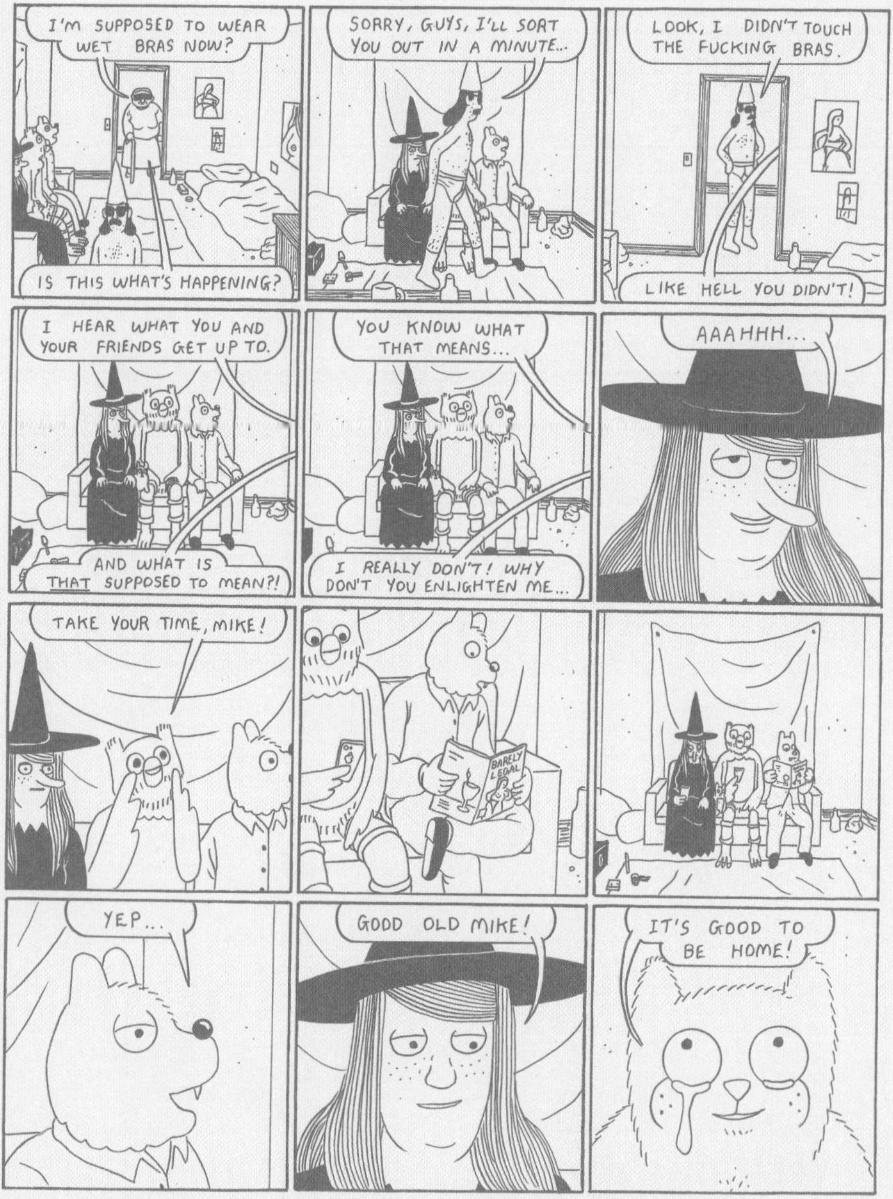
I'M SUPPOSED TO WEAR WET BRAS NOW?
IS THIS WHAT'S HAPPENING?
SORRY, GUYS, I'LL SORT YOU OUT IN A MINUTE...
LOOK, I DIDN'T TOUCH THE FUCKING BRAS.
LIKE HELL YOU DIDN'T!
I HEAR WHAT YOU AND YOUR FRIENDS GET UP TO.
AND WHAT IS THAT SUPPOSED TO MEAN?!
YOU KNOW WHAT THAT MEANS...
I REALLY DON'T! WHY DON'T YOU ENLIGHTEN ME...
AAAHHH...
TAKE YOUR TIME, MIKE!
BARELY LEGAL
YEP...
GOOD OLD MIKE!
IT'S GOOD TO BE HOME!

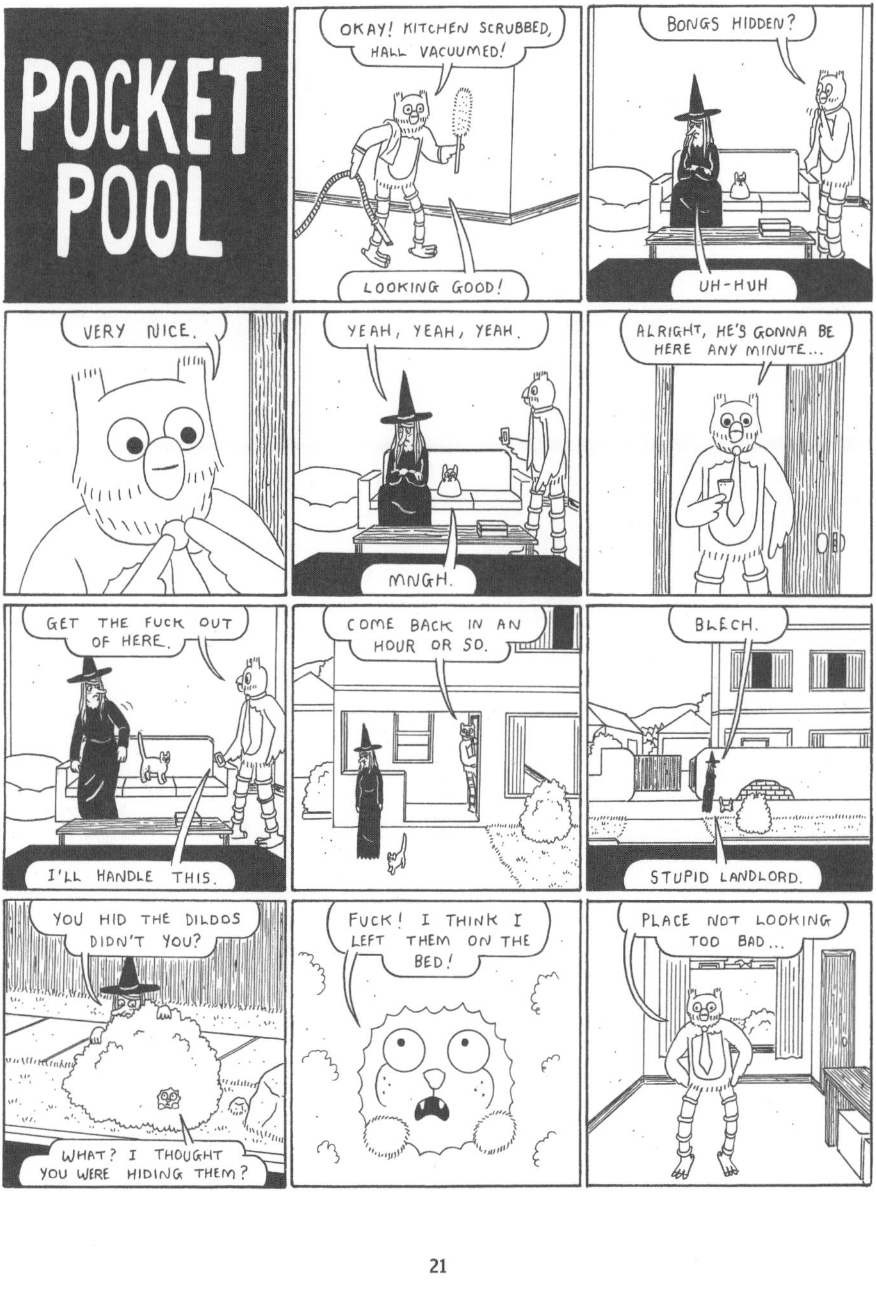
POCKET POOL
OKAY! KITCHEN SCRUBBED, HALL VACUUMED!
LOOKING GOOD!
BONGS HIDDEN?
UH-HUH
VERY NICE.
YEAH, YEAH, YEAH.
MNGH.
ALRIGHT, HE'S GONNA BE HERE ANY MINUTE...
GET THE FUCK OUT OF HERE.
I'LL HANDLE THIS.
COME BACK IN AN HOUR OR SO.
BLECH.
STUPID LANDLORD.
YOU HID THE DILDOS DIDN'T YOU?
WHAT? I THOUGHT YOU WERE HIDING THEM?
FUCK! I THINK I LEFT THEM ON THE BED!
PLACE NOT LOOKING TOO BAD...

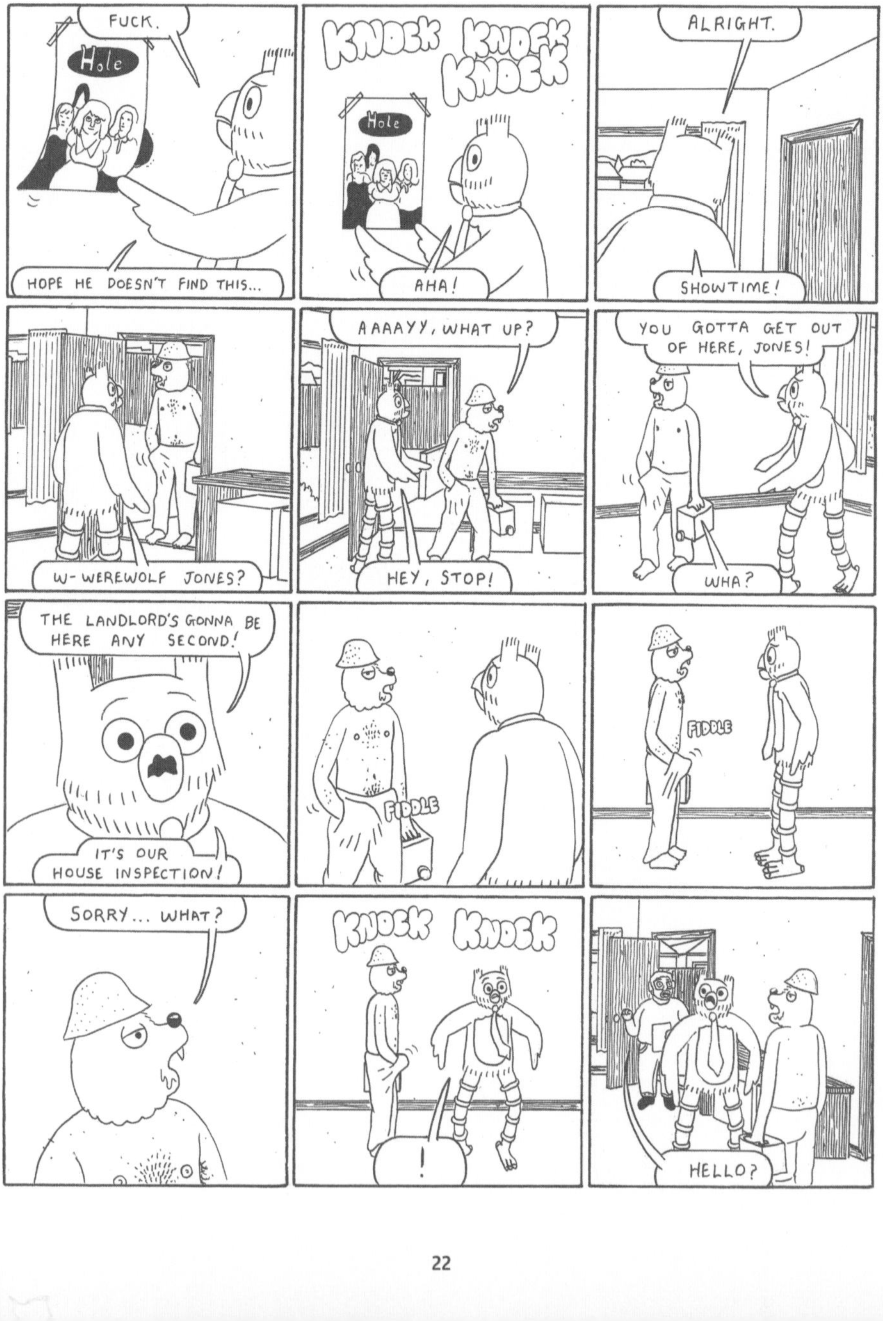
FUCK.
Hole
HOPE HE DOESN'T FIND THIS...
KNOCK KNOCK KNOCK
Hole
AHA!
ALRIGHT.
SHOWTIME!
W-WEREWOLF JONES?
AAAAYY, WHAT UP?
HEY, STOP!
YOU GOTTA GET OUT OF HERE, JONES!
WHA?
THE LANDLORD'S GONNA BE HERE ANY SECOND!
IT'S OUR HOUSE INSPECTION!
FIDDLE
FIDDLE
SORRY... WHAT?
KNOCK KNOCK
!
HELLO?

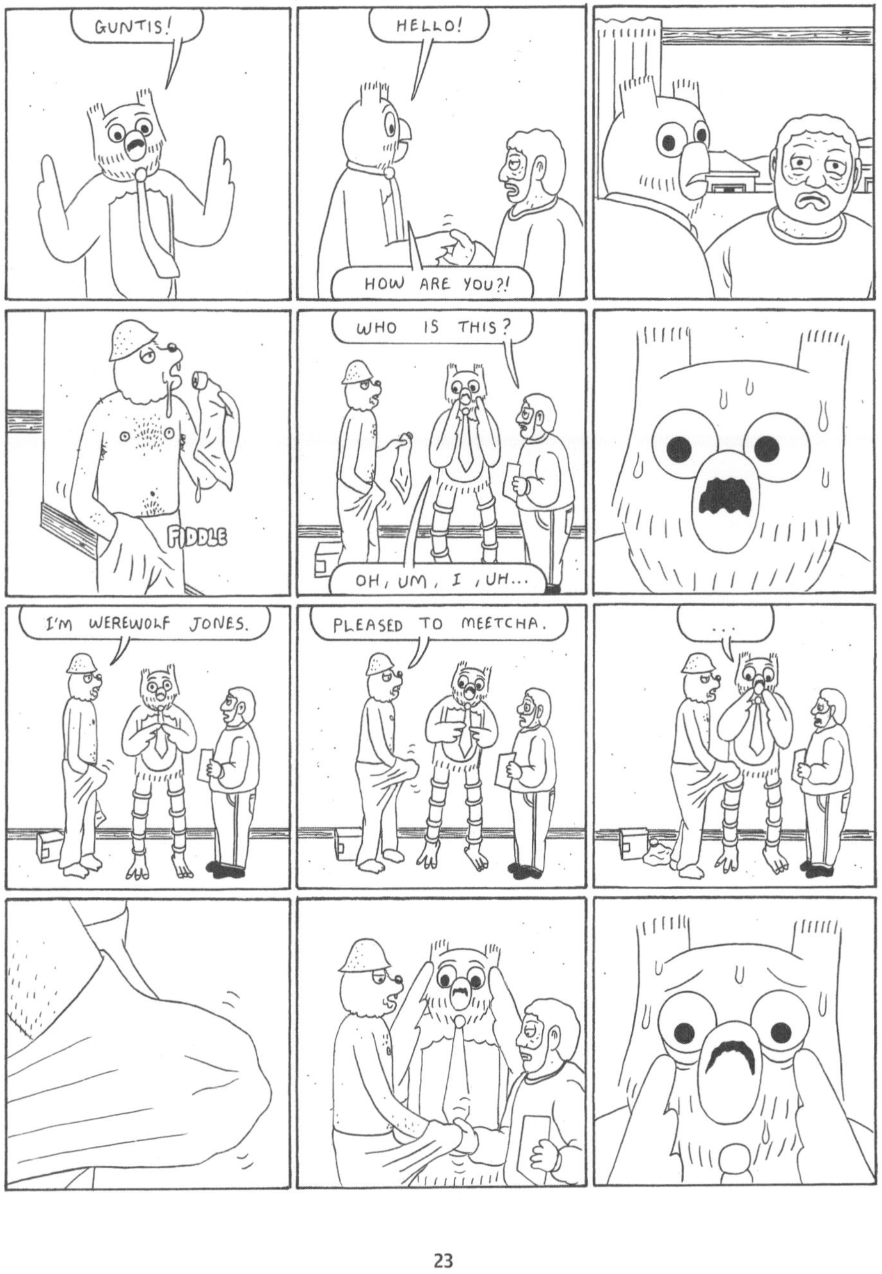
GUNTIS!
HELLO!
HOW ARE YOU?!
FIDDLE
WHO IS THIS?
OH, UM, I, UH...
I'M WEREWOLF JONES.
PLEASED TO MEETCHA.
...

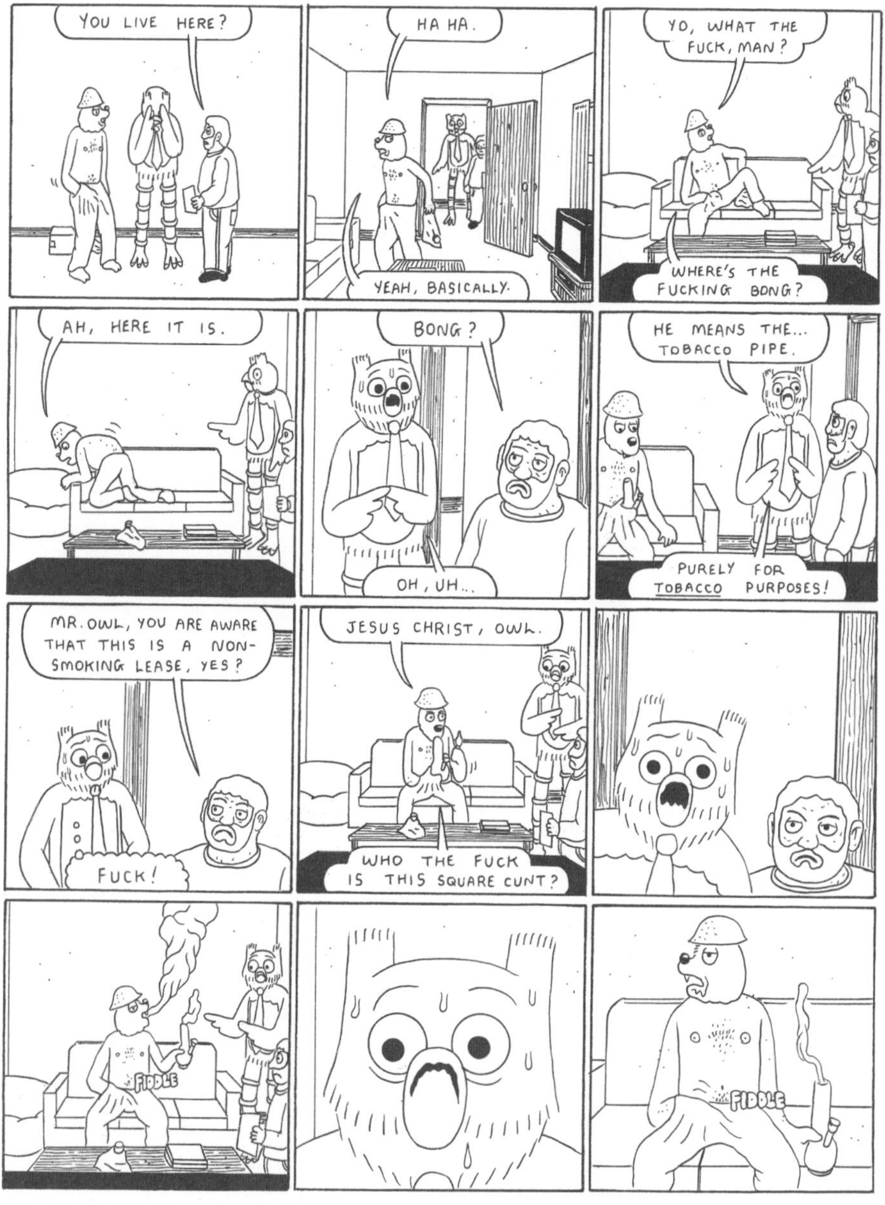

YOU LIVE HERE?
HA HA.
YEAH, BASICALLY.
YO, WHAT THE FUCK, MAN?
WHERE'S THE FUCKING BONG?
AH, HERE IT IS.
BONG?
OH, UH..
HE MEANS THE... TOBACCO PIPE.
PURELY FOR TOBACCO PURPOSES!
MR. OWL, YOU ARE AWARE THAT THIS IS A NON-SMOKING LEASE, YES?
FUCK!
JESUS CHRIST, OWL.
WHO THE FUCK IS THIS SQUARE CUNT?
FIDDLE
FIDDLE

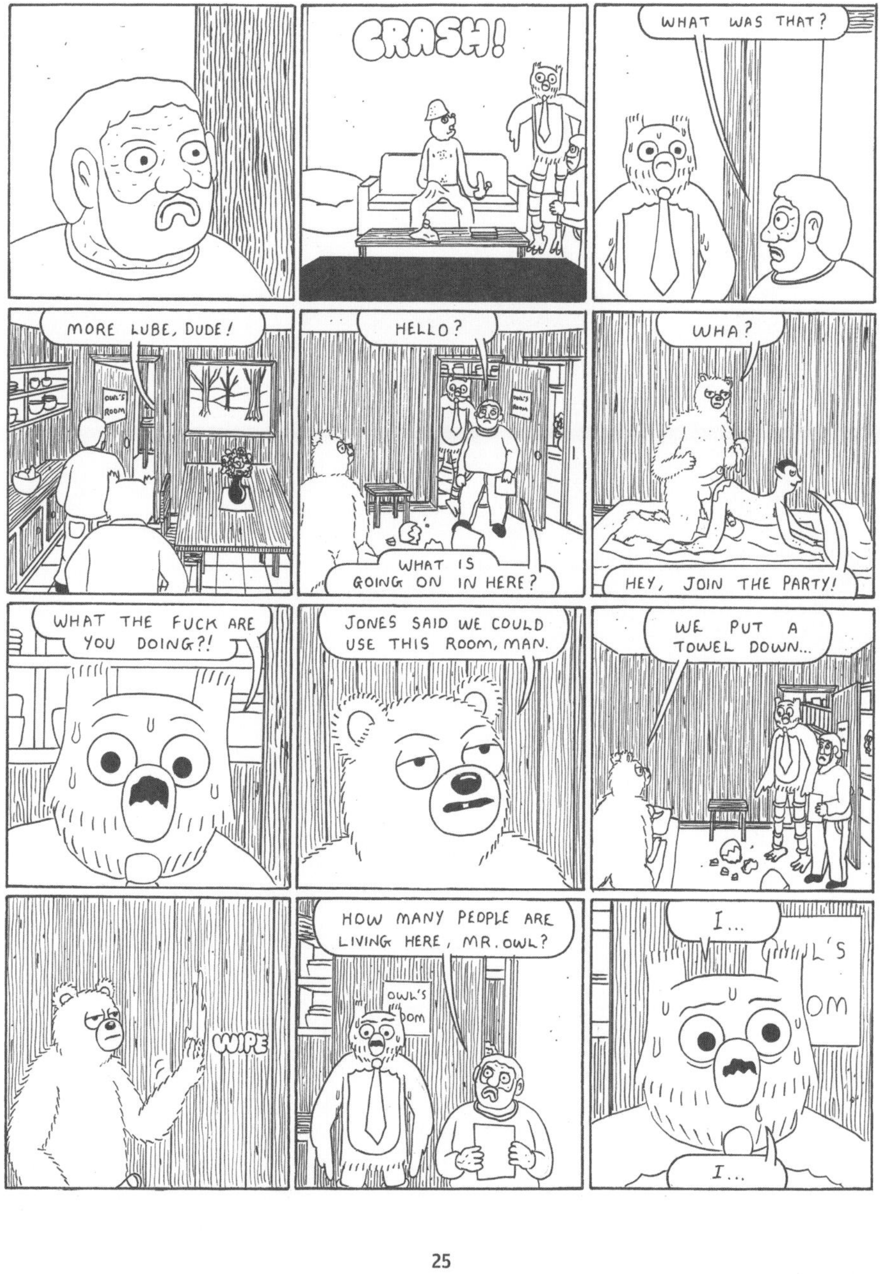
CRASH!
WHAT WAS THAT?
MORE LUBE, DUDE!
OWL'S ROOM
HELLO?
WHAT IS GOING ON IN HERE?
WHA?
HEY, JOIN THE PARTY!
WHAT THE FUCK ARE YOU DOING?!
JONES SAID WE COULD USE THIS ROOM, MAN.
WE PUT A TOWEL DOWN...
WIPE
HOW MANY PEOPLE ARE LIVING HERE, MR. OWL?
I...
I...

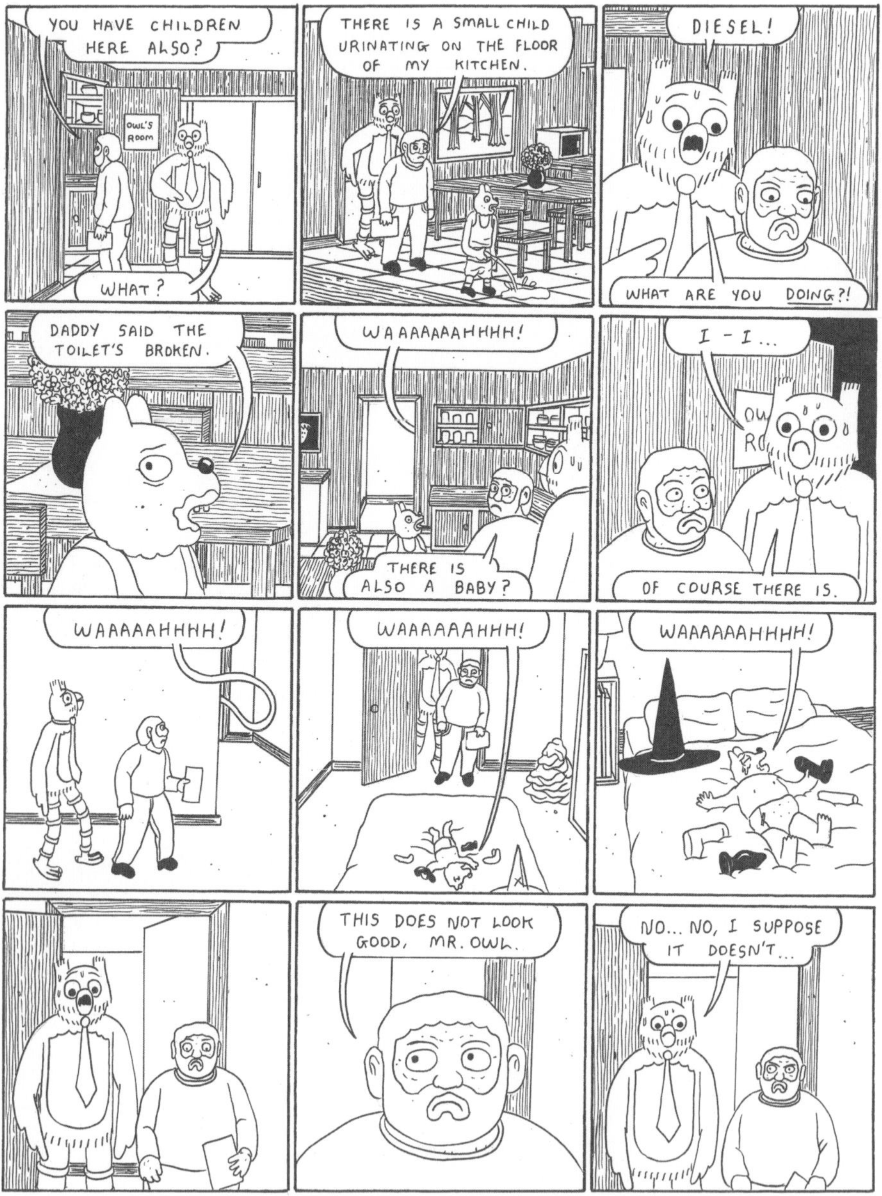
YOU HAVE CHILDREN HERE ALSO?
OWL'S ROOM
WHAT?
THERE IS A SMALL CHILD URINATING ON THE FLOOR OF MY KITCHEN.
DIESEL!
WHAT ARE YOU DOING?!
DADDY SAID THE TOILET'S BROKEN.
WAAAAAAAHHHH!
THERE IS ALSO A BABY?
I - I...
OF COURSE THERE IS.
WAAAAAHHHH!
WAAAAAAAHHH!
WAAAAAAAHHHH!
THIS DOES NOT LOOK GOOD, MR. OWL.
NO... NO, I SUPPOSE IT DOESN'T...

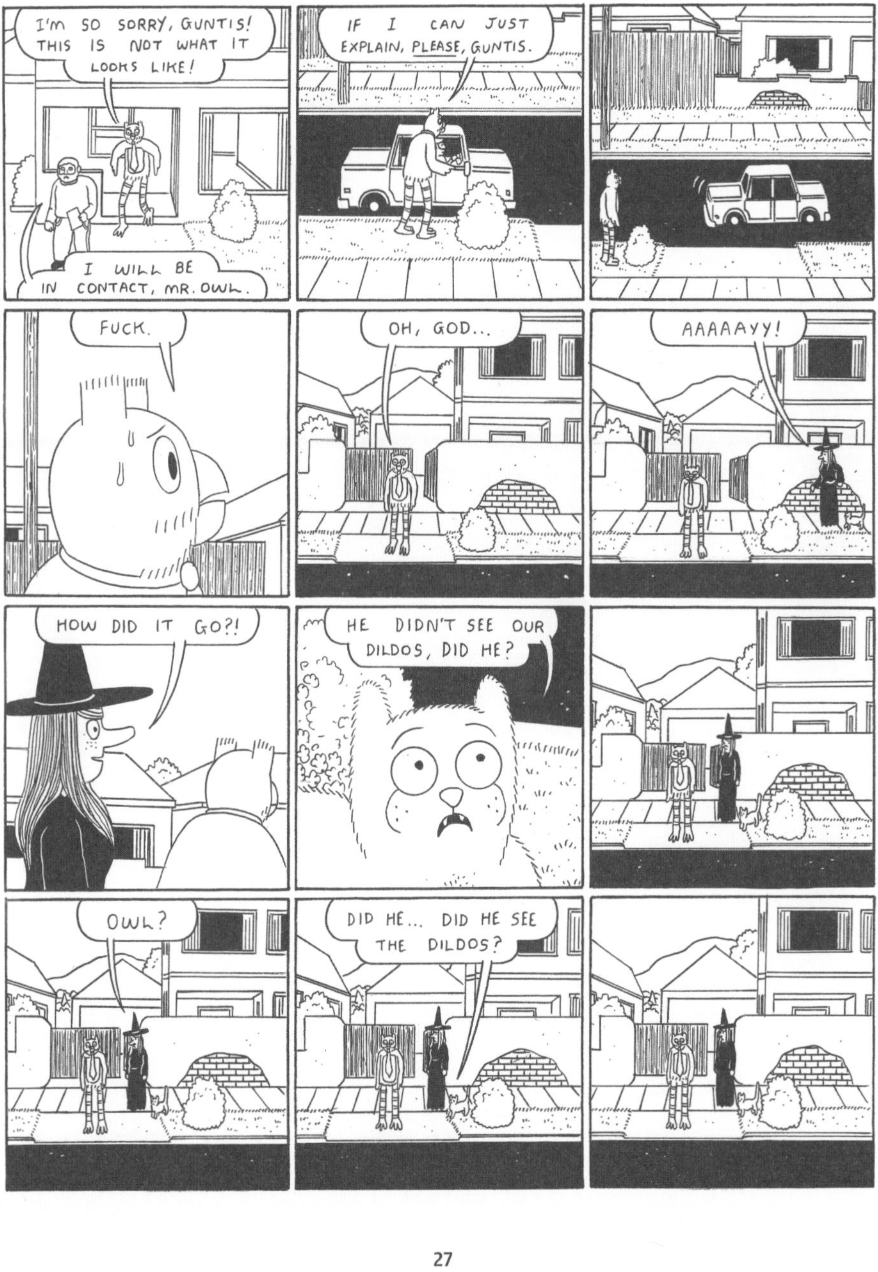
I'M SO SORRY, GUNTIS! THIS IS NOT WHAT IT LOOKS LIKE!
I WILL BE IN CONTACT, MR. OWL.
IF I CAN JUST EXPLAIN, PLEASE, GUNTIS.
FUCK.
OH, GOD...
AAAAAYY!
HOW DID IT GO?!
HE DIDN'T SEE OUR DILDOS, DID HE?
OWL?
DID HE... DID HE SEE THE DILDOS?

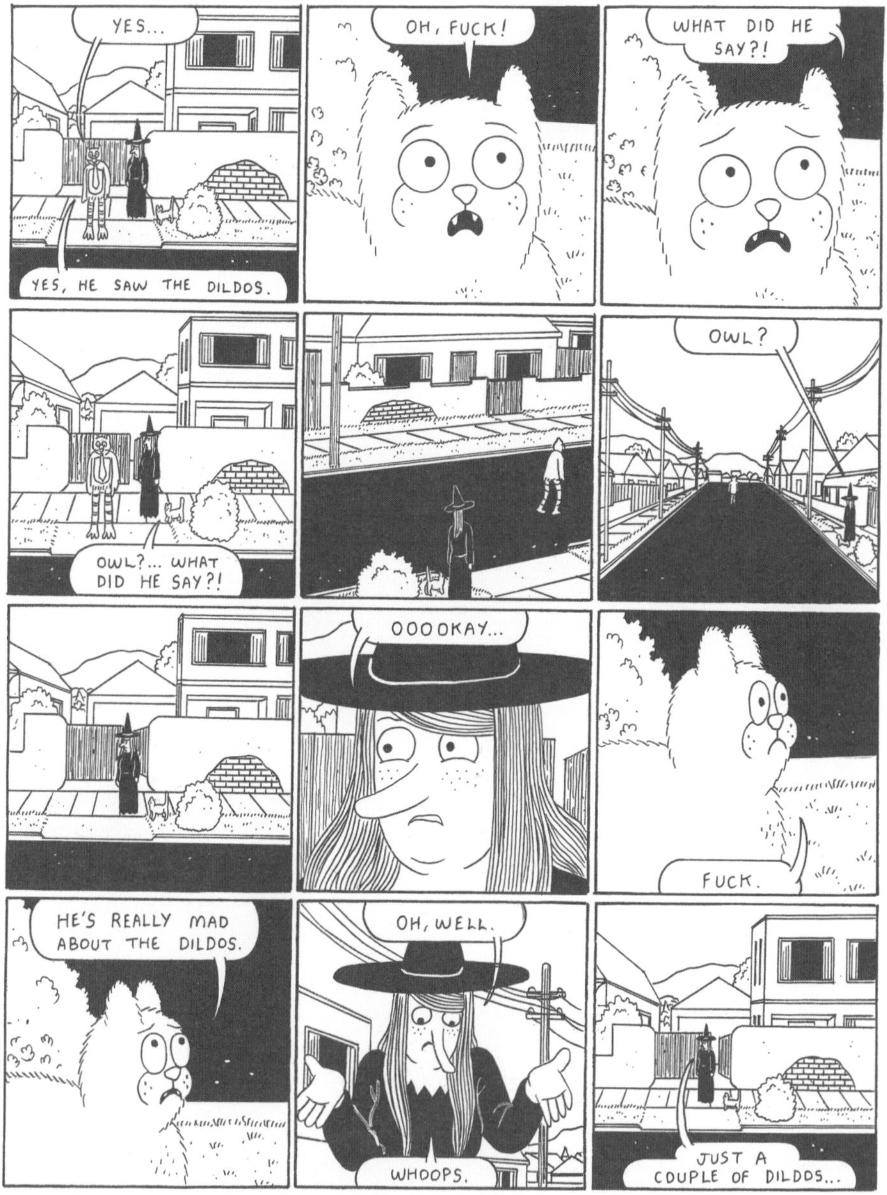
YES...
YES, HE SAW THE DILDOS.
OH, FUCK!
WHAT DID HE SAY?!
OWL?... WHAT DID HE SAY?!
OWL?
OOOOKAY...
FUCK.
HE'S REALLY MAD ABOUT THE DILDOS.
OH, WELL.
WHOOPS.
JUST A COUPLE OF DILDOS...

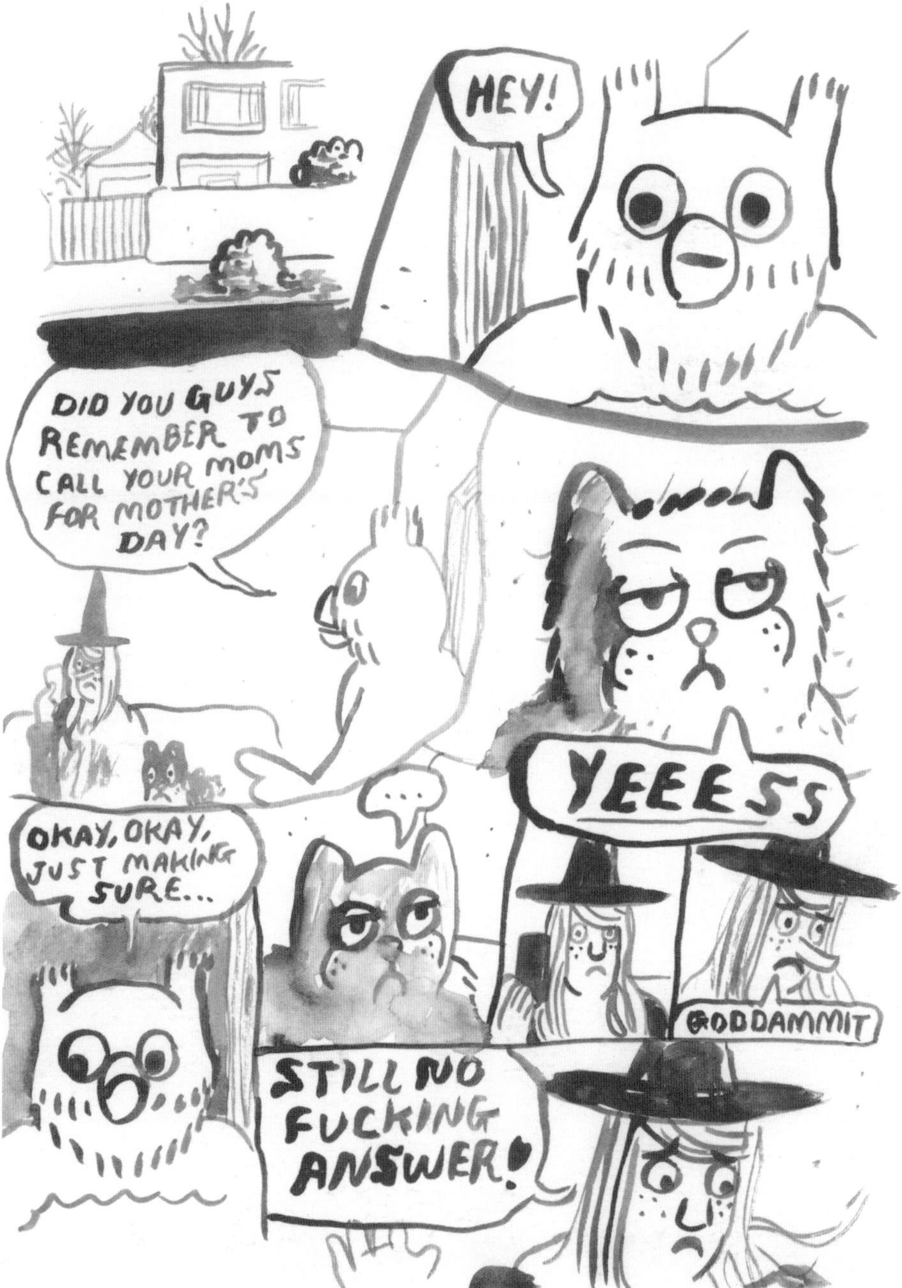
HEY!
DID YOU GUYS REMEMBER TO CALL YOUR MOMS FOR MOTHER'S DAY?
YEEESS
GODDAMMIT
...
OKAY, OKAY, JUST MAKING SURE...
STILL NO FUCKING ANSWER!

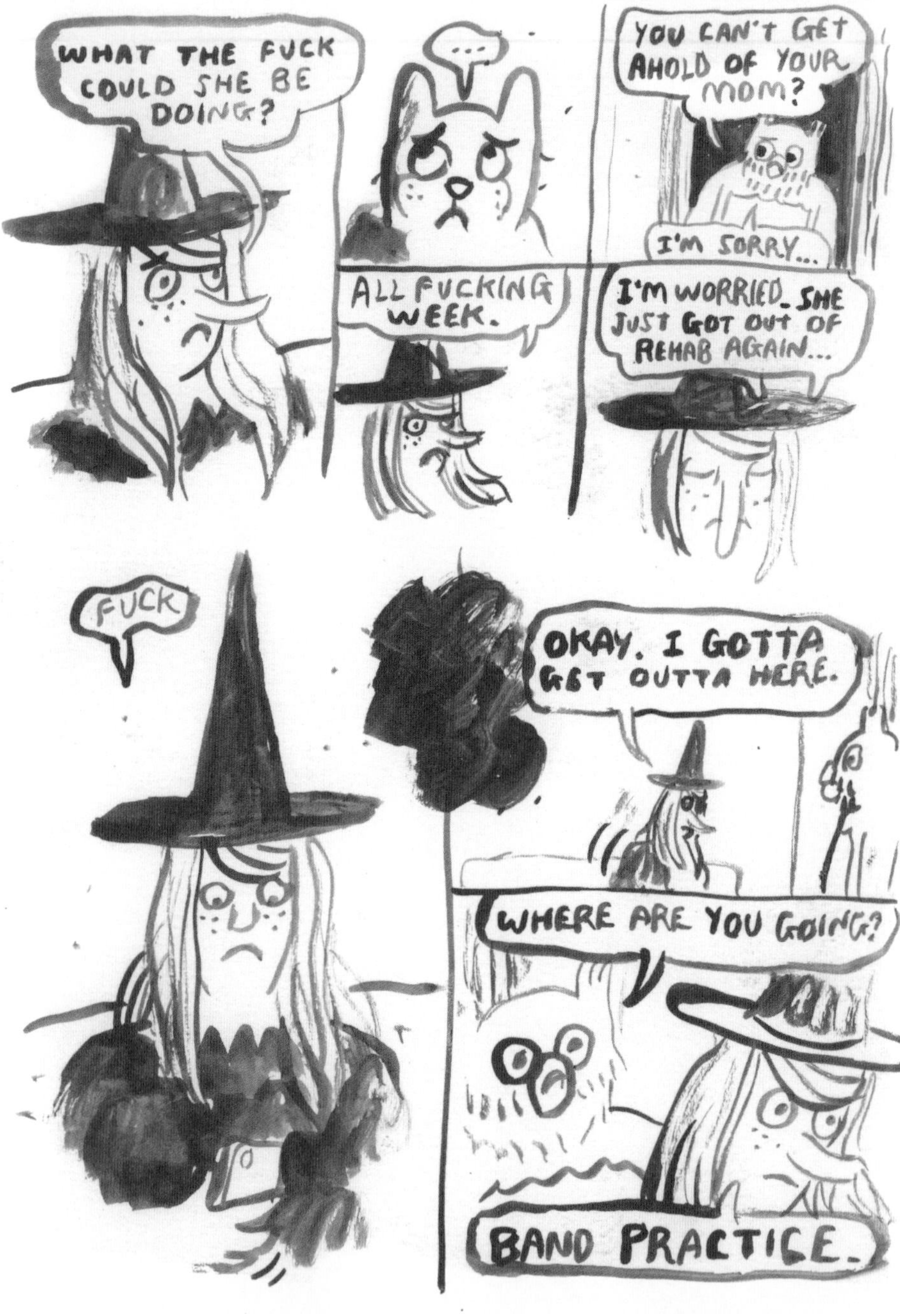
WHAT THE FUCK COULD SHE BE DOING?
...
YOU CAN'T GET AHOLD OF YOUR MOM?
I'M SORRY...
ALL FUCKING WEEK.
I'M WORRIED. SHE JUST GOT OUT OF REHAB AGAIN...
FUCK
OKAY. I GOTTA GET OUTTA HERE.
WHERE ARE YOU GOING?
BAND PRACTICE.

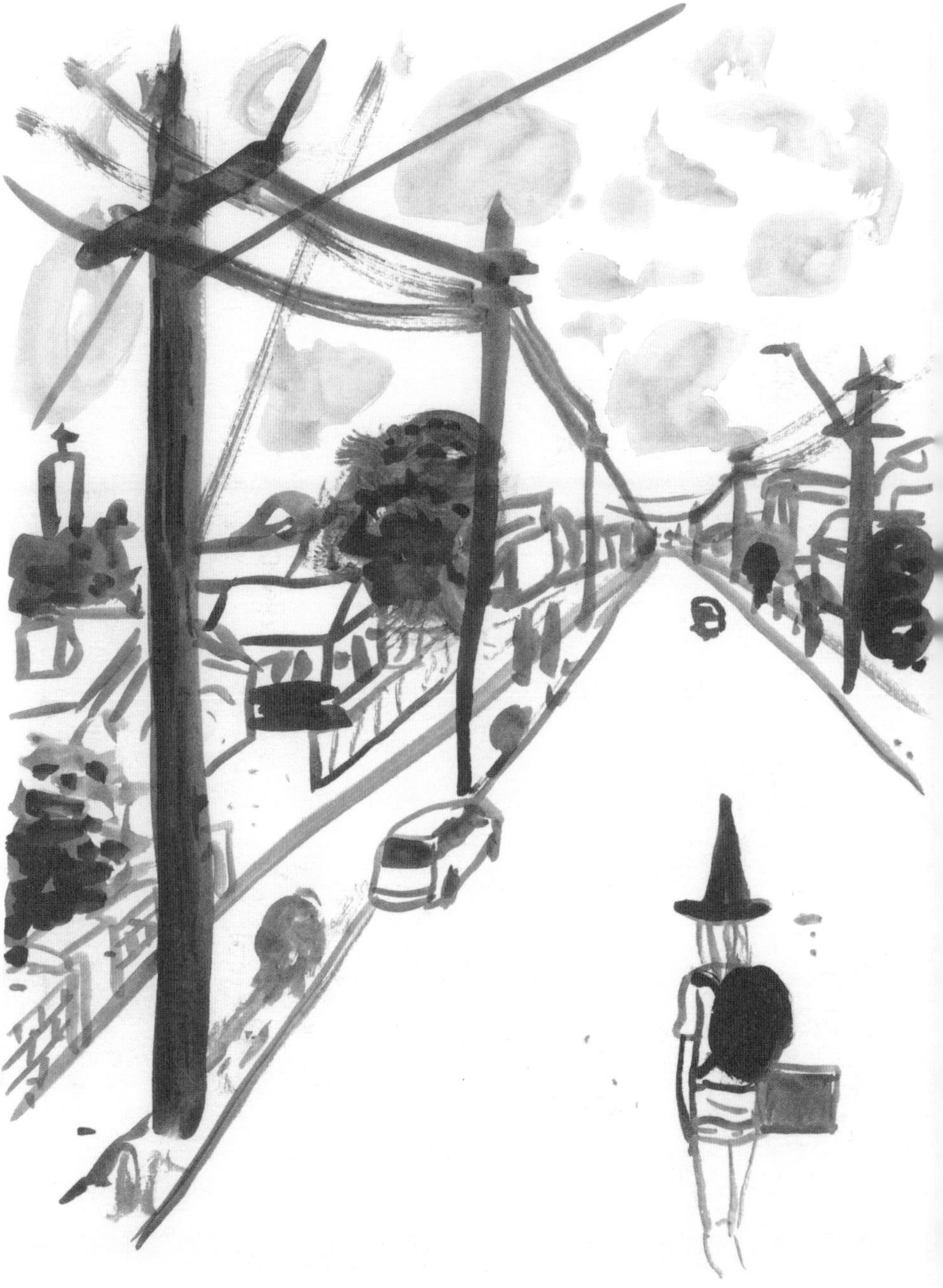

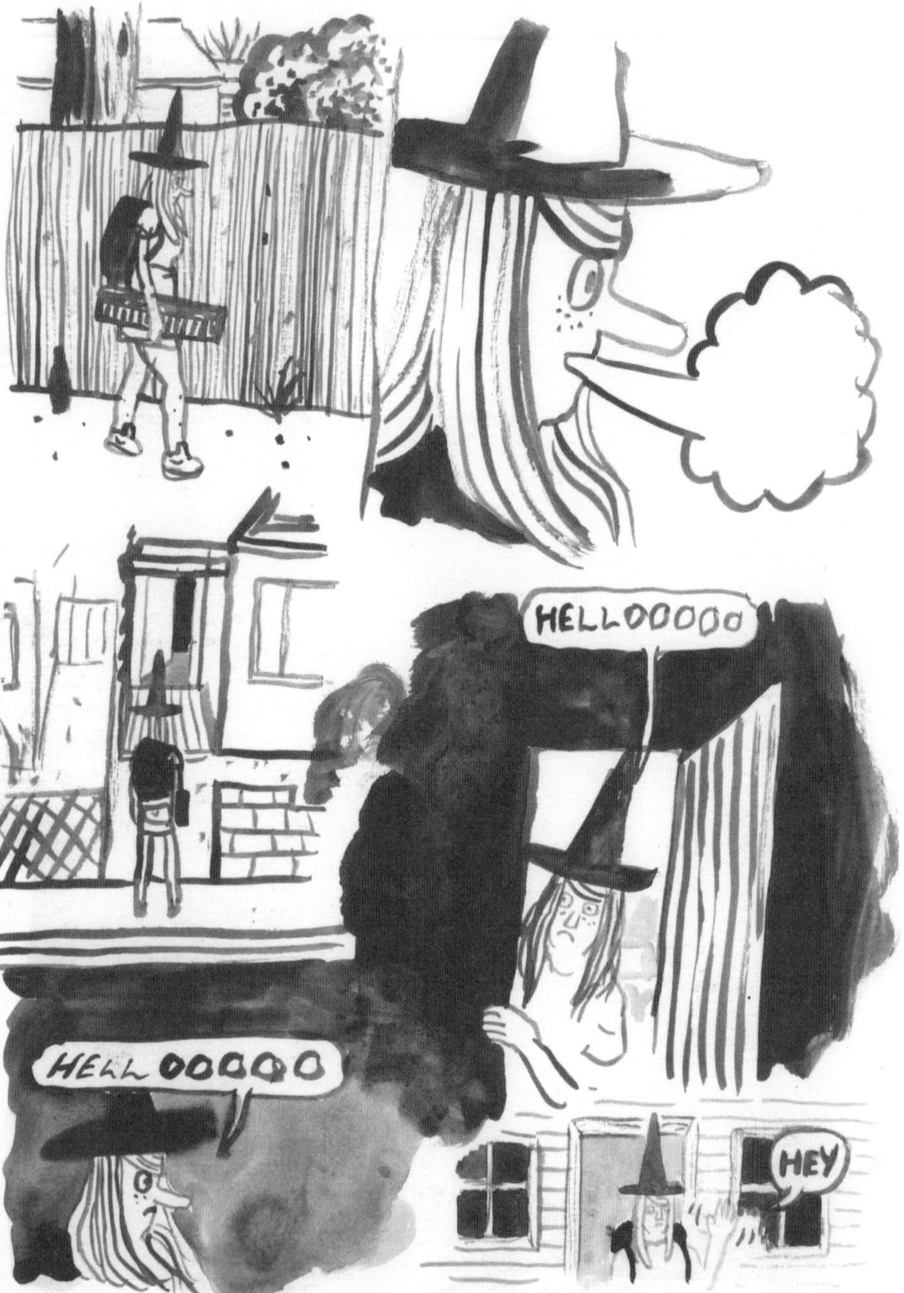
HELLOOOOO
HELLOOOOO
HEY

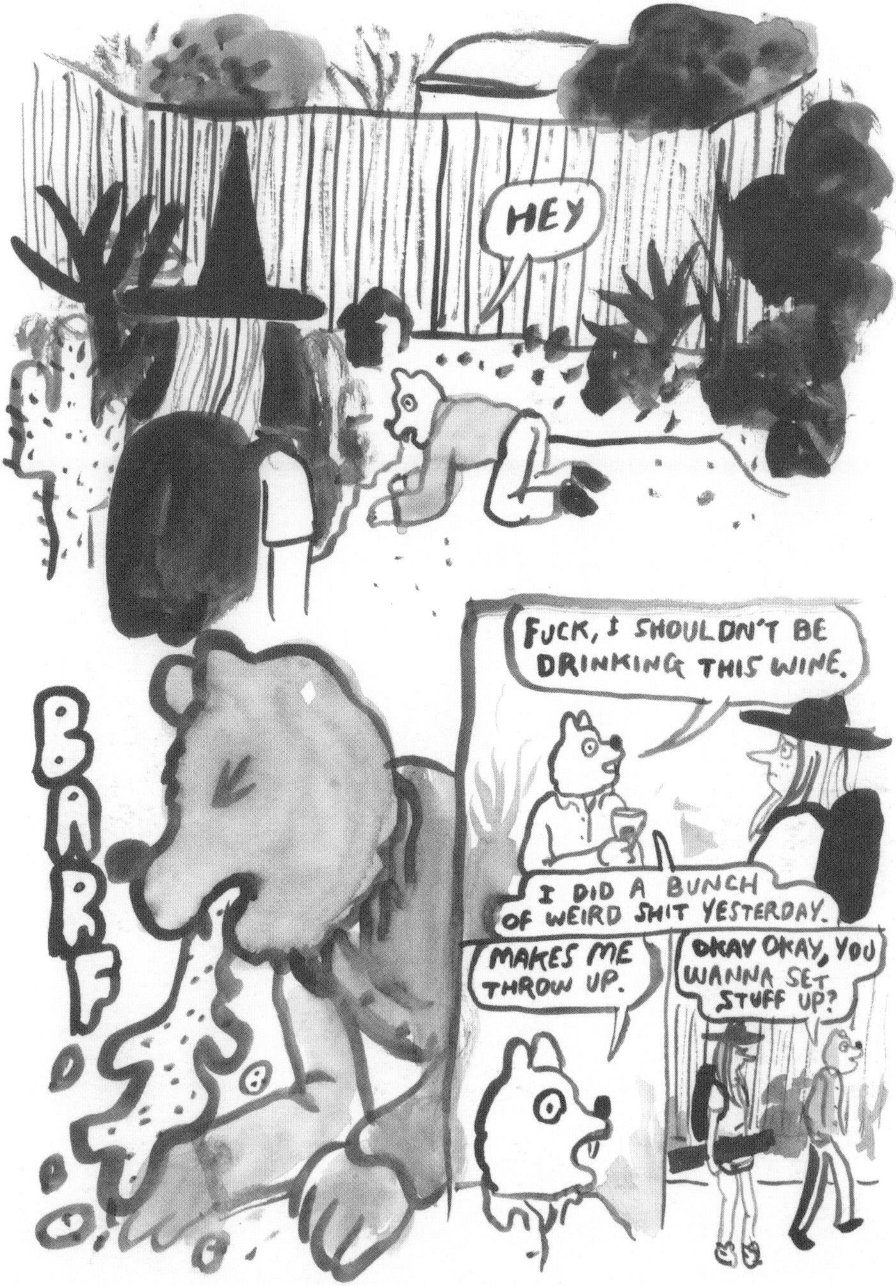
HEY
BARF
FUCK, I SHOULDN'T BE DRINKING THIS WINE.
I DID A BUNCH OF WEIRD SHIT YESTERDAY.
MAKES ME THROW UP.
OKAY OKAY, YOU WANNA SET STUFF UP?

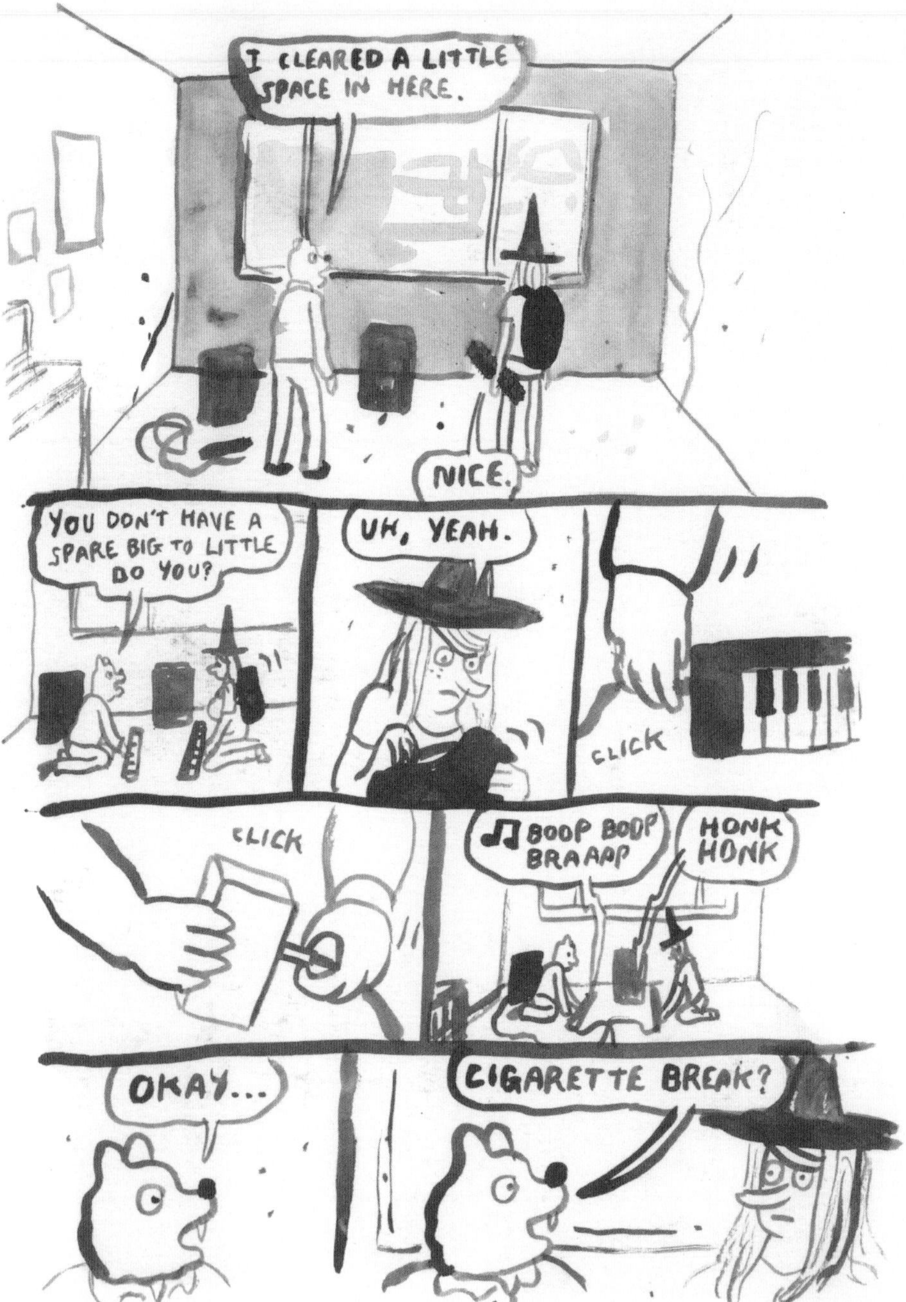
I CLEARED A LITTLE SPACE IN HERE.
NICE.
YOU DON'T HAVE A SPARE BIG TO LITTLE DO YOU?
UH, YEAH.
CLICK
CLICK
♫ BOOP BOOP BRAAAP
HONK HONK
OKAY...
CIGARETTE BREAK?

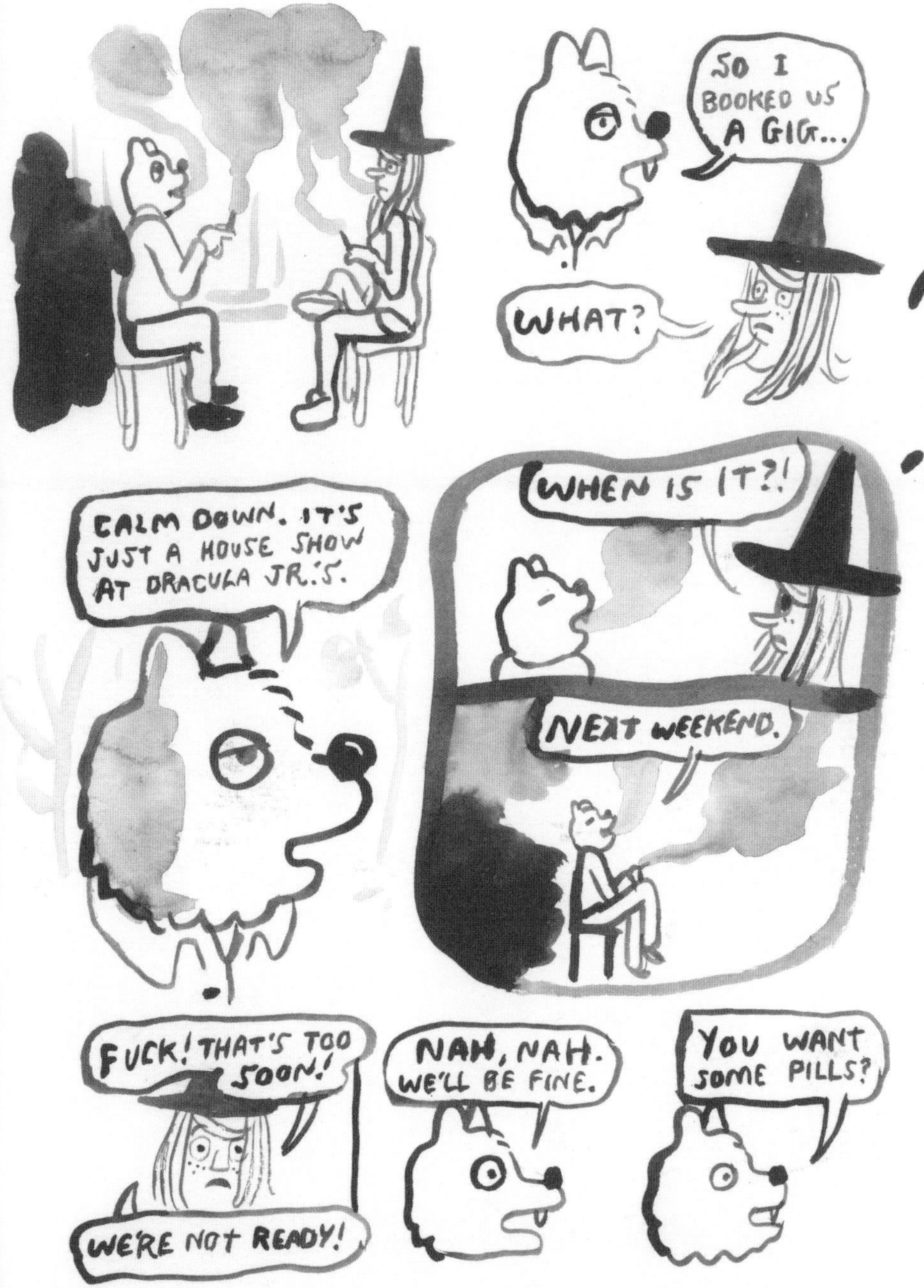
SO I BOOKED US A GIG...
WHAT?
CALM DOWN. IT'S JUST A HOUSE SHOW AT DRACULA JR.'S.
WHEN IS IT?!
NEXT WEEKEND.
FUCK! THAT'S TOO SOON!
WE'RE NOT READY!
NAH, NAH. WE'LL BE FINE.
YOU WANT SOME PILLS?

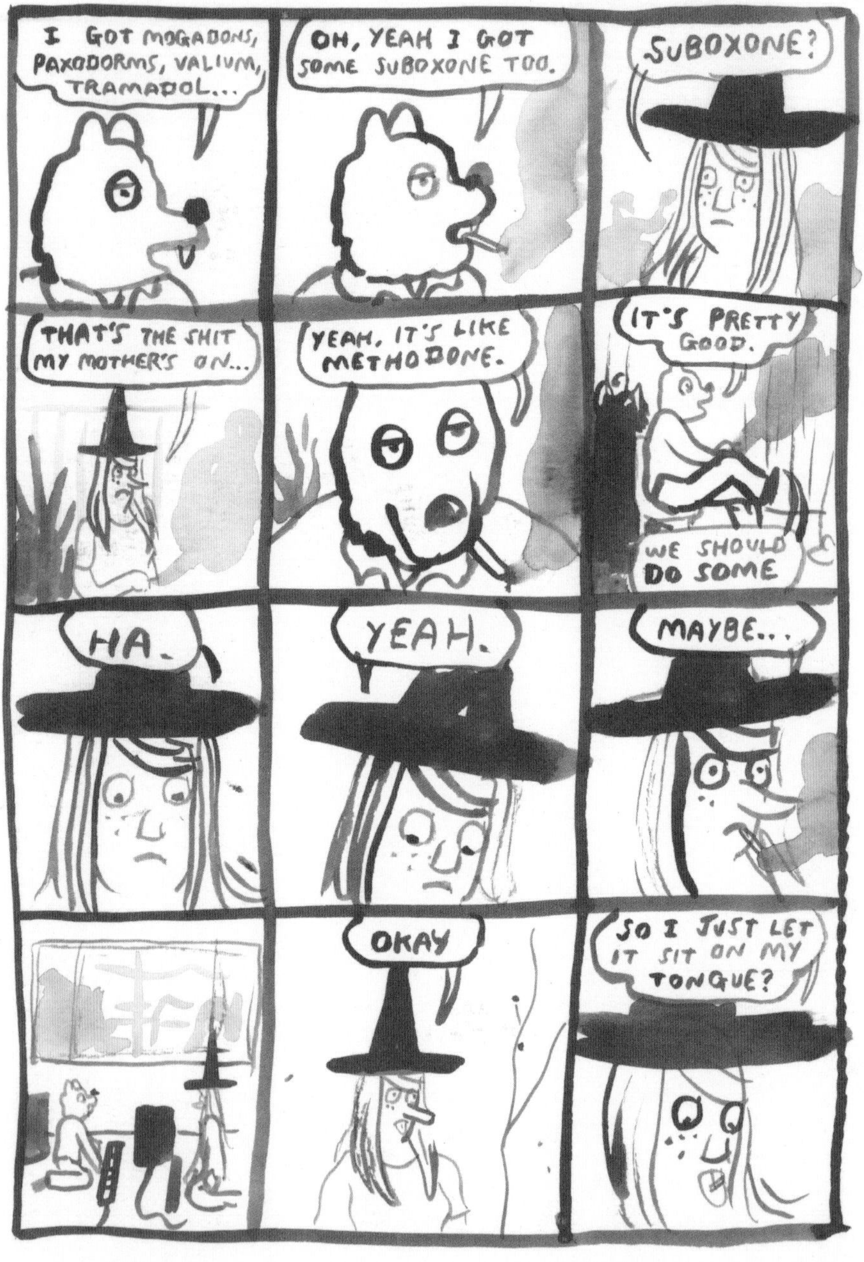
I GOT MOGADONS, PAXODORMS, VALIUM, TRAMADOL...
OH, YEAH I GOT SOME SUBOXONE TOO.
SUBOXONE?
THAT'S THE SHIT MY MOTHER'S ON...
YEAH, IT'S LIKE METHODONE.
IT'S PRETTY GOOD.
WE SHOULD DO SOME
HA.
YEAH.
MAYBE...
OKAY
SO I JUST LET IT SIT ON MY TONGUE?

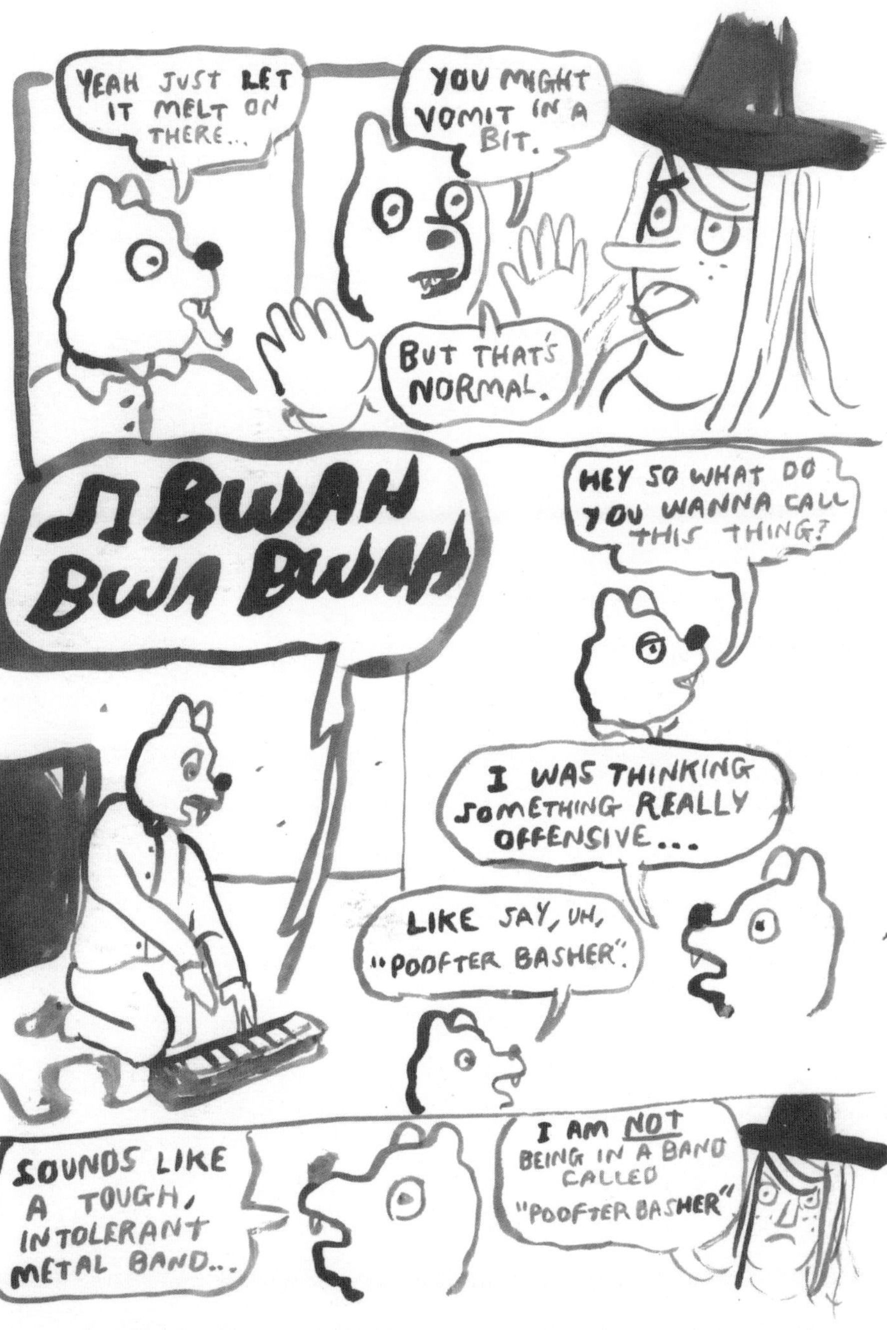
YEAH JUST LET IT MELT ON THERE...
YOU MIGHT VOMIT IN A BIT.
BUT THAT'S NORMAL.
♫ BWAH BWA BWAH
HEY SO WHAT DO YOU WANNA CALL THIS THING?
I WAS THINKING SOMETHING REALLY OFFENSIVE...
LIKE SAY, UH, "POOFTER BASHER".
SOUNDS LIKE A TOUGH, INTOLERANT METAL BAND...
I AM NOT BEING IN A BAND CALLED "POOFTER BASHER"

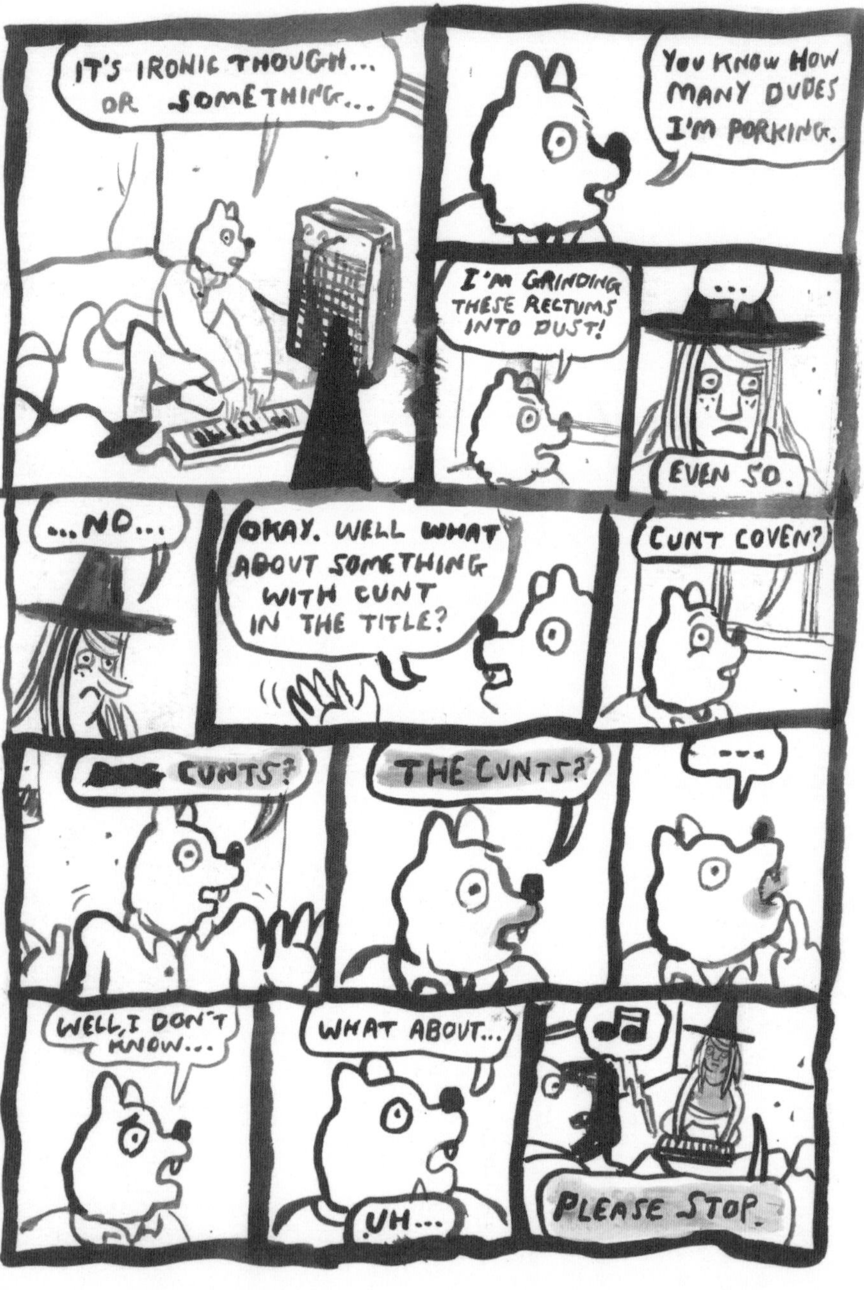
IT'S IRONIC THOUGH... OR SOMETHING...
YOU KNOW HOW MANY DUDES I'M PORKING.
I'M GRINDING THESE RECTUMS INTO DUST!
...
EVEN SO.
...NO...
OKAY. WELL WHAT ABOUT SOMETHING WITH CUNT IN THE TITLE?
CUNT COVEN?
[redacted] CUNTS?
THE CUNTS?
...
WELL, I DON'T KNOW...
WHAT ABOUT...
UH...
PLEASE STOP.

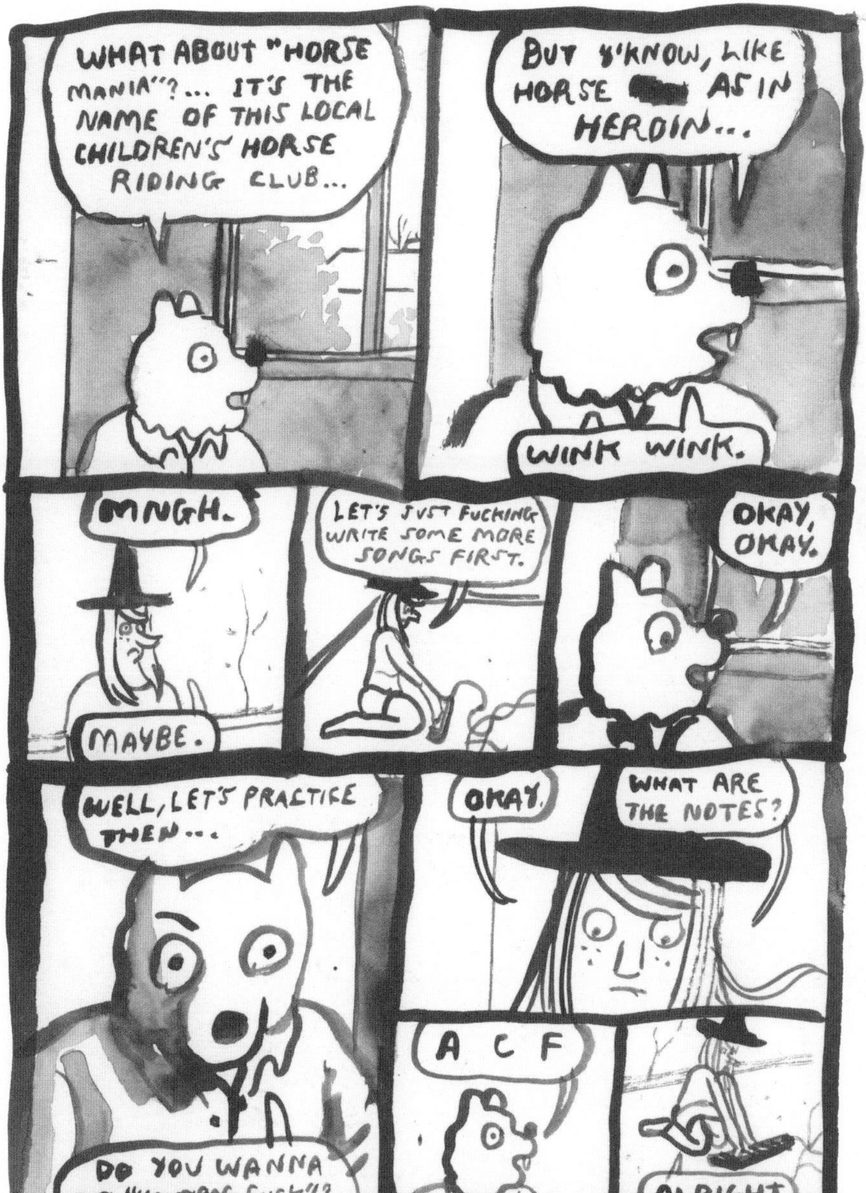
WHAT ABOUT "HORSE MANIA"?... IT'S THE NAME OF THIS LOCAL CHILDREN'S HORSE RIDING CLUB...
BUT Y'KNOW, LIKE HORSE [redacted] AS IN HEROIN...
WINK WINK.
MNGH.
MAYBE.
LET'S JUST FUCKING WRITE SOME MORE SONGS FIRST.
OKAY, OKAY.
WELL, LET'S PRACTICE THEN...
DO YOU WANNA DO "HANDBAG FUCK"?
OKAY.
WHAT ARE THE NOTES?
A C F
ALRIGHT

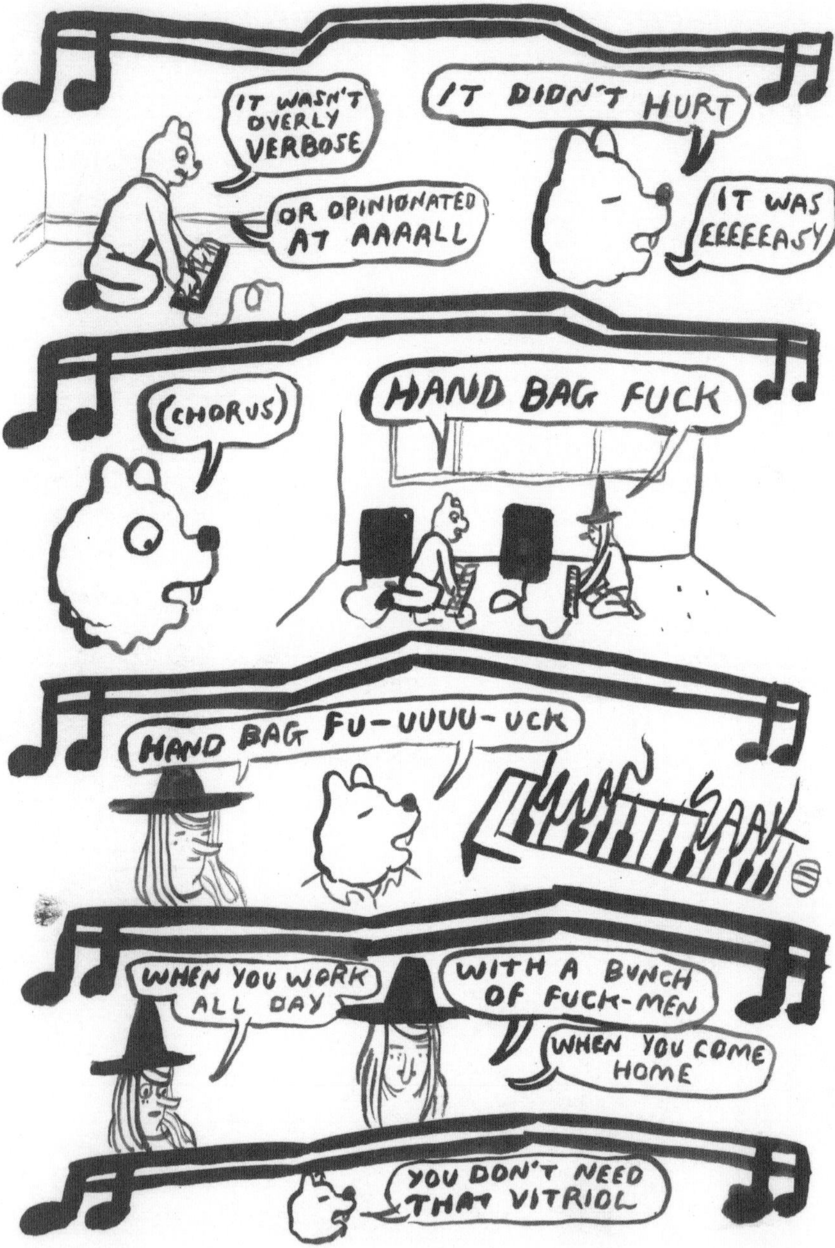
IT WASN'T OVERLY VERBOSE
OR OPINIONATED AT AAAALL
IT DIDN'T HURT
IT WAS EEEEEASY
(CHORUS)
HAND BAG FUCK
HAND BAG FU-UUUU-UCK
WHEN YOU WORK ALL DAY
WITH A BUNCH OF FUCK-MEN
WHEN YOU COME HOME
YOU DON'T NEED THAT VITRIOL

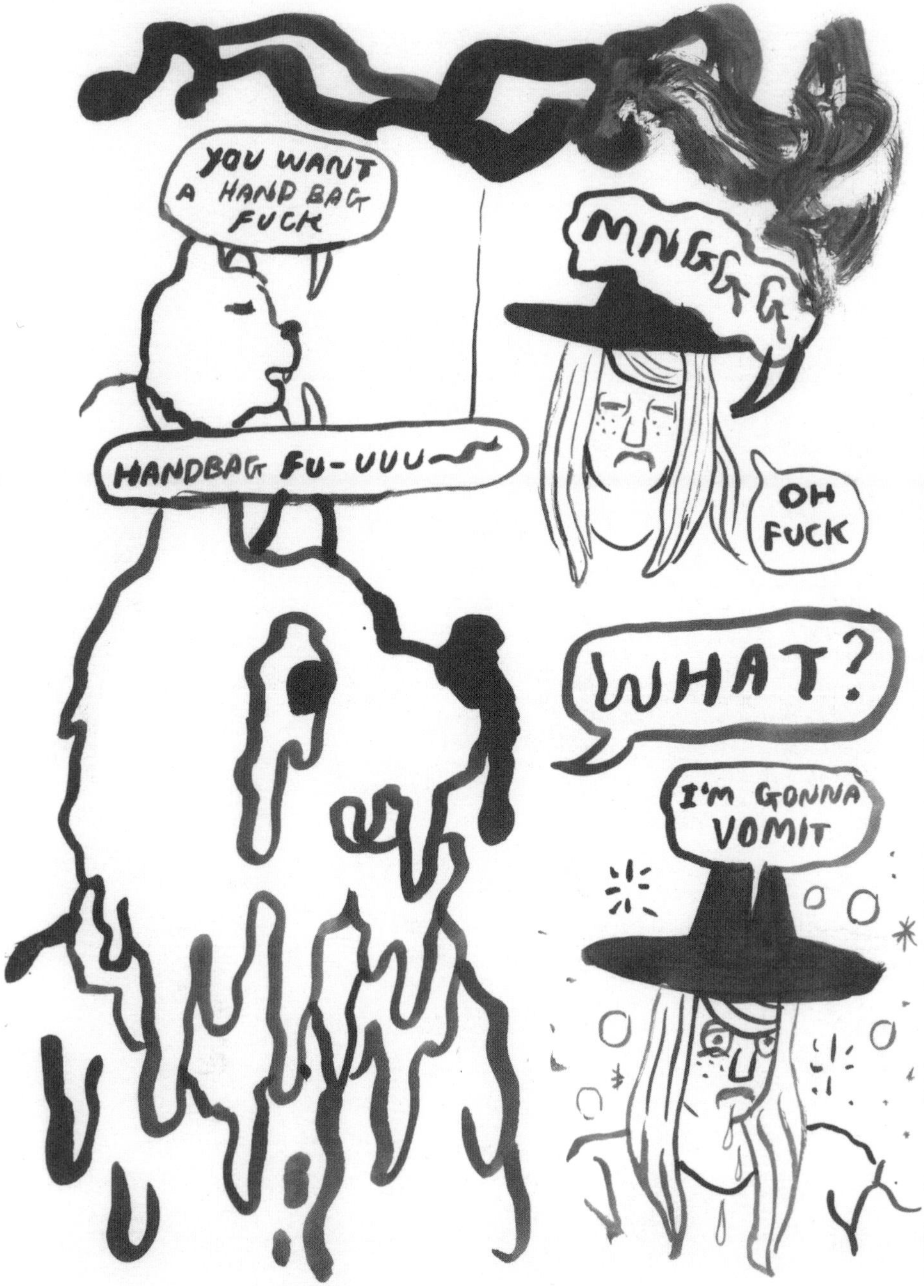
YOU WANT A HAND BAG FUCK
HANDBAG FU-UUU~
MNGGGG
OH FUCK
WHAT?
I'M GONNA VOMIT

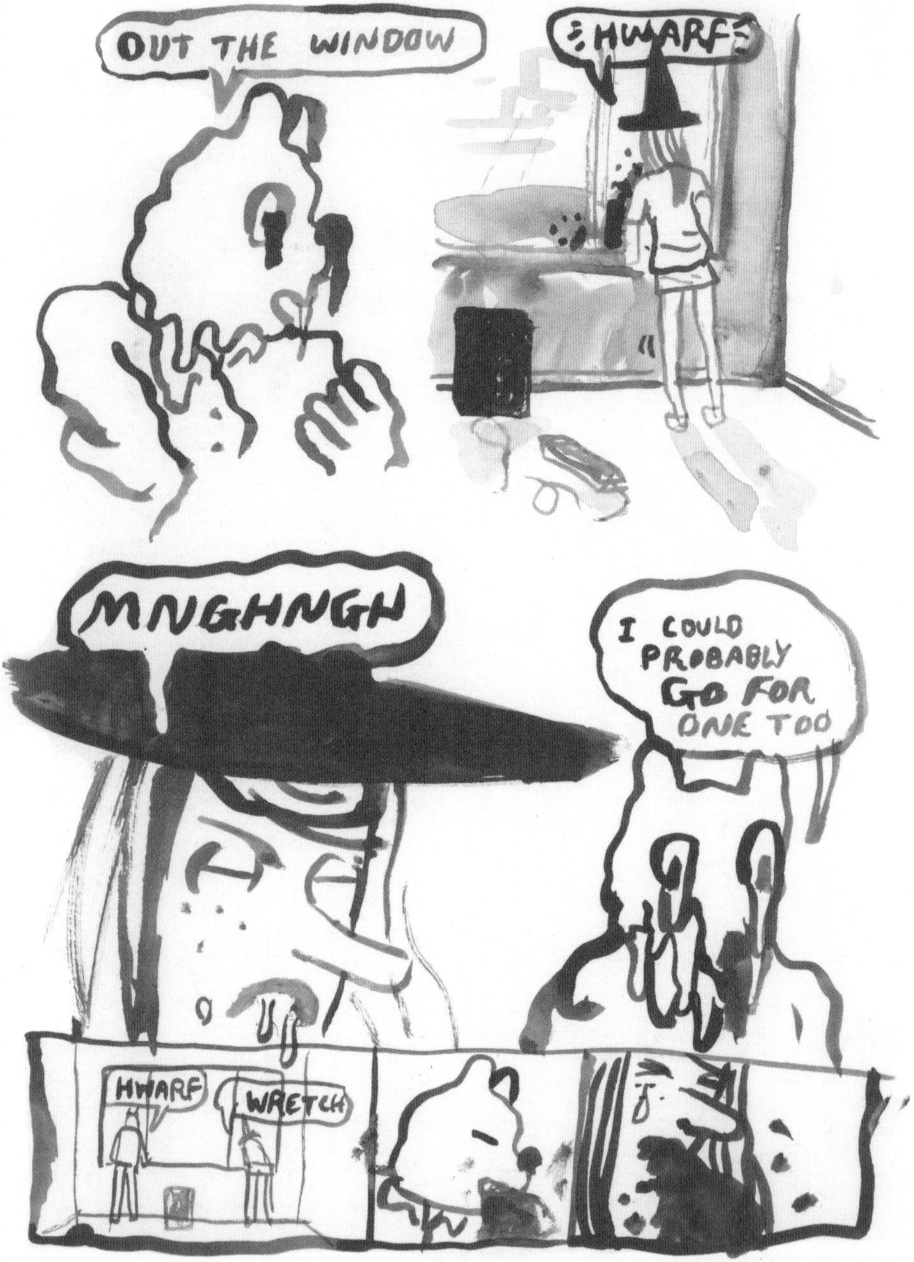

OUT THE WINDOW
HWARF
MNGHNGH
I COULD PROBABLY GO FOR ONE TOO
HWARF
WRETCH

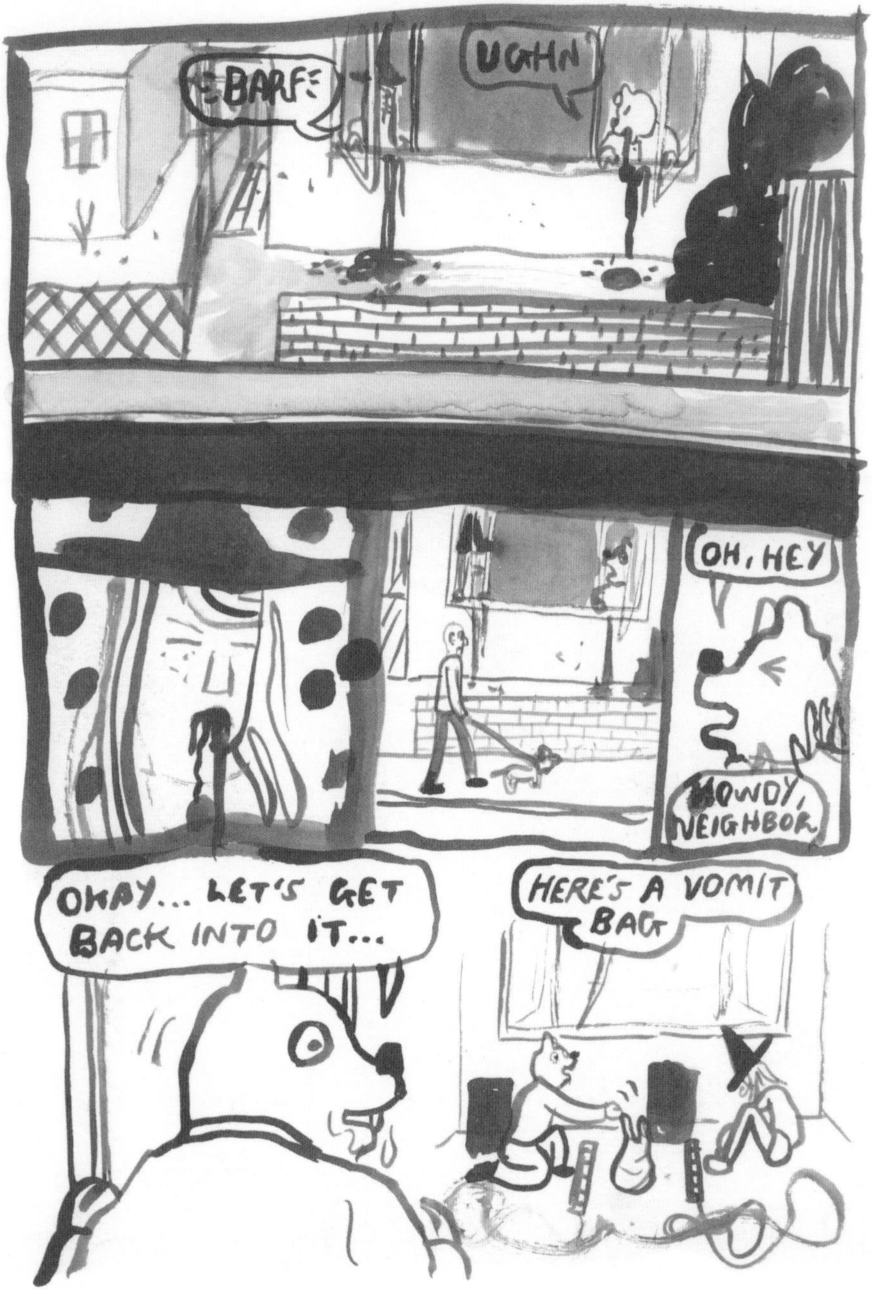
BARF
UGHN
OH, HEY
HOWDY, NEIGHBOR
OKAY... LET'S GET BACK INTO IT...
HERE'S A VOMIT BAG

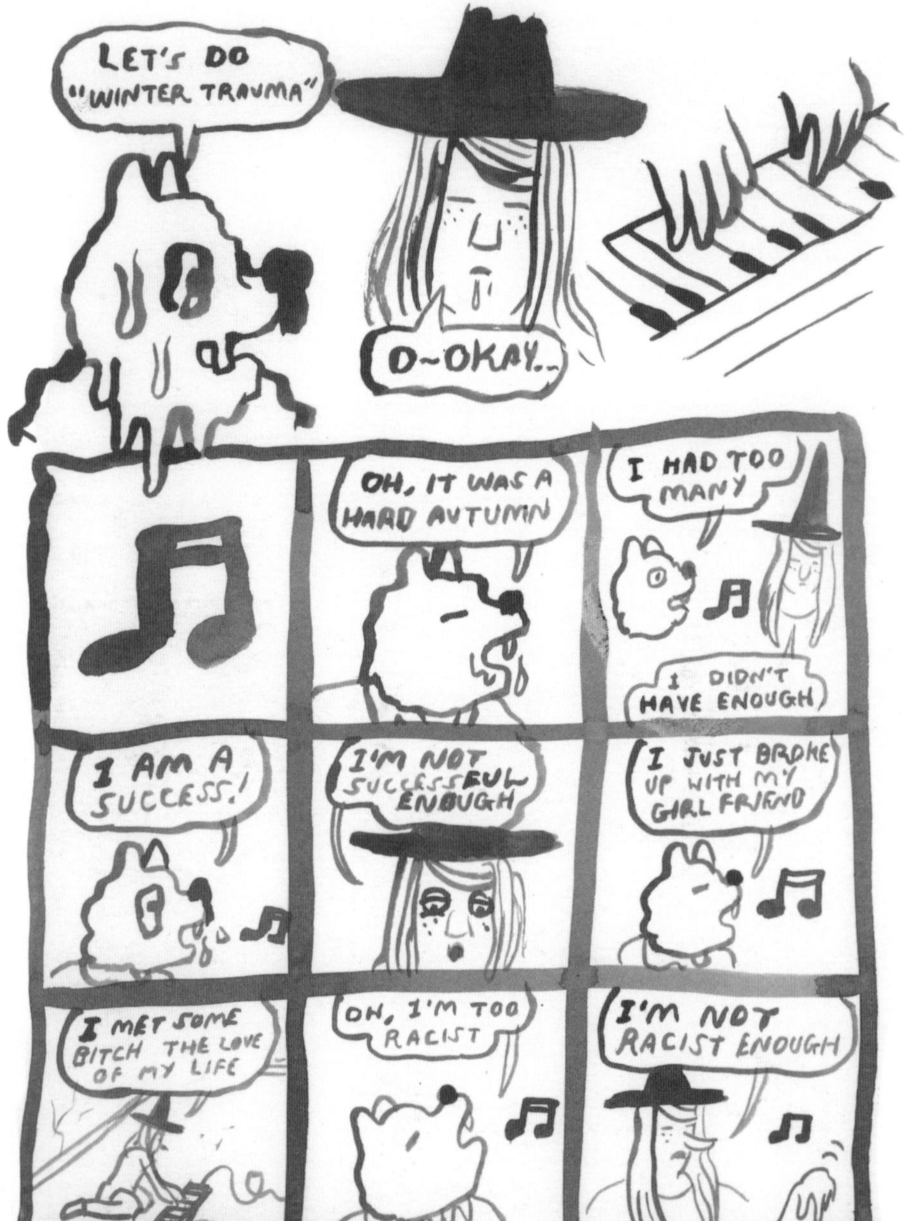
LET'S DO "WINTER TRAUMA"
O~OKAY...
OH, IT WAS A HARD AUTUMN
I HAD TOO MANY
I DIDN'T HAVE ENOUGH
I AM A SUCCESS!
I'M NOT SUCCESSFUL ENOUGH
I JUST BROKE UP WITH MY GIRL FRIEND
I MET SOME BITCH THE LOVE OF MY LIFE
OH, I'M TOO RACIST
I'M NOT RACIST ENOUGH

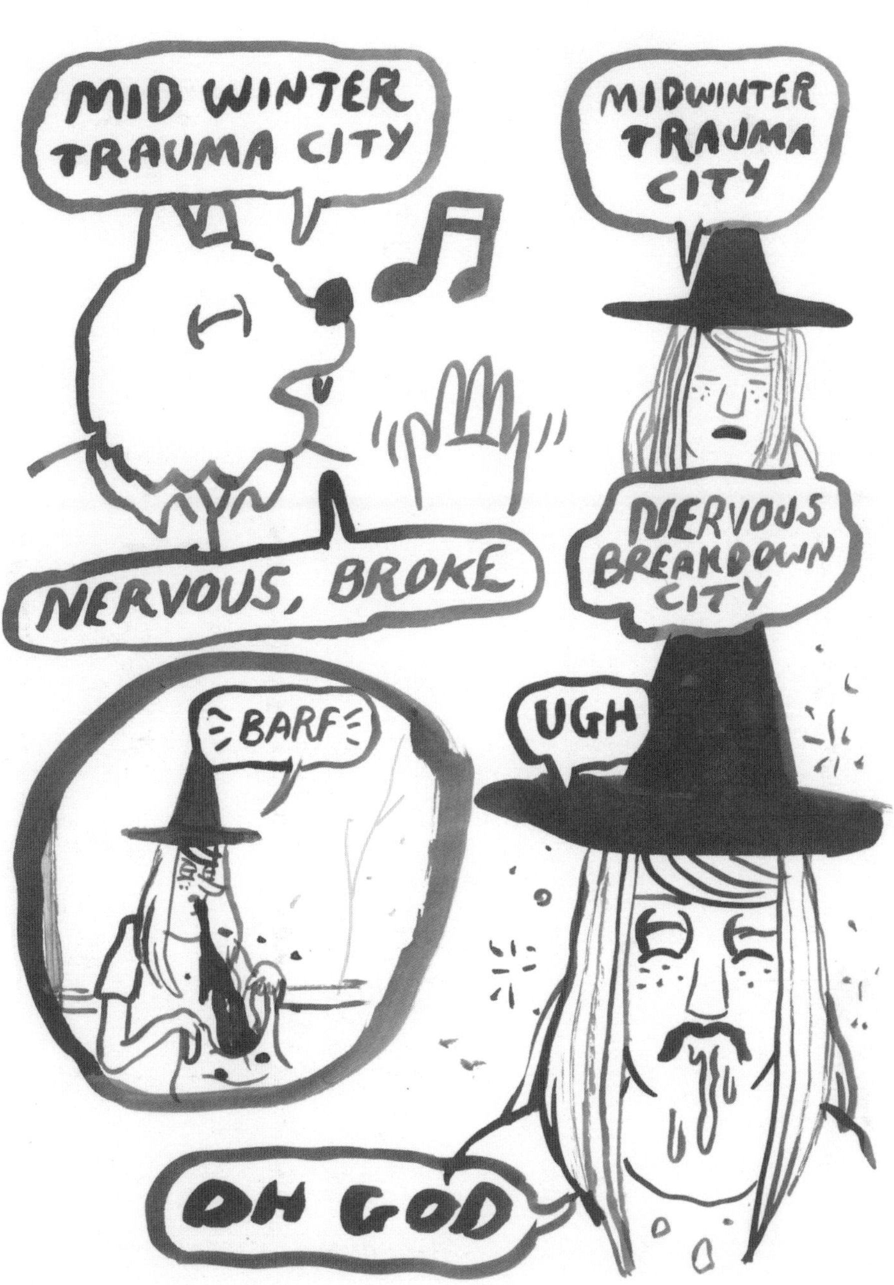
MID WINTER TRAUMA CITY
NERVOUS, BROKE
MIDWINTER TRAUMA CITY
NERVOUS BREAKDOWN CITY
BARF
UGH
OH GOD

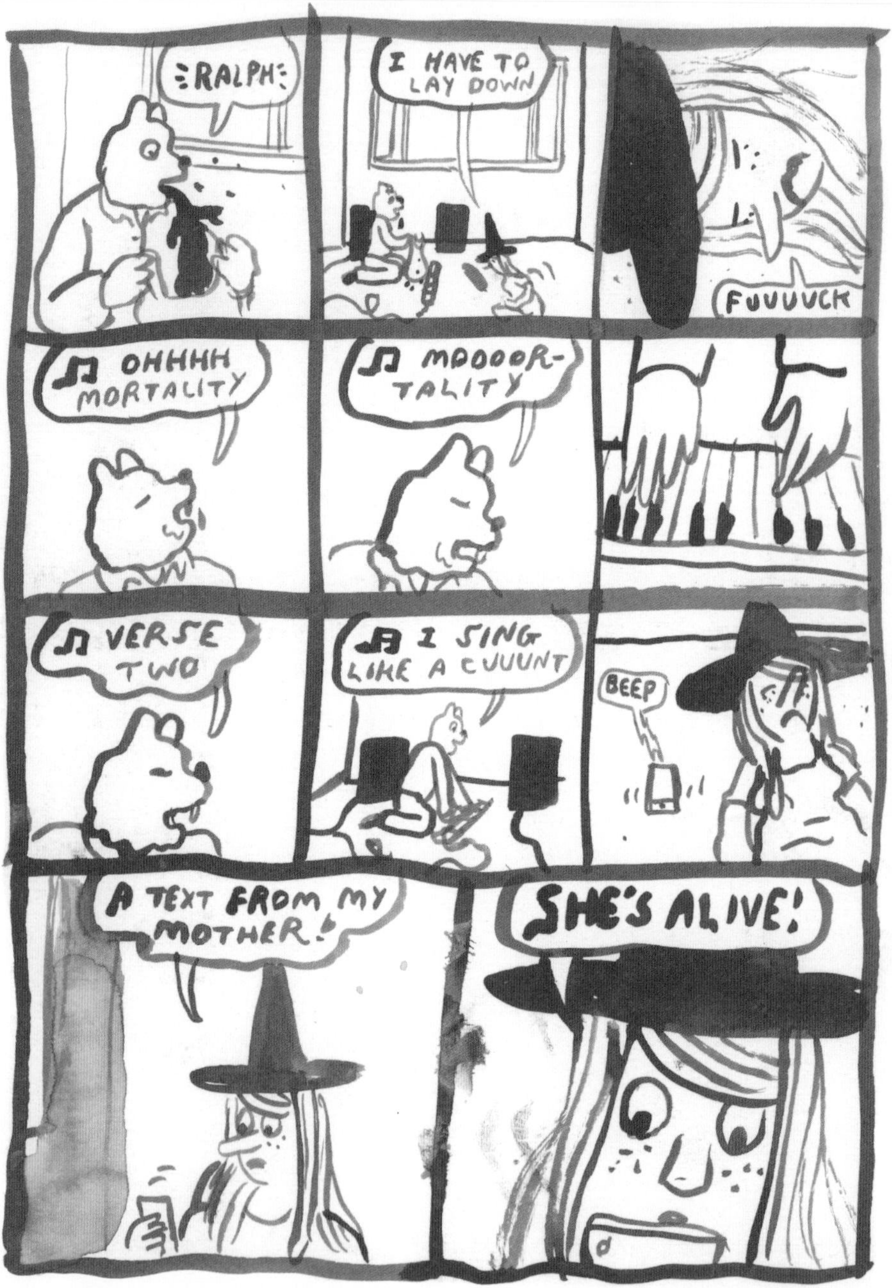
RALPH
I HAVE TO LAY DOWN
FUUUUCK
OHHHH MORTALITY
MOOOOR-TALITY
VERSE TWO
I SING LIKE A CUUUNT
BEEP
A TEXT FROM MY MOTHER!
SHE'S ALIVE!

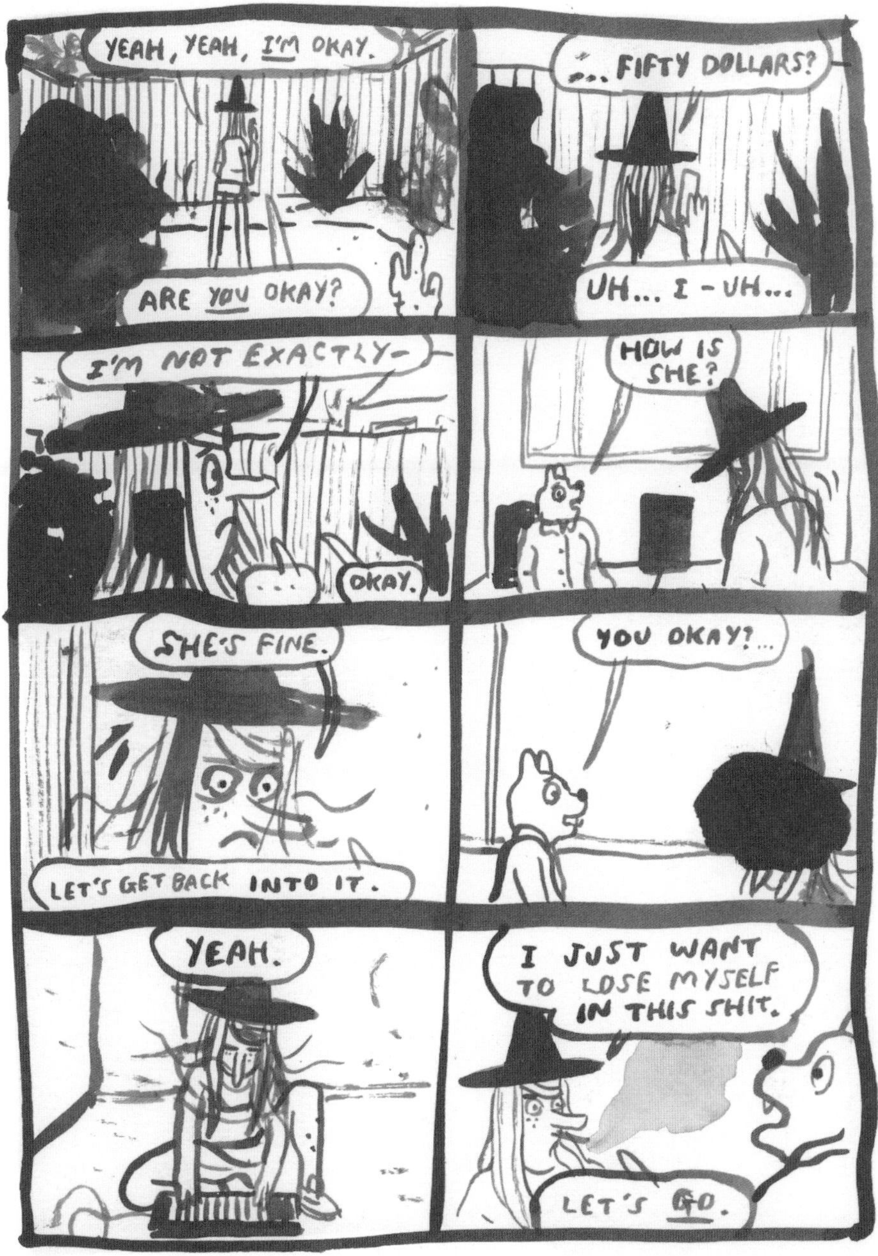
YEAH, YEAH, I'M OKAY.
ARE YOU OKAY?
... FIFTY DOLLARS?
UH... I-UH...
I'M NOT EXACTLY-
...
OKAY.
HOW IS SHE?
SHE'S FINE.
LET'S GET BACK INTO IT.
YOU OKAY?...
YEAH.
I JUST WANT TO LOSE MYSELF IN THIS SHIT.
LET'S GO.

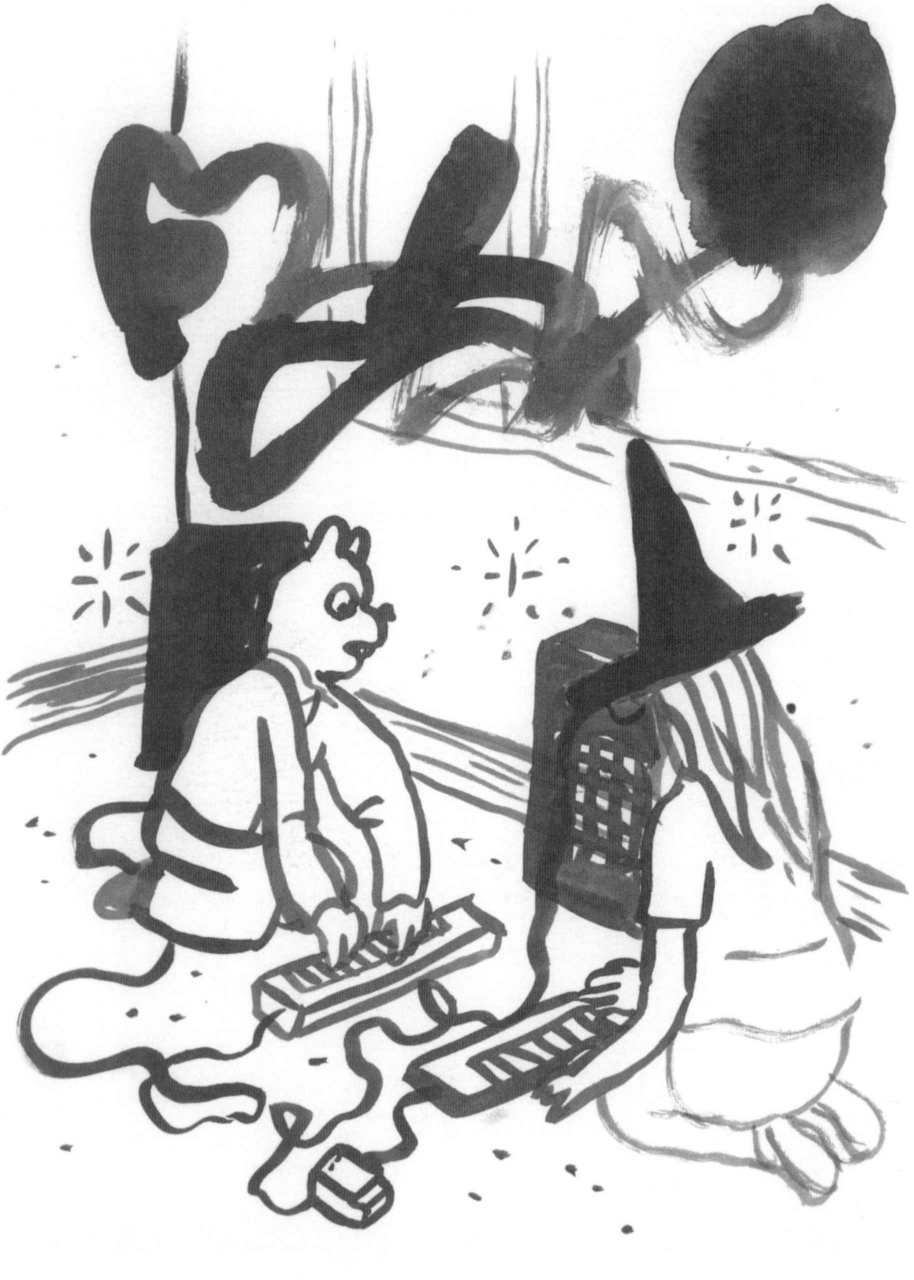

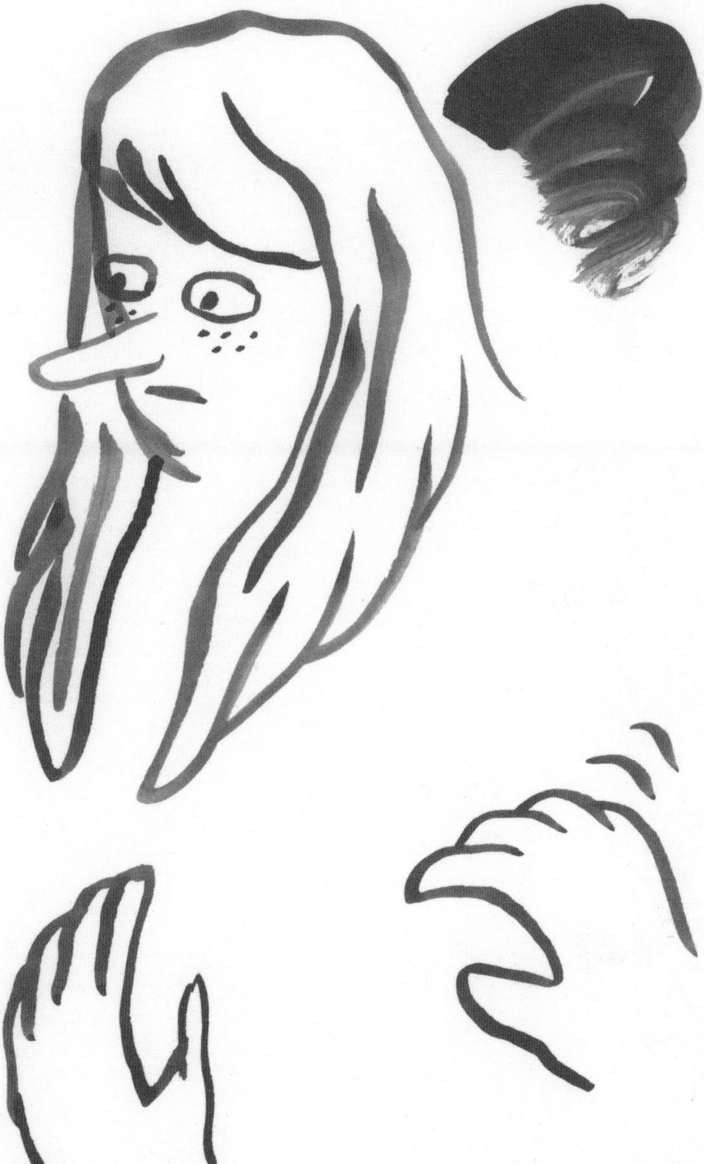

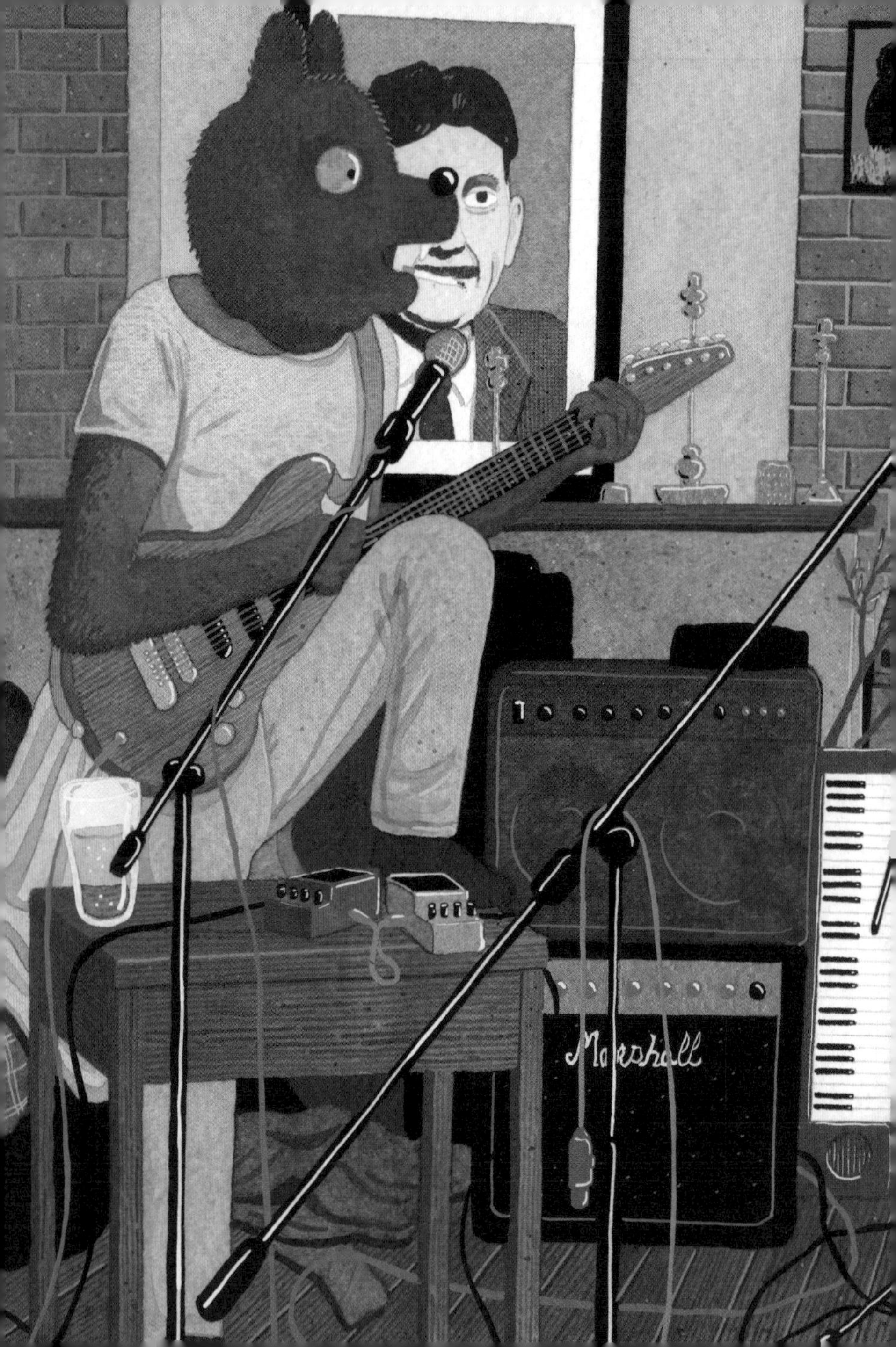
Marshall

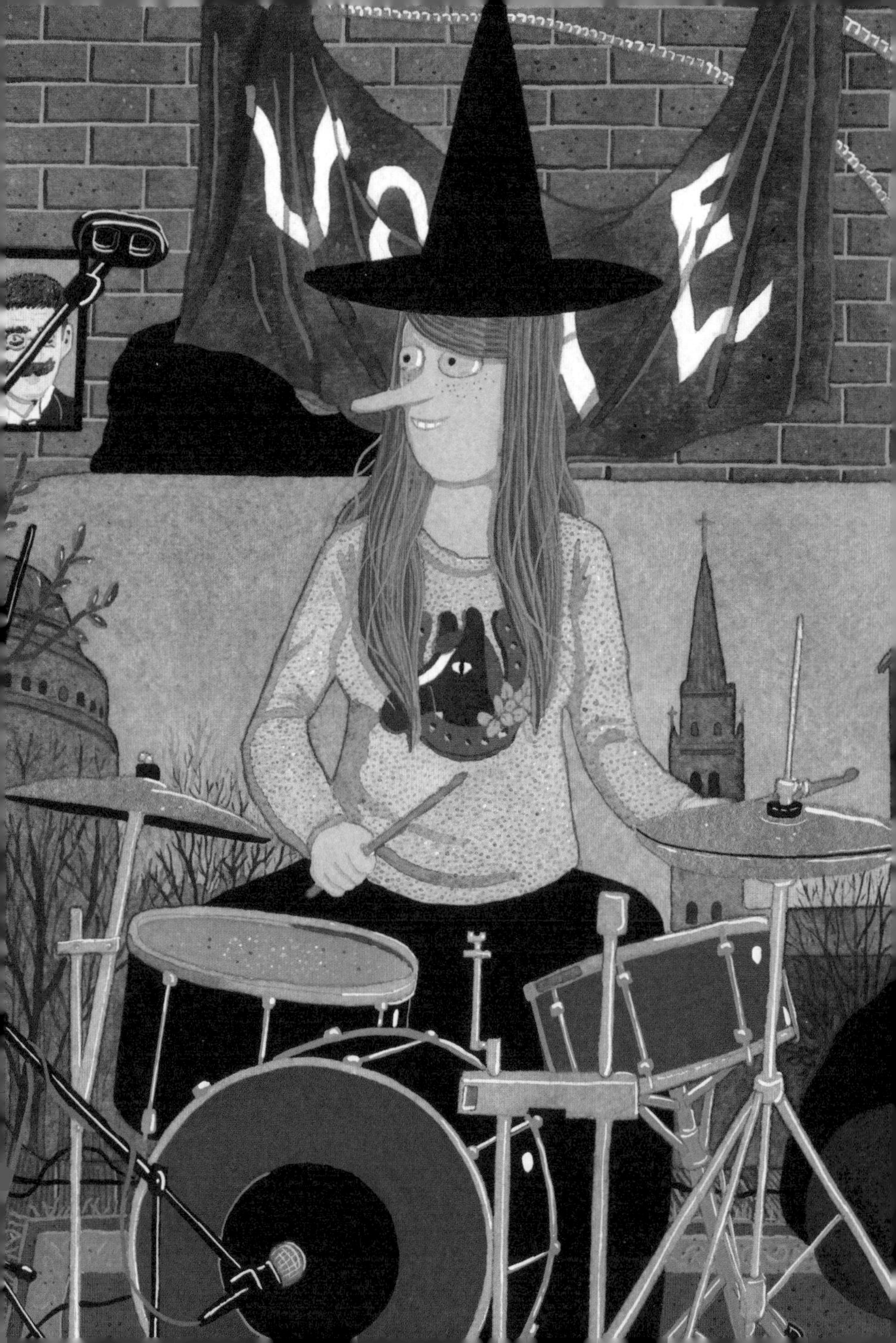

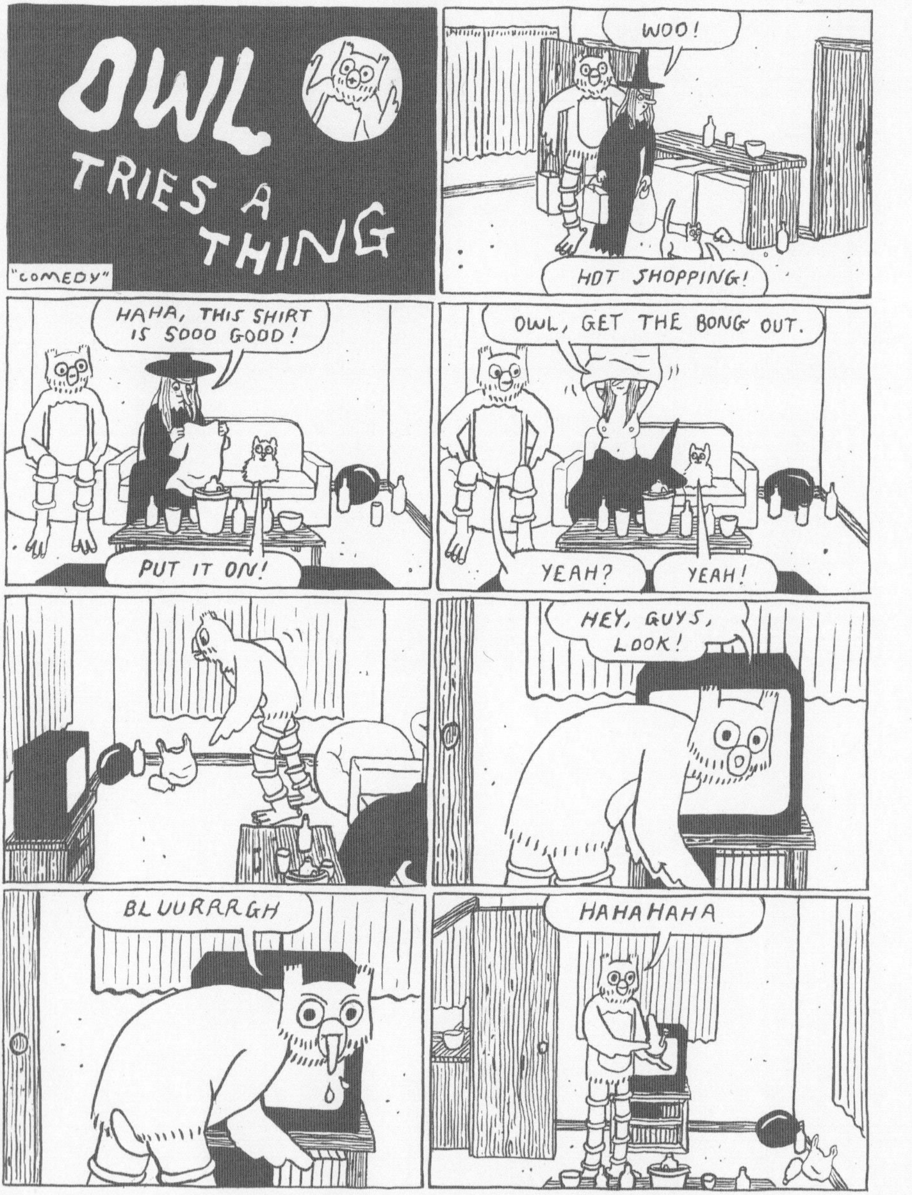
OWL TRIES A THING
"COMEDY"
WOO!
HOT SHOPPING!
HAHA, THIS SHIRT IS SOOO GOOD!
PUT IT ON!
OWL, GET THE BONG OUT.
YEAH?
YEAH!
HEY, GUYS, LOOK!
BLUURRRGH
HAHAHAHA

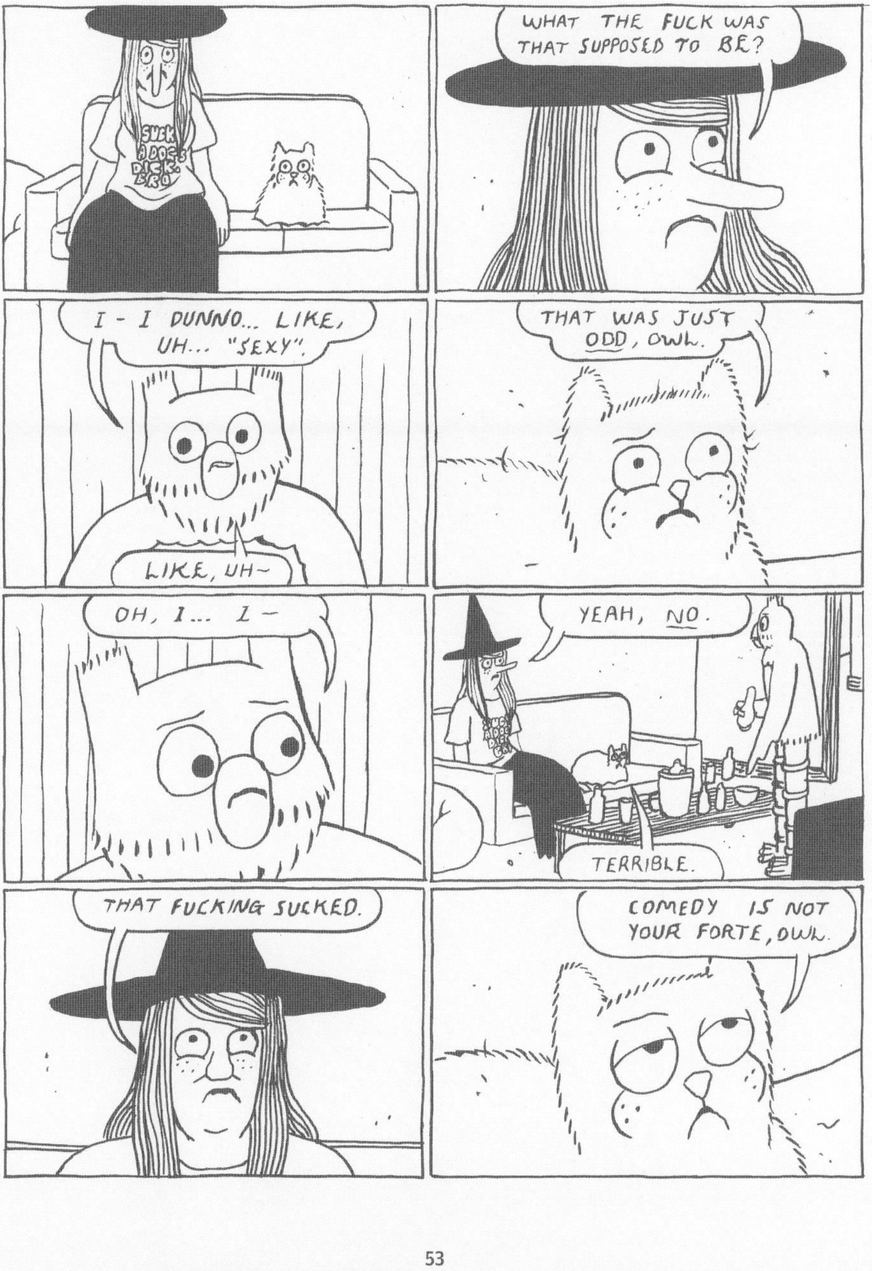
WHAT THE FUCK WAS THAT SUPPOSED TO BE?
I - I DUNNO... LIKE, UH... "SEXY".
LIKE, UH~
THAT WAS JUST ODD, OWL.
OH, I... I~
YEAH, NO.
TERRIBLE.
THAT FUCKING SUCKED.
COMEDY IS NOT YOUR FORTE, OWL.

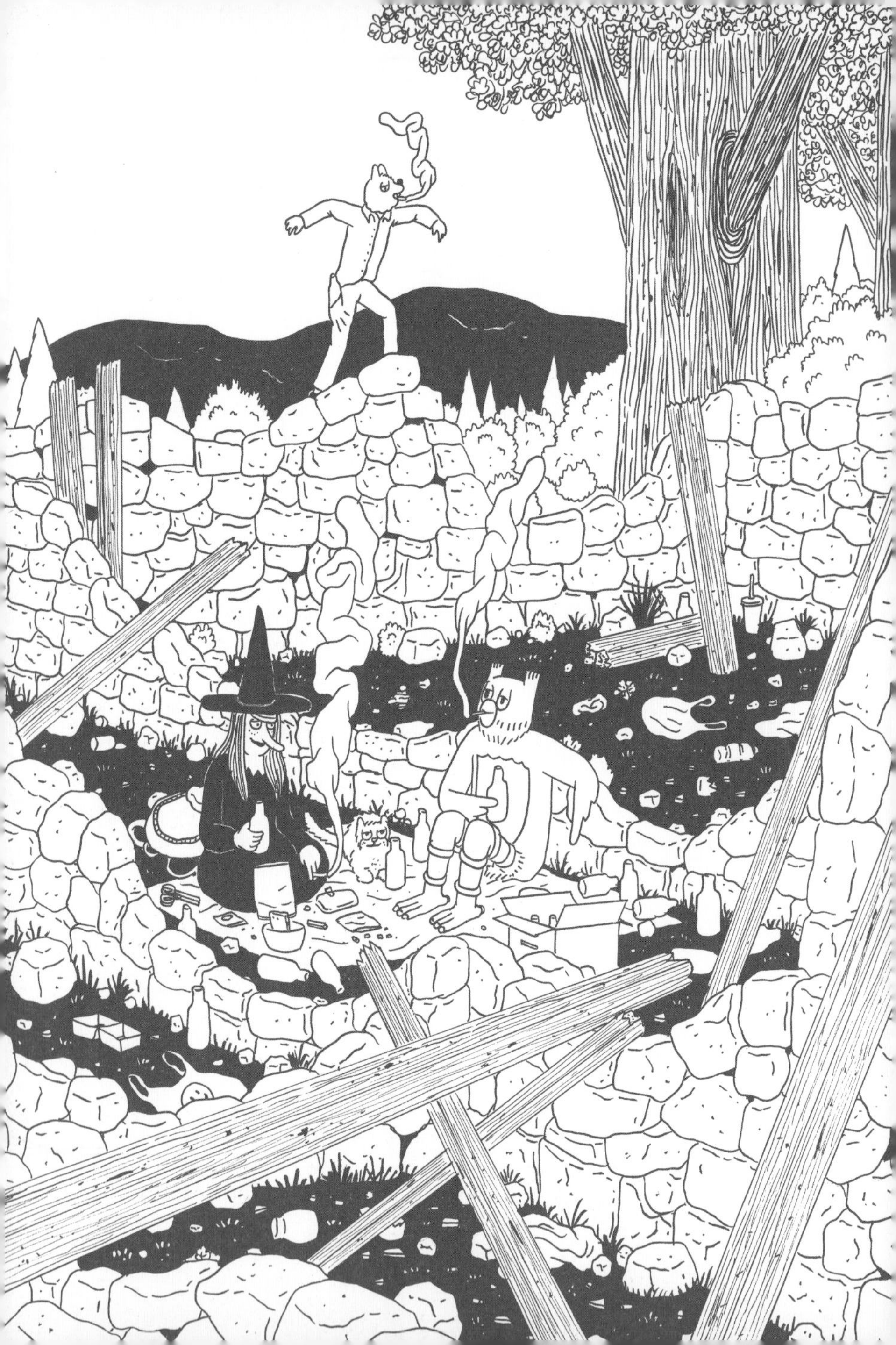

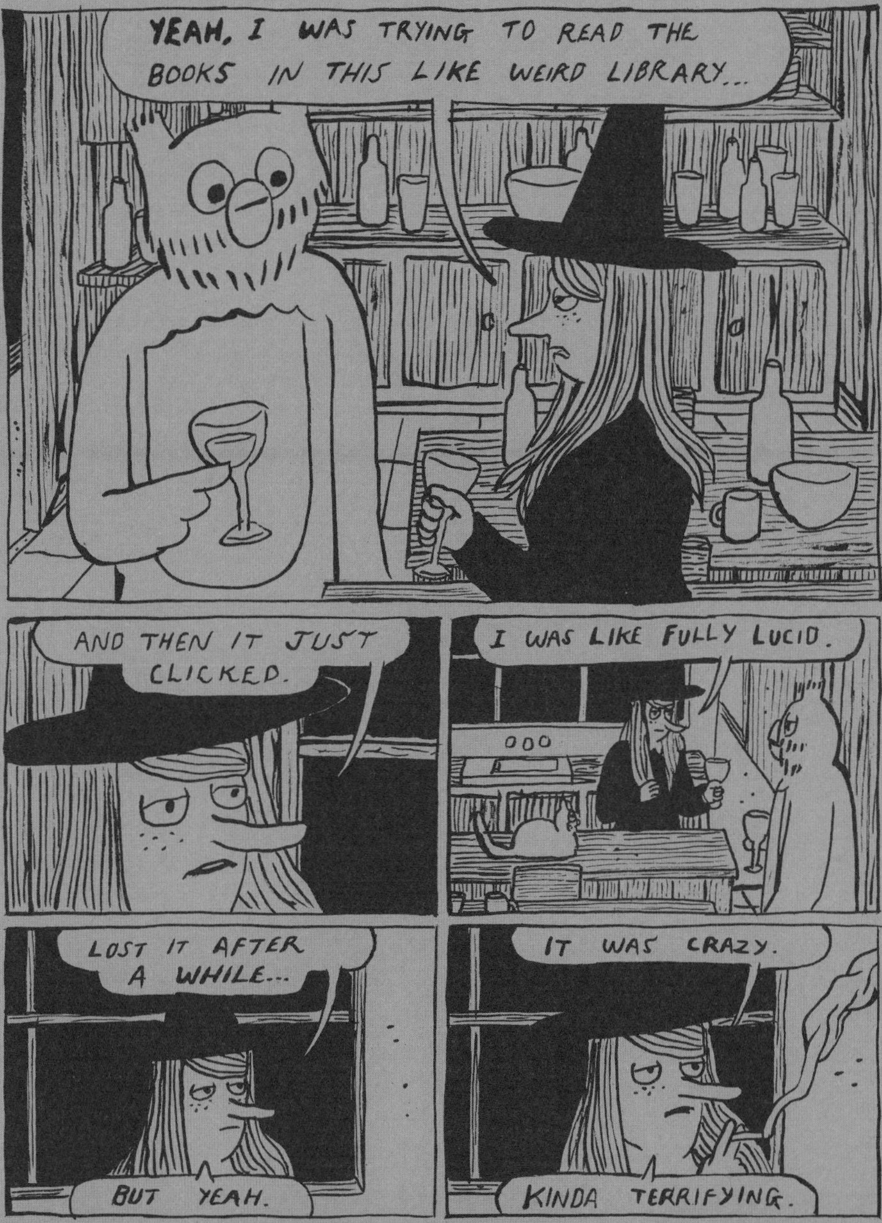
YEAH, I WAS TRYING TO READ THE BOOKS IN THIS LIKE WEIRD LIBRARY...
AND THEN IT JUST CLICKED.
I WAS LIKE FULLY LUCID.
LOST IT AFTER A WHILE...
BUT YEAH.
IT WAS CRAZY.
KINDA TERRIFYING.

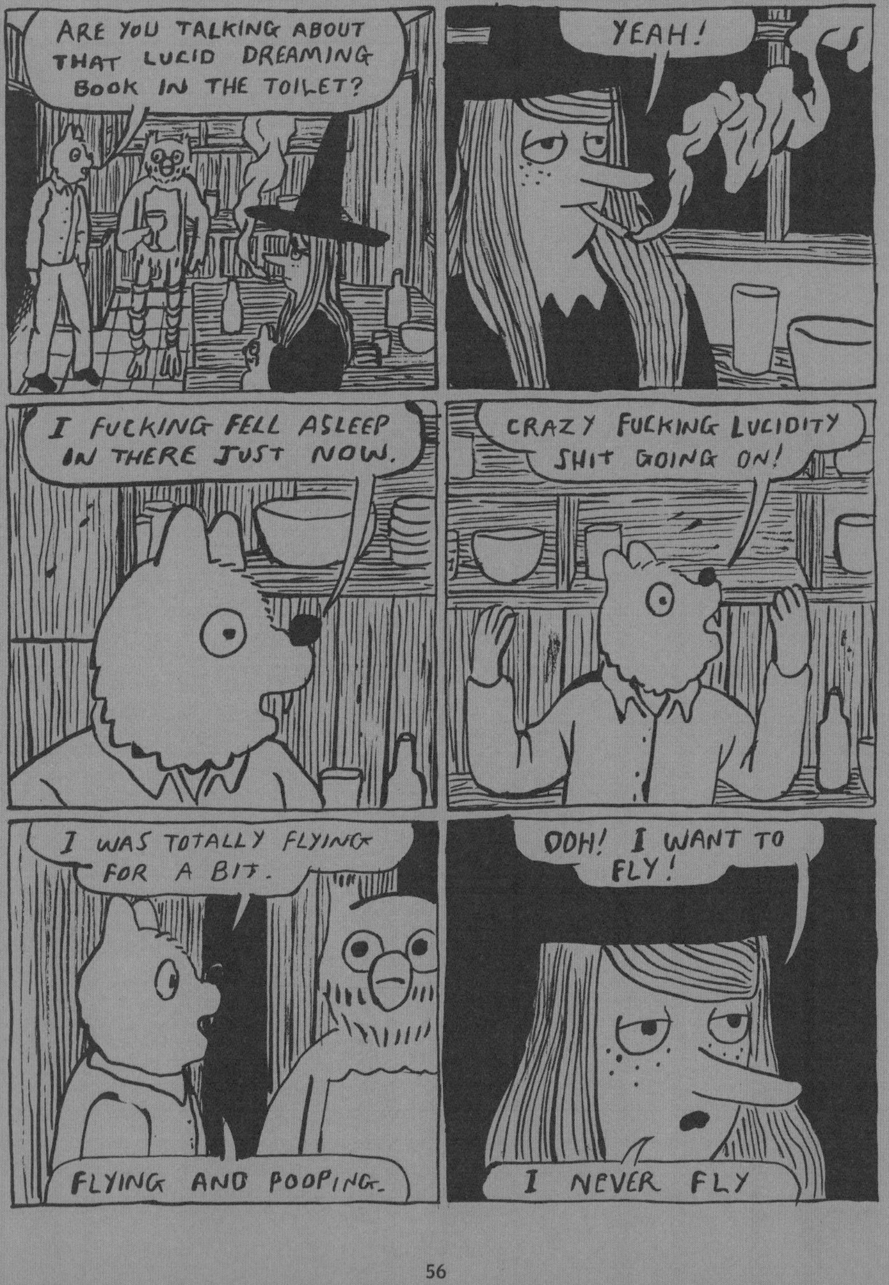
ARE YOU TALKING ABOUT THAT LUCID DREAMING BOOK IN THE TOILET?
YEAH!
I FUCKING FELL ASLEEP IN THERE JUST NOW.
CRAZY FUCKING LUCIDITY SHIT GOING ON!
I WAS TOTALLY FLYING FOR A BIT.
FLYING AND POOPING.
OOH! I WANT TO FLY!
I NEVER FLY

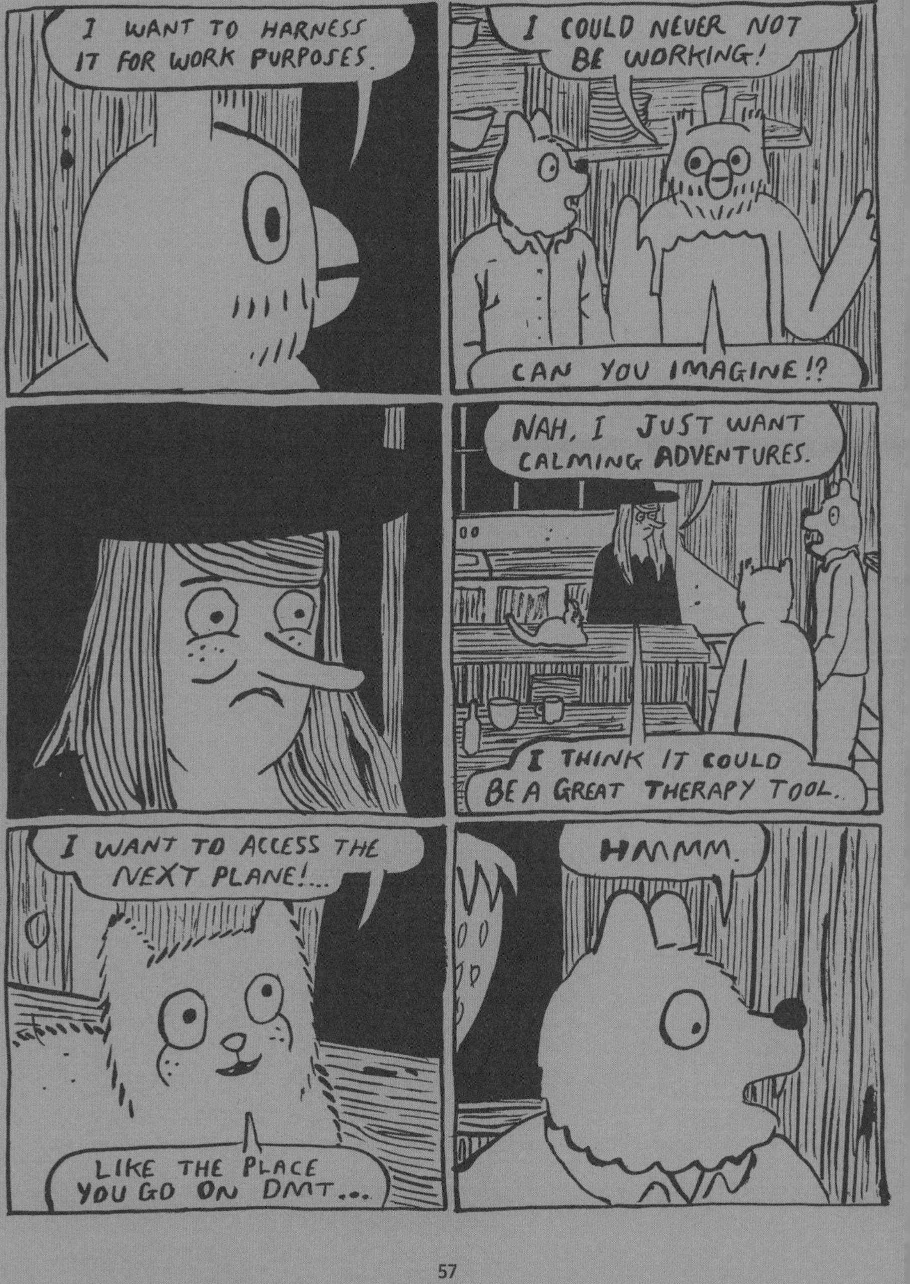
I WANT TO HARNESS IT FOR WORK PURPOSES.
I COULD NEVER NOT BE WORKING!
CAN YOU IMAGINE!?
NAH, I JUST WANT CALMING ADVENTURES.
I THINK IT COULD BE A GREAT THERAPY TOOL.
I WANT TO ACCESS THE NEXT PLANE!...
LIKE THE PLACE YOU GO ON DMT...
HMMM.

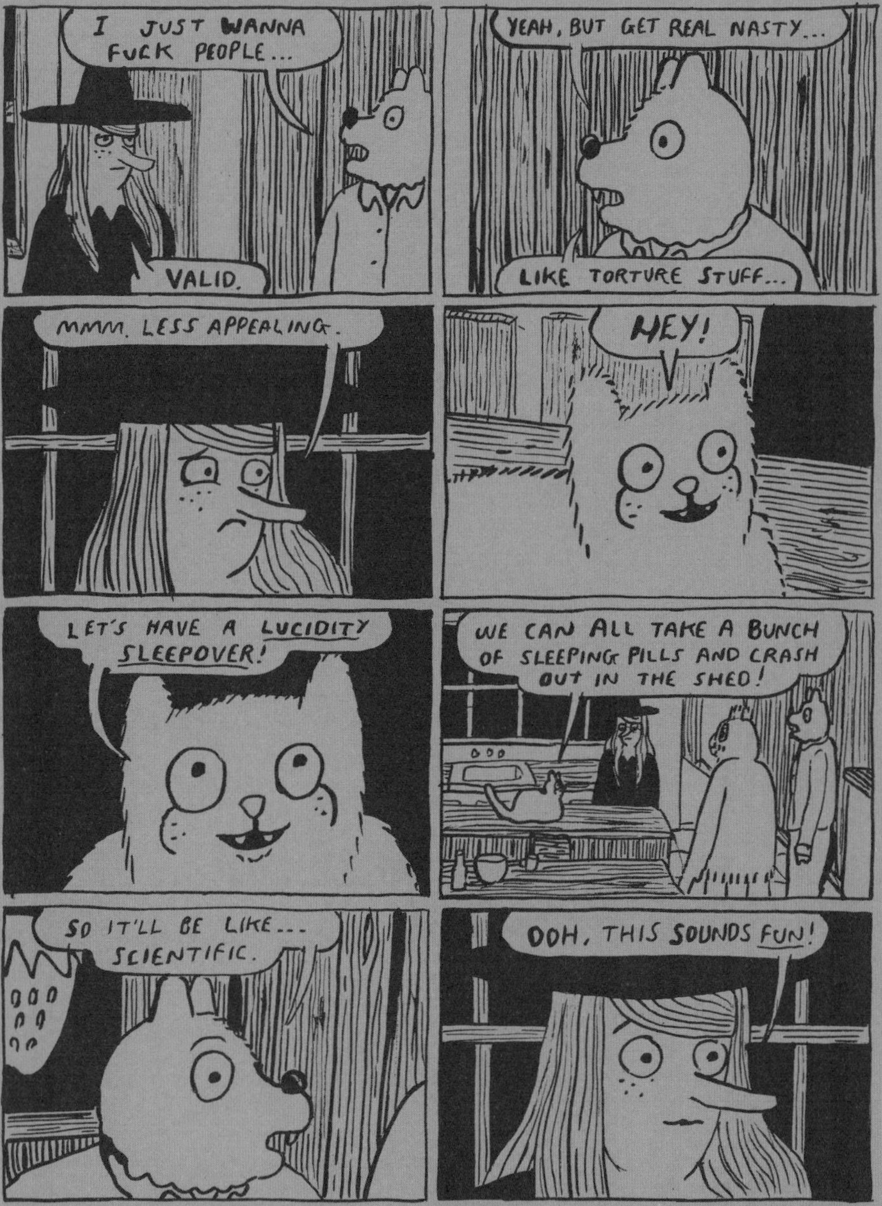
I JUST WANNA FUCK PEOPLE...
VALID.
YEAH, BUT GET REAL NASTY...
LIKE TORTURE STUFF...
MMM. LESS APPEALING.
HEY!
LET'S HAVE A LUCIDITY SLEEPOVER!
WE CAN ALL TAKE A BUNCH OF SLEEPING PILLS AND CRASH OUT IN THE SHED!
SO IT'LL BE LIKE... SCIENTIFIC.
OOH, THIS SOUNDS FUN!

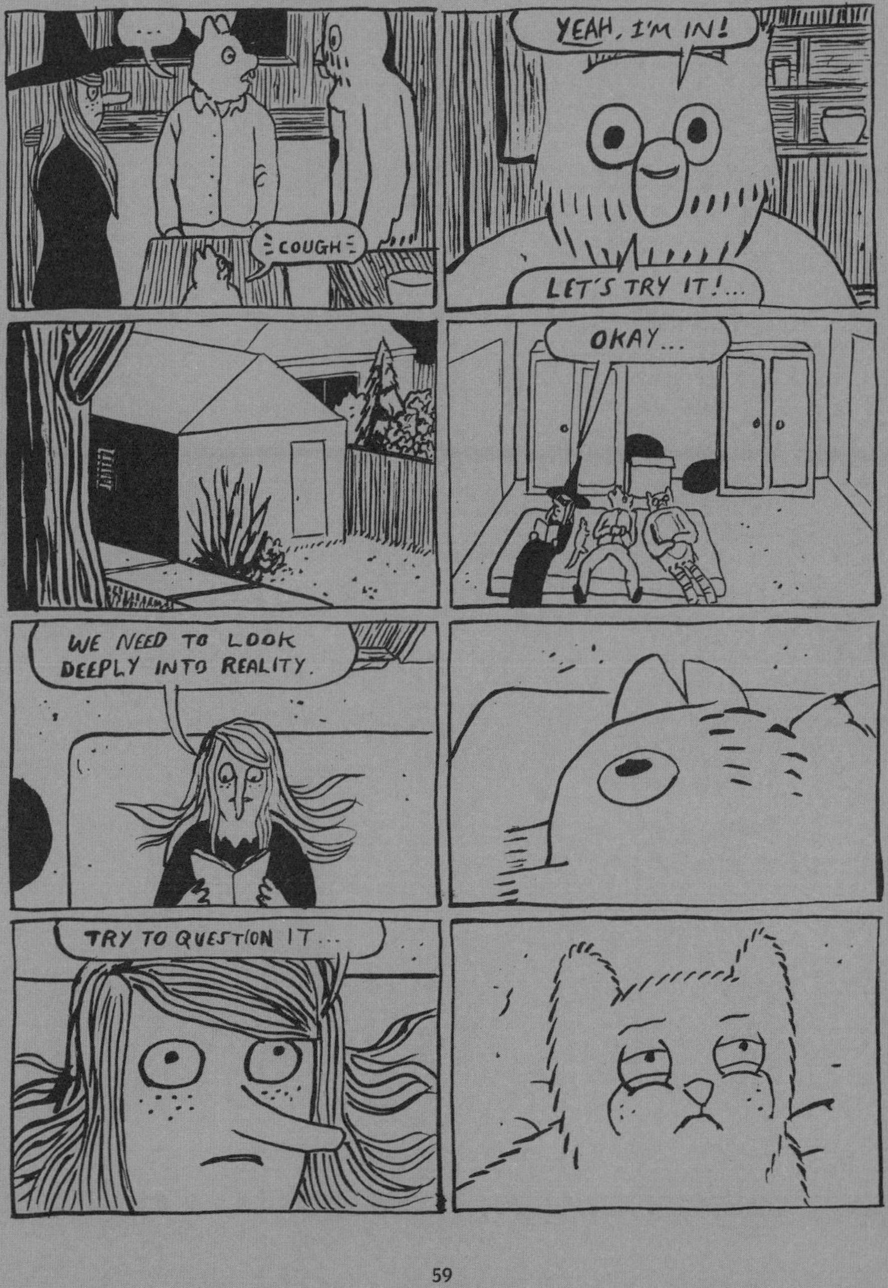
...
COUGH
YEAH, I'M IN!
LET'S TRY IT!...
OKAY...
WE NEED TO LOOK DEEPLY INTO REALITY.
TRY TO QUESTION IT...

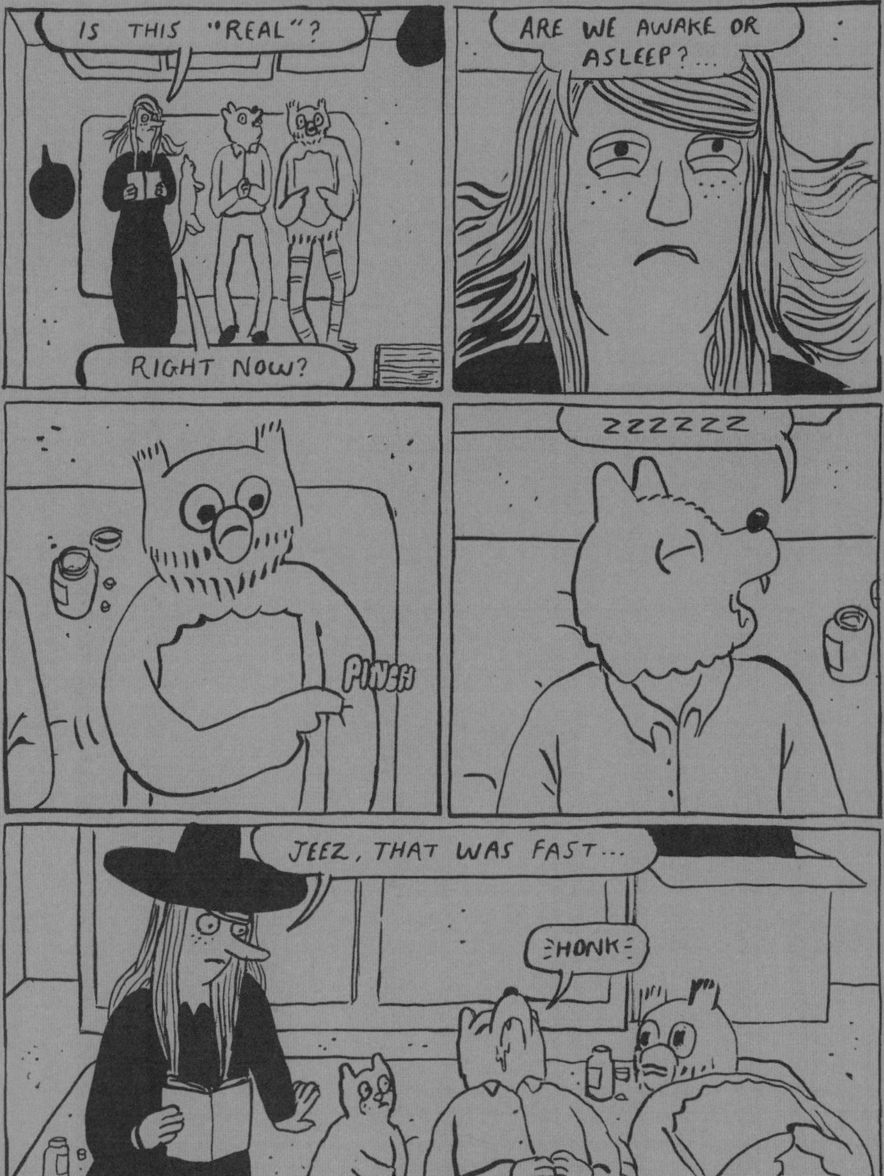

IS THIS "REAL"?
RIGHT NOW?
ARE WE AWAKE OR ASLEEP?...
PINCH
ZZZZZZ
JEEZ, THAT WAS FAST...
HONK

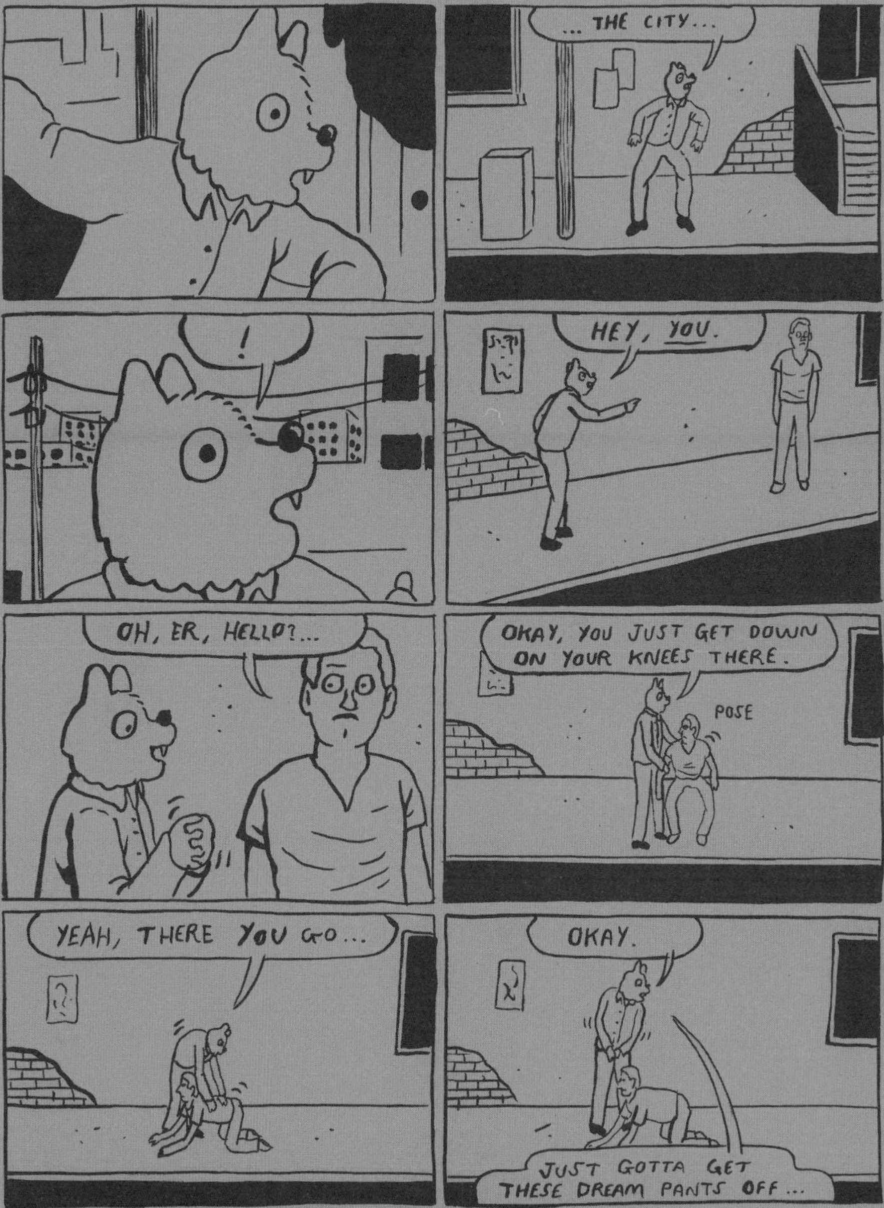
... THE CITY...
!
HEY, YOU.
OH, ER, HELLO?...
OKAY, YOU JUST GET DOWN ON YOUR KNEES THERE.
POSE
YEAH, THERE YOU GO...
OKAY.
JUST GOTTA GET THESE DREAM PANTS OFF...

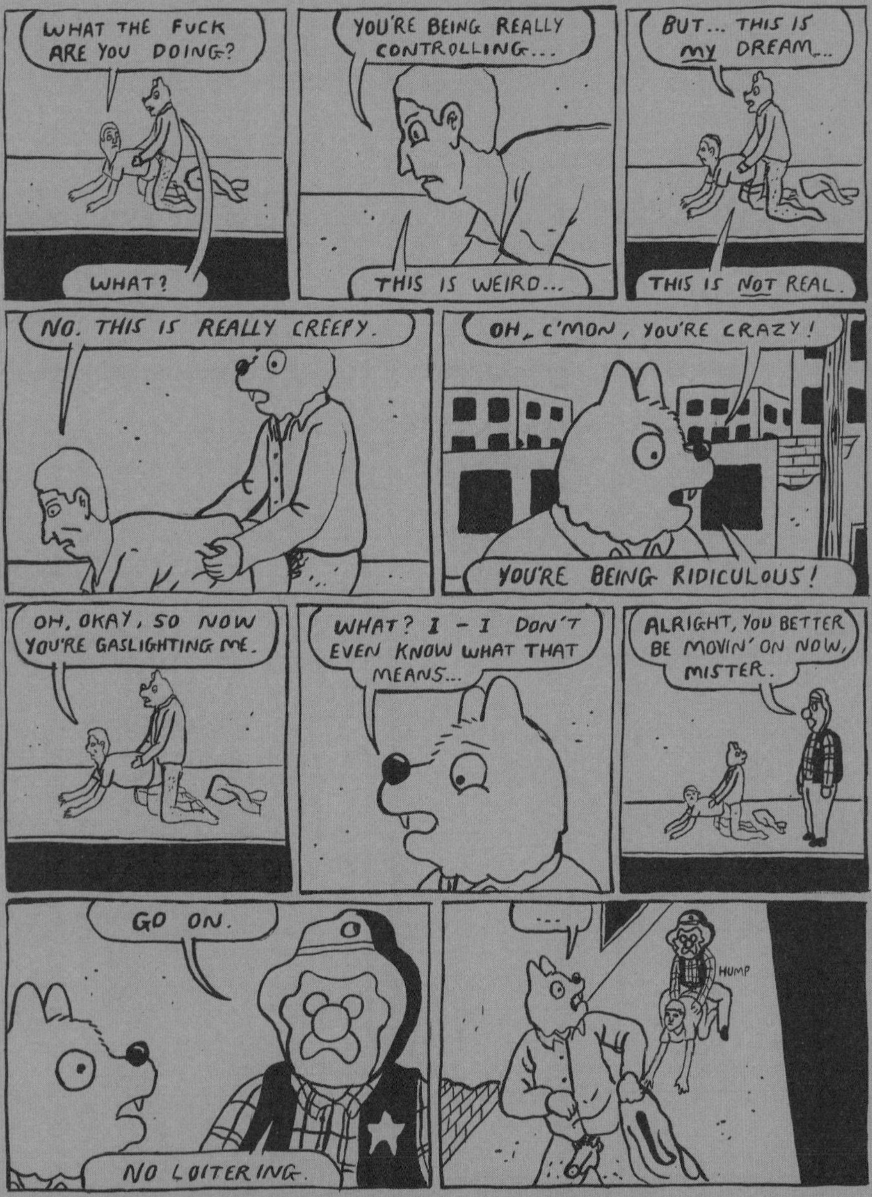
WHAT THE FUCK ARE YOU DOING?
WHAT?
YOU'RE BEING REALLY CONTROLLING...
THIS IS WEIRD...
BUT... THIS IS MY DREAM...
THIS IS NOT REAL.
NO. THIS IS REALLY CREEPY.
OH, C'MON, YOU'RE CRAZY!
YOU'RE BEING RIDICULOUS!
OH, OKAY, SO NOW YOU'RE GASLIGHTING ME.
WHAT? I - I DON'T EVEN KNOW WHAT THAT MEANS...
ALRIGHT, YOU BETTER BE MOVIN' ON NOW, MISTER.
GO ON.
NO LOITERING.
...
HUMP

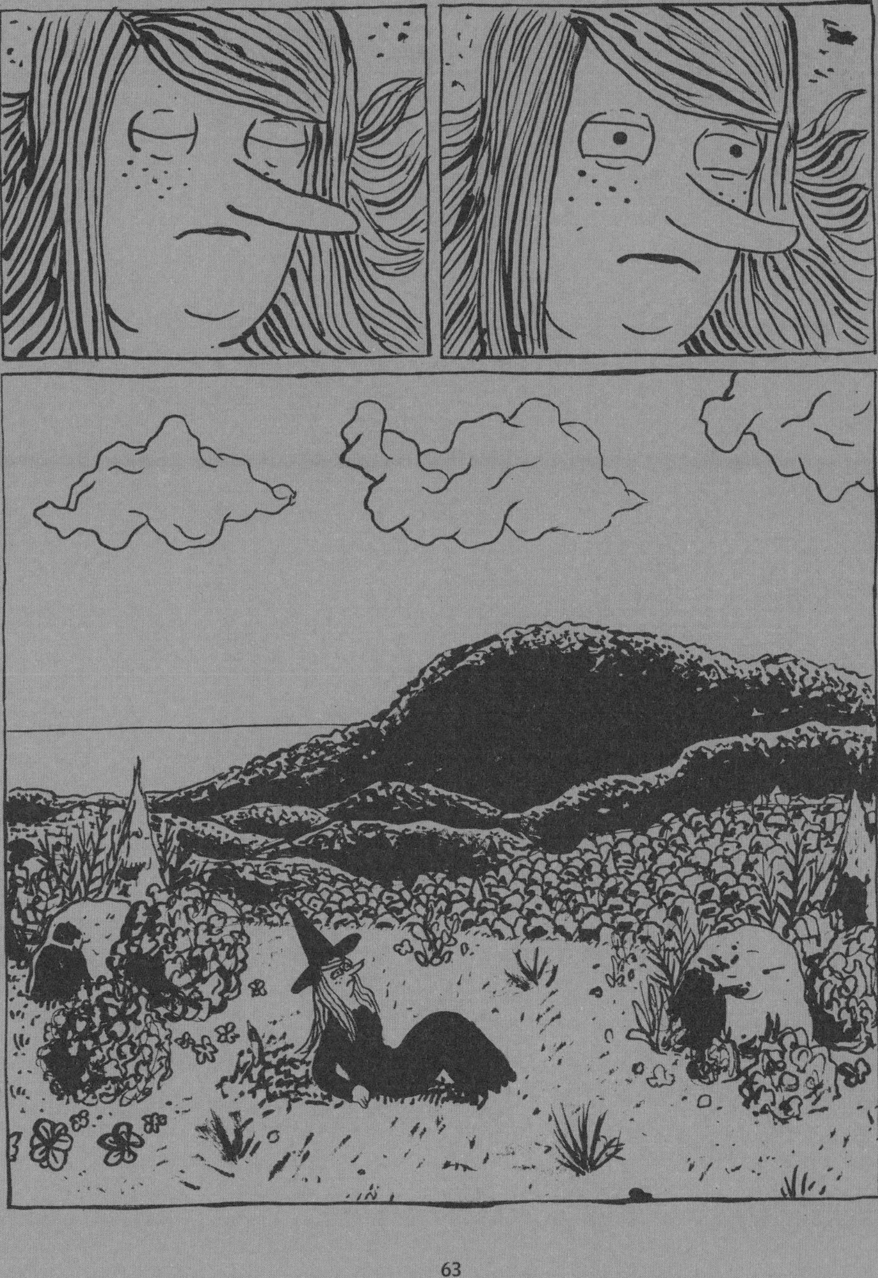

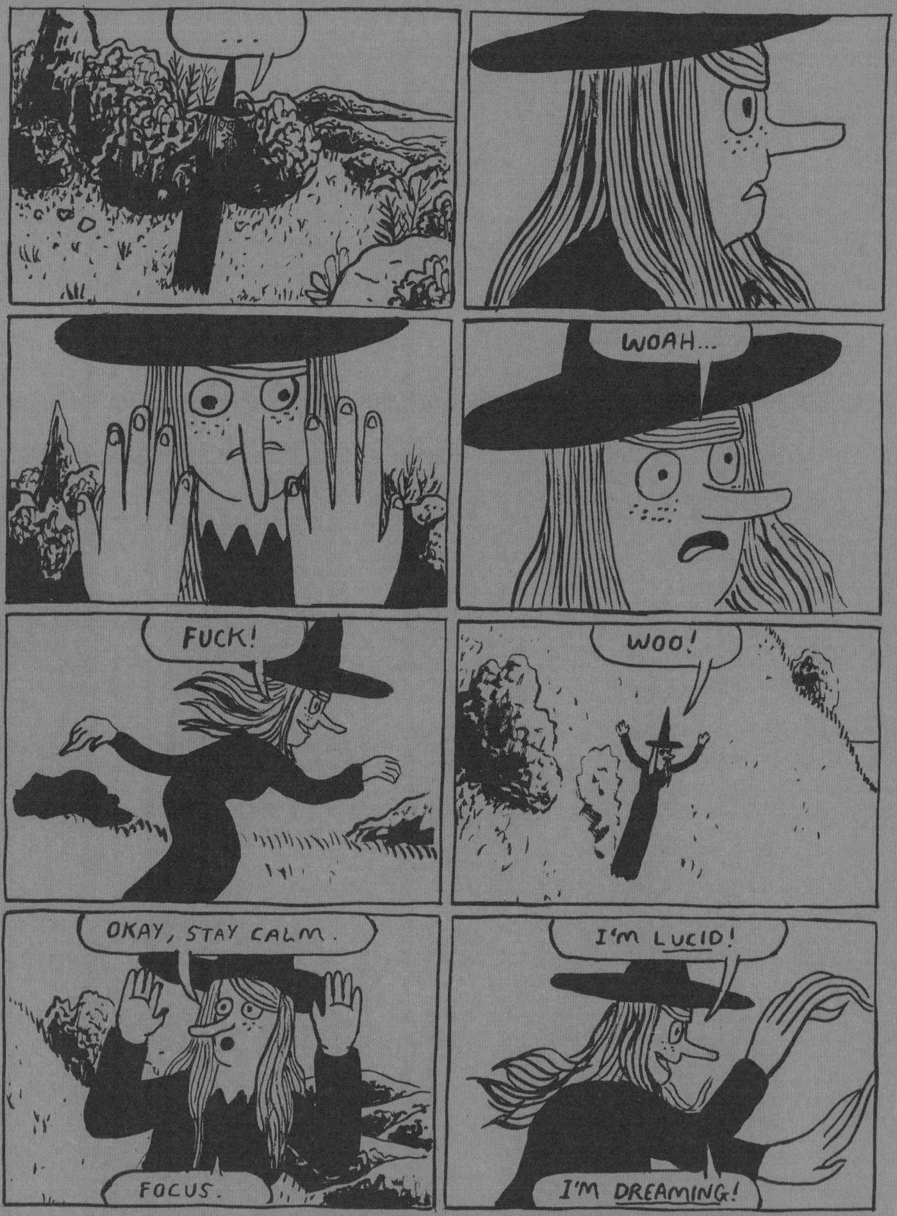
...
WOAH...
FUCK!
WOO!
OKAY, STAY CALM.
FOCUS.
I'M LUCID!
I'M DREAMING!

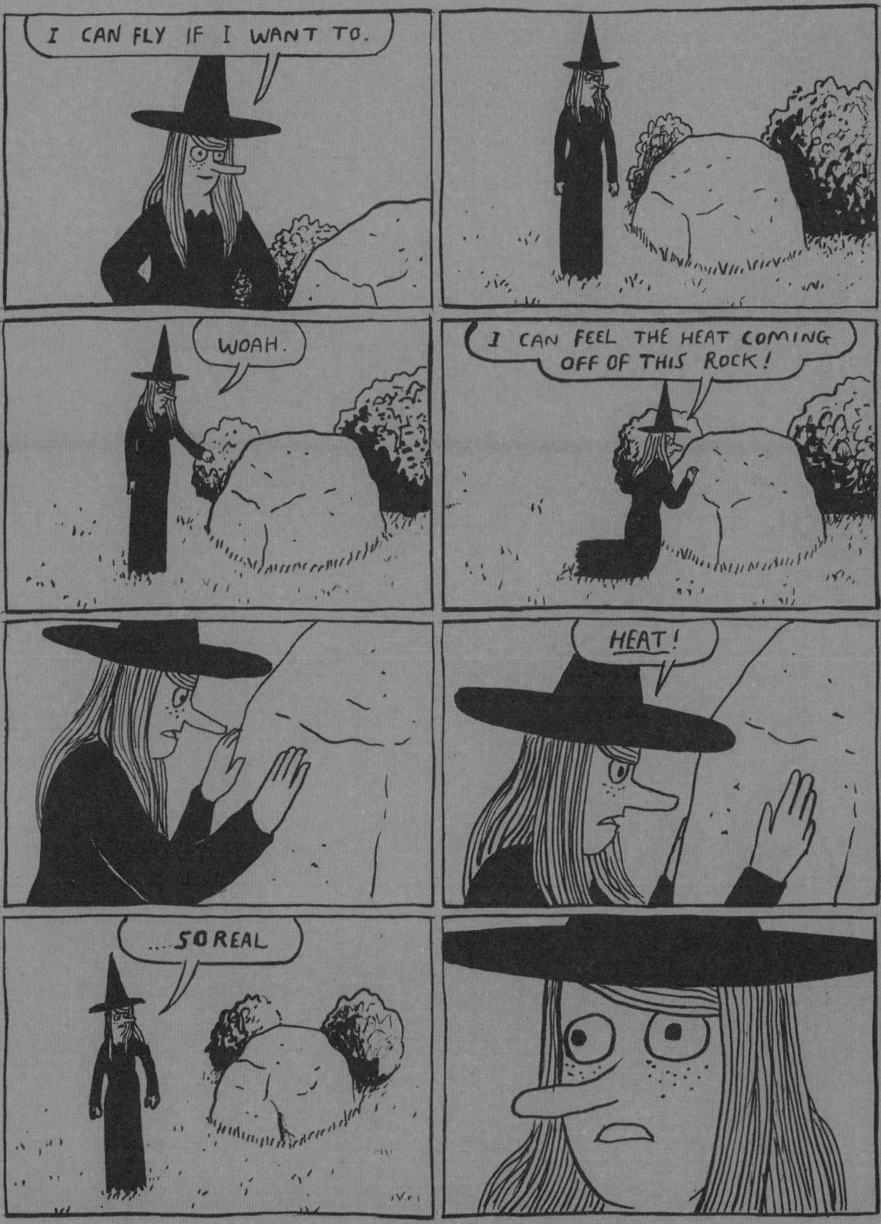
I CAN FLY IF I WANT TO.
WOAH.
I CAN FEEL THE HEAT COMING OFF OF THIS ROCK!
HEAT!
....SO REAL

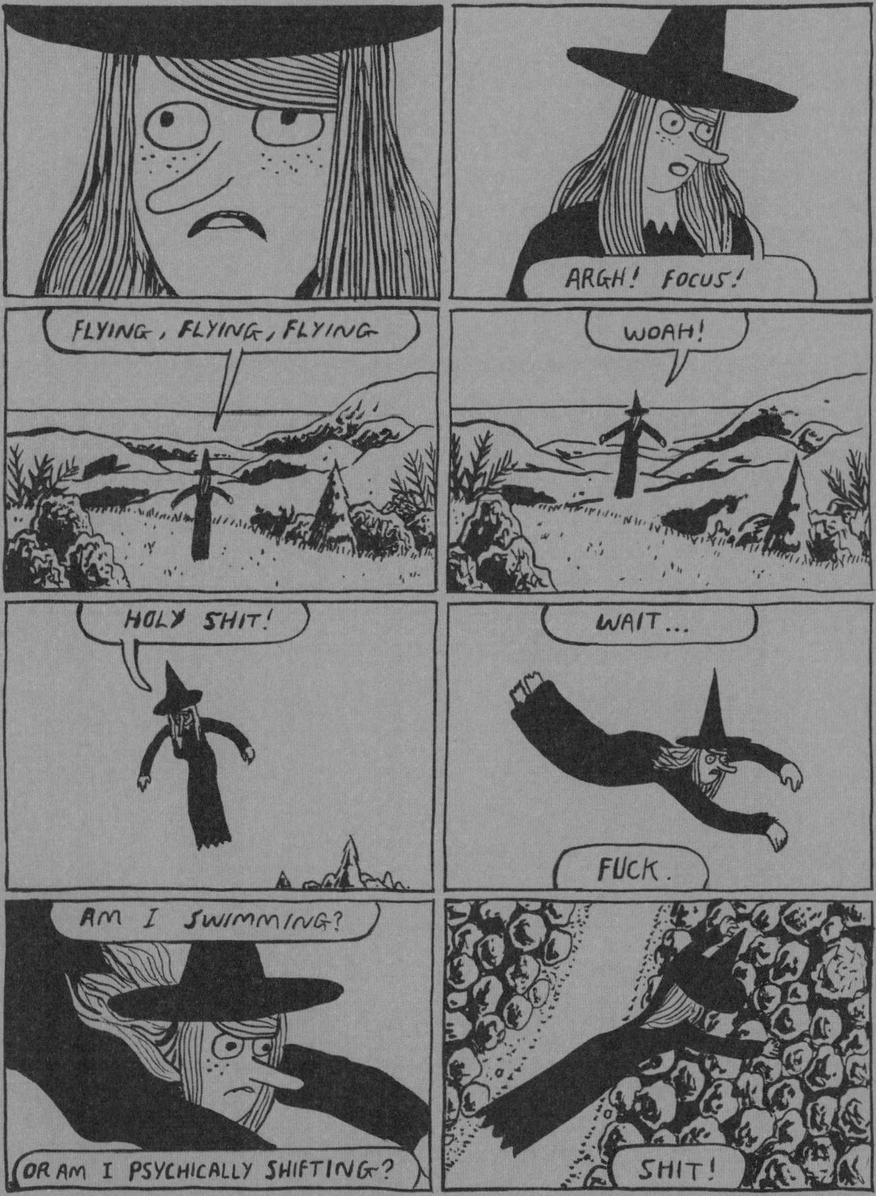
ARGH! FOCUS!
FLYING, FLYING, FLYING
WOAH!
HOLY SHIT!
WAIT...
FUCK.
AM I SWIMMING?
OR AM I PSYCHICALLY SHIFTING?
SHIT!

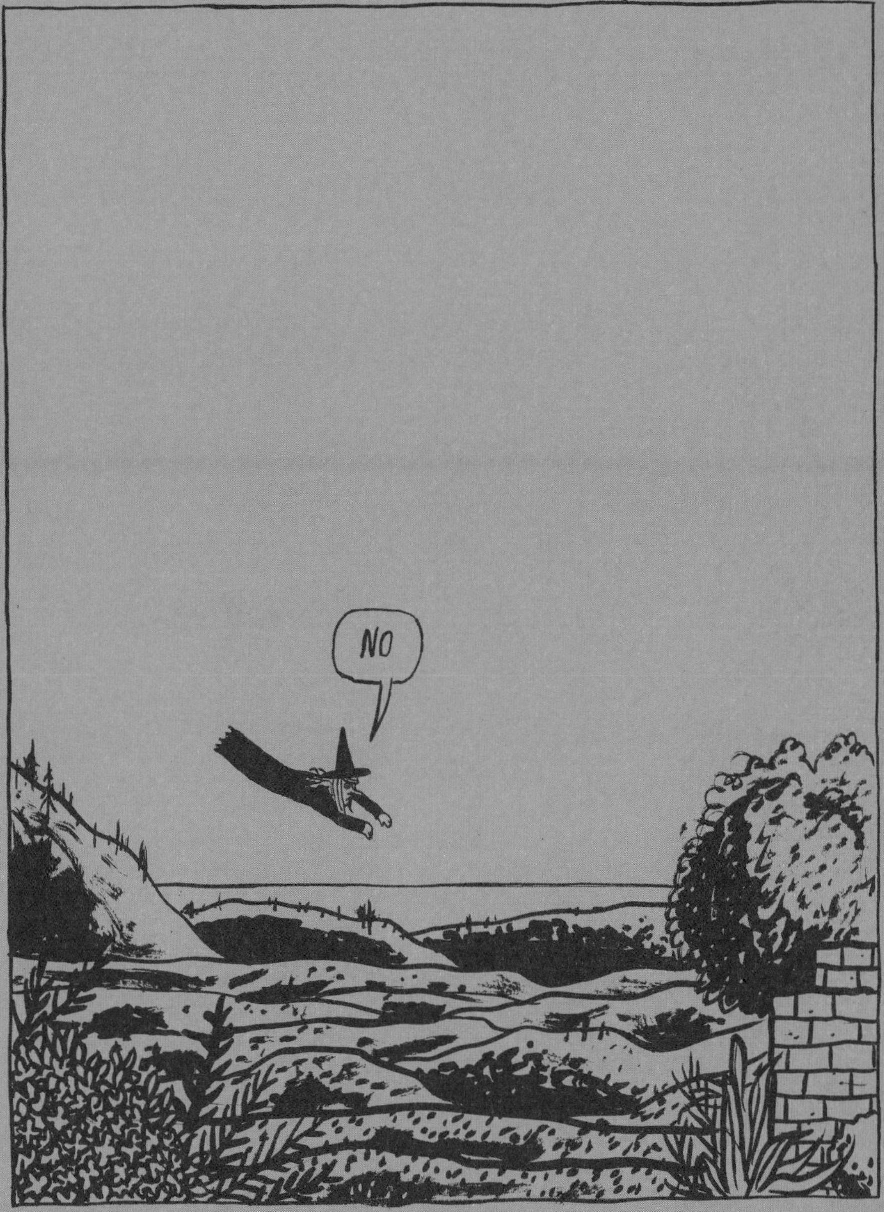
NO

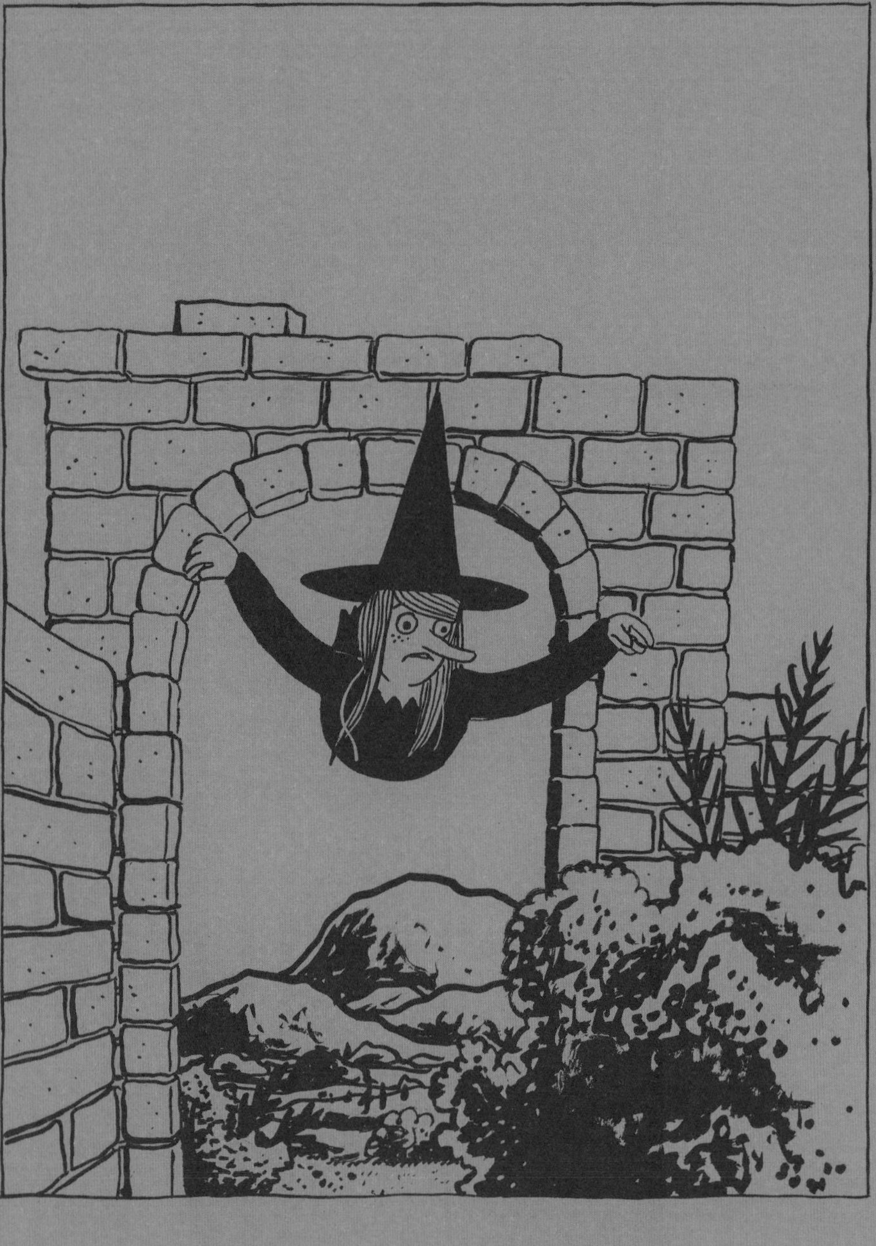

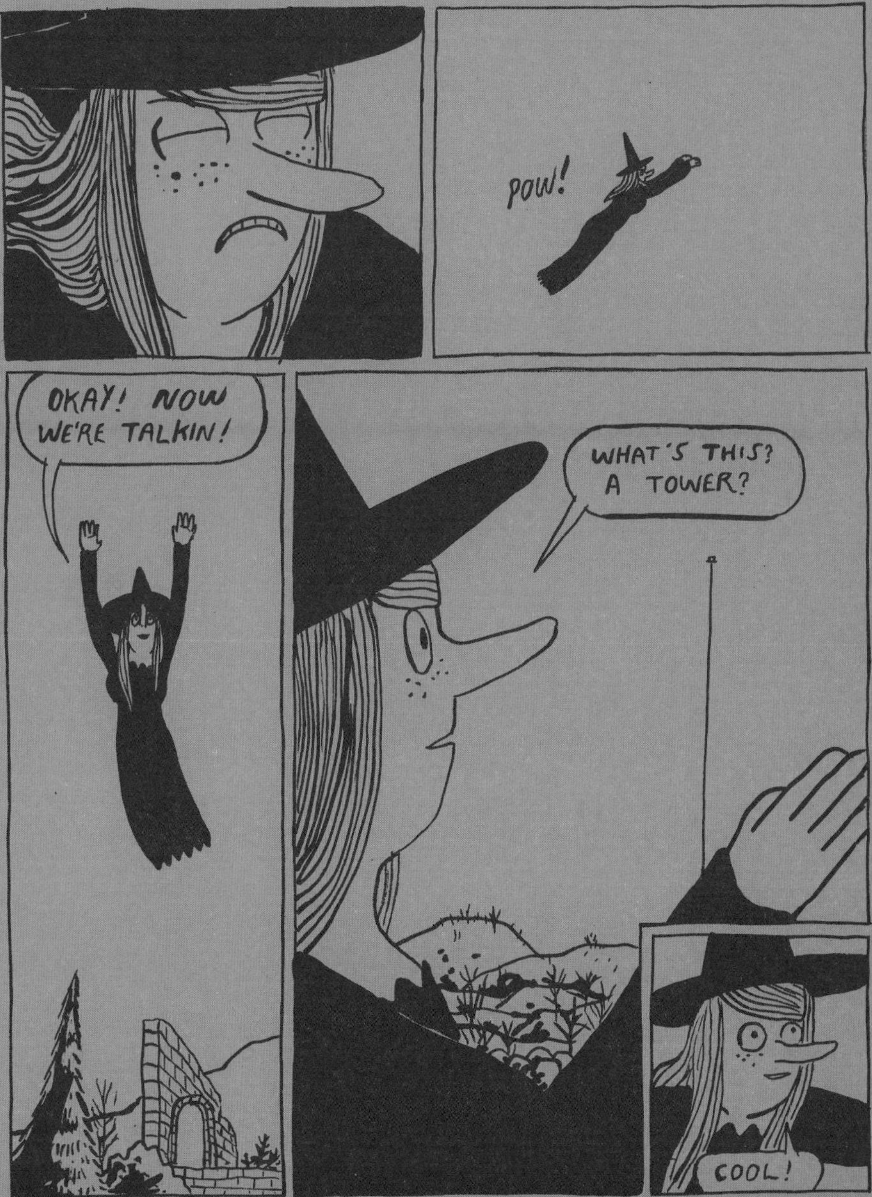
POW!
OKAY! NOW WE'RE TALKIN!
WHAT'S THIS? A TOWER?
COOL!

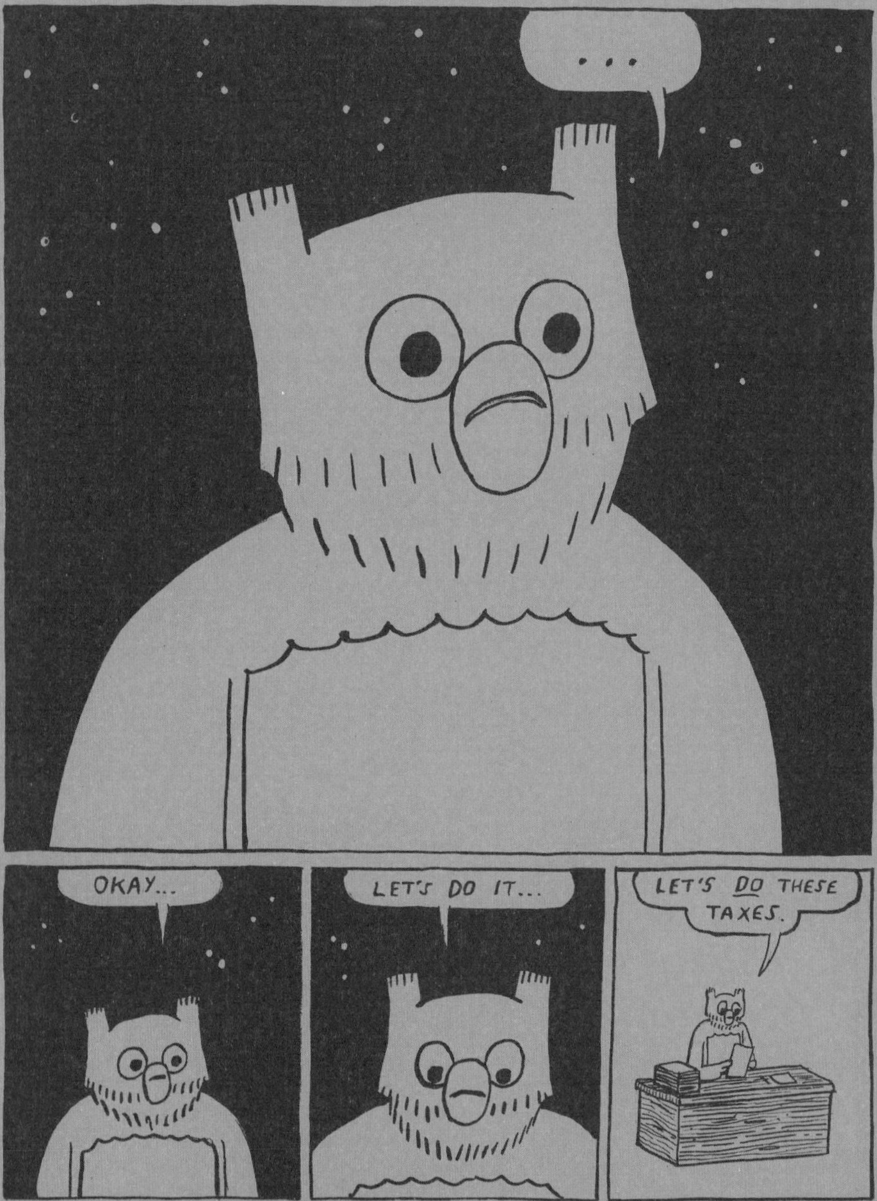
...
OKAY...
LET'S DO IT...
LET'S DO THESE TAXES.

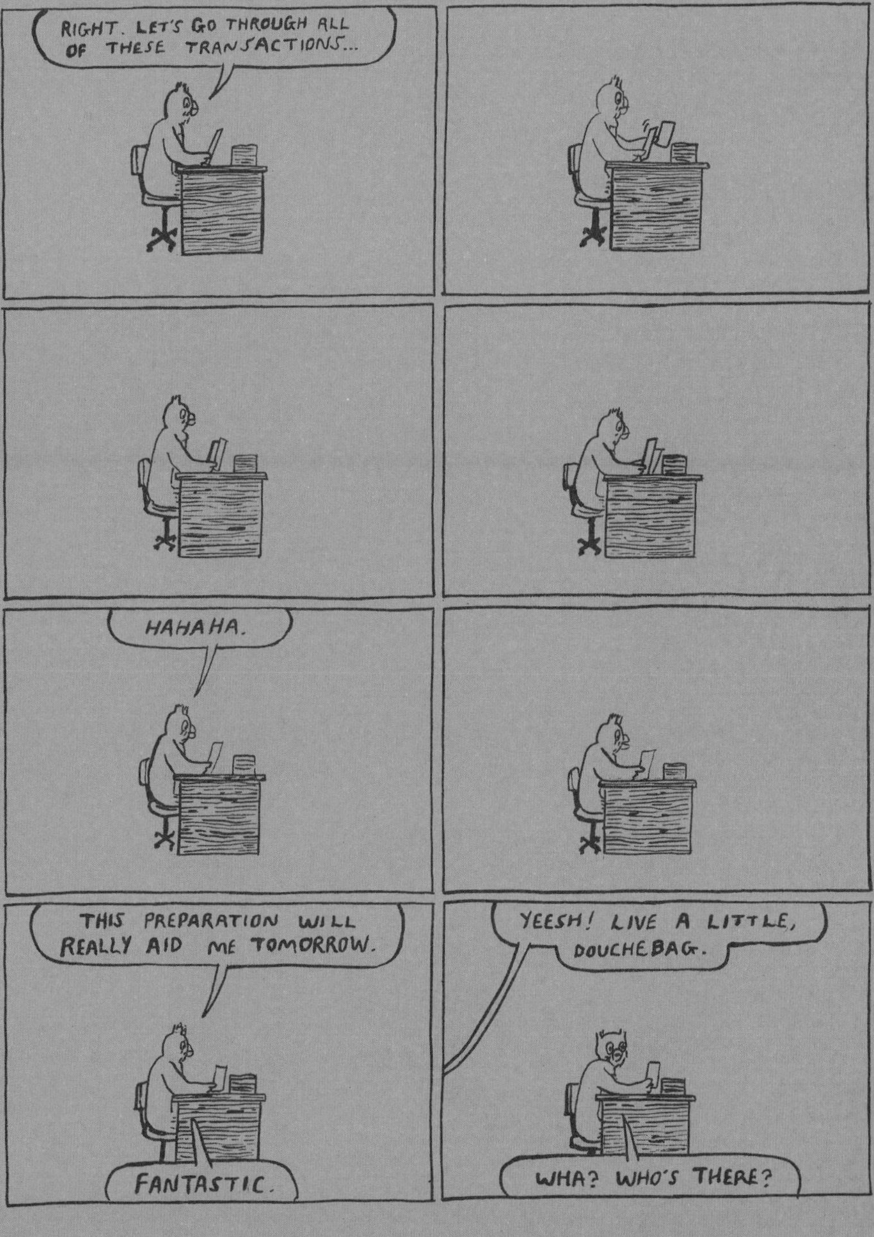
RIGHT. LET'S GO THROUGH ALL OF THESE TRANSACTIONS...
HAHAHA.
THIS PREPARATION WILL REALLY AID ME TOMORROW.
FANTASTIC.
YEESH! LIVE A LITTLE, DOUCHEBAG.
WHA? WHO'S THERE?

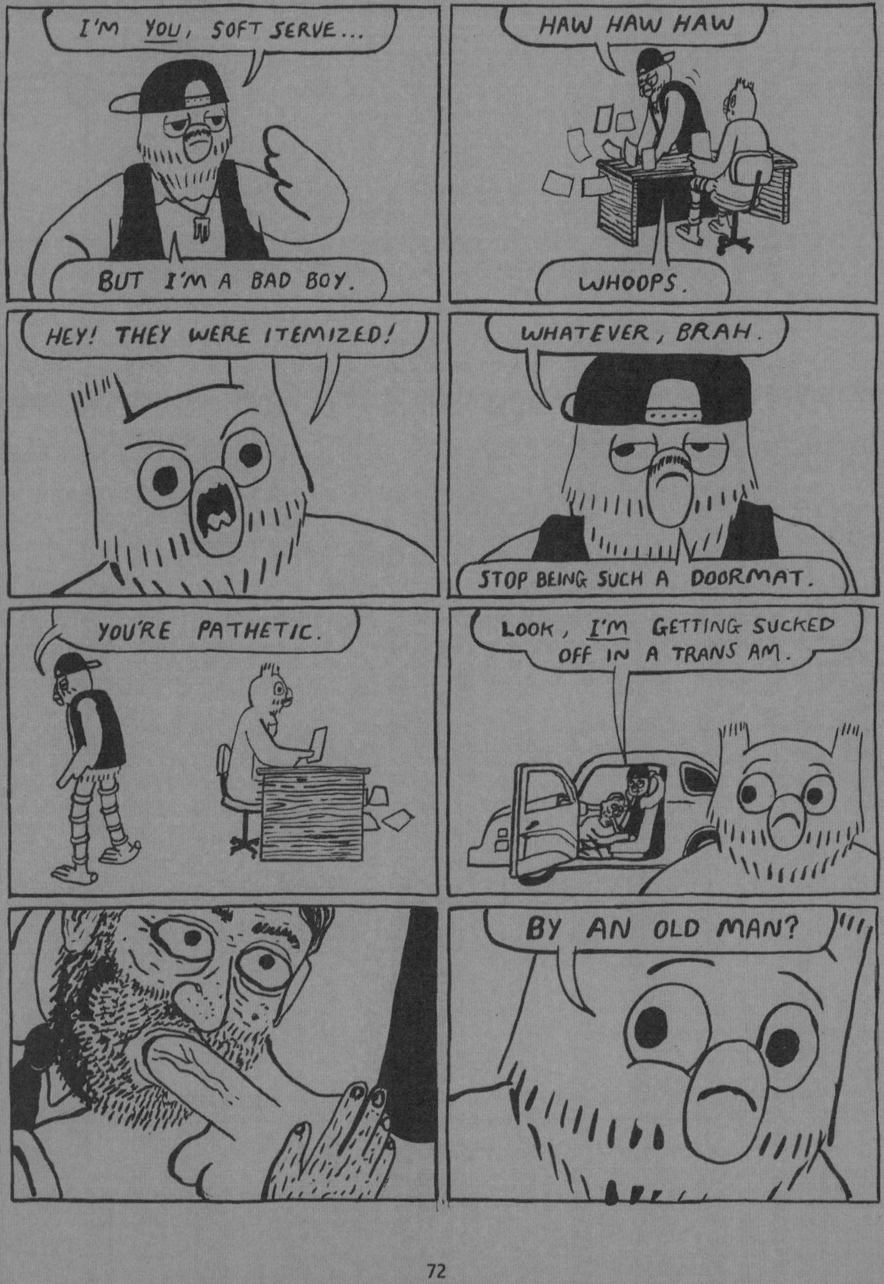
I'M YOU, SOFT SERVE...
BUT I'M A BAD BOY.
HAW HAW HAW
WHOOPS.
HEY! THEY WERE ITEMIZED!
WHATEVER, BRAH.
STOP BEING SUCH A DOORMAT.
YOU'RE PATHETIC.
LOOK, I'M GETTING SUCKED OFF IN A TRANS AM.
BY AN OLD MAN?

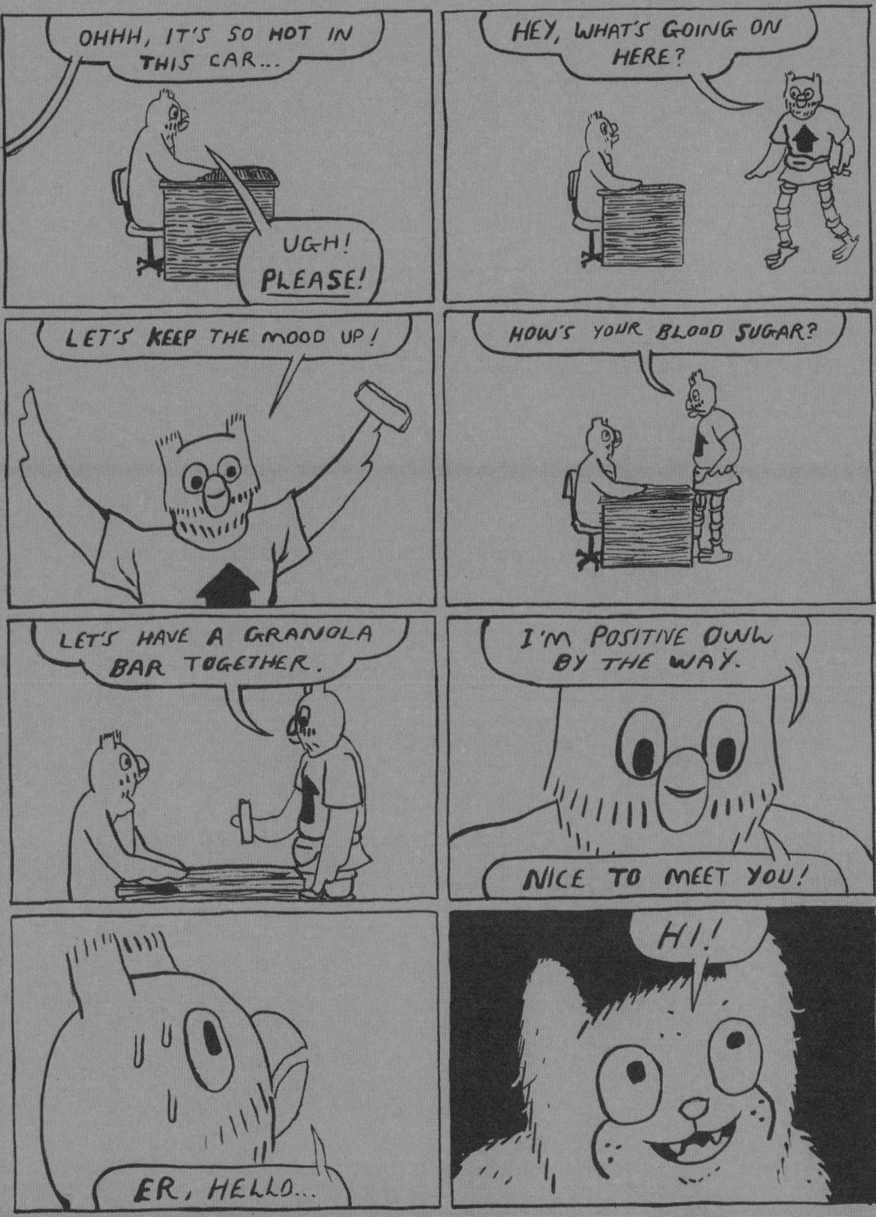
OHHH, IT'S SO HOT IN THIS CAR...
UGH! PLEASE!
HEY, WHAT'S GOING ON HERE?
LET'S KEEP THE MOOD UP!
HOW'S YOUR BLOOD SUGAR?
LET'S HAVE A GRANOLA BAR TOGETHER.
I'M POSITIVE OWL BY THE WAY.
NICE TO MEET YOU!
ER, HELLO...
HI!

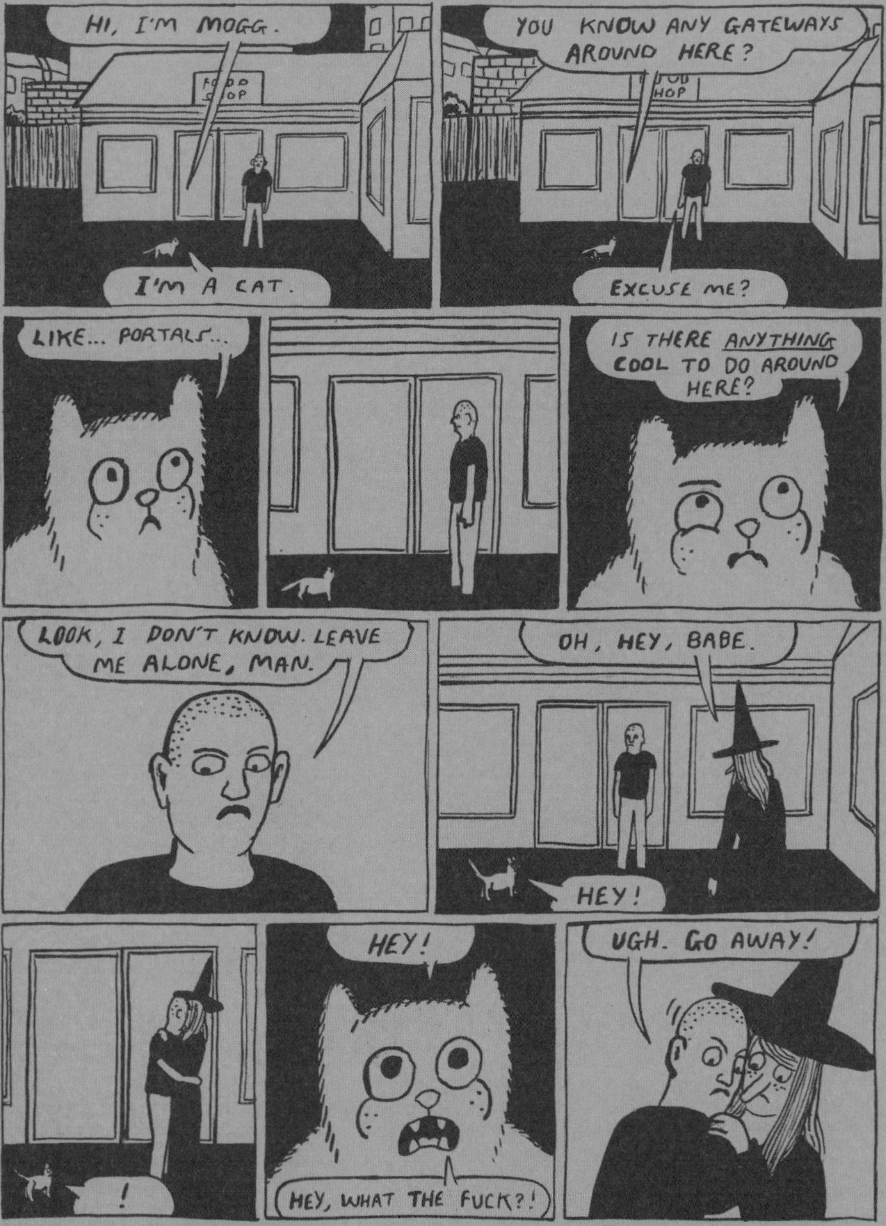
HI, I'M MOGG.
FOOD SHOP
I'M A CAT.
YOU KNOW ANY GATEWAYS AROUND HERE?
EXCUSE ME?
LIKE... PORTALS...
IS THERE ANYTHING COOL TO DO AROUND HERE?
LOOK, I DON'T KNOW. LEAVE ME ALONE, MAN.
OH, HEY, BABE.
HEY!
!
HEY!
HEY, WHAT THE FUCK?!
UGH. GO AWAY!

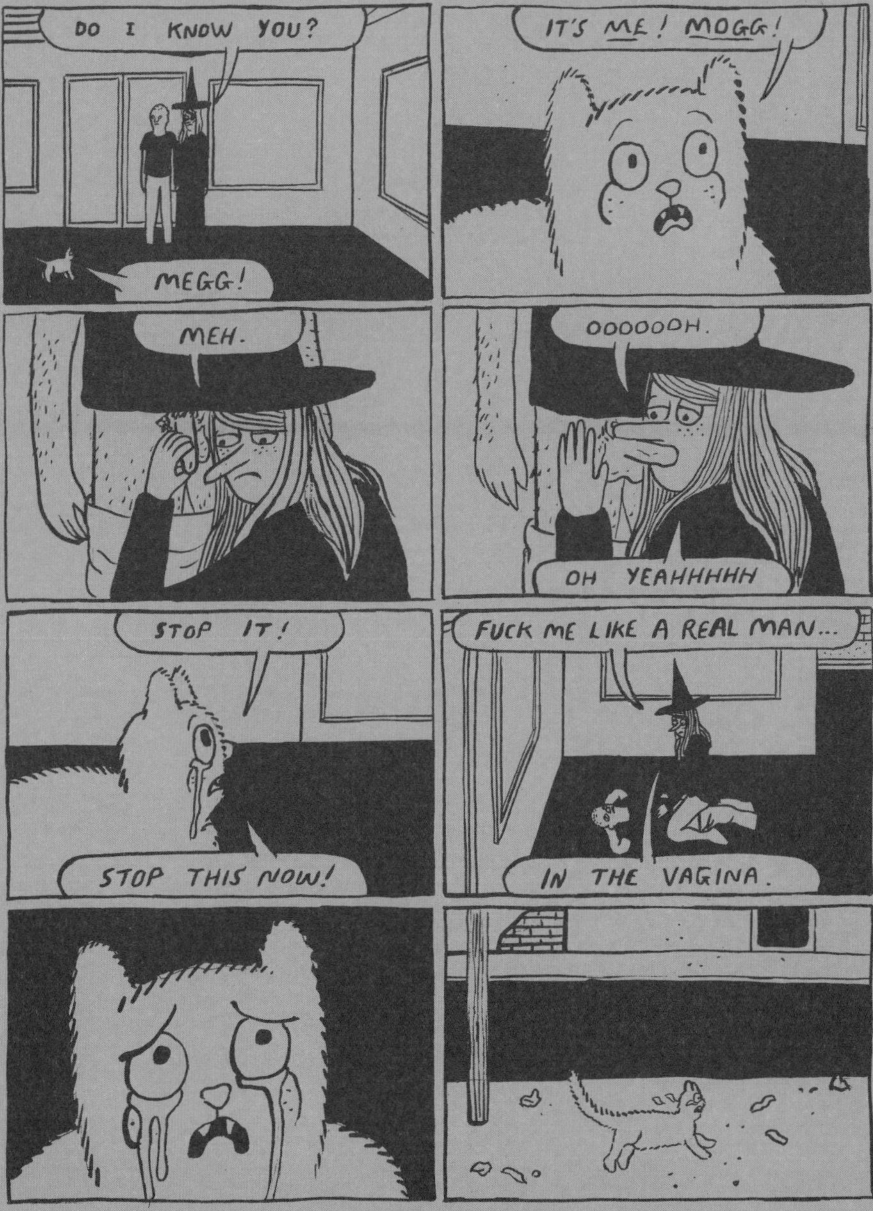
DO I KNOW YOU?
MEGG!
IT'S ME! MOGG!
MEH.
OOOOOOH.
OH YEAHHHHH
STOP IT!
STOP THIS NOW!
FUCK ME LIKE A REAL MAN...
IN THE VAGINA.

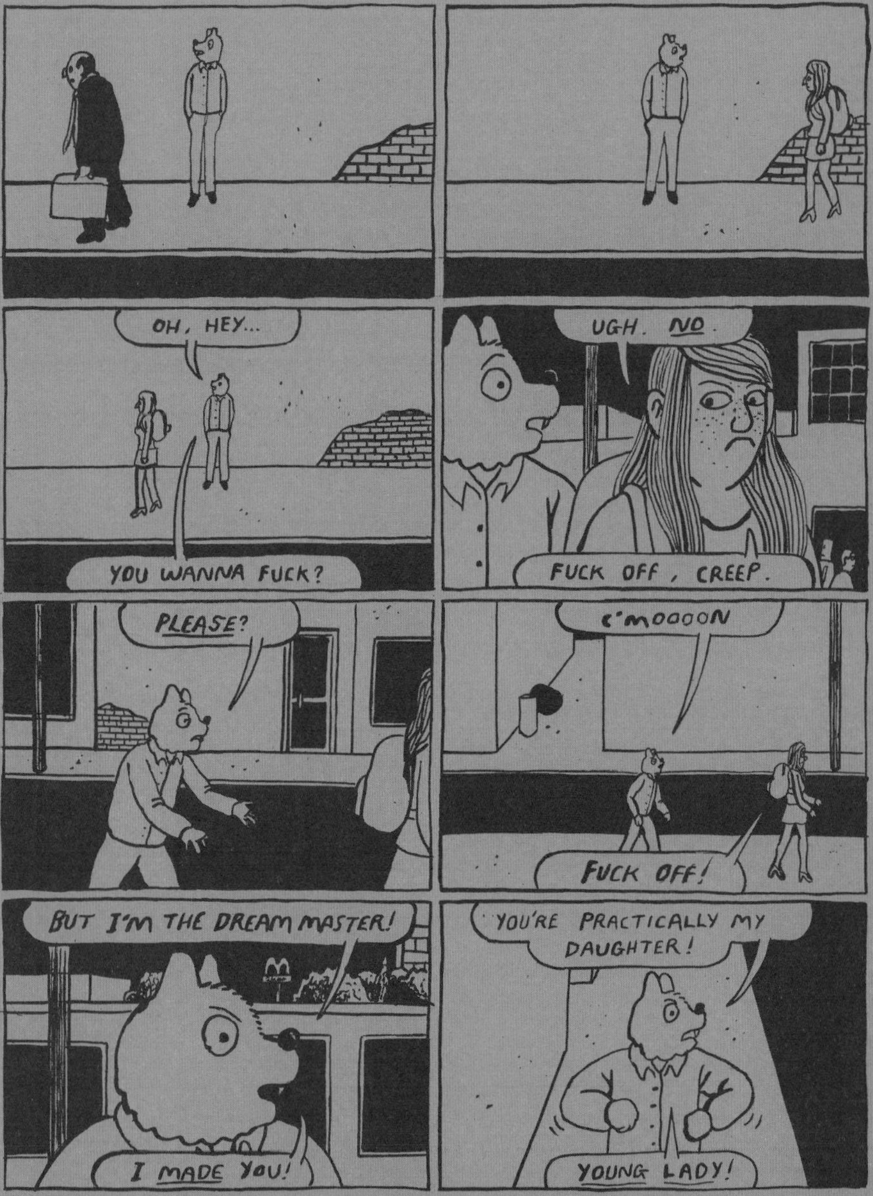
OH, HEY...
YOU WANNA FUCK?
UGH. NO.
FUCK OFF, CREEP.
PLEASE?
C'MOOOON
FUCK OFF!
BUT I'M THE DREAM MASTER!
I MADE YOU!
YOU'RE PRACTICALLY MY DAUGHTER!
YOUNG LADY!

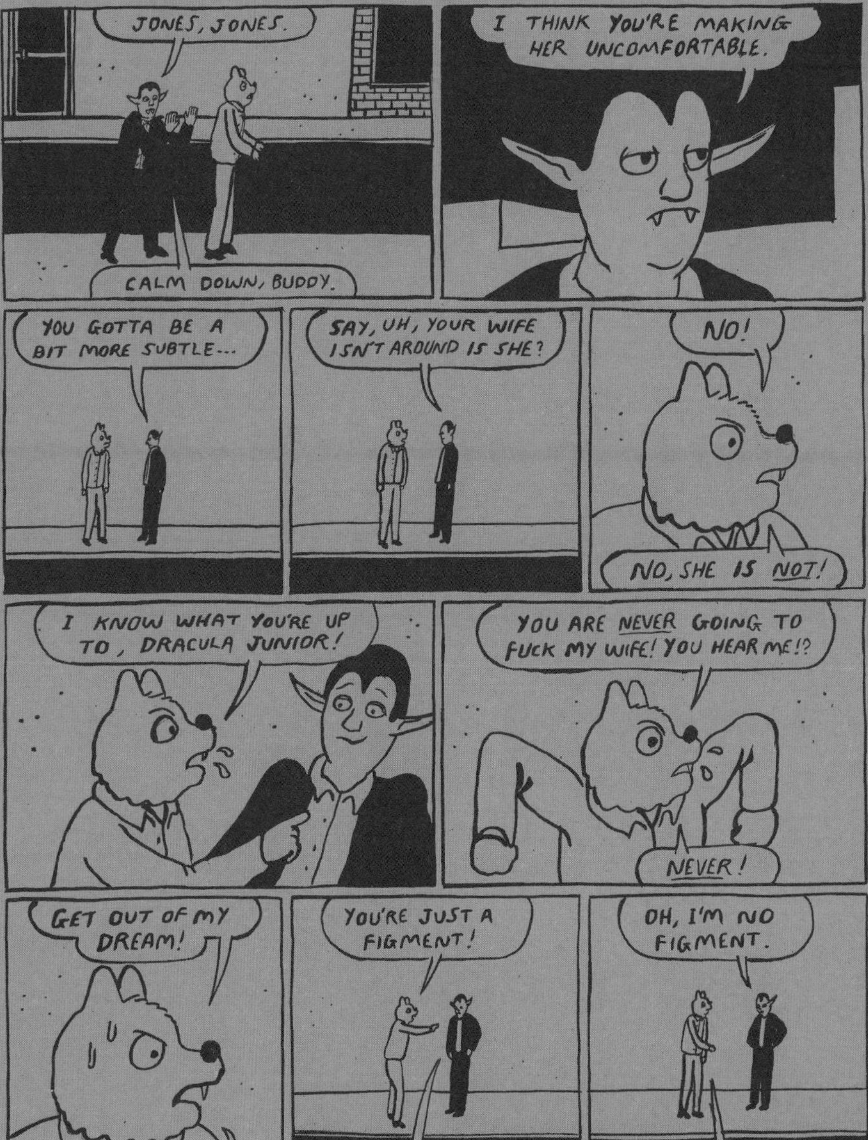
JONES, JONES.
CALM DOWN, BUDDY.
I THINK YOU'RE MAKING HER UNCOMFORTABLE.
YOU GOTTA BE A BIT MORE SUBTLE...
SAY, UH, YOUR WIFE ISN'T AROUND IS SHE?
NO!
NO, SHE IS NOT!
I KNOW WHAT YOU'RE UP TO, DRACULA JUNIOR!
YOU ARE NEVER GOING TO FUCK MY WIFE! YOU HEAR ME!?
NEVER!
GET OUT OF MY DREAM!
I BANISH YOU!
YOU'RE JUST A FIGMENT!
HAHAHAHA
OH, I'M NO FIGMENT.
WHA-?

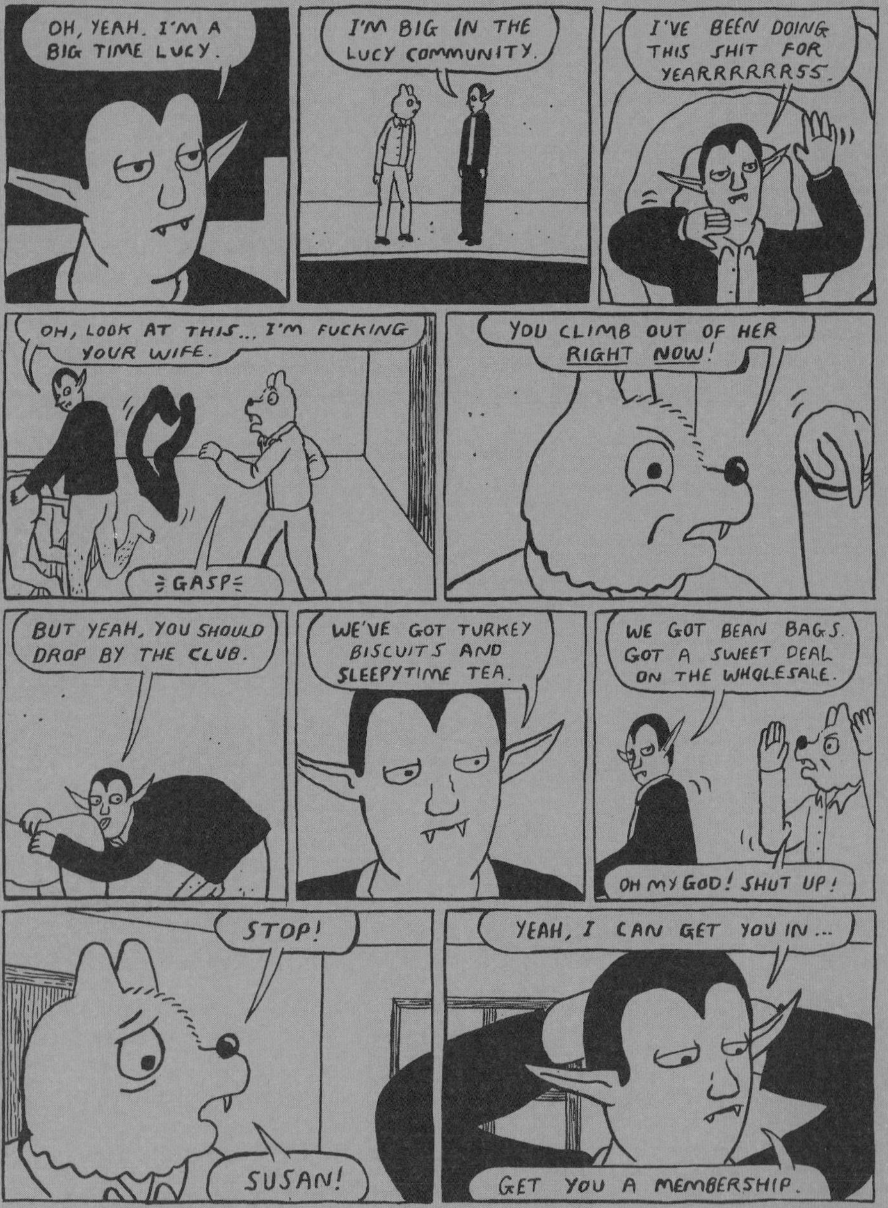
OH, YEAH. I'M A BIG TIME LUCY.
I'M BIG IN THE LUCY COMMUNITY.
I'VE BEEN DOING THIS SHIT FOR YEARRRRRRSS.
OH, LOOK AT THIS... I'M FUCKING YOUR WIFE.
GASP
YOU CLIMB OUT OF HER RIGHT NOW!
BUT YEAH, YOU SHOULD DROP BY THE CLUB.
WE'VE GOT TURKEY BISCUITS AND SLEEPYTIME TEA.
WE GOT BEAN BAGS. GOT A SWEET DEAL ON THE WHOLESALE.
OH MY GOD! SHUT UP!
STOP!
SUSAN!
YEAH, I CAN GET YOU IN...
GET YOU A MEMBERSHIP.

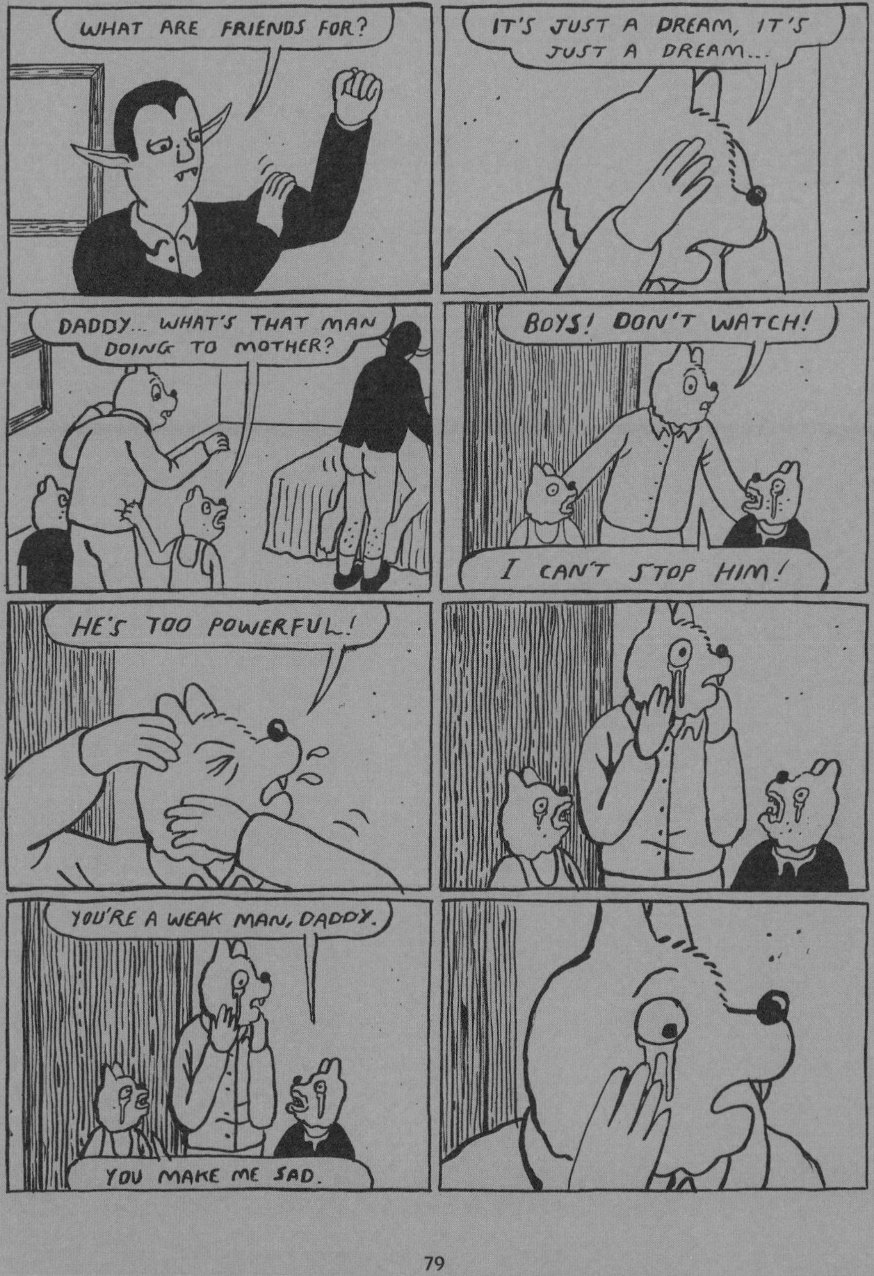
WHAT ARE FRIENDS FOR?
IT'S JUST A DREAM, IT'S JUST A DREAM...
DADDY... WHAT'S THAT MAN DOING TO MOTHER?
BOYS! DON'T WATCH!
I CAN'T STOP HIM!
HE'S TOO POWERFUL!
YOU'RE A WEAK MAN, DADDY.
YOU MAKE ME SAD.

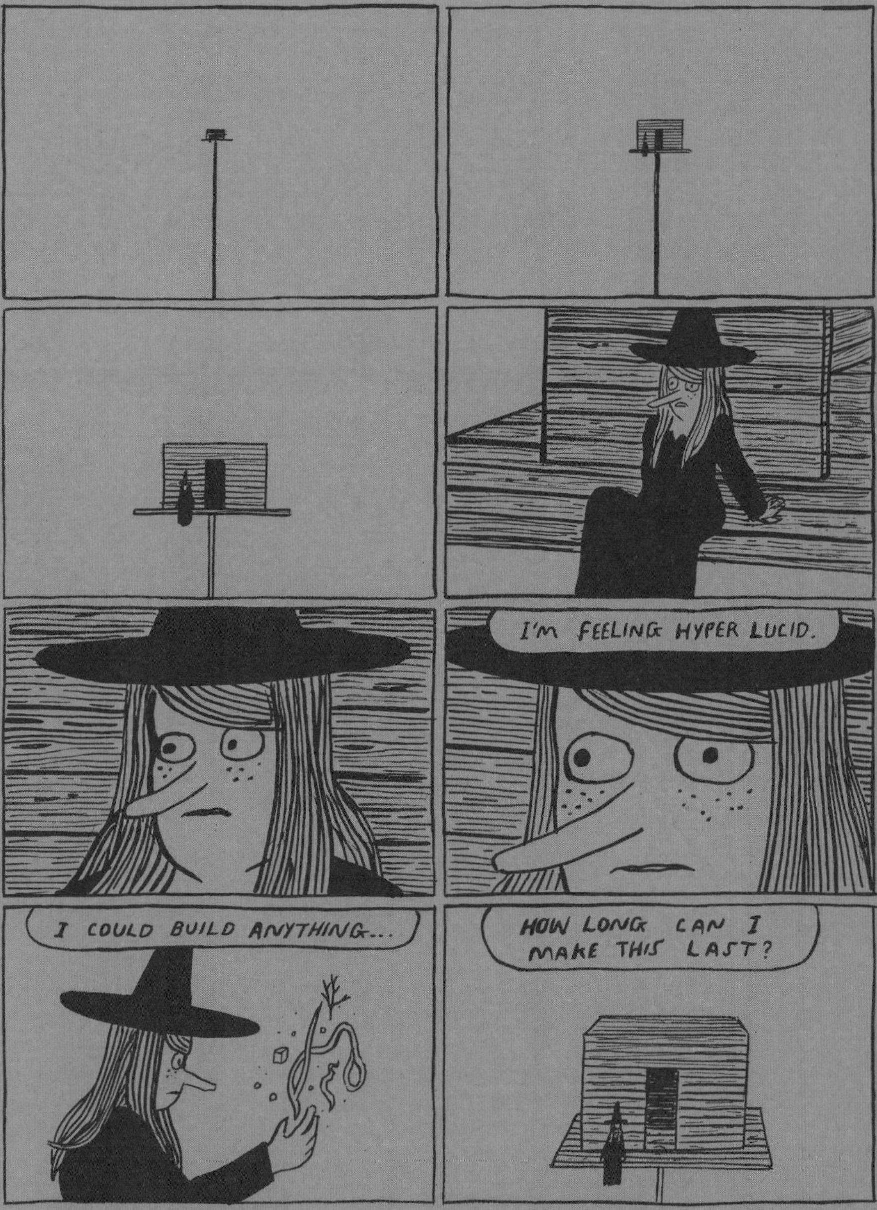
I'M FEELING HYPER LUCID.
I COULD BUILD ANYTHING...
HOW LONG CAN I MAKE THIS LAST?

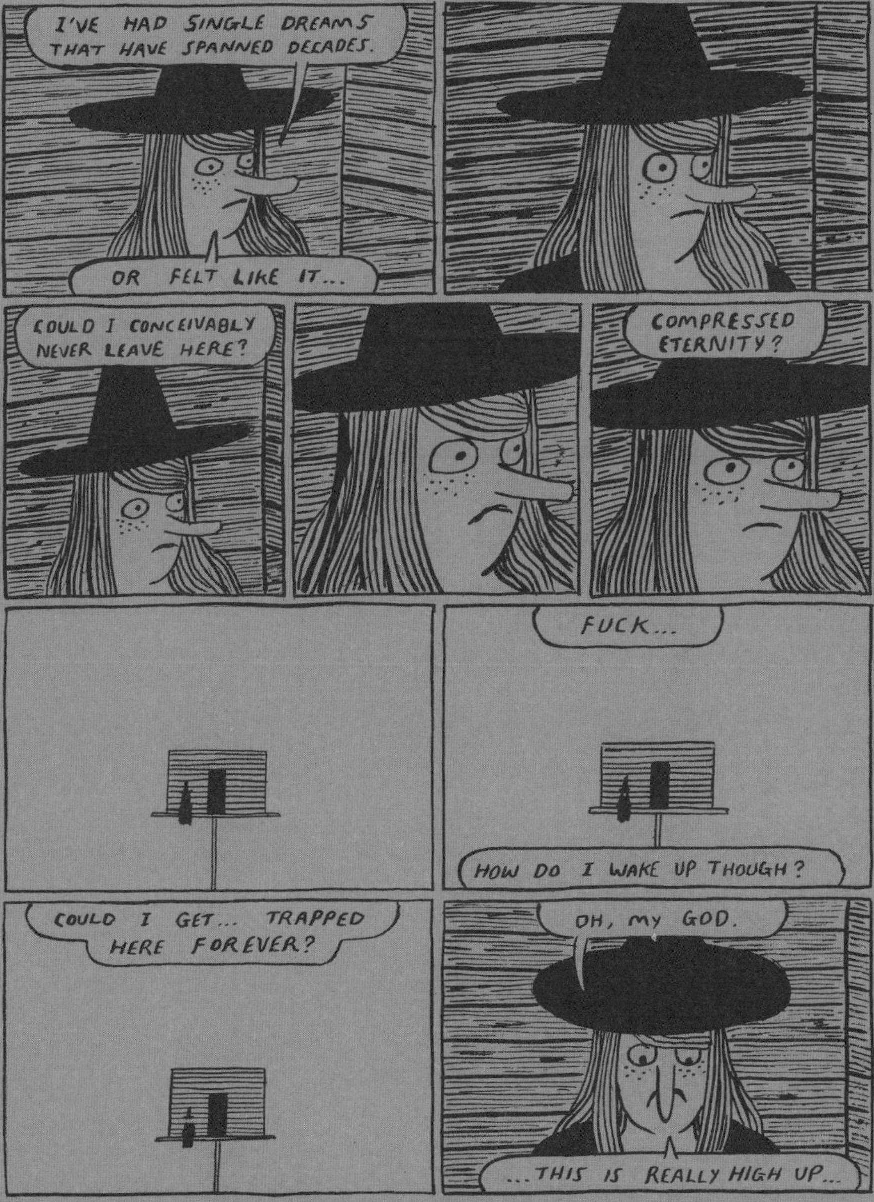
I'VE HAD SINGLE DREAMS THAT HAVE SPANNED DECADES.
OR FELT LIKE IT...
COULD I CONCEIVABLY NEVER LEAVE HERE?
COMPRESSED ETERNITY?
FUCK...
HOW DO I WAKE UP THOUGH?
COULD I GET... TRAPPED HERE FOREVER?
OH, MY GOD.
...THIS IS REALLY HIGH UP...

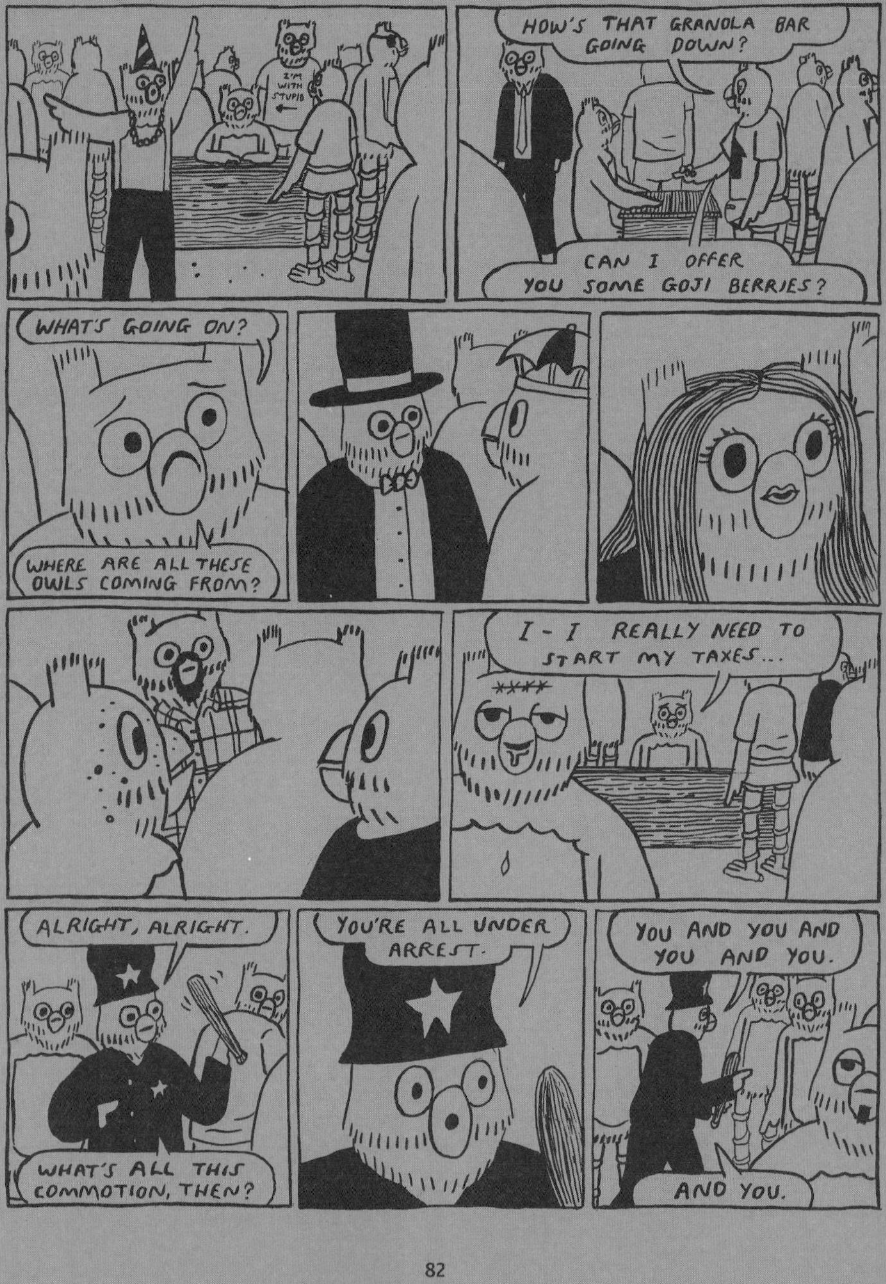
I'M WITH STUPID
HOW'S THAT GRANOLA BAR GOING DOWN?
CAN I OFFER YOU SOME GOJI BERRIES?
WHAT'S GOING ON?
WHERE ARE ALL THESE OWLS COMING FROM?
I - I REALLY NEED TO START MY TAXES...
ALRIGHT, ALRIGHT.
WHAT'S ALL THIS COMMOTION, THEN?
YOU'RE ALL UNDER ARREST.
YOU AND YOU AND YOU AND YOU.
AND YOU.

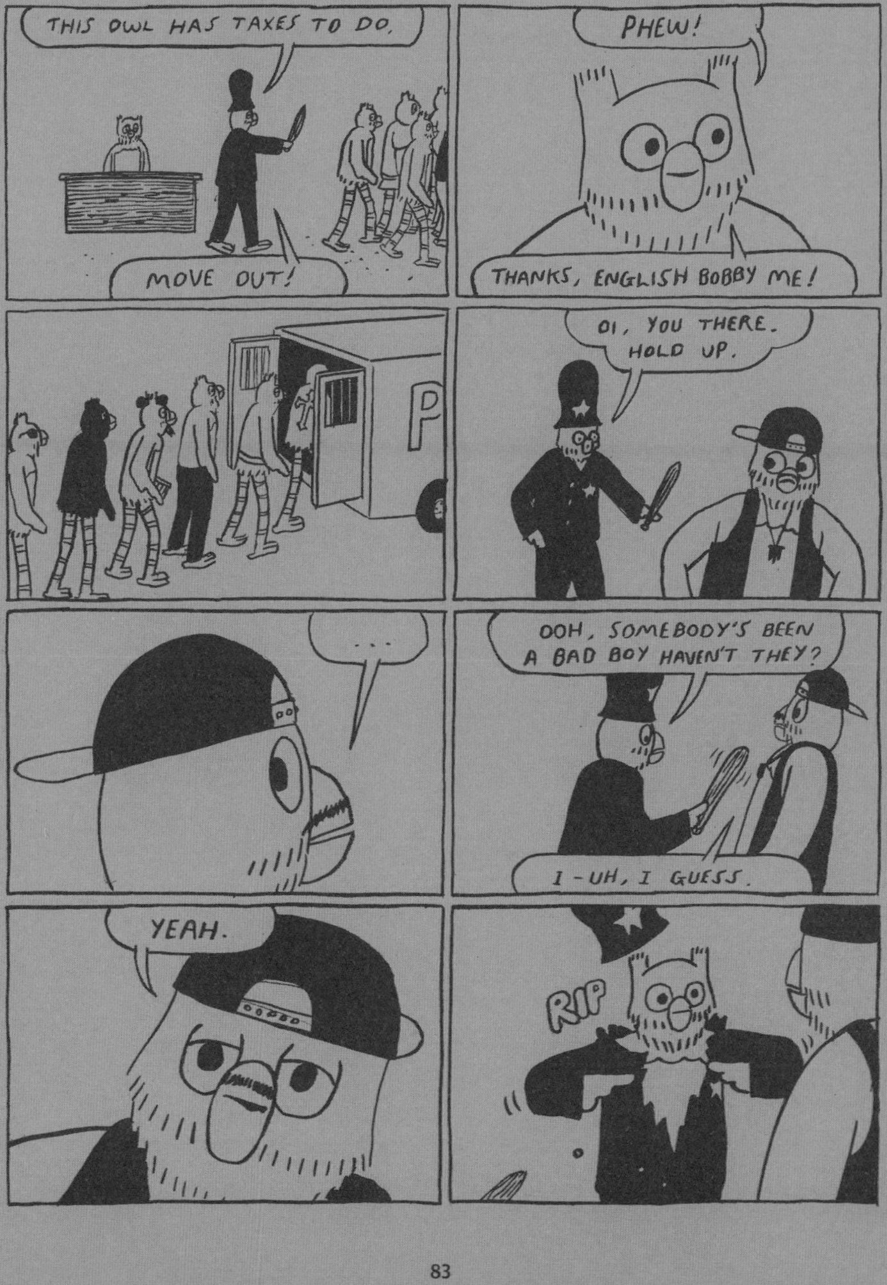
THIS OWL HAS TAXES TO DO.
MOVE OUT!
PHEW!
THANKS, ENGLISH BOBBY ME!
P
OI, YOU THERE. HOLD UP.
. . .
OOH, SOMEBODY'S BEEN A BAD BOY HAVEN'T THEY?
I - UH, I GUESS.
YEAH.
RIP

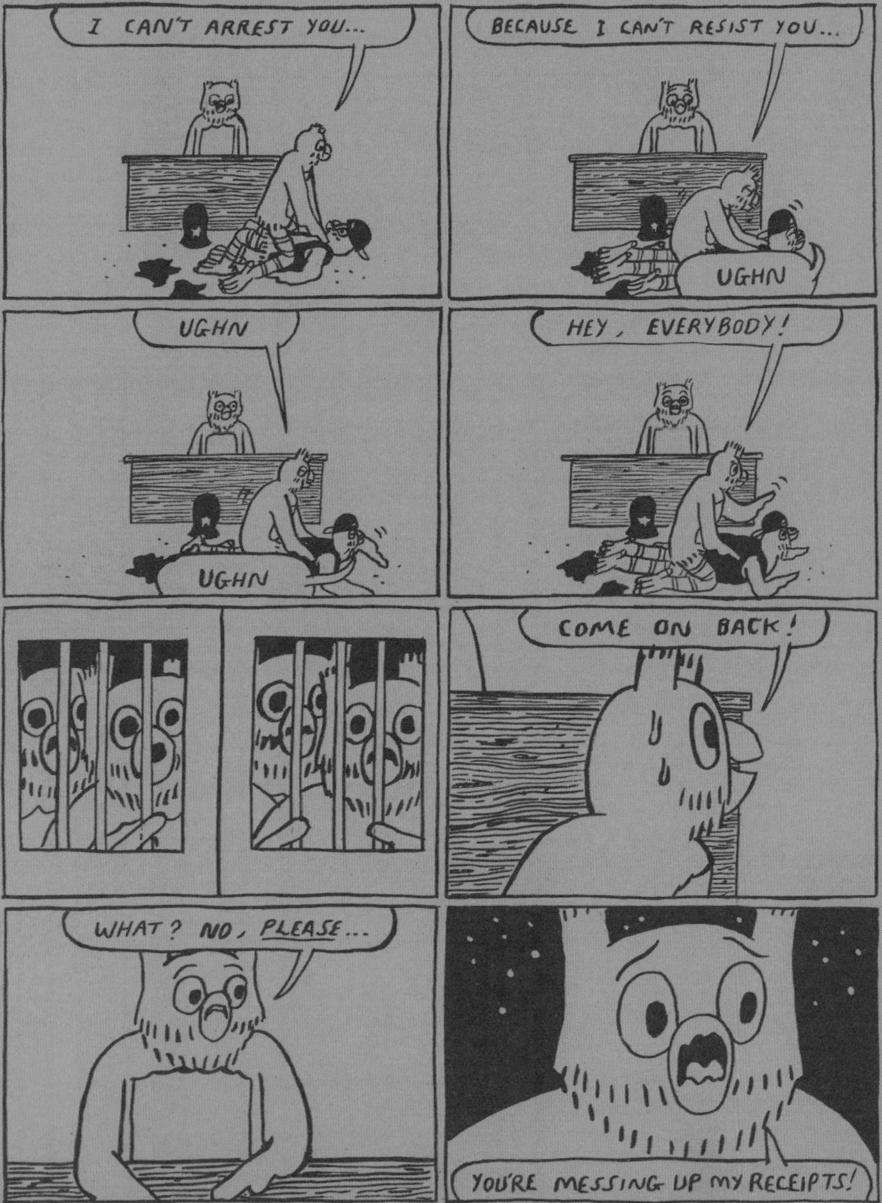
I CAN'T ARREST YOU...
BECAUSE I CAN'T RESIST YOU...
UGHN
UGHN
UGHN
HEY, EVERYBODY!
COME ON BACK!
WHAT? NO, PLEASE...
YOU'RE MESSING UP MY RECEIPTS!

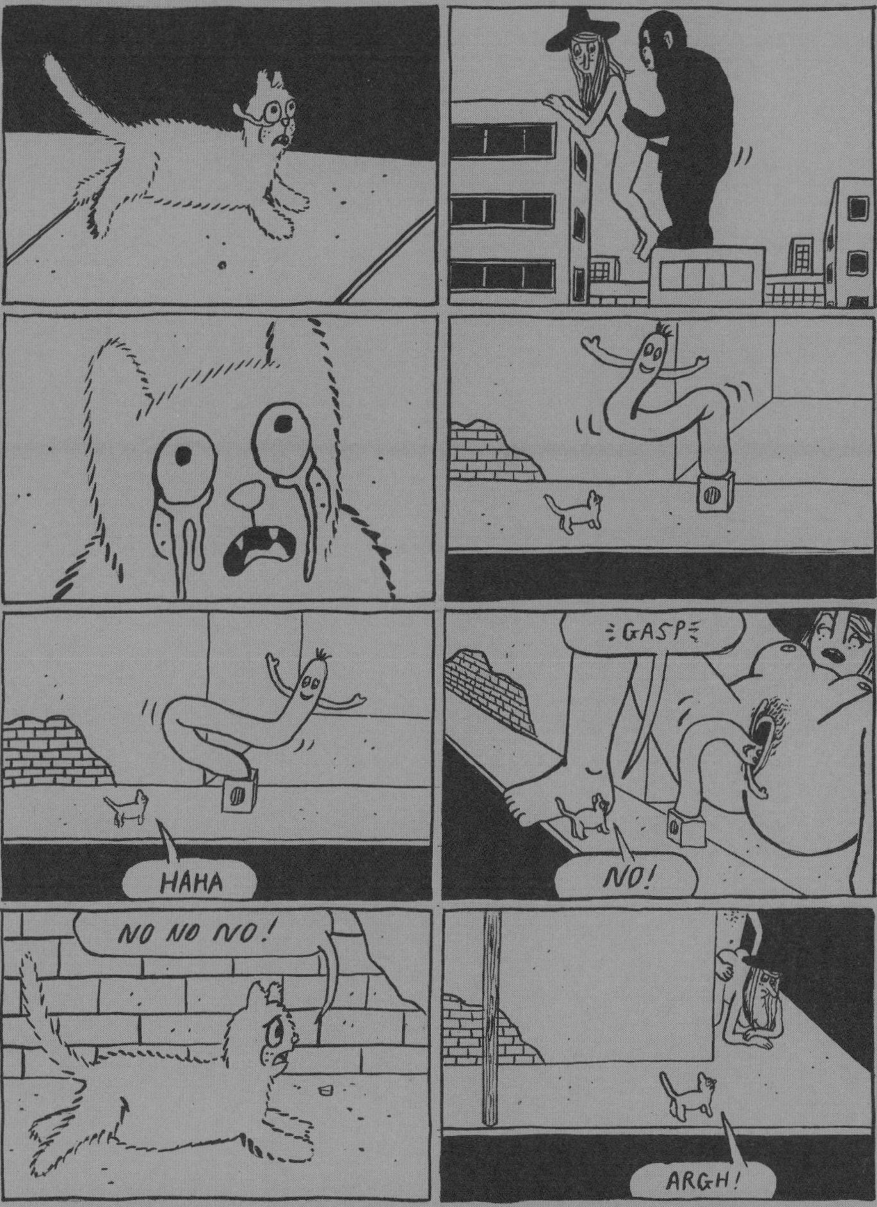
HAHA
GASP
NO!
NO NO NO!
ARGH!

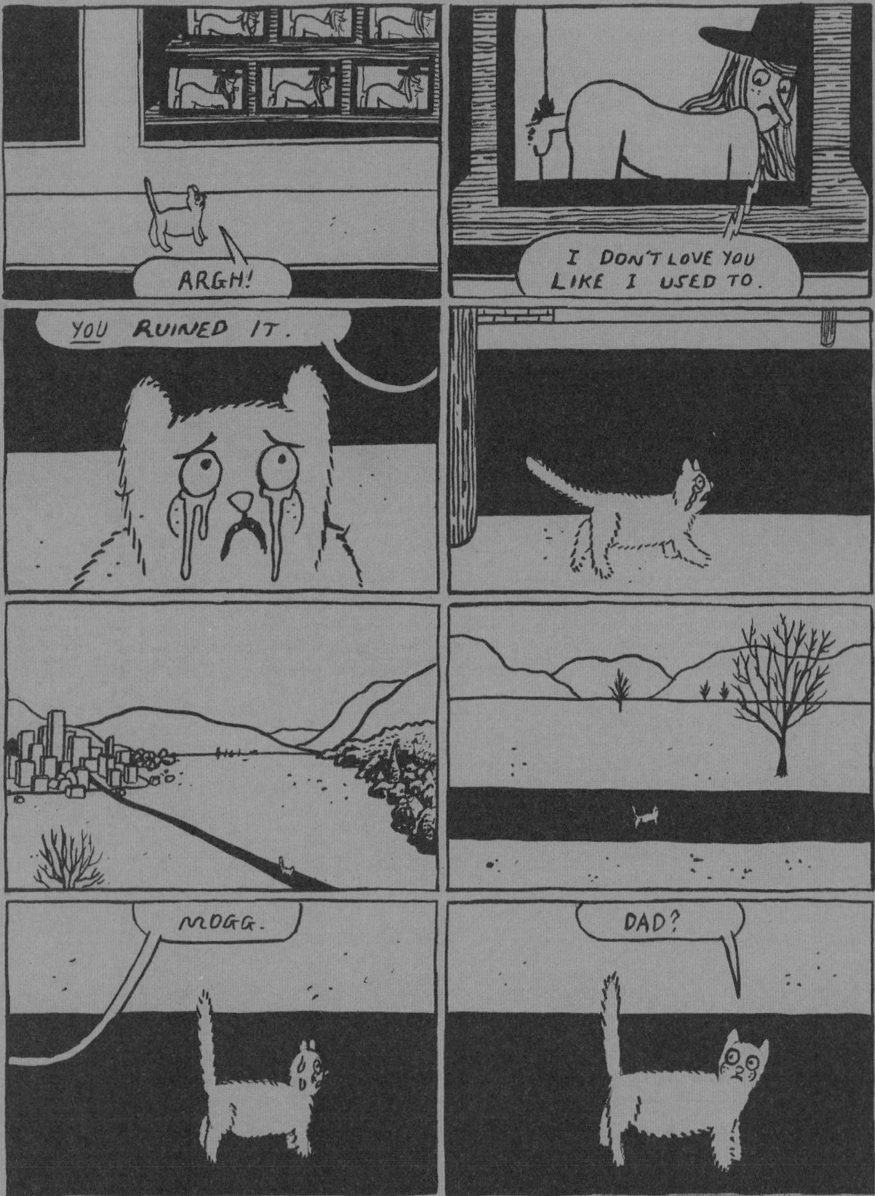
ARGH!
I DON'T LOVE YOU LIKE I USED TO.
YOU RUINED IT.
MOGG.
DAD?

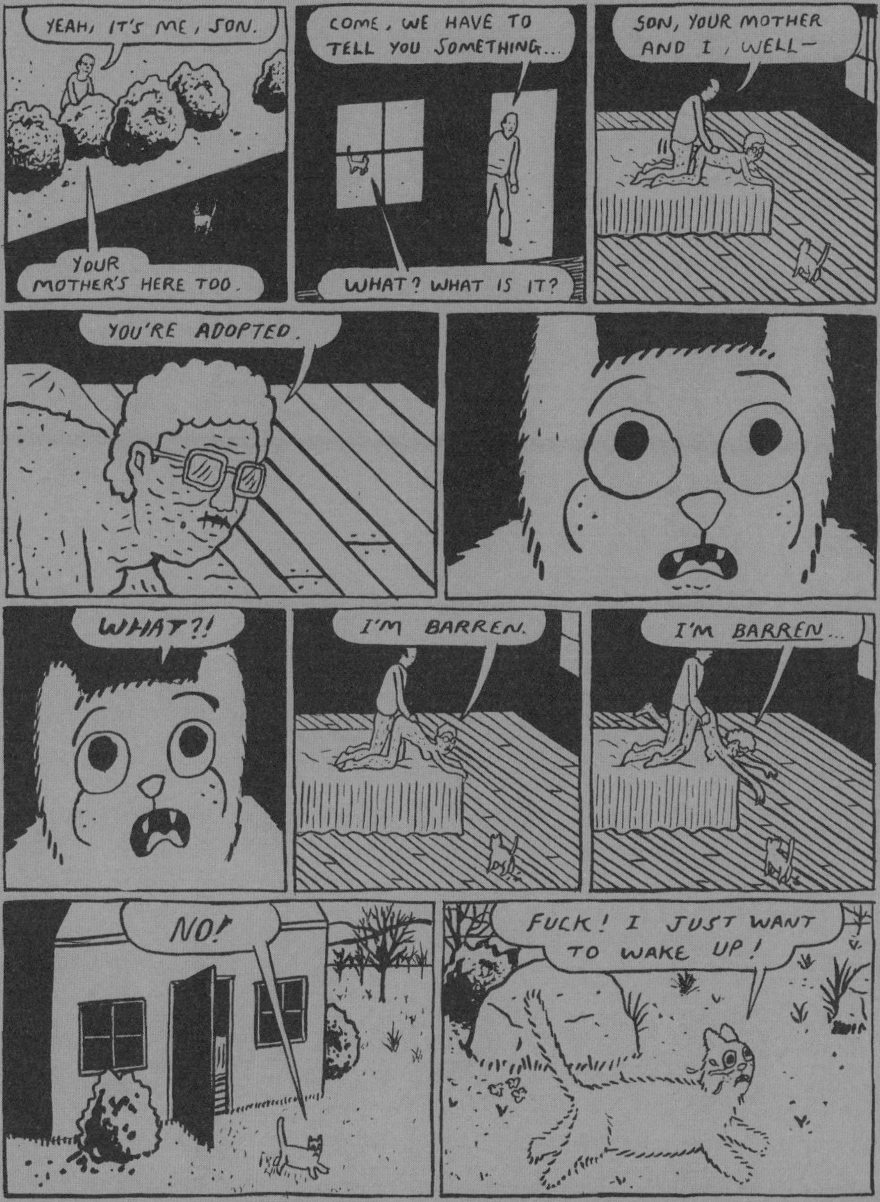
YEAH, IT'S ME, SON.
YOUR MOTHER'S HERE TOO.
COME, WE HAVE TO TELL YOU SOMETHING...
WHAT? WHAT IS IT?
SON, YOUR MOTHER AND I, WELL—
YOU'RE ADOPTED.
WHAT?!
I'M BARREN.
I'M BARREN...
NO!
FUCK! I JUST WANT TO WAKE UP!

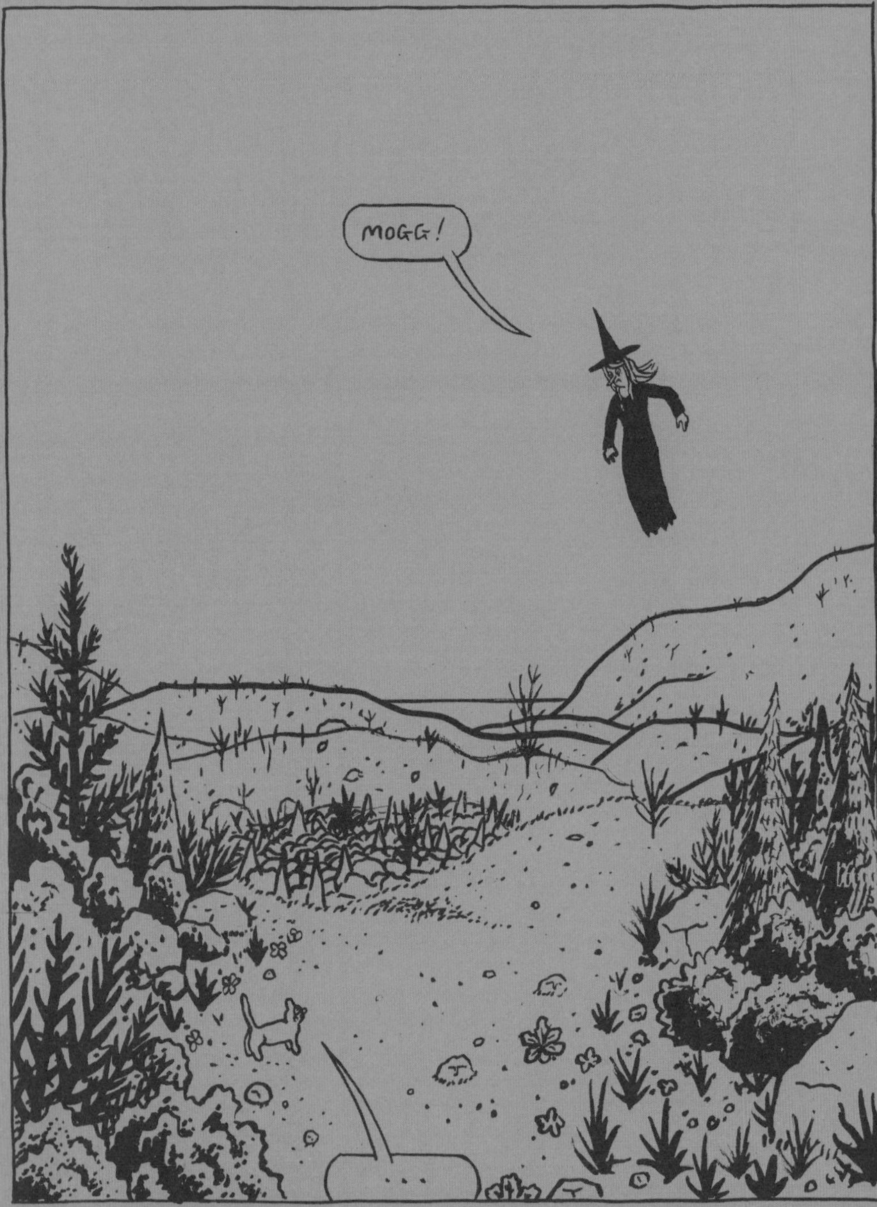
MOGG!
...

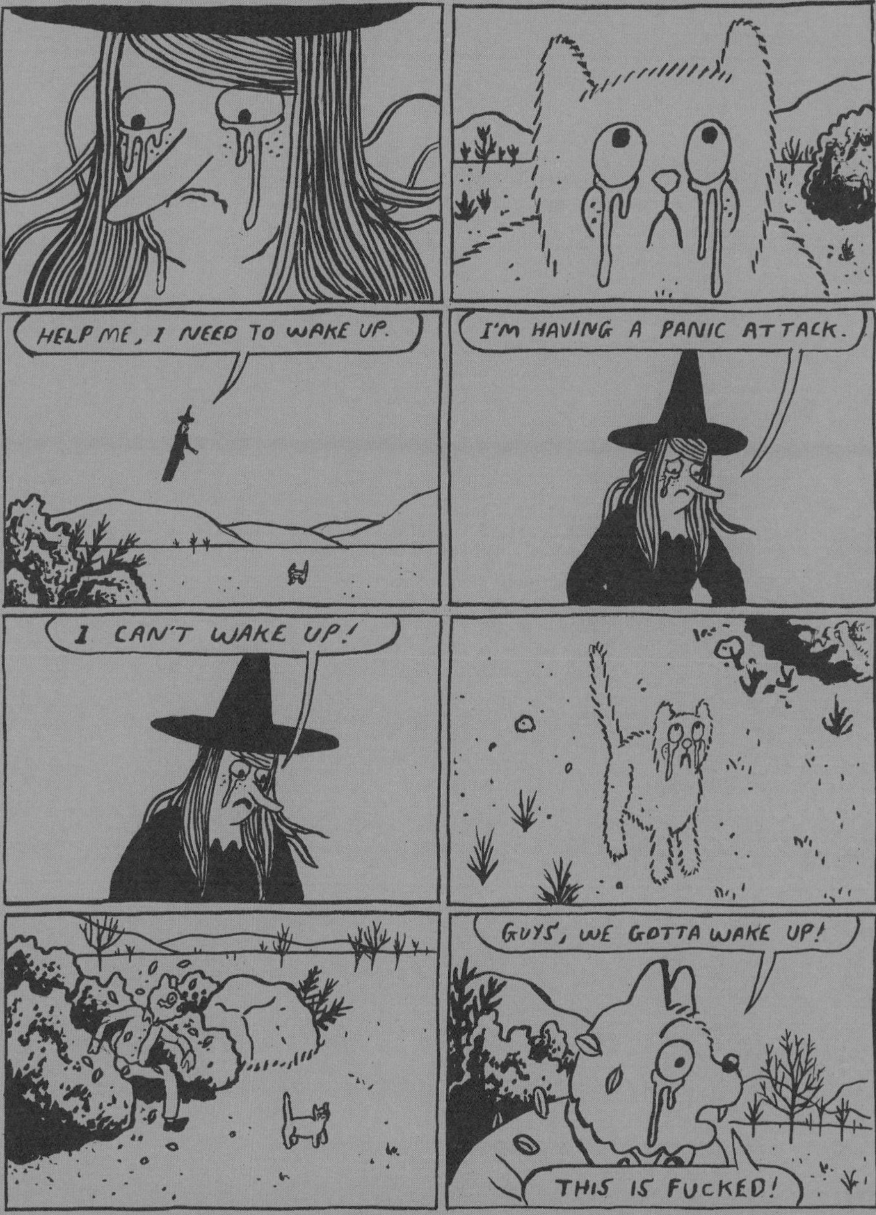
HELP ME, I NEED TO WAKE UP.
I'M HAVING A PANIC ATTACK.
I CAN'T WAKE UP!
GUYS, WE GOTTA WAKE UP!
THIS IS FUCKED!

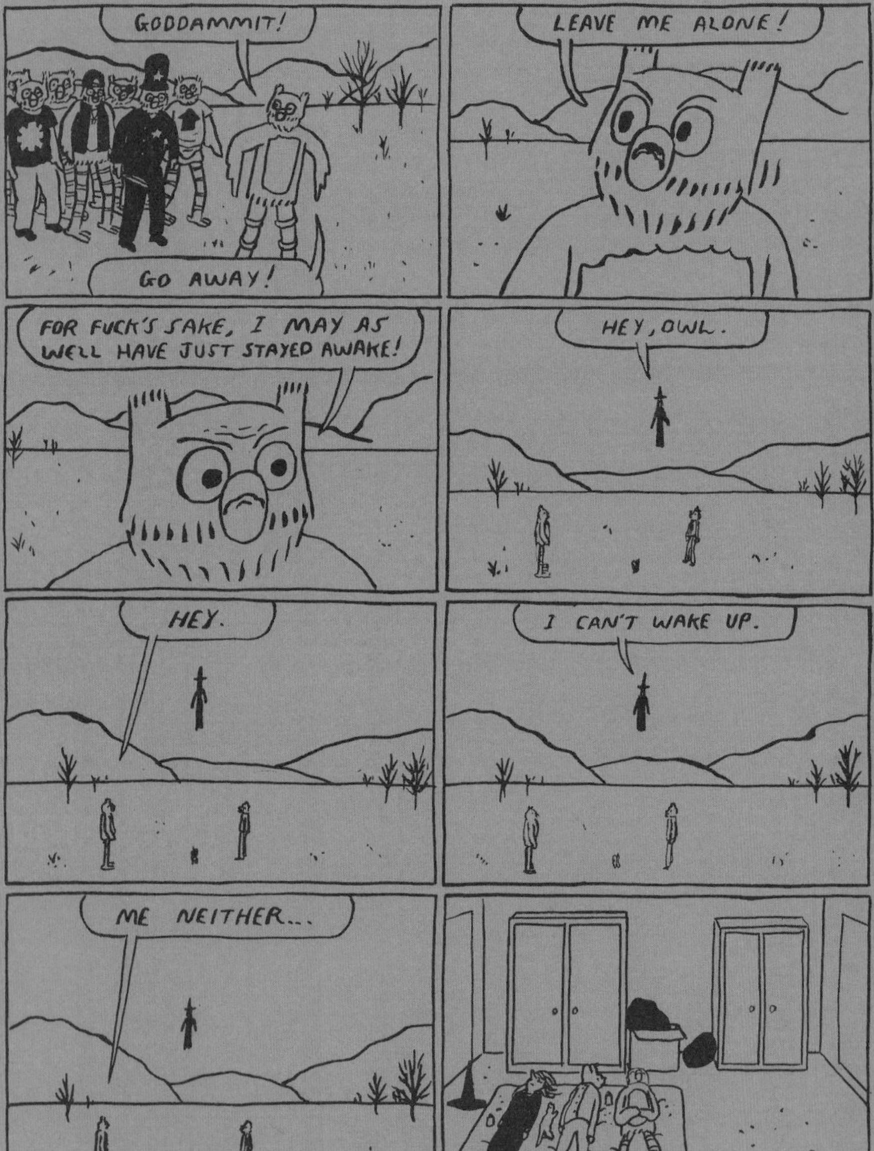
GODDAMMIT!
GO AWAY!
LEAVE ME ALONE!
FOR FUCK'S SAKE, I MAY AS WELL HAVE JUST STAYED AWAKE!
HEY, OWL.
HEY.
I CAN'T WAKE UP.
ME NEITHER...

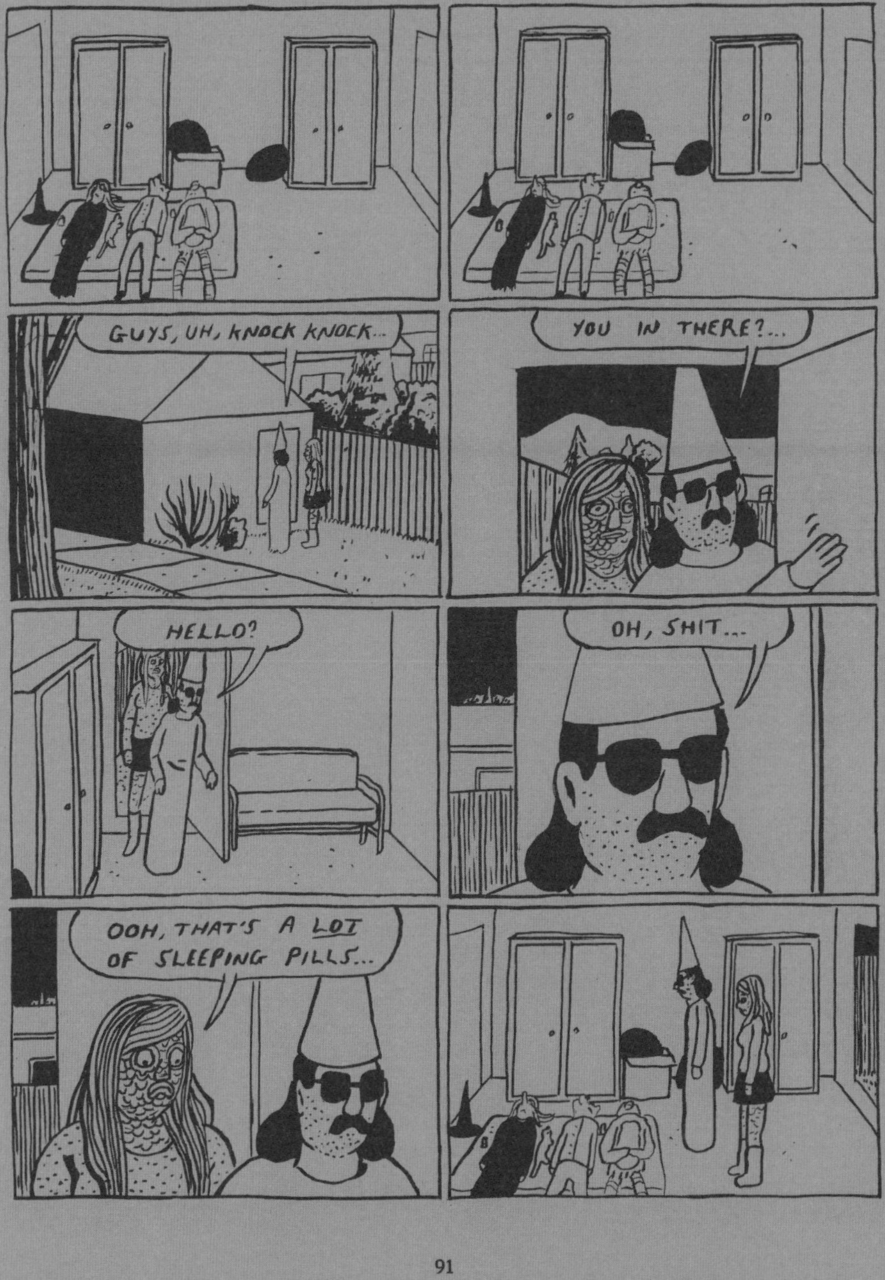
GUYS, UH, KNOCK KNOCK...
YOU IN THERE?...
HELLO?
OH, SHIT...
OOH, THAT'S A LOT OF SLEEPING PILLS...

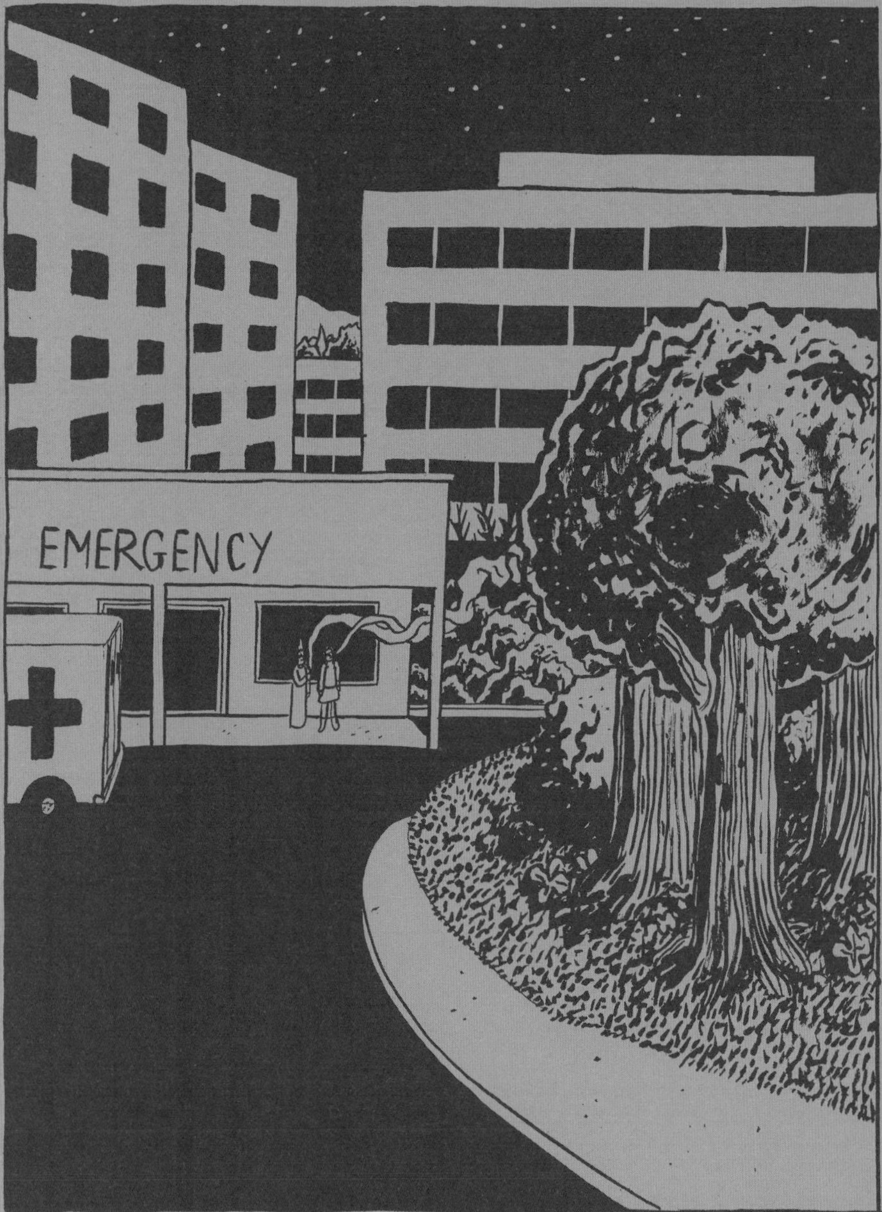
EMERGENCY

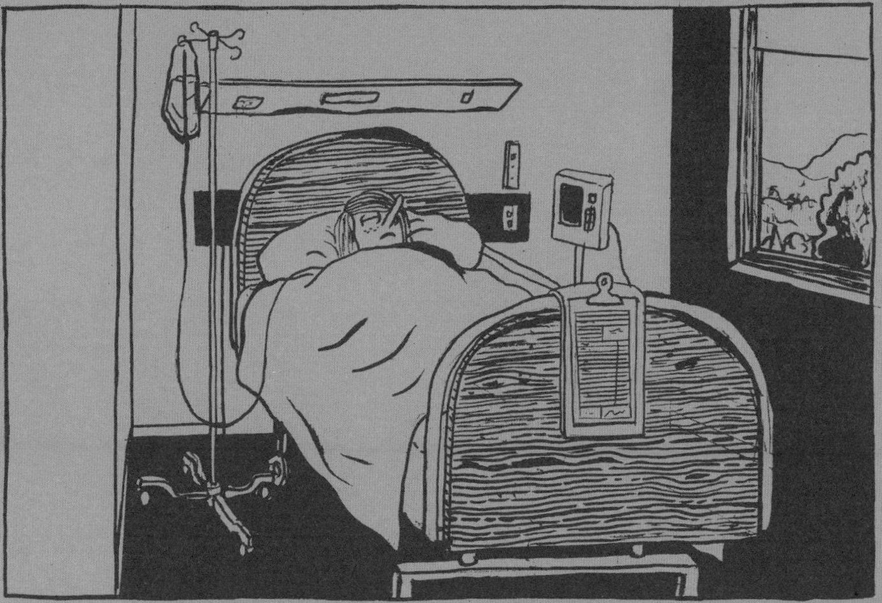

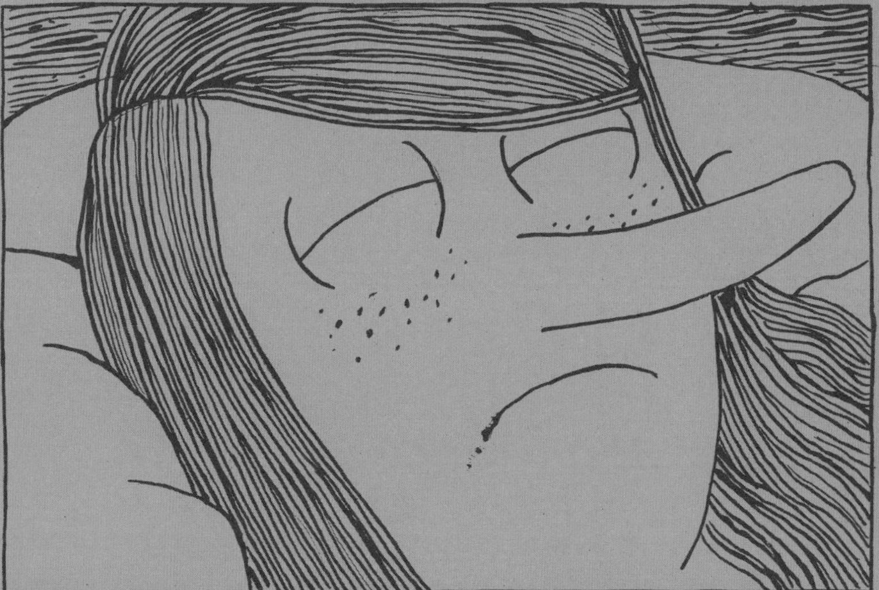

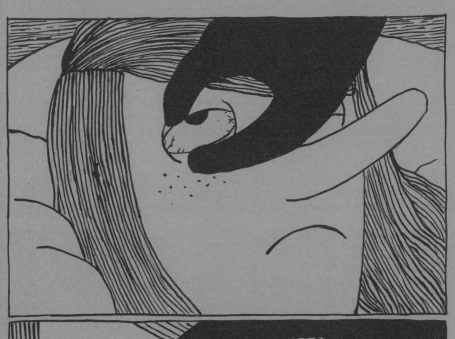

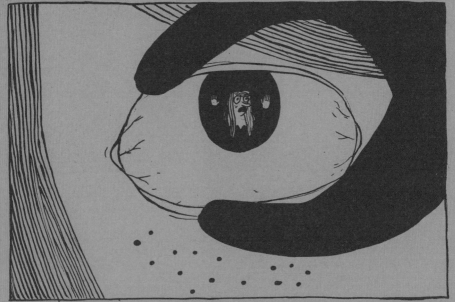

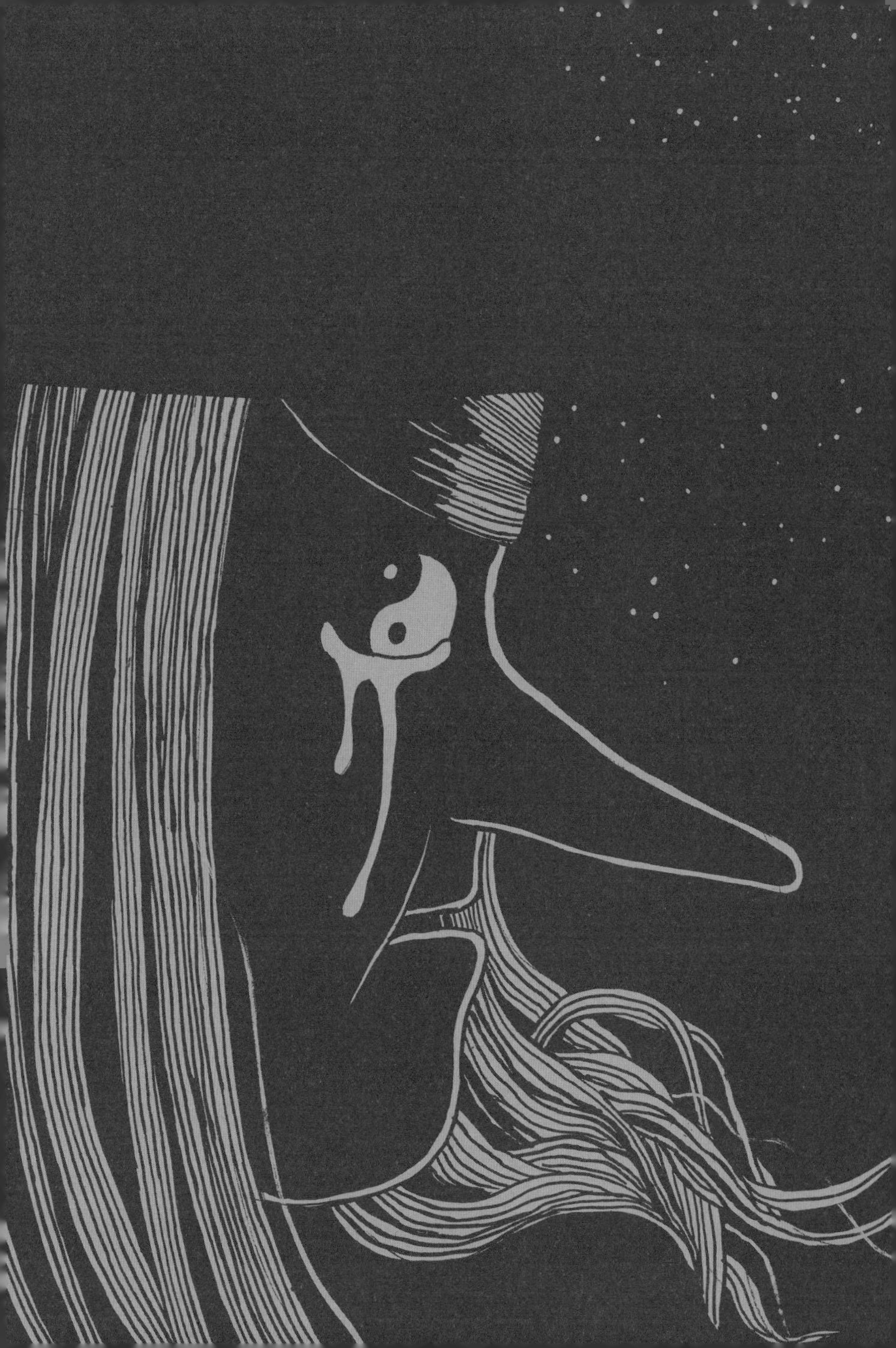

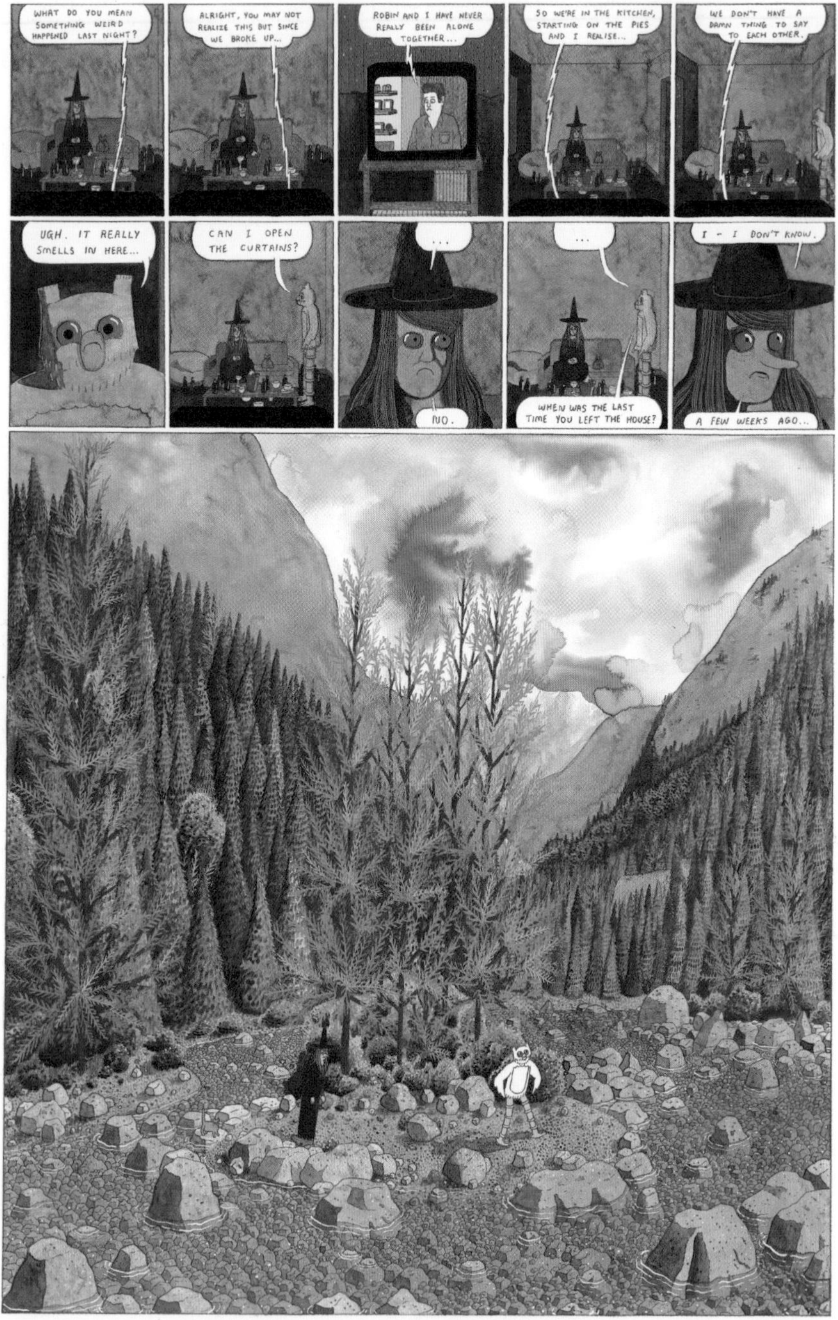
WHAT DO YOU MEAN SOMETHING WEIRD HAPPENED LAST NIGHT?
ALRIGHT, YOU MAY NOT REALIZE THIS BUT SINCE WE BROKE UP...
ROBIN AND I HAVE NEVER REALLY BEEN ALONE TOGETHER...
SO WE'RE IN THE KITCHEN, STARTING ON THE PIES AND I REALISE...
WE DON'T HAVE A DAMN THING TO SAY TO EACH OTHER.
UGH. IT REALLY SMELLS IN HERE...
CAN I OPEN THE CURTAINS?
...
NO.
...
WHEN WAS THE LAST TIME YOU LEFT THE HOUSE?
I - I DON'T KNOW.
A FEW WEEKS AGO...

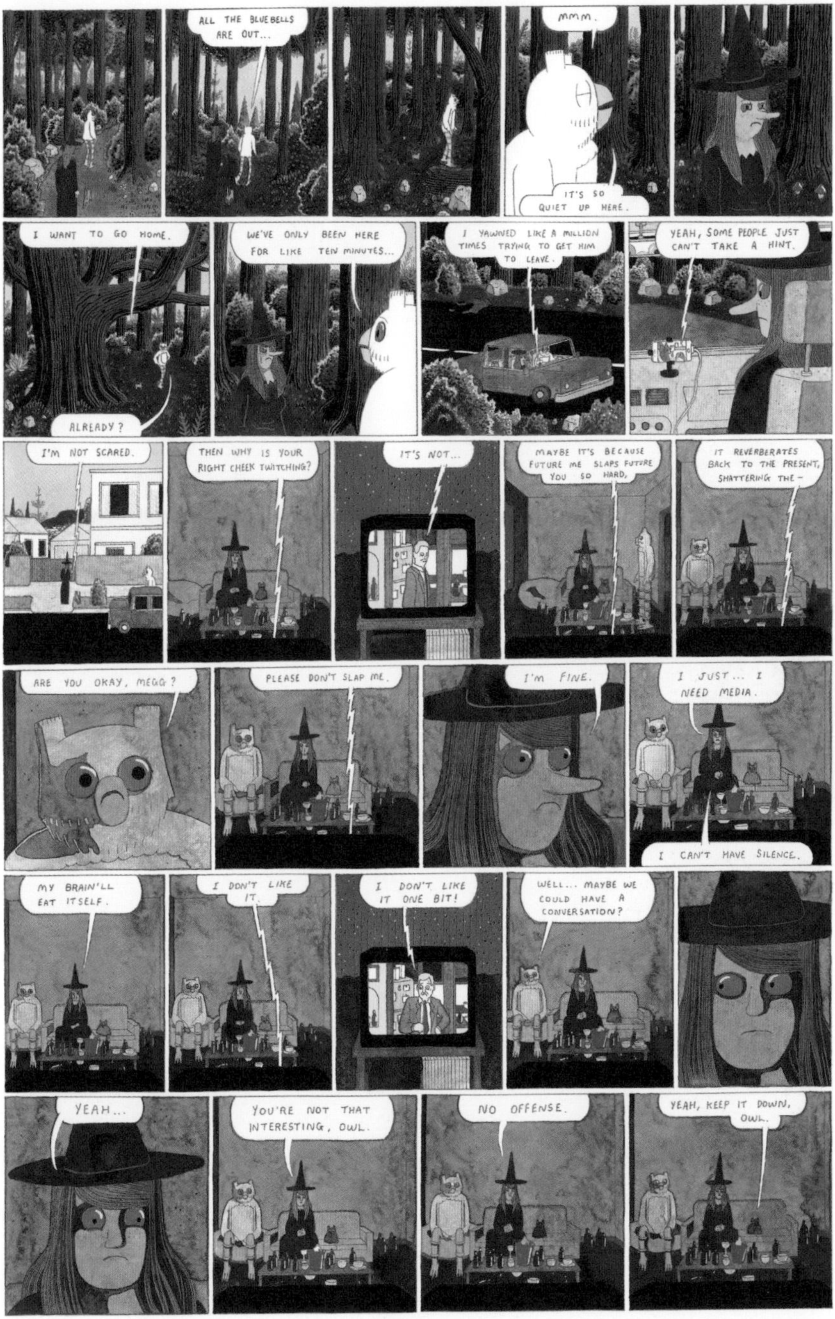
ALL THE BLUEBELLS ARE OUT...
MMM.
IT'S SO QUIET UP HERE.
I WANT TO GO HOME.
ALREADY?
WE'VE ONLY BEEN HERE FOR LIKE TEN MINUTES...
I YAWNED LIKE A MILLION TIMES TRYING TO GET HIM TO LEAVE.
YEAH, SOME PEOPLE JUST CAN'T TAKE A HINT.
I'M NOT SCARED.
THEN WHY IS YOUR RIGHT CHEEK TWITCHING?
IT'S NOT...
MAYBE IT'S BECAUSE FUTURE ME SLAPS FUTURE YOU SO HARD,
IT REVERBERATES BACK TO THE PRESENT, SHATTERING THE—
ARE YOU OKAY, MEGG?
PLEASE DON'T SLAP ME.
I'M FINE.
I JUST... I NEED MEDIA.
I CAN'T HAVE SILENCE.
MY BRAIN'LL EAT ITSELF.
I DON'T LIKE IT.
I DON'T LIKE IT ONE BIT!
WELL... MAYBE WE COULD HAVE A CONVERSATION?
YEAH...
YOU'RE NOT THAT INTERESTING, OWL.
NO OFFENSE.
YEAH, KEEP IT DOWN, OWL.

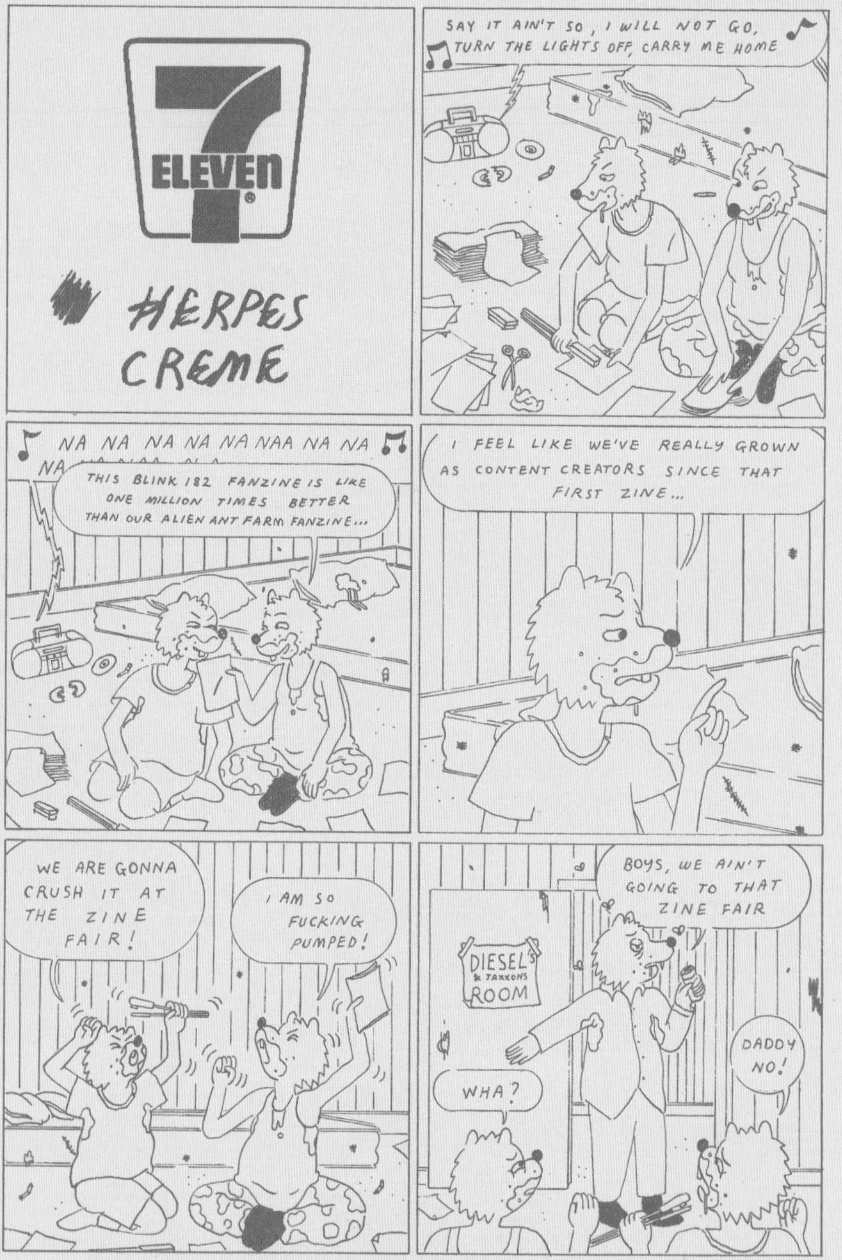
ELEVEN
HERPES CREME
SAY IT AIN'T SO, I WILL NOT GO, TURN THE LIGHTS OFF, CARRY ME HOME
NA NA NA NA NA NAA NA NA
THIS BLINK 182 FANZINE IS LIKE ONE MILLION TIMES BETTER THAN OUR ALIEN ANT FARM FANZINE...
I FEEL LIKE WE'VE REALLY GROWN AS CONTENT CREATORS SINCE THAT FIRST ZINE...
WE ARE GONNA CRUSH IT AT THE ZINE FAIR!
I AM SO FUCKING PUMPED!
BOYS, WE AIN'T GOING TO THAT ZINE FAIR
DIESEL'S & JAXXONS ROOM
WHA?
DADDY NO!

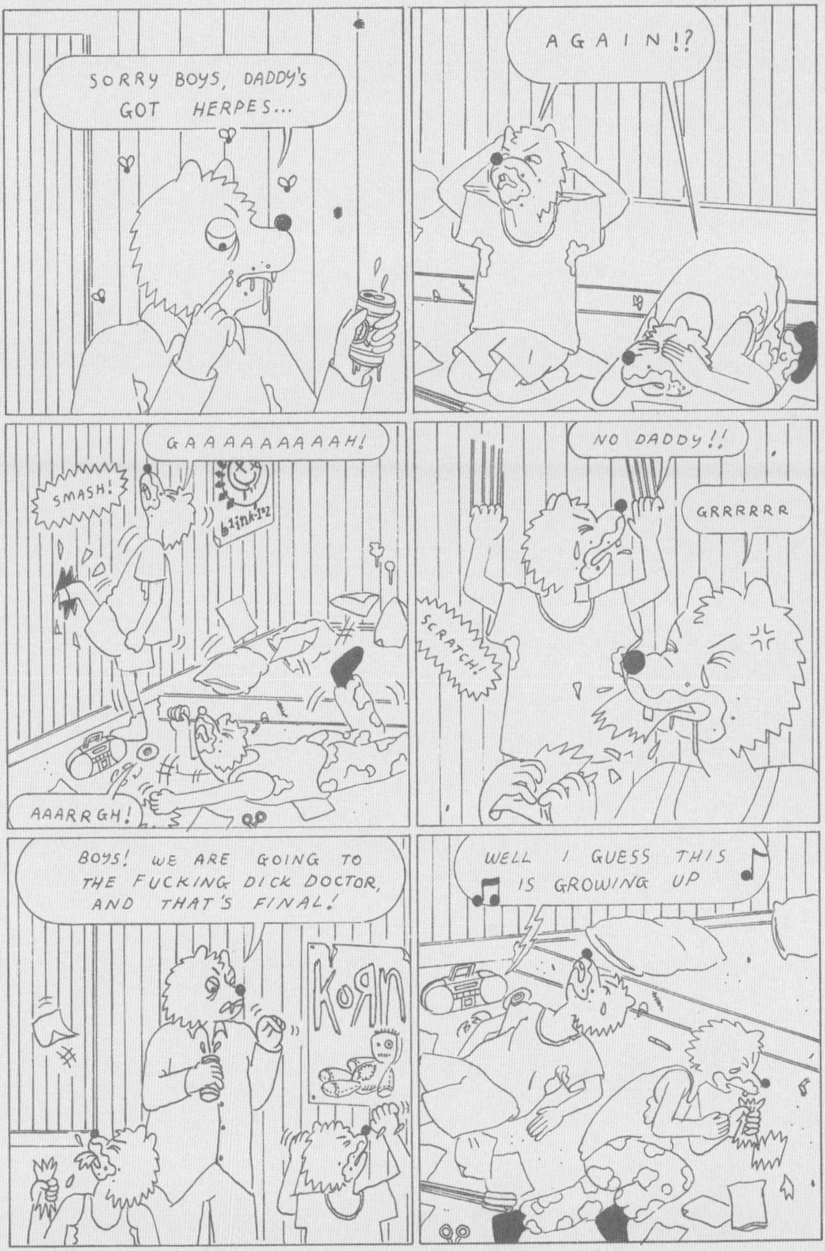
SORRY BOYS, DADDY'S GOT HERPES...
AGAIN!?
GAAAAAAAAAH!
SMASH!
blink-182
AAARRGH!
NO DADDY!!
GRRRRRR
SCRATCH!
BOYS! WE ARE GOING TO THE FUCKING DICK DOCTOR, AND THAT'S FINAL!
KoRN
WELL I GUESS THIS IS GROWING UP

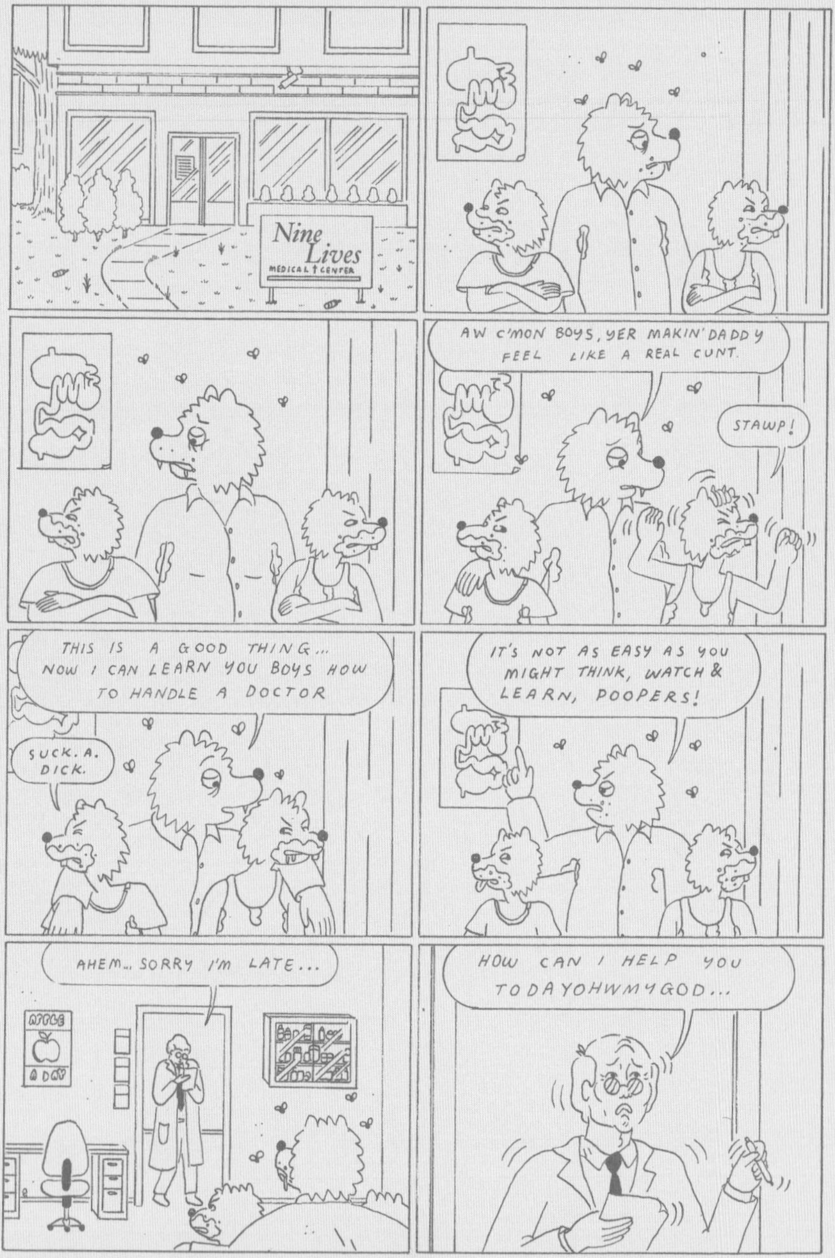
Nine Lives
MEDICAL CENTER
AW C'MON BOYS, YER MAKIN' DADDY FEEL LIKE A REAL CUNT.
STAWP!
THIS IS A GOOD THING... NOW I CAN LEARN YOU BOYS HOW TO HANDLE A DOCTOR
SUCK. A. DICK.
IT'S NOT AS EASY AS YOU MIGHT THINK, WATCH & LEARN, POOPERS!
AHEM... SORRY I'M LATE...
HOW CAN I HELP YOU TODAYOHWMYGOD...

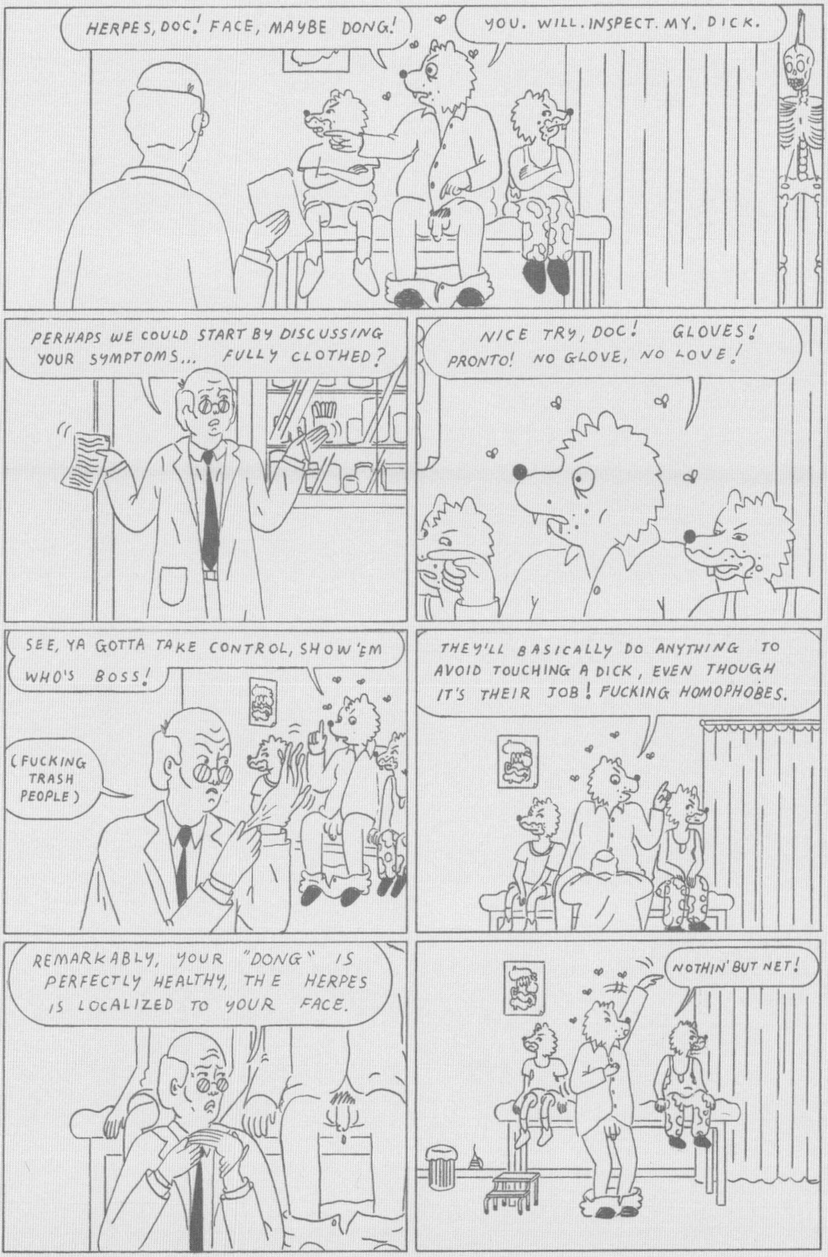
HERPES, DOC! FACE, MAYBE DONG!
YOU. WILL. INSPECT. MY. DICK.
PERHAPS WE COULD START BY DISCUSSING YOUR SYMPTOMS... FULLY CLOTHED?
NICE TRY, DOC! GLOVES! PRONTO! NO GLOVE, NO LOVE!
SEE, YA GOTTA TAKE CONTROL, SHOW 'EM WHO'S BOSS!
(FUCKING TRASH PEOPLE)
THEY'LL BASICALLY DO ANYTHING TO AVOID TOUCHING A DICK, EVEN THOUGH IT'S THEIR JOB! FUCKING HOMOPHOBES.
REMARKABLY, YOUR "DONG" IS PERFECTLY HEALTHY, THE HERPES IS LOCALIZED TO YOUR FACE.
NOTHIN' BUT NET!

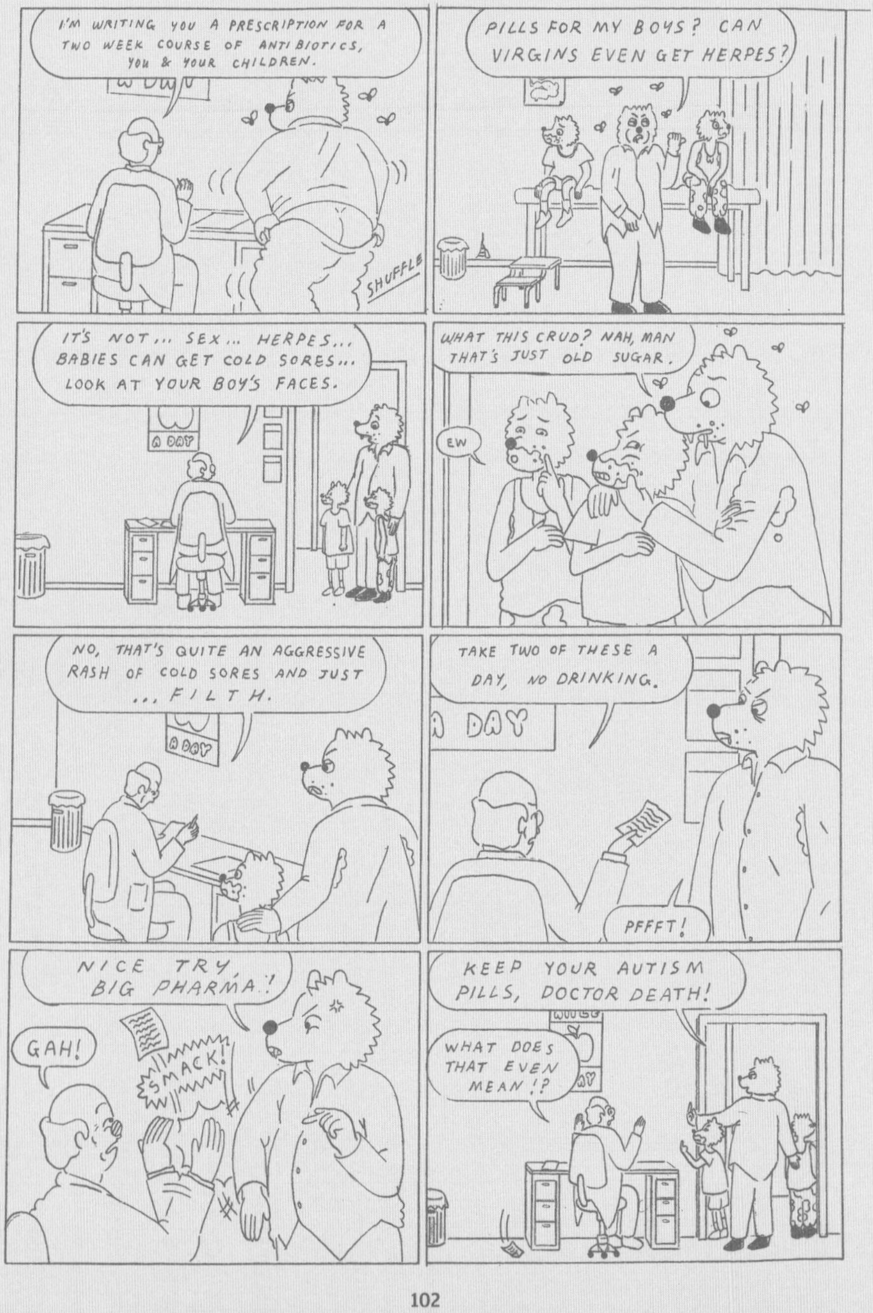
I'M WRITING YOU A PRESCRIPTION FOR A TWO WEEK COURSE OF ANTIBIOTICS, YOU & YOUR CHILDREN.
SHUFFLE
PILLS FOR MY BOYS? CAN VIRGINS EVEN GET HERPES?
IT'S NOT... SEX... HERPES... BABIES CAN GET COLD SORES... LOOK AT YOUR BOY'S FACES.
A DAY
WHAT THIS CRUD? NAH, MAN THAT'S JUST OLD SUGAR.
EW
NO, THAT'S QUITE AN AGGRESSIVE RASH OF COLD SORES AND JUST ..., FILTH.
A DAY
TAKE TWO OF THESE A DAY, NO DRINKING.
A DAY
PFFFT!
NICE TRY, BIG PHARMA!
GAH!
SMACK!
KEEP YOUR AUTISM PILLS, DOCTOR DEATH!
WHAT DOES THAT EVEN MEAN!?

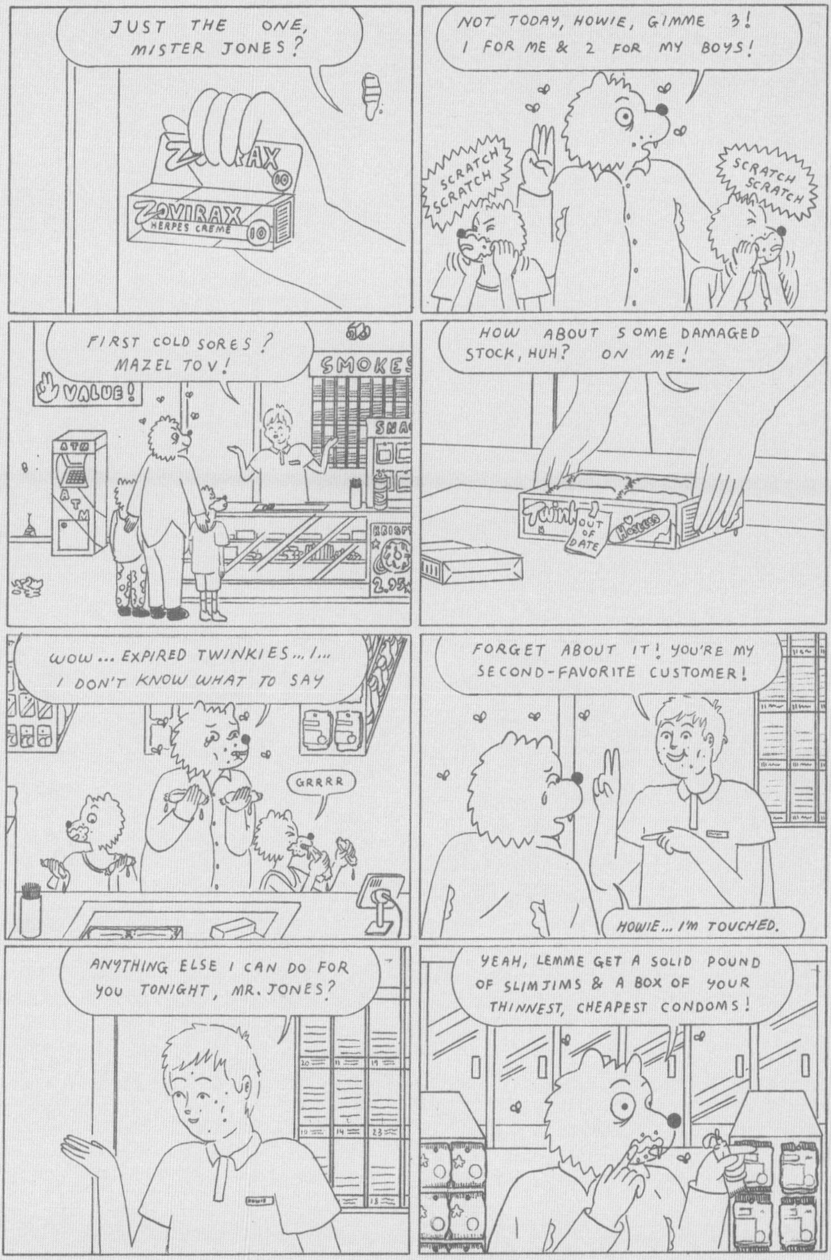
JUST THE ONE, MISTER JONES?
ZOVIRAX 10
ZOVIRAX HERPES CREME 10
NOT TODAY, HOWIE, GIMME 3! 1 FOR ME & 2 FOR MY BOYS!
SCRATCH SCRATCH
SCRATCH SCRATCH
FIRST COLD SORES? MAZEL TOV!
SMOKES
VALUE!
ATM
ATM
2.95
HOW ABOUT SOME DAMAGED STOCK, HUH? ON ME!
OUT OF DATE
WOW... EXPIRED TWINKIES... I... I DON'T KNOW WHAT TO SAY
GRRRR
FORGET ABOUT IT! YOU'RE MY SECOND-FAVORITE CUSTOMER!
HOWIE... I'M TOUCHED.
ANYTHING ELSE I CAN DO FOR YOU TONIGHT, MR. JONES?
YEAH, LEMME GET A SOLID POUND OF SLIMJIMS & A BOX OF YOUR THINNEST, CHEAPEST CONDOMS!

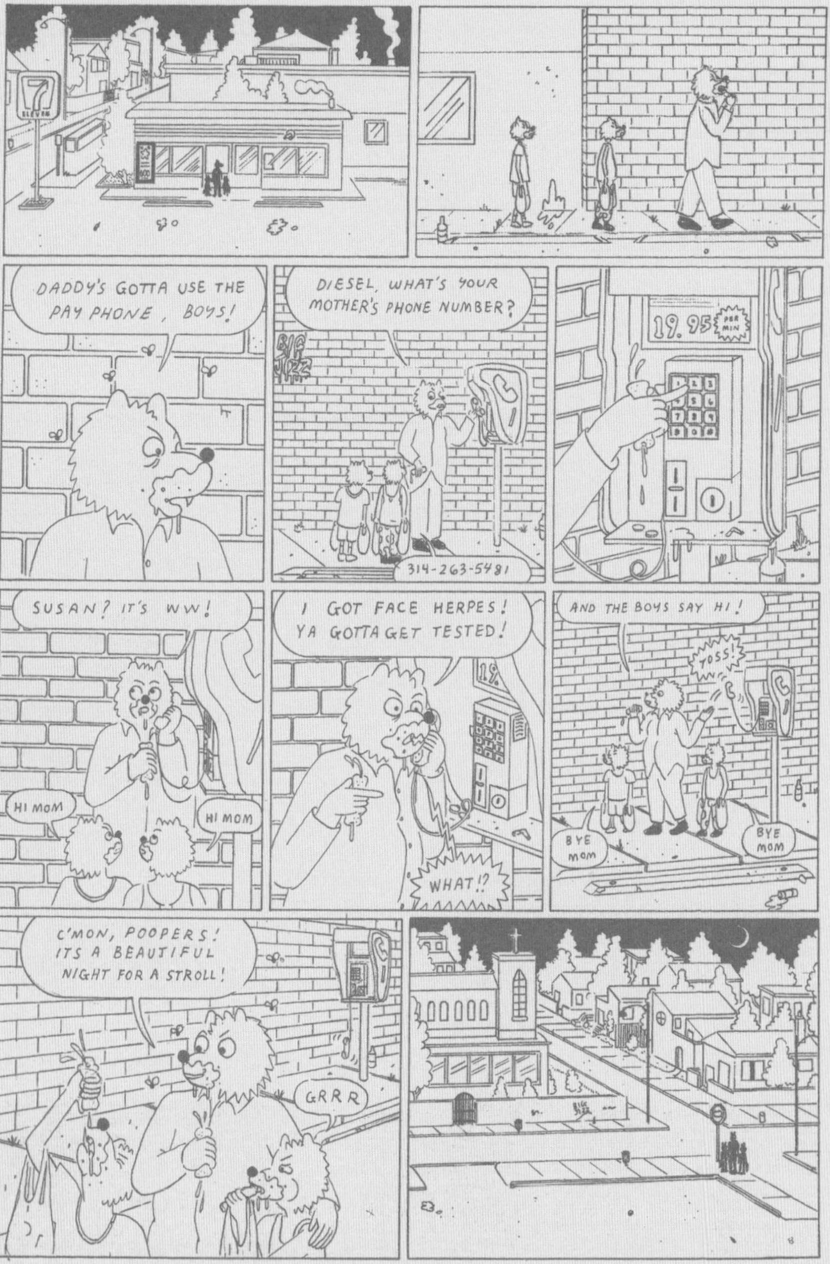
ELEVEN
DADDY'S GOTTA USE THE PAY PHONE, BOYS!
DIESEL, WHAT'S YOUR MOTHER'S PHONE NUMBER?
BIG JIZZ
314-263-5481
19.95 PER MIN
SUSAN? IT'S WW!
HI MOM
HI MOM
I GOT FACE HERPES! YA GOTTA GET TESTED!
WHAT!?
AND THE BOYS SAY HI!
TOSS!
BYE MOM
BYE MOM
C'MON, POOPERS! ITS A BEAUTIFUL NIGHT FOR A STROLL!
GRRR

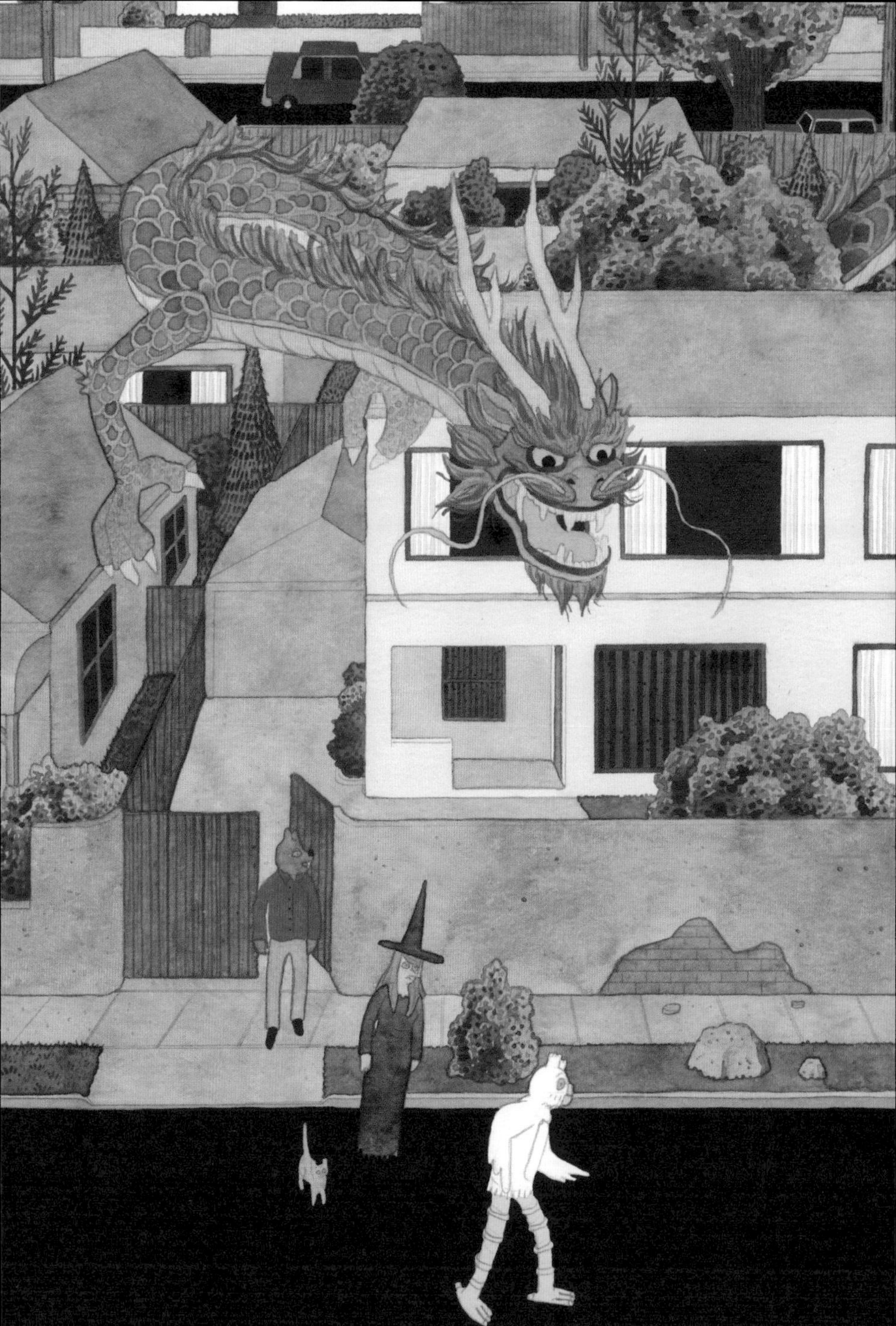

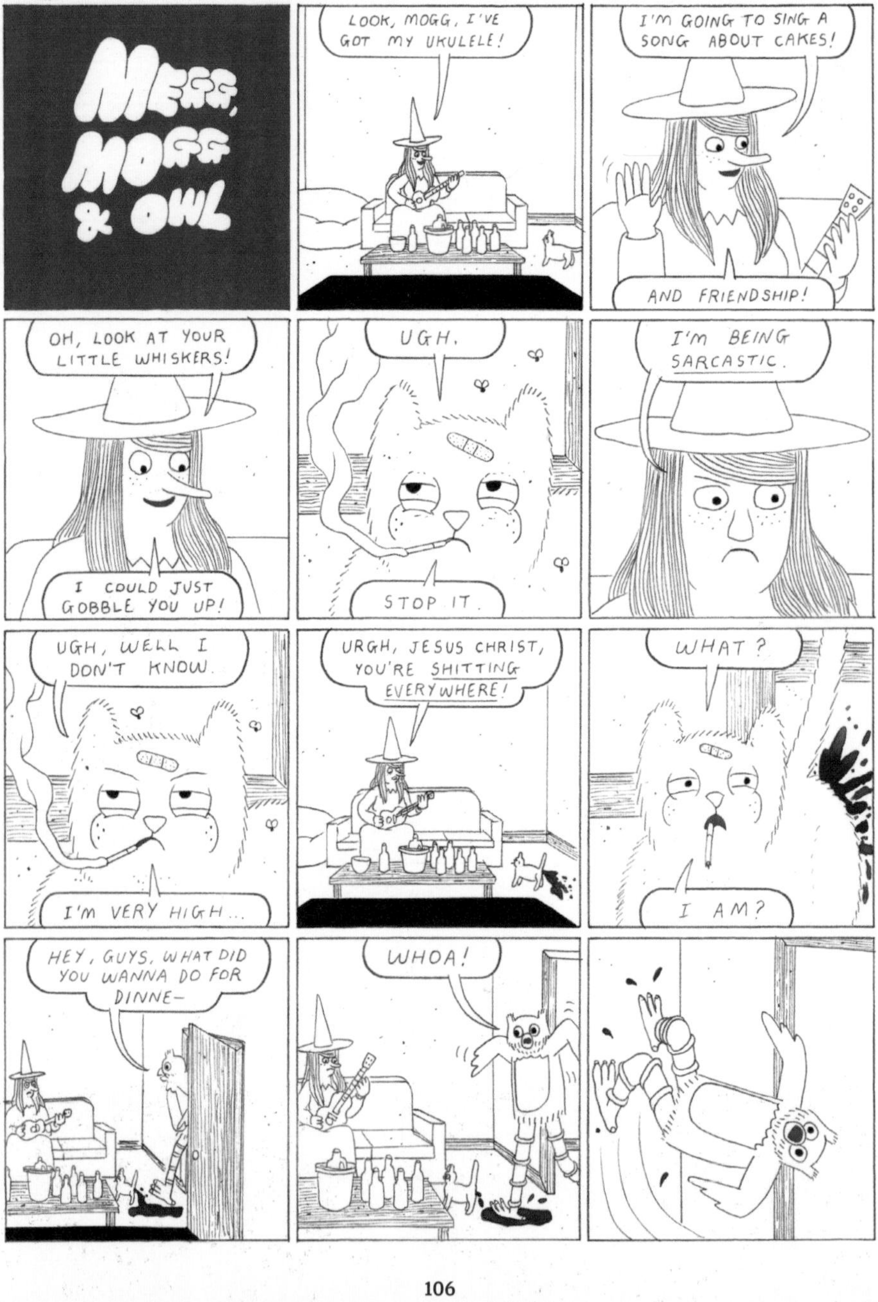
MEGG, MOGG & OWL
LOOK, MOGG, I'VE GOT MY UKULELE!
I'M GOING TO SING A SONG ABOUT CAKES!
AND FRIENDSHIP!
OH, LOOK AT YOUR LITTLE WHISKERS!
I COULD JUST GOBBLE YOU UP!
UGH.
STOP IT.
I'M BEING SARCASTIC.
UGH, WELL I DON'T KNOW.
I'M VERY HIGH...
URGH, JESUS CHRIST, YOU'RE SHITTING EVERYWHERE!
WHAT?
I AM?
HEY, GUYS, WHAT DID YOU WANNA DO FOR DINNE-
WHOA!

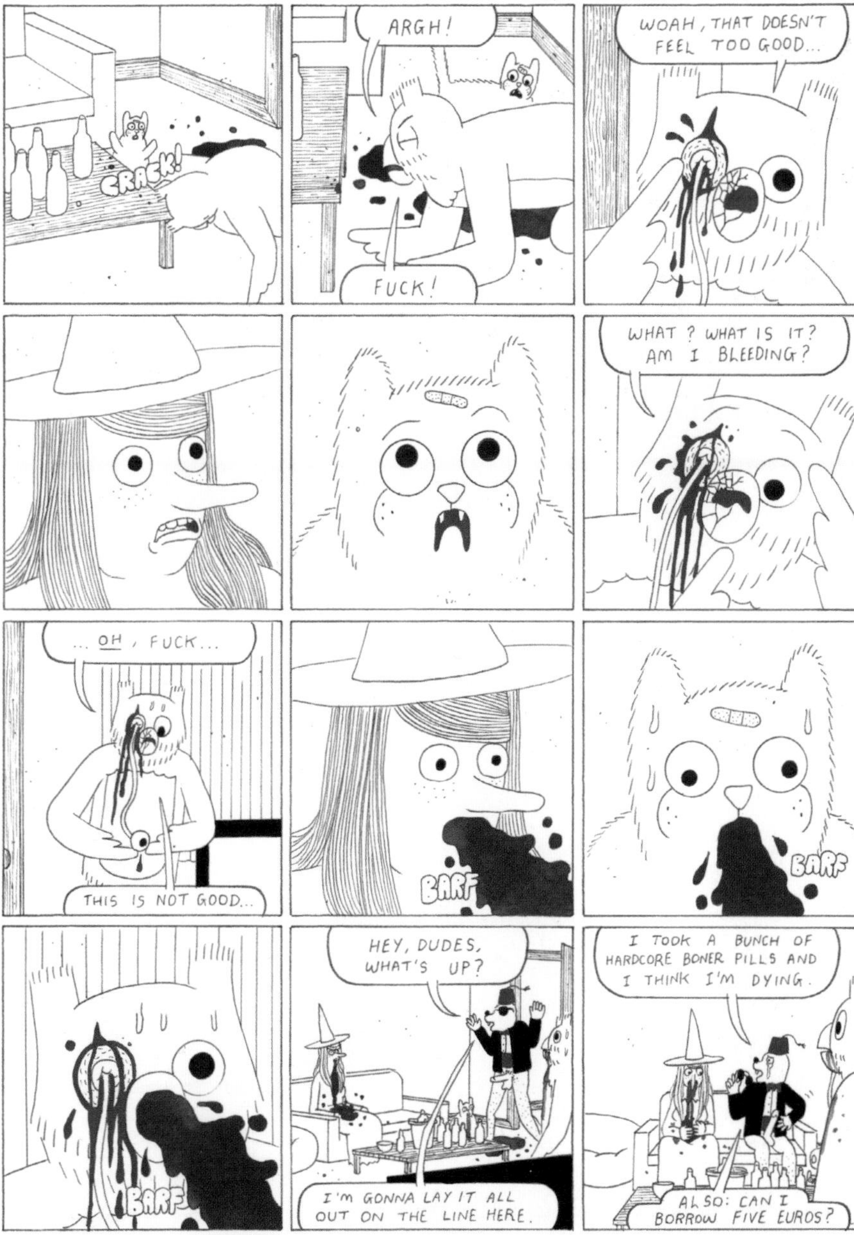
CRACK!
ARGH!
FUCK!
WOAH, THAT DOESN'T FEEL TOO GOOD...
WHAT? WHAT IS IT? AM I BLEEDING?
... OH, FUCK...
THIS IS NOT GOOD...
BARF
BARF
BARF
HEY, DUDES, WHAT'S UP?
I'M GONNA LAY IT ALL OUT ON THE LINE HERE.
I TOOK A BUNCH OF HARDCORE BONER PILLS AND I THINK I'M DYING.
ALSO: CAN I BORROW FIVE EUROS?

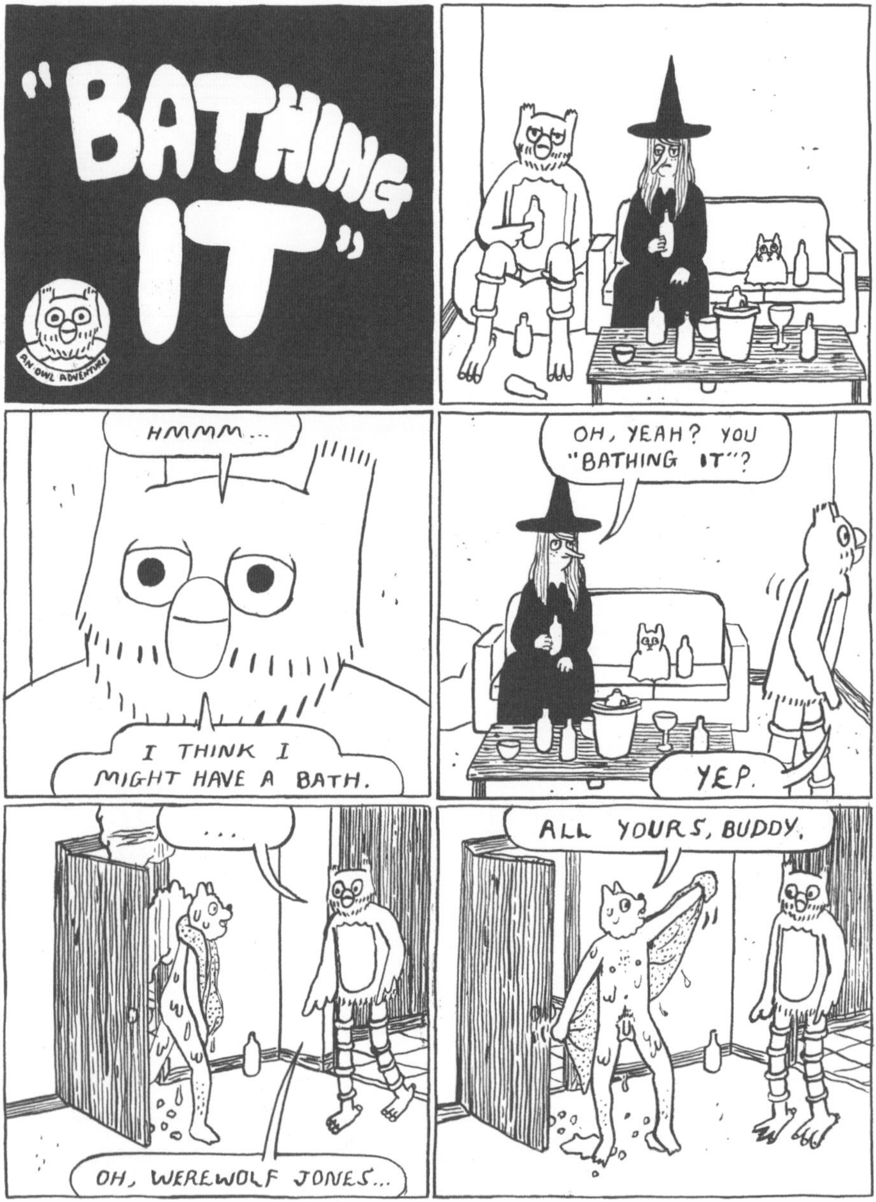
"BATHING IT"
AN OWL ADVENTURE
HMMM...
I THINK I MIGHT HAVE A BATH.
OH, YEAH? YOU "BATHING IT"?
YEP.
...
OH, WEREWOLF JONES...
ALL YOURS, BUDDY.

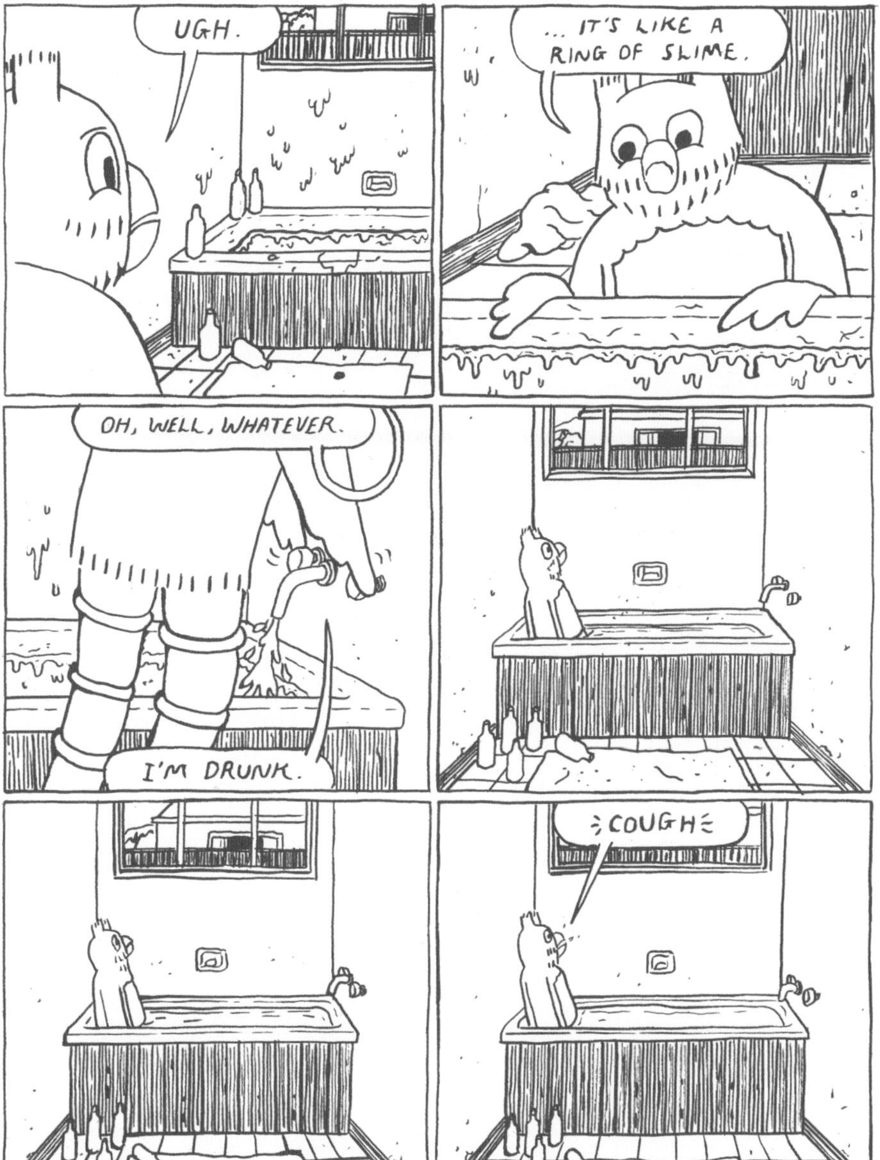
UGH.
... IT'S LIKE A RING OF SLIME.
OH, WELL, WHATEVER.
I'M DRUNK.
COUGH

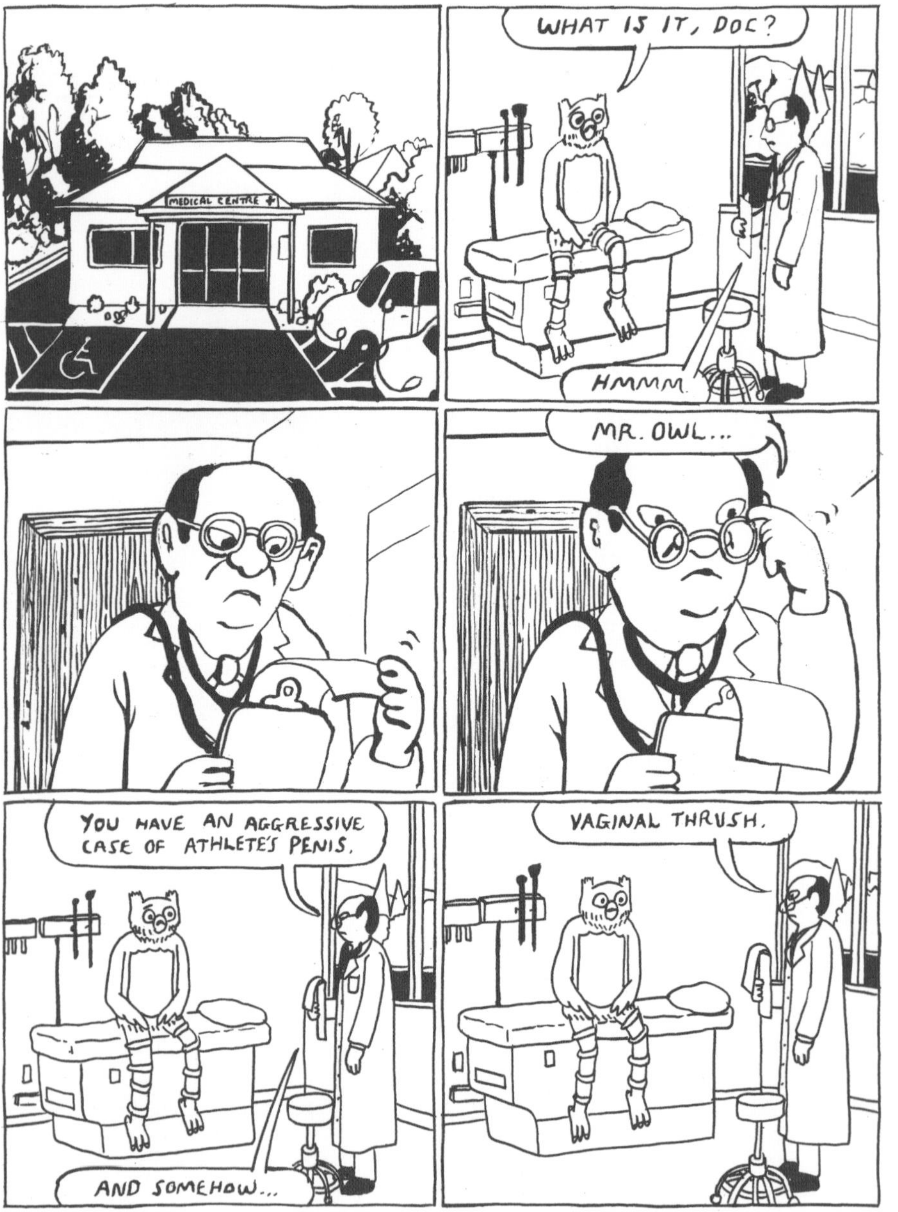
MEDICAL CENTRE
WHAT IS IT, DOC?
HMMM.
MR. OWL...
YOU HAVE AN AGGRESSIVE CASE OF ATHLETE'S PENIS.
AND SOMEHOW...
VAGINAL THRUSH.

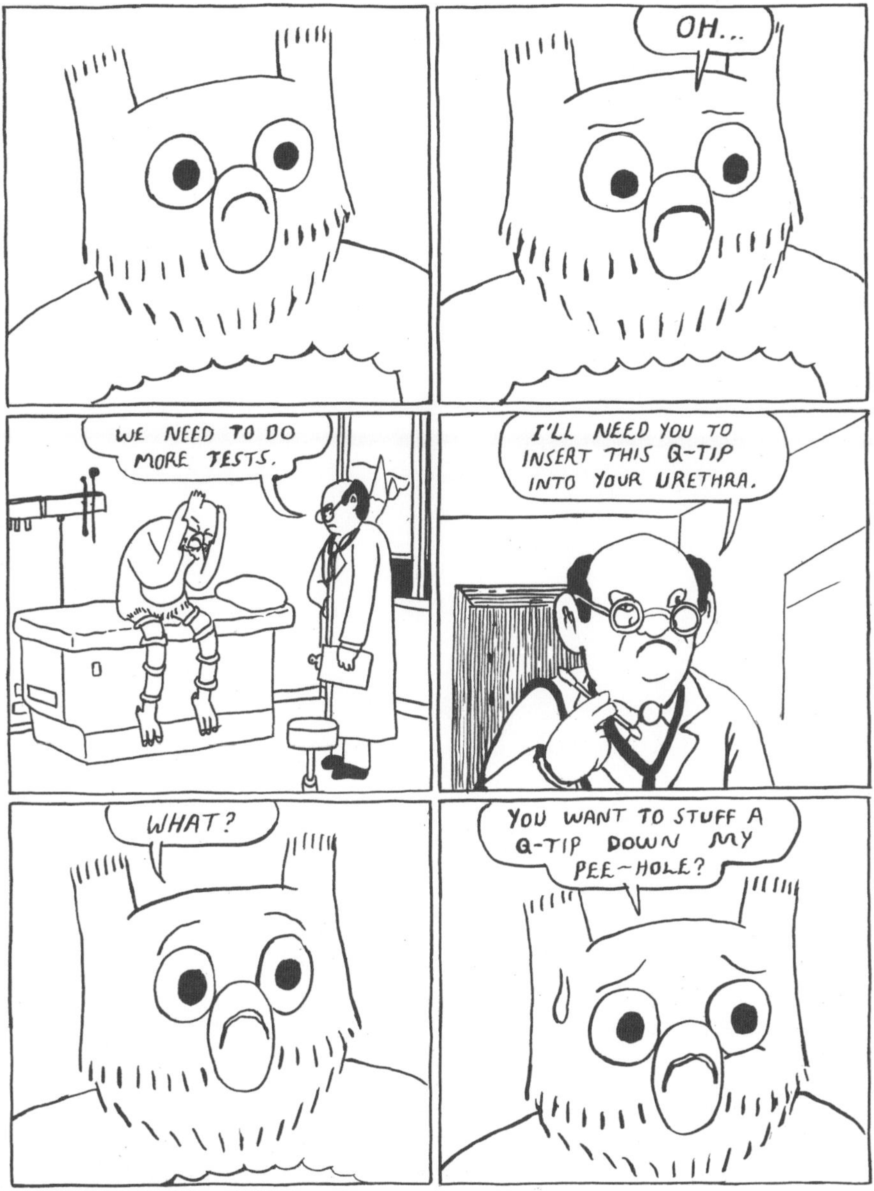
OH...
WE NEED TO DO MORE TESTS.
I'LL NEED YOU TO INSERT THIS Q-TIP INTO YOUR URETHRA.
WHAT?
YOU WANT TO STUFF A Q-TIP DOWN MY PEE-HOLE?

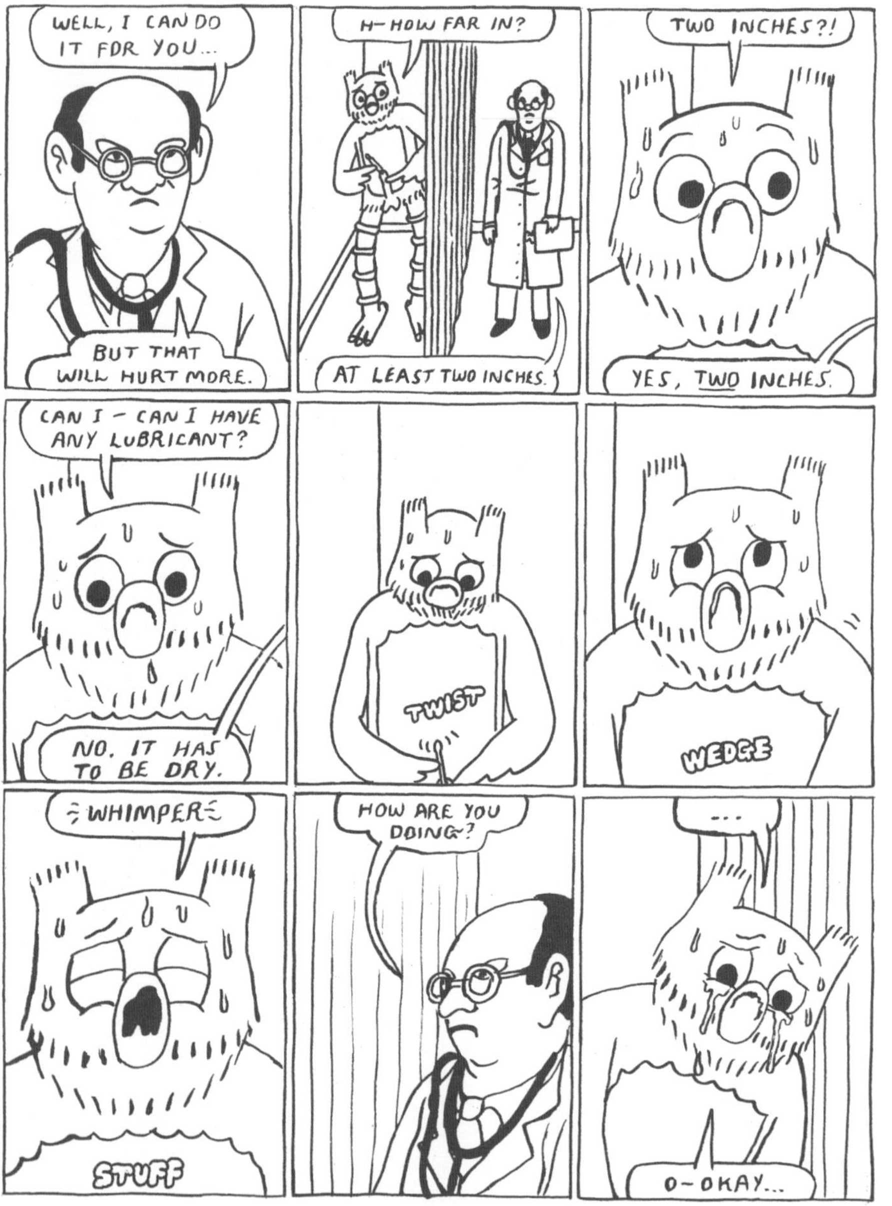
WELL, I CAN DO IT FOR YOU...
BUT THAT WILL HURT MORE.
H-HOW FAR IN?
AT LEAST TWO INCHES.
TWO INCHES?!
YES, TWO INCHES.
CAN I - CAN I HAVE ANY LUBRICANT?
NO. IT HAS TO BE DRY.
TWIST
WEDGE
WHIMPER
STUFF
HOW ARE YOU DOING?
...
O-OKAY...

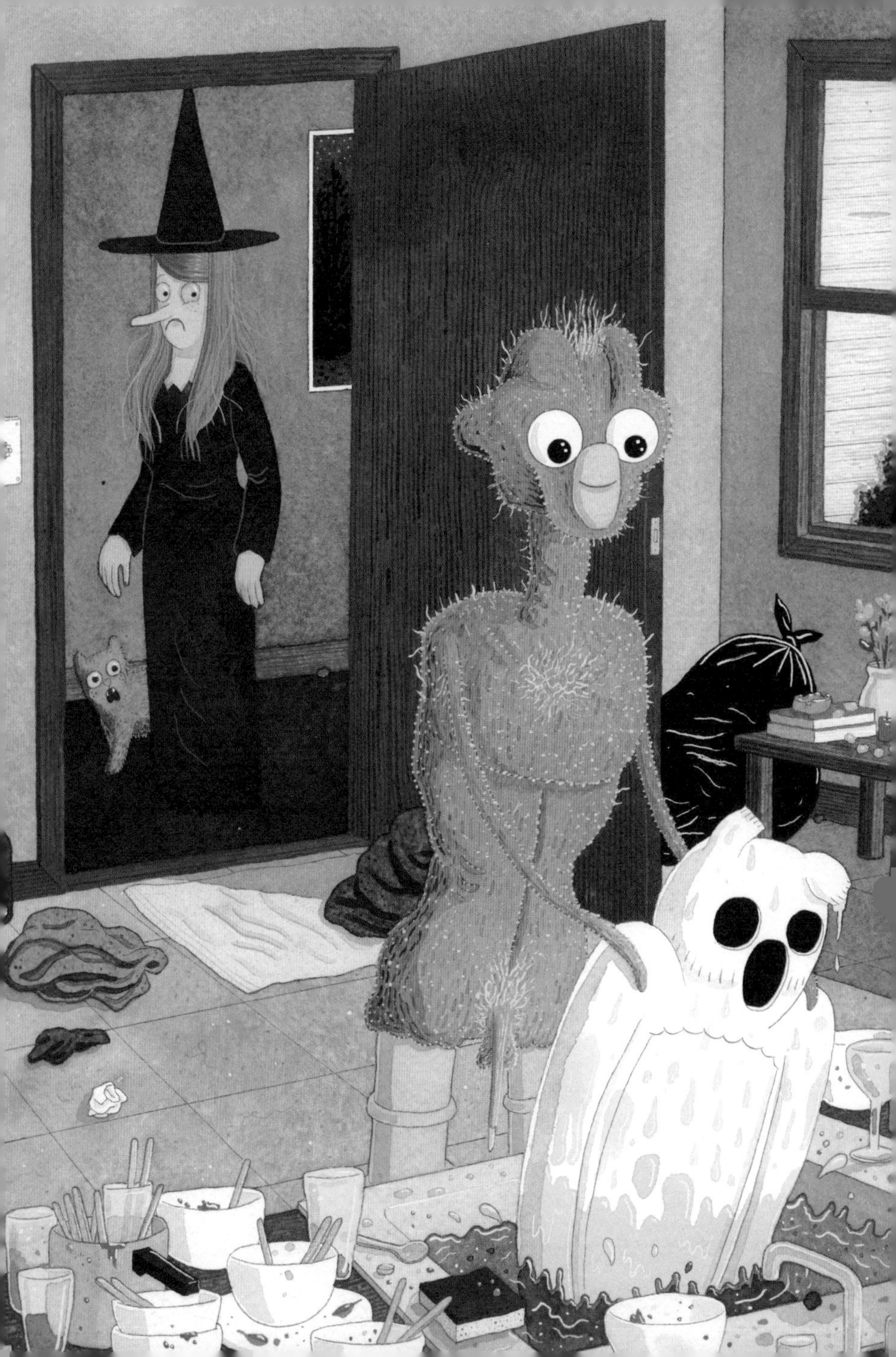

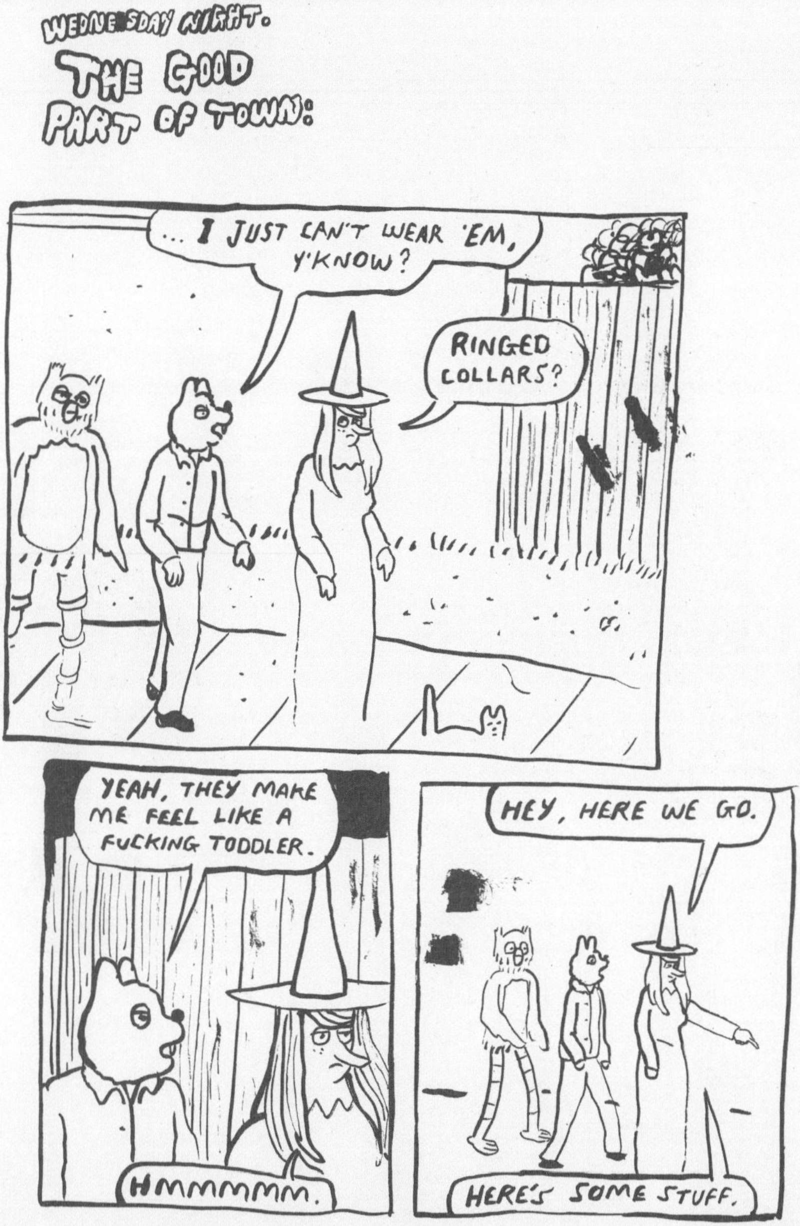
WEDNESDAY NIGHT.
THE GOOD PART OF TOWN:
... I JUST CAN'T WEAR 'EM, Y'KNOW?
RINGED COLLARS?
YEAH, THEY MAKE ME FEEL LIKE A FUCKING TODDLER.
HMMMMMM.
HEY, HERE WE GO.
HERE'S SOME STUFF.

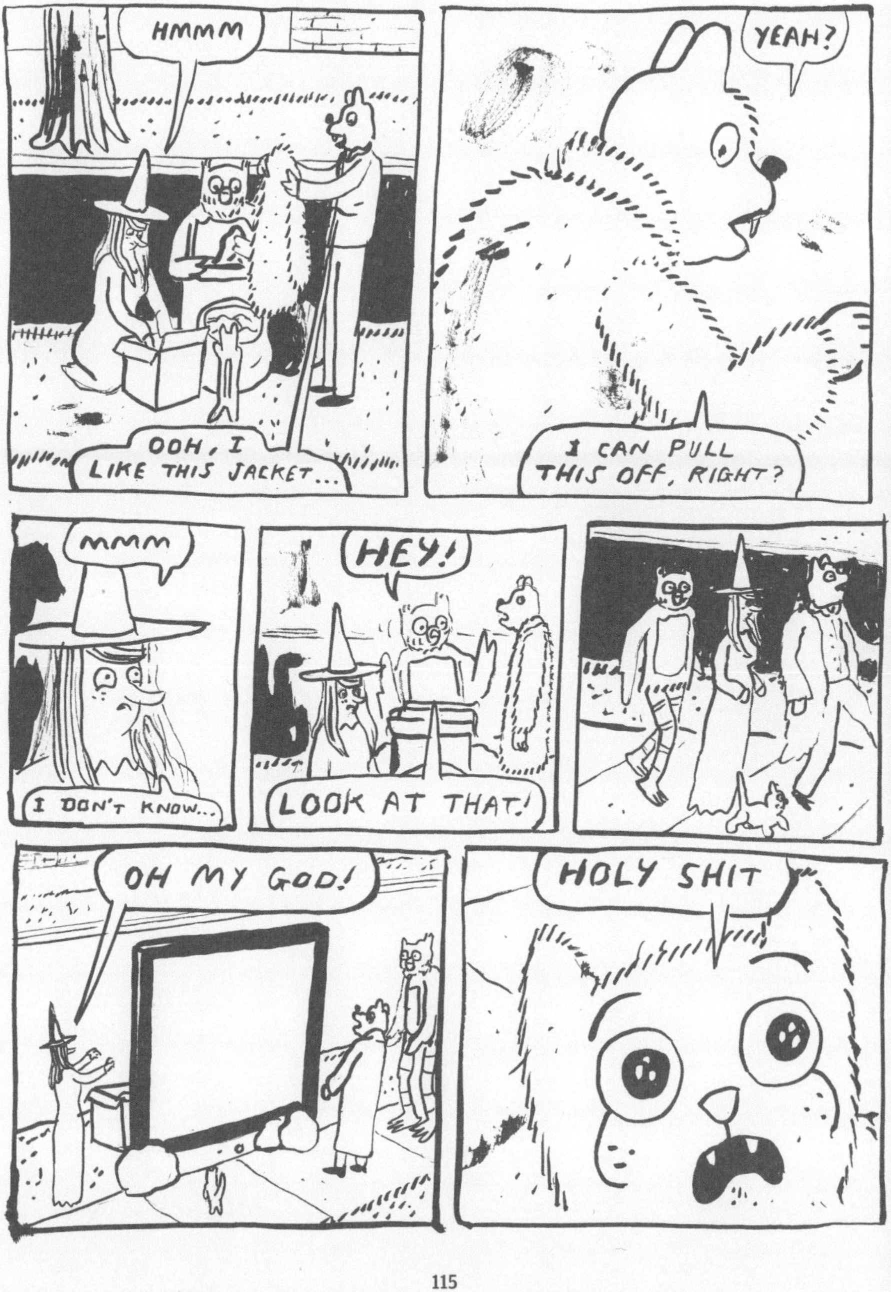
HMMM
OOH, I LIKE THIS JACKET...
YEAH?
I CAN PULL THIS OFF, RIGHT?
MMM
I DON'T KNOW...
HEY!
LOOK AT THAT!
OH MY GOD!
HOLY SHIT

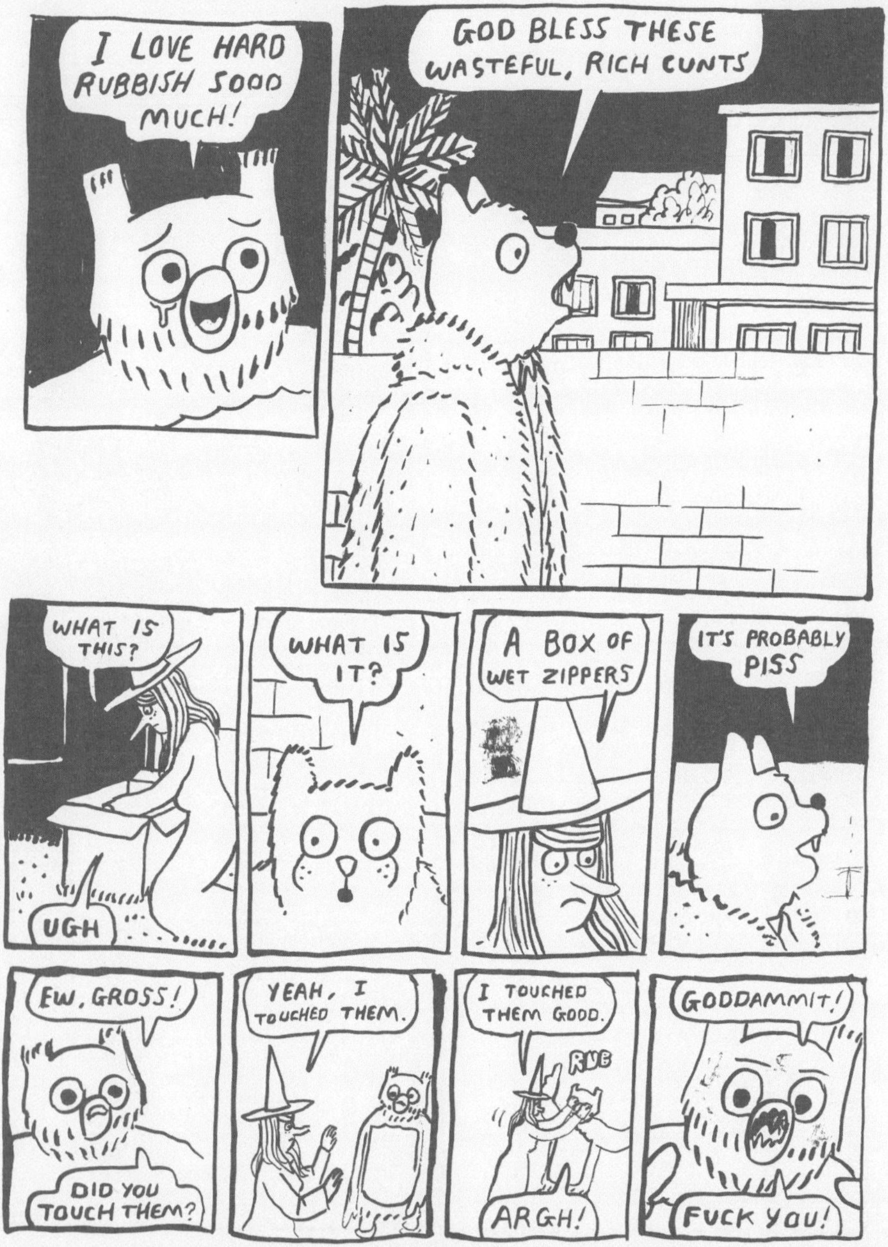
I LOVE HARD RUBBISH SOOO MUCH!
GOD BLESS THESE WASTEFUL, RICH CUNTS
WHAT IS THIS?
UGH
WHAT IS IT?
A BOX OF WET ZIPPERS
IT'S PROBABLY PISS
EW, GROSS!
DID YOU TOUCH THEM?
YEAH, I TOUCHED THEM.
I TOUCHED THEM GOOD.
RUB
ARGH!
GODDAMMIT!
FUCK YOU!

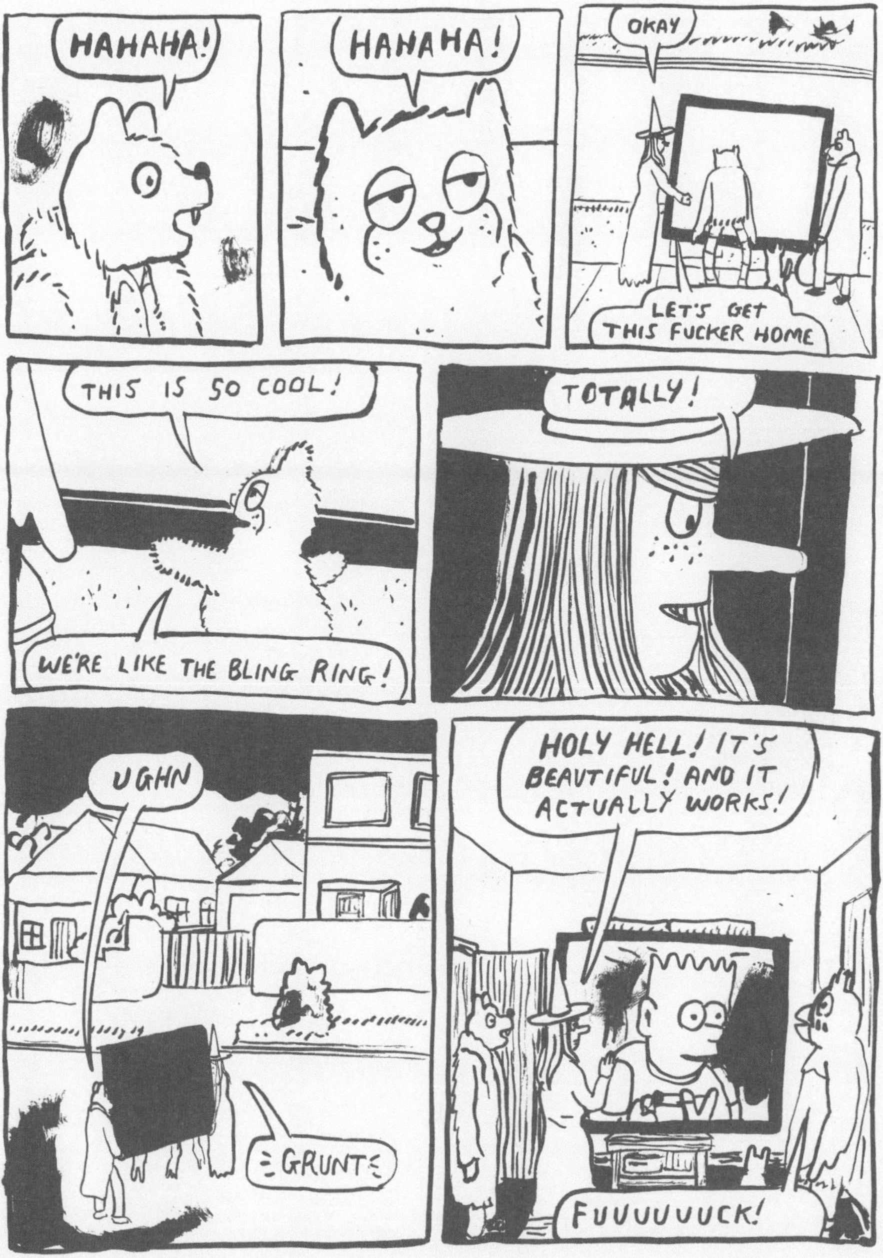
HAHAHA!
HAHAHA!
OKAY
LET'S GET THIS FUCKER HOME
THIS IS SO COOL!
WE'RE LIKE THE BLING RING!
TOTALLY!
UGHN
GRUNT
HOLY HELL! IT'S BEAUTIFUL! AND IT ACTUALLY WORKS!
FUUUUUUCK!

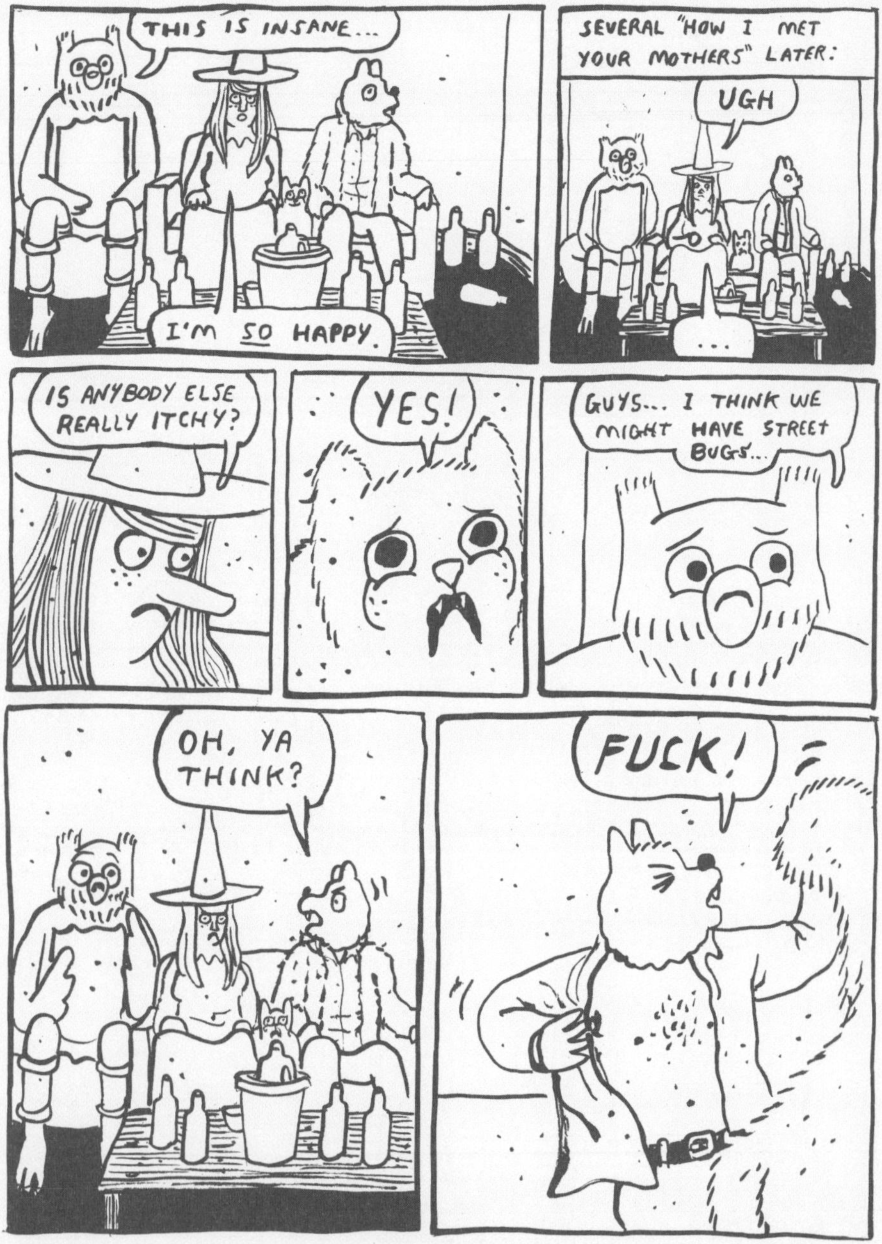
THIS IS INSANE...
I'M SO HAPPY.
SEVERAL "HOW I MET YOUR MOTHERS" LATER:
UGH
...
IS ANYBODY ELSE REALLY ITCHY?
YES!
GUYS... I THINK WE MIGHT HAVE STREET BUGS...
OH, YA THINK?
FUCK!

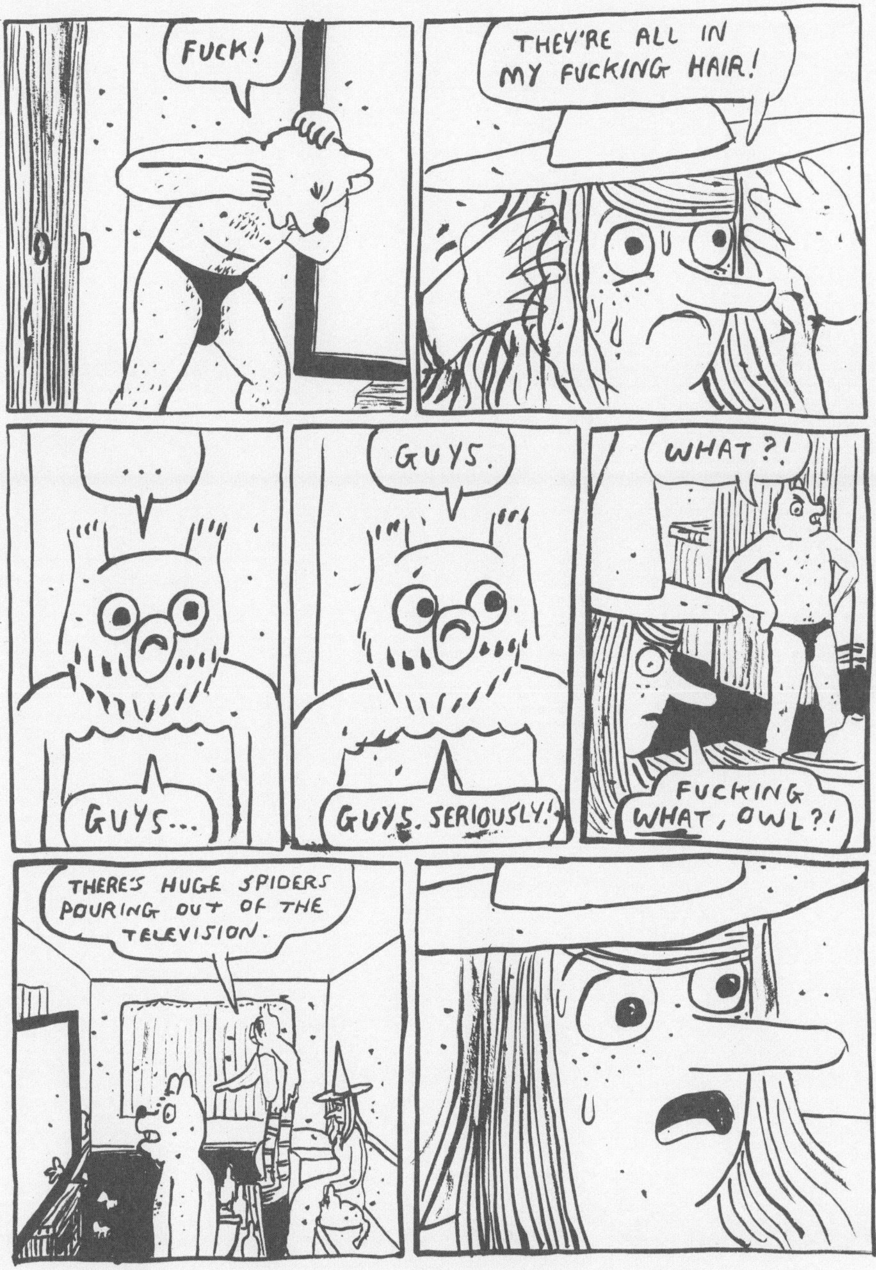
FUCK!
THEY'RE ALL IN MY FUCKING HAIR!
...
GUYS...
GUYS.
GUYS. SERIOUSLY!
WHAT?!
FUCKING WHAT, OWL?!
THERE'S HUGE SPIDERS POURING OUT OF THE TELEVISION.

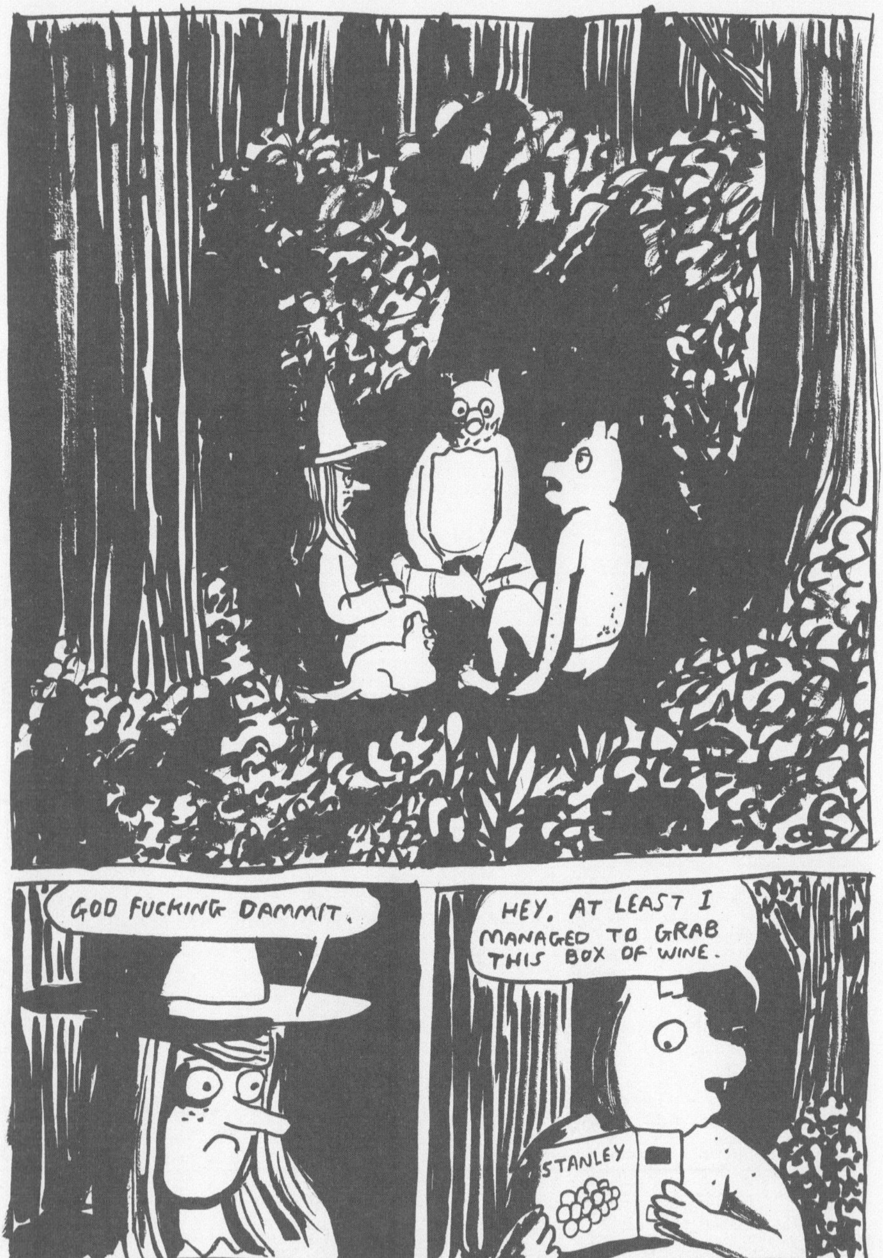
GOD FUCKING DAMMIT.
HEY, AT LEAST I MANAGED TO GRAB THIS BOX OF WINE.
STANLEY

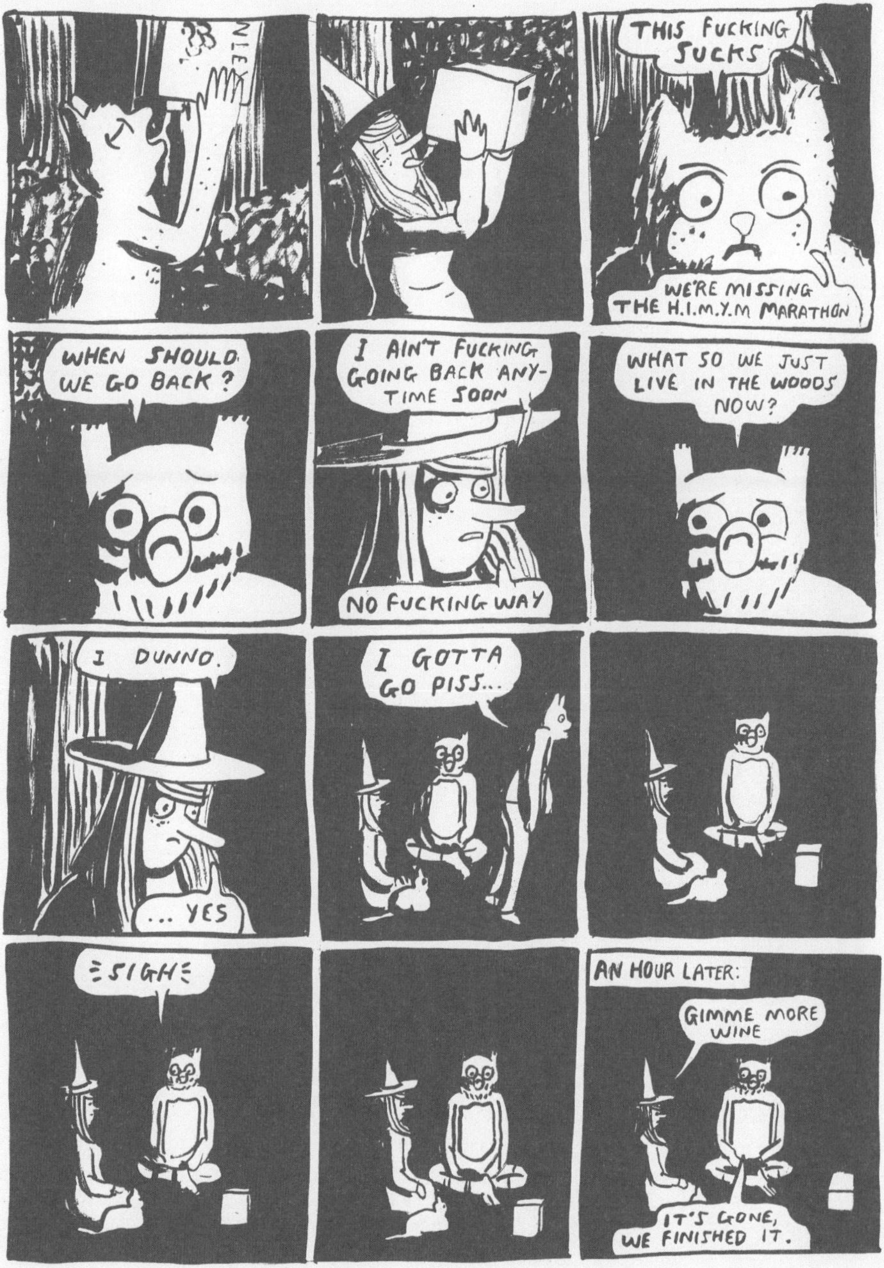
THIS FUCKING SUCKS
WE'RE MISSING THE H.I.M.Y.M MARATHON
WHEN SHOULD WE GO BACK?
I AIN'T FUCKING GOING BACK ANY-TIME SOON
NO FUCKING WAY
WHAT SO WE JUST LIVE IN THE WOODS NOW?
I DUNNO.
... YES
I GOTTA GO PISS...
SIGH
AN HOUR LATER:
GIMME MORE WINE
IT'S GONE, WE FINISHED IT.

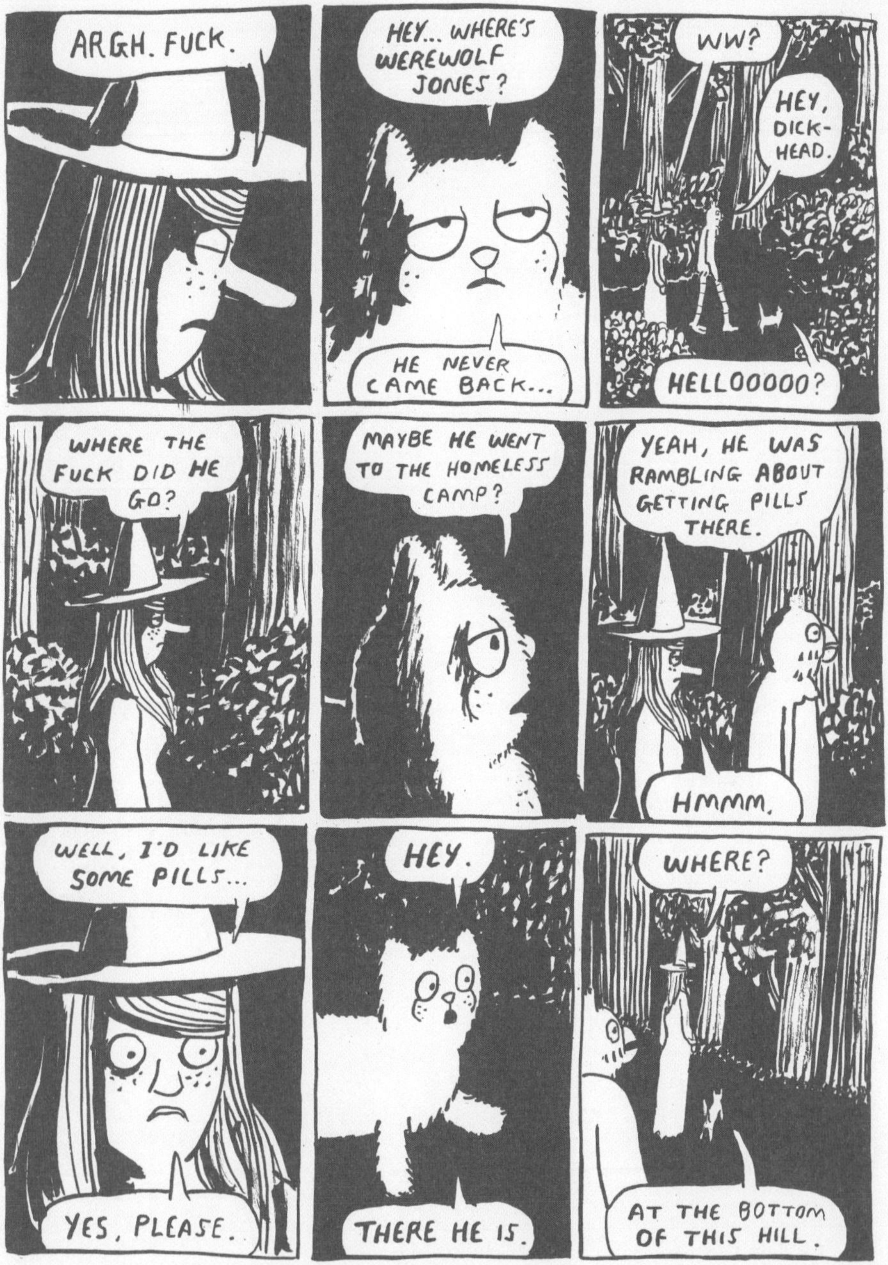
ARGH. FUCK.
HEY... WHERE'S WEREWOLF JONES?
HE NEVER CAME BACK...
WW?
HEY, DICK-HEAD.
HELLOOOOO?
WHERE THE FUCK DID HE GO?
MAYBE HE WENT TO THE HOMELESS CAMP?
YEAH, HE WAS RAMBLING ABOUT GETTING PILLS THERE.
HMMM.
WELL, I'D LIKE SOME PILLS...
YES, PLEASE.
HEY.
THERE HE IS.
WHERE?
AT THE BOTTOM OF THIS HILL.

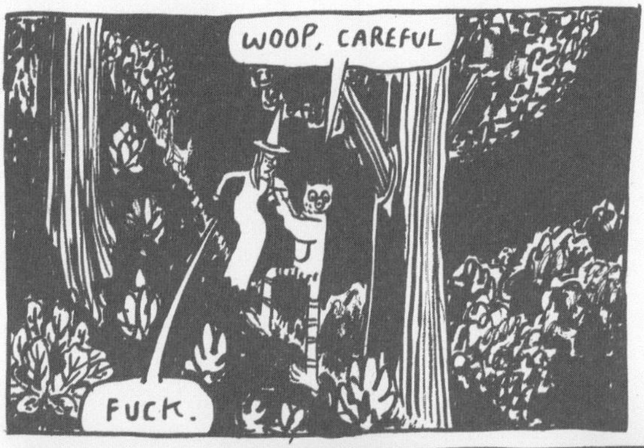
WOOP, CAREFUL
FUCK.

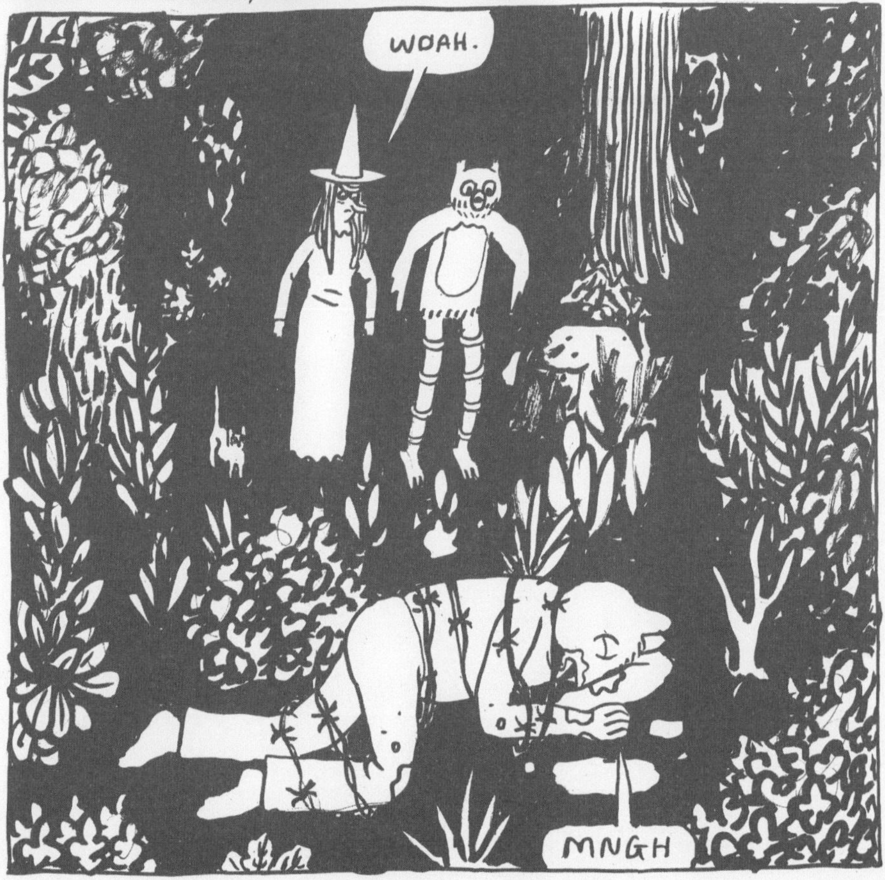
WOAH.
MNGH

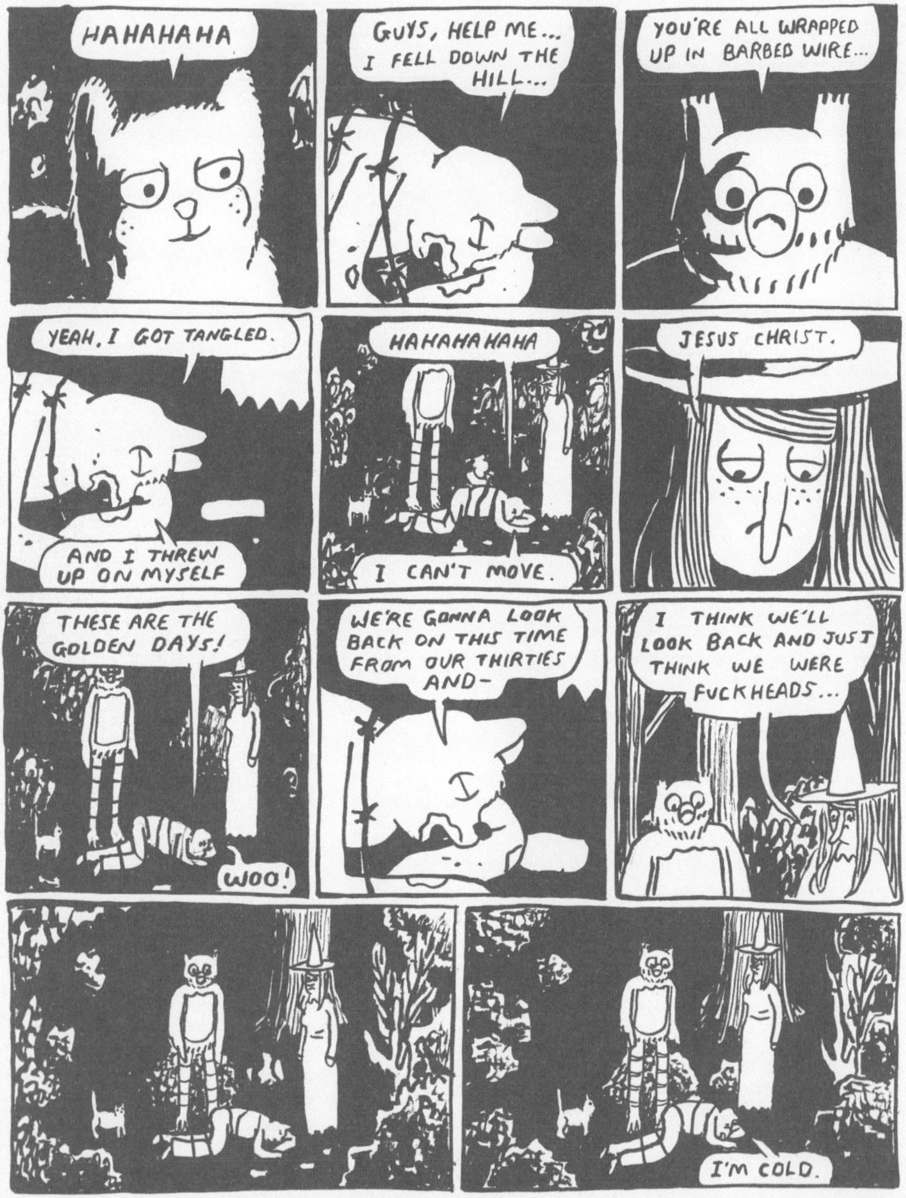
HAHAHAHA
GUYS, HELP ME... I FELL DOWN THE HILL...
YOU'RE ALL WRAPPED UP IN BARBED WIRE...
YEAH, I GOT TANGLED.
AND I THREW UP ON MYSELF
HAHAHAHAHA
I CAN'T MOVE.
JESUS CHRIST.
THESE ARE THE GOLDEN DAYS!
WOO!
WE'RE GONNA LOOK BACK ON THIS TIME FROM OUR THIRTIES AND-
I THINK WE'LL LOOK BACK AND JUST THINK WE WERE FUCKHEADS...
I'M COLD.

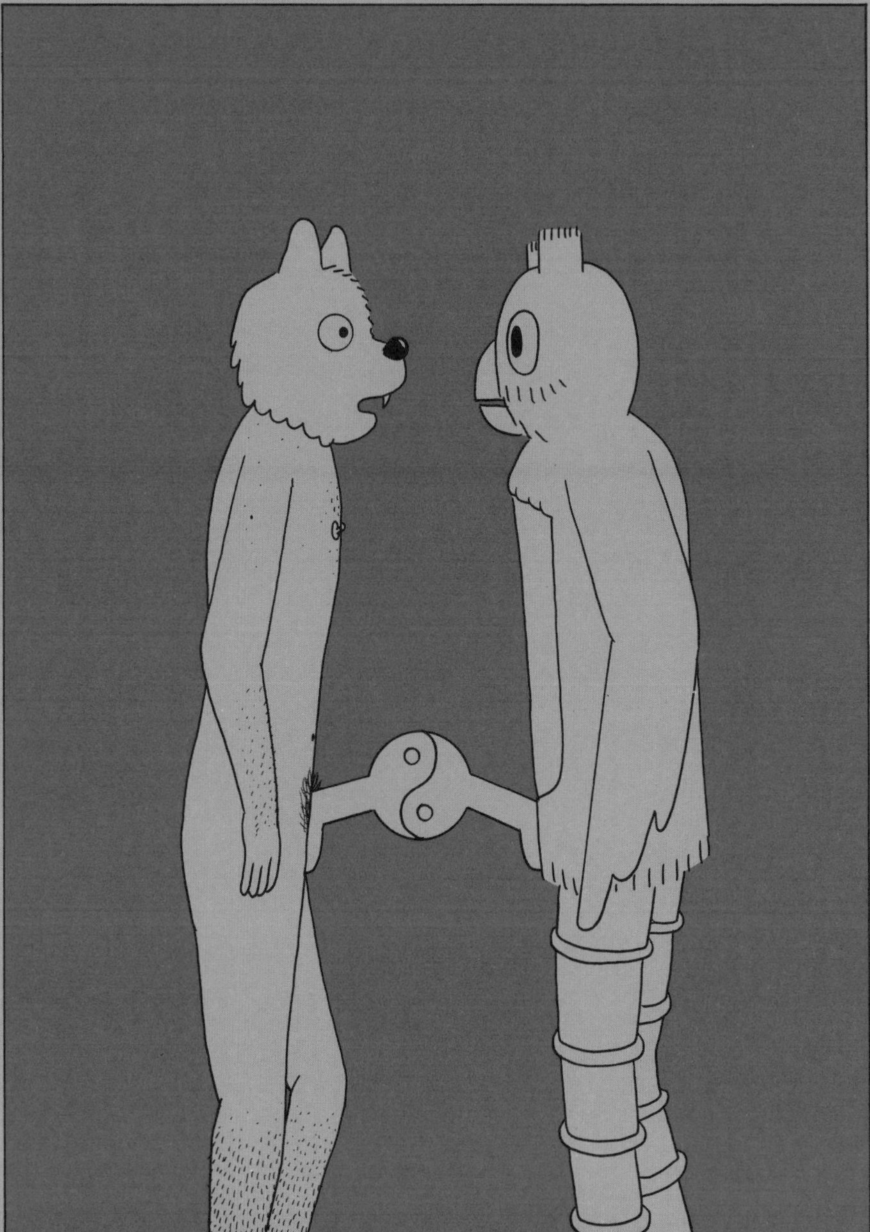

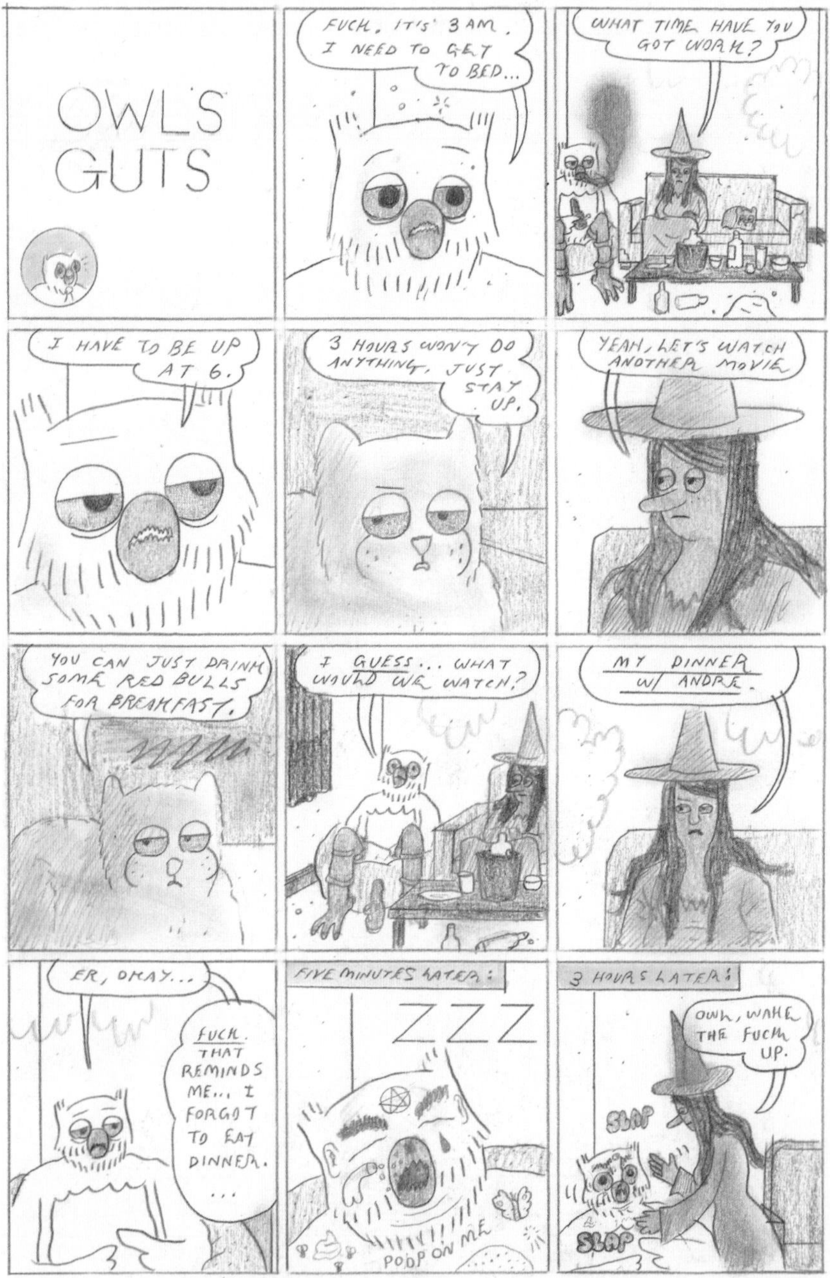
OWLS GUTS
FUCK, IT'S 3 AM. I NEED TO GET TO BED...
WHAT TIME HAVE YOU GOT WORK?
I HAVE TO BE UP AT 6.
3 HOURS WON'T DO ANYTHING, JUST STAY UP.
YEAH, LET'S WATCH ANOTHER MOVIE
YOU CAN JUST DRINK SOME RED BULLS FOR BREAKFAST.
I GUESS... WHAT WOULD WE WATCH?
MY DINNER W/ ANDRE.
ER, OKAY...
FUCK. THAT REMINDS ME... I FORGOT TO EAT DINNER. ...
FIVE MINUTES LATER:
ZZZ
POOP ON ME
3 HOURS LATER:
OWL, WAKE THE FUCK UP.
SLAP
SLAP

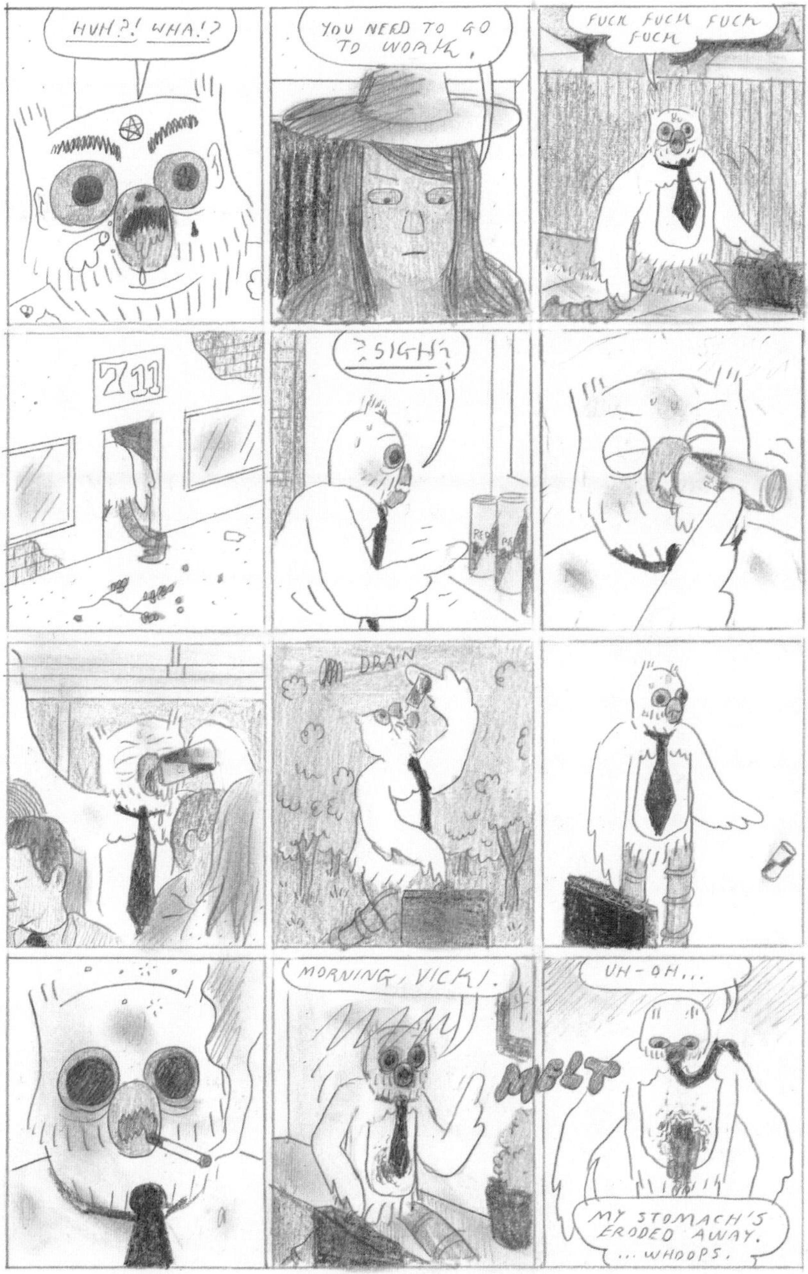
HUH?! WHA!?
YOU NEED TO GO TO WORK.
FUCK FUCK FUCK FUCK
711
SIGH
DRAIN
MORNING, VICKI.
MELT
UH-OH...
MY STOMACH'S ERODED AWAY. ...WHOOPS.

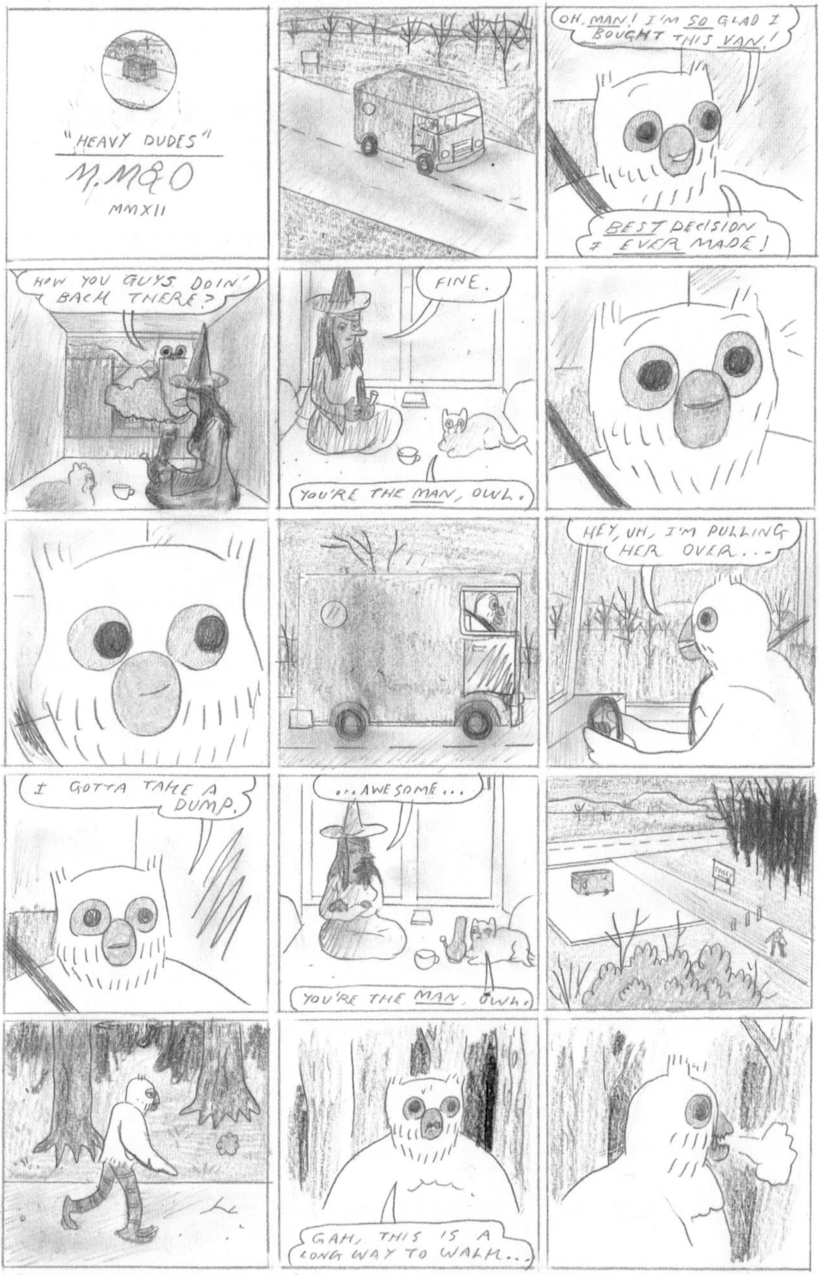
"HEAVY DUDES"
M.M&O
MMXII
OH, MAN! I'M SO GLAD I BOUGHT THIS VAN!
BEST DECISION I EVER MADE!
HOW YOU GUYS DOIN' BACK THERE?
FINE.
YOU'RE THE MAN, OWL.
HEY, UH, I'M PULLING HER OVER...
I GOTTA TAKE A DUMP.
...AWESOME...
YOU'RE THE MAN, OWL.
GAH, THIS IS A LONG WAY TO WALK...

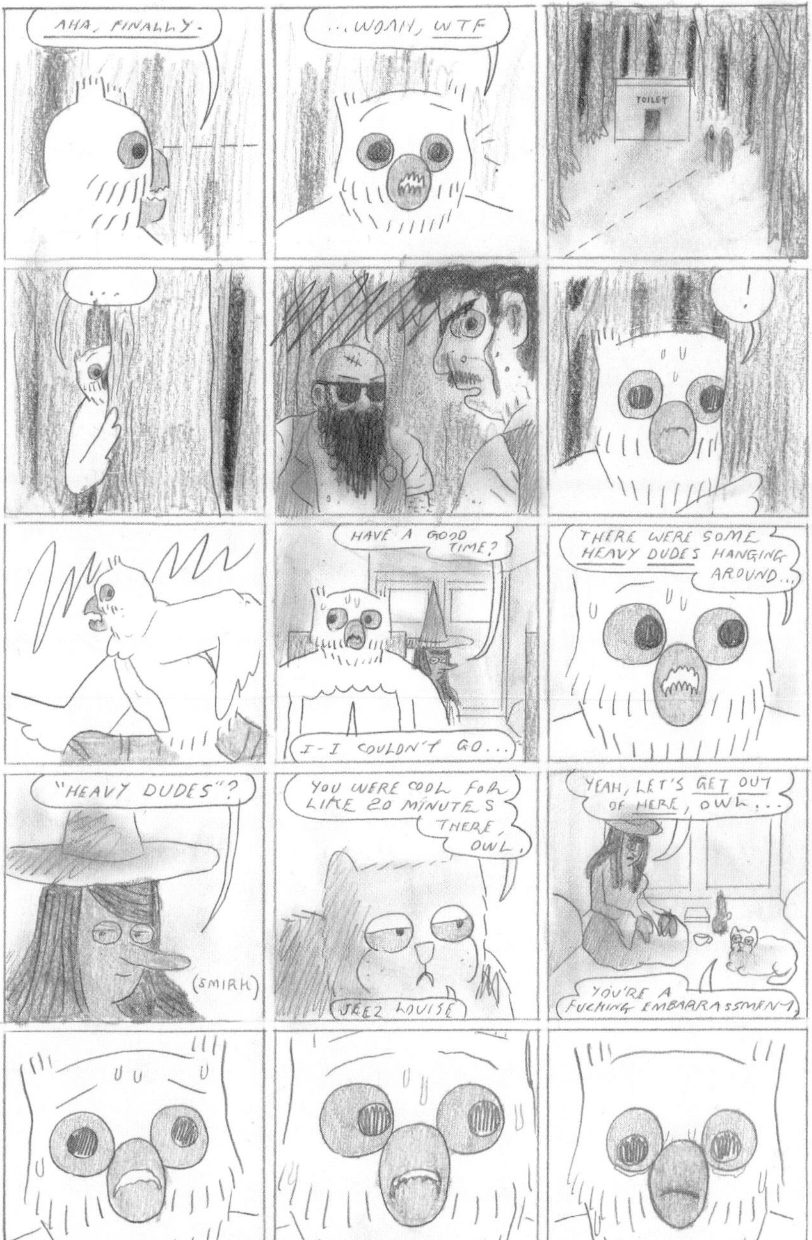
AHA, FINALLY.
...WOAH, WTF
TOILET
...
!
HAVE A GOOD TIME?
I-I COULDN'T GO...
THERE WERE SOME HEAVY DUDES HANGING AROUND...
"HEAVY DUDES"?
(SMIRK)
YOU WERE COOL FOR LIKE 20 MINUTES THERE, OWL.
JEEZ LOUISE
YEAH, LET'S GET OUT OF HERE, OWL...
YOU'RE A FUCKING EMBARRASSMENT

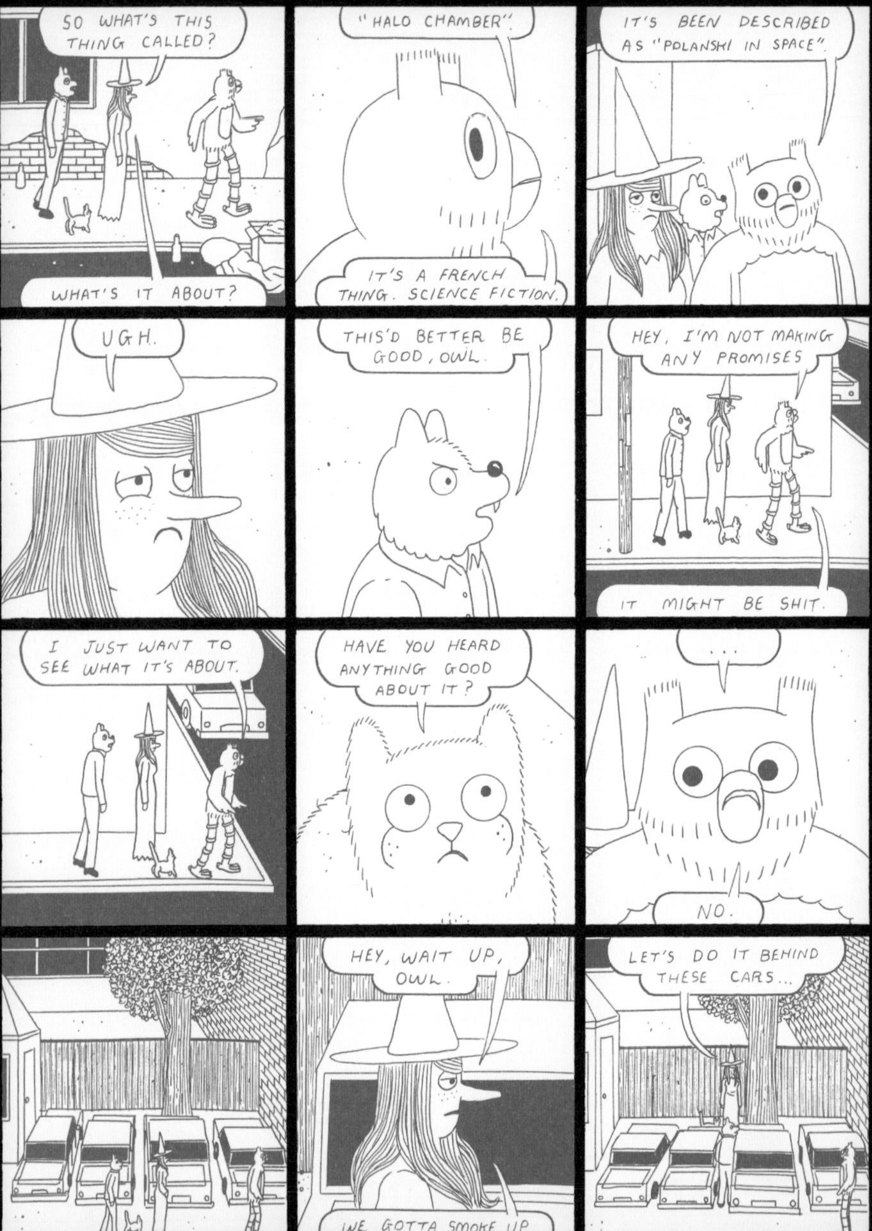
SO WHAT'S THIS THING CALLED?
WHAT'S IT ABOUT?
"HALO CHAMBER".
IT'S A FRENCH THING. SCIENCE FICTION.
IT'S BEEN DESCRIBED AS "POLANSKI IN SPACE".
UGH.
THIS'D BETTER BE GOOD, OWL.
HEY, I'M NOT MAKING ANY PROMISES
IT MIGHT BE SHIT.
I JUST WANT TO SEE WHAT IT'S ABOUT.
HAVE YOU HEARD ANYTHING GOOD ABOUT IT?
...
NO.
HEY, WAIT UP, OWL.
WE GOTTA SMOKE UP.
LET'S DO IT BEHIND THESE CARS...

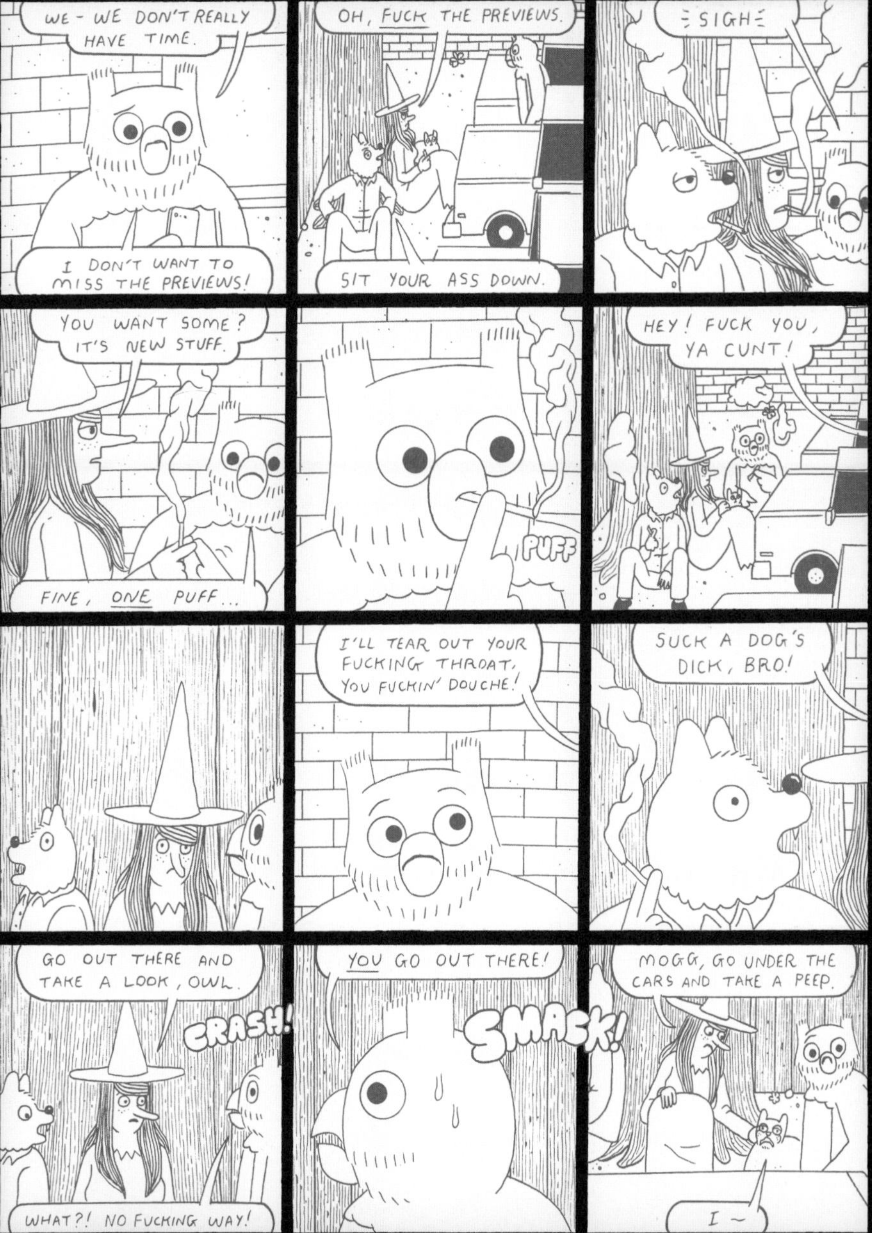

WE - WE DON'T REALLY HAVE TIME.
I DON'T WANT TO MISS THE PREVIEWS!
OH, FUCK THE PREVIEWS.
SIT YOUR ASS DOWN.
SIGH
YOU WANT SOME? IT'S NEW STUFF.
FINE, ONE PUFF...
PUFF
HEY! FUCK YOU, YA CUNT!
I'LL TEAR OUT YOUR FUCKING THROAT, YOU FUCKIN' DOUCHE!
SUCK A DOG'S DICK, BRO!
GO OUT THERE AND TAKE A LOOK, OWL.
CRASH!
WHAT?! NO FUCKING WAY!
YOU GO OUT THERE!
SMACK!
MOGG, GO UNDER THE CARS AND TAKE A PEEP.
I ~

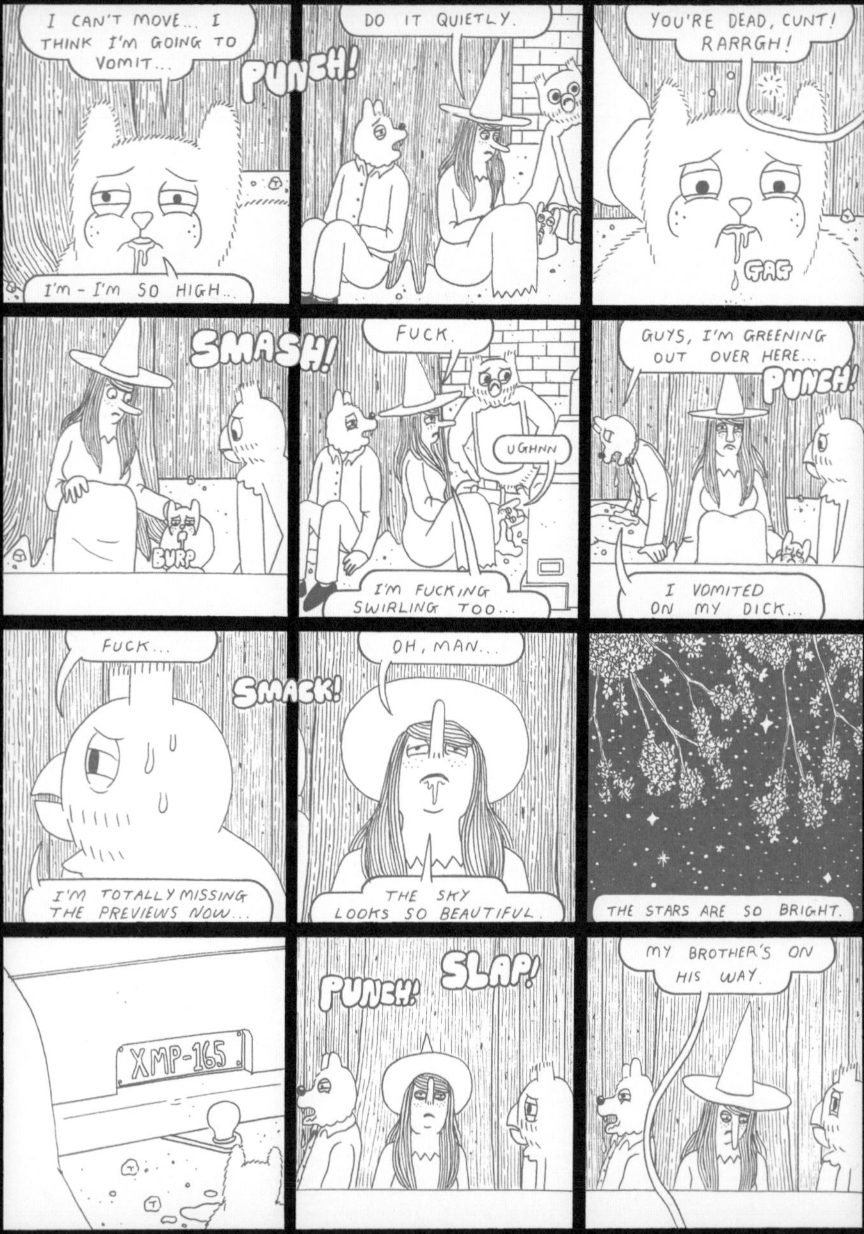
I CAN'T MOVE... I THINK I'M GOING TO VOMIT...
I'M - I'M SO HIGH...
PUNCH!
DO IT QUIETLY.
YOU'RE DEAD, CUNT! RARRGH!
GAG
SMASH!
BURP
FUCK.
UGHNN
I'M FUCKING SWIRLING TOO...
GUYS, I'M GREENING OUT OVER HERE...
PUNCH!
I VOMITED ON MY DICK...
FUCK...
SMACK!
I'M TOTALLY MISSING THE PREVIEWS NOW...
OH, MAN...
THE SKY LOOKS SO BEAUTIFUL.
THE STARS ARE SO BRIGHT.
XMP-165
PUNCH!
SLAP!
MY BROTHER'S ON HIS WAY.

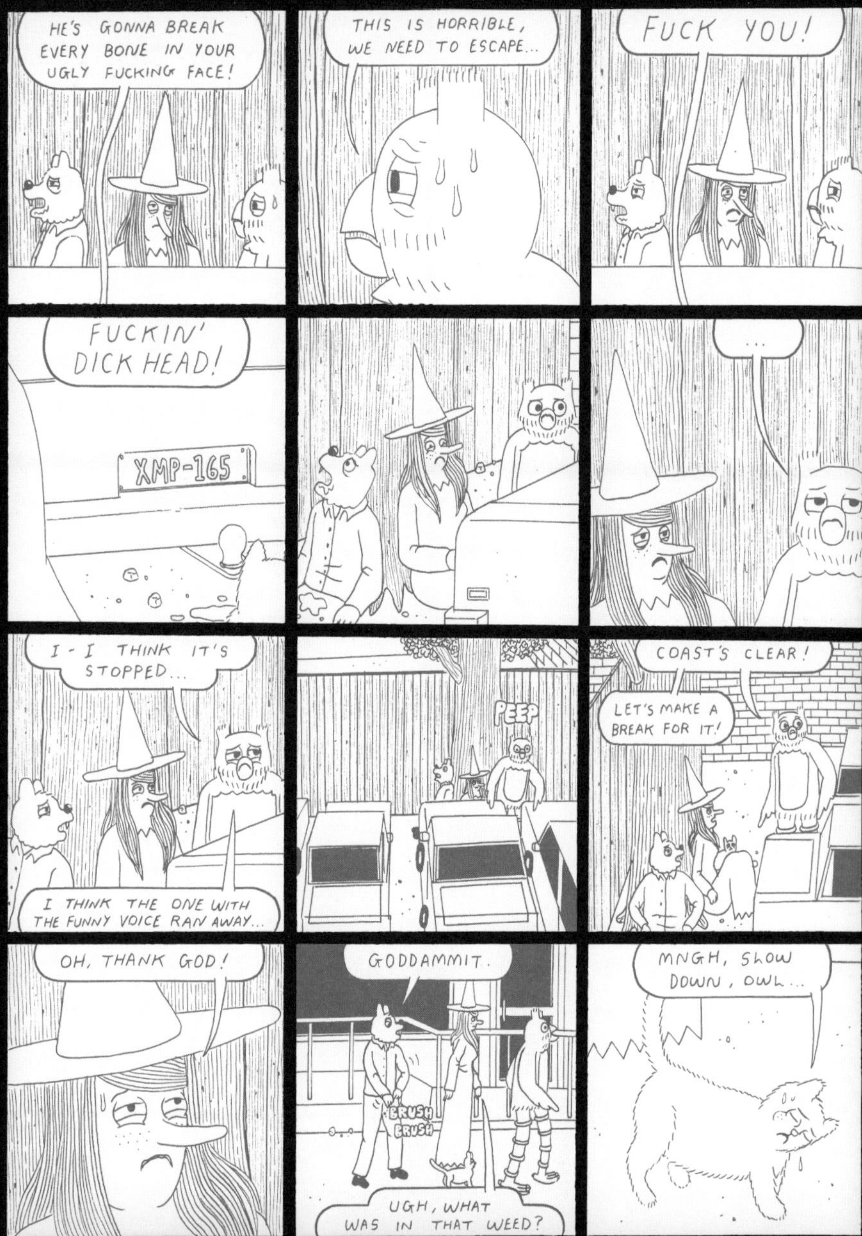
HE'S GONNA BREAK EVERY BONE IN YOUR UGLY FUCKING FACE!
THIS IS HORRIBLE, WE NEED TO ESCAPE...
FUCK YOU!
FUCKIN' DICK HEAD!
XMP-165
...
I-I THINK IT'S STOPPED...
I THINK THE ONE WITH THE FUNNY VOICE RAN AWAY...
PEEP
COAST'S CLEAR!
LET'S MAKE A BREAK FOR IT!
OH, THANK GOD!
GODDAMMIT.
BRUSH BRUSH
UGH, WHAT WAS IN THAT WEED?
MNGH, SLOW DOWN, OWL...

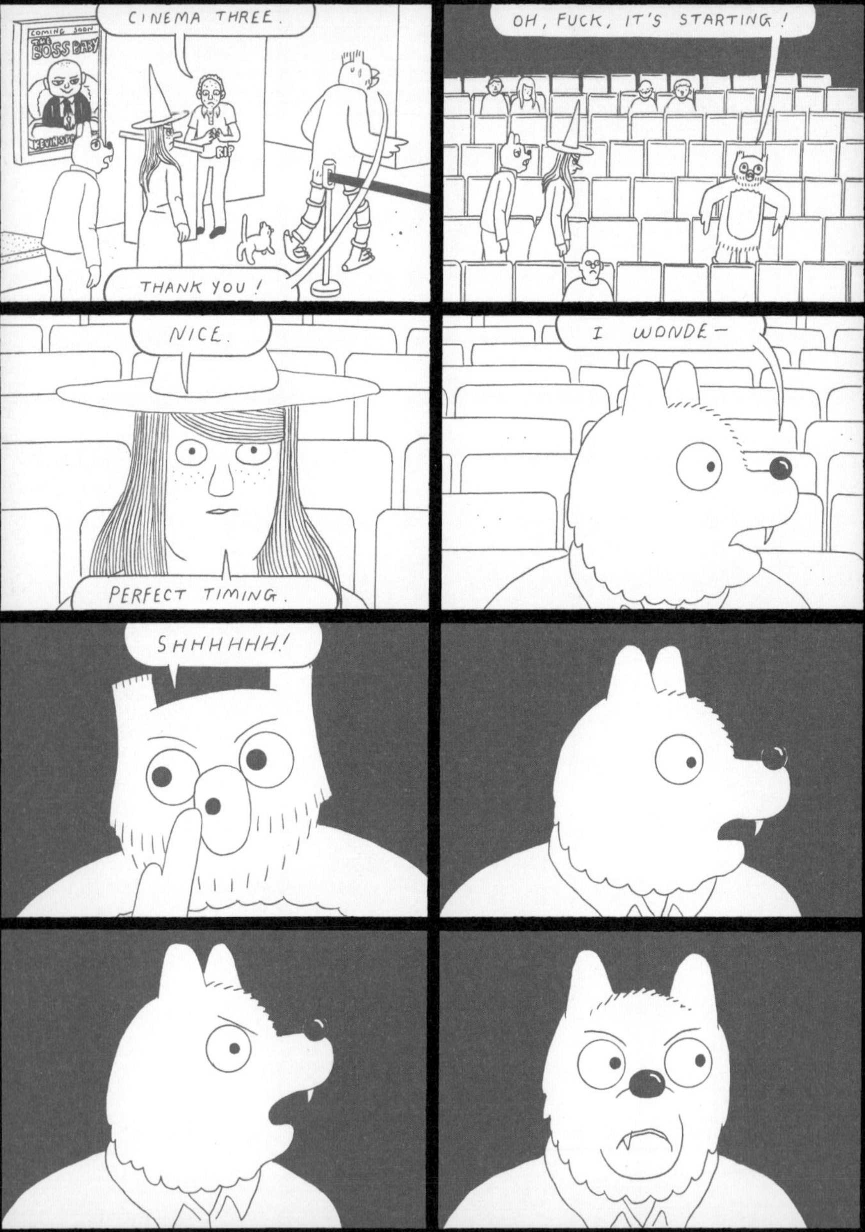

CINEMA THREE.
THANK YOU!
OH, FUCK, IT'S STARTING!
NICE.
PERFECT TIMING.
I WONDE-
SHHHHHH!

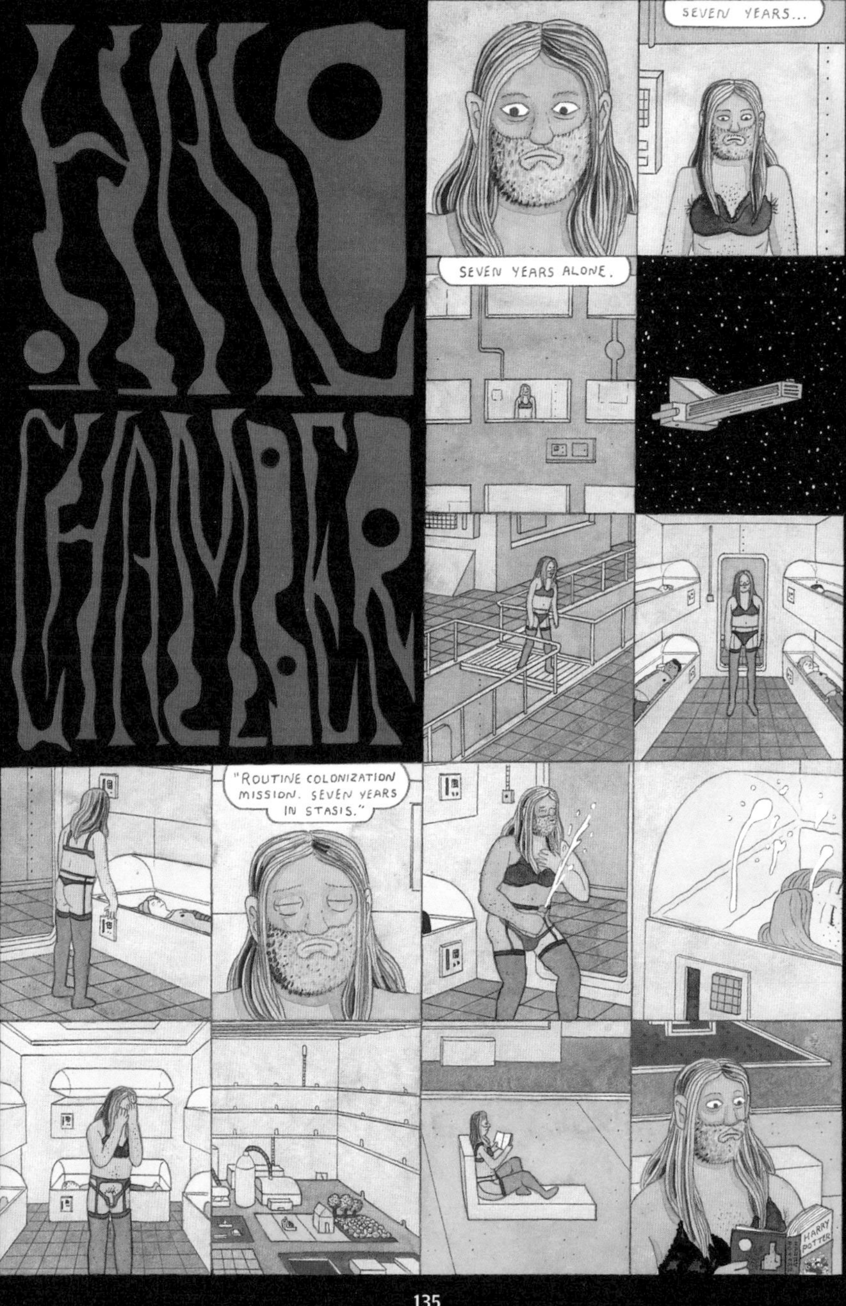
SEVEN YEARS...
SEVEN YEARS ALONE.
"ROUTINE COLONIZATION MISSION. SEVEN YEARS IN STASIS."
HARRY POTTER

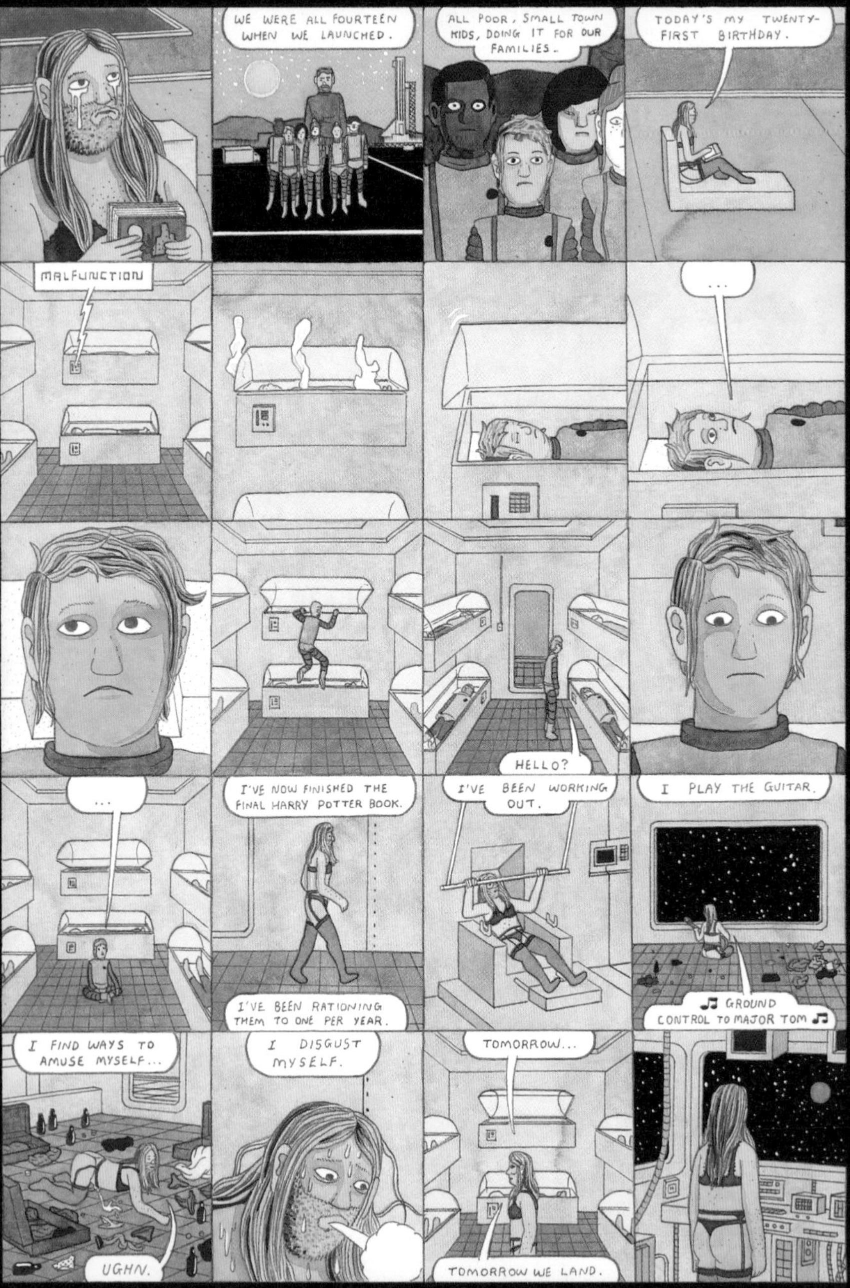
WE WERE ALL FOURTEEN WHEN WE LAUNCHED.
ALL POOR, SMALL TOWN KIDS, DOING IT FOR OUR FAMILIES.
TODAY'S MY TWENTY-FIRST BIRTHDAY.
MALFUNCTION
...
HELLO?
...
I'VE NOW FINISHED THE FINAL HARRY POTTER BOOK.
I'VE BEEN RATIONING THEM TO ONE PER YEAR.
I'VE BEEN WORKING OUT.
I PLAY THE GUITAR.
♫ GROUND CONTROL TO MAJOR TOM ♫
I FIND WAYS TO AMUSE MYSELF...
UGHN.
I DISGUST MYSELF.
TOMORROW...
TOMORROW WE LAND.

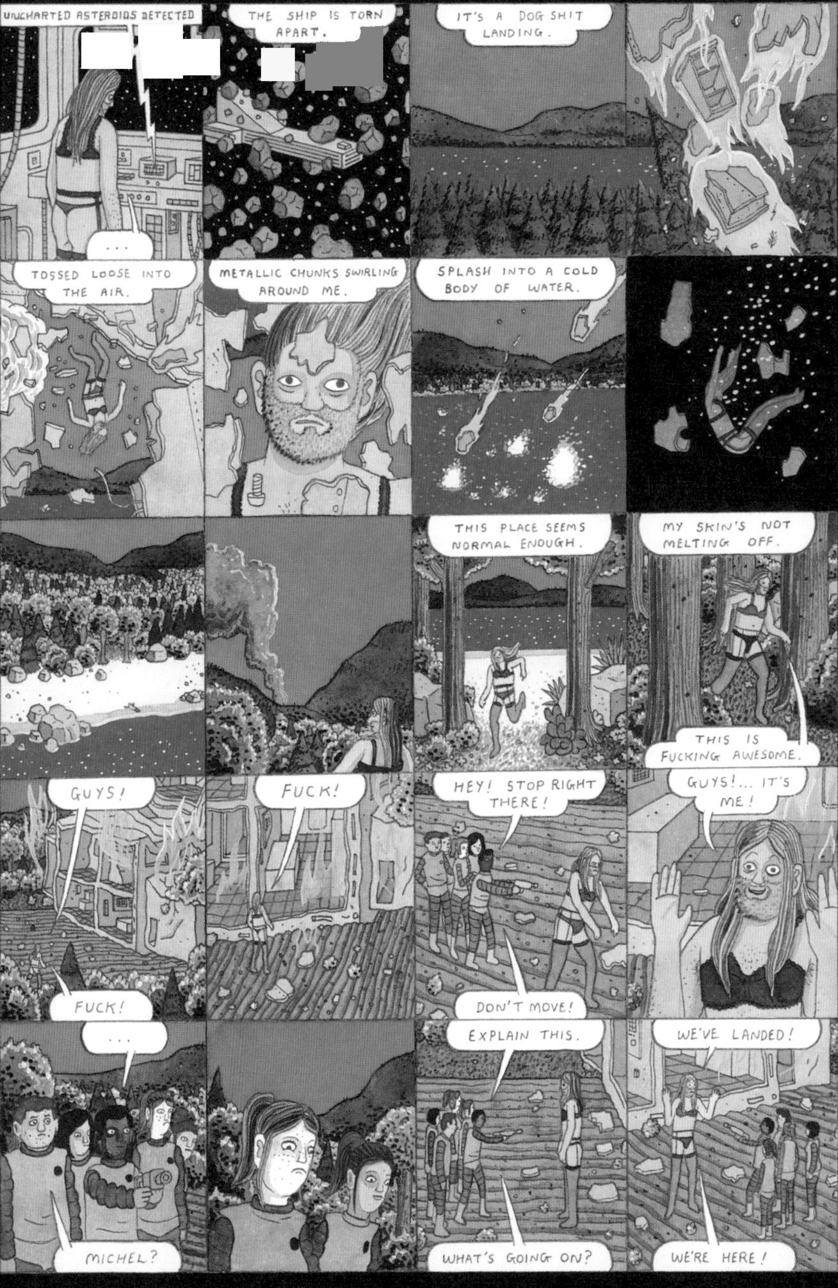
UNCHARTED ASTEROIDS DETECTED
...
THE SHIP IS TORN APART.
IT'S A DOG SHIT LANDING.
TOSSED LOOSE INTO THE AIR.
METALLIC CHUNKS SWIRLING AROUND ME.
SPLASH INTO A COLD BODY OF WATER.
THIS PLACE SEEMS NORMAL ENOUGH.
MY SKIN'S NOT MELTING OFF.
THIS IS FUCKING AWESOME.
GUYS!
FUCK!
FUCK!
HEY! STOP RIGHT THERE!
DON'T MOVE!
GUYS!... IT'S ME!
...
MICHEL?
EXPLAIN THIS.
WHAT'S GOING ON?
WE'VE LANDED!
WE'RE HERE!

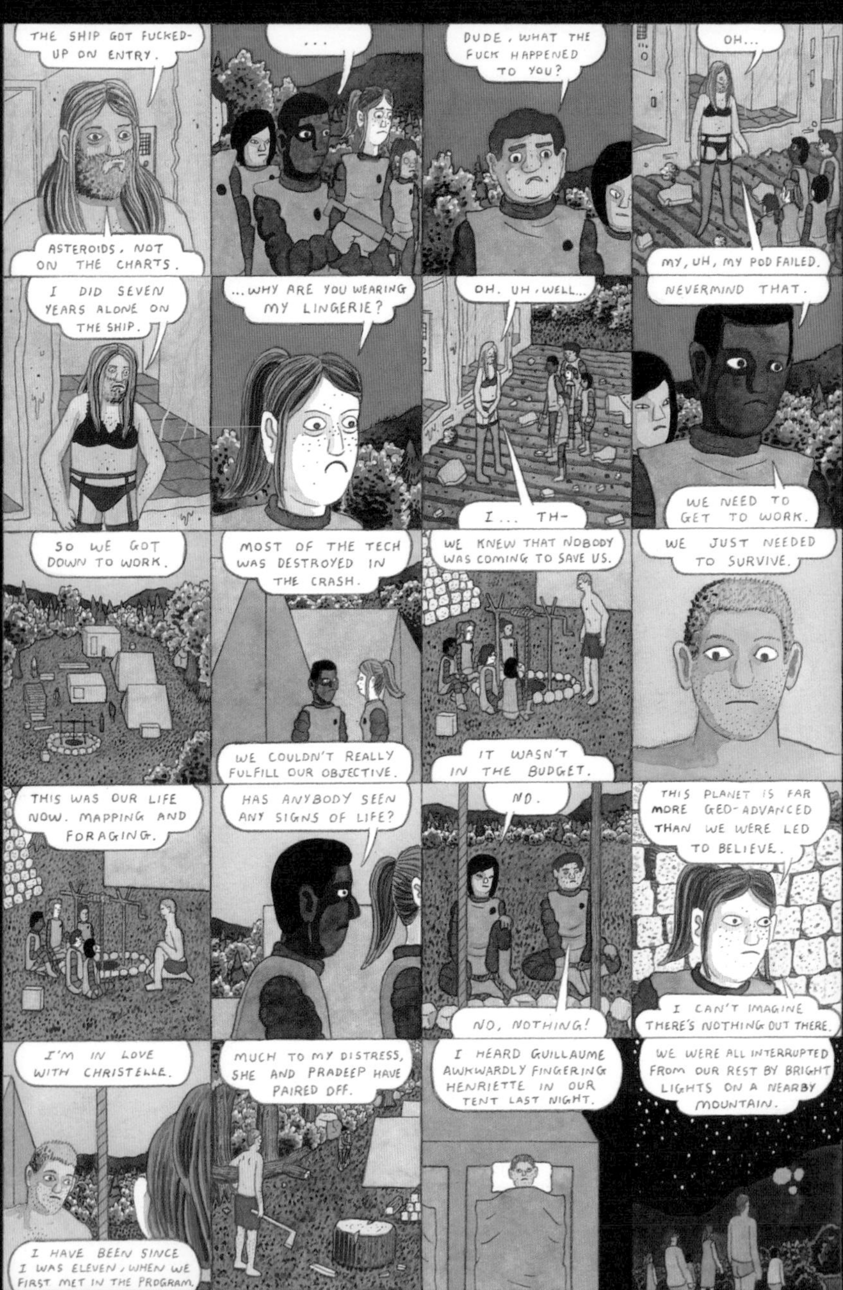
THE SHIP GOT FUCKED-UP ON ENTRY.
ASTEROIDS, NOT ON THE CHARTS.
...
DUDE, WHAT THE FUCK HAPPENED TO YOU?
OH...
MY, UH, MY POD FAILED.
I DID SEVEN YEARS ALONE ON THE SHIP.
...WHY ARE YOU WEARING MY LINGERIE?
OH. UH, WELL...
I... TH-
NEVERMIND THAT.
WE NEED TO GET TO WORK.
SO WE GOT DOWN TO WORK.
MOST OF THE TECH WAS DESTROYED IN THE CRASH.
WE COULDN'T REALLY FULFILL OUR OBJECTIVE.
WE KNEW THAT NOBODY WAS COMING TO SAVE US.
IT WASN'T IN THE BUDGET.
WE JUST NEEDED TO SURVIVE.
THIS WAS OUR LIFE NOW. MAPPING AND FORAGING.
HAS ANYBODY SEEN ANY SIGNS OF LIFE?
NO.
NO, NOTHING!
THIS PLANET IS FAR MORE GEO-ADVANCED THAN WE WERE LED TO BELIEVE.
I CAN'T IMAGINE THERE'S NOTHING OUT THERE.
I'M IN LOVE WITH CHRISTELLE.
I HAVE BEEN SINCE I WAS ELEVEN, WHEN WE FIRST MET IN THE PROGRAM.
MUCH TO MY DISTRESS, SHE AND PRADEEP HAVE PAIRED OFF.
I HEARD GUILLAUME AWKWARDLY FINGERING HENRIETTE IN OUR TENT LAST NIGHT.
WE WERE ALL INTERRUPTED FROM OUR REST BY BRIGHT LIGHTS ON A NEARBY MOUNTAIN.

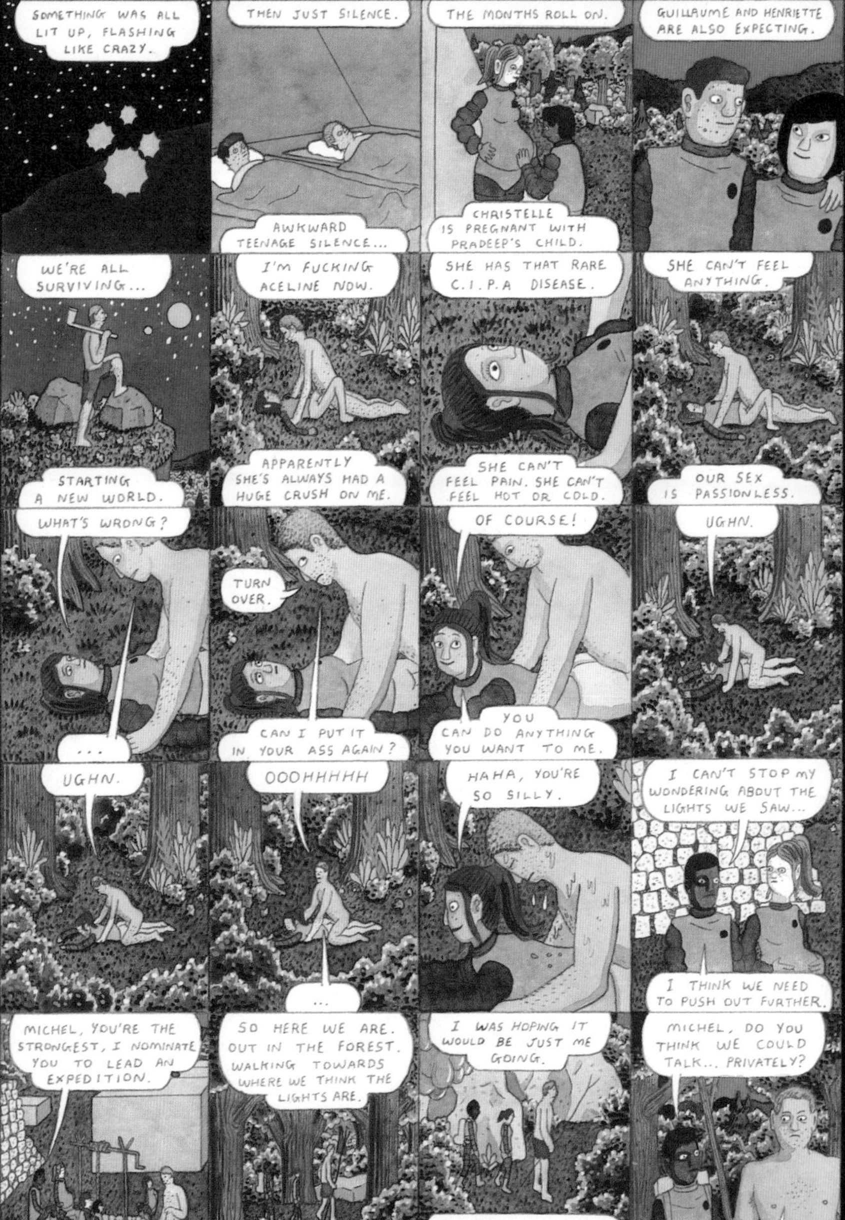

SOMETHING WAS ALL LIT UP, FLASHING LIKE CRAZY.
THEN JUST SILENCE.
AWKWARD TEENAGE SILENCE...
THE MONTHS ROLL ON.
CHRISTELLE IS PREGNANT WITH PRADEEP'S CHILD.
GUILLAUME AND HENRIETTE ARE ALSO EXPECTING.
WE'RE ALL SURVIVING...
STARTING A NEW WORLD.
I'M FUCKING ACELINE NOW.
APPARENTLY SHE'S ALWAYS HAD A HUGE CRUSH ON ME.
SHE HAS THAT RARE C.I.P.A DISEASE.
SHE CAN'T FEEL PAIN. SHE CAN'T FEEL HOT OR COLD.
SHE CAN'T FEEL ANYTHING.
OUR SEX IS PASSIONLESS.
WHAT'S WRONG?
...
TURN OVER.
CAN I PUT IT IN YOUR ASS AGAIN?
OF COURSE!
YOU CAN DO ANYTHING YOU WANT TO ME.
UGHN.
UGHN.
OOOHHHHH
...
HAHA, YOU'RE SO SILLY.
I CAN'T STOP MY WONDERING ABOUT THE LIGHTS WE SAW...
I THINK WE NEED TO PUSH OUT FURTHER.
MICHEL, YOU'RE THE STRONGEST, I NOMINATE YOU TO LEAD AN EXPEDITION.
SO HERE WE ARE. OUT IN THE FOREST. WALKING TOWARDS WHERE WE THINK THE LIGHTS ARE.
I WAS HOPING IT WOULD BE JUST ME GOING.
BUT ACELINE INSISTED ON COMING AND THEN PRADEEP DEMANDED HE COME ALSO.
MICHEL, DO YOU THINK WE COULD TALK... PRIVATELY?
WHAT?...

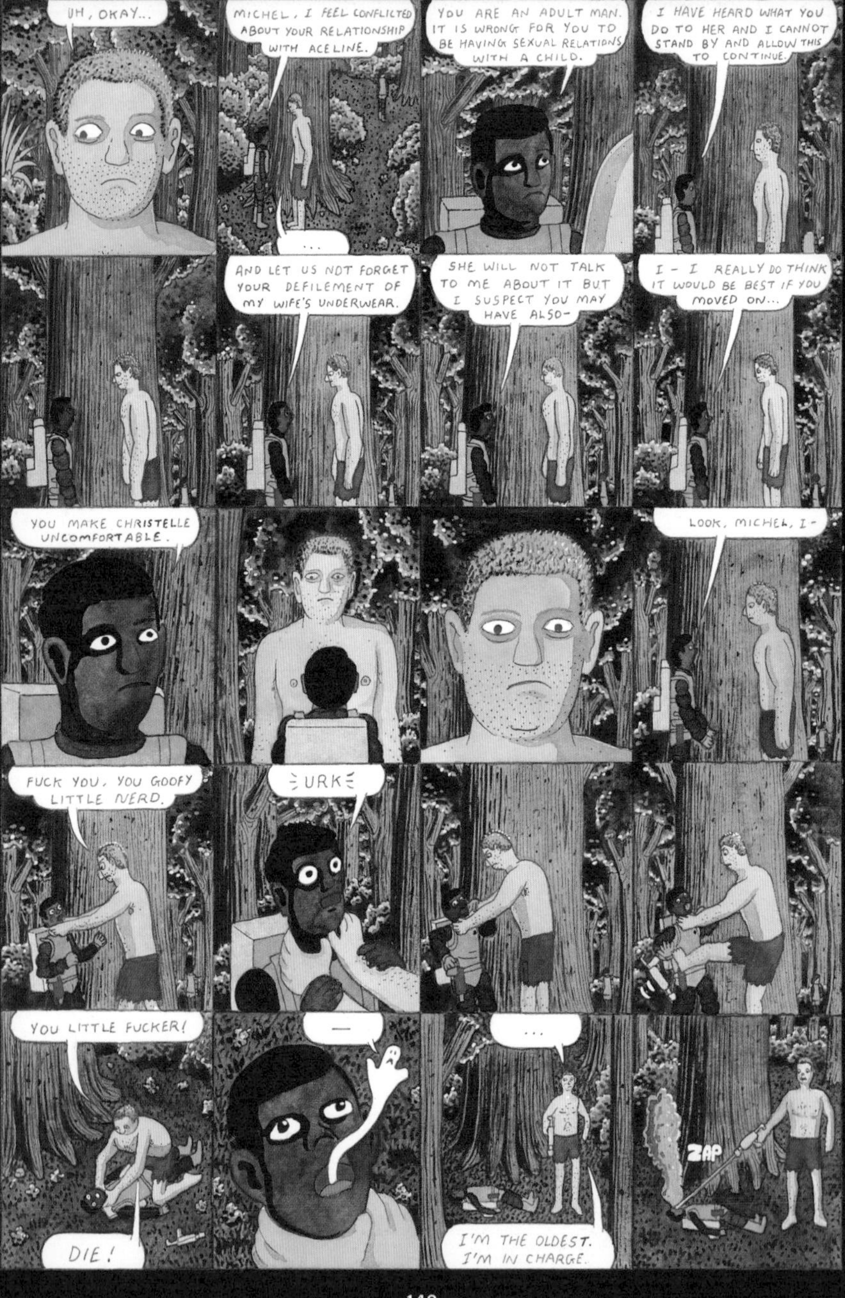
UH, OKAY...
MICHEL, I FEEL CONFLICTED ABOUT YOUR RELATIONSHIP WITH ACELINE.
...
YOU ARE AN ADULT MAN. IT IS WRONG FOR YOU TO BE HAVING SEXUAL RELATIONS WITH A CHILD.
I HAVE HEARD WHAT YOU DO TO HER AND I CANNOT STAND BY AND ALLOW THIS TO CONTINUE.
AND LET US NOT FORGET YOUR DEFILEMENT OF MY WIFE'S UNDERWEAR.
SHE WILL NOT TALK TO ME ABOUT IT BUT I SUSPECT YOU MAY HAVE ALSO-
I - I REALLY DO THINK IT WOULD BE BEST IF YOU MOVED ON...
YOU MAKE CHRISTELLE UNCOMFORTABLE.
LOOK, MICHEL, I-
FUCK YOU, YOU GOOFY LITTLE NERD.
URK
YOU LITTLE FUCKER!
DIE!
—
...
I'M THE OLDEST. I'M IN CHARGE.
ZAP

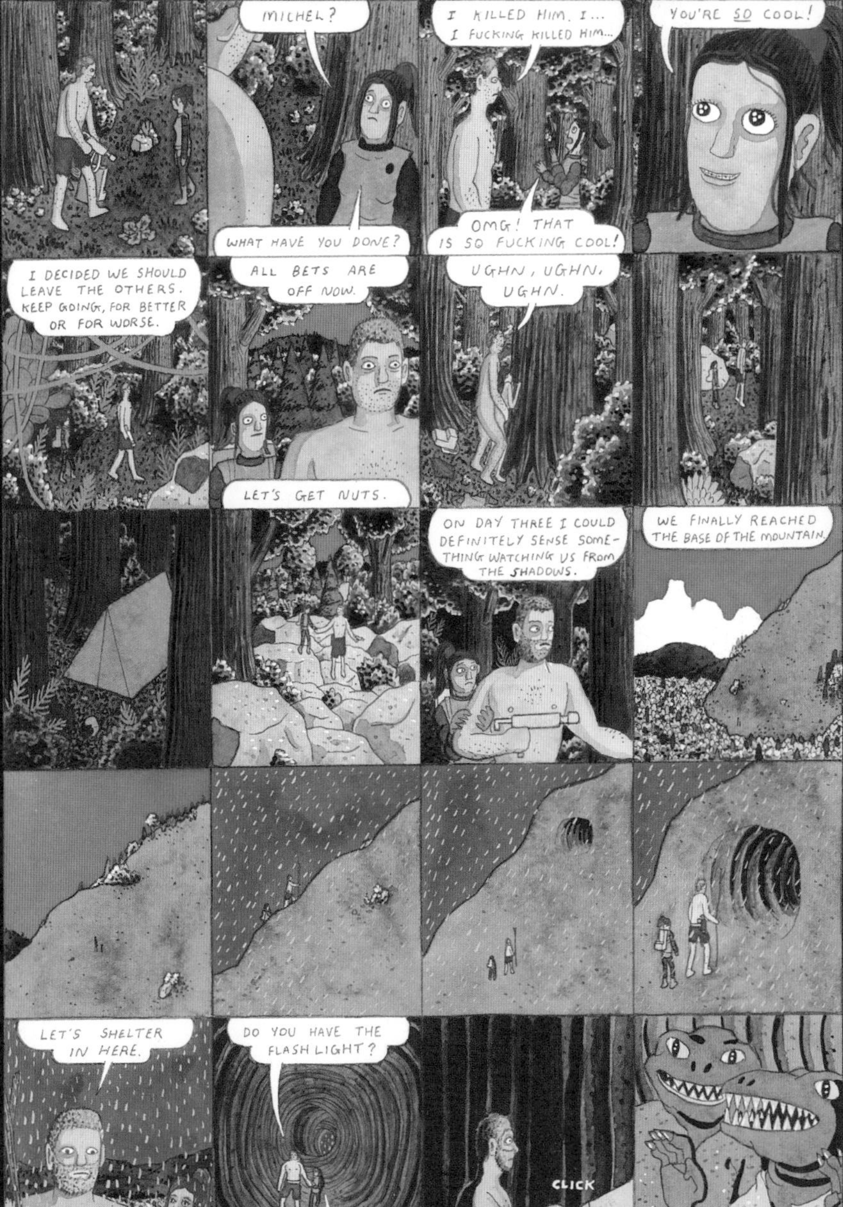
MICHEL?
WHAT HAVE YOU DONE?
I KILLED HIM. I... I FUCKING KILLED HIM...
OMG! THAT IS SO FUCKING COOL!
YOU'RE SO COOL!
I DECIDED WE SHOULD LEAVE THE OTHERS. KEEP GOING, FOR BETTER OR FOR WORSE.
ALL BETS ARE OFF NOW.
LET'S GET NUTS.
UGHN, UGHN, UGHN.
ON DAY THREE I COULD DEFINITELY SENSE SOMETHING WATCHING US FROM THE SHADOWS.
WE FINALLY REACHED THE BASE OF THE MOUNTAIN.
LET'S SHELTER IN HERE.
DO YOU HAVE THE FLASHLIGHT?
YEAH, HERE YOU ARE.
CLICK

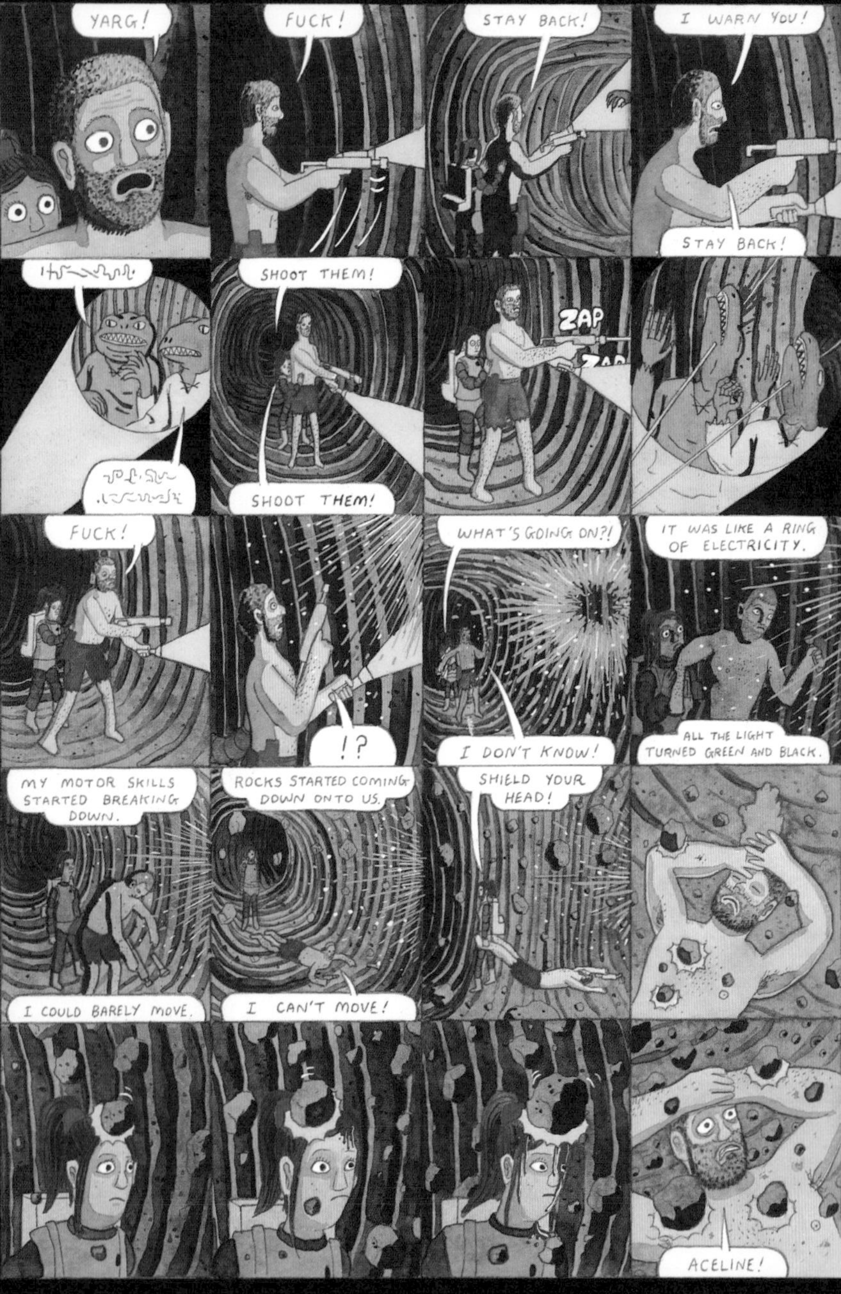
YARG!
FUCK!
STAY BACK!
I WARN YOU!
STAY BACK!
SHOOT THEM!
SHOOT THEM!
ZAP
FUCK!
!?
WHAT'S GOING ON?!
I DON'T KNOW!
IT WAS LIKE A RING OF ELECTRICITY.
ALL THE LIGHT TURNED GREEN AND BLACK.
MY MOTOR SKILLS STARTED BREAKING DOWN.
I COULD BARELY MOVE.
ROCKS STARTED COMING DOWN ONTO US.
I CAN'T MOVE!
SHIELD YOUR HEAD!
ACELINE!

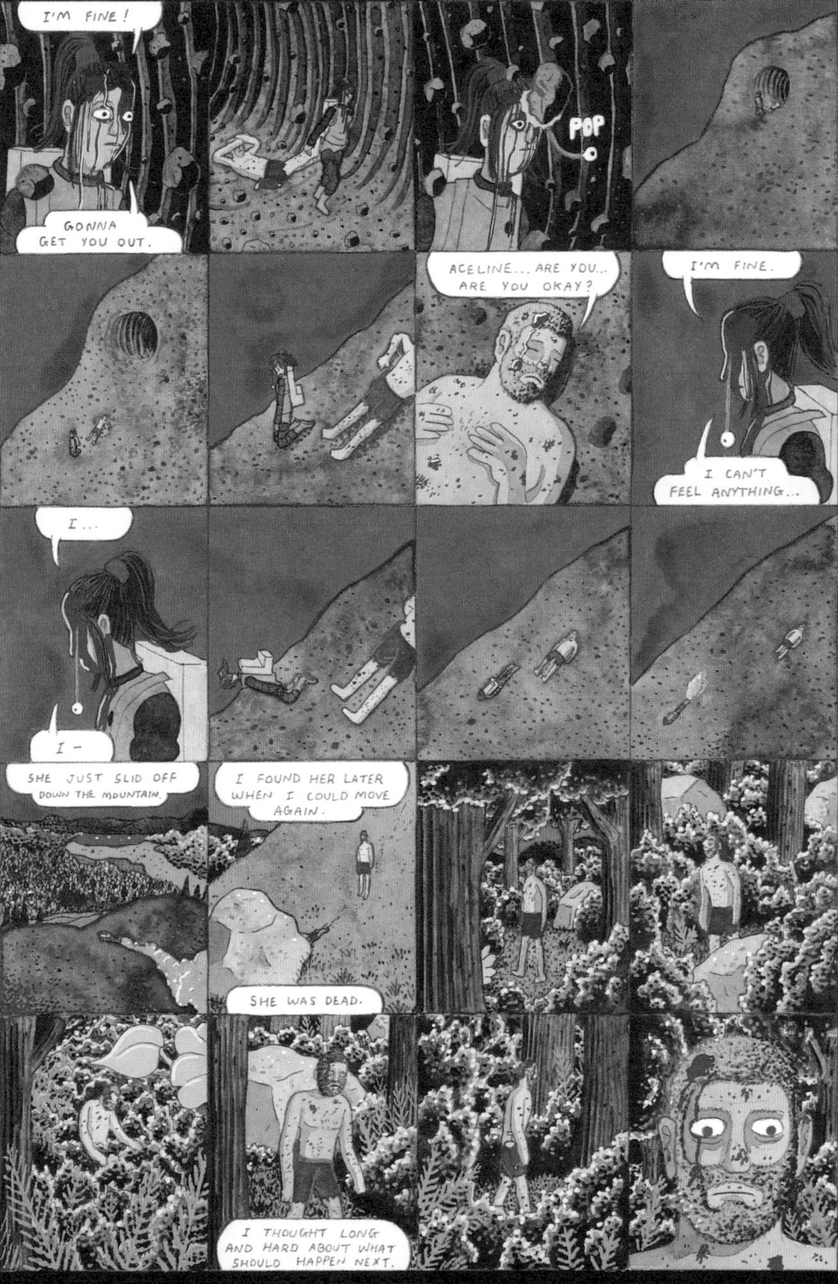
I'M FINE!
GONNA GET YOU OUT.
POP
ACELINE... ARE YOU... ARE YOU OKAY?
I'M FINE.
I CAN'T FEEL ANYTHING...
I...
I -
SHE JUST SLID OFF DOWN THE MOUNTAIN.
I FOUND HER LATER WHEN I COULD MOVE AGAIN.
SHE WAS DEAD.
I THOUGHT LONG AND HARD ABOUT WHAT SHOULD HAPPEN NEXT.

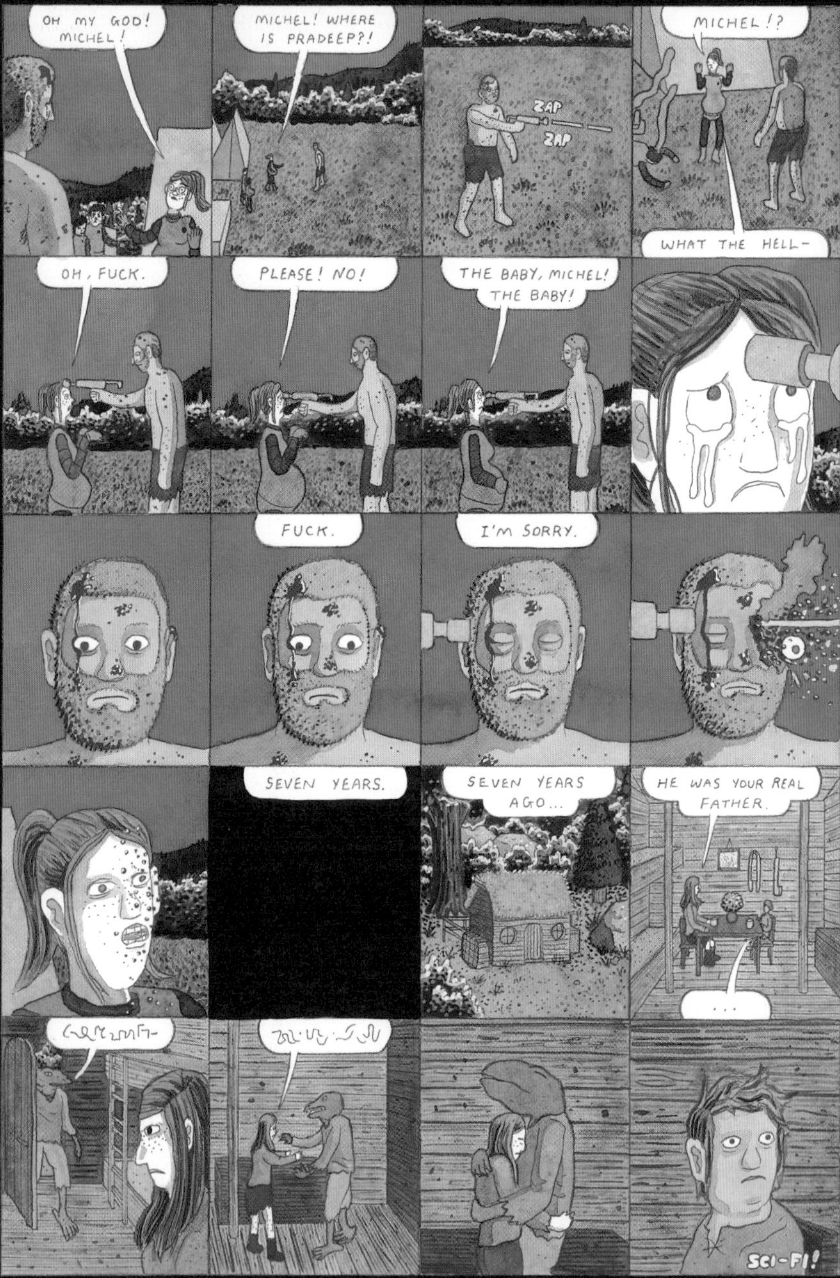
OH MY GOD! MICHEL!
MICHEL! WHERE IS PRADEEP?!
ZAP
ZAP
MICHEL!?
WHAT THE HELL-
OH, FUCK.
PLEASE! NO!
THE BABY, MICHEL! THE BABY!
FUCK.
I'M SORRY.
SEVEN YEARS.
SEVEN YEARS AGO...
HE WAS YOUR REAL FATHER.
...
SCI-FI!

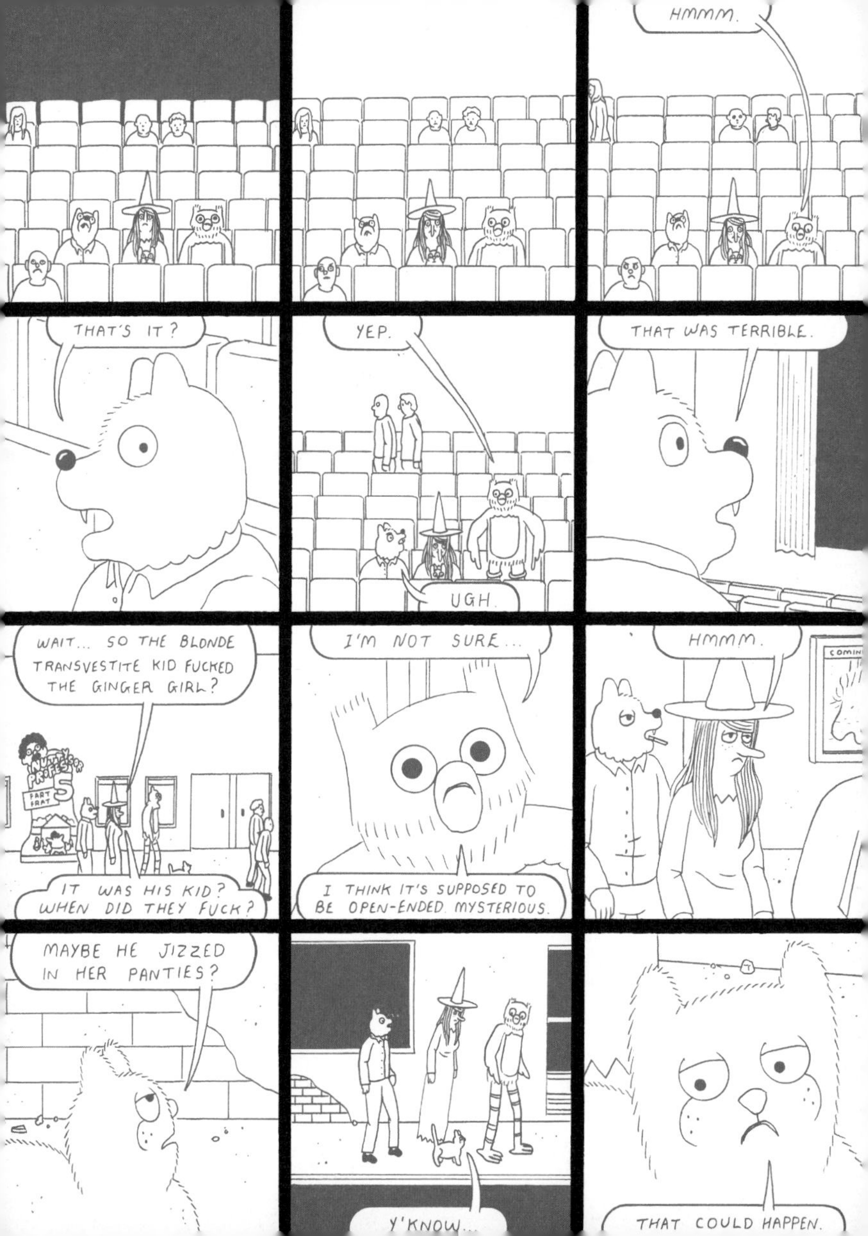
HMMM.
THAT'S IT?
YEP.
UGH.
THAT WAS TERRIBLE.
WAIT... SO THE BLONDE TRANSVESTITE KID FUCKED THE GINGER GIRL?
NUTTY PROFESSOR 5
FART FRAT
IT WAS HIS KID? WHEN DID THEY FUCK?
I'M NOT SURE...
I THINK IT'S SUPPOSED TO BE OPEN-ENDED. MYSTERIOUS.
HMMM.
MAYBE HE JIZZED IN HER PANTIES?
Y'KNOW...
THAT COULD HAPPEN.

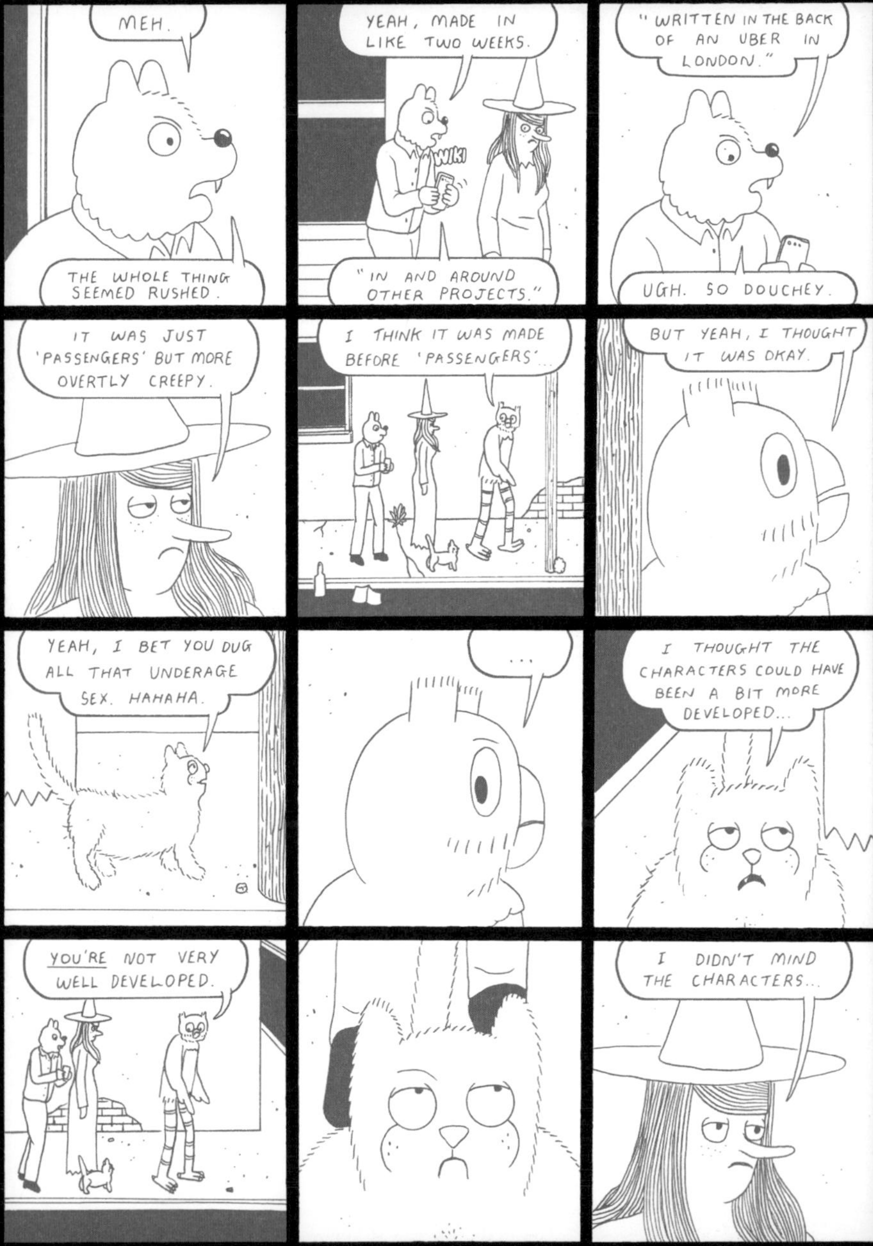
MEH.
THE WHOLE THING SEEMED RUSHED.
YEAH, MADE IN LIKE TWO WEEKS.
WIKI
"IN AND AROUND OTHER PROJECTS."
"WRITTEN IN THE BACK OF AN UBER IN LONDON."
UGH. SO DOUCHEY.
IT WAS JUST 'PASSENGERS' BUT MORE OVERTLY CREEPY.
I THINK IT WAS MADE BEFORE 'PASSENGERS'...
BUT YEAH, I THOUGHT IT WAS OKAY.
YEAH, I BET YOU DUG ALL THAT UNDERAGE SEX. HAHAHA.
...
I THOUGHT THE CHARACTERS COULD HAVE BEEN A BIT MORE DEVELOPED...
YOU'RE NOT VERY WELL DEVELOPED.
I DIDN'T MIND THE CHARACTERS...

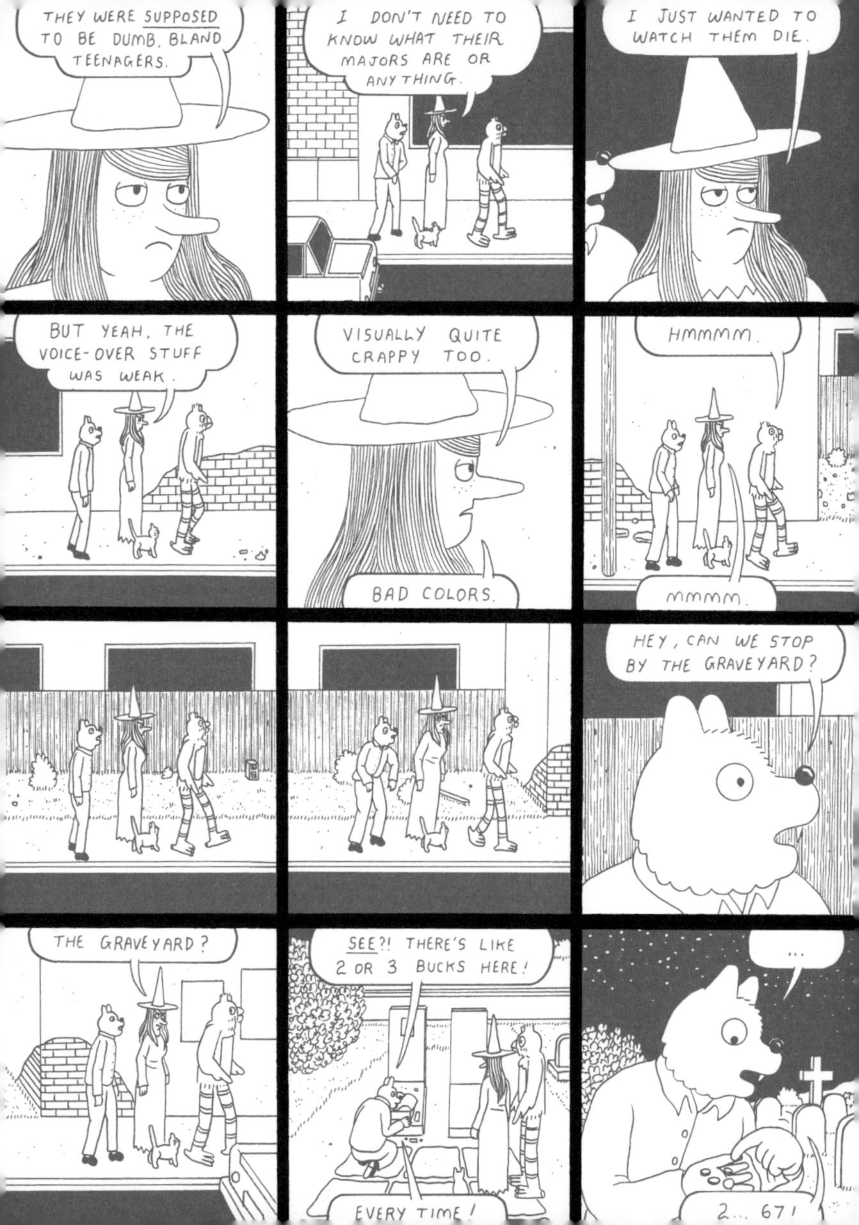
THEY WERE SUPPOSED TO BE DUMB, BLAND TEENAGERS.
I DON'T NEED TO KNOW WHAT THEIR MAJORS ARE OR ANYTHING.
I JUST WANTED TO WATCH THEM DIE.
BUT YEAH, THE VOICE-OVER STUFF WAS WEAK.
VISUALLY QUITE CRAPPY TOO.
BAD COLORS.
HMMMM.
MMMM.
HEY, CAN WE STOP BY THE GRAVEYARD?
THE GRAVEYARD?
SEE?! THERE'S LIKE 2 OR 3 BUCKS HERE!
EVERY TIME!
...
2... 67!

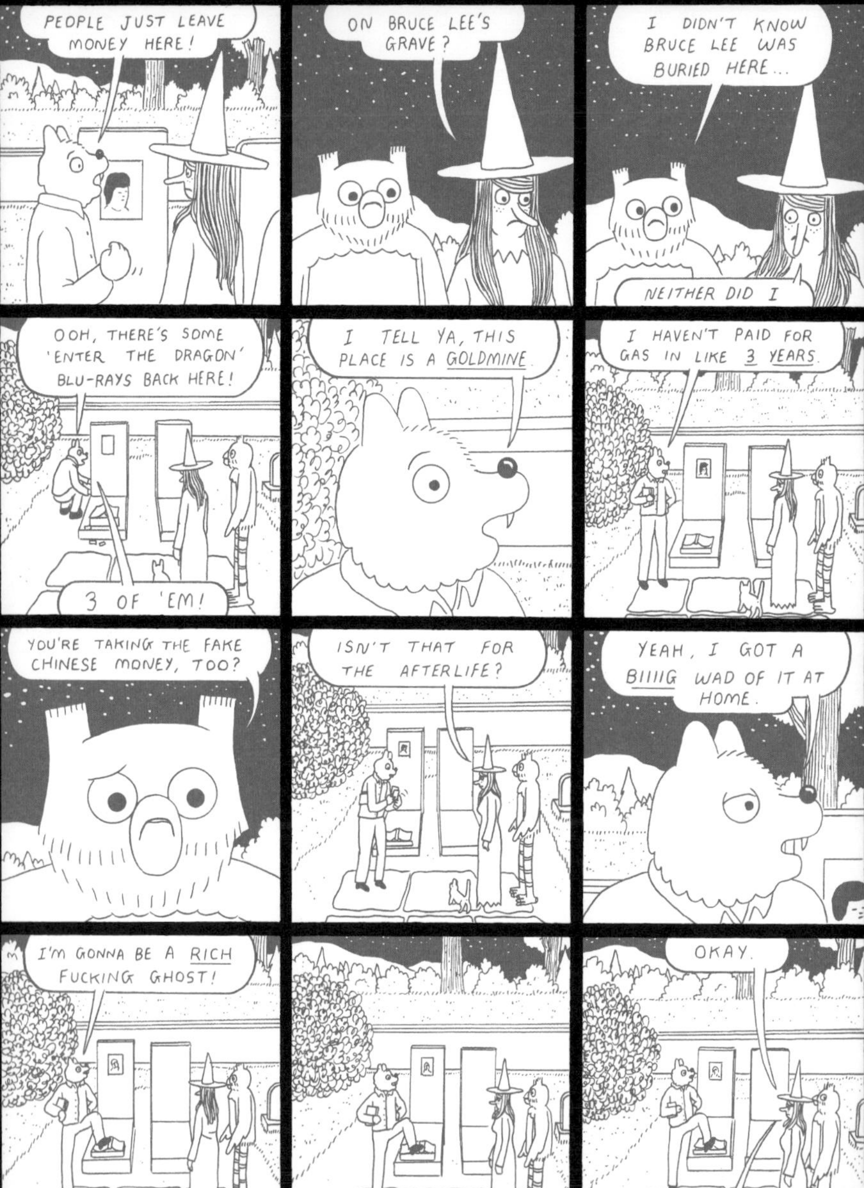
PEOPLE JUST LEAVE MONEY HERE!
ON BRUCE LEE'S GRAVE?
I DIDN'T KNOW BRUCE LEE WAS BURIED HERE...
NEITHER DID I
OOH, THERE'S SOME 'ENTER THE DRAGON' BLU-RAYS BACK HERE!
3 OF 'EM!
I TELL YA, THIS PLACE IS A GOLDMINE
I HAVEN'T PAID FOR GAS IN LIKE 3 YEARS
YOU'RE TAKING THE FAKE CHINESE MONEY, TOO?
ISN'T THAT FOR THE AFTERLIFE?
YEAH, I GOT A BIIIG WAD OF IT AT HOME.
I'M GONNA BE A RICH FUCKING GHOST!
OKAY.
LET'S GO HOME.

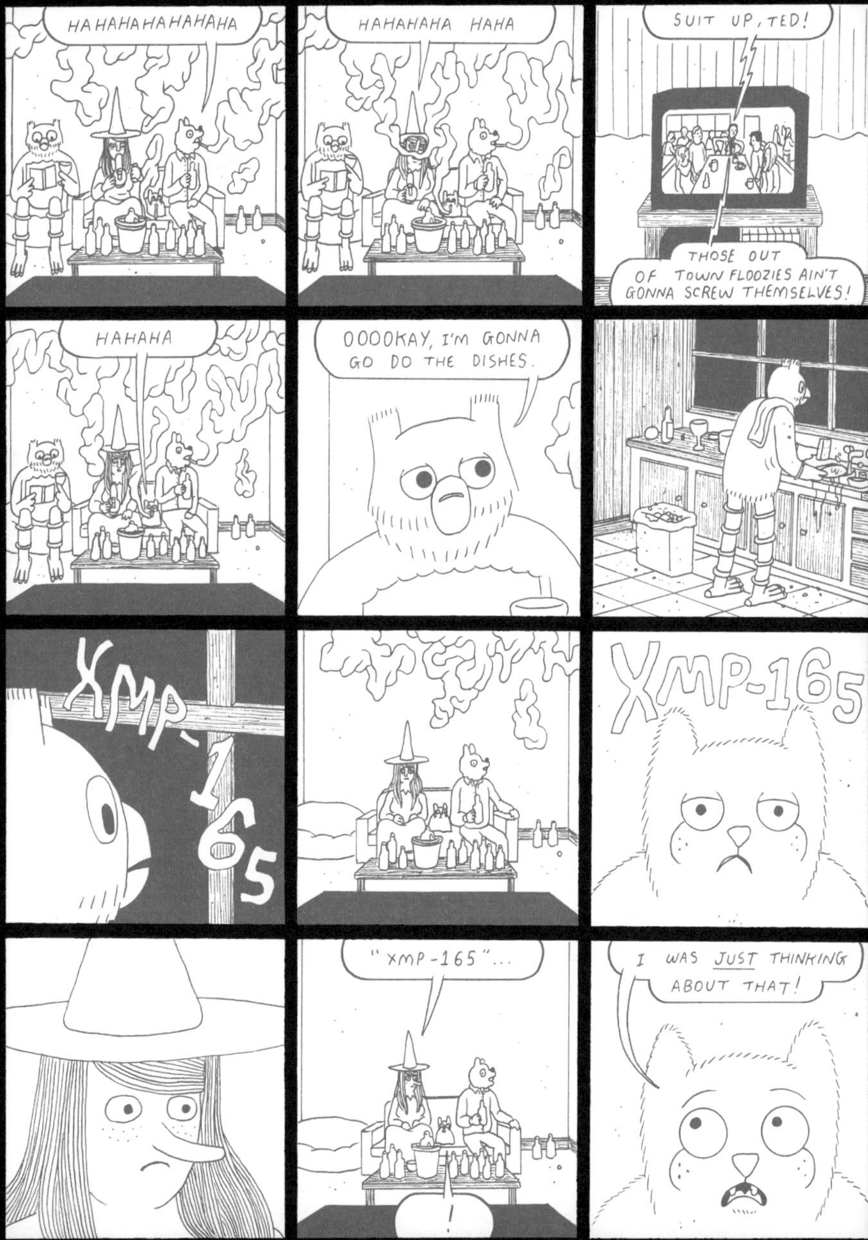
HAHAHAHAHAHAHA
HAHAHAHA HAHA
SUIT UP, TED!
THOSE OUT OF TOWN FLOOZIES AIN'T GONNA SCREW THEMSELVES!
HAHAHA
OOOOKAY, I'M GONNA GO DO THE DISHES.
XMP-165
XMP-165
"XMP-165"...
!
I WAS JUST THINKING ABOUT THAT!

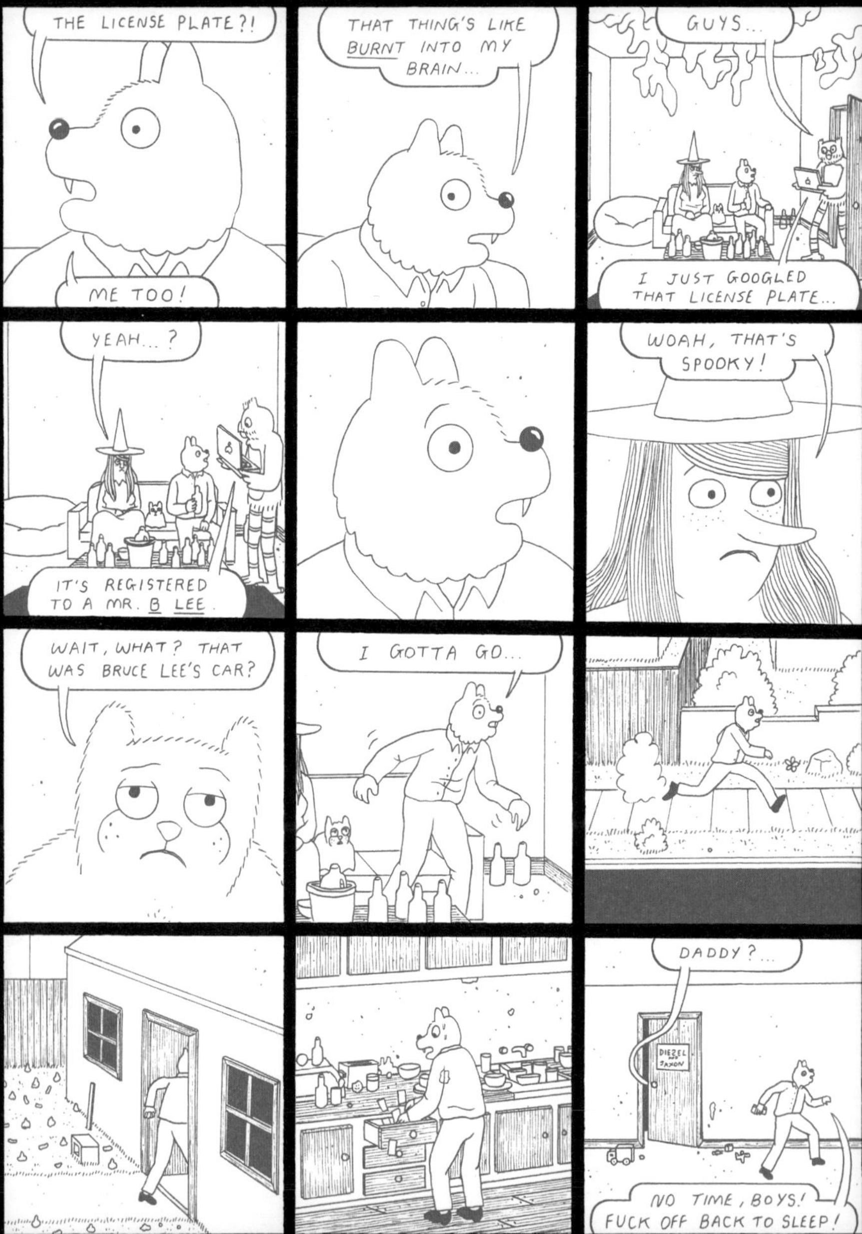

THE LICENSE PLATE?!
ME TOO!
THAT THING'S LIKE BURNT INTO MY BRAIN...
GUYS...
I JUST GOOGLED THAT LICENSE PLATE...
YEAH...?
IT'S REGISTERED TO A MR. B LEE.
WOAH, THAT'S SPOOKY!
WAIT, WHAT? THAT WAS BRUCE LEE'S CAR?
I GOTTA GO...
DADDY?...
DIEZEL AND SAXON
NO TIME, BOYS! FUCK OFF BACK TO SLEEP!

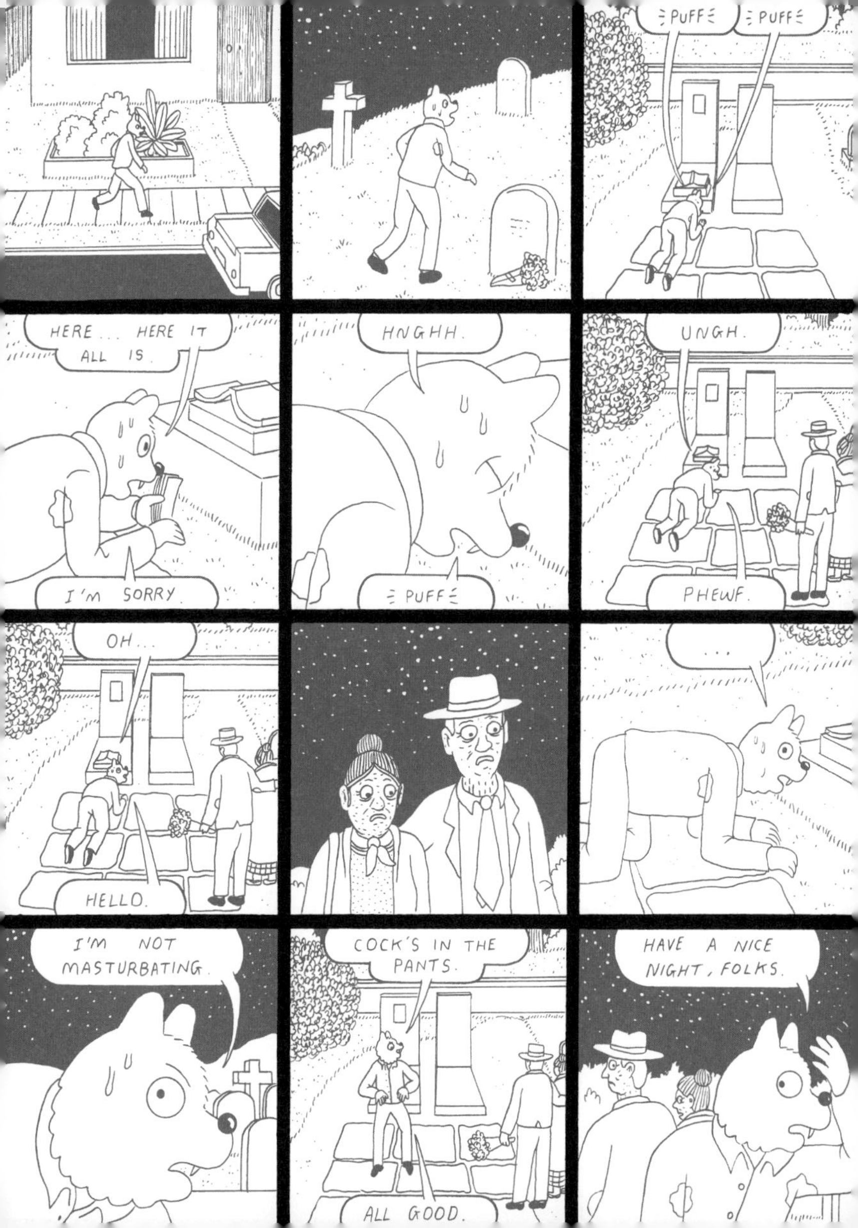
PUFF
PUFF
HERE... HERE IT ALL IS.
I'M SORRY.
HNGHH.
PUFF
UNGH.
PHEWF.
OH...
HELLO.
...
I'M NOT MASTURBATING.
COCK'S IN THE PANTS.
ALL GOOD.
HAVE A NICE NIGHT, FOLKS.

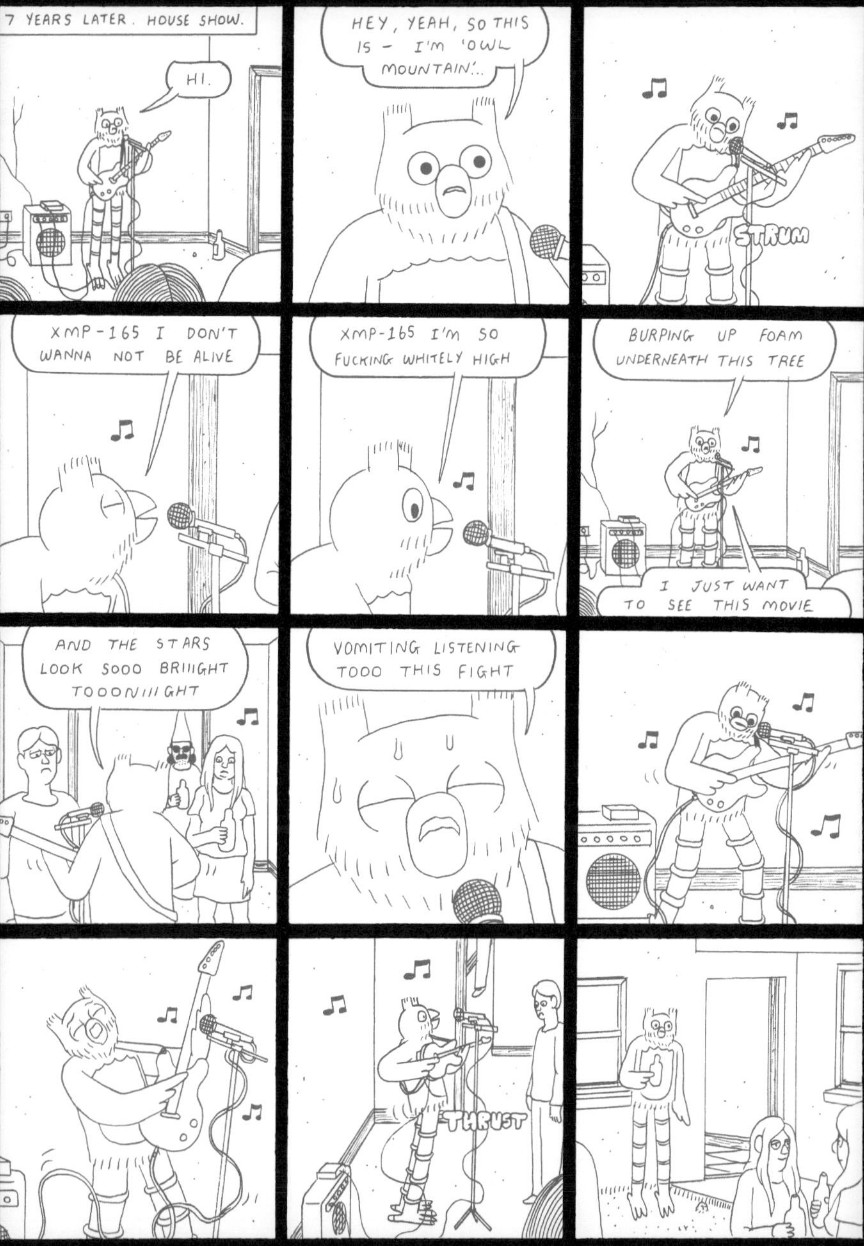

7 YEARS LATER. HOUSE SHOW.
HI.
HEY, YEAH, SO THIS IS - I'M 'OWL MOUNTAIN'...
STRUM
XMP-165 I DON'T WANNA NOT BE ALIVE
XMP-165 I'M SO FUCKING WHITELY HIGH
BURPING UP FOAM UNDERNEATH THIS TREE
I JUST WANT TO SEE THIS MOVIE
AND THE STARS LOOK SOOO BRIIIGHT TOOONIIIGHT
VOMITING LISTENING TOOO THIS FIGHT
THRUST

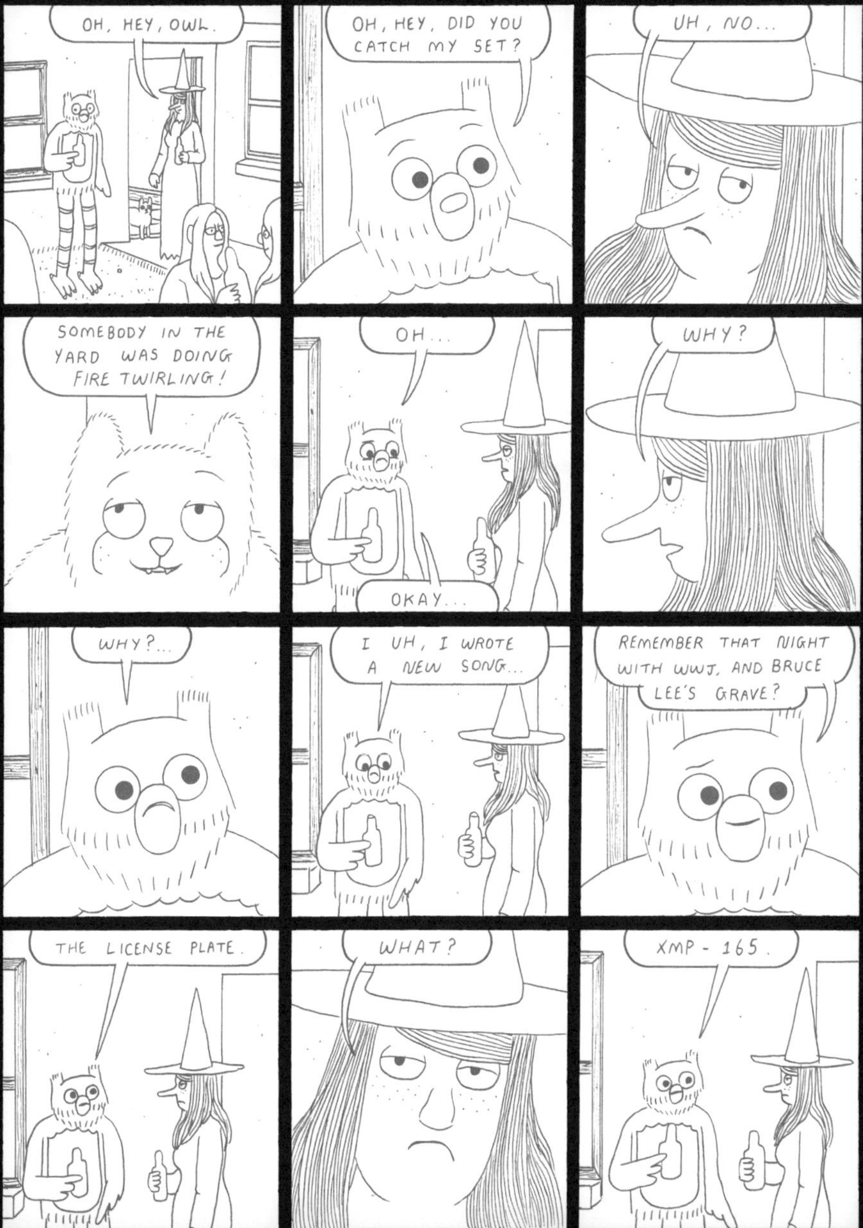

OH, HEY, OWL.
OH, HEY, DID YOU CATCH MY SET?
UH, NO...
SOMEBODY IN THE YARD WAS DOING FIRE TWIRLING!
OH...
OKAY...
WHY?
WHY?...
I UH, I WROTE A NEW SONG...
REMEMBER THAT NIGHT WITH WWJ, AND BRUCE LEE'S GRAVE?
THE LICENSE PLATE.
WHAT?
XMP - 165.

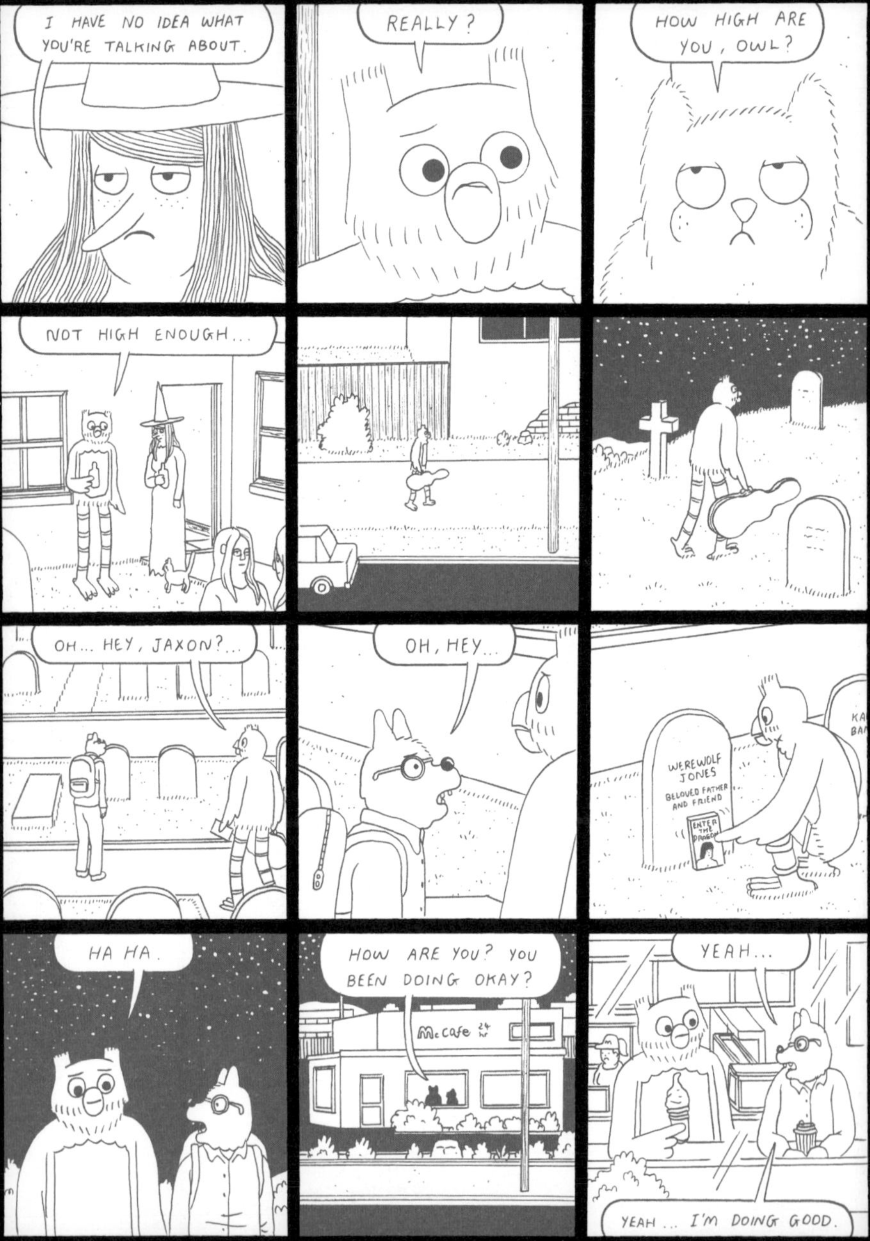
I HAVE NO IDEA WHAT YOU'RE TALKING ABOUT.
REALLY?
HOW HIGH ARE YOU, OWL?
NOT HIGH ENOUGH...
OH... HEY, JAXON?...
OH, HEY...
WEREWOLF JONES
BELOVED FATHER AND FRIEND
ENTER THE DRAGON
HA HA.
HOW ARE YOU? YOU BEEN DOING OKAY?
McCafe 24 hr
YEAH...
YEAH... I'M DOING GOOD.

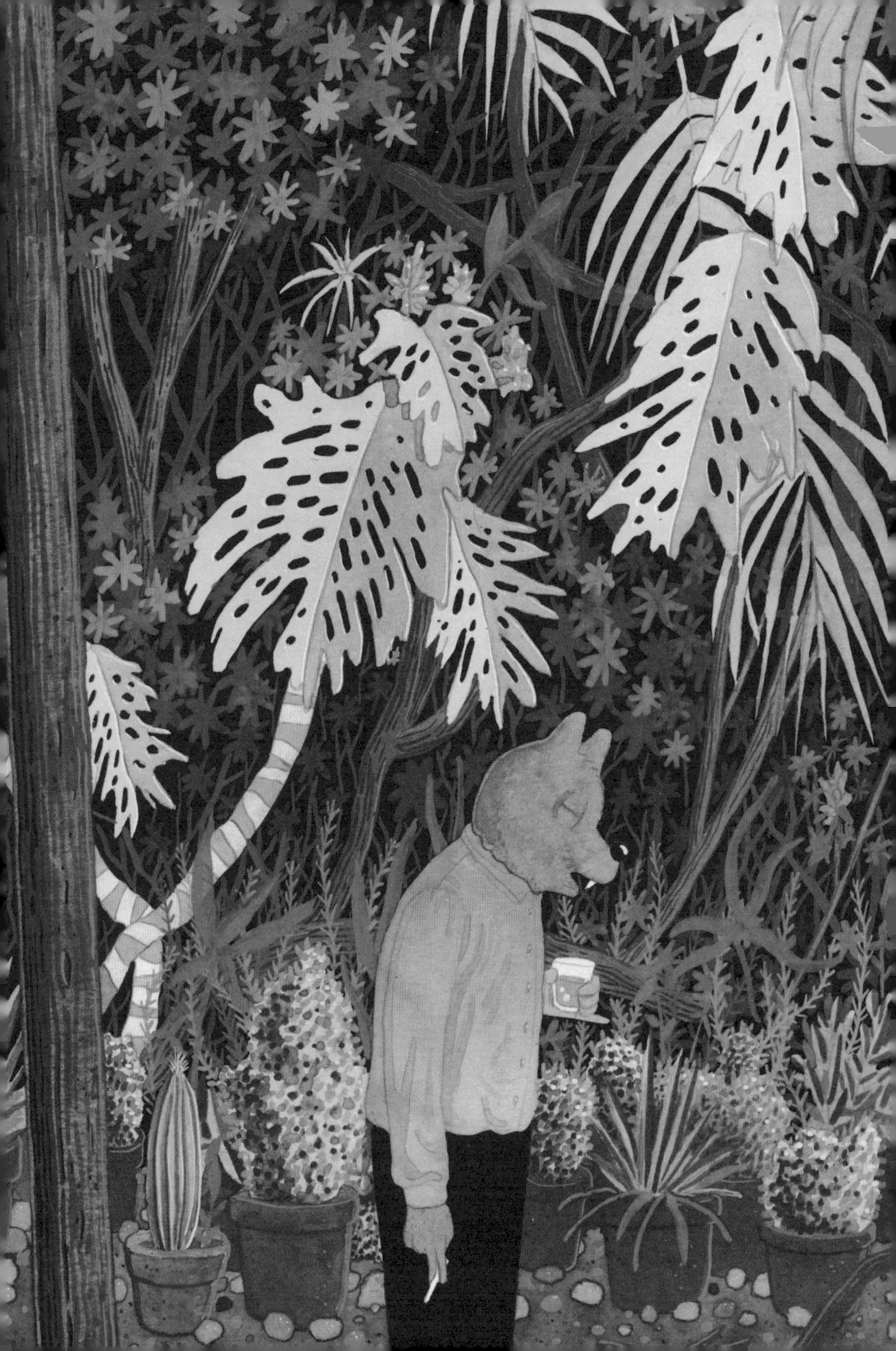

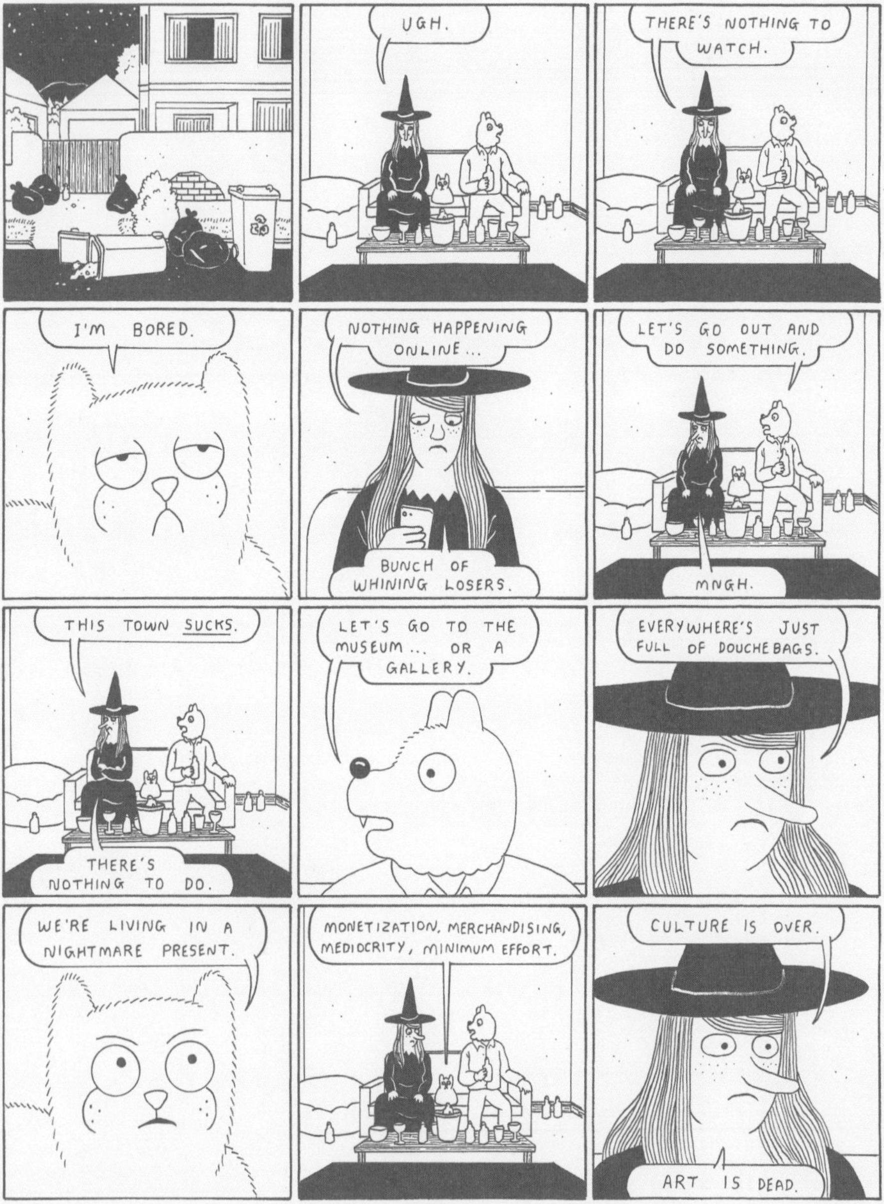

UGH.
THERE'S NOTHING TO WATCH.
I'M BORED.
NOTHING HAPPENING ONLINE...
BUNCH OF WHINING LOSERS.
LET'S GO OUT AND DO SOMETHING.
MNGH.
THIS TOWN SUCKS.
THERE'S NOTHING TO DO.
LET'S GO TO THE MUSEUM... OR A GALLERY.
EVERYWHERE'S JUST FULL OF DOUCHEBAGS.
WE'RE LIVING IN A NIGHTMARE PRESENT.
MONETIZATION, MERCHANDISING, MEDIOCRITY, MINIMUM EFFORT.
CULTURE IS OVER.
ART IS DEAD.

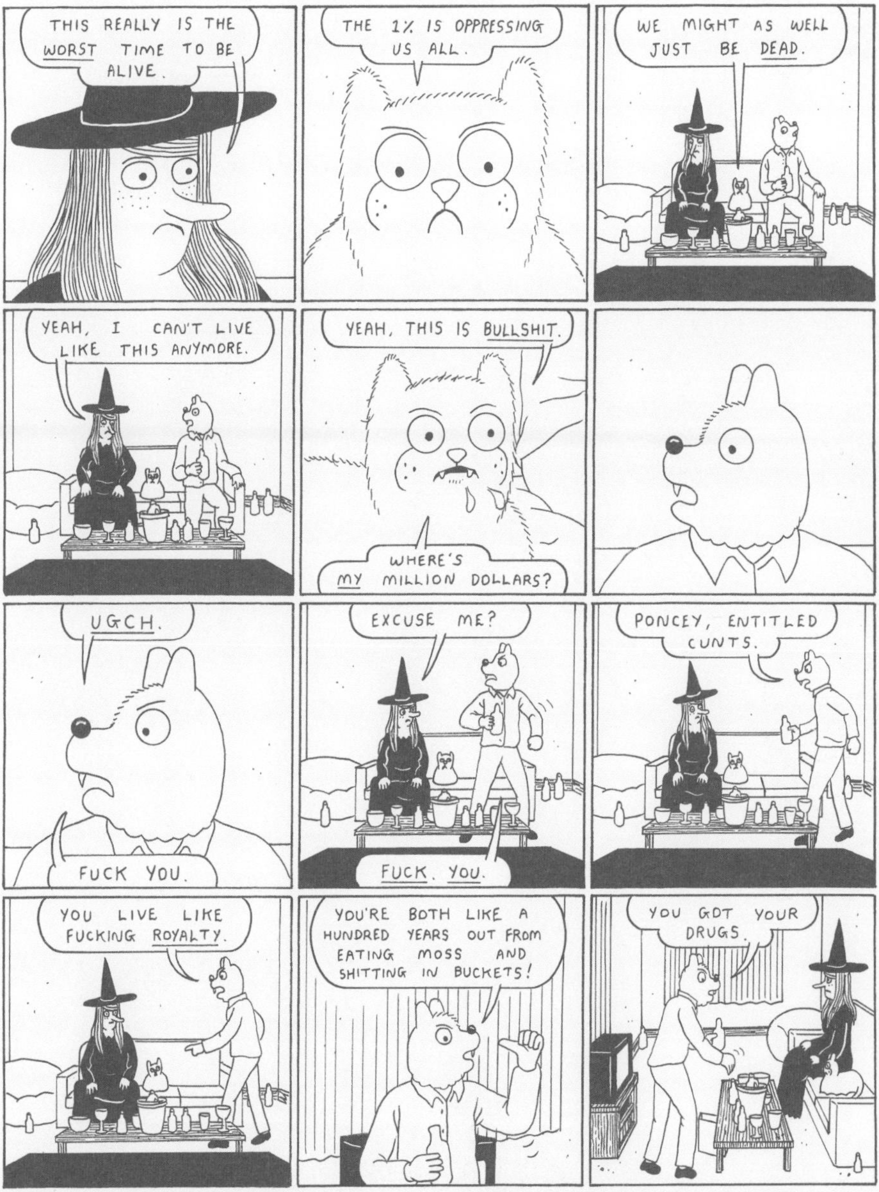
THIS REALLY IS THE WORST TIME TO BE ALIVE.
THE 1% IS OPPRESSING US ALL.
WE MIGHT AS WELL JUST BE DEAD.
YEAH, I CAN'T LIVE LIKE THIS ANYMORE.
YEAH, THIS IS BULLSHIT.
WHERE'S MY MILLION DOLLARS?
UGCH.
FUCK YOU.
EXCUSE ME?
FUCK. YOU.
PONCEY, ENTITLED CUNTS.
YOU LIVE LIKE FUCKING ROYALTY.
YOU'RE BOTH LIKE A HUNDRED YEARS OUT FROM EATING MOSS AND SHITTING IN BUCKETS!
YOU GOT YOUR DRUGS.

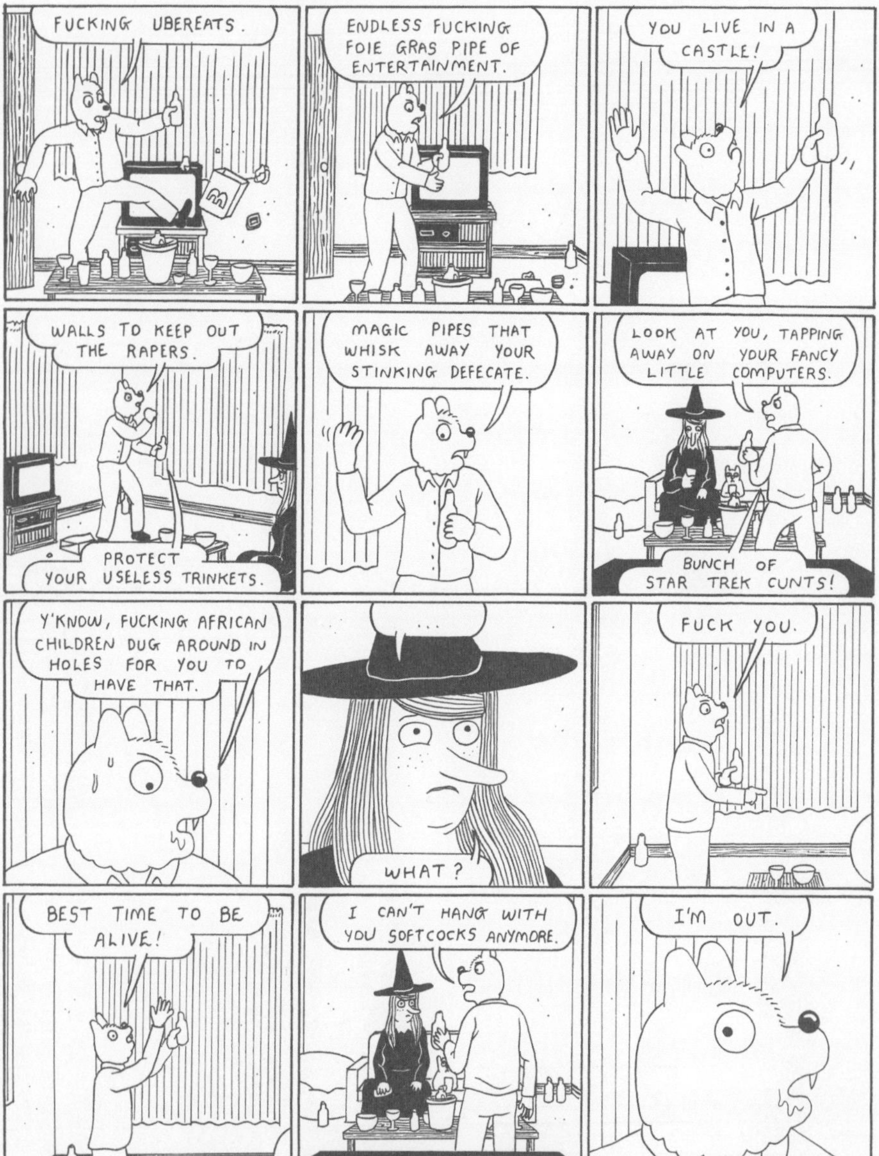
FUCKING UBEREATS.
ENDLESS FUCKING FOIE GRAS PIPE OF ENTERTAINMENT.
YOU LIVE IN A CASTLE!
WALLS TO KEEP OUT THE RAPERS.
PROTECT YOUR USELESS TRINKETS.
MAGIC PIPES THAT WHISK AWAY YOUR STINKING DEFECATE.
LOOK AT YOU, TAPPING AWAY ON YOUR FANCY LITTLE COMPUTERS.
BUNCH OF STAR TREK CUNTS!
Y'KNOW, FUCKING AFRICAN CHILDREN DUG AROUND IN HOLES FOR YOU TO HAVE THAT.
...
WHAT?
FUCK YOU.
BEST TIME TO BE ALIVE!
I CAN'T HANG WITH YOU SOFTCOCKS ANYMORE.
I'M OUT.

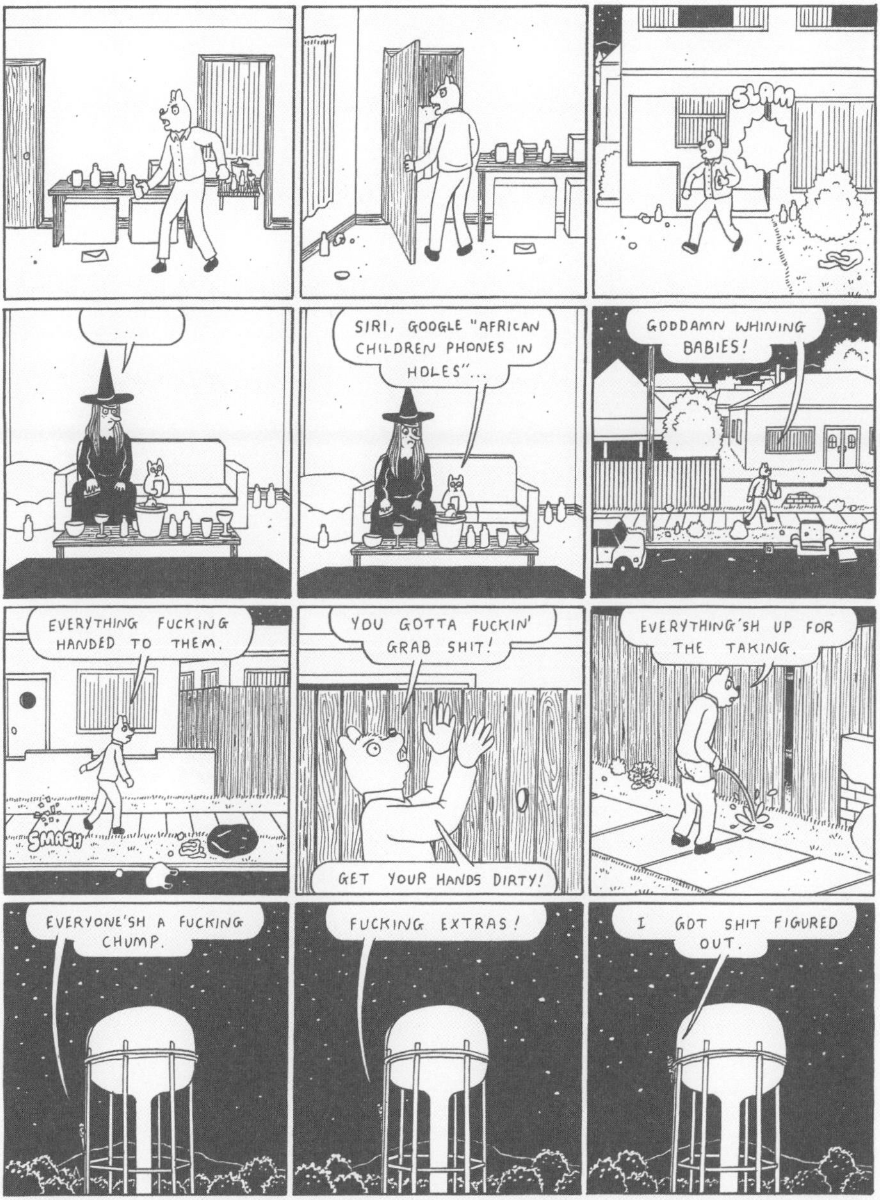
SLAM
...
SIRI, GOOGLE "AFRICAN CHILDREN PHONES IN HOLES"...
GODDAMN WHINING BABIES!
EVERYTHING FUCKING HANDED TO THEM.
SMASH
YOU GOTTA FUCKIN' GRAB SHIT!
GET YOUR HANDS DIRTY!
EVERYTHING'SH UP FOR THE TAKING.
EVERYONE'SH A FUCKING CHUMP.
FUCKING EXTRAS!
I GOT SHIT FIGURED OUT.

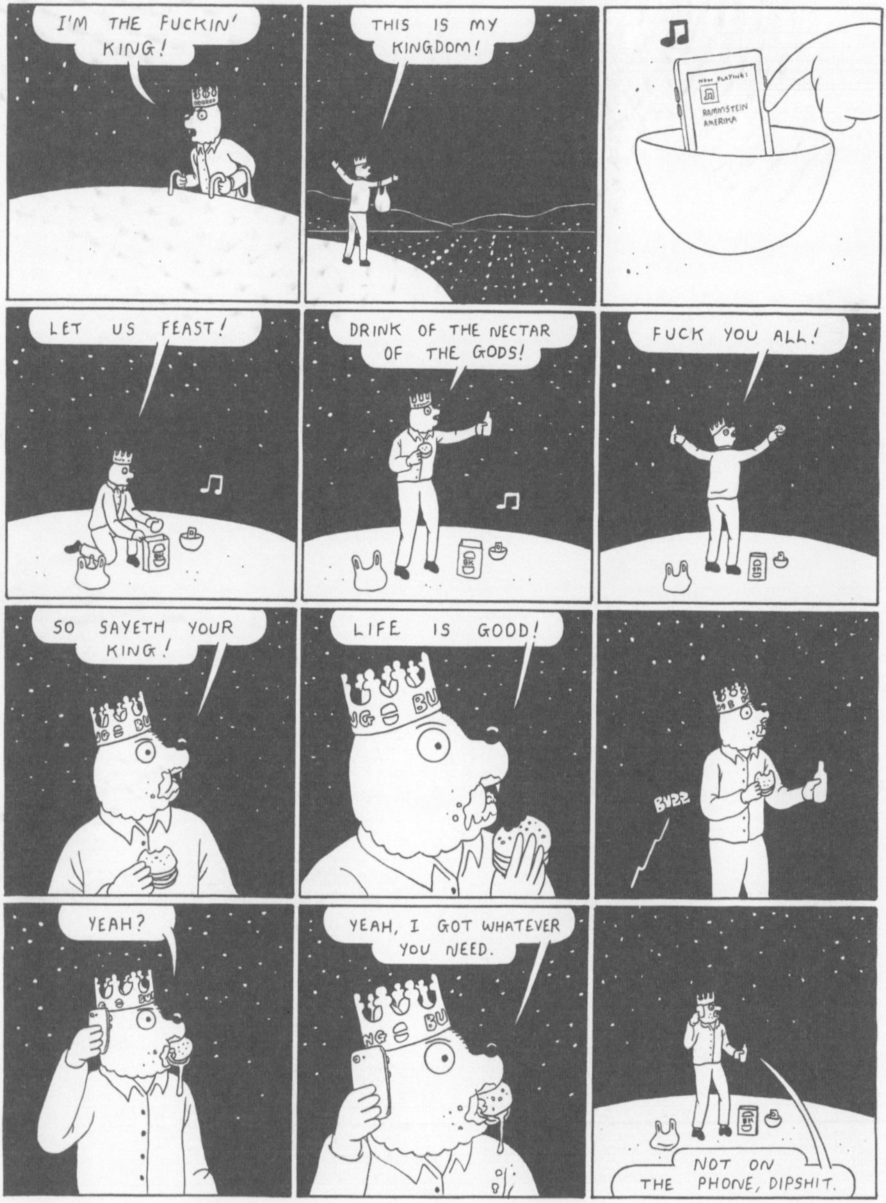
I'M THE FUCKIN' KING!
THIS IS MY KINGDOM!
NOW PLAYING:
RAMMSTEIN
AMERIKA
LET US FEAST!
DRINK OF THE NECTAR OF THE GODS!
FUCK YOU ALL!
SO SAYETH YOUR KING!
LIFE IS GOOD!
BUZZ
YEAH?
YEAH, I GOT WHATEVER YOU NEED.
NOT ON THE PHONE, DIPSHIT.

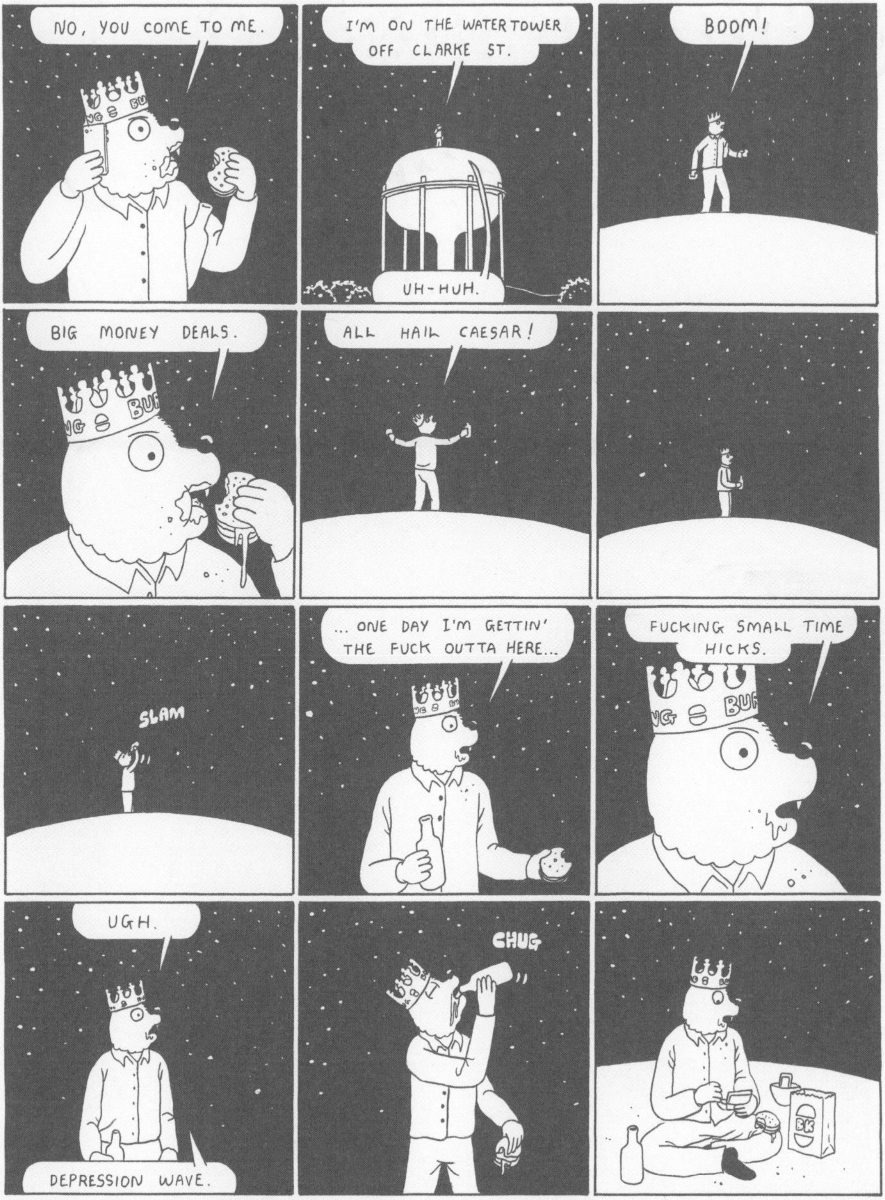
NO, YOU COME TO ME.
I'M ON THE WATERTOWER OFF CLARKE ST.
UH-HUH.
BOOM!
BIG MONEY DEALS.
ALL HAIL CAESAR!
SLAM
... ONE DAY I'M GETTIN' THE FUCK OUTTA HERE...
FUCKING SMALL TIME HICKS.
UGH.
DEPRESSION WAVE.
CHUG
BK

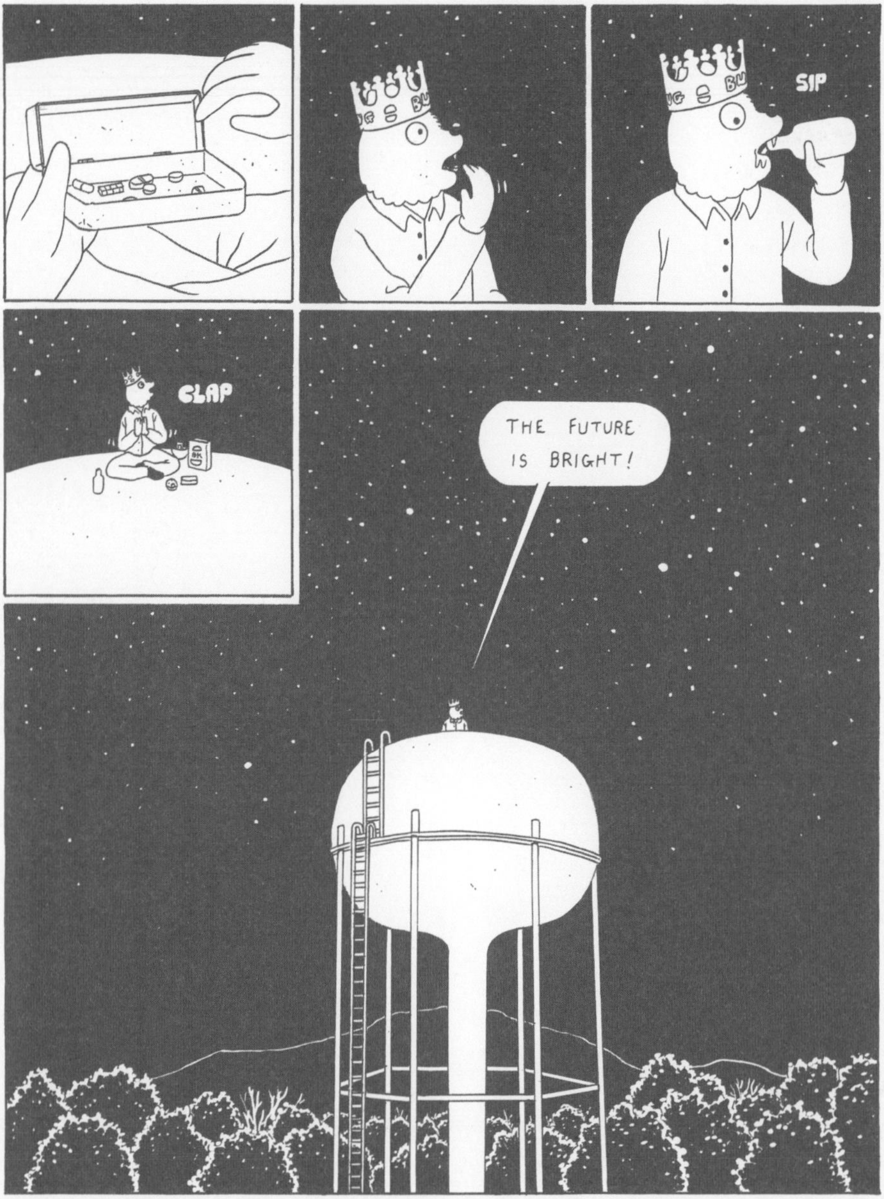
SIP
CLAP
THE FUTURE IS BRIGHT!

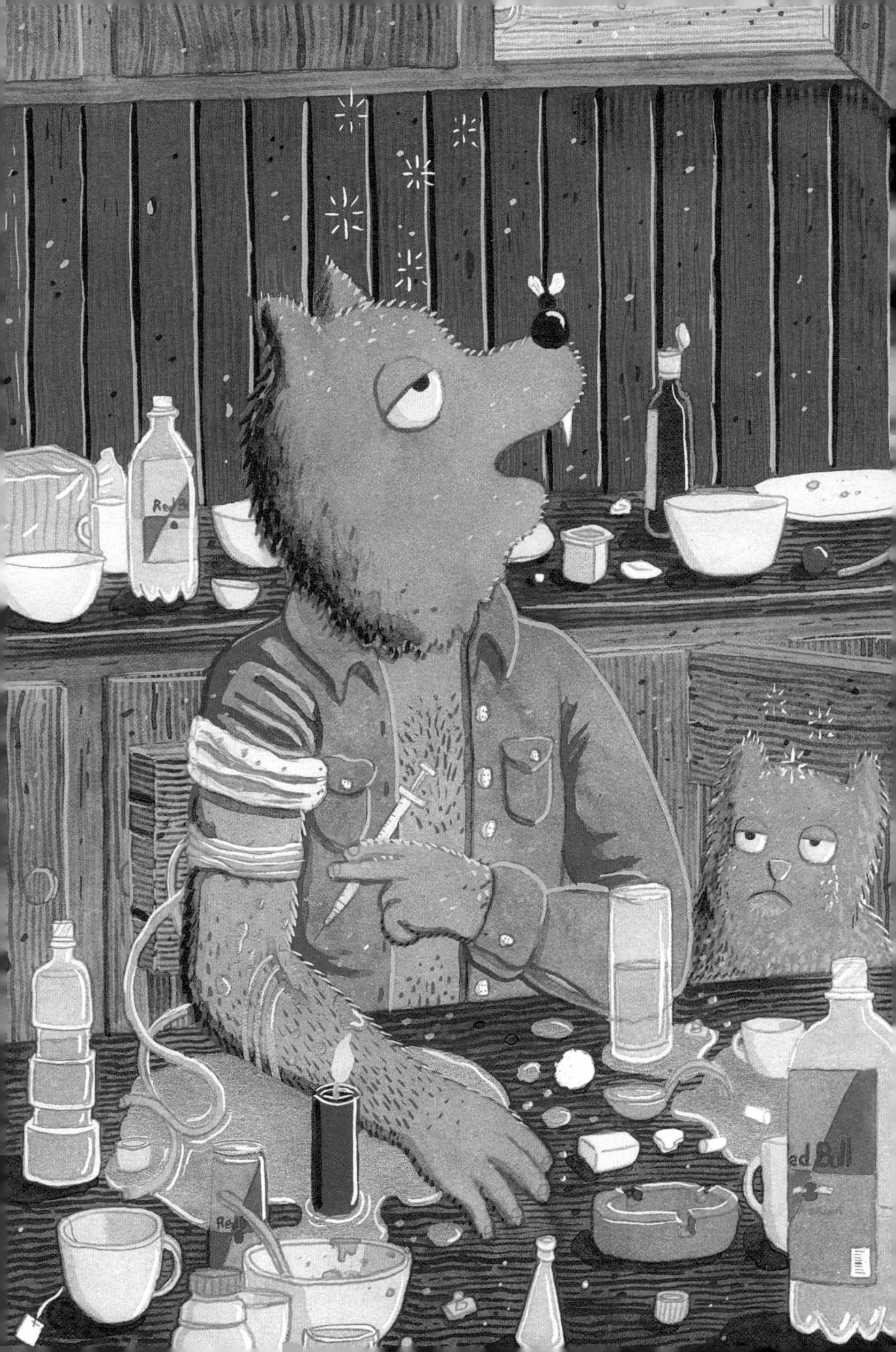
ed Bull

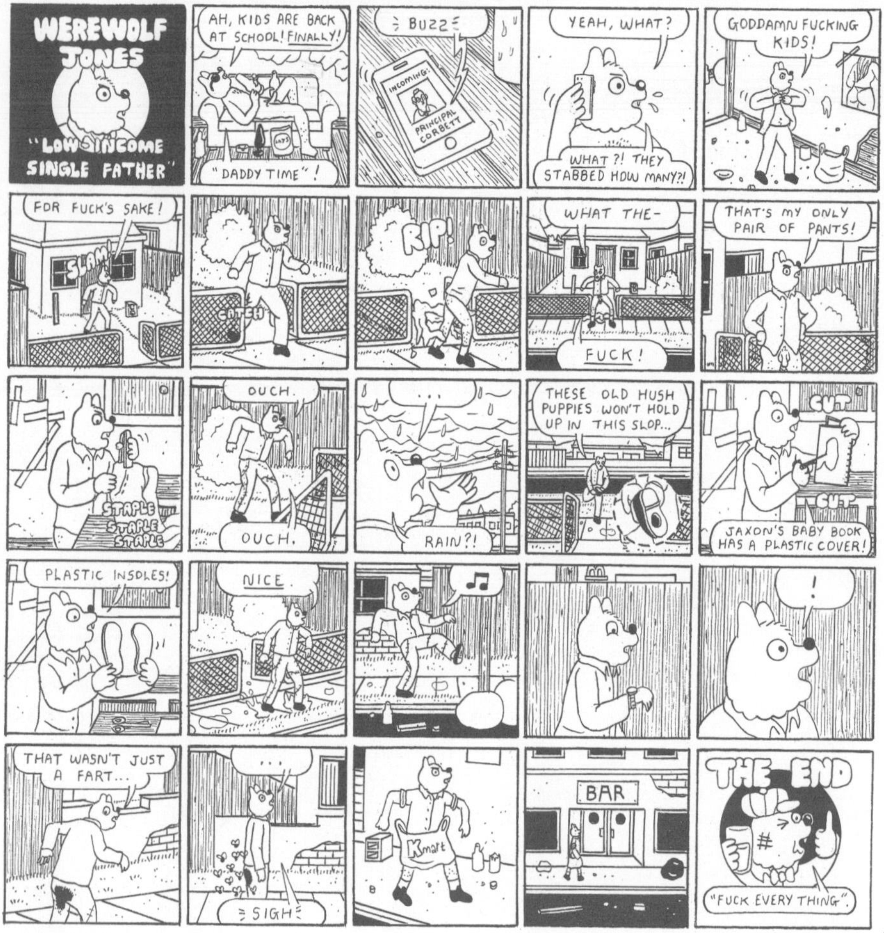
WEREWOLF JONES
"LOW INCOME SINGLE FATHER"
AH, KIDS ARE BACK AT SCHOOL! FINALLY!
"DADDY TIME"!
BUZZ
INCOMING:
PRINCIPAL CORBETT
YEAH, WHAT?
WHAT?! THEY STABBED HOW MANY?!
GODDAMN FUCKING KIDS!
FOR FUCK'S SAKE!
SLAM!
CATCH
RIP!
WHAT THE-
FUCK!
THAT'S MY ONLY PAIR OF PANTS!
STAPLE
STAPLE
STAPLE
OUCH.
OUCH.
...
RAIN?!
THESE OLD HUSH PUPPIES WON'T HOLD UP IN THIS SLOP...
CUT
CUT
JAXON'S BABY BOOK HAS A PLASTIC COVER!
PLASTIC INSOLES!
NICE.
!
THAT WASN'T JUST A FART...
...
SIGH
Kmart
BAR
THE END
"FUCK EVERY THING".

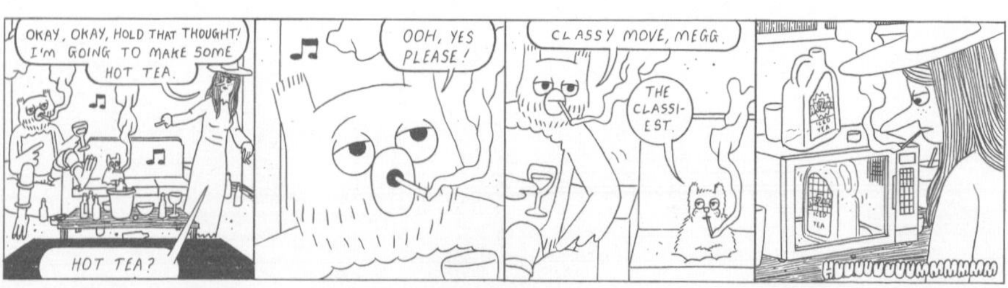
OKAY, OKAY, HOLD THAT THOUGHT! I'M GOING TO MAKE SOME HOT TEA.
HOT TEA?
OOH, YES PLEASE!
CLASSY MOVE, MEGG.
THE CLASSI-EST.
ICED TEA
HUUUUUUUUMMMMMMMM

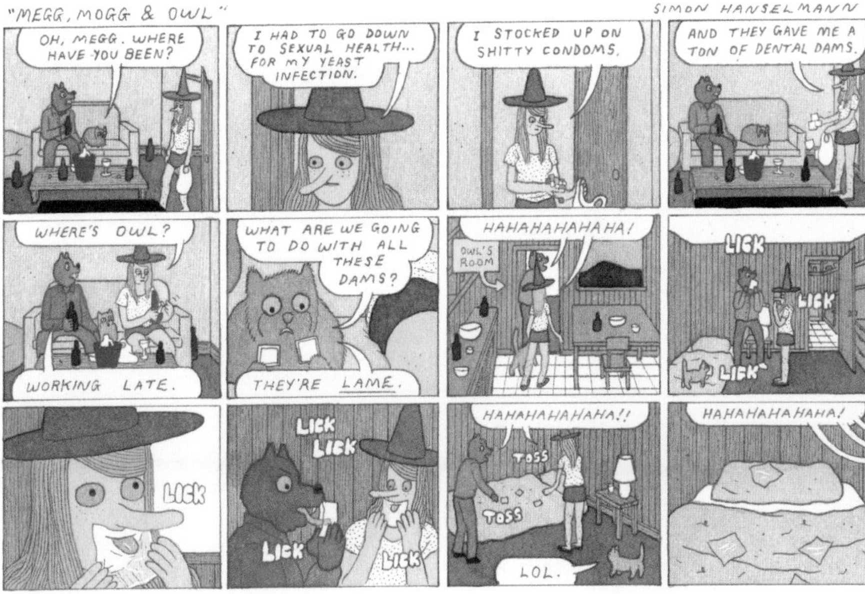
"MEGG, MOGG & OWL"
SIMON HANSELMANN
OH, MEGG. WHERE HAVE YOU BEEN?
I HAD TO GO DOWN TO SEXUAL HEALTH... FOR MY YEAST INFECTION.
I STOCKED UP ON SHITTY CONDOMS.
AND THEY GAVE ME A TON OF DENTAL DAMS.
WHERE'S OWL?
WORKING LATE.
WHAT ARE WE GOING TO DO WITH ALL THESE DAMS?
THEY'RE LAME.
HAHAHAHAHAHAHA!
OWL'S ROOM
LICK
LICK
LICK
LICK
LICK
LICK
LICK
LICK
HAHAHAHAHAHAHA!!
TOSS
TOSS
LOL.
HAHAHAHAHAHAHA!

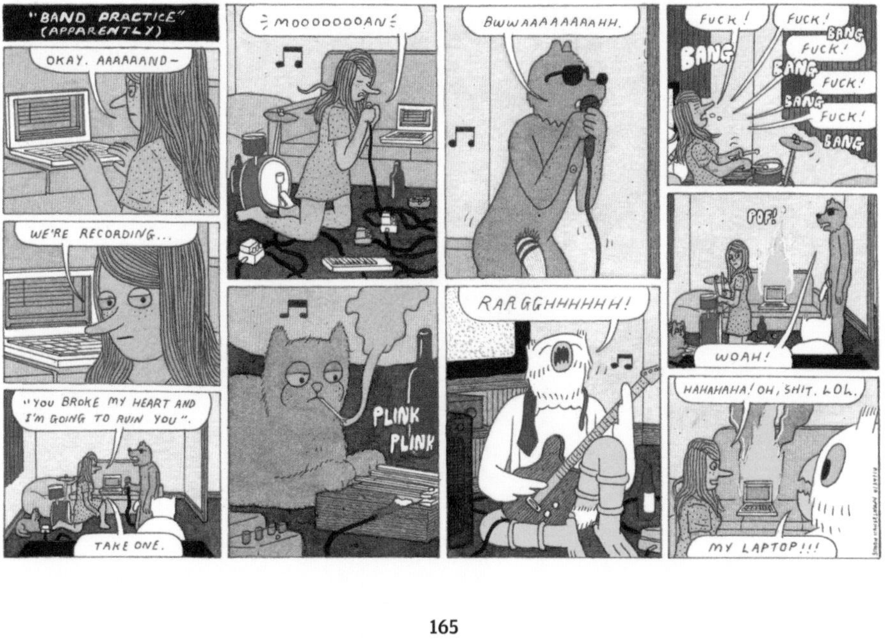
"BAND PRACTICE" (APPARENTLY)
OKAY. AAAAAAND—
WE'RE RECORDING...
"YOU BROKE MY HEART AND I'M GOING TO RUIN YOU".
TAKE ONE.
MOOOOOOOAN
PLINK
PLINK
BWWAAAAAAAAHH.
RARGGHHHHHH!
FUCK!
FUCK!
BANG
FUCK!
BANG
BANG
FUCK!
BANG
FUCK!
BANG
POF!
WOAH!
HAHAHAHA! OH, SHIT. LOL.
MY LAPTOP!!!

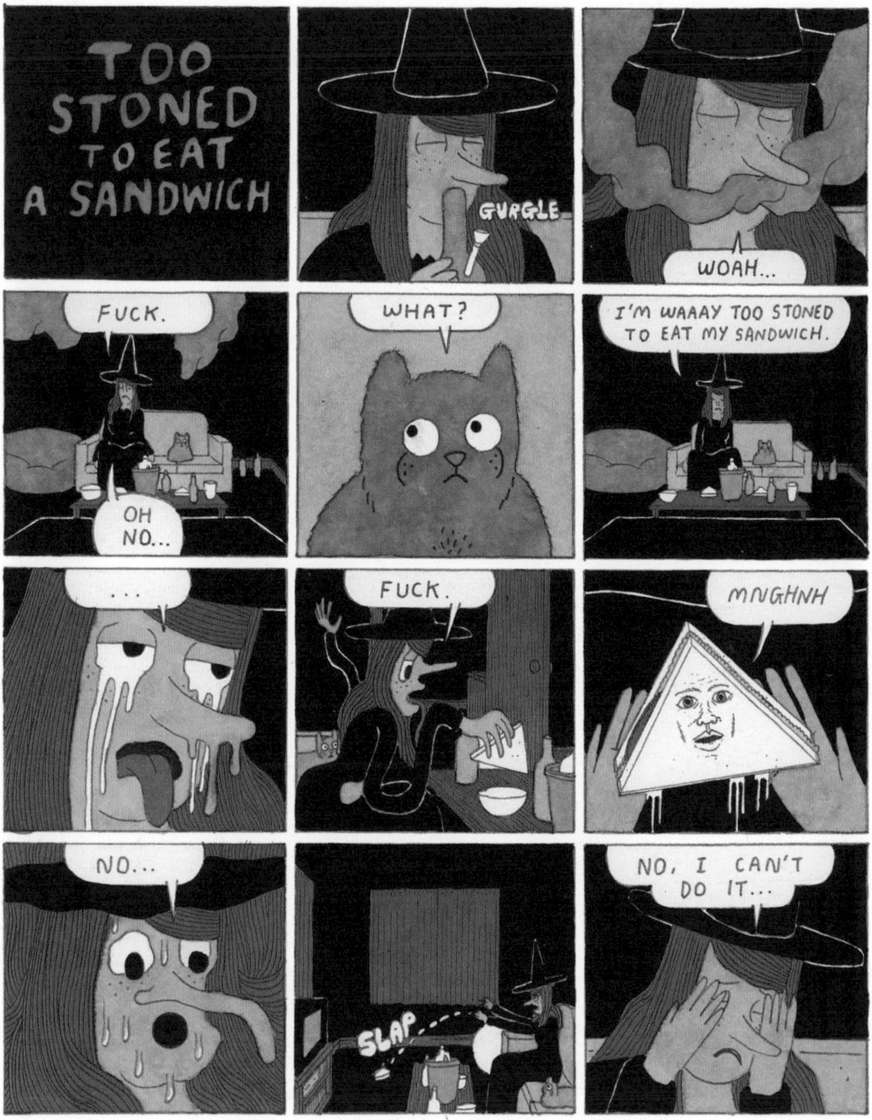
TOO STONED TO EAT A SANDWICH
GURGLE
WOAH...
FUCK.
OH NO...
WHAT?
I'M WAAAY TOO STONED TO EAT MY SANDWICH.
...
FUCK.
MNGHNH
NO...
SLAP
NO, I CAN'T DO IT...

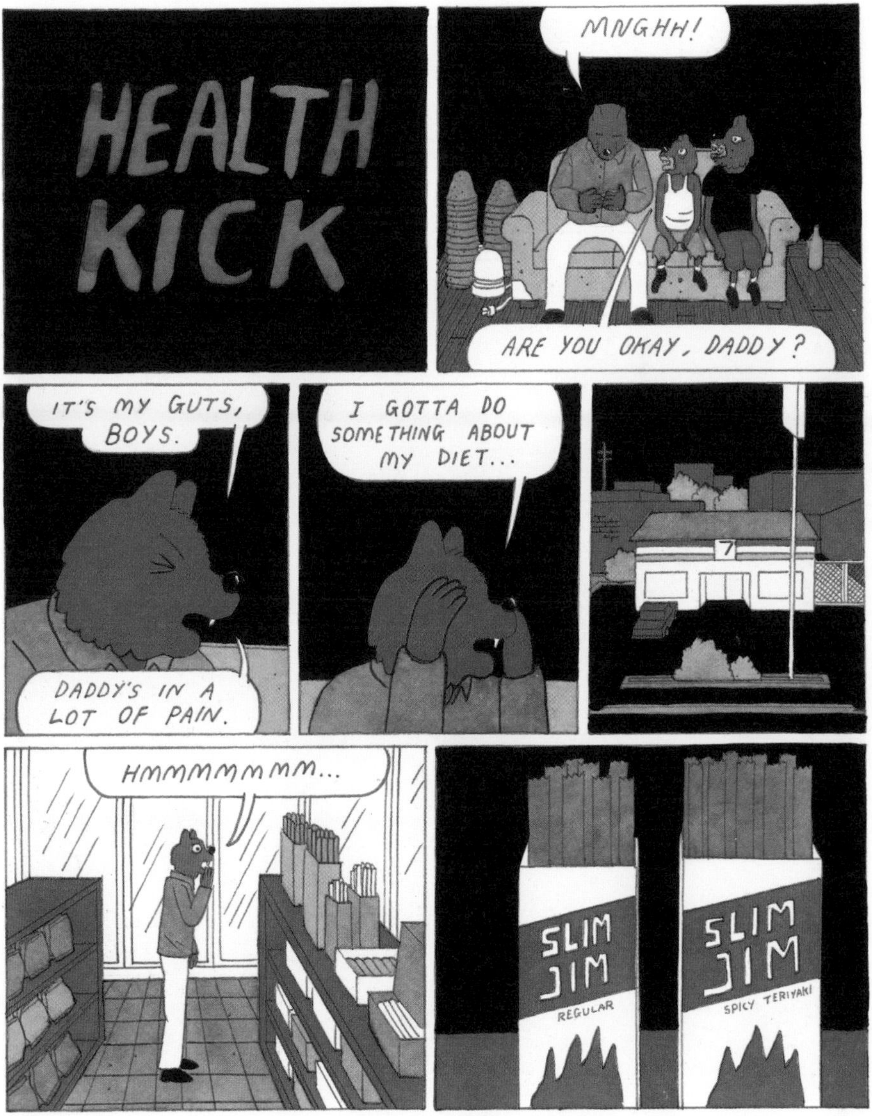
HEALTH KICK
MNGHH!
ARE YOU OKAY, DADDY?
IT'S MY GUTS, BOYS.
DADDY'S IN A LOT OF PAIN.
I GOTTA DO SOMETHING ABOUT MY DIET...
7
HMMMMMMM...
SLIM JIM
REGULAR
SLIM JIM
SPICY TERIYAKI

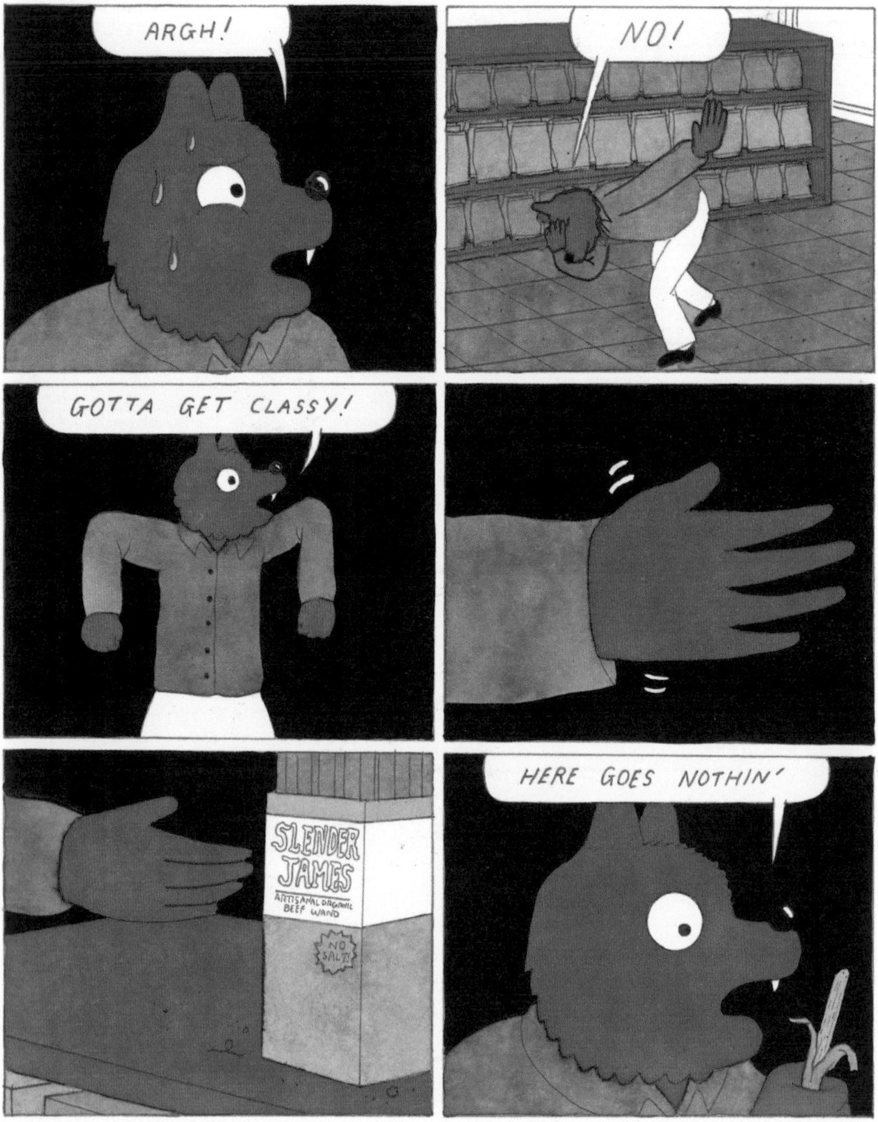
ARGH!
NO!
GOTTA GET CLASSY!
SLENDER JAMES
ARTISANAL ORGANIC BEEF WAND
NO SALT!
HERE GOES NOTHIN'

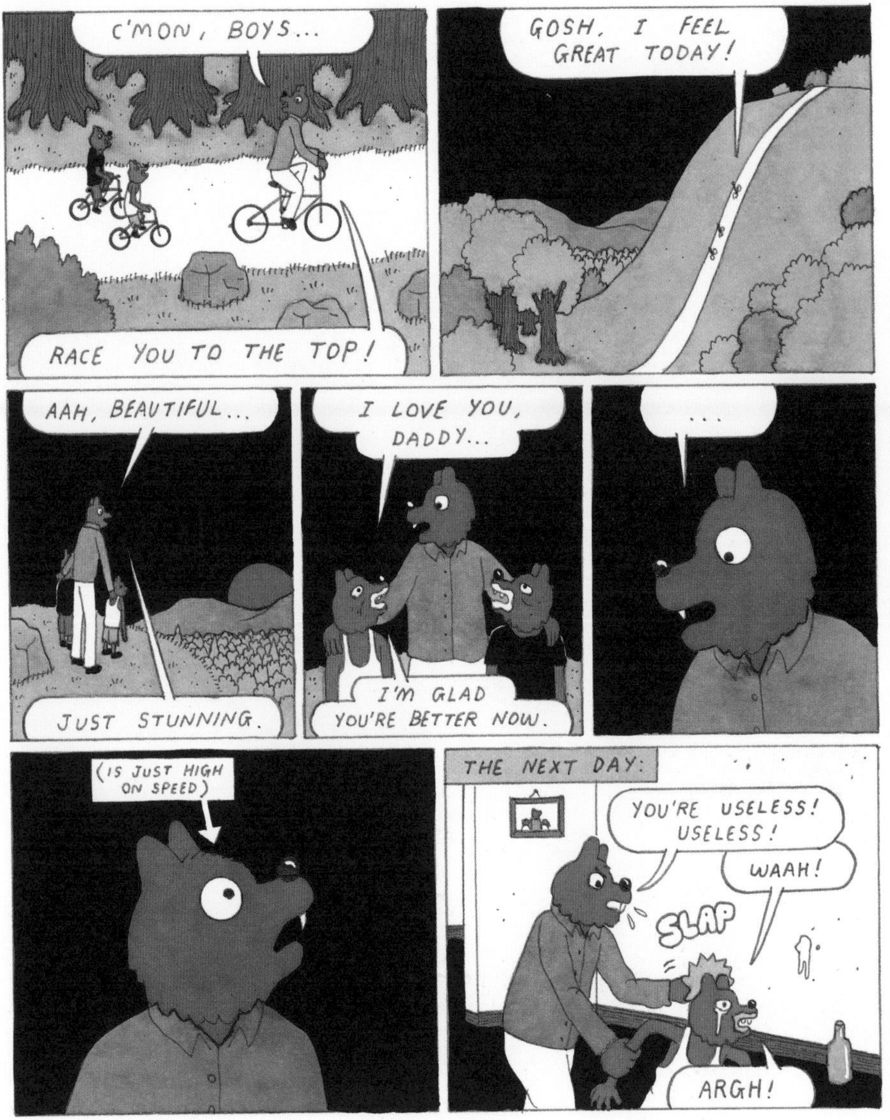
C'MON, BOYS...
RACE YOU TO THE TOP!
GOSH, I FEEL GREAT TODAY!
AAH, BEAUTIFUL...
JUST STUNNING.
I LOVE YOU, DADDY...
I'M GLAD YOU'RE BETTER NOW.
...
(IS JUST HIGH ON SPEED)
THE NEXT DAY:
YOU'RE USELESS! USELESS!
WAAH!
SLAP
ARGH!

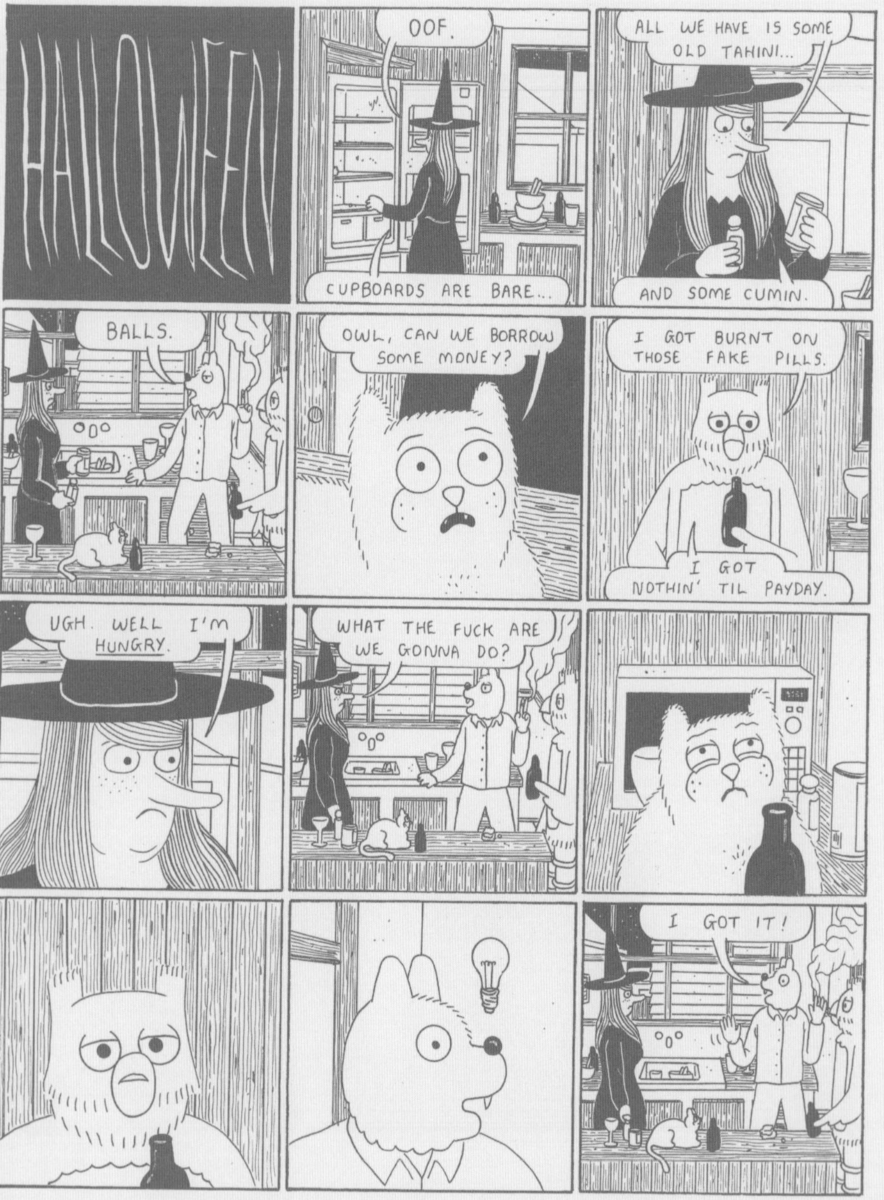
HALLOWEEN
OOF.
CUPBOARDS ARE BARE...
ALL WE HAVE IS SOME OLD TAHINI...
AND SOME CUMIN.
BALLS.
OWL, CAN WE BORROW SOME MONEY?
I GOT BURNT ON THOSE FAKE PILLS.
I GOT NOTHIN' TIL PAYDAY.
UGH. WELL I'M HUNGRY.
WHAT THE FUCK ARE WE GONNA DO?
I GOT IT!

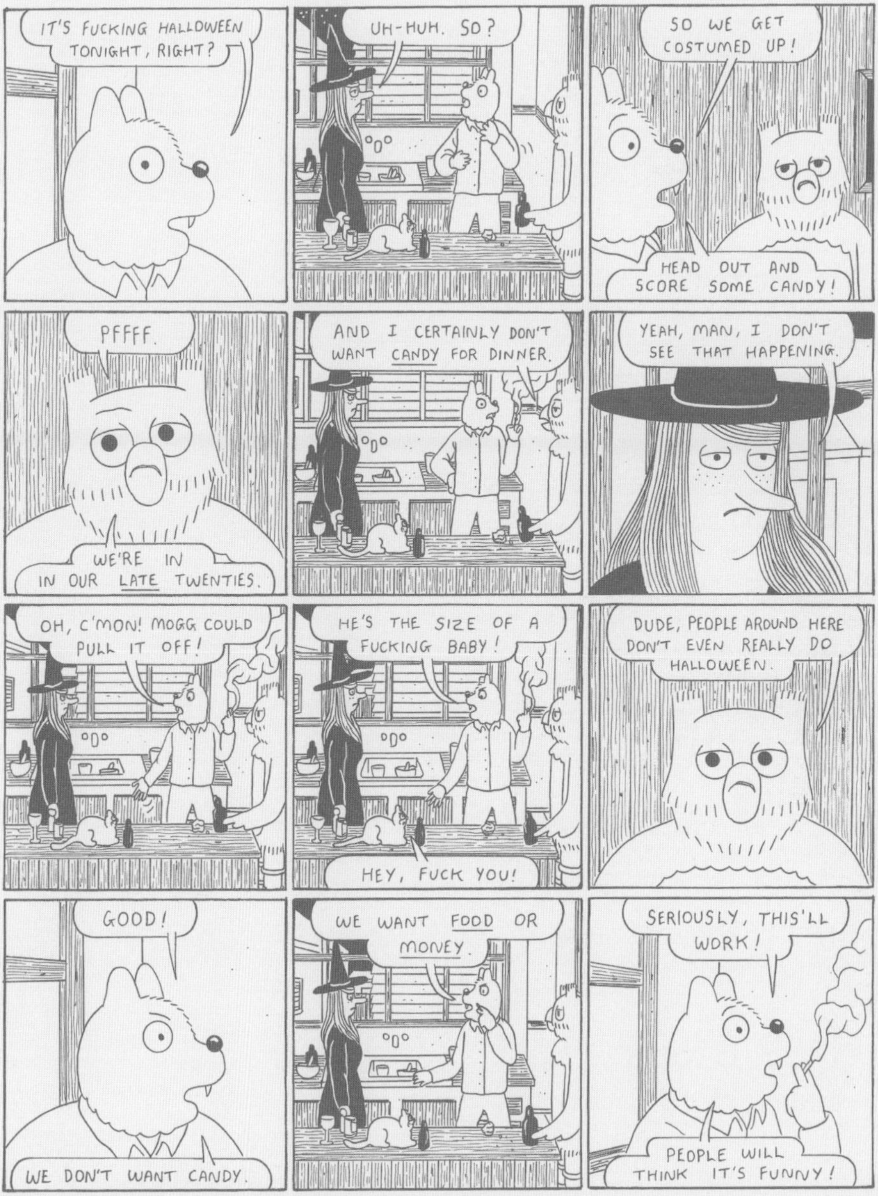
IT'S FUCKING HALLOWEEN TONIGHT, RIGHT?
UH-HUH. SO?
SO WE GET COSTUMED UP!
HEAD OUT AND SCORE SOME CANDY!
PFFFF.
WE'RE IN IN OUR LATE TWENTIES.
AND I CERTAINLY DON'T WANT CANDY FOR DINNER.
YEAH, MAN, I DON'T SEE THAT HAPPENING.
OH, C'MON! MOGG COULD PULL IT OFF!
HE'S THE SIZE OF A FUCKING BABY!
HEY, FUCK YOU!
DUDE, PEOPLE AROUND HERE DON'T EVEN REALLY DO HALLOWEEN.
GOOD!
WE DON'T WANT CANDY.
WE WANT FOOD OR MONEY.
SERIOUSLY, THIS'LL WORK!
PEOPLE WILL THINK IT'S FUNNY!

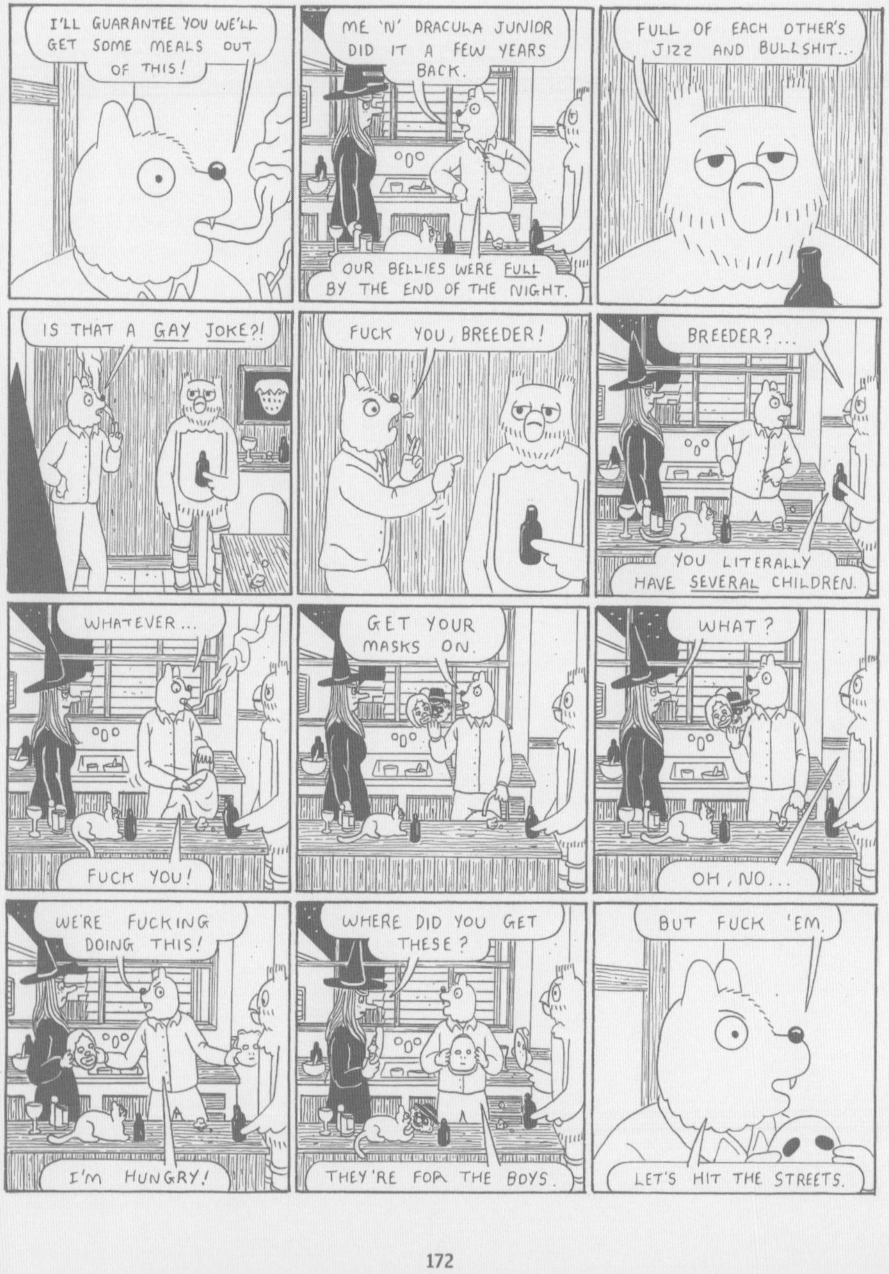
I'LL GUARANTEE YOU WE'LL GET SOME MEALS OUT OF THIS!
ME 'N' DRACULA JUNIOR DID IT A FEW YEARS BACK.
OUR BELLIES WERE FULL BY THE END OF THE NIGHT.
FULL OF EACH OTHER'S JIZZ AND BULLSHIT...
IS THAT A GAY JOKE?!
FUCK YOU, BREEDER!
BREEDER?...
YOU LITERALLY HAVE SEVERAL CHILDREN.
WHATEVER...
FUCK YOU!
GET YOUR MASKS ON.
WHAT?
OH, NO...
WE'RE FUCKING DOING THIS!
I'M HUNGRY!
WHERE DID YOU GET THESE?
THEY'RE FOR THE BOYS.
BUT FUCK 'EM.
LET'S HIT THE STREETS.

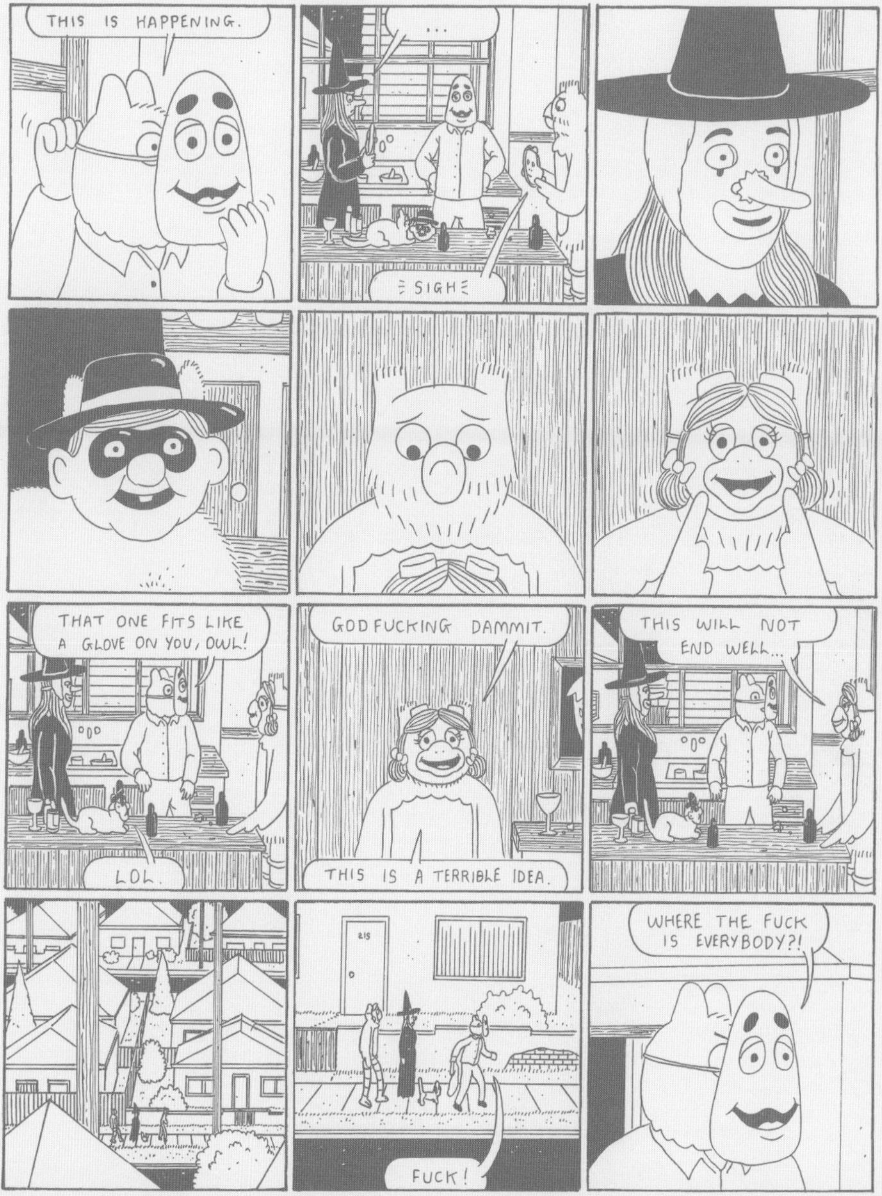

THIS IS HAPPENING.
...
≡ SIGH ≡
THAT ONE FITS LIKE A GLOVE ON YOU, OWL!
LOL.
GODFUCKING DAMMIT.
THIS IS A TERRIBLE IDEA.
THIS WILL NOT END WELL...
FUCK!
WHERE THE FUCK IS EVERYBODY?!

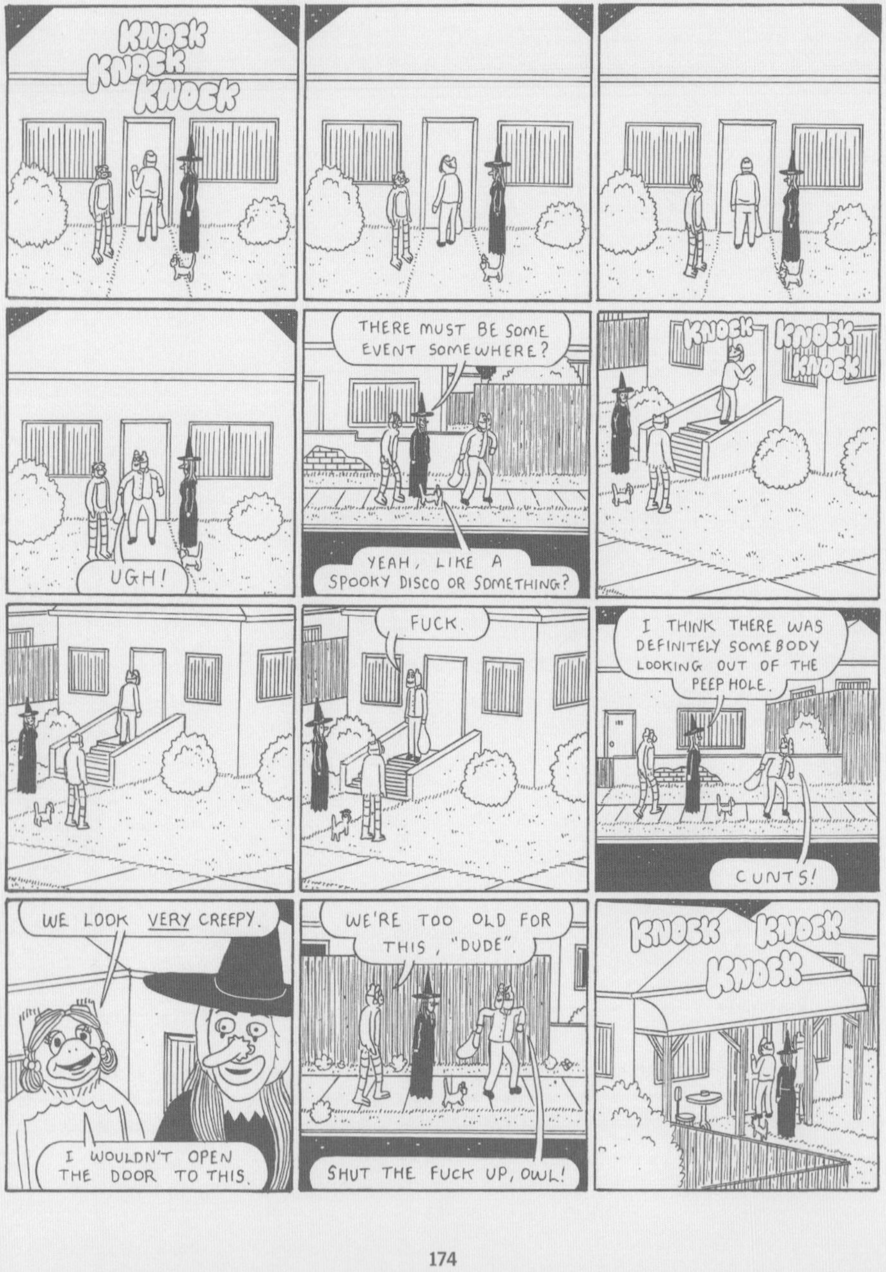
KNOCK
KNOCK
KNOCK
THERE MUST BE SOME EVENT SOMEWHERE?
UGH!
YEAH, LIKE A SPOOKY DISCO OR SOMETHING?
KNOCK KNOCK KNOCK
FUCK.
I THINK THERE WAS DEFINITELY SOMEBODY LOOKING OUT OF THE PEEP HOLE.
CUNTS!
WE LOOK VERY CREEPY.
I WOULDN'T OPEN THE DOOR TO THIS.
WE'RE TOO OLD FOR THIS, "DUDE".
SHUT THE FUCK UP, OWL!
KNOCK KNOCK KNOCK

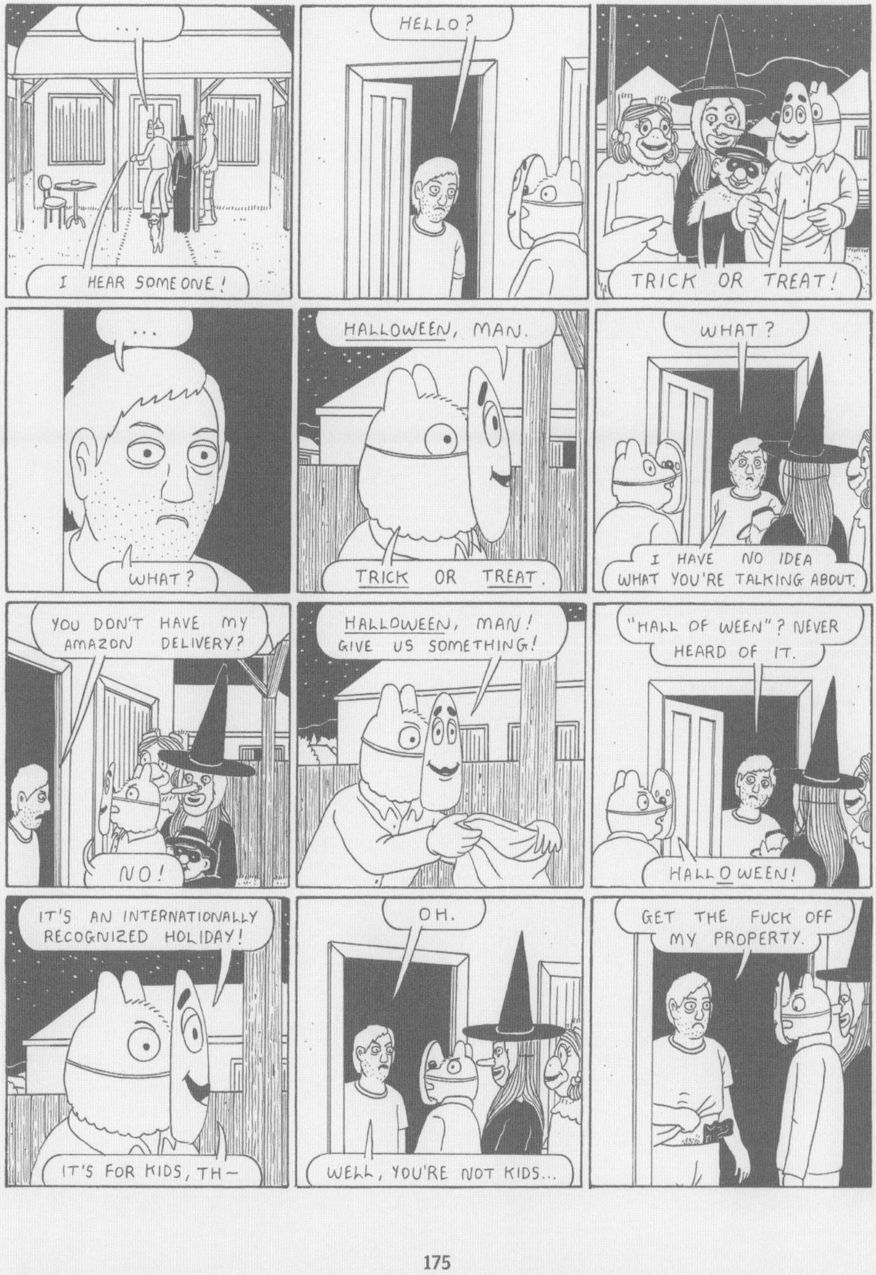
...
I HEAR SOMEONE!
HELLO?
TRICK OR TREAT!
...
WHAT?
HALLOWEEN, MAN.
TRICK OR TREAT.
WHAT?
I HAVE NO IDEA WHAT YOU'RE TALKING ABOUT.
YOU DON'T HAVE MY AMAZON DELIVERY?
NO!
HALLOWEEN, MAN! GIVE US SOMETHING!
"HALL OF WEEN"? NEVER HEARD OF IT.
HALLOWEEN!
IT'S AN INTERNATIONALLY RECOGNIZED HOLIDAY!
IT'S FOR KIDS, TH—
OH.
WELL, YOU'RE NOT KIDS...
GET THE FUCK OFF MY PROPERTY.

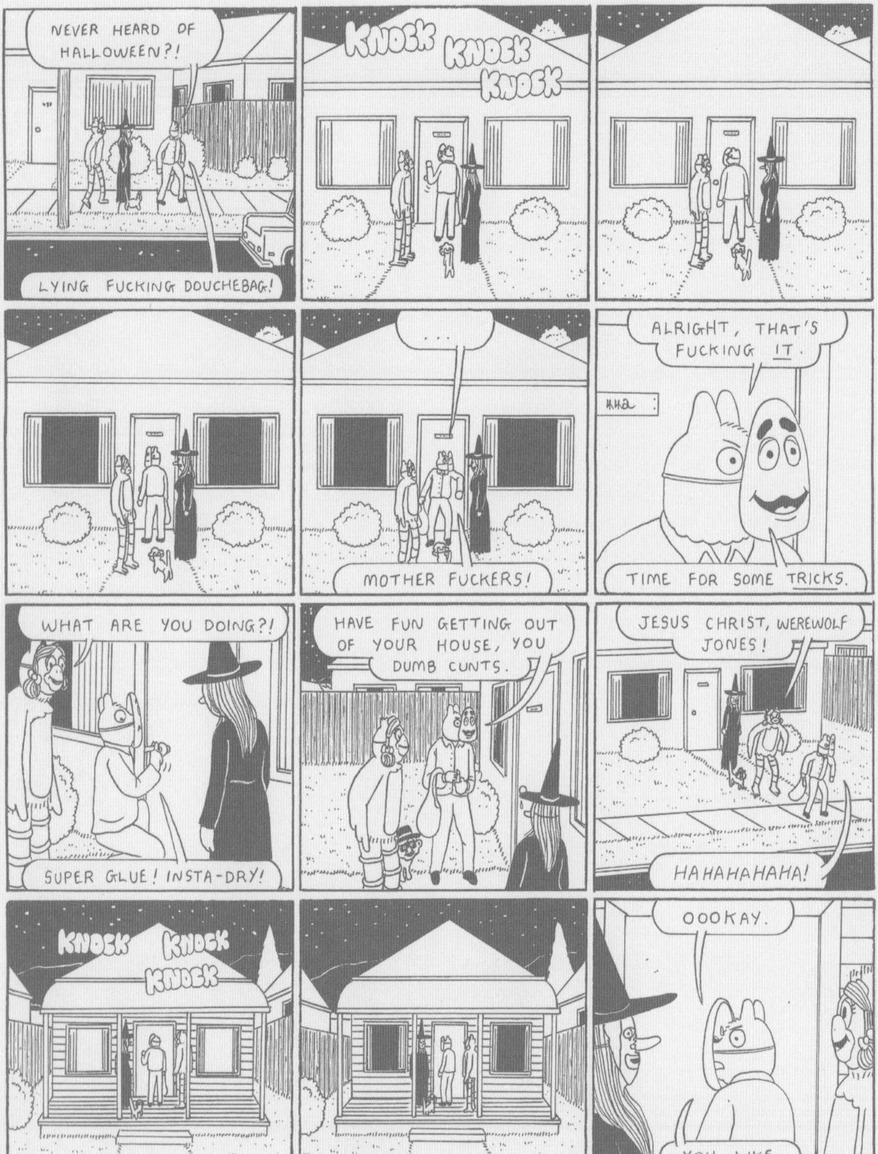
NEVER HEARD OF HALLOWEEN?!
LYING FUCKING DOUCHEBAG!
KNOCK KNOCK KNOCK
...
MOTHER FUCKERS!
ALRIGHT, THAT'S FUCKING IT.
TIME FOR SOME TRICKS.
WHAT ARE YOU DOING?!
SUPER GLUE! INSTA-DRY!
HAVE FUN GETTING OUT OF YOUR HOUSE, YOU DUMB CUNTS.
JESUS CHRIST, WEREWOLF JONES!
HAHAHAHAHA!
KNOCK KNOCK KNOCK
OOOKAY.
YOU LIKE TURNING YOUR LIGHTS OFF?

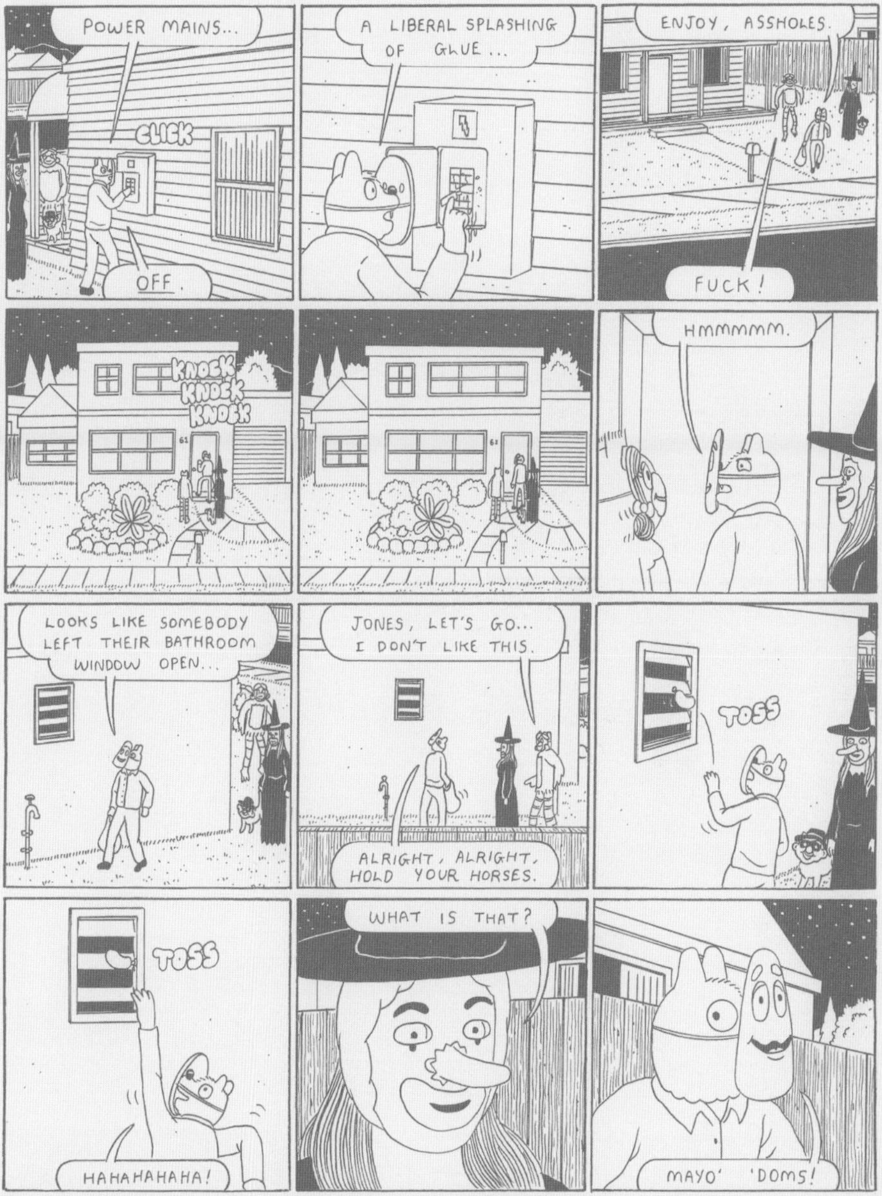
POWER MAINS...
CLICK
OFF.
A LIBERAL SPLASHING OF GLUE...
ENJOY, ASSHOLES.
FUCK!
KNOCK KNOCK KNOCK
HMMMMM.
LOOKS LIKE SOMEBODY LEFT THEIR BATHROOM WINDOW OPEN...
JONES, LET'S GO... I DON'T LIKE THIS.
ALRIGHT, ALRIGHT, HOLD YOUR HORSES.
TOSS
TOSS
HAHAHAHAHA!
WHAT IS THAT?
MAYO' 'DOMS!

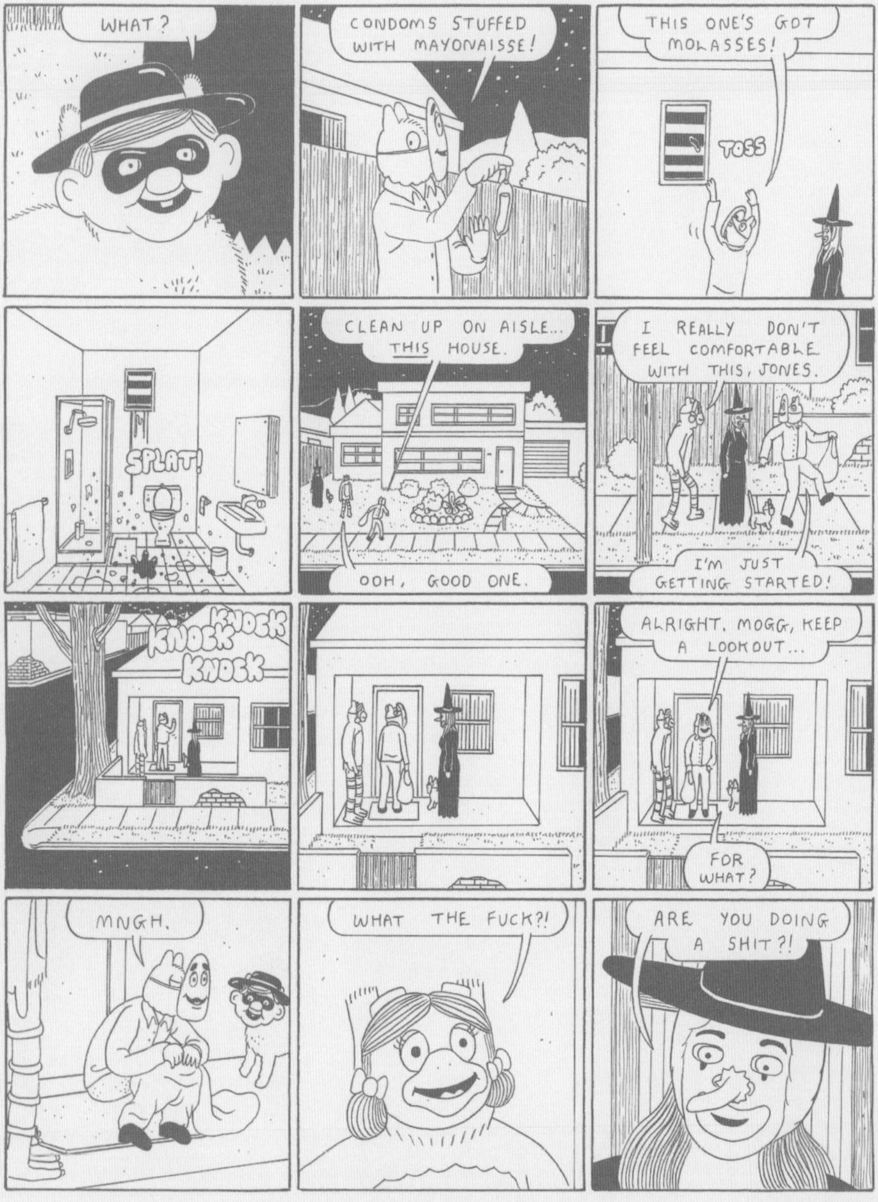
WHAT?
CONDOMS STUFFED WITH MAYONAISSE!
THIS ONE'S GOT MOLASSES!
TOSS
SPLAT!
CLEAN UP ON AISLE... THIS HOUSE.
OOH, GOOD ONE.
I REALLY DON'T FEEL COMFORTABLE WITH THIS, JONES.
I'M JUST GETTING STARTED!
KNOCK
KNOCK
KNOCK
ALRIGHT, MOGG, KEEP A LOOKOUT...
FOR WHAT?
MNGH.
WHAT THE FUCK?!
ARE YOU DOING A SHIT?!

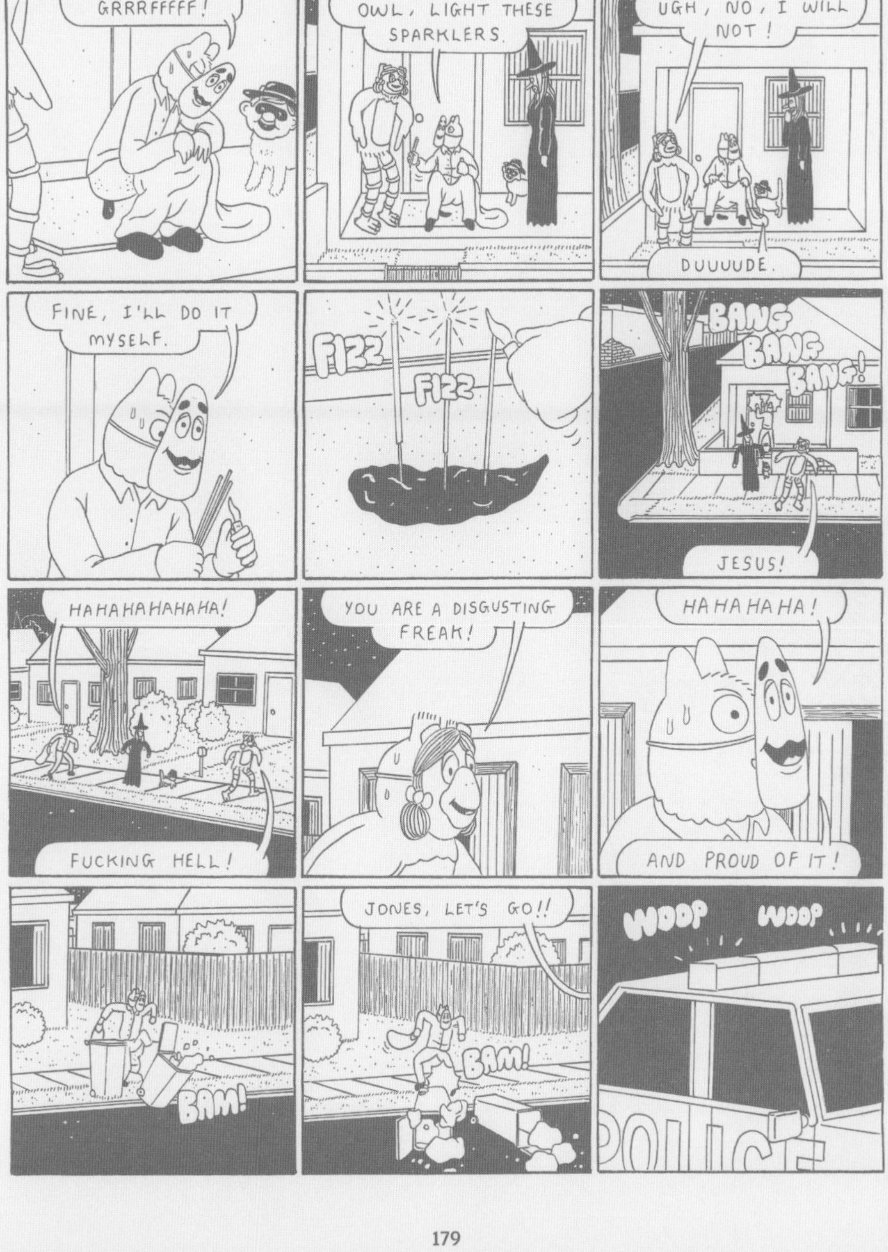
GRRRFFFFF!
OWL, LIGHT THESE SPARKLERS.
UGH, NO, I WILL NOT!
DUUUUDE.
FINE, I'LL DO IT MYSELF.
FIZZ
FIZZ
BANG
BANG
BANG!
JESUS!
HAHAHAHAHAHA!
FUCKING HELL!
YOU ARE A DISGUSTING FREAK!
HAHAHAHA!
AND PROUD OF IT!
BAM!
JONES, LET'S GO!!
BAM!
WOOP
WOOP
POLICE

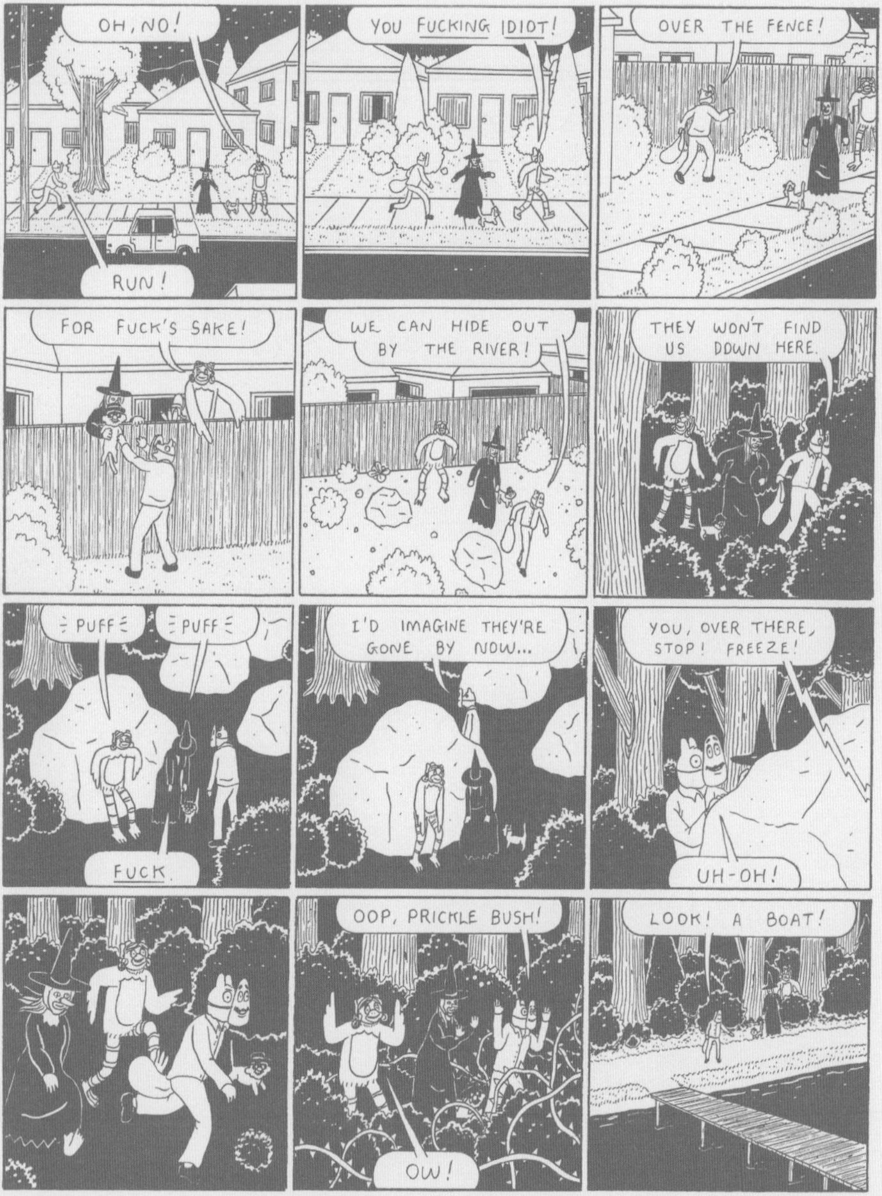

OH, NO!
RUN!
YOU FUCKING IDIOT!
OVER THE FENCE!
FOR FUCK'S SAKE!
WE CAN HIDE OUT BY THE RIVER!
THEY WON'T FIND US DOWN HERE.
PUFF
PUFF
FUCK
I'D IMAGINE THEY'RE GONE BY NOW...
YOU, OVER THERE, STOP! FREEZE!
UH-OH!
OOP, PRICKLE BUSH!
OW!
LOOK! A BOAT!

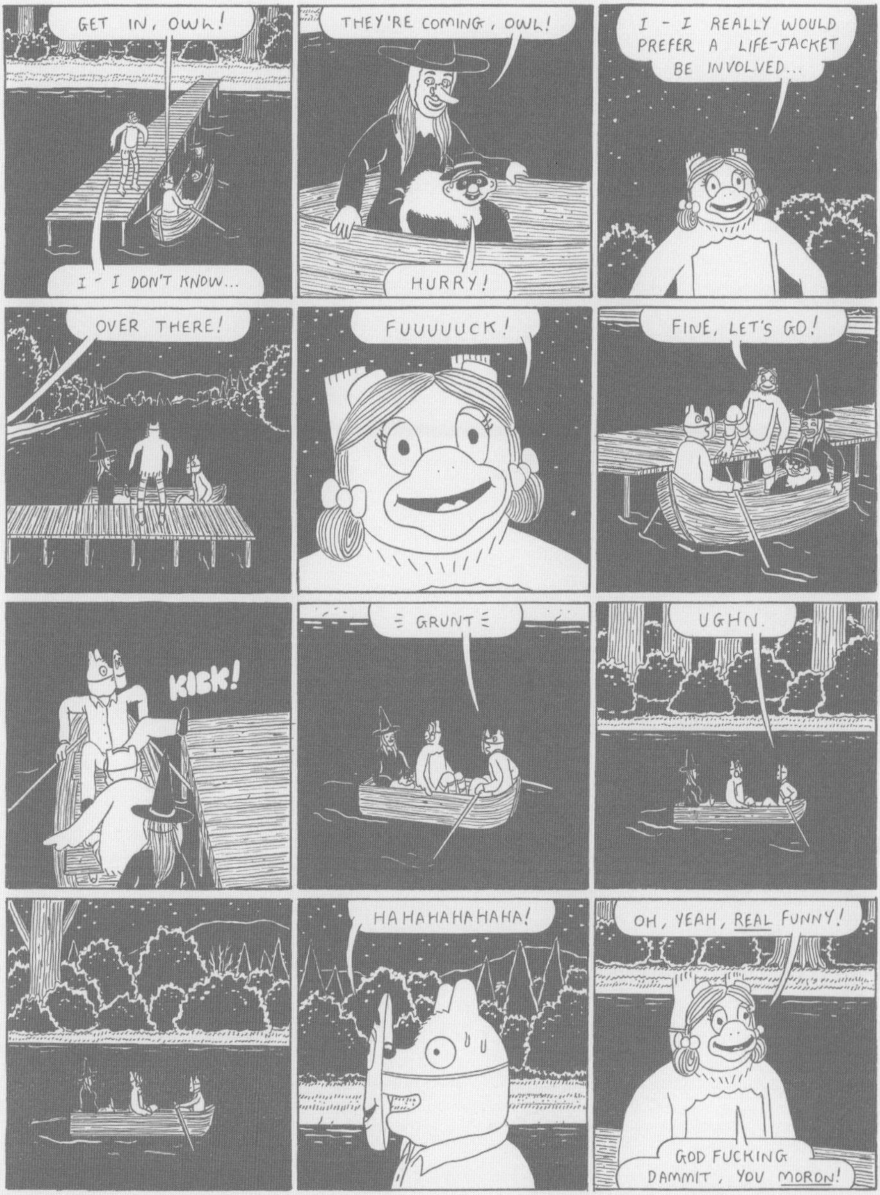
GET IN, OWL!
I - I DON'T KNOW...
THEY'RE COMING, OWL!
HURRY!
I - I REALLY WOULD PREFER A LIFE-JACKET BE INVOLVED...
OVER THERE!
FUUUUUCK!
FINE, LET'S GO!
KICK!
GRUNT
UGHN.
HAHAHAHAHAHA!
OH, YEAH, REAL FUNNY!
GOD FUCKING DAMMIT, YOU MORON!

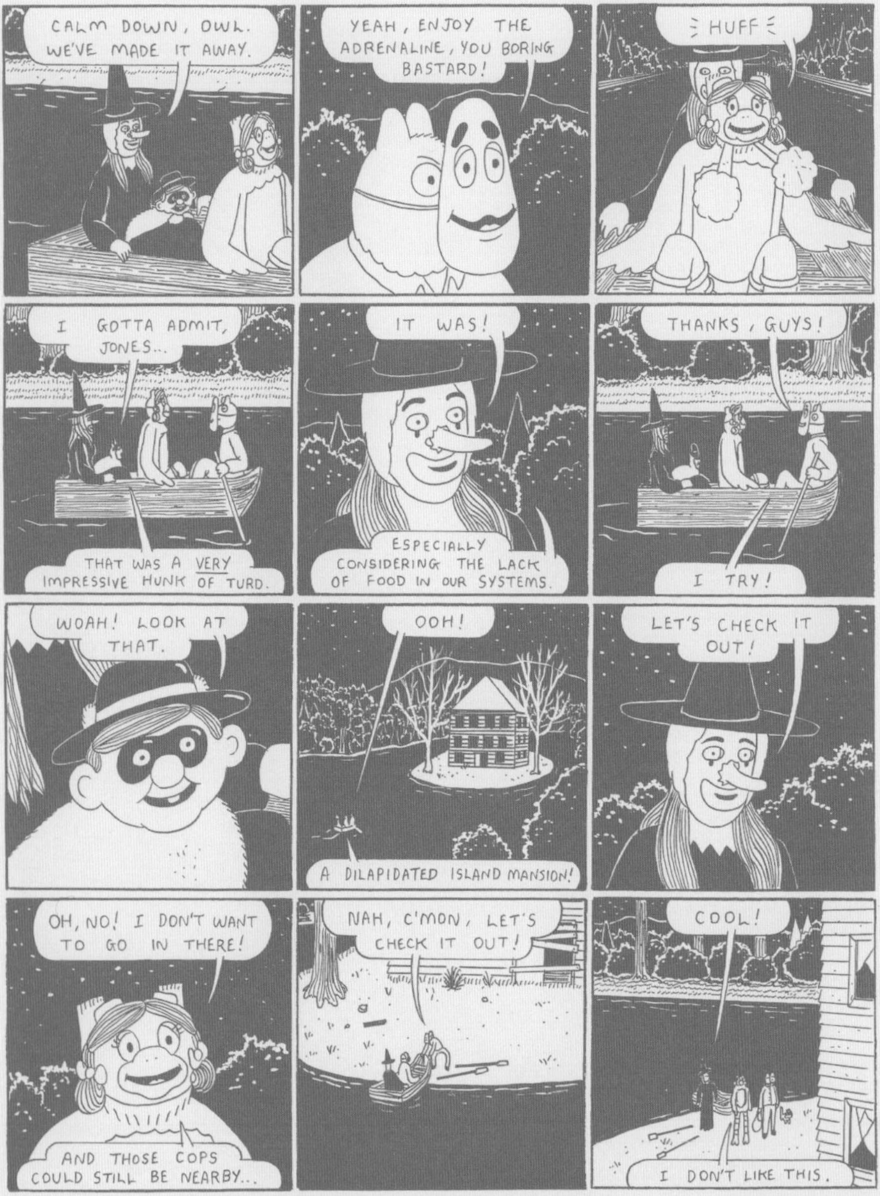
CALM DOWN, OWL. WE'VE MADE IT AWAY.
YEAH, ENJOY THE ADRENALINE, YOU BORING BASTARD!
HUFF
I GOTTA ADMIT, JONES...
THAT WAS A VERY IMPRESSIVE HUNK OF TURD.
IT WAS!
ESPECIALLY CONSIDERING THE LACK OF FOOD IN OUR SYSTEMS.
THANKS, GUYS!
I TRY!
WOAH! LOOK AT THAT.
OOH!
A DILAPIDATED ISLAND MANSION!
LET'S CHECK IT OUT!
OH, NO! I DON'T WANT TO GO IN THERE!
AND THOSE COPS COULD STILL BE NEARBY...
NAH, C'MON, LET'S CHECK IT OUT!
COOL!
I DON'T LIKE THIS.

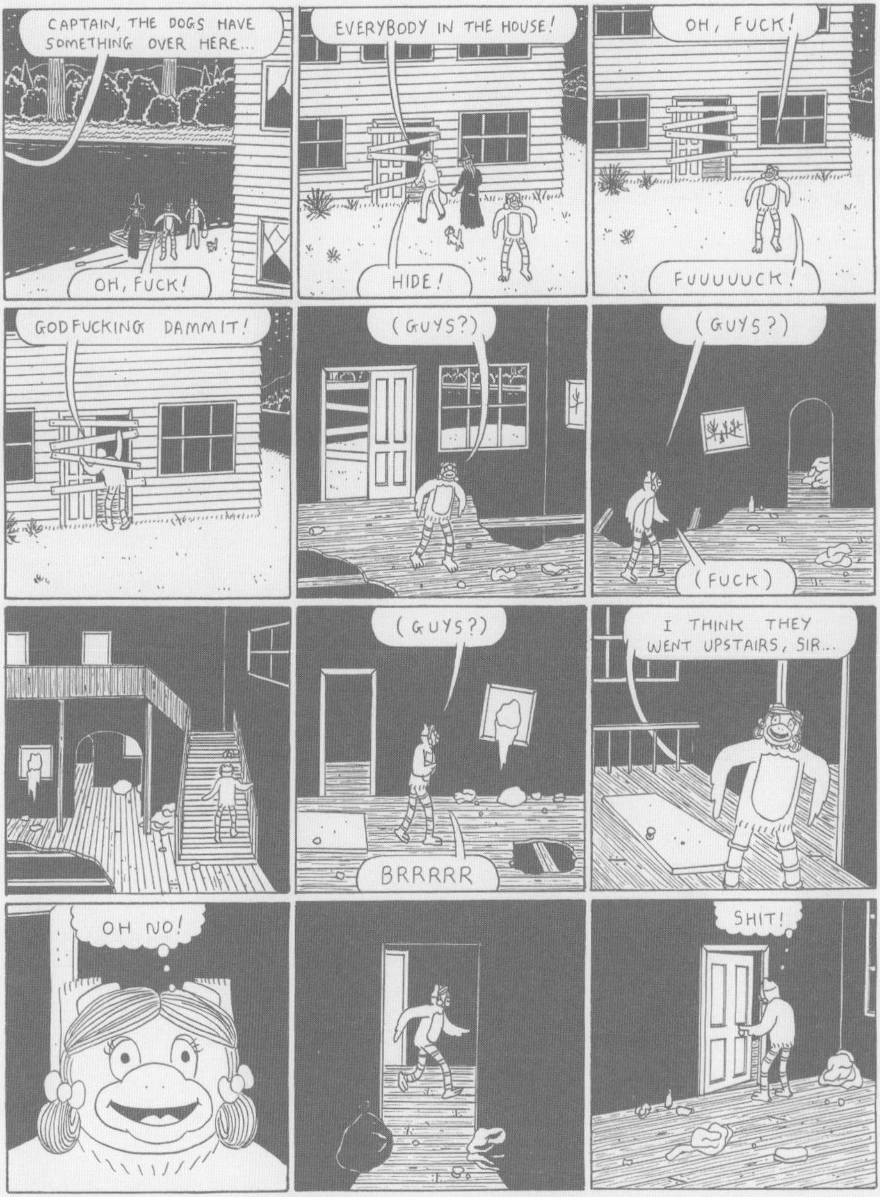
CAPTAIN, THE DOGS HAVE SOMETHING OVER HERE...
OH, FUCK!
EVERYBODY IN THE HOUSE!
HIDE!
OH, FUCK!
FUUUUUCK!
GODFUCKING DAMMIT!
(GUYS?)
(GUYS?)
(FUCK)
(GUYS?)
BRRRRR
I THINK THEY WENT UPSTAIRS, SIR...
OH NO!
SHIT!

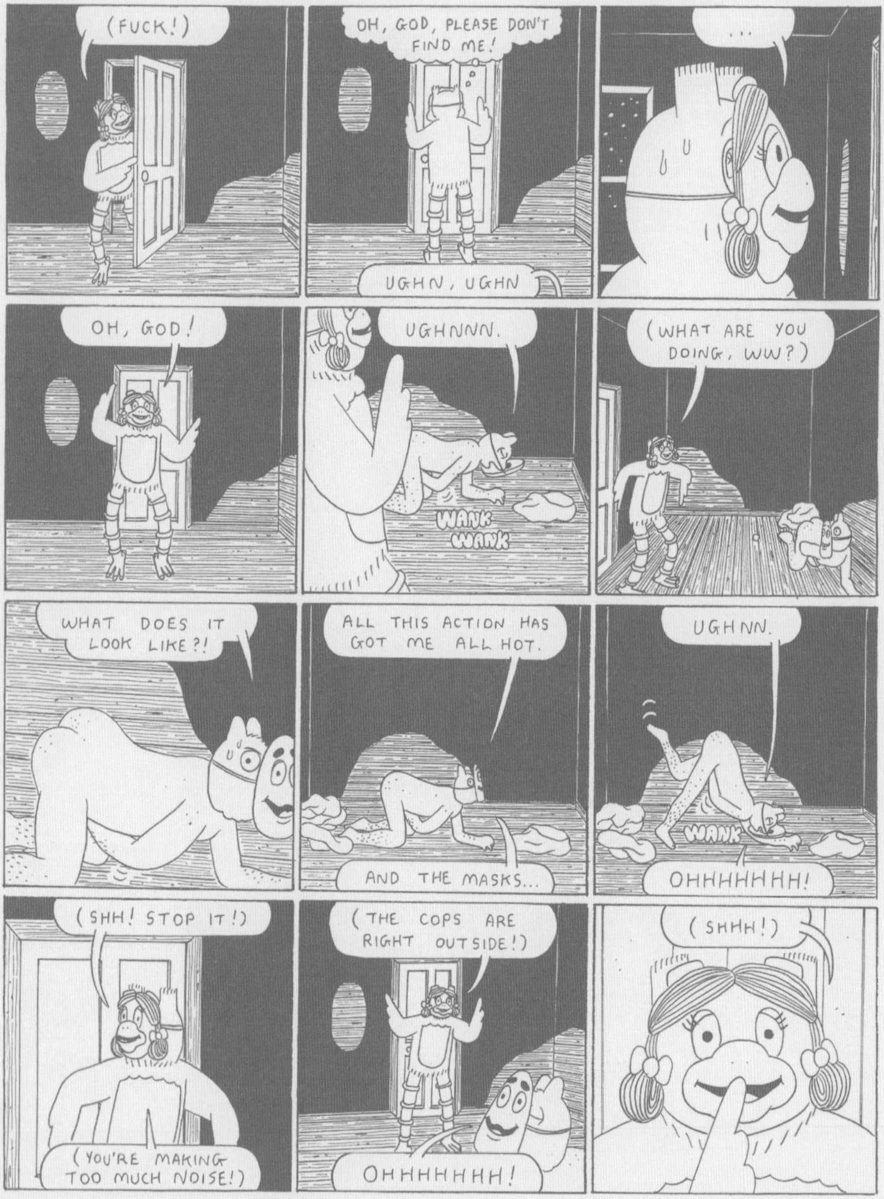

(FUCK!)
OH, GOD, PLEASE DON'T FIND ME!
UGHN, UGHN
. . .
OH, GOD!
UGHNNN.
WANK
WANK
(WHAT ARE YOU DOING, WW?)
WHAT DOES IT LOOK LIKE?!
ALL THIS ACTION HAS GOT ME ALL HOT.
AND THE MASKS...
UGHNN.
WANK
OHHHHHHH!
(SHH! STOP IT!)
(YOU'RE MAKING TOO MUCH NOISE!)
(THE COPS ARE RIGHT OUTSIDE!)
OHHHHHHH!
(SHHH!)

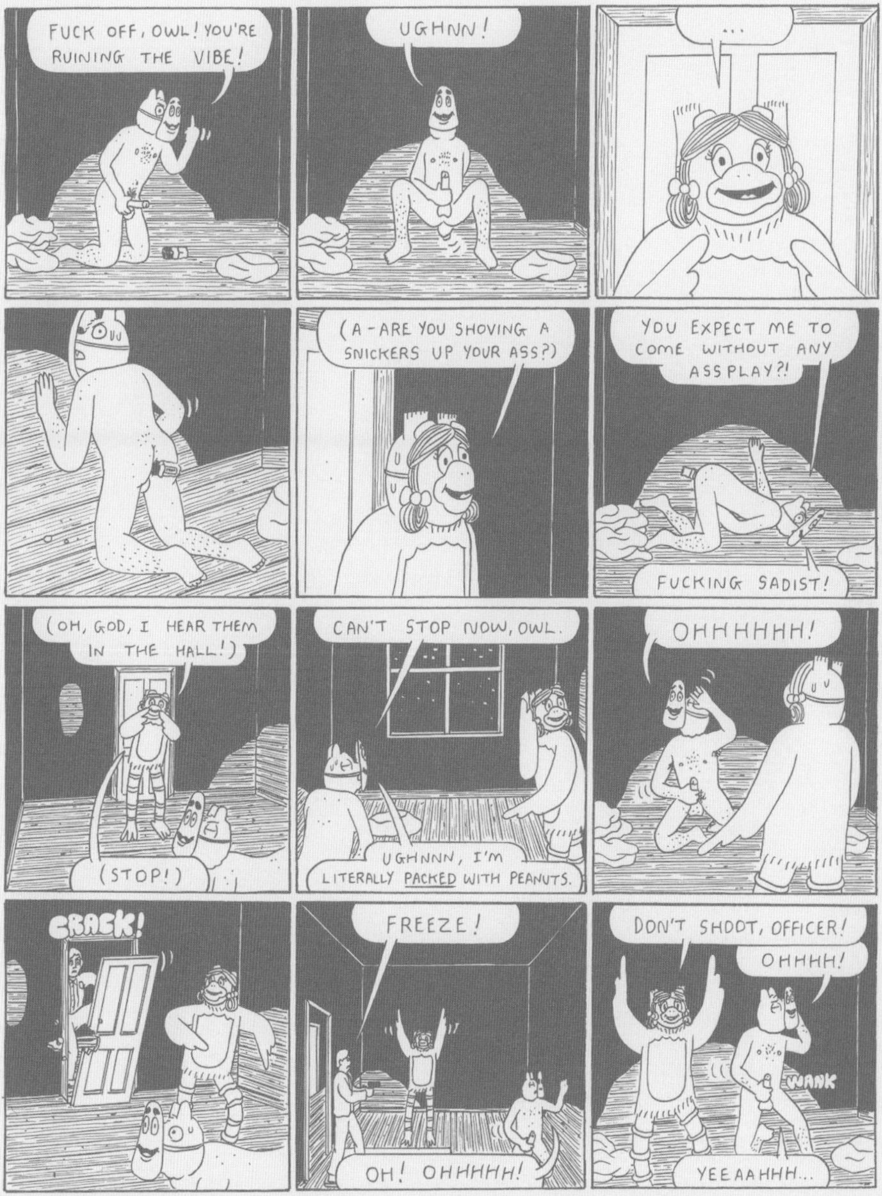
FUCK OFF, OWL! YOU'RE RUINING THE VIBE!
UGHNN!
...
(A-ARE YOU SHOVING A SNICKERS UP YOUR ASS?)
YOU EXPECT ME TO COME WITHOUT ANY ASSPLAY?!
FUCKING SADIST!
(OH, GOD, I HEAR THEM IN THE HALL!)
(STOP!)
CAN'T STOP NOW, OWL.
UGHNNN, I'M LITERALLY PACKED WITH PEANUTS.
OHHHHHH!
CRACK!
FREEZE!
OH! OHHHHH!
DON'T SHOOT, OFFICER!
OHHHH!
WANK
YEEAAHHH...

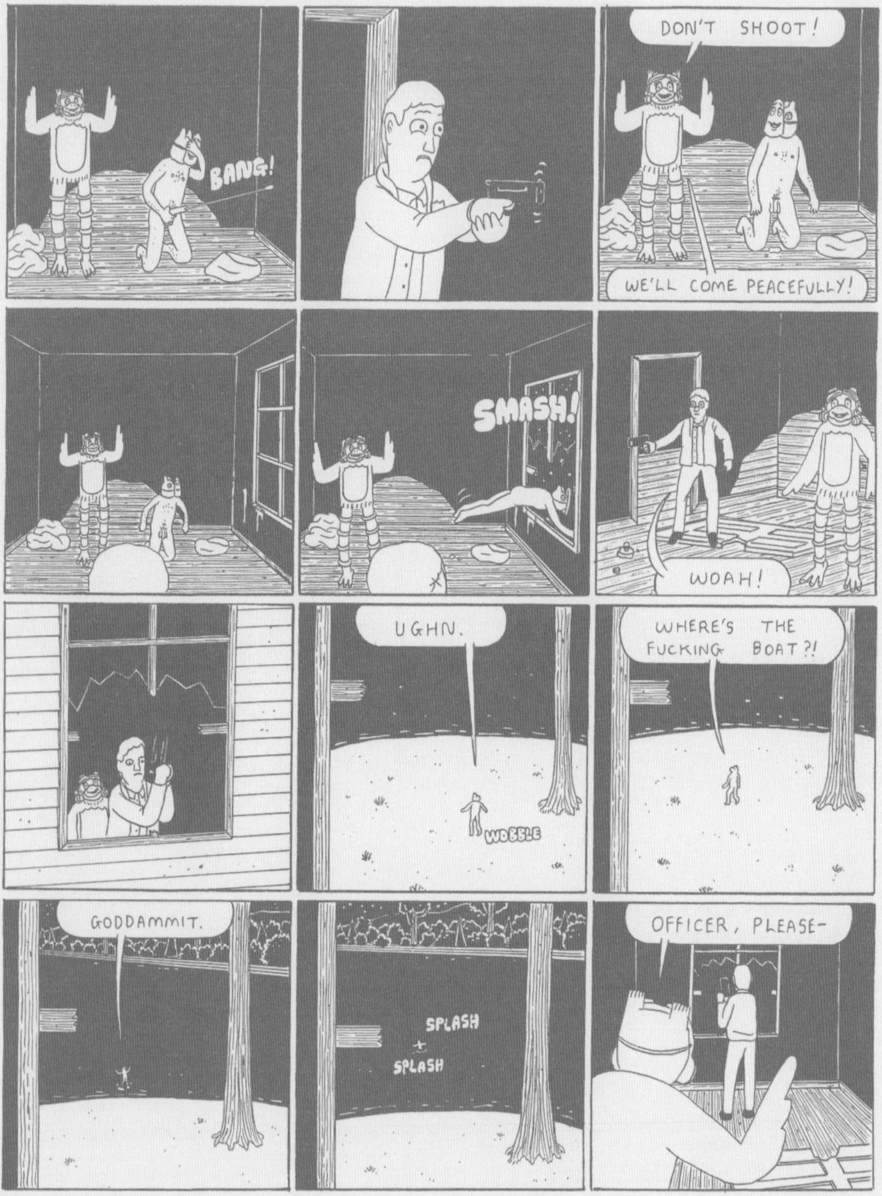
BANG!
DON'T SHOOT!
WE'LL COME PEACEFULLY!
SMASH!
WOAH!
UGHN.
WOBBLE
WHERE'S THE FUCKING BOAT?!
GODDAMMIT.
SPLASH
SPLASH
OFFICER, PLEASE-

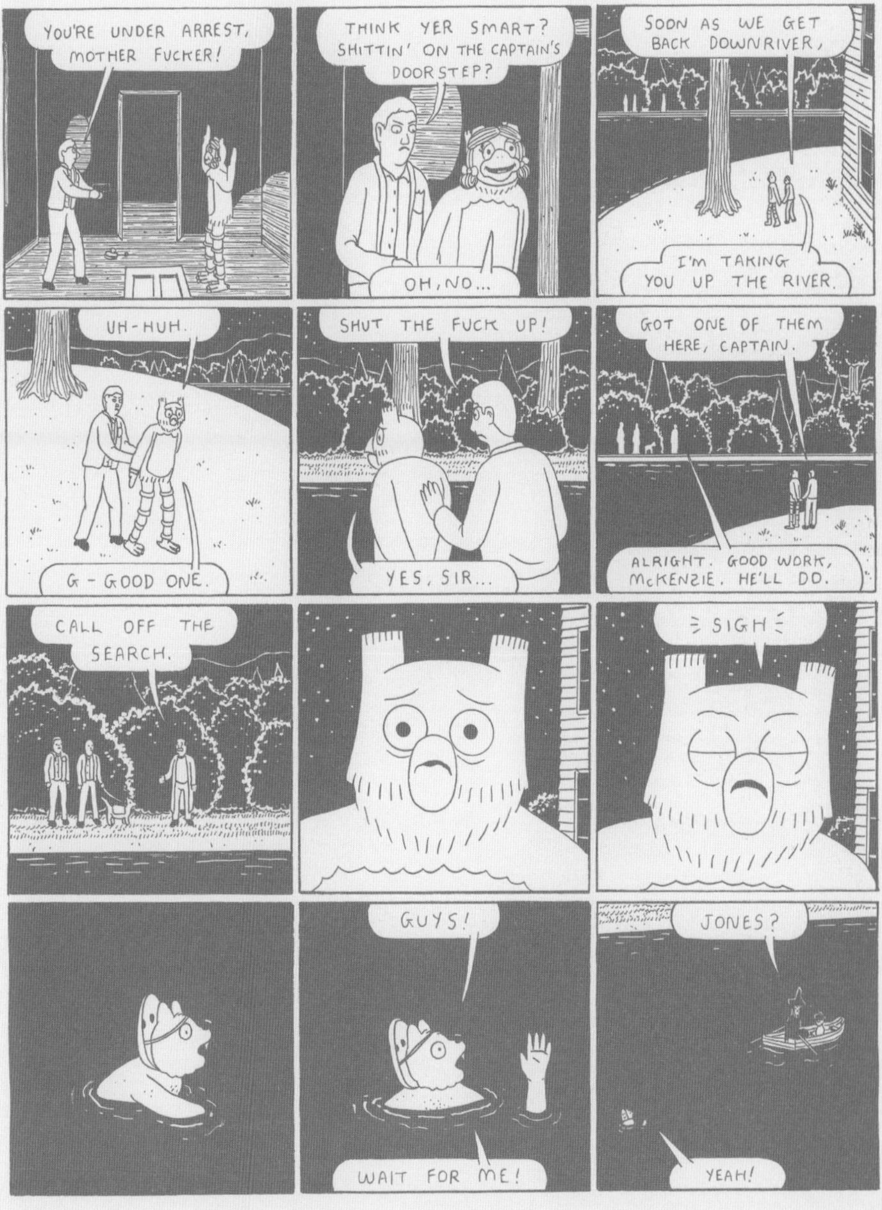
YOU'RE UNDER ARREST, MOTHER FUCKER!
THINK YER SMART? SHITTIN' ON THE CAPTAIN'S DOORSTEP?
OH, NO...
SOON AS WE GET BACK DOWNRIVER,
I'M TAKING YOU UP THE RIVER.
UH-HUH.
G-GOOD ONE.
SHUT THE FUCK UP!
YES, SIR...
GOT ONE OF THEM HERE, CAPTAIN.
ALRIGHT. GOOD WORK, McKENZIE. HE'LL DO.
CALL OFF THE SEARCH.
SIGH
GUYS!
WAIT FOR ME!
JONES?
YEAH!

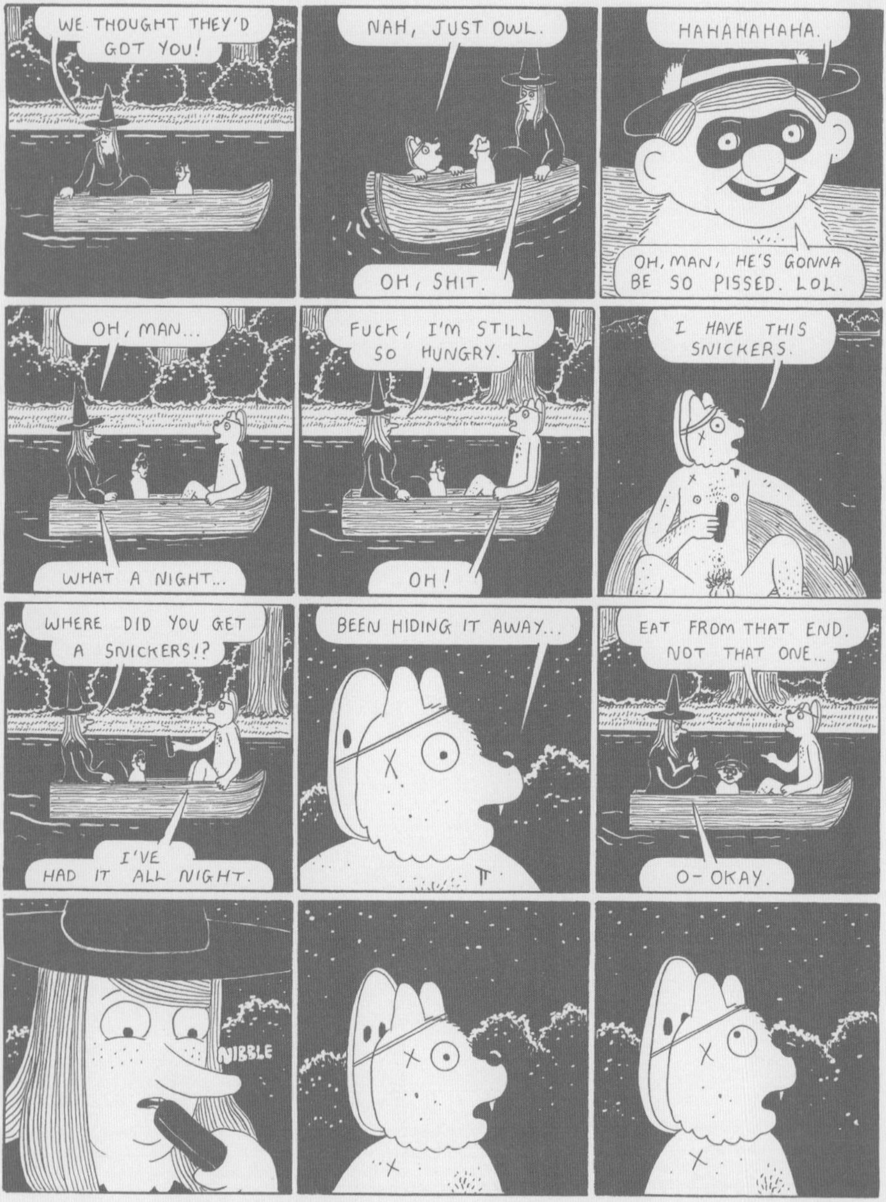
WE THOUGHT THEY'D GOT YOU!
NAH, JUST OWL.
OH, SHIT.
HAHAHAHAHA.
OH, MAN, HE'S GONNA BE SO PISSED. LOL.
OH, MAN...
WHAT A NIGHT...
FUCK, I'M STILL SO HUNGRY.
OH!
I HAVE THIS SNICKERS.
WHERE DID YOU GET A SNICKERS!?
I'VE HAD IT ALL NIGHT.
BEEN HIDING IT AWAY...
EAT FROM THAT END. NOT THAT ONE...
O-OKAY.
NIBBLE

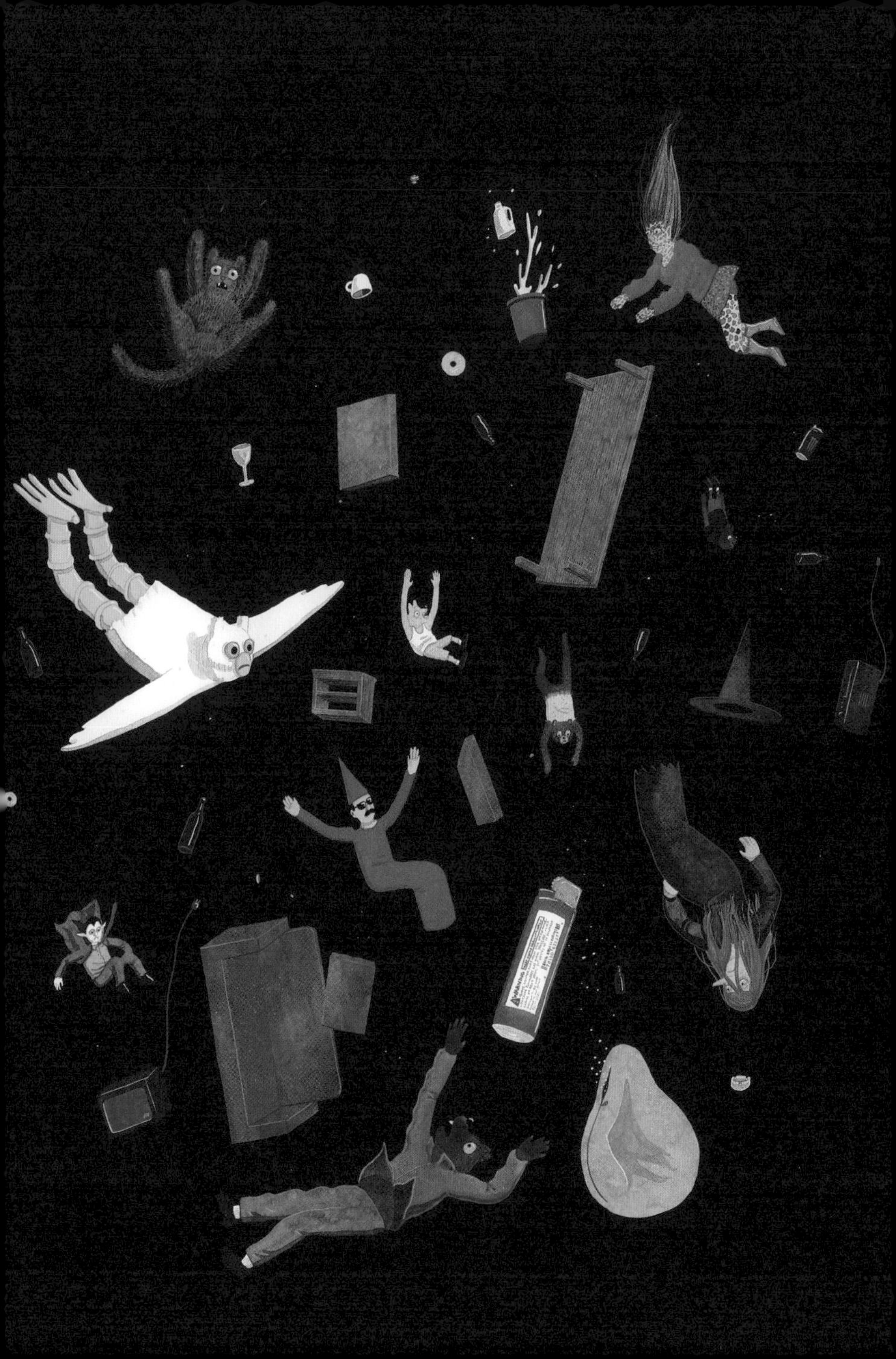
WARNING

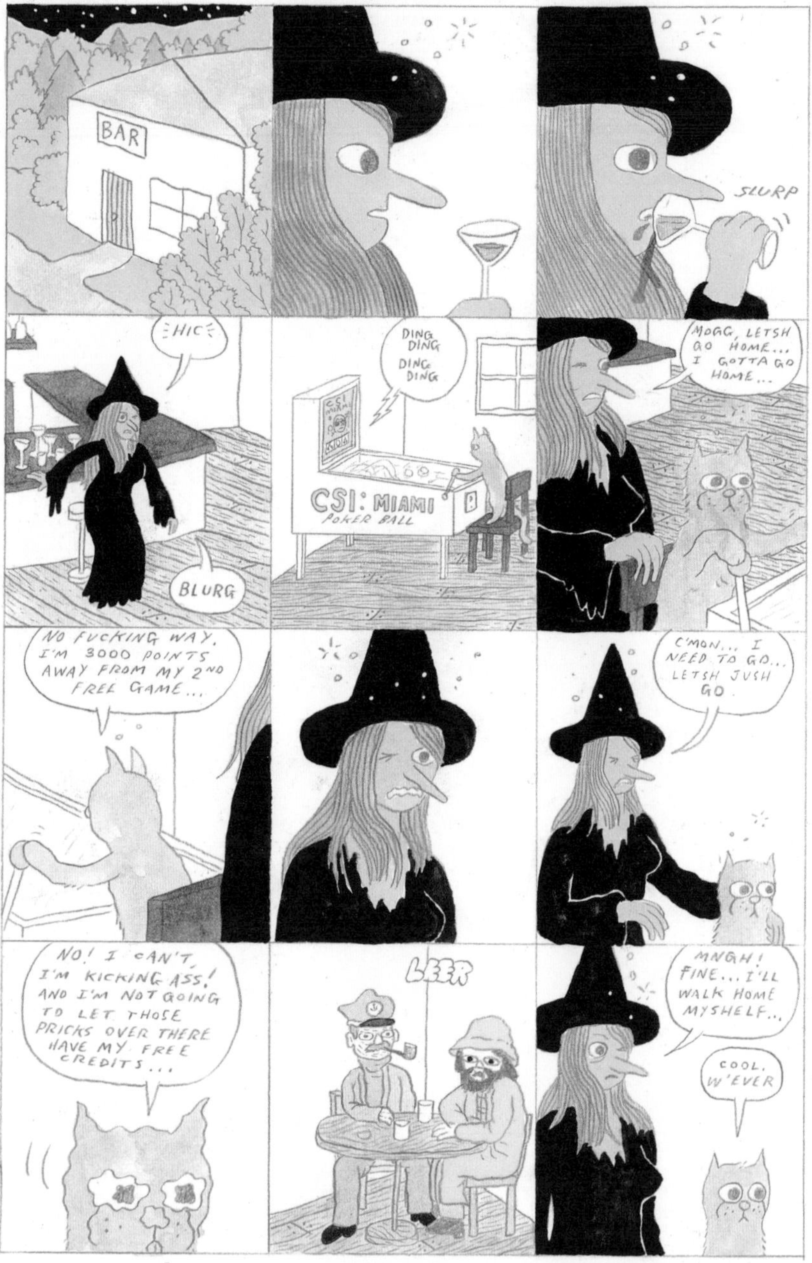
BAR
SLURP
HIC
BLURG
DING DING DING DING
CSI MIAMI
CSI: MIAMI POKER BALL
MOGG, LETSH GO HOME... I GOTTA GO HOME...
NO FUCKING WAY. I'M 3000 POINTS AWAY FROM MY 2ND FREE GAME...
C'MON... I NEED TO GO... LETSH JUSH GO
NO! I CAN'T, I'M KICKING ASS! AND I'M NOT GOING TO LET THOSE PRICKS OVER THERE HAVE MY FREE CREDITS...
LEER
MNGH! FINE... I'LL WALK HOME MYSHELF...
COOL. W'EVER

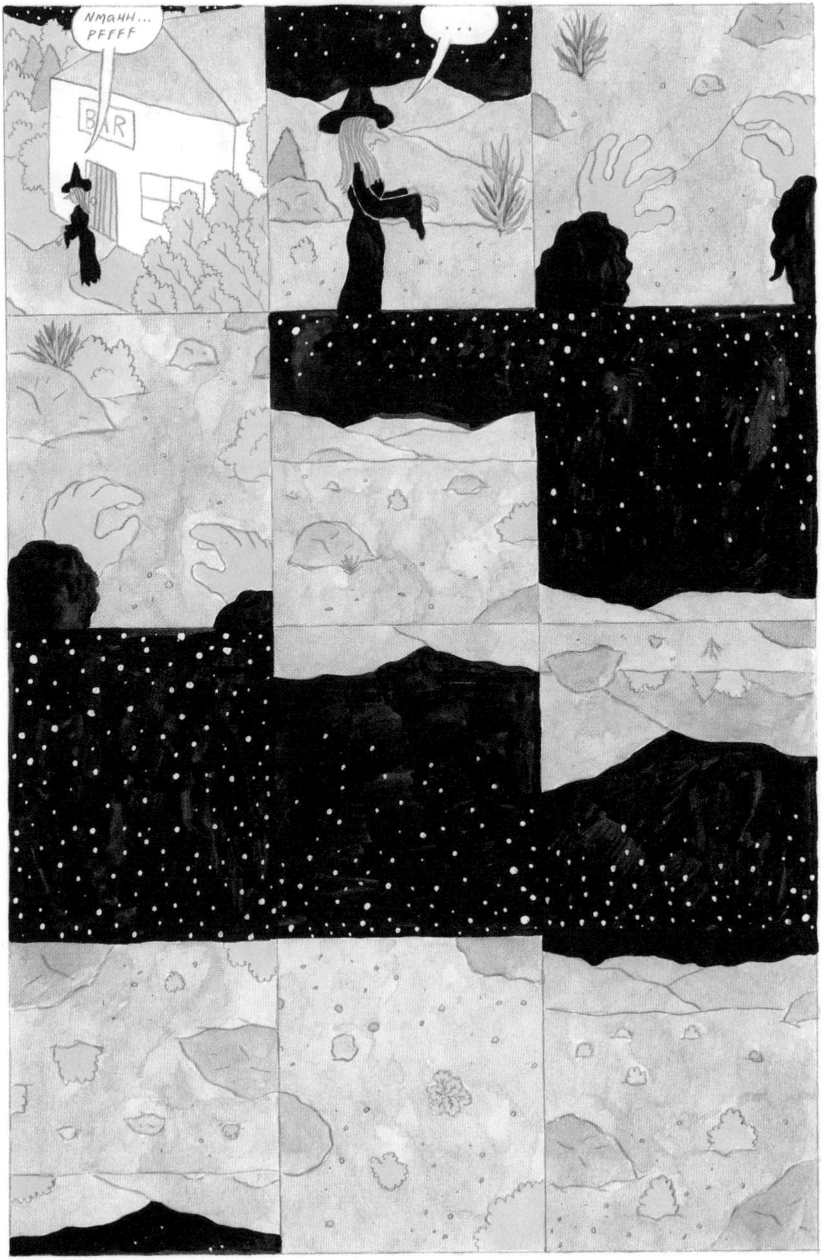
NMAHH...
PFFFF
...

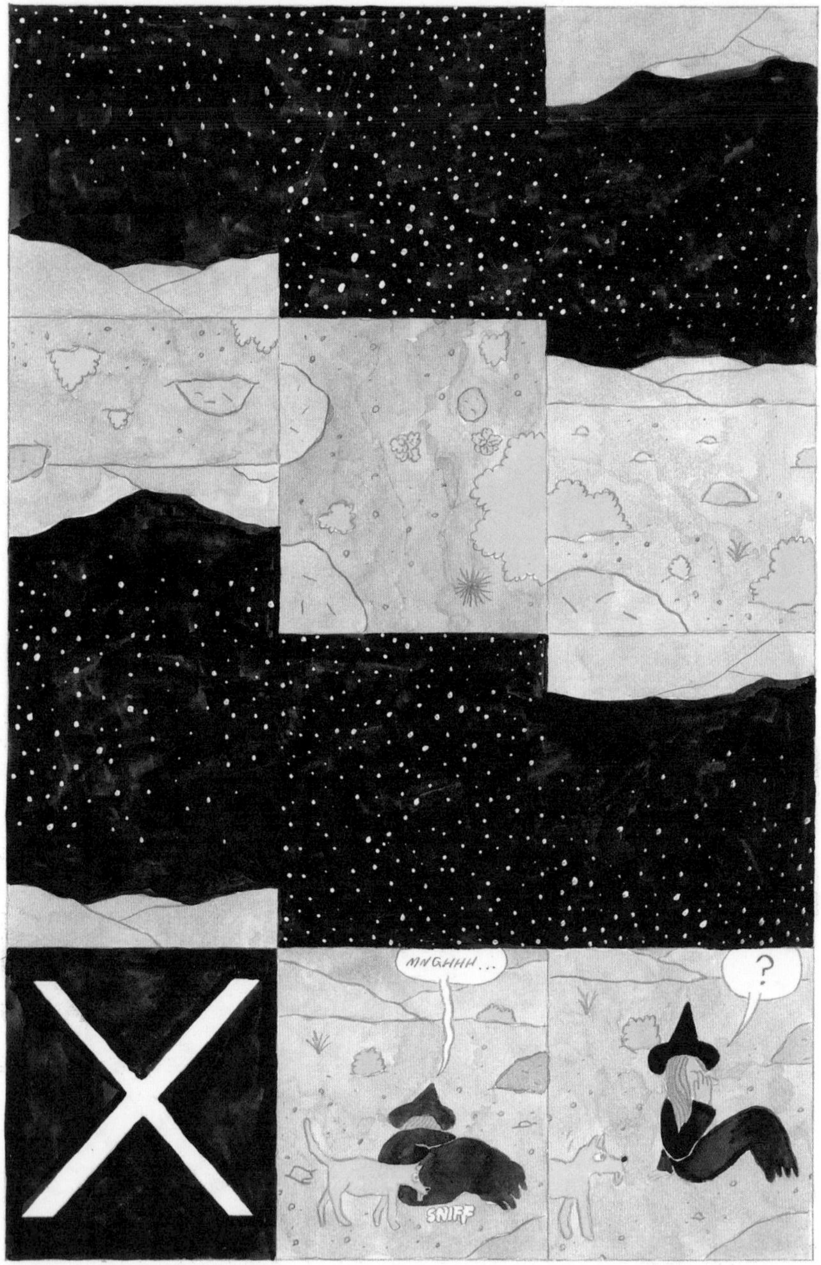
X
MNGHHH...
SNIFF
?

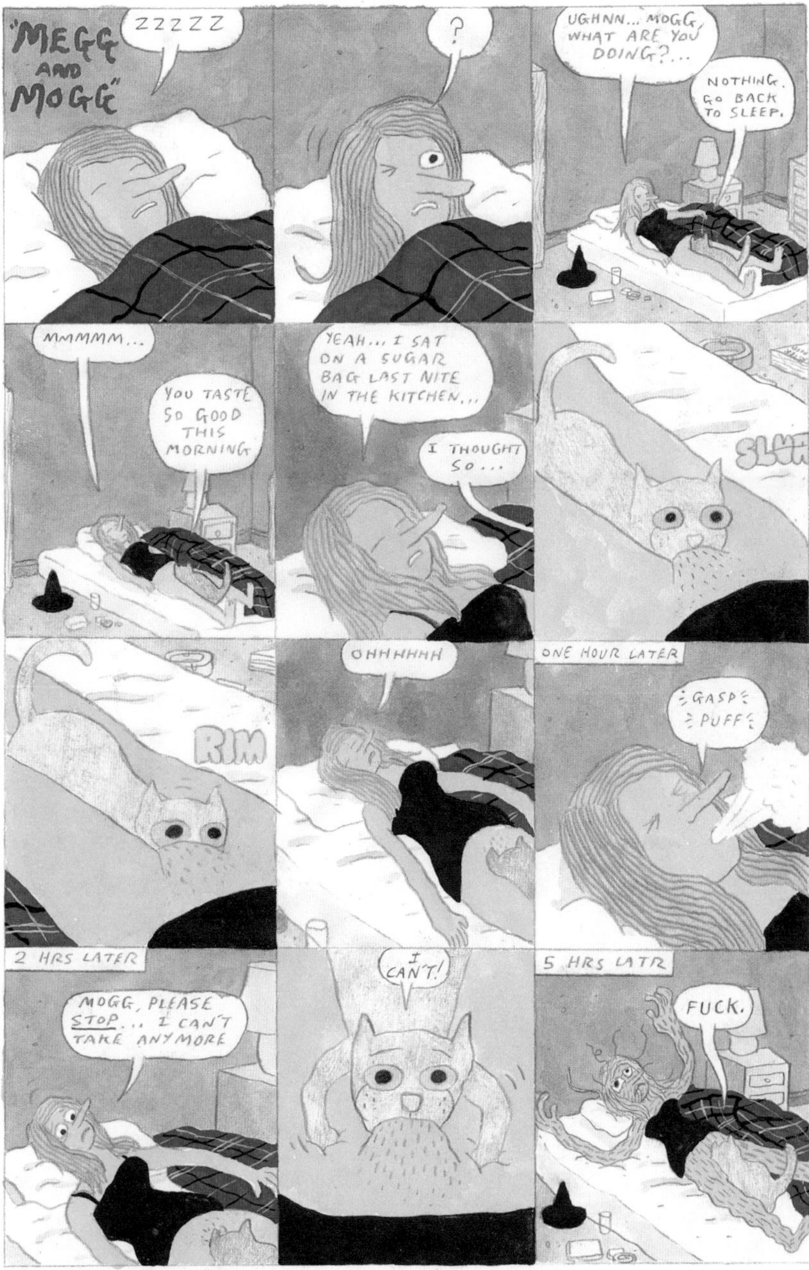
"MEGG AND MOGG"
ZZZZZ
?
UGHNN... MOGG, WHAT ARE YOU DOING?...
NOTHING. GO BACK TO SLEEP.
MMMMM...
YOU TASTE SO GOOD THIS MORNING
YEAH... I SAT ON A SUGAR BAG LAST NITE IN THE KITCHEN...
I THOUGHT SO...
SLURP
RIM
OHHHHHH
ONE HOUR LATER
GASP PUFF
2 HRS LATER
MOGG, PLEASE STOP... I CAN'T TAKE ANYMORE
I CAN'T!
5 HRS LATR
FUCK.

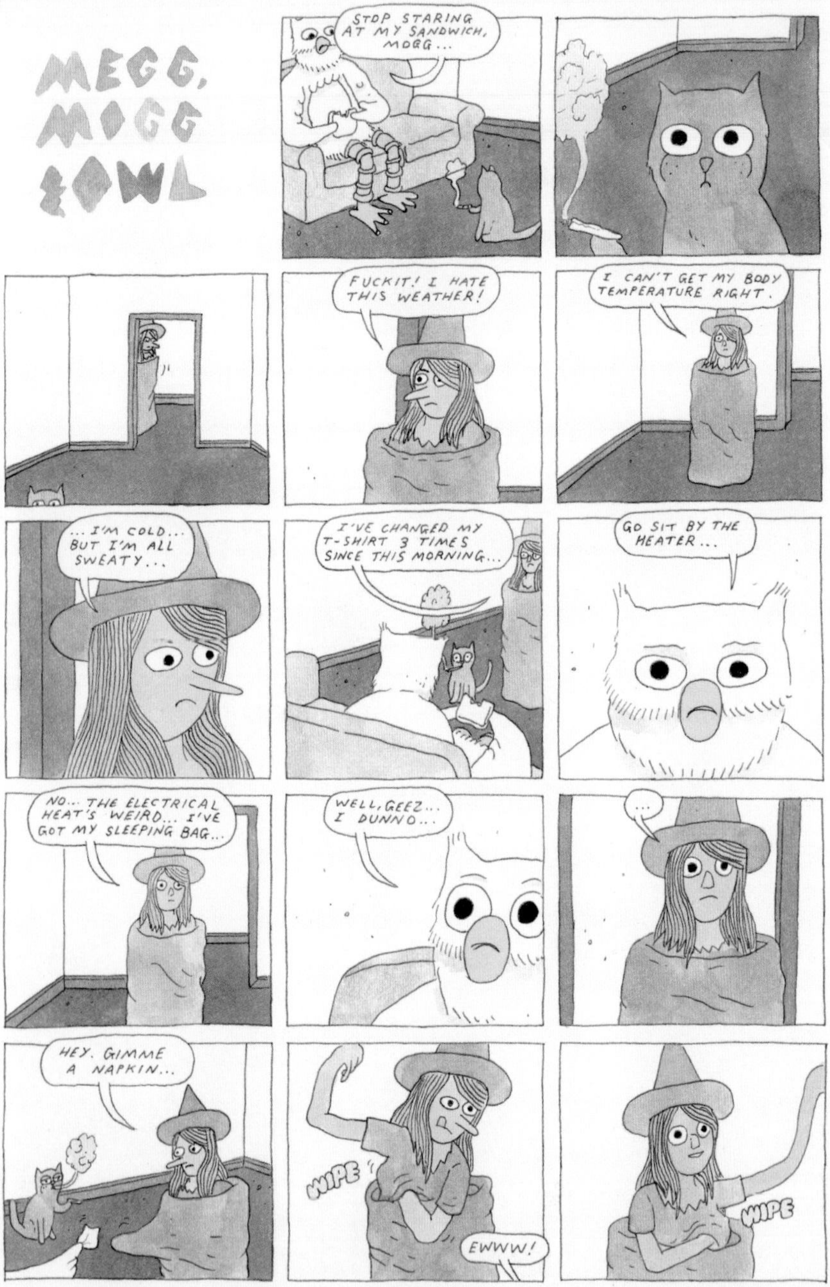
MEGG, MOGG & OWL
STOP STARING AT MY SANDWICH, MOGG...
FUCKIT! I HATE THIS WEATHER!
I CAN'T GET MY BODY TEMPERATURE RIGHT.
... I'M COLD... BUT I'M ALL SWEATY...
I'VE CHANGED MY T-SHIRT 3 TIMES SINCE THIS MORNING...
GO SIT BY THE HEATER...
NO... THE ELECTRICAL HEAT'S WEIRD... I'VE GOT MY SLEEPING BAG...
WELL, GEEZ... I DUNNO...
...
HEY. GIMME A NAPKIN...
WIPE
EWWW!
WIPE

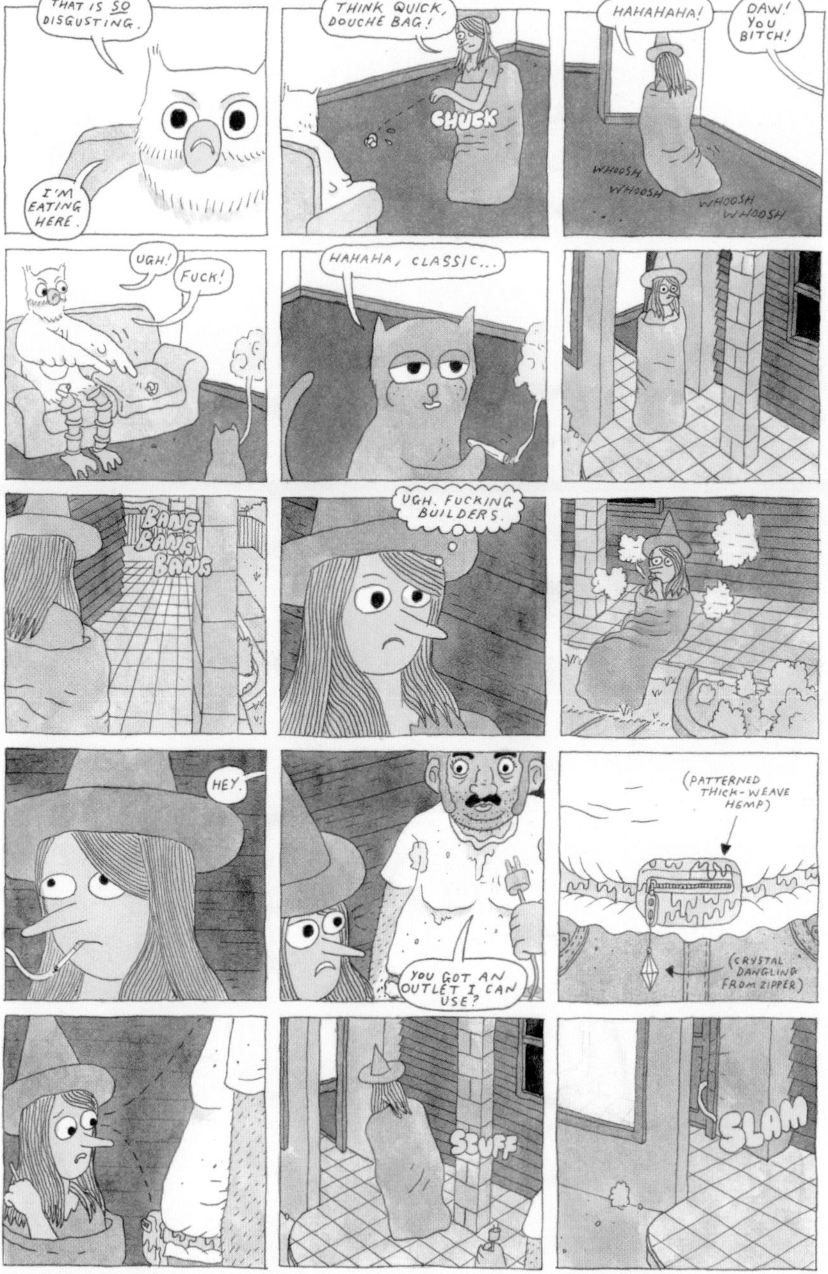
THAT IS SO DISGUSTING.
I'M EATING HERE.
THINK QUICK, DOUCHE BAG!
CHUCK
HAHAHAHA!
DAW! YOU BITCH!
WHOOSH
WHOOSH
WHOOSH
WHOOSH
UGH!
FUCK!
HAHAHA, CLASSIC...
BANG
BANG
BANG
UGH. FUCKING BUILDERS.
HEY.
YOU GOT AN OUTLET I CAN USE?
(PATTERNED THICK-WEAVE HEMP)
(CRYSTAL DANGLING FROM ZIPPER)
SCUFF
SLAM

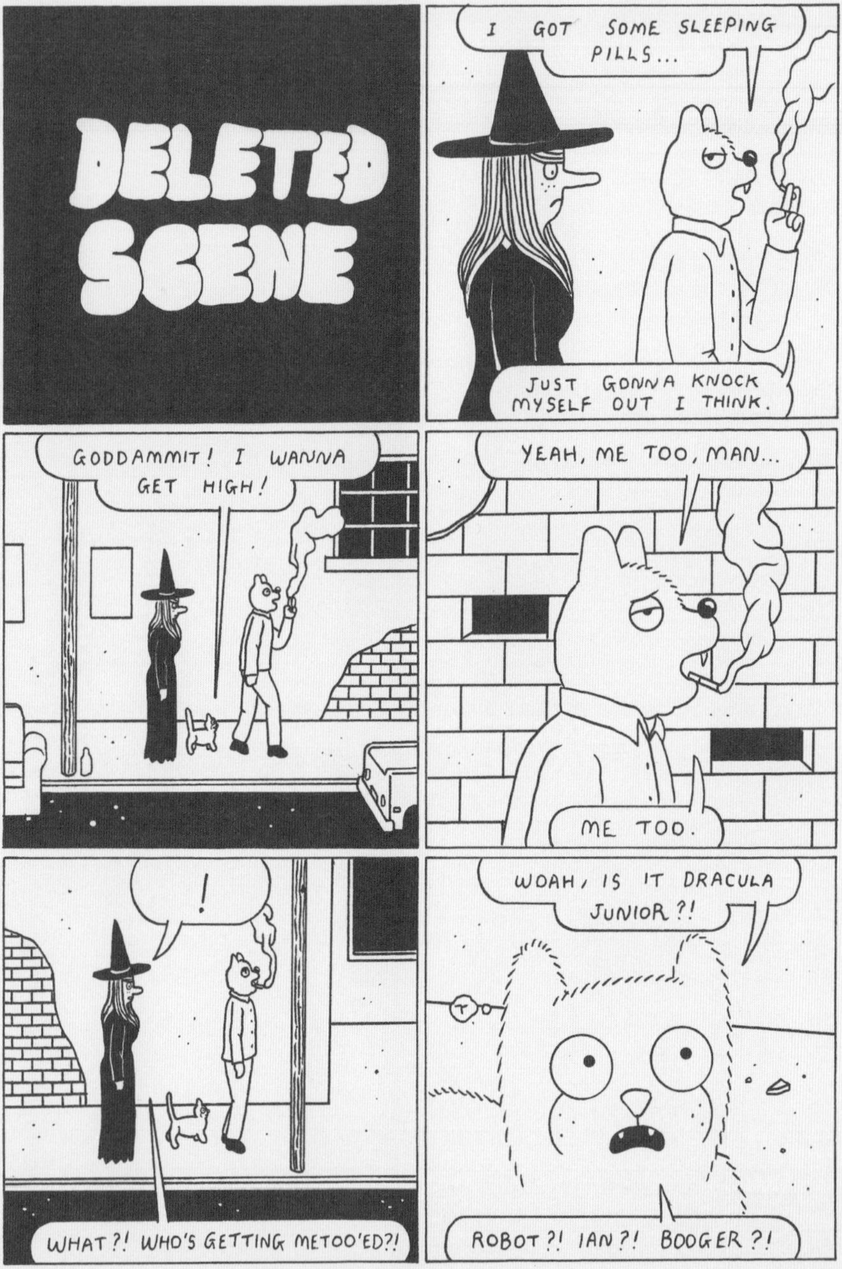
DELETED SCENE
I GOT SOME SLEEPING PILLS...
JUST GONNA KNOCK MYSELF OUT I THINK.
GODDAMMIT! I WANNA GET HIGH!
YEAH, ME TOO, MAN...
ME TOO.
!
WHAT?! WHO'S GETTING METOO'ED?!
WOAH, IS IT DRACULA JUNIOR?!
ROBOT?! IAN?! BOOGER?!

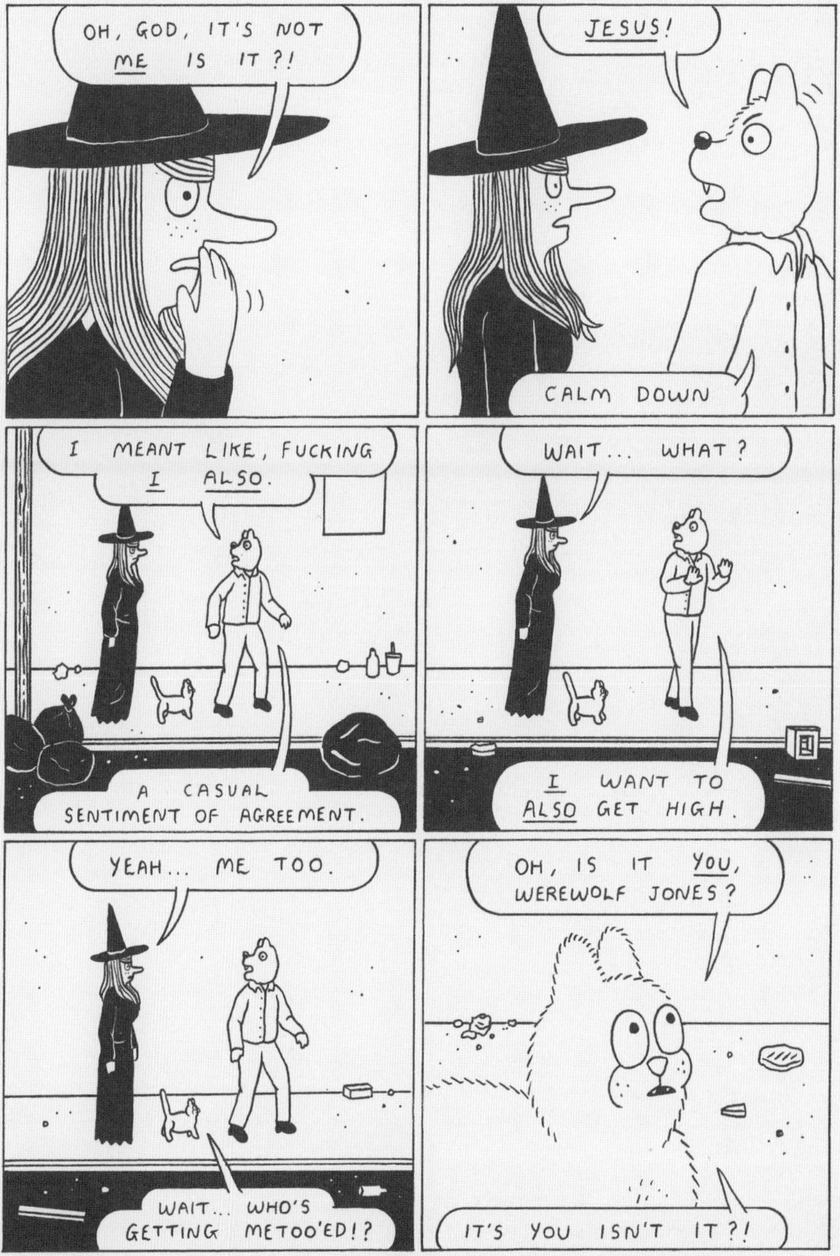
OH, GOD, IT'S NOT ME IS IT?!
JESUS!
CALM DOWN
I MEANT LIKE, FUCKING I ALSO.
A CASUAL SENTIMENT OF AGREEMENT.
WAIT... WHAT?
I WANT TO ALSO GET HIGH.
YEAH... ME TOO.
WAIT... WHO'S GETTING METOO'ED!?
OH, IS IT YOU, WEREWOLF JONES?
IT'S YOU ISN'T IT?!

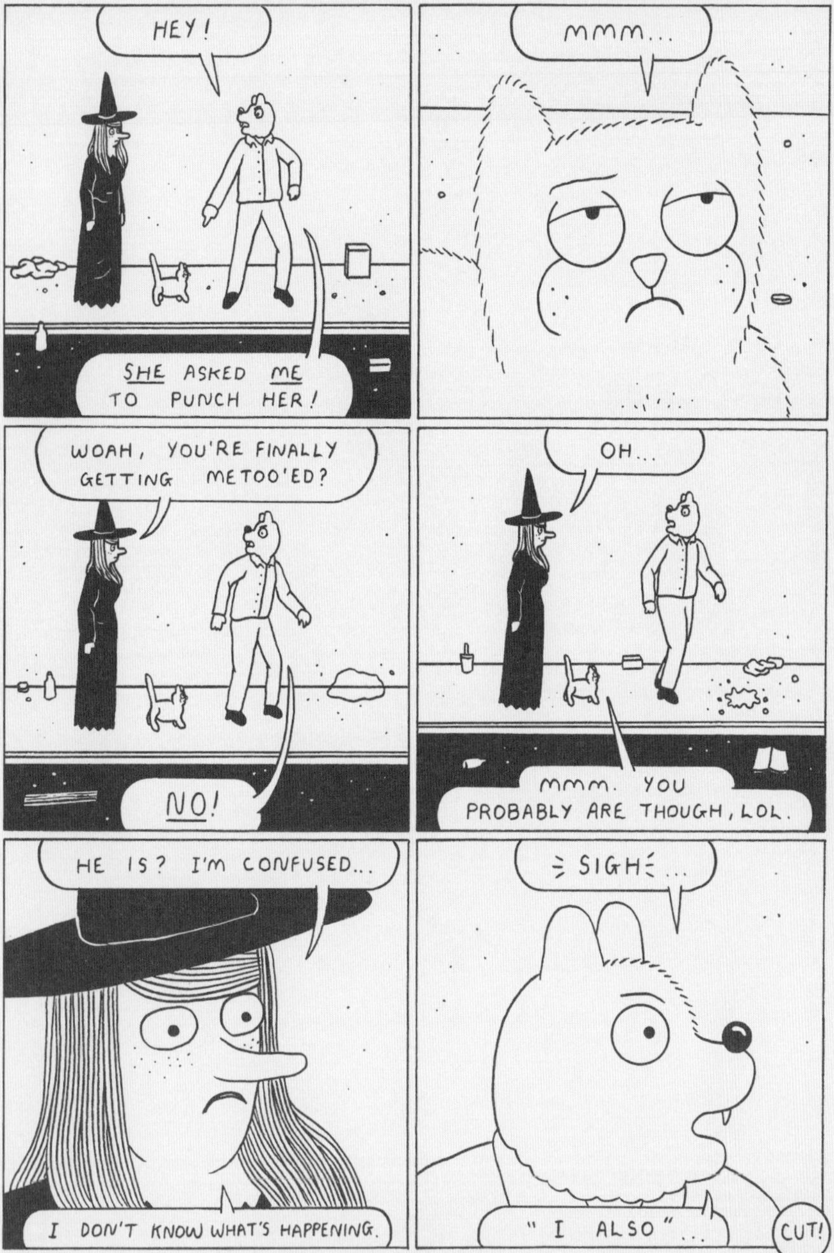
HEY!
SHE ASKED ME TO PUNCH HER!
MMM...
WOAH, YOU'RE FINALLY GETTING METOO'ED?
NO!
OH...
MMM. YOU PROBABLY ARE THOUGH, LOL.
HE IS? I'M CONFUSED...
I DON'T KNOW WHAT'S HAPPENING.
SIGH...
"I ALSO"...
CUT!

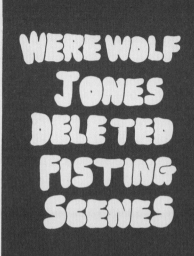

WERE WOLF JONES DELETED FISTING SCENES

PUMPKIN

ANIME PILLOW W/ WITCHES HAT

JAXON'S SCHOOL SHOES

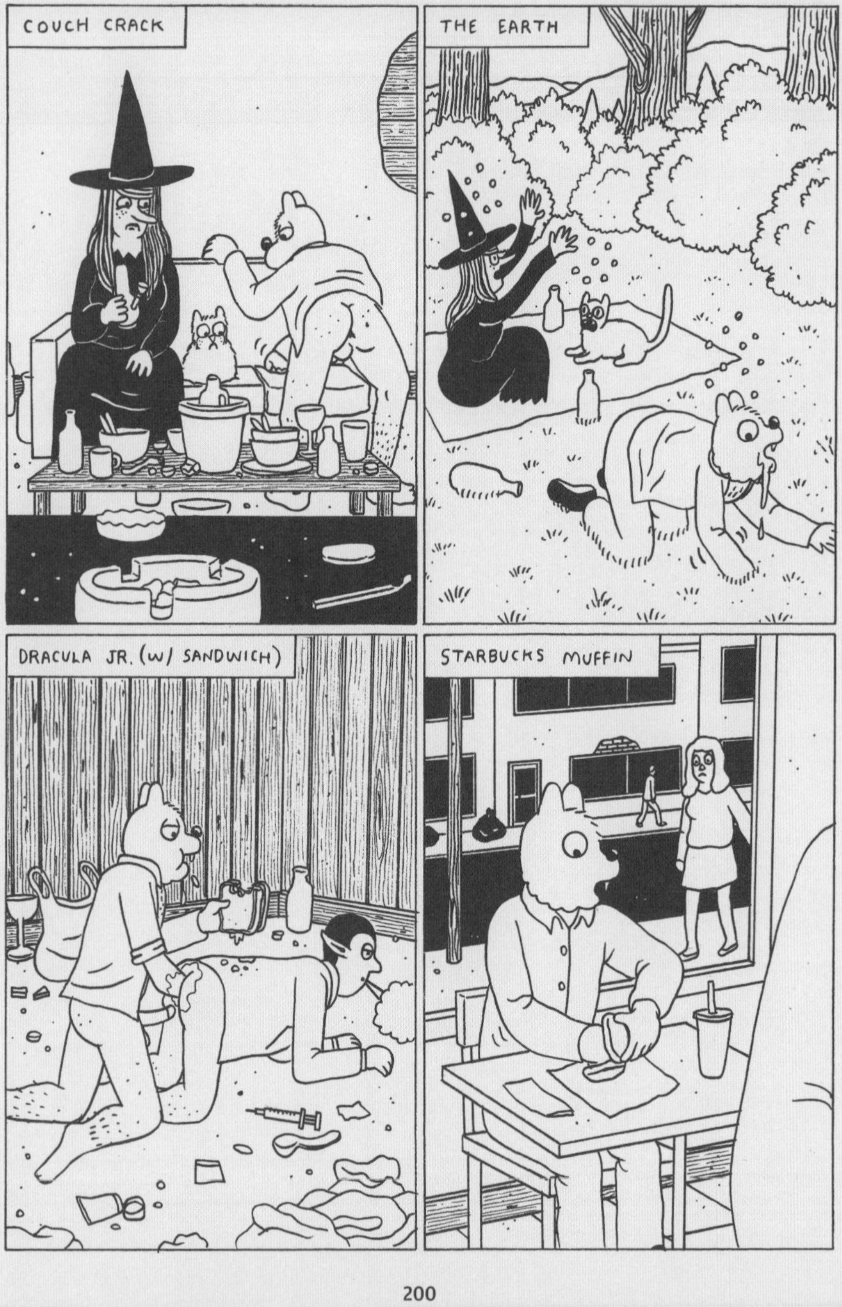
COUCH CRACK
THE EARTH
DRACULA JR. (W/ SANDWICH)
STARBUCKS MUFFIN

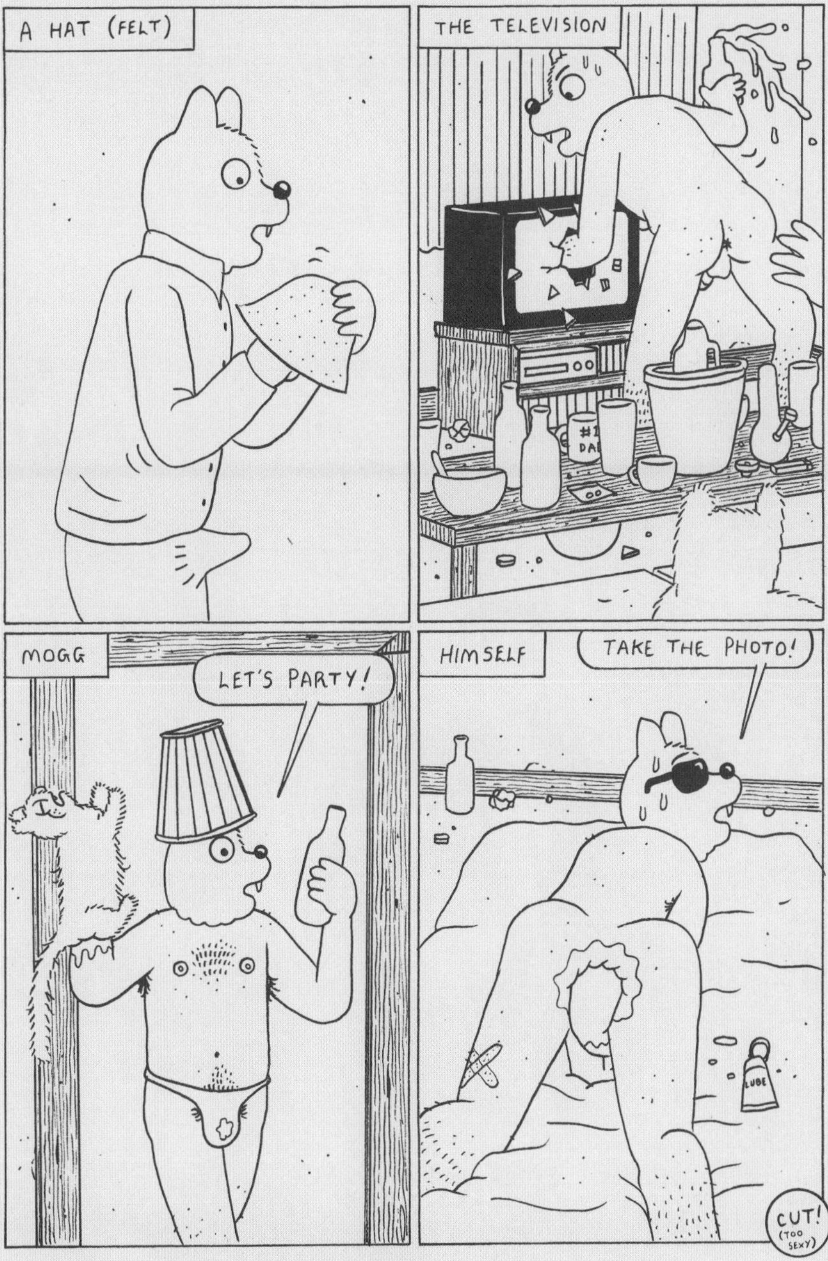
A HAT (FELT)
THE TELEVISION
MOGG
LET'S PARTY!
HIMSELF
TAKE THE PHOTO!
LUBE
CUT! (TOO SEXY)

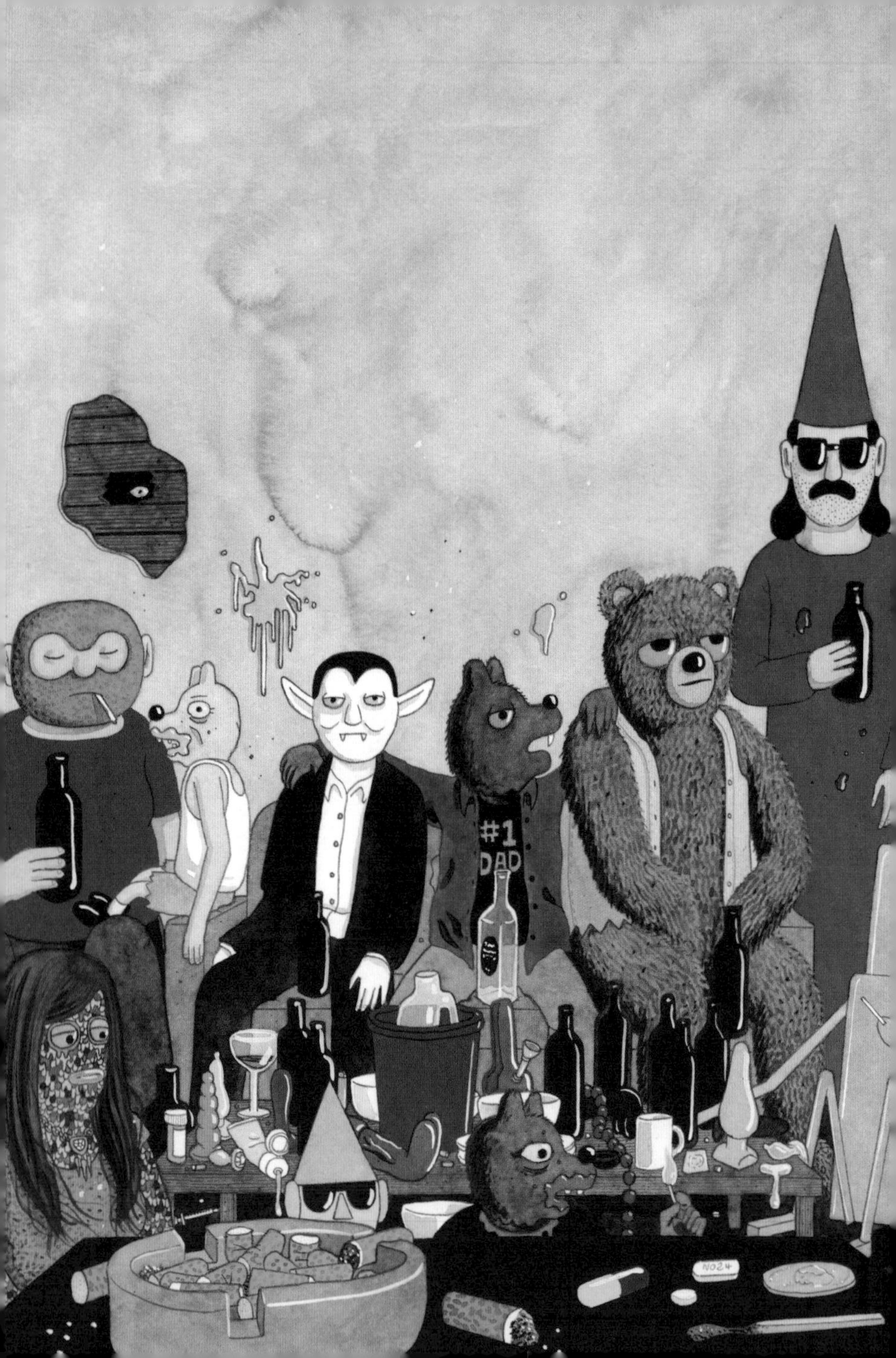
#1
DAD

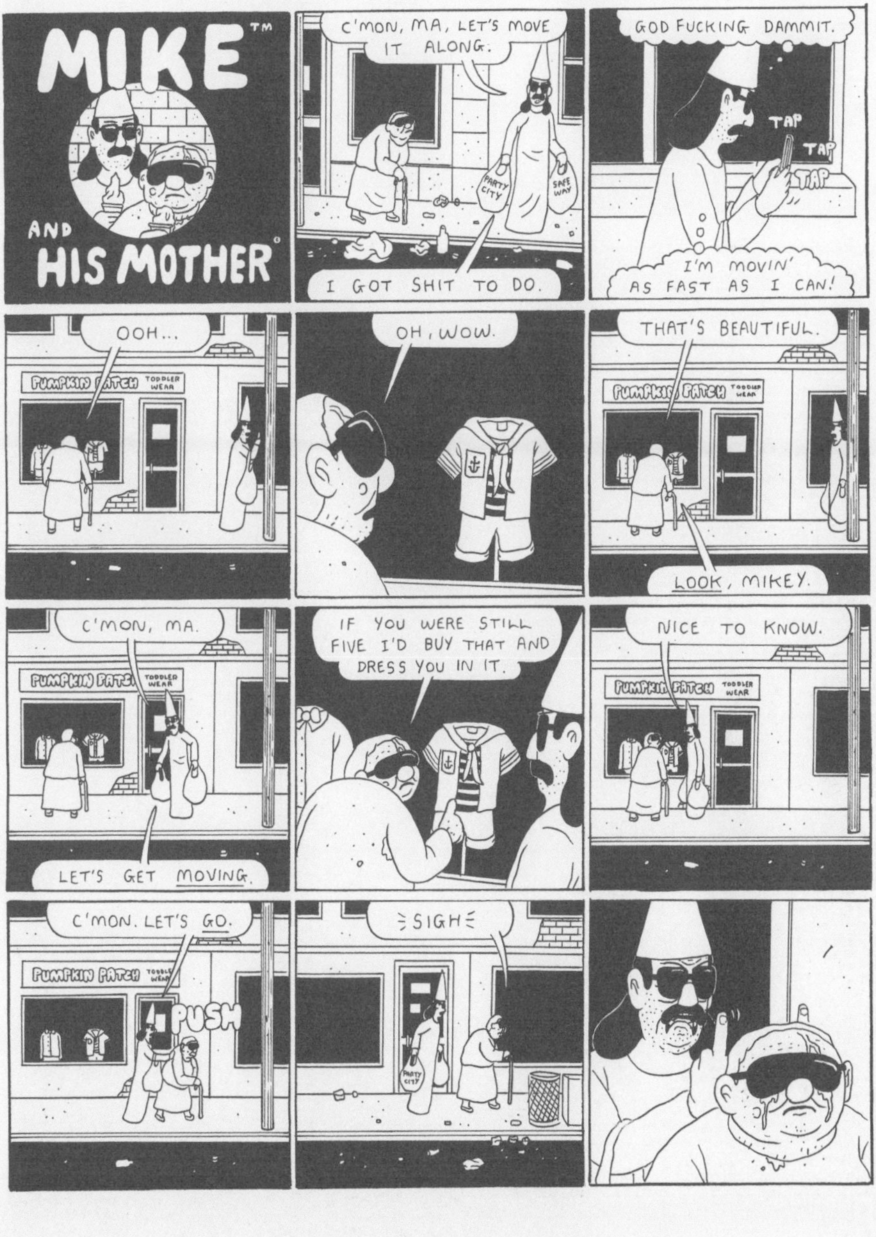
MIKE™
AND
HIS MOTHER
C'MON, MA, LET'S MOVE IT ALONG.
PARTY CITY
SAFE WAY
I GOT SHIT TO DO.
GOD FUCKING DAMMIT.
TAP
TAP
TAP
I'M MOVIN' AS FAST AS I CAN!
OOH...
PUMPKIN PATCH TODDLER WEAR
OH, WOW.
THAT'S BEAUTIFUL.
PUMPKIN PATCH TODDLER WEAR
LOOK, MIKEY.
C'MON, MA.
PUMPKIN PATCH TODDLER WEAR
LET'S GET MOVING.
IF YOU WERE STILL FIVE I'D BUY THAT AND DRESS YOU IN IT.
NICE TO KNOW.
PUMPKIN PATCH TODDLER WEAR
C'MON. LET'S GO.
PUMPKIN PATCH
PUSH
SIGH
PARTY CITY

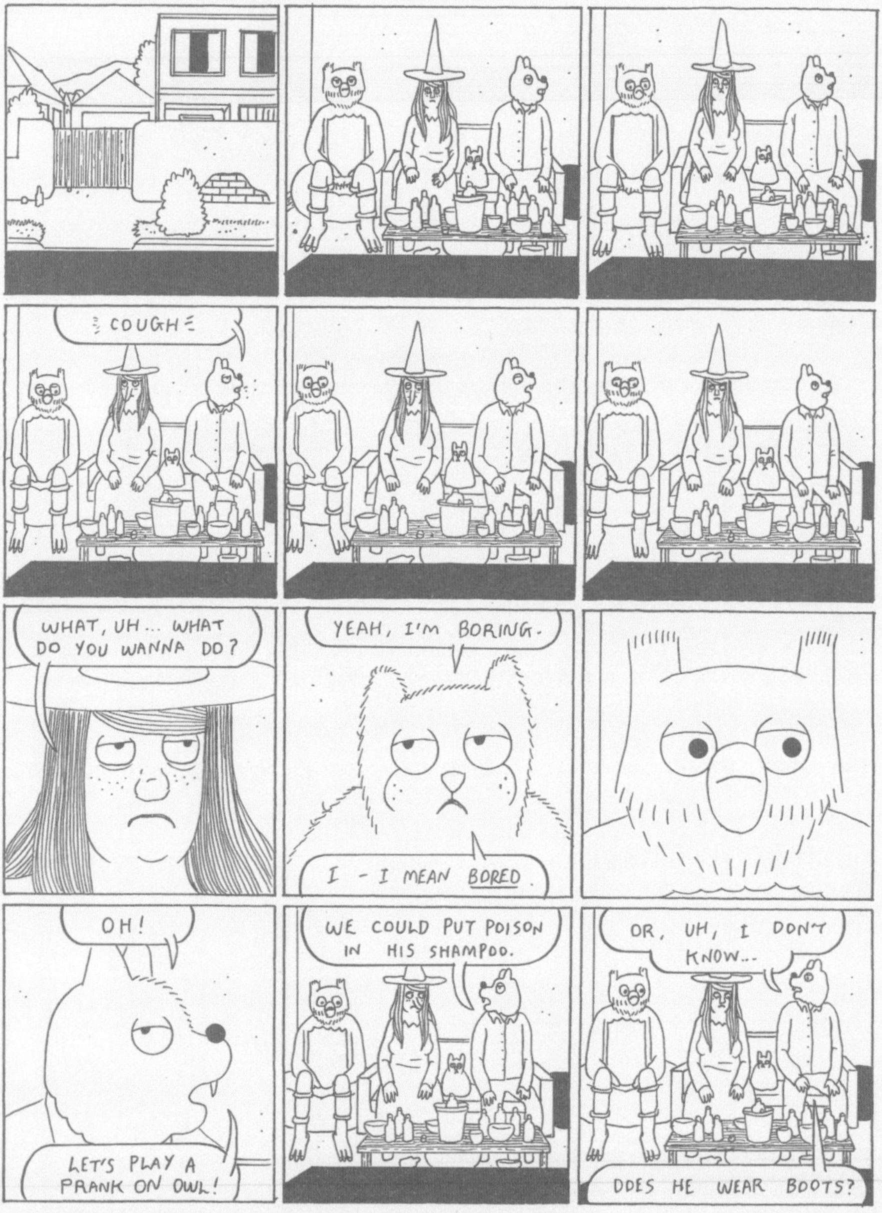
COUGH
WHAT, UH... WHAT DO YOU WANNA DO?
YEAH, I'M BORING.
I - I MEAN BORED.
OH!
LET'S PLAY A PRANK ON OWL!
WE COULD PUT POISON IN HIS SHAMPOO.
OR, UH, I DON'T KNOW...
DOES HE WEAR BOOTS?

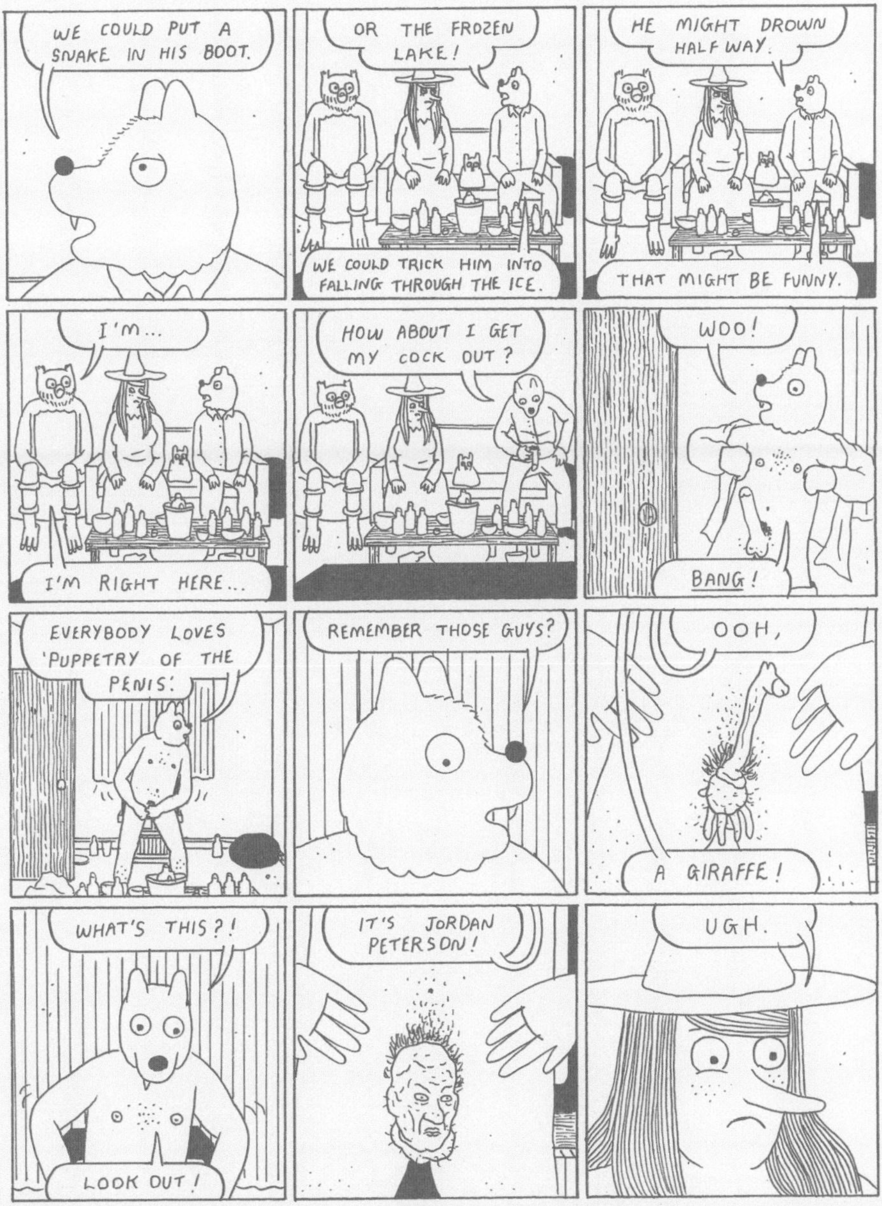

WE COULD PUT A SNAKE IN HIS BOOT.
OR THE FROZEN LAKE!
WE COULD TRICK HIM INTO FALLING THROUGH THE ICE.
HE MIGHT DROWN HALF WAY.
THAT MIGHT BE FUNNY.
I'M...
I'M RIGHT HERE...
HOW ABOUT I GET MY COCK OUT?
WOO!
BANG!
EVERYBODY LOVES 'PUPPETRY OF THE PENIS.'
REMEMBER THOSE GUYS?
OOH,
A GIRAFFE!
WHAT'S THIS?!
LOOK OUT!
IT'S JORDAN PETERSON!
UGH.

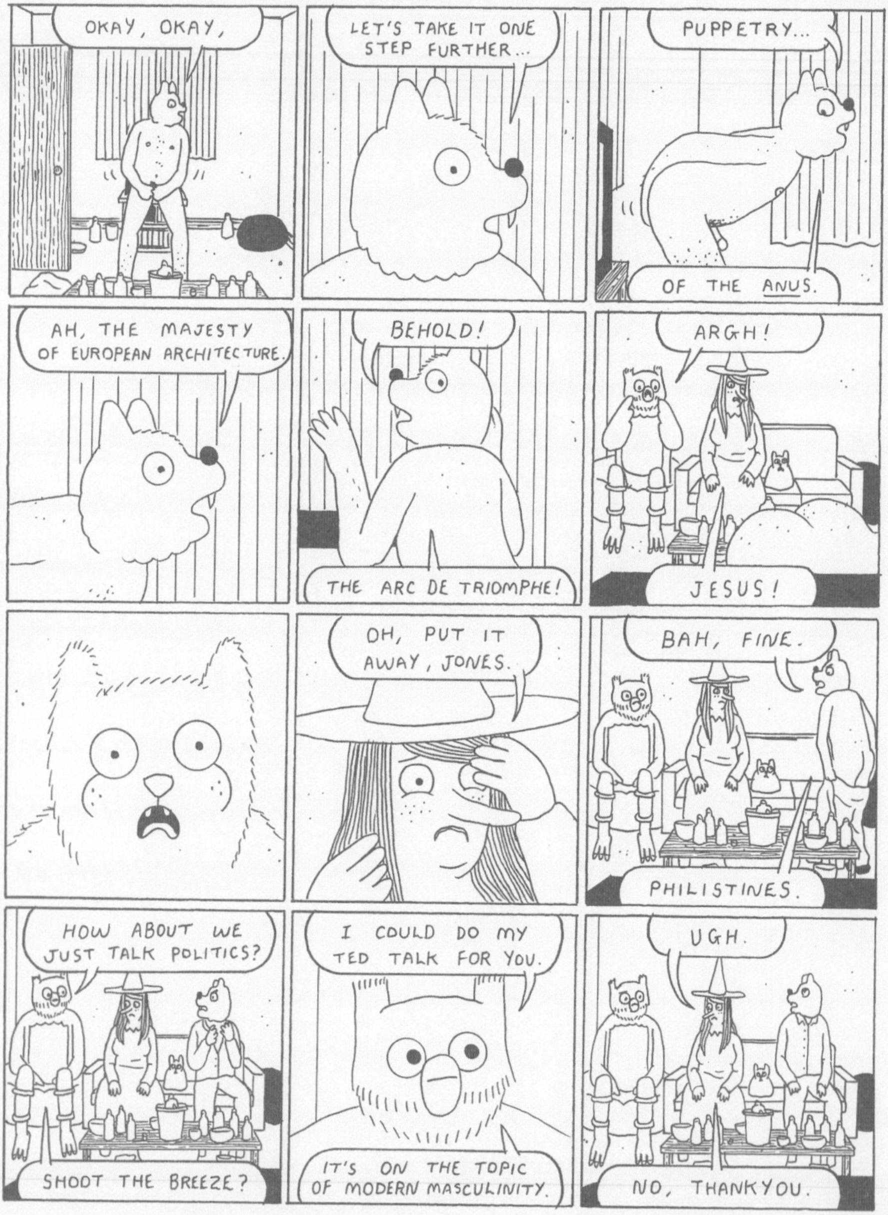
OKAY, OKAY,
LET'S TAKE IT ONE STEP FURTHER...
PUPPETRY...
OF THE ANUS.
AH, THE MAJESTY OF EUROPEAN ARCHITECTURE.
BEHOLD!
THE ARC DE TRIOMPHE!
ARGH!
JESUS!
OH, PUT IT AWAY, JONES.
BAH, FINE.
PHILISTINES.
HOW ABOUT WE JUST TALK POLITICS?
SHOOT THE BREEZE?
I COULD DO MY TED TALK FOR YOU.
IT'S ON THE TOPIC OF MODERN MASCULINITY.
UGH.
NO, THANKYOU.

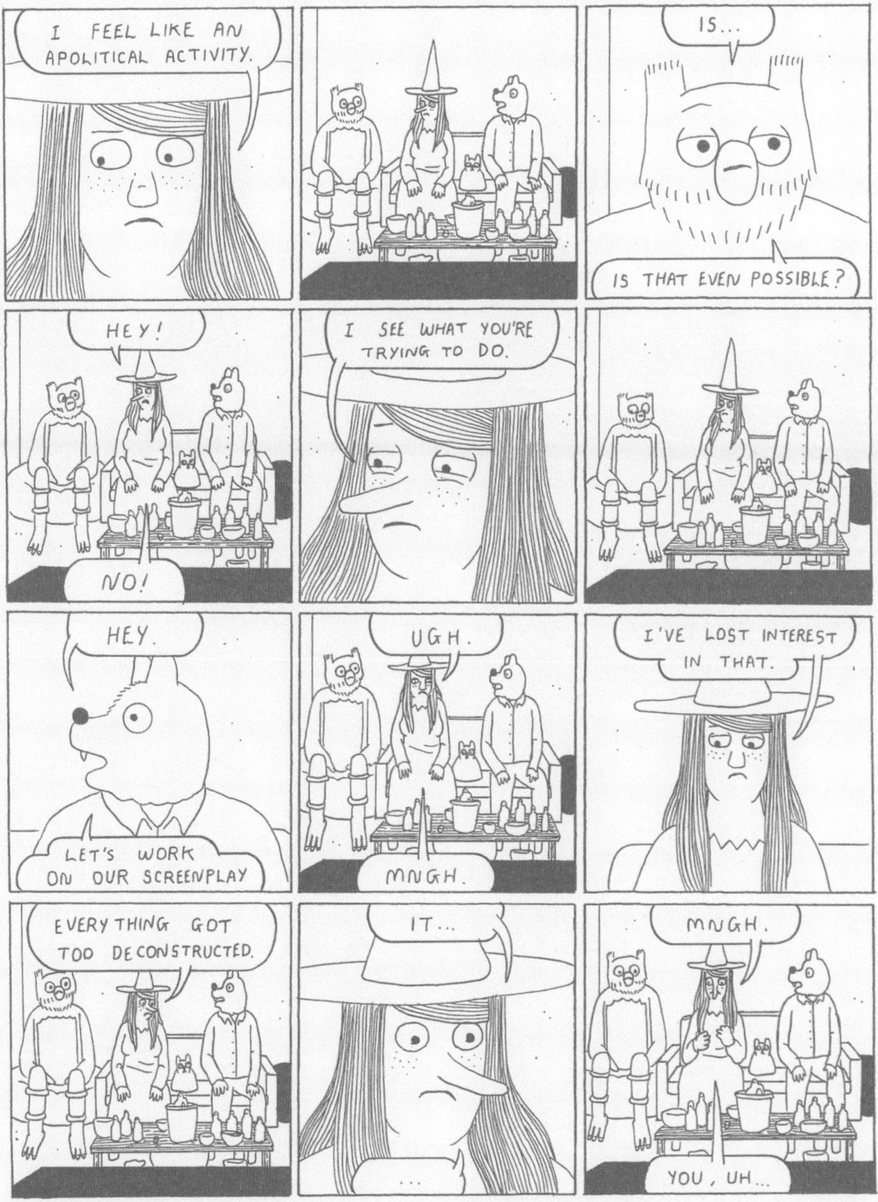
I FEEL LIKE AN APOLITICAL ACTIVITY.
IS...
IS THAT EVEN POSSIBLE?
HEY!
NO!
I SEE WHAT YOU'RE TRYING TO DO.
HEY.
LET'S WORK ON OUR SCREENPLAY
UGH.
MNGH.
I'VE LOST INTEREST IN THAT.
EVERYTHING GOT TOO DECONSTRUCTED.
IT...
...
MNGH.
YOU, UH...

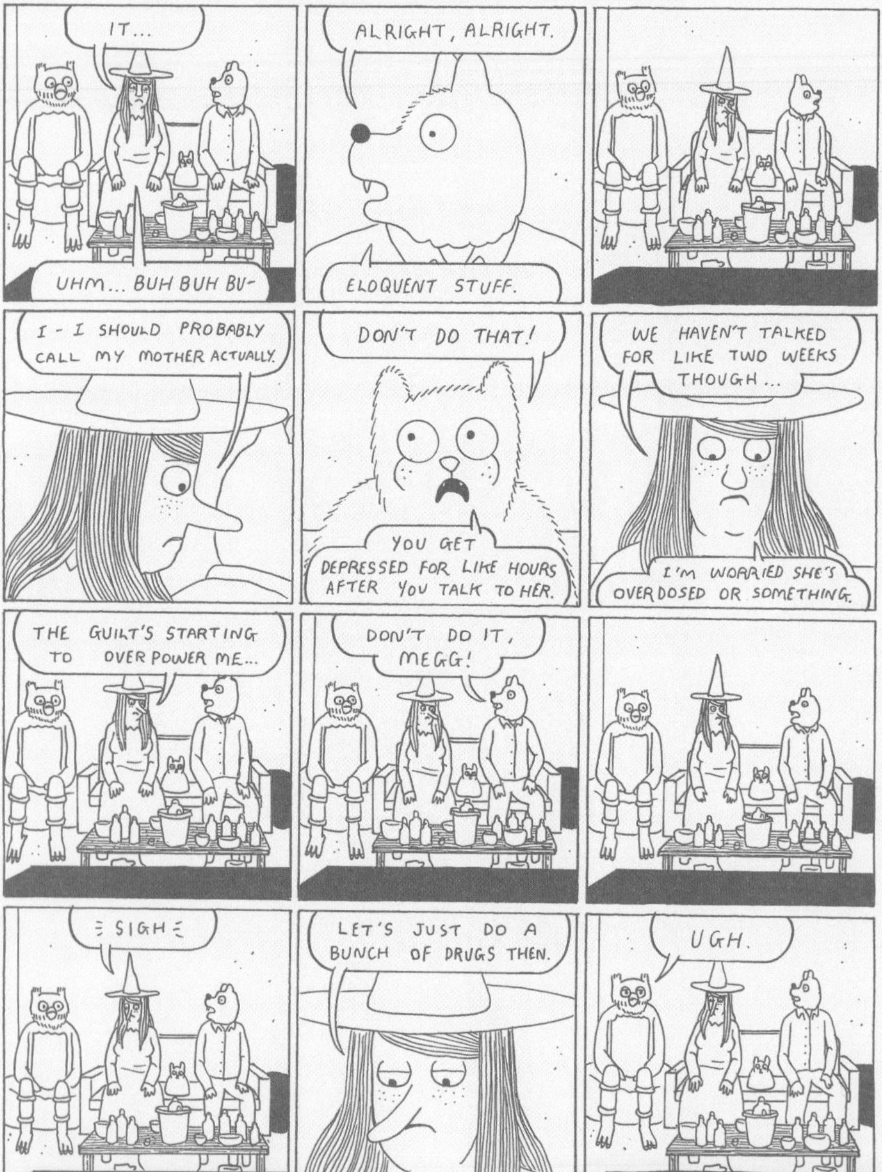
IT...
UHM... BUH BUH BU-
ALRIGHT, ALRIGHT.
ELOQUENT STUFF.
I - I SHOULD PROBABLY CALL MY MOTHER ACTUALLY.
DON'T DO THAT!
YOU GET DEPRESSED FOR LIKE HOURS AFTER YOU TALK TO HER.
WE HAVEN'T TALKED FOR LIKE TWO WEEKS THOUGH...
I'M WORRIED SHE'S OVERDOSED OR SOMETHING.
THE GUILT'S STARTING TO OVERPOWER ME...
DON'T DO IT, MEGG!
SIGH
LET'S JUST DO A BUNCH OF DRUGS THEN.
UGH.

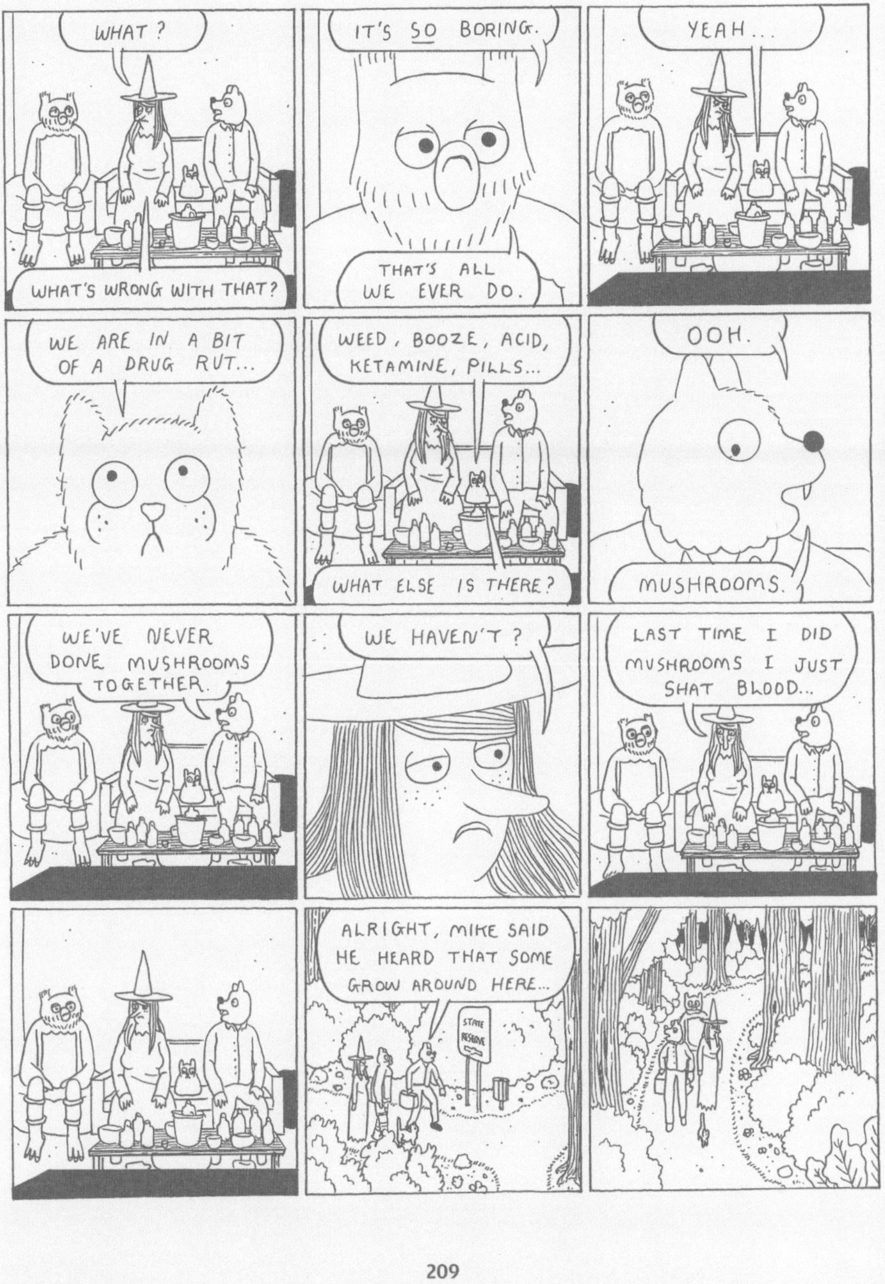
WHAT?
WHAT'S WRONG WITH THAT?
IT'S SO BORING.
THAT'S ALL WE EVER DO.
YEAH...
WE ARE IN A BIT OF A DRUG RUT...
WEED, BOOZE, ACID, KETAMINE, PILLS...
WHAT ELSE IS THERE?
OOH.
MUSHROOMS.
WE'VE NEVER DONE MUSHROOMS TOGETHER.
WE HAVEN'T?
LAST TIME I DID MUSHROOMS I JUST SHAT BLOOD...
ALRIGHT, MIKE SAID HE HEARD THAT SOME GROW AROUND HERE...
STATE RESERVE

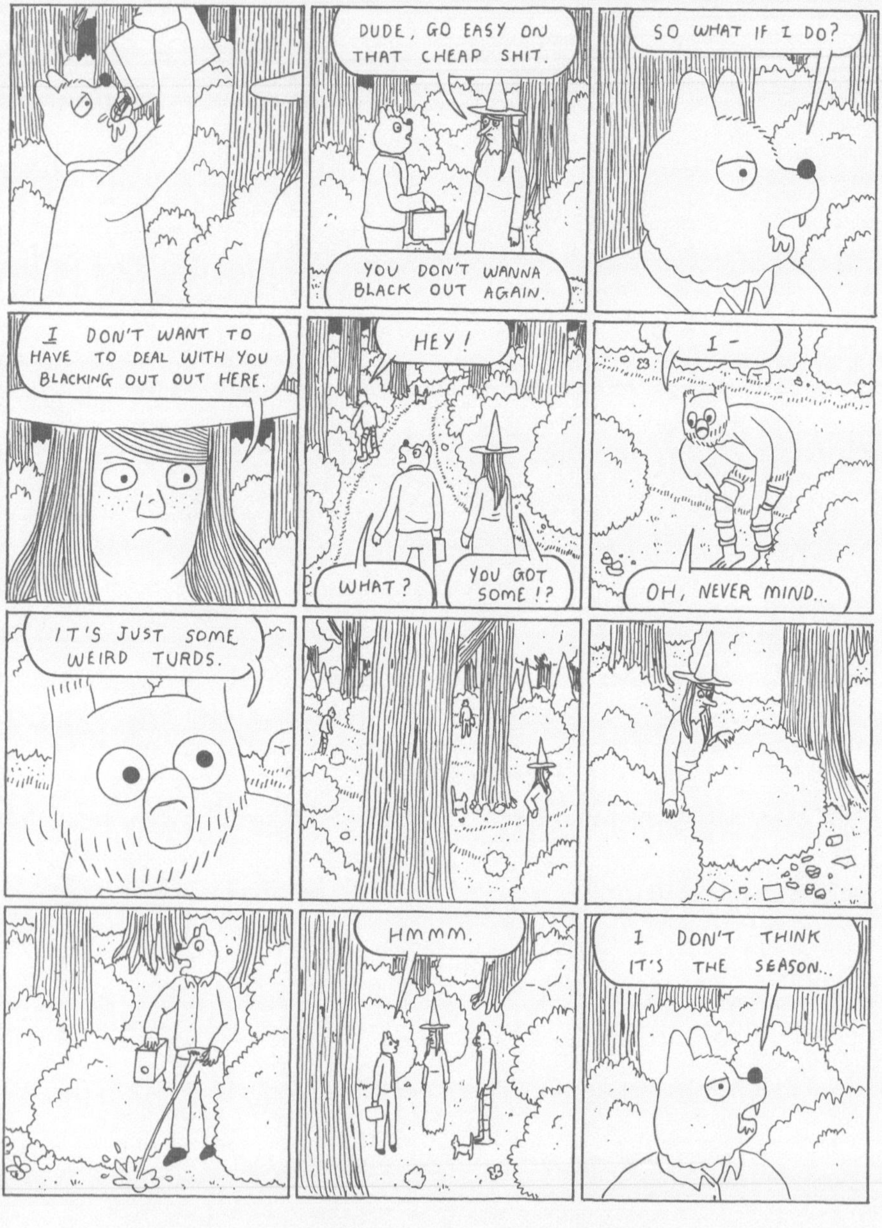
DUDE, GO EASY ON THAT CHEAP SHIT.
YOU DON'T WANNA BLACK OUT AGAIN.
SO WHAT IF I DO?
I DON'T WANT TO HAVE TO DEAL WITH YOU BLACKING OUT OUT HERE.
HEY!
WHAT?
YOU GOT SOME!?
I -
OH, NEVER MIND...
IT'S JUST SOME WEIRD TURDS.
HMMM.
I DON'T THINK IT'S THE SEASON...

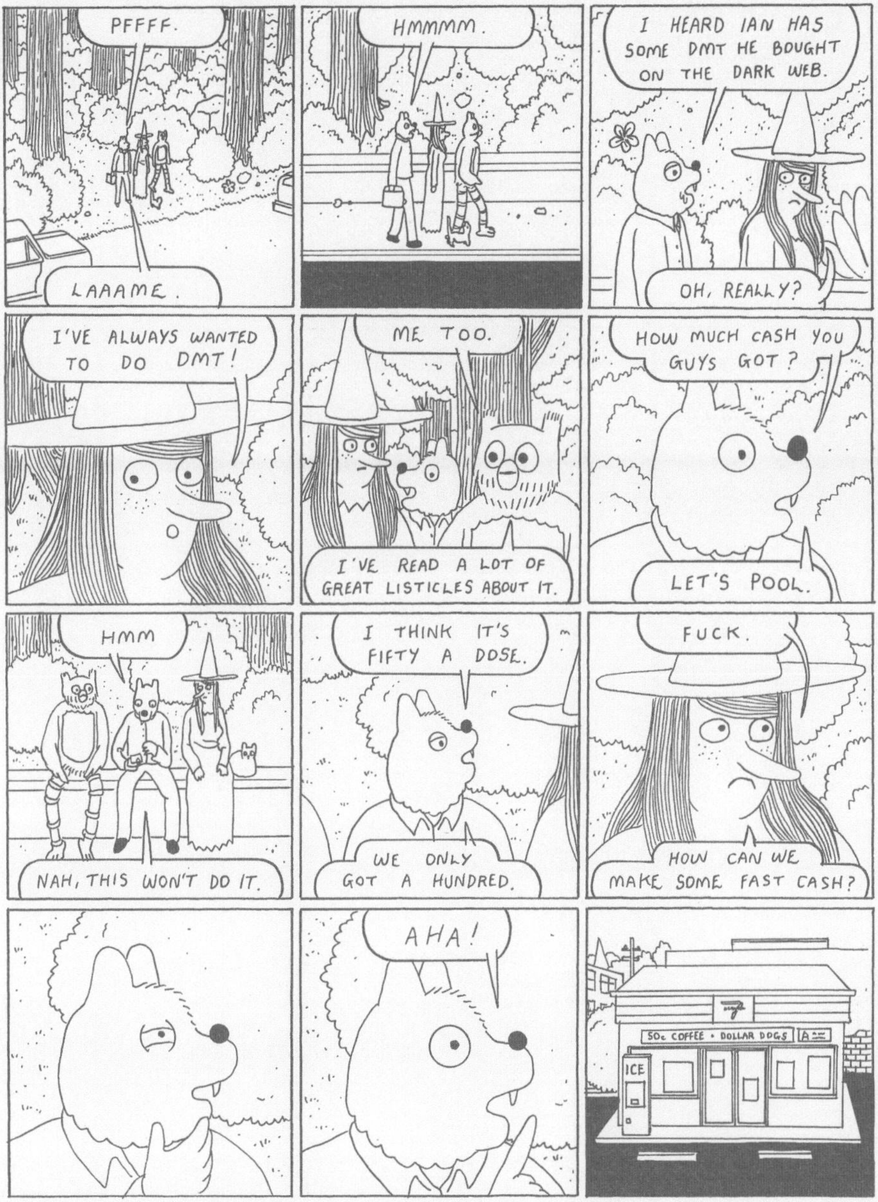
PFFFF.
LAAAME.
HMMMM.
I HEARD IAN HAS SOME DMT HE BOUGHT ON THE DARK WEB.
OH, REALLY?
I'VE ALWAYS WANTED TO DO DMT!
ME TOO.
I'VE READ A LOT OF GREAT LISTICLES ABOUT IT.
HOW MUCH CASH YOU GUYS GOT?
LET'S POOL.
HMM
NAH, THIS WON'T DO IT.
I THINK IT'S FIFTY A DOSE.
WE ONLY GOT A HUNDRED.
FUCK.
HOW CAN WE MAKE SOME FAST CASH?
AHA!
50¢ COFFEE • DOLLAR DOGS
ICE

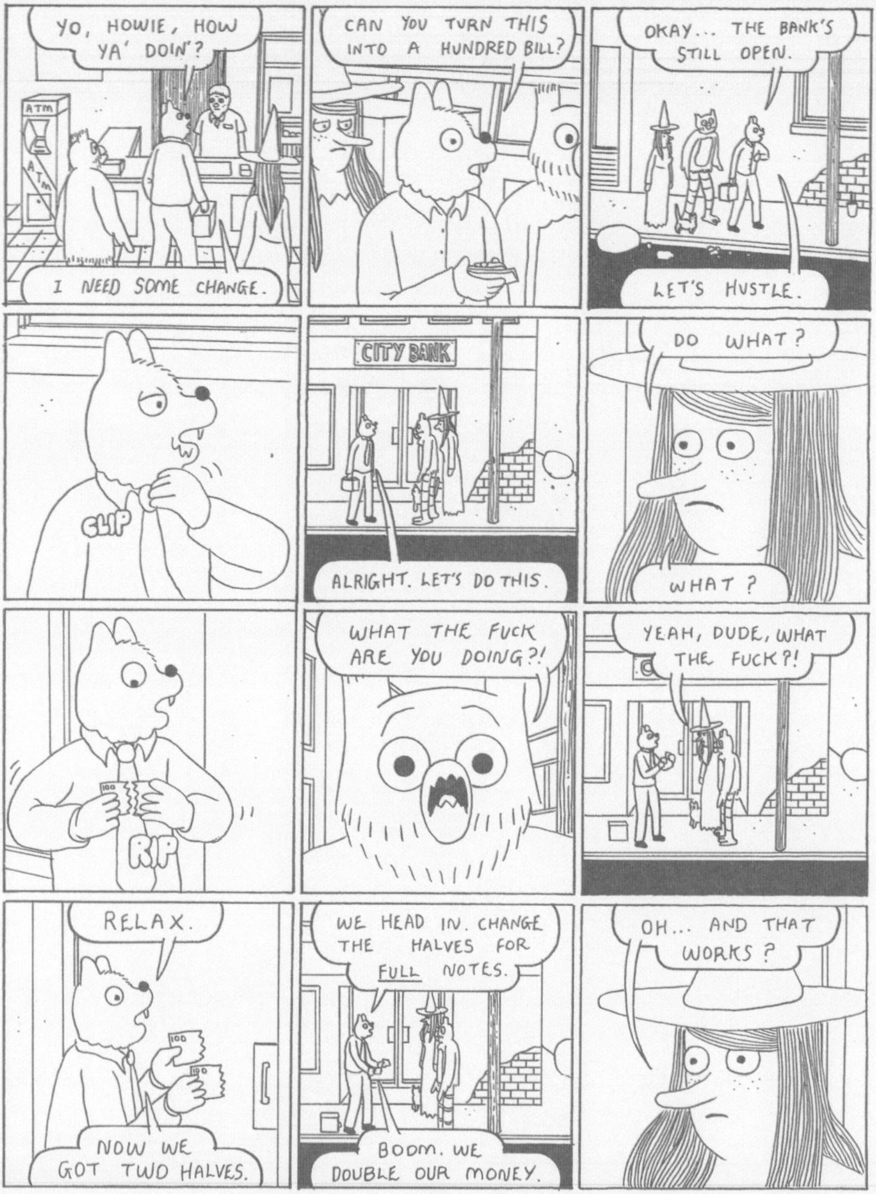
YO, HOWIE, HOW YA' DOIN'?
I NEED SOME CHANGE.
CAN YOU TURN THIS INTO A HUNDRED BILL?
OKAY... THE BANK'S STILL OPEN.
LET'S HUSTLE.
CLIP
CITY BANK
ALRIGHT. LET'S DO THIS.
DO WHAT?
WHAT?
RIP
WHAT THE FUCK ARE YOU DOING?!
YEAH, DUDE, WHAT THE FUCK?!
RELAX.
NOW WE GOT TWO HALVES.
WE HEAD IN. CHANGE THE HALVES FOR FULL NOTES.
BOOM. WE DOUBLE OUR MONEY.
OH... AND THAT WORKS?

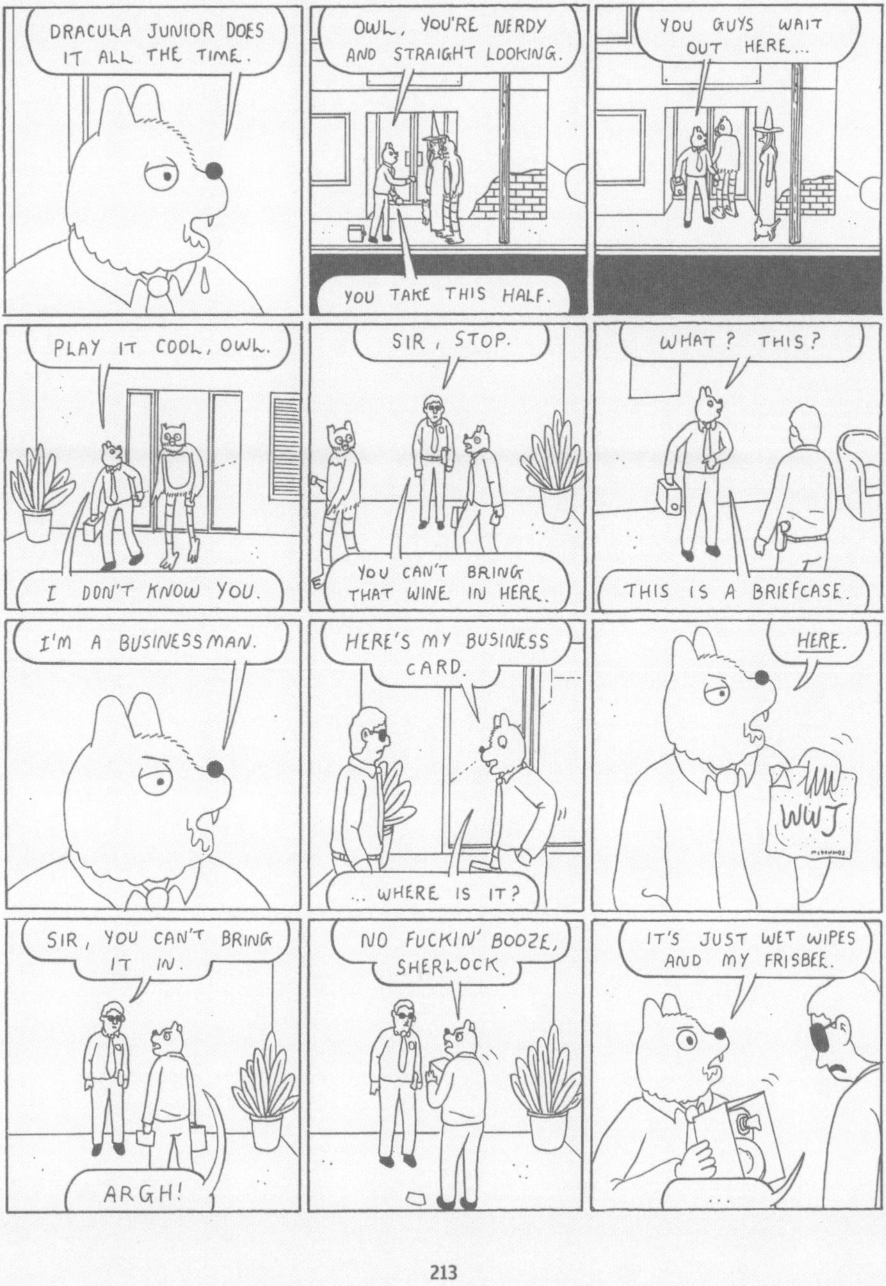
DRACULA JUNIOR DOES IT ALL THE TIME.
OWL, YOU'RE NERDY AND STRAIGHT LOOKING.
YOU TAKE THIS HALF.
YOU GUYS WAIT OUT HERE...
PLAY IT COOL, OWL.
I DON'T KNOW YOU.
SIR, STOP.
YOU CAN'T BRING THAT WINE IN HERE.
WHAT? THIS?
THIS IS A BRIEFCASE.
I'M A BUSINESSMAN.
HERE'S MY BUSINESS CARD.
... WHERE IS IT?
HERE.
WWJ
SIR, YOU CAN'T BRING IT IN.
ARGH!
NO FUCKIN' BOOZE, SHERLOCK.
IT'S JUST WET WIPES AND MY FRISBEE.
...

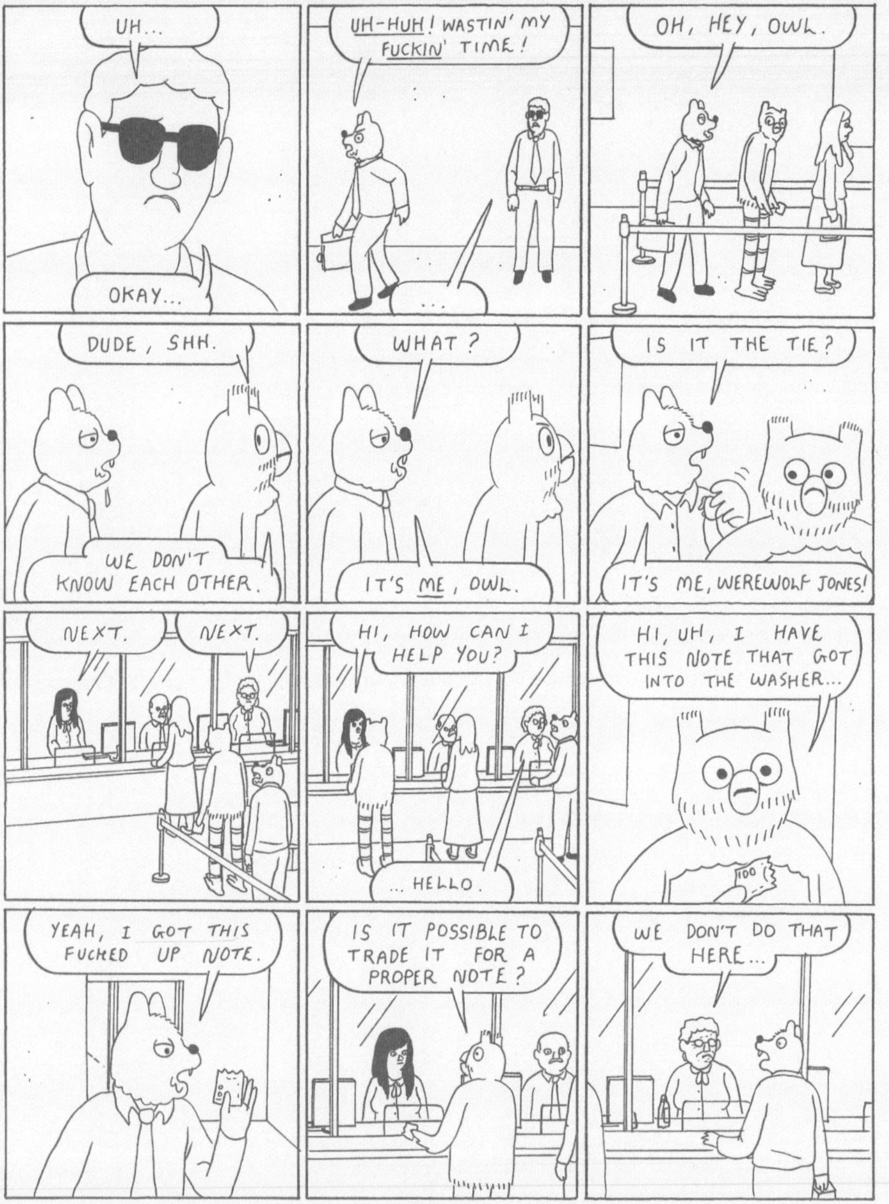
UH...
OKAY...
UH-HUH! WASTIN' MY FUCKIN' TIME!
...
OH, HEY, OWL.
DUDE, SHH.
WE DON'T KNOW EACH OTHER.
WHAT?
IT'S ME, OWL.
IS IT THE TIE?
IT'S ME, WEREWOLF JONES!
NEXT.
NEXT.
HI, HOW CAN I HELP YOU?
... HELLO.
HI, UH, I HAVE THIS NOTE THAT GOT INTO THE WASHER...
100
YEAH, I GOT THIS FUCKED UP NOTE.
IS IT POSSIBLE TO TRADE IT FOR A PROPER NOTE?
WE DON'T DO THAT HERE...

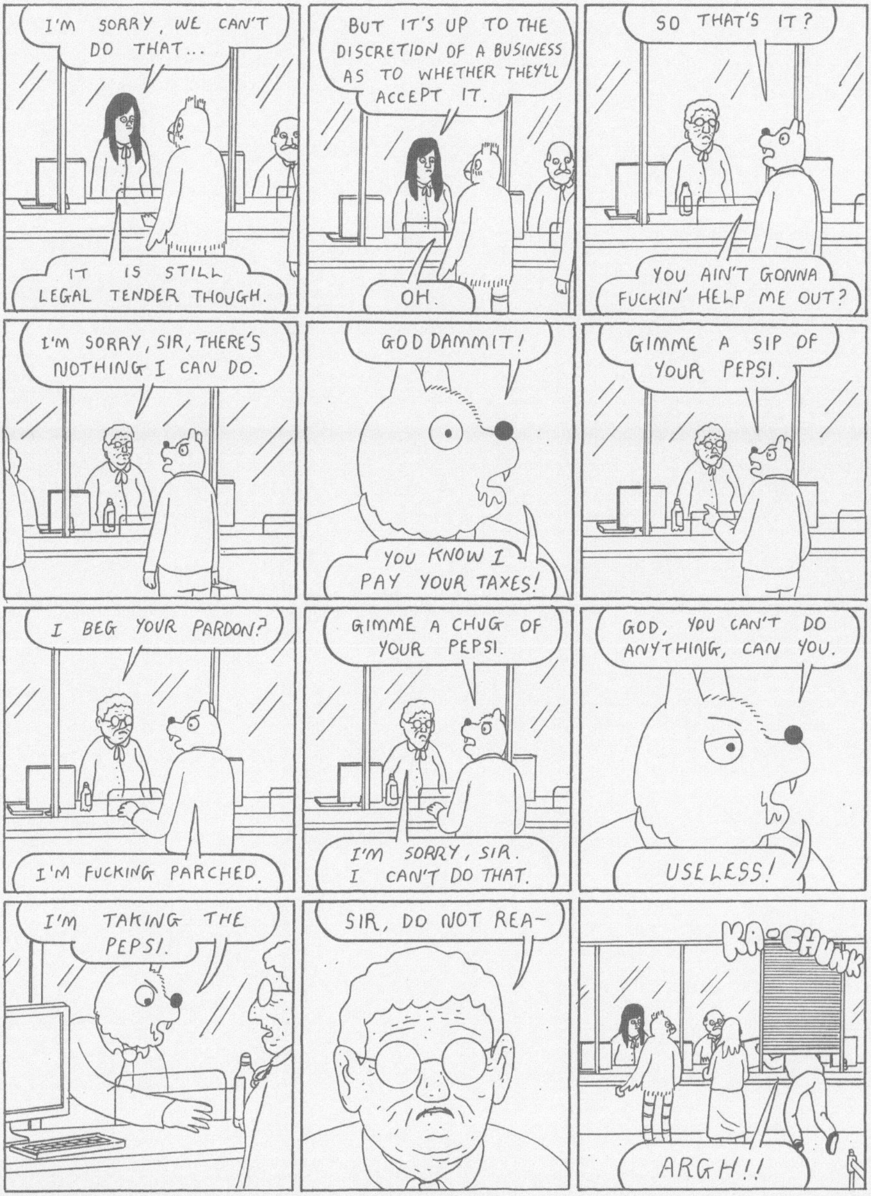
I'M SORRY, WE CAN'T DO THAT...
IT IS STILL LEGAL TENDER THOUGH.
BUT IT'S UP TO THE DISCRETION OF A BUSINESS AS TO WHETHER THEY'LL ACCEPT IT.
OH.
SO THAT'S IT?
YOU AIN'T GONNA FUCKIN' HELP ME OUT?
I'M SORRY, SIR, THERE'S NOTHING I CAN DO.
GODDAMMIT!
YOU KNOW I PAY YOUR TAXES!
GIMME A SIP OF YOUR PEPSI.
I BEG YOUR PARDON?
I'M FUCKING PARCHED.
GIMME A CHUG OF YOUR PEPSI.
I'M SORRY, SIR. I CAN'T DO THAT.
GOD, YOU CAN'T DO ANYTHING, CAN YOU.
USELESS!
I'M TAKING THE PEPSI.
SIR, DO NOT REA-
KA-CHUNK
ARGH!!

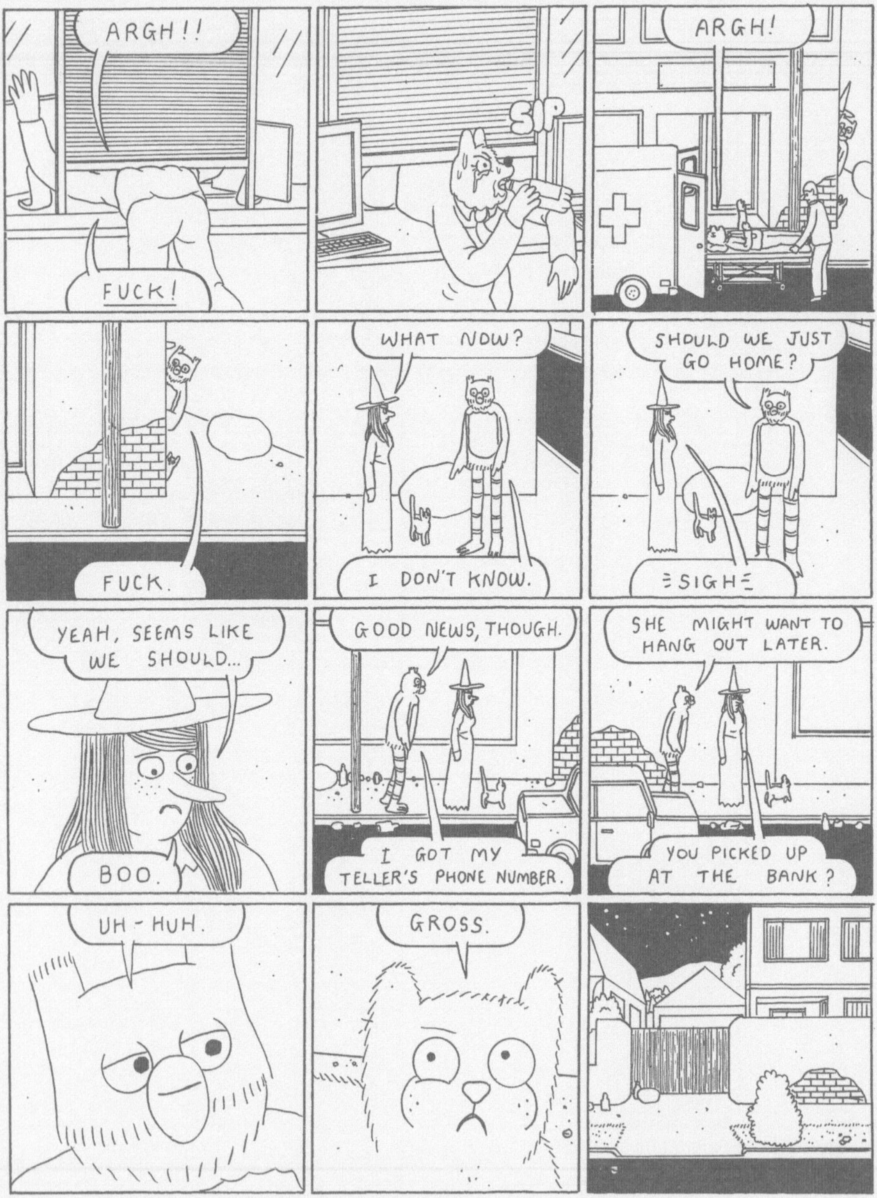
ARGH!!
FUCK!
SIP
ARGH!
FUCK.
WHAT NOW?
I DON'T KNOW.
SHOULD WE JUST GO HOME?
SIGH
YEAH, SEEMS LIKE WE SHOULD...
BOO.
GOOD NEWS, THOUGH.
I GOT MY TELLER'S PHONE NUMBER.
SHE MIGHT WANT TO HANG OUT LATER.
YOU PICKED UP AT THE BANK?
UH-HUH.
GROSS.

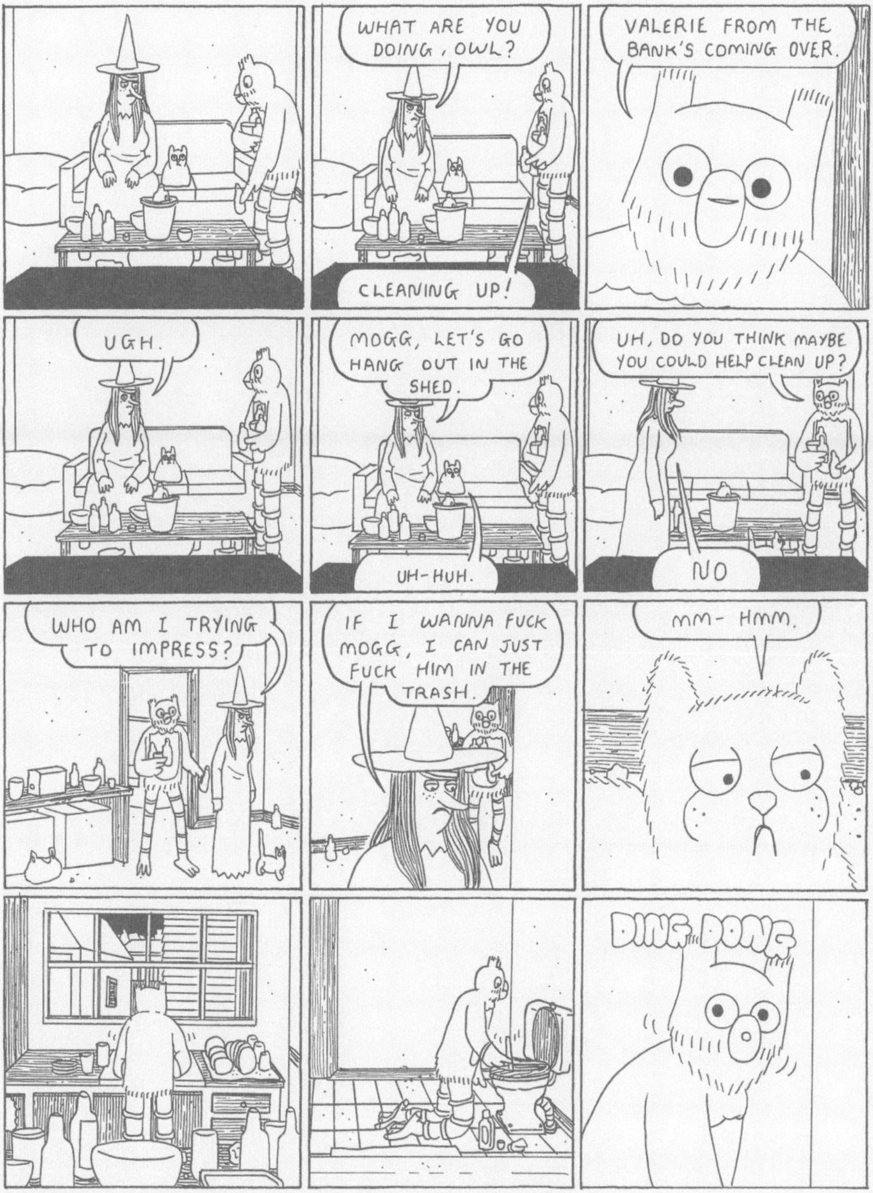
WHAT ARE YOU DOING, OWL?
CLEANING UP!
VALERIE FROM THE BANK'S COMING OVER.
UGH.
MOGG, LET'S GO HANG OUT IN THE SHED.
UH-HUH.
UH, DO YOU THINK MAYBE YOU COULD HELP CLEAN UP?
NO
WHO AM I TRYING TO IMPRESS?
IF I WANNA FUCK MOGG, I CAN JUST FUCK HIM IN THE TRASH.
MM-HMM.
DING DONG

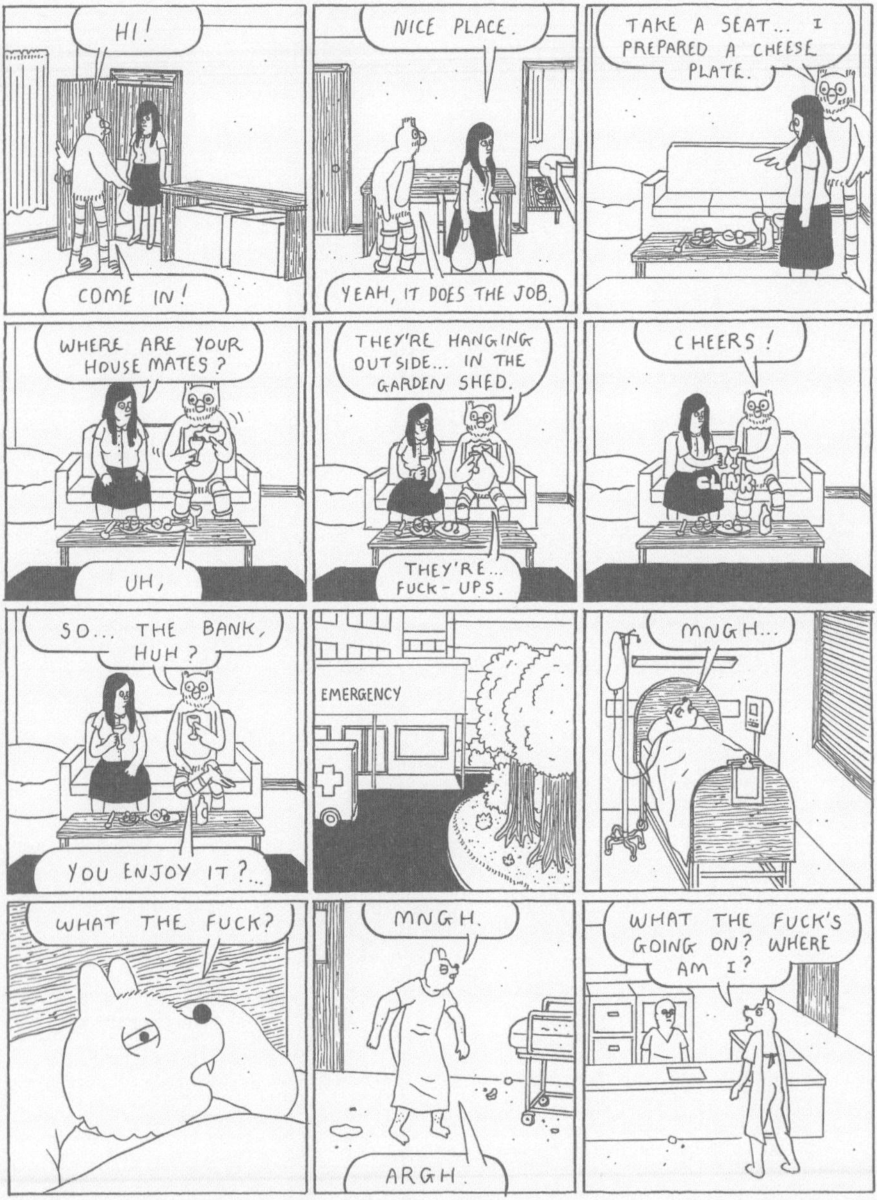
HI!
COME IN!
NICE PLACE.
YEAH, IT DOES THE JOB.
TAKE A SEAT... I PREPARED A CHEESE PLATE.
WHERE ARE YOUR HOUSE MATES?
UH,
THEY'RE HANGING OUTSIDE... IN THE GARDEN SHED.
THEY'RE... FUCK-UPS.
CHEERS!
CLINK
SO... THE BANK, HUH?
YOU ENJOY IT?...
EMERGENCY
MNGH...
WHAT THE FUCK?
MNGH.
ARGH.
WHAT THE FUCK'S GOING ON? WHERE AM I?

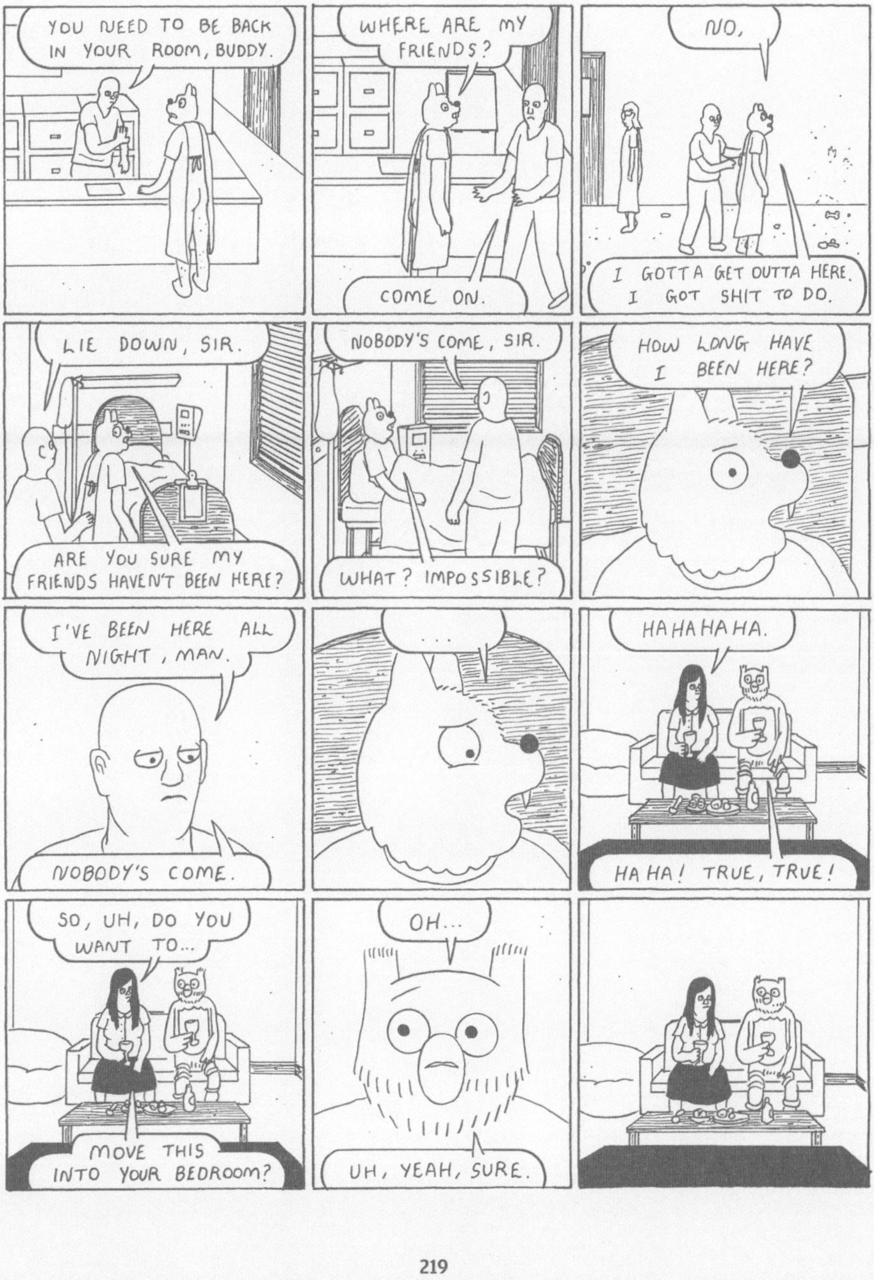
YOU NEED TO BE BACK IN YOUR ROOM, BUDDY.
WHERE ARE MY FRIENDS?
COME ON.
NO,
I GOTTA GET OUTTA HERE. I GOT SHIT TO DO.
LIE DOWN, SIR.
ARE YOU SURE MY FRIENDS HAVEN'T BEEN HERE?
NOBODY'S COME, SIR.
WHAT? IMPOSSIBLE?
HOW LONG HAVE I BEEN HERE?
I'VE BEEN HERE ALL NIGHT, MAN.
NOBODY'S COME.
...
HAHAHAHA.
HAHA! TRUE, TRUE!
SO, UH, DO YOU WANT TO...
MOVE THIS INTO YOUR BEDROOM?
OH...
UH, YEAH, SURE.

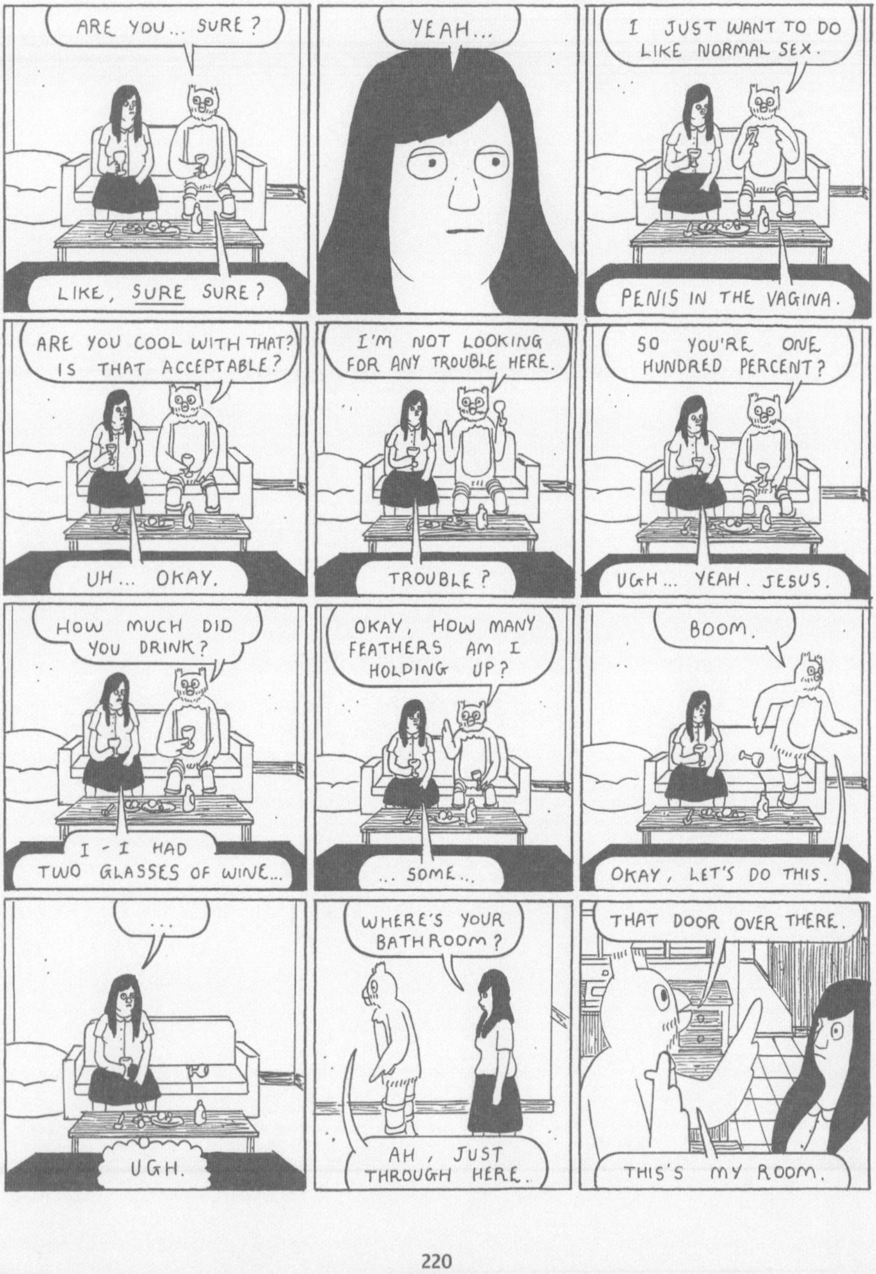
ARE YOU... SURE?
LIKE, SURE SURE?
YEAH...
I JUST WANT TO DO LIKE NORMAL SEX.
PENIS IN THE VAGINA.
ARE YOU COOL WITH THAT? IS THAT ACCEPTABLE?
UH... OKAY.
I'M NOT LOOKING FOR ANY TROUBLE HERE.
TROUBLE?
SO YOU'RE ONE HUNDRED PERCENT?
UGH... YEAH. JESUS.
HOW MUCH DID YOU DRINK?
I-I HAD TWO GLASSES OF WINE...
OKAY, HOW MANY FEATHERS AM I HOLDING UP?
... SOME...
BOOM.
OKAY, LET'S DO THIS.
...
UGH.
WHERE'S YOUR BATHROOM?
AH, JUST THROUGH HERE.
THAT DOOR OVER THERE.
THIS'S MY ROOM.

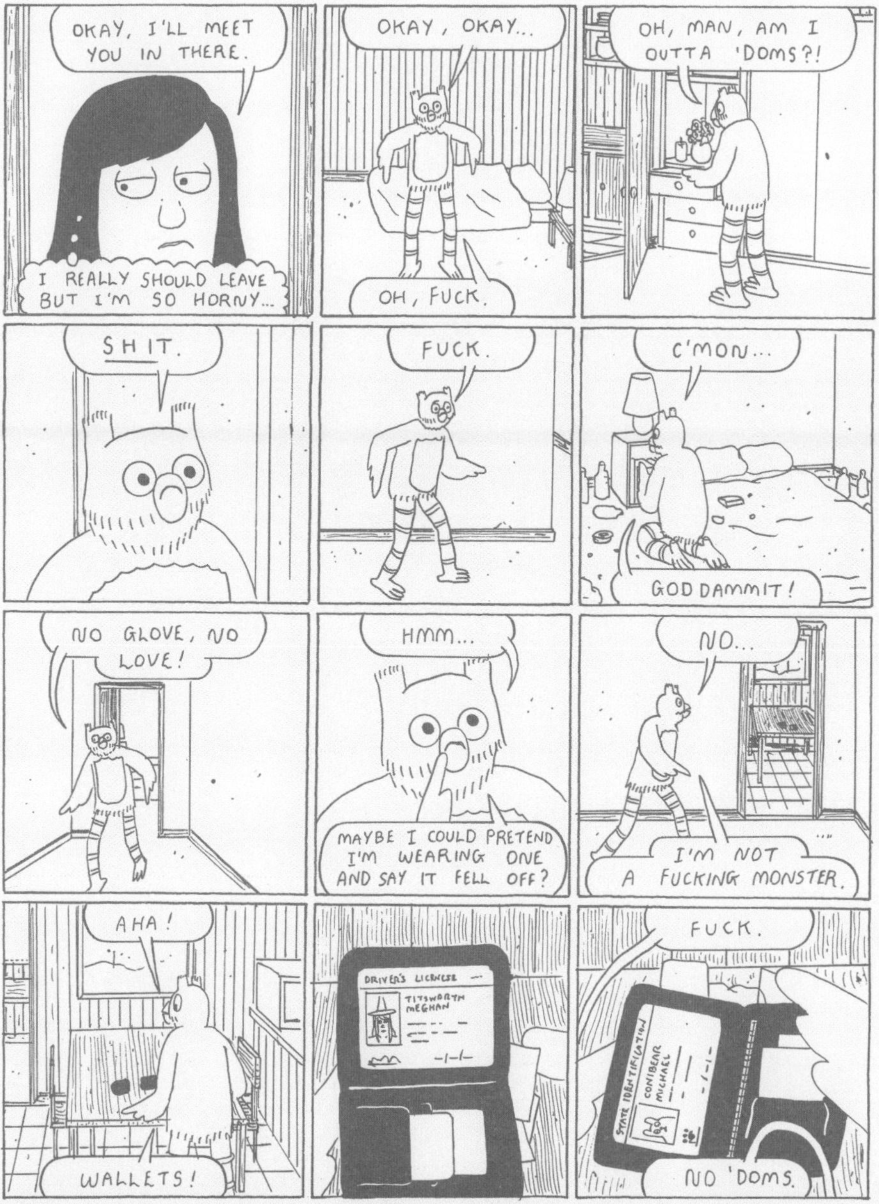
OKAY, I'LL MEET YOU IN THERE.
I REALLY SHOULD LEAVE BUT I'M SO HORNY...
OKAY, OKAY...
OH, FUCK.
OH, MAN, AM I OUTTA 'DOMS?!
SHIT.
FUCK.
C'MON...
GODDAMMIT!
NO GLOVE, NO LOVE!
HMM...
MAYBE I COULD PRETEND I'M WEARING ONE AND SAY IT FELL OFF?
NO...
I'M NOT A FUCKING MONSTER.
AHA!
WALLETS!
DRIVER'S LICENSE
TITSWORTH MEGHAN
FUCK.
STATE IDENTIFICATION
CONIBEAR MICHAEL
NO 'DOMS.

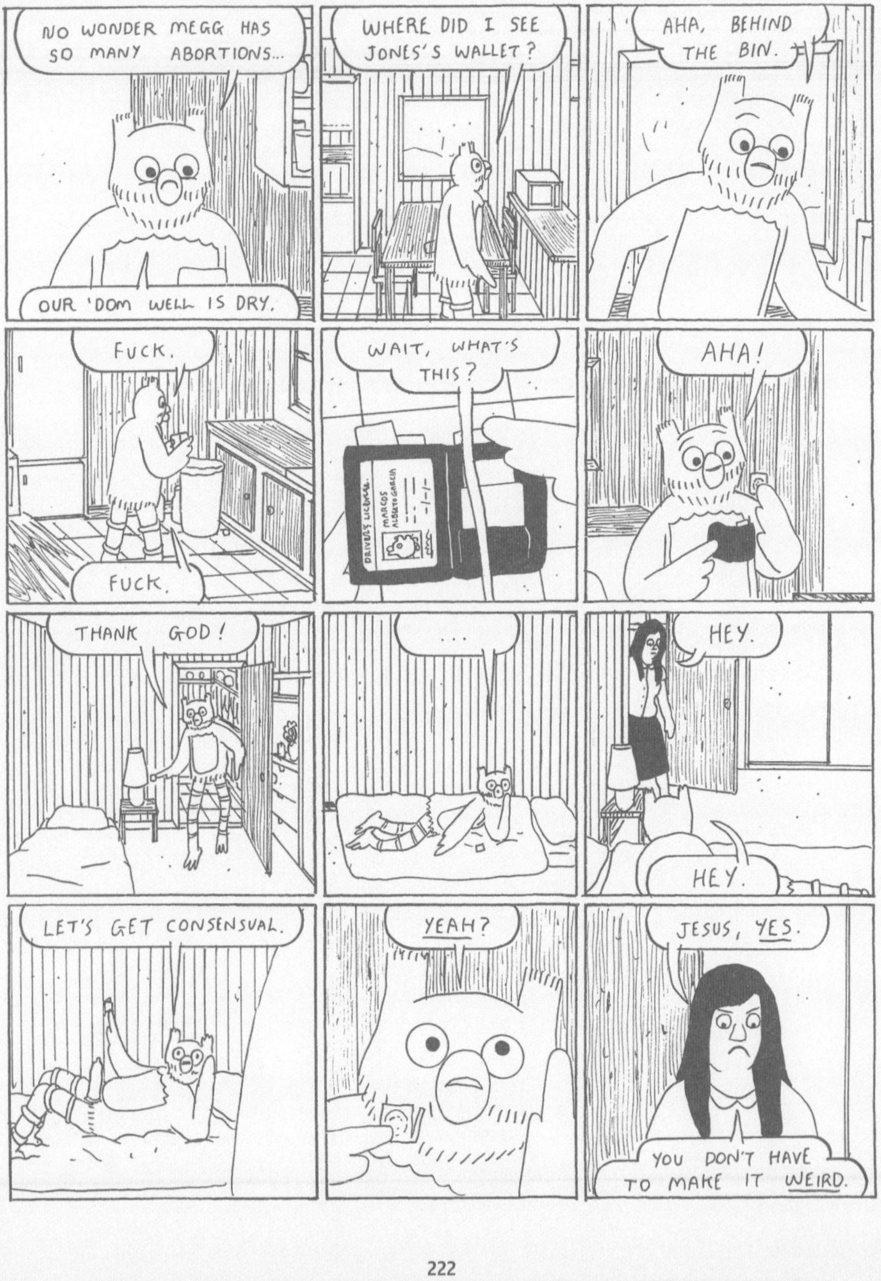
NO WONDER MEGG HAS SO MANY ABORTIONS...
OUR 'DOM WELL IS DRY.
WHERE DID I SEE JONES'S WALLET?
AHA, BEHIND THE BIN.
FUCK.
FUCK.
WAIT, WHAT'S THIS?
AHA!
THANK GOD!
...
HEY.
HEY.
LET'S GET CONSENSUAL.
YEAH?
JESUS, YES.
YOU DON'T HAVE TO MAKE IT WEIRD.

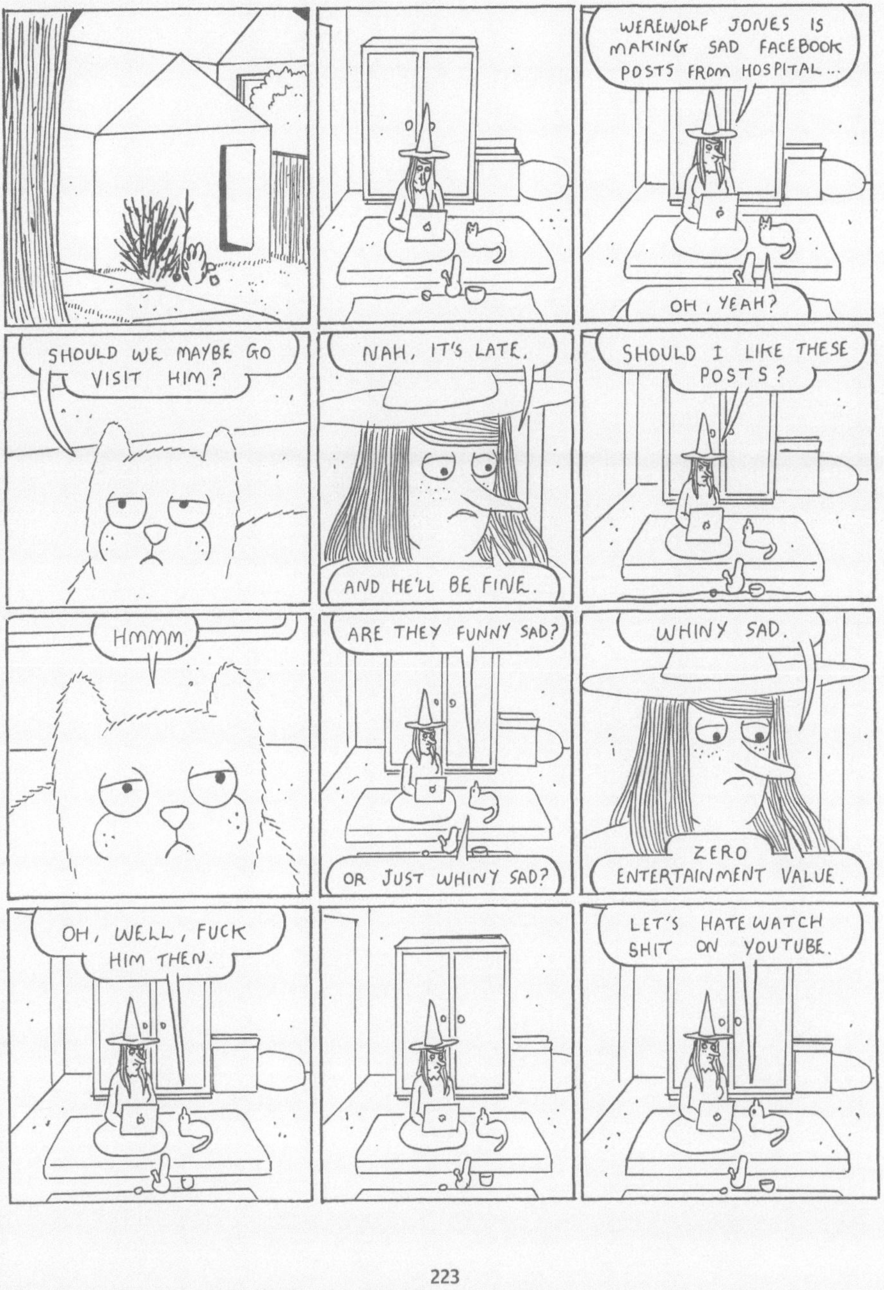
WEREWOLF JONES IS MAKING SAD FACEBOOK POSTS FROM HOSPITAL...
OH, YEAH?
SHOULD WE MAYBE GO VISIT HIM?
NAH, IT'S LATE.
AND HE'LL BE FINE.
SHOULD I LIKE THESE POSTS?
HMMM.
ARE THEY FUNNY SAD?
OR JUST WHINY SAD?
WHINY SAD.
ZERO ENTERTAINMENT VALUE.
OH, WELL, FUCK HIM THEN.
LET'S HATE WATCH SHIT ON YOUTUBE.

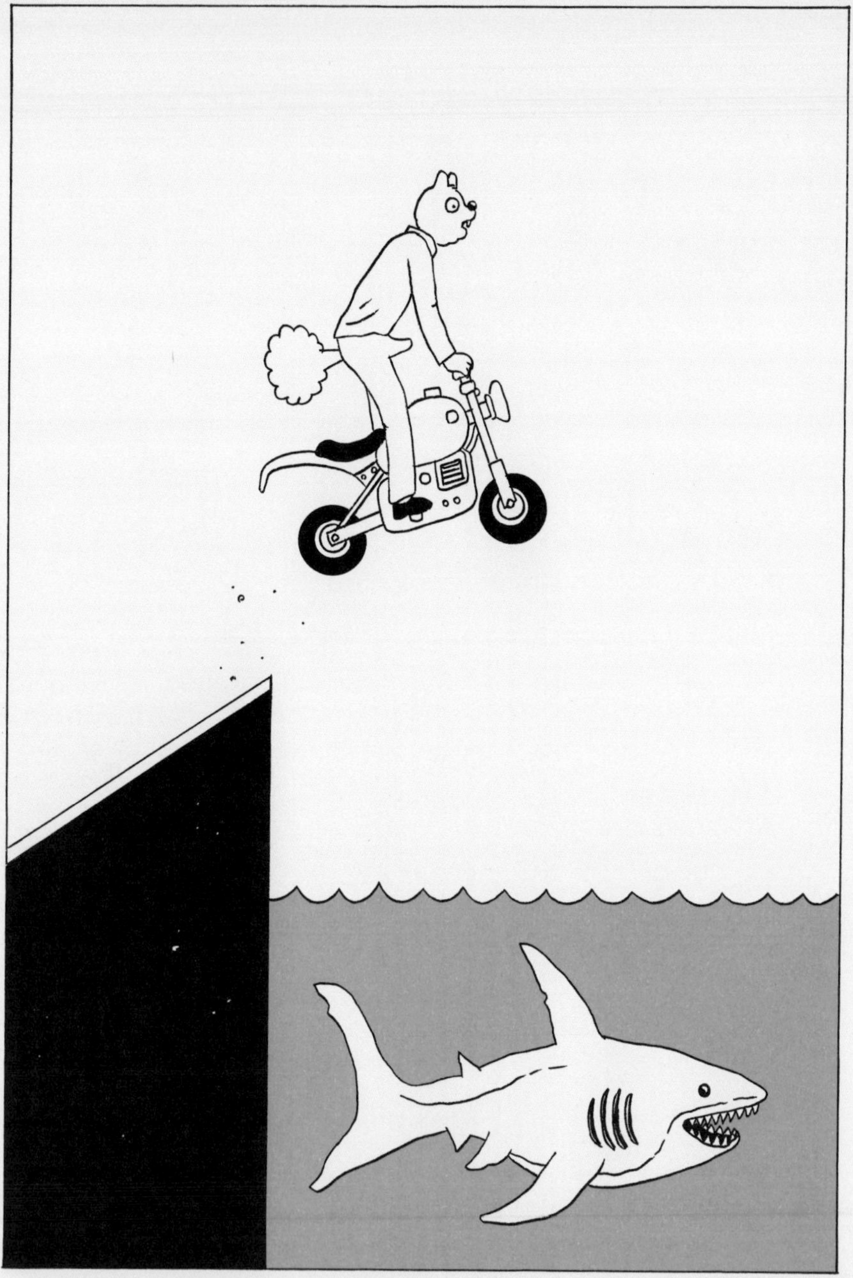

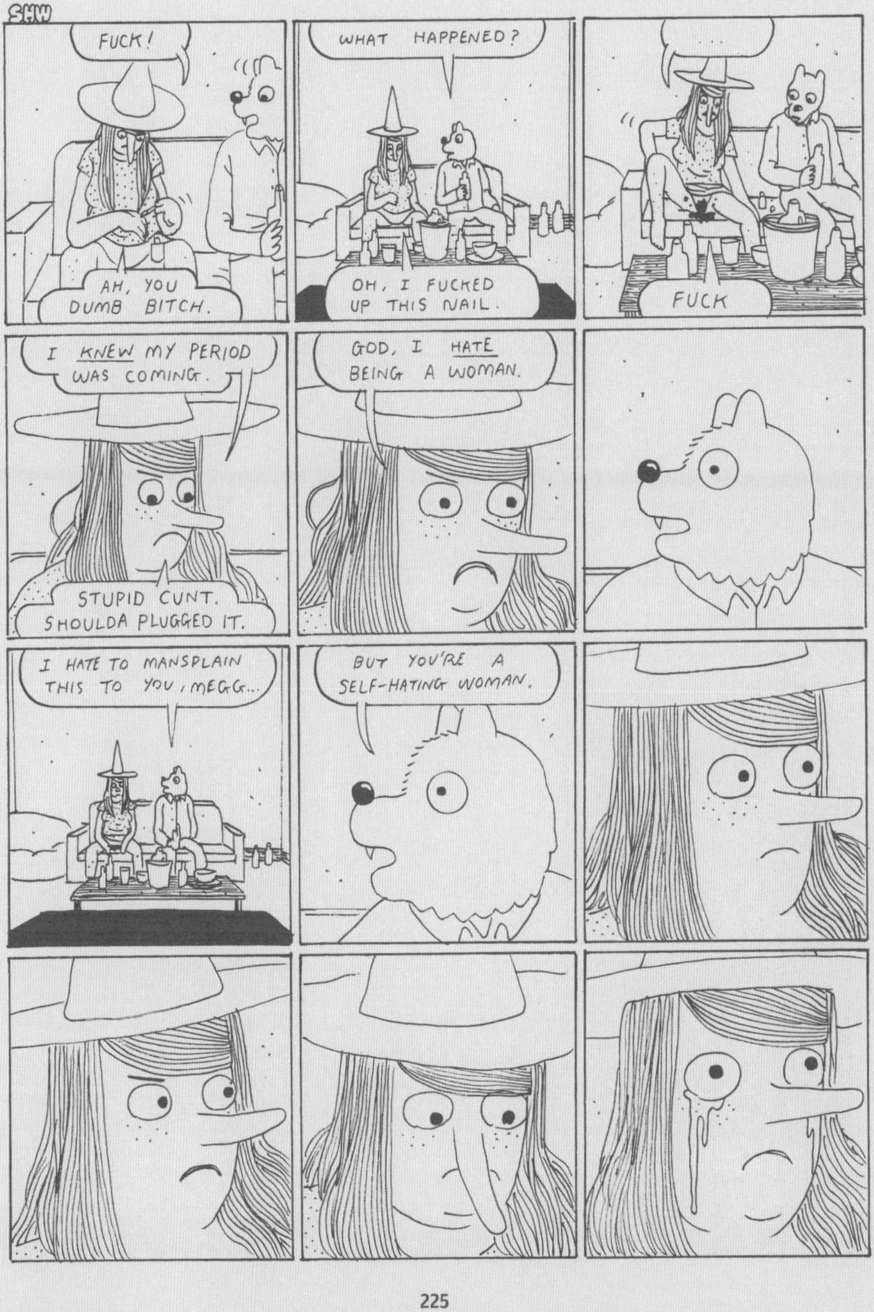
SHW
FUCK!
AH, YOU DUMB BITCH.
WHAT HAPPENED?
OH, I FUCKED UP THIS NAIL.
...
FUCK
I KNEW MY PERIOD WAS COMING.
STUPID CUNT. SHOULDA PLUGGED IT.
GOD, I HATE BEING A WOMAN.
I HATE TO MANSPLAIN THIS TO YOU, MEGG...
BUT YOU'RE A SELF-HATING WOMAN.

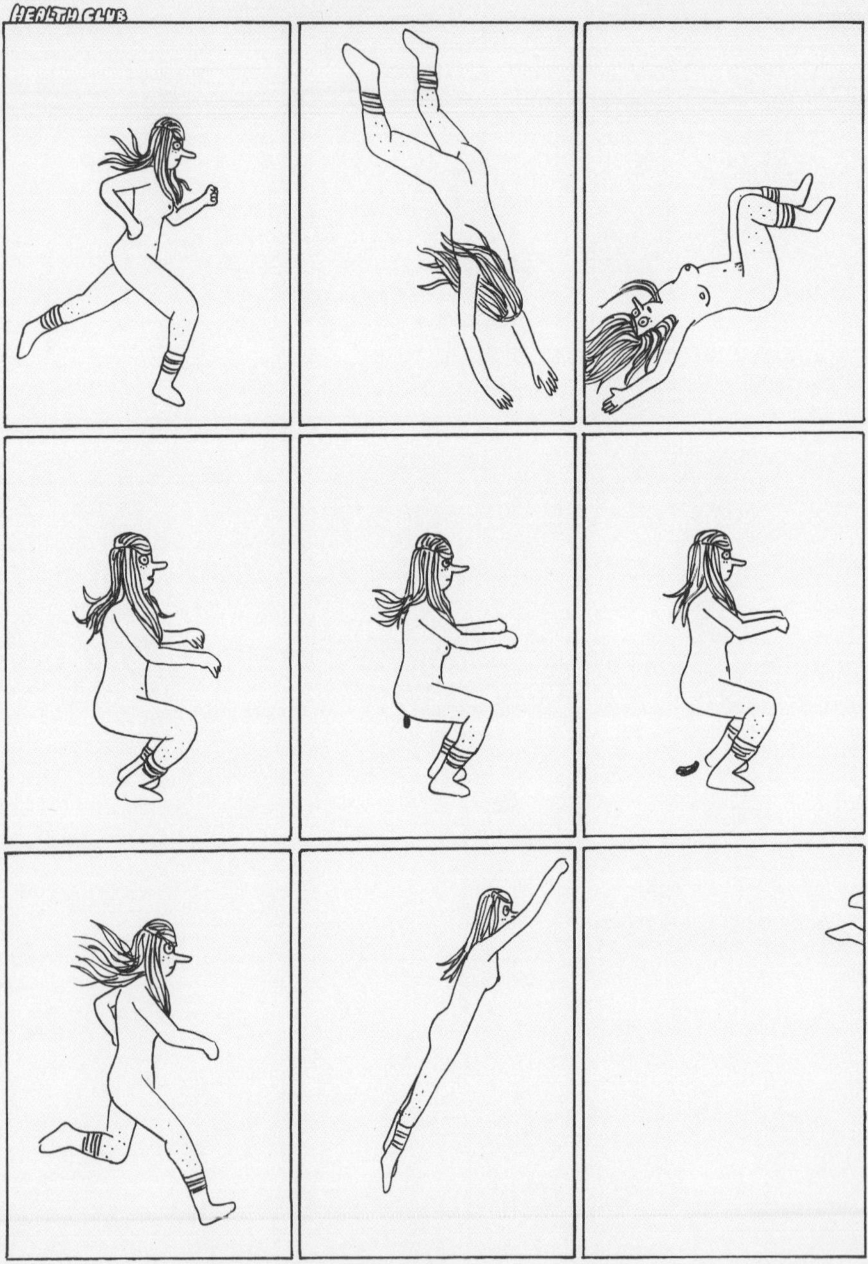
HEALTH CLUB

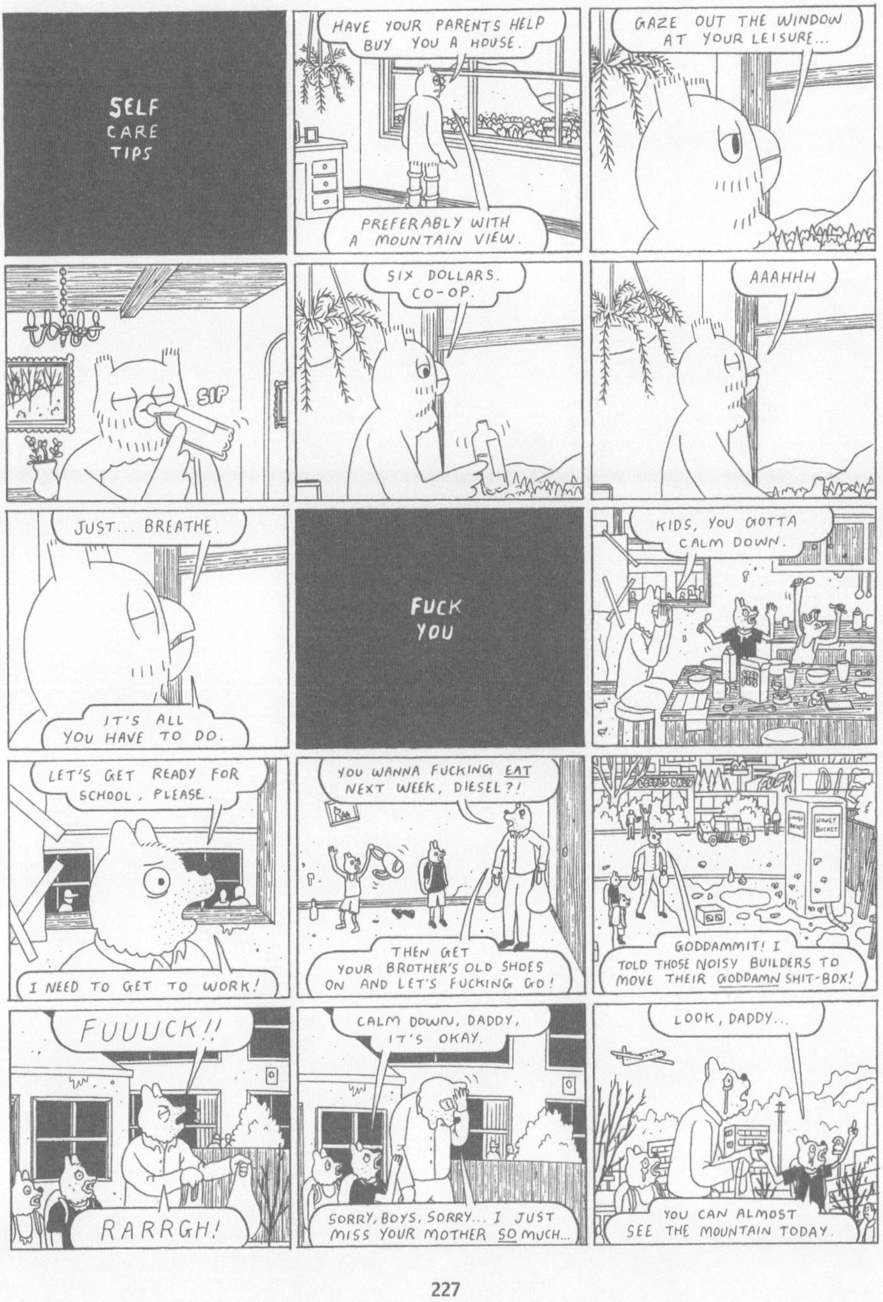
SELF
CARE
TIPS
HAVE YOUR PARENTS HELP BUY YOU A HOUSE.
PREFERABLY WITH A MOUNTAIN VIEW.
GAZE OUT THE WINDOW AT YOUR LEISURE...
SIP
SIX DOLLARS. CO-OP.
AAAHHH
JUST... BREATHE.
IT'S ALL YOU HAVE TO DO.
FUCK
YOU
KIDS, YOU GOTTA CALM DOWN.
LET'S GET READY FOR SCHOOL, PLEASE.
I NEED TO GET TO WORK!
YOU WANNA FUCKING EAT NEXT WEEK, DIESEL?!
THEN GET YOUR BROTHER'S OLD SHOES ON AND LET'S FUCKING GO!
GODDAMMIT! I TOLD THOSE NOISY BUILDERS TO MOVE THEIR GODDAMN SHIT-BOX!
FUUUCK!!
RARRGH!
CALM DOWN, DADDY, IT'S OKAY.
SORRY, BOYS, SORRY... I JUST MISS YOUR MOTHER SO MUCH...
LOOK, DADDY...
YOU CAN ALMOST SEE THE MOUNTAIN TODAY.

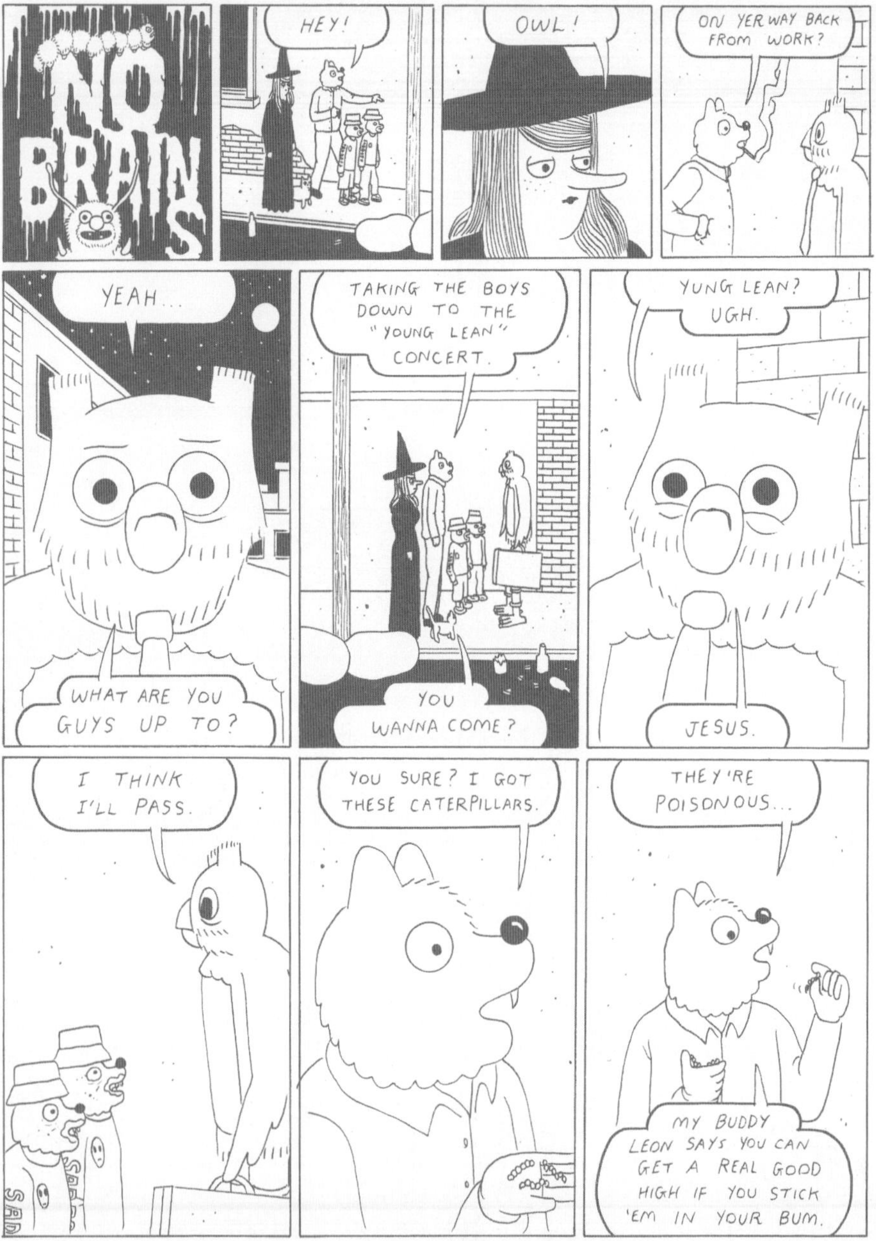
NO BRAINS
HEY!
OWL!
ON YER WAY BACK FROM WORK?
YEAH...
WHAT ARE YOU GUYS UP TO?
TAKING THE BOYS DOWN TO THE "YOUNG LEAN" CONCERT.
YOU WANNA COME?
YUNG LEAN? UGH.
JESUS.
I THINK I'LL PASS.
YOU SURE? I GOT THESE CATERPILLARS.
THEY'RE POISONOUS...
MY BUDDY LEON SAYS YOU CAN GET A REAL GOOD HIGH IF YOU STICK 'EM IN YOUR BUM.

...
YEAH, UH, I'LL SEE YOU GUYS AT HOME.
FINE.
MORE FOR ME.
GET 'EM IN THERE, BOYS!
♫ LEAN DOOOO-OOOOOER
SHOUTOUT THAIBOY DIGITAL
FUCK.
I GOTTA GET SOME AIR...
3 HOURS LATER:
WWJ!?
DADDY?!
WHERE THE FUCK DID HE GO?
OH...
DEPARTMENT OF JUSTICE
FEDERAL BUREAU OF INVESTIGATION
"WINNERS DON'T USE DRUGS"
WILLIAM S. SESSIONS
DIRECTOR, FBI.

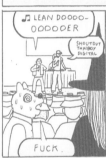

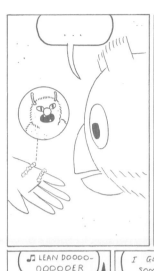

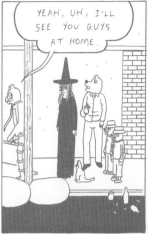

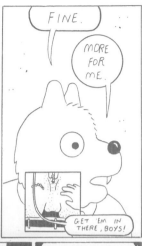

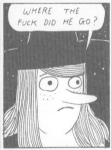

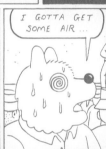

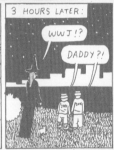

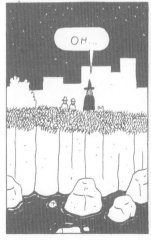

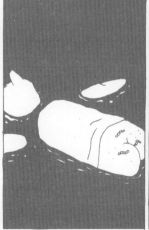

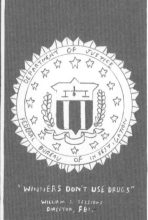

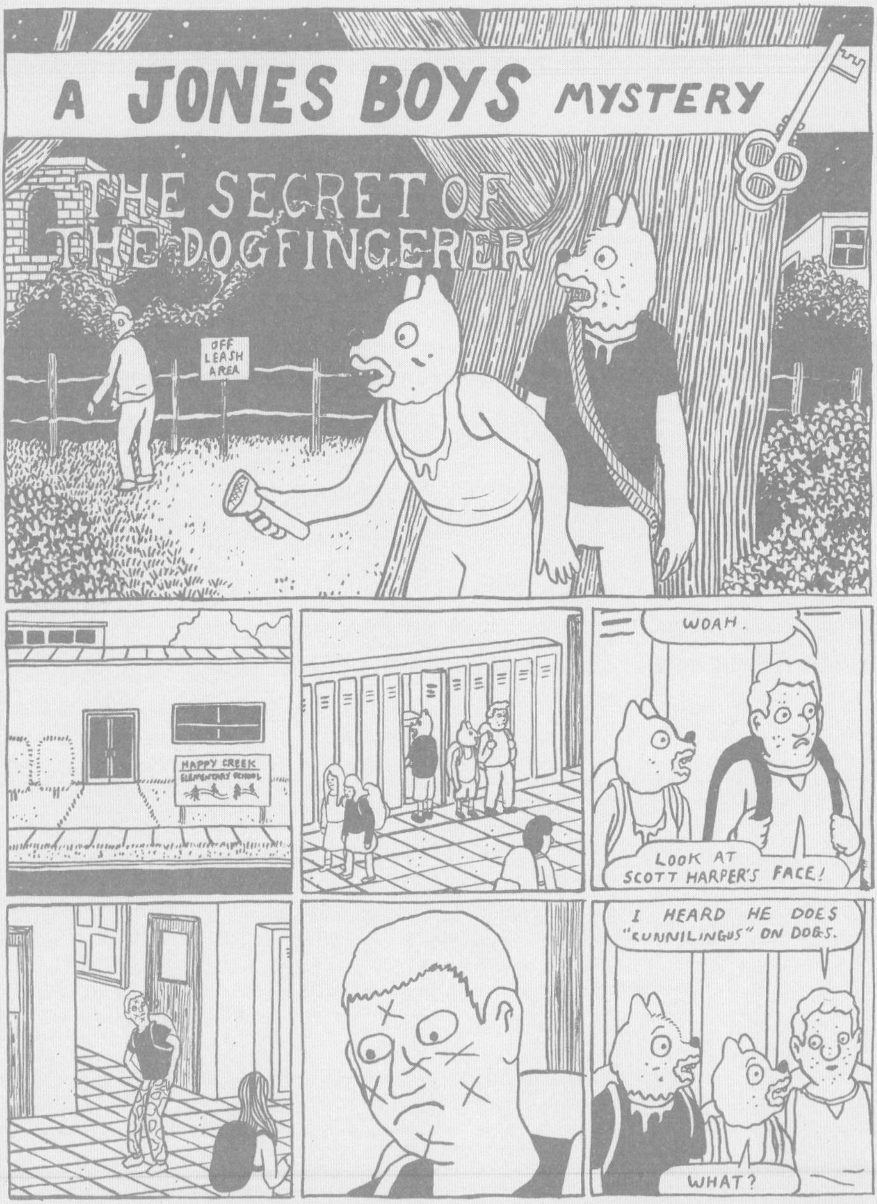
A JONES BOYS MYSTERY
THE SECRET OF THE DOGFINGERER
OFF LEASH AREA
HAPPY CREEK ELEMENTARY SCHOOL
WOAH.
LOOK AT SCOTT HARPER'S FACE!
I HEARD HE DOES "CUNNILINGUS" ON DOGS.
WHAT?

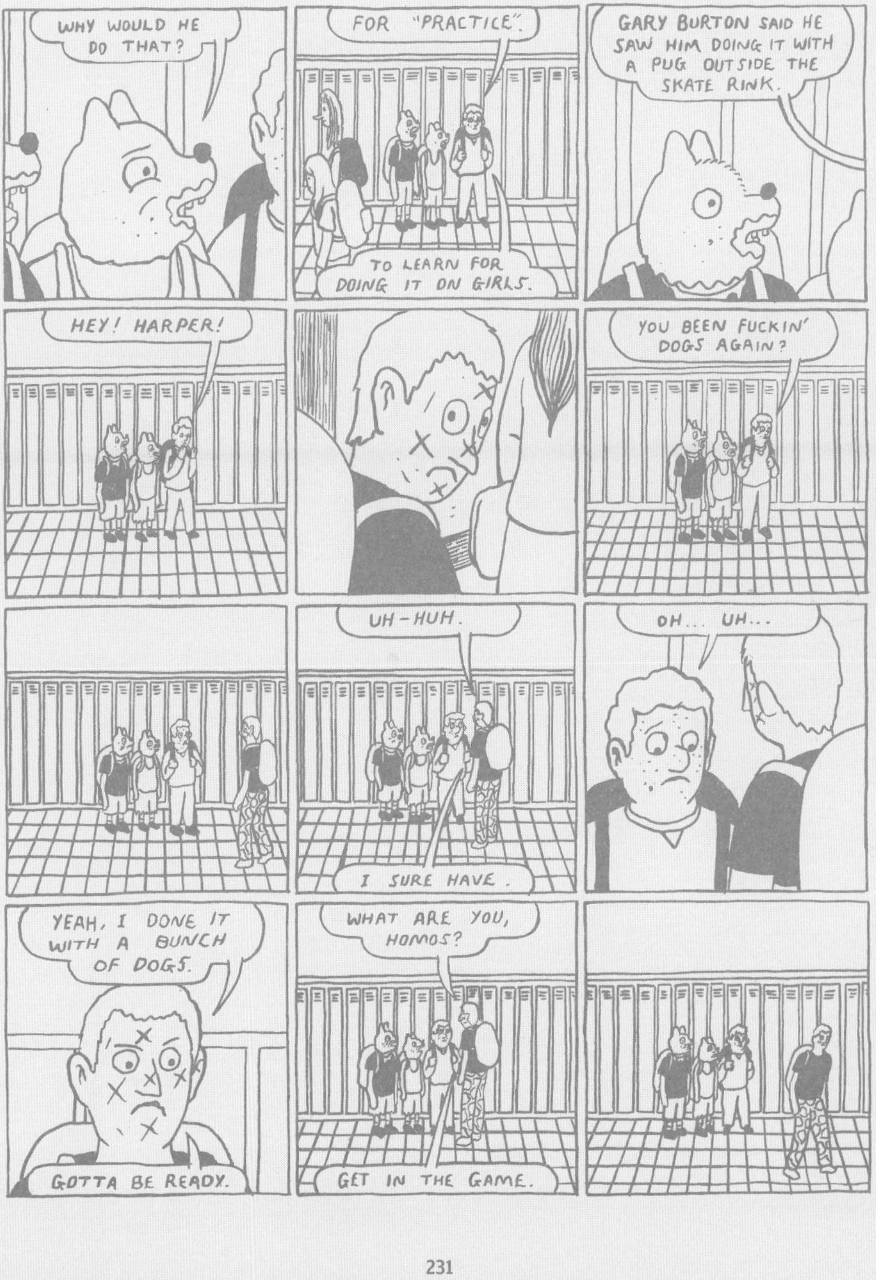
WHY WOULD HE DO THAT?
FOR "PRACTICE".
TO LEARN FOR DOING IT ON GIRLS.
GARY BURTON SAID HE SAW HIM DOING IT WITH A PUG OUTSIDE THE SKATE RINK.
HEY! HARPER!
YOU BEEN FUCKIN' DOGS AGAIN?
UH-HUH.
I SURE HAVE.
OH... UH...
YEAH, I DONE IT WITH A BUNCH OF DOGS.
GOTTA BE READY.
WHAT ARE YOU, HOMOS?
GET IN THE GAME.

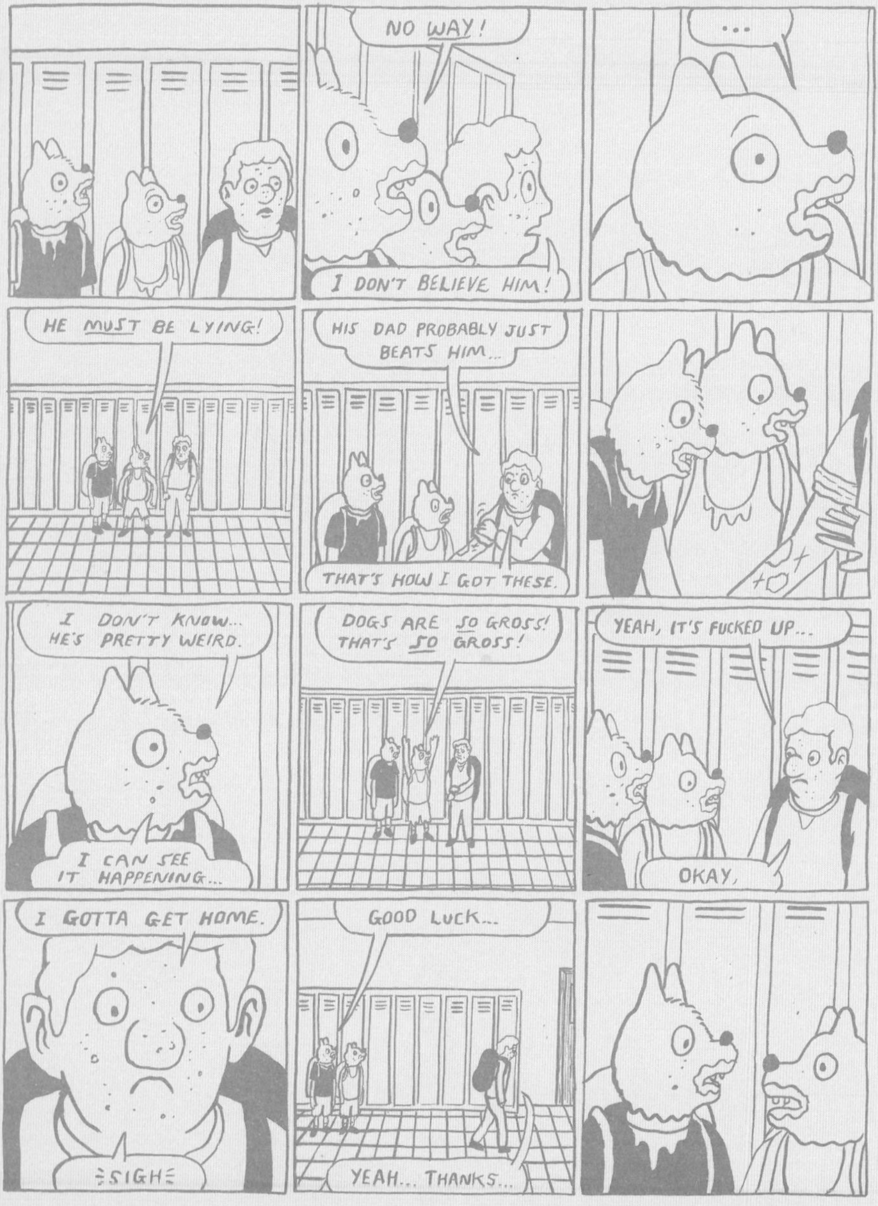
NO WAY!
I DON'T BELIEVE HIM!
...
HE MUST BE LYING!
HIS DAD PROBABLY JUST BEATS HIM...
THAT'S HOW I GOT THESE.
I DON'T KNOW... HE'S PRETTY WEIRD.
I CAN SEE IT HAPPENING...
DOGS ARE SO GROSS! THAT'S SO GROSS!
YEAH, IT'S FUCKED UP...
OKAY.
I GOTTA GET HOME.
SIGH
GOOD LUCK...
YEAH... THANKS...

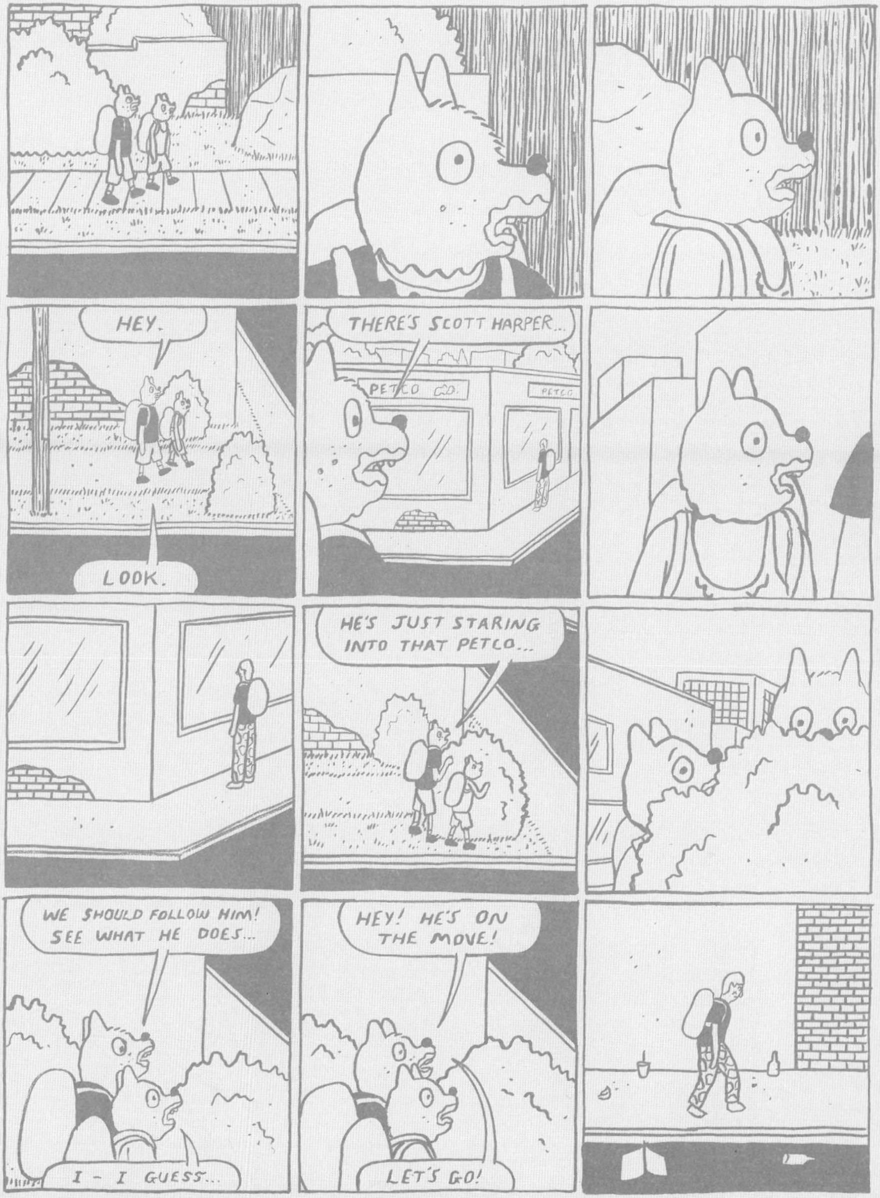
HEY.
LOOK.
THERE'S SCOTT HARPER...
PETCO
PETCO
HE'S JUST STARING INTO THAT PETCO...
WE SHOULD FOLLOW HIM! SEE WHAT HE DOES...
I - I GUESS...
HEY! HE'S ON THE MOVE!
LET'S GO!

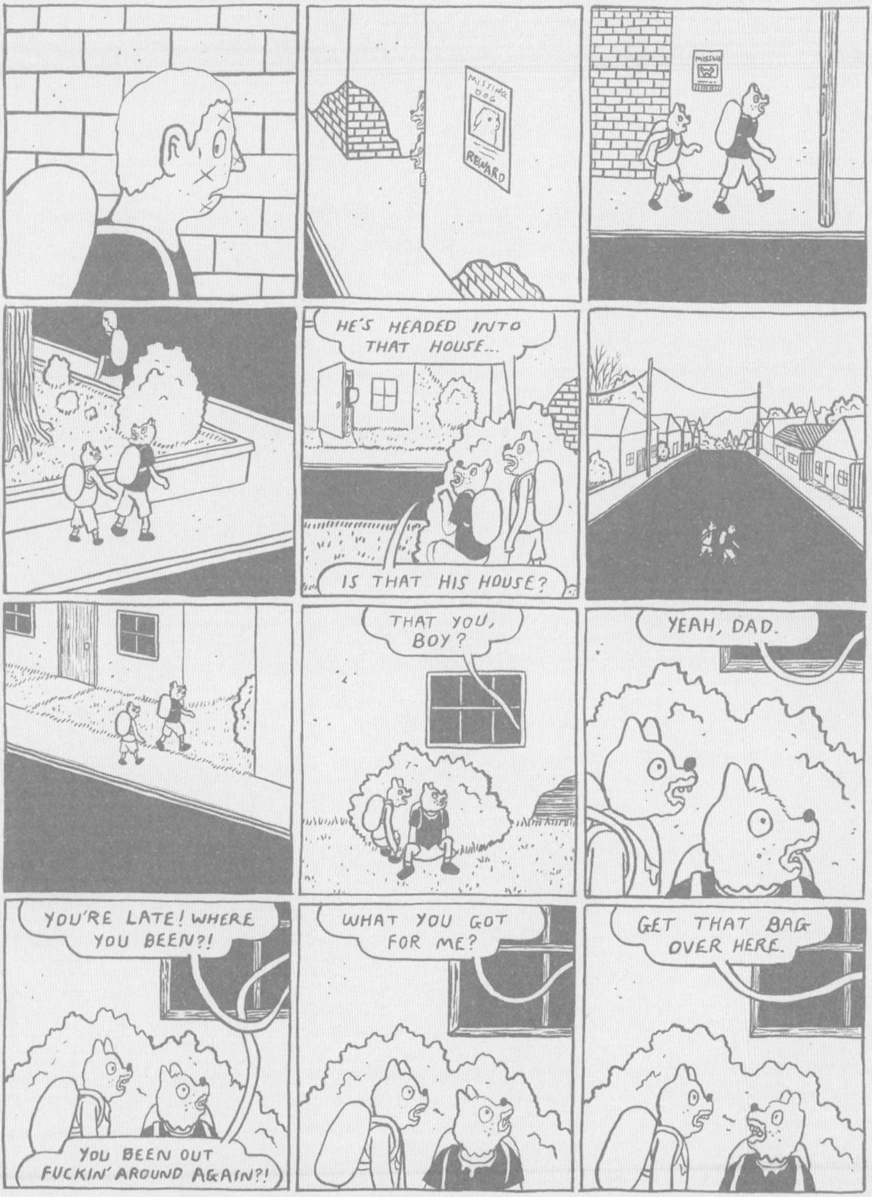
MISSING DOG
REWARD
MISSING
HE'S HEADED INTO THAT HOUSE...
IS THAT HIS HOUSE?
THAT YOU, BOY?
YEAH, DAD.
YOU'RE LATE! WHERE YOU BEEN?!
YOU BEEN OUT FUCKIN' AROUND AGAIN?!
WHAT YOU GOT FOR ME?
GET THAT BAG OVER HERE.

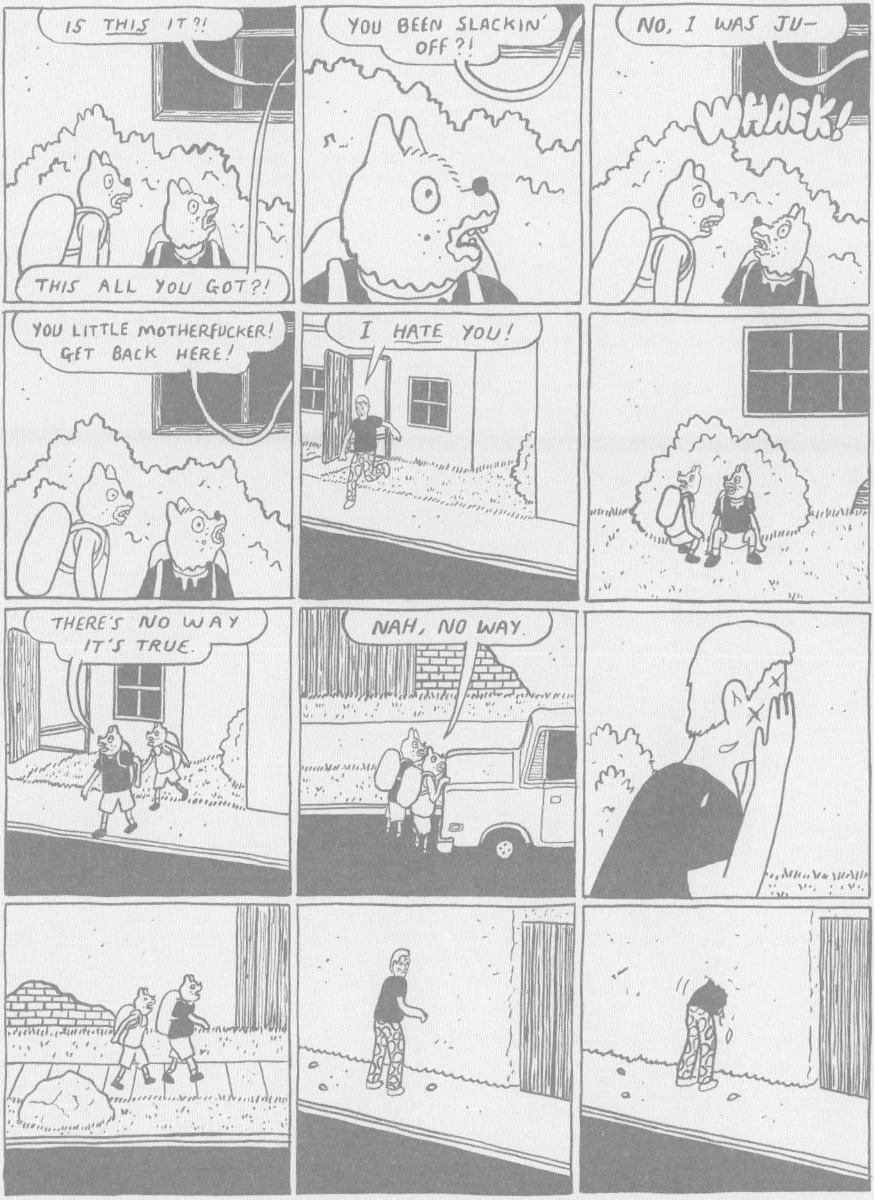
IS THIS IT?!
THIS ALL YOU GOT?!
YOU BEEN SLACKIN' OFF?!
NO, I WAS JU—
WHACK!
YOU LITTLE MOTHERFUCKER! GET BACK HERE!
I HATE YOU!
THERE'S NO WAY IT'S TRUE.
NAH, NO WAY.

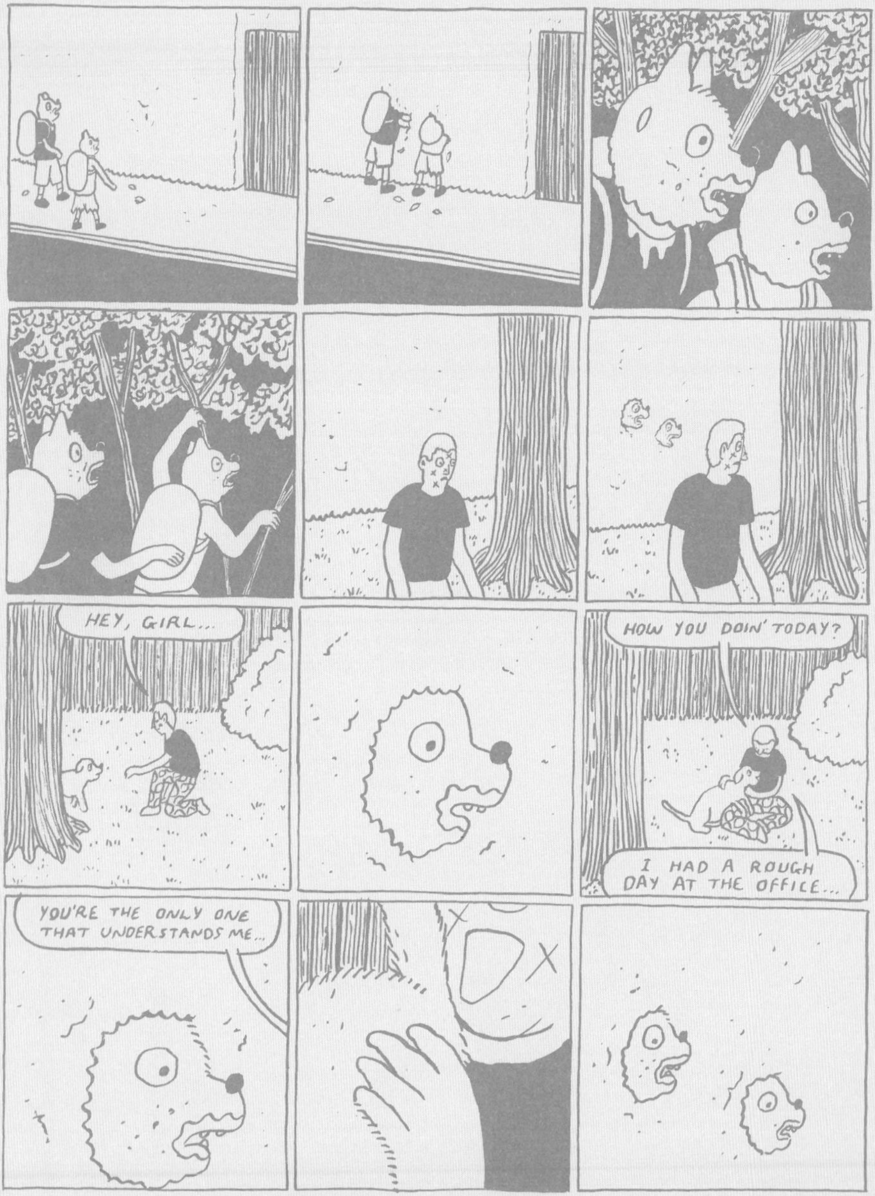
HEY, GIRL...
HOW YOU DOIN' TODAY?
I HAD A ROUGH DAY AT THE OFFICE...
YOU'RE THE ONLY ONE THAT UNDERSTANDS ME...

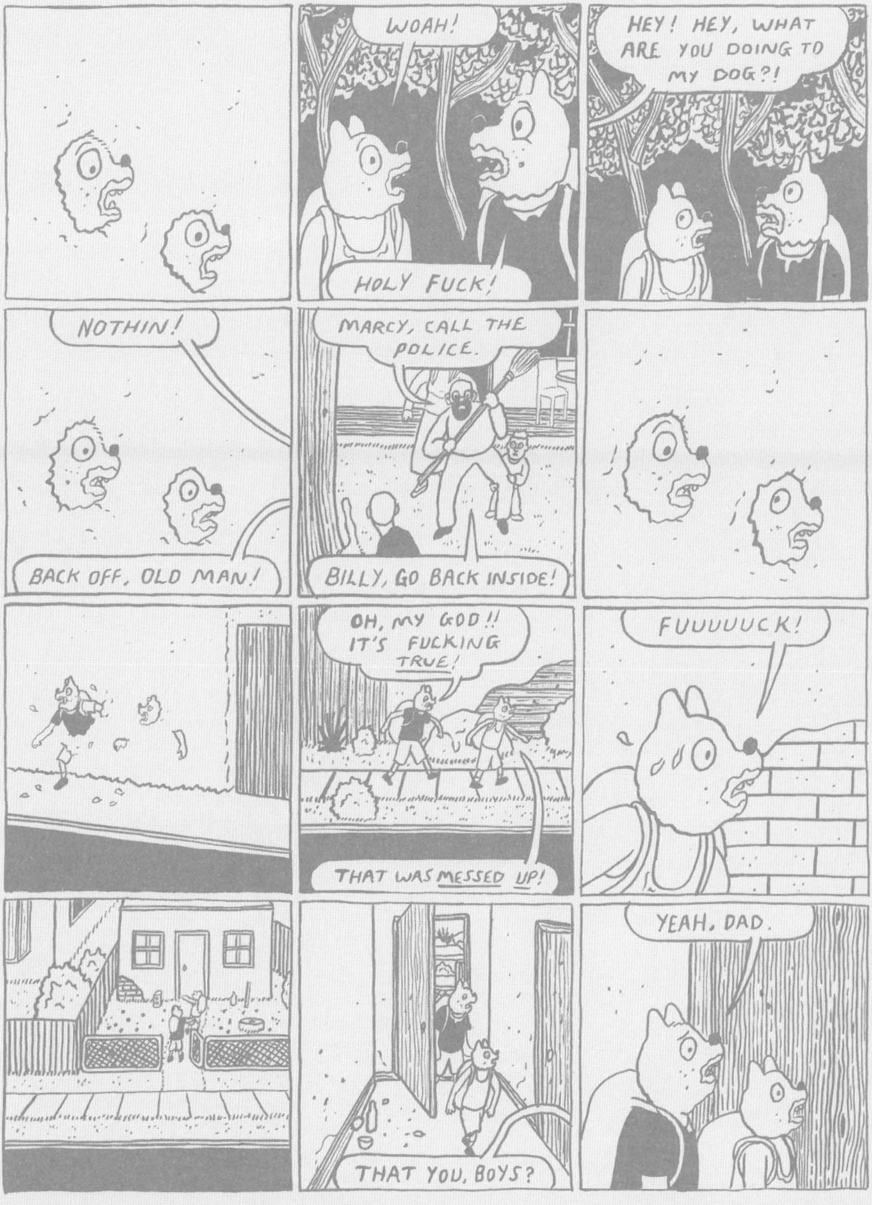
WOAH!
HOLY FUCK!
HEY! HEY, WHAT ARE YOU DOING TO MY DOG?!
NOTHIN!
BACK OFF, OLD MAN!
MARCY, CALL THE POLICE.
BILLY, GO BACK INSIDE!
OH, MY GOD!! IT'S FUCKING TRUE!
THAT WAS MESSED UP!
FUUUUUCK!
THAT YOU, BOYS?
YEAH, DAD.

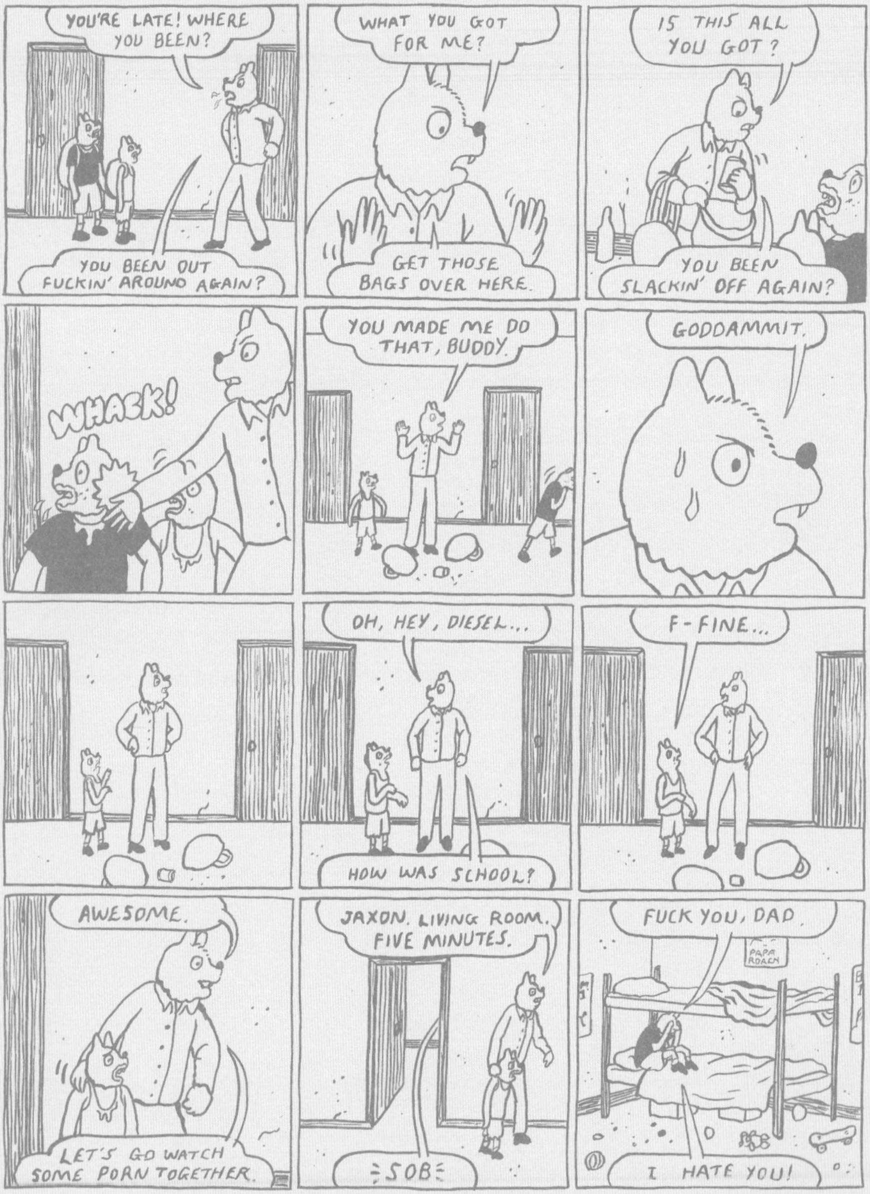
YOU'RE LATE! WHERE YOU BEEN?
YOU BEEN OUT FUCKIN' AROUND AGAIN?
WHAT YOU GOT FOR ME?
GET THOSE BAGS OVER HERE.
IS THIS ALL YOU GOT?
YOU BEEN SLACKIN' OFF AGAIN?
WHACK!
YOU MADE ME DO THAT, BUDDY.
GODDAMMIT.
OH, HEY, DIESEL...
HOW WAS SCHOOL?
F-FINE...
AWESOME.
LET'S GO WATCH SOME PORN TOGETHER.
JAXON. LIVING ROOM. FIVE MINUTES.
SOB
FUCK YOU, DAD.
PAPA ROACH
I HATE YOU!

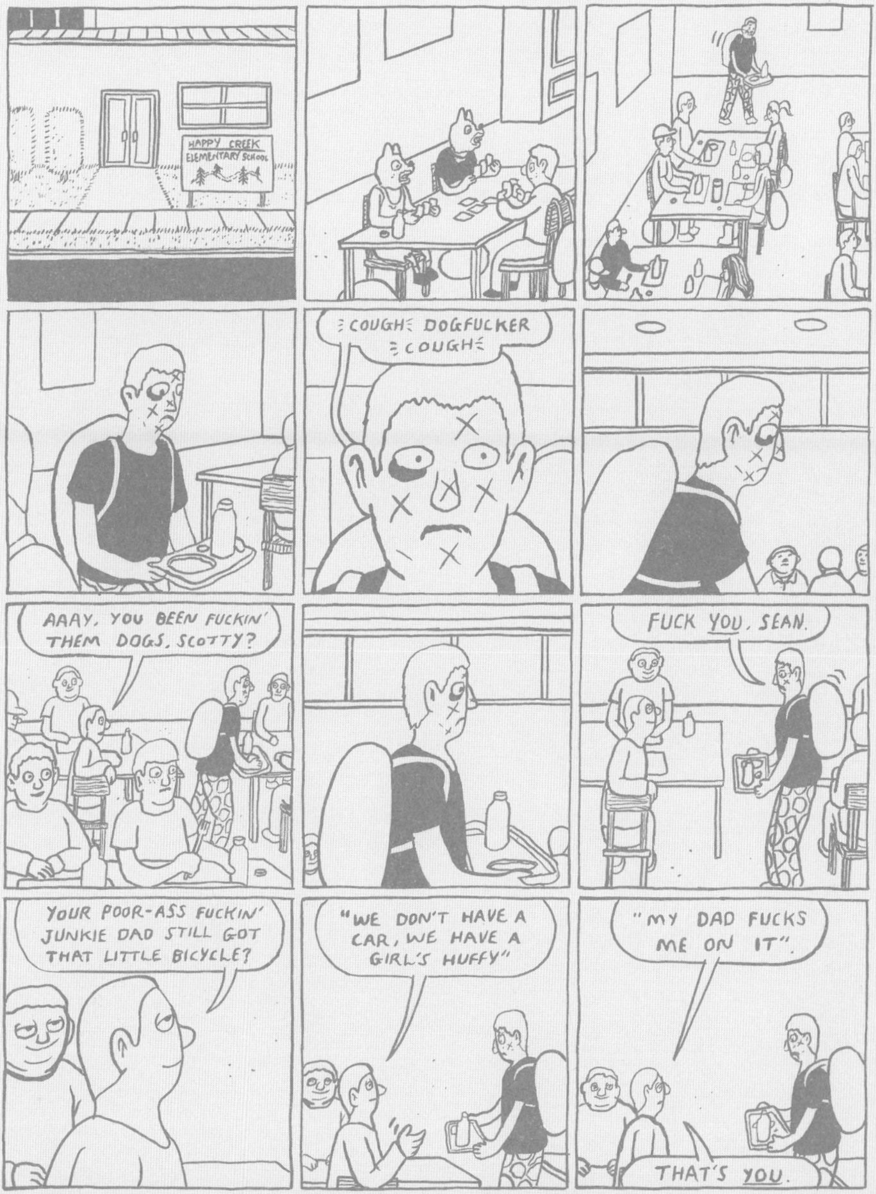
HAPPY CREEK ELEMENTARY SCHOOL
COUGH DOGFUCKER COUGH
AAAY, YOU BEEN FUCKIN' THEM DOGS, SCOTTY?
FUCK YOU, SEAN.
YOUR POOR-ASS FUCKIN' JUNKIE DAD STILL GOT THAT LITTLE BICYCLE?
"WE DON'T HAVE A CAR, WE HAVE A GIRL'S HUFFY"
"MY DAD FUCKS ME ON IT".
THAT'S YOU.

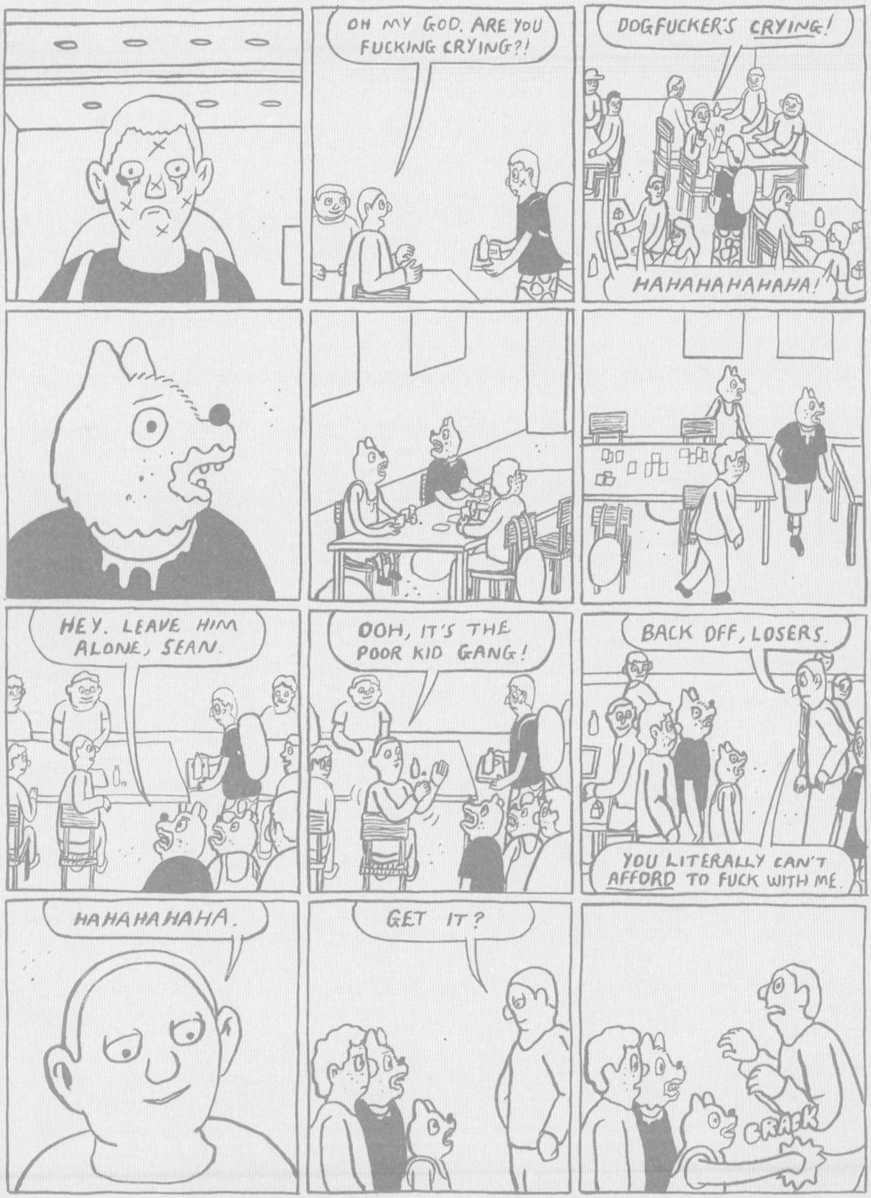

OH MY GOD. ARE YOU FUCKING CRYING?!
DOGFUCKER'S CRYING!
HAHAHAHAHAHA!
HEY. LEAVE HIM ALONE, SEAN.
OOH, IT'S THE POOR KID GANG!
BACK OFF, LOSERS.
YOU LITERALLY CAN'T AFFORD TO FUCK WITH ME.
HAHAHAHAHA.
GET IT?
CRACK

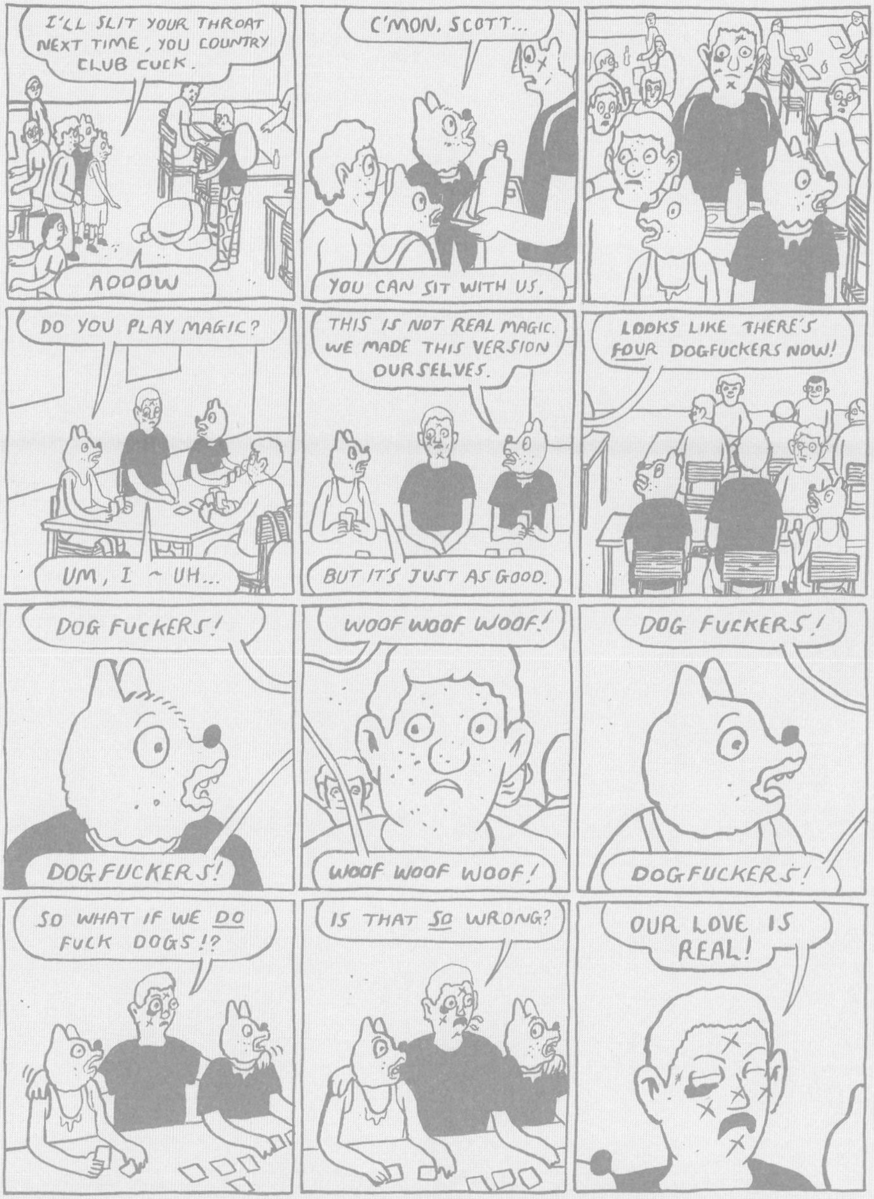
I'LL SLIT YOUR THROAT NEXT TIME, YOU COUNTRY CLUB CUCK.
AOOOW
C'MON, SCOTT...
YOU CAN SIT WITH US.
DO YOU PLAY MAGIC?
UM, I ~ UH...
THIS IS NOT REAL MAGIC. WE MADE THIS VERSION OURSELVES.
BUT IT'S JUST AS GOOD.
LOOKS LIKE THERE'S FOUR DOGFUCKERS NOW!
DOG FUCKERS!
DOGFUCKERS!
WOOF WOOF WOOF!
WOOF WOOF WOOF!
DOG FUCKERS!
DOGFUCKERS!
SO WHAT IF WE DO FUCK DOGS!?
IS THAT SO WRONG?
OUR LOVE IS REAL!

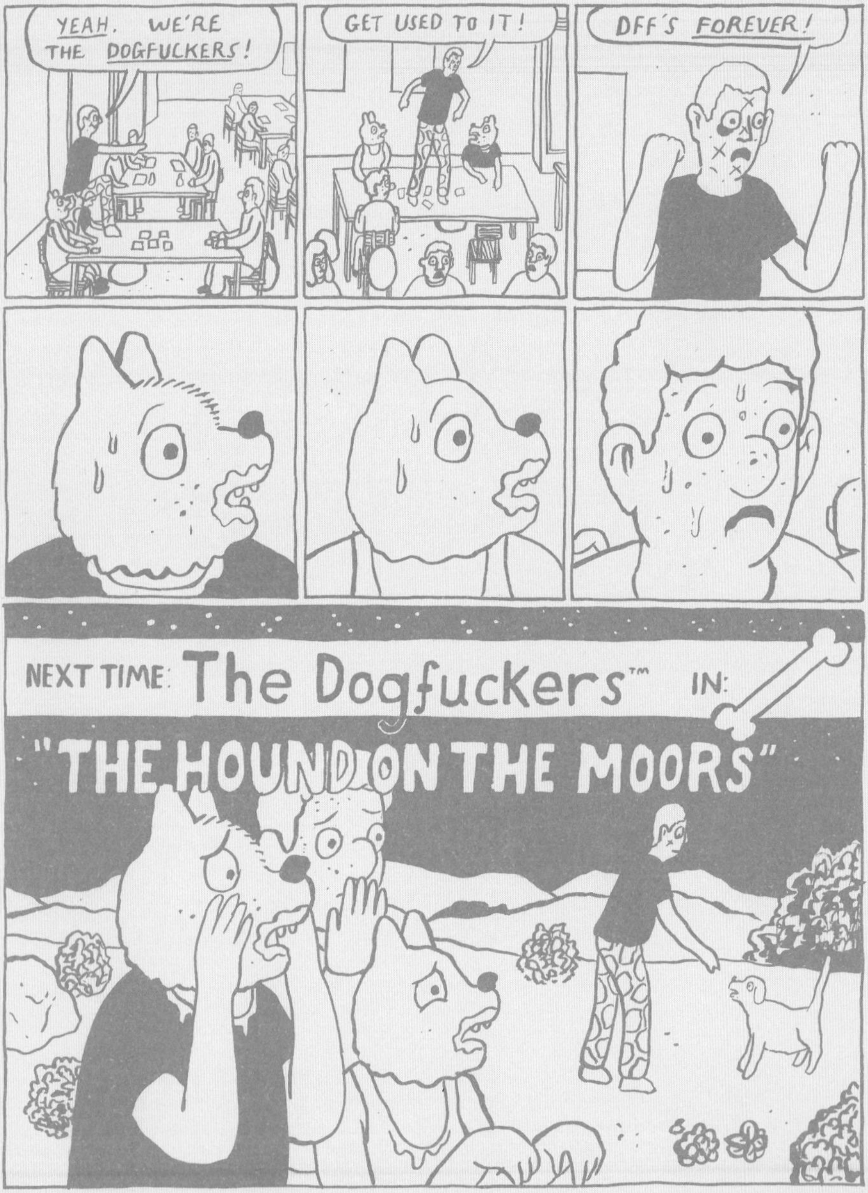
YEAH. WE'RE THE DOGFUCKERS!
GET USED TO IT!
DFF'S FOREVER!
NEXT TIME: The Dogfuckers™ IN:
"THE HOUND ON THE MOORS"

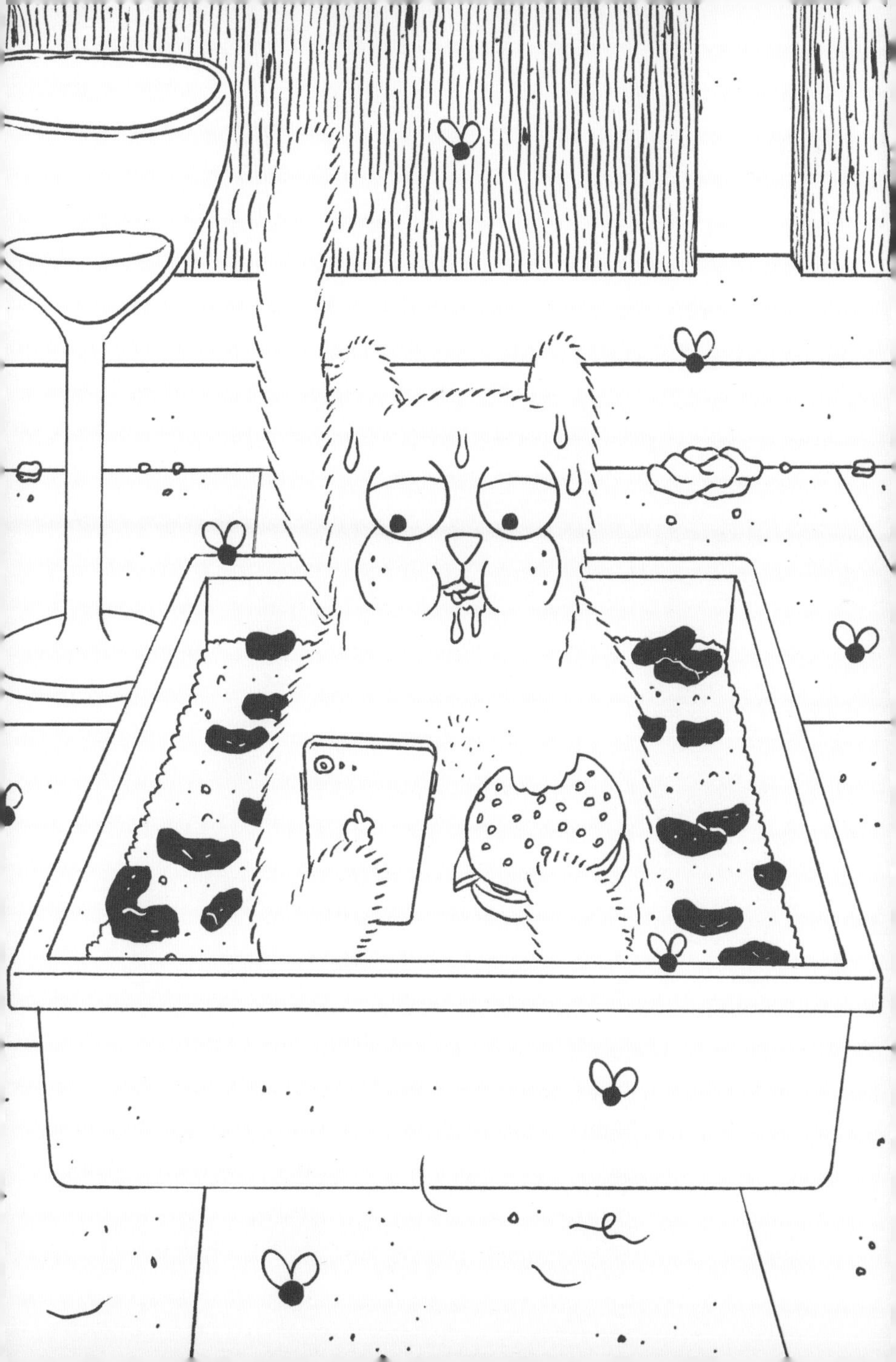

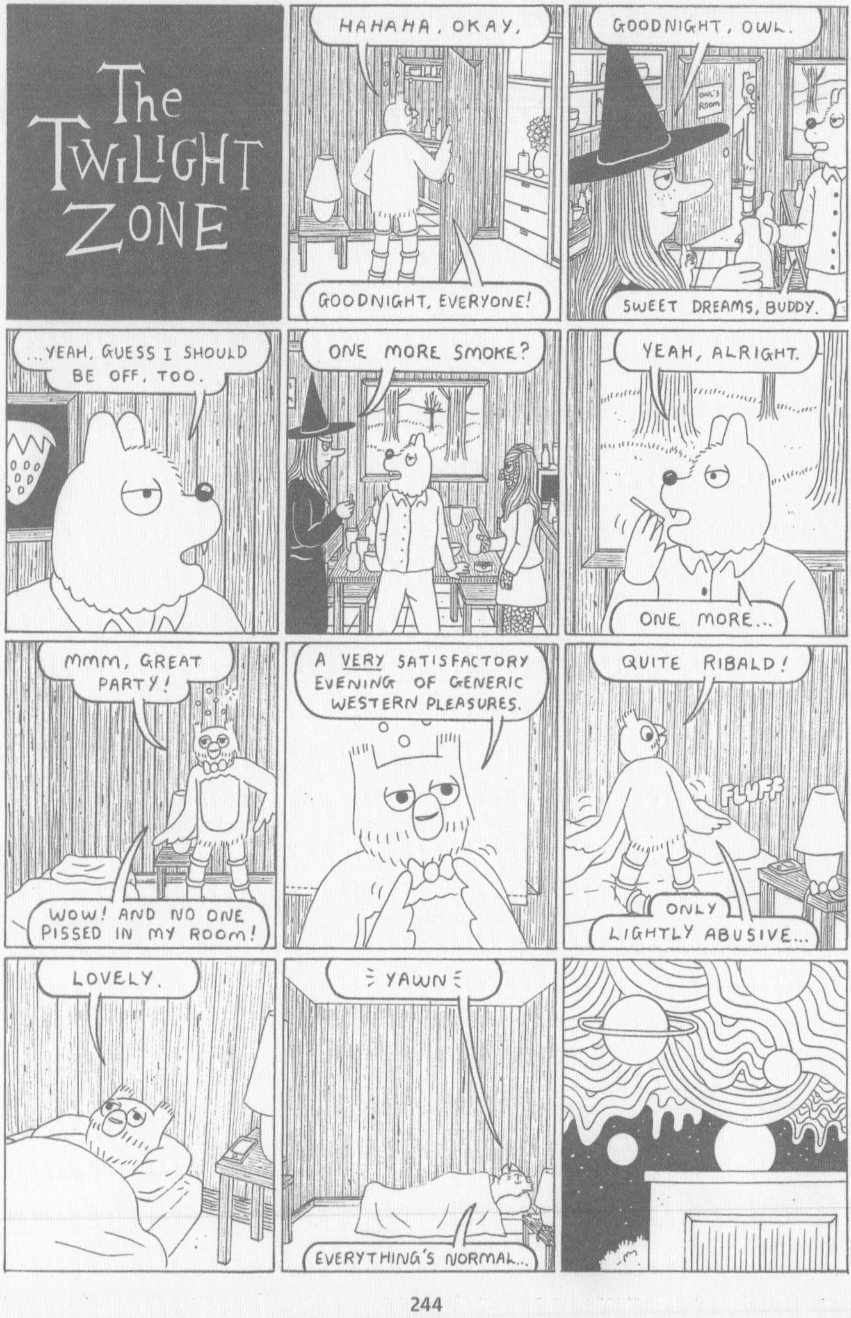
The Twilight Zone
HAHAHA, OKAY,
GOODNIGHT, EVERYONE!
GOODNIGHT, OWL.
OWL'S ROOM
SWEET DREAMS, BUDDY.
...YEAH, GUESS I SHOULD BE OFF, TOO.
ONE MORE SMOKE?
YEAH, ALRIGHT.
ONE MORE...
MMM, GREAT PARTY!
WOW! AND NO ONE PISSED IN MY ROOM!
A VERY SATISFACTORY EVENING OF GENERIC WESTERN PLEASURES.
QUITE RIBALD!
FLUFF
ONLY LIGHTLY ABUSIVE...
LOVELY.
YAWN
EVERYTHING'S NORMAL...

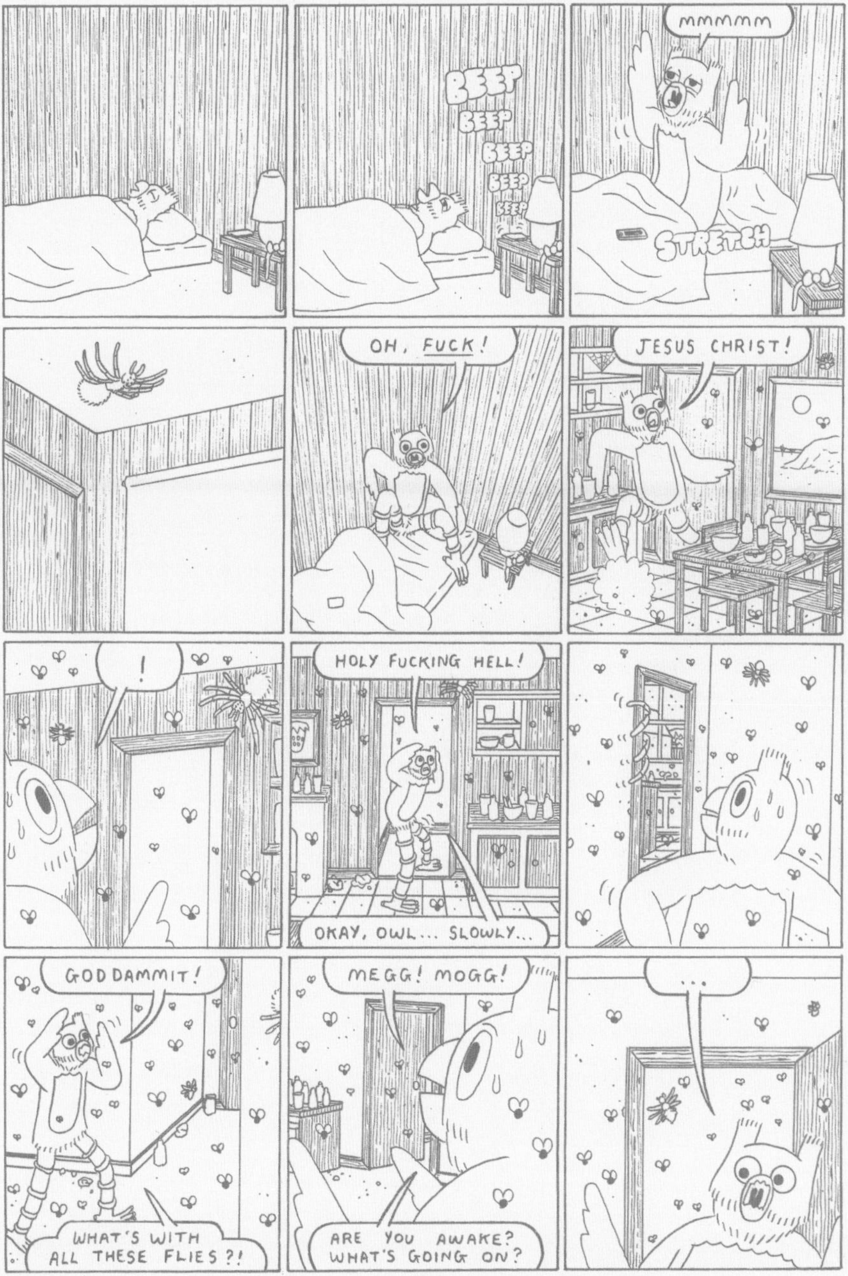
BEEP
BEEP
BEEP
BEEP
BEEP
MMMMM
STRETCH
OH, FUCK!
JESUS CHRIST!
!
HOLY FUCKING HELL!
OKAY, OWL... SLOWLY...
GODDAMMIT!
WHAT'S WITH ALL THESE FLIES?!
MEGG! MOGG!
ARE YOU AWAKE? WHAT'S GOING ON?
...

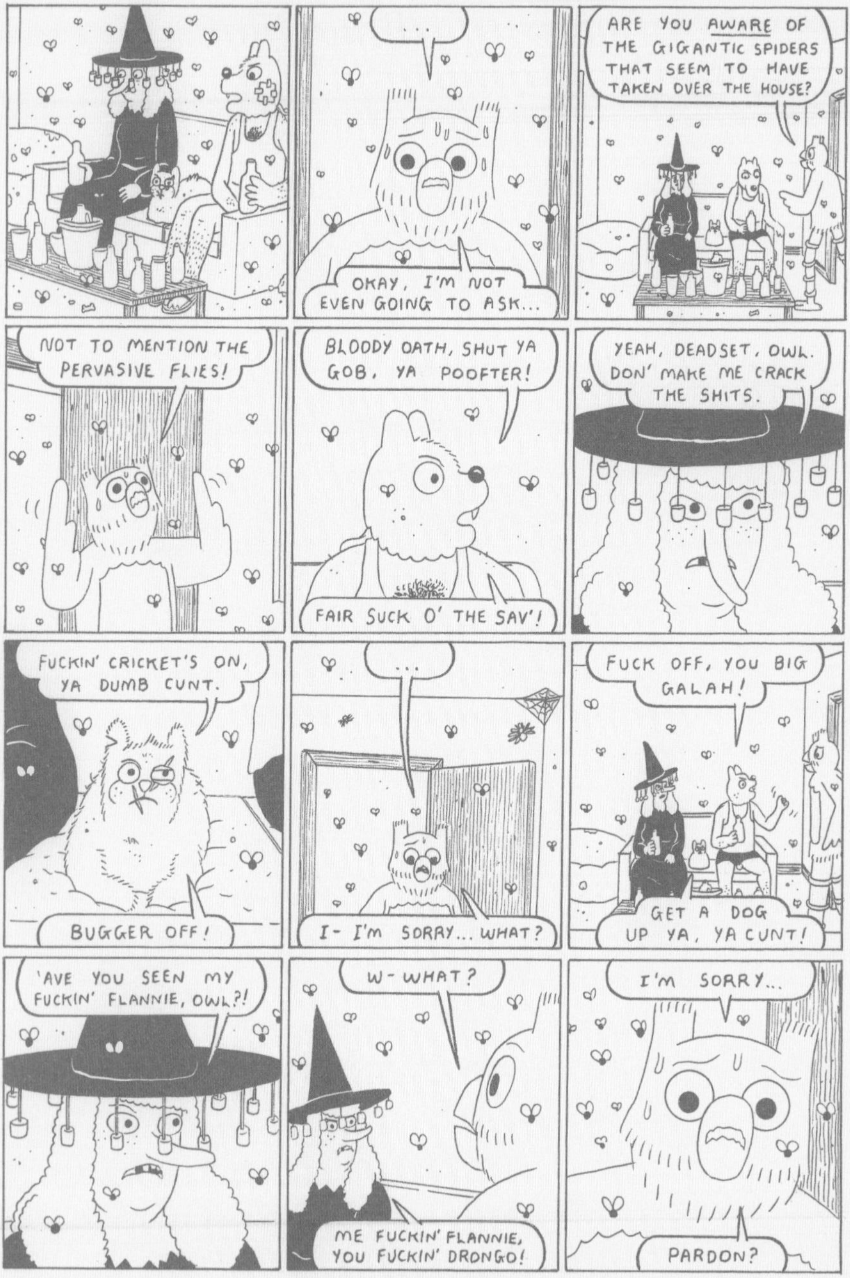

...
OKAY, I'M NOT EVEN GOING TO ASK...
ARE YOU AWARE OF THE GIGANTIC SPIDERS THAT SEEM TO HAVE TAKEN OVER THE HOUSE?
NOT TO MENTION THE PERVASIVE FLIES!
BLOODY OATH, SHUT YA GOB, YA POOFTER!
FAIR SUCK O' THE SAV'!
YEAH, DEADSET, OWL. DON' MAKE ME CRACK THE SHITS.
FUCKIN' CRICKET'S ON, YA DUMB CUNT.
BUGGER OFF!
...
I- I'M SORRY... WHAT?
FUCK OFF, YOU BIG GALAH!
GET A DOG UP YA, YA CUNT!
'AVE YOU SEEN MY FUCKIN' FLANNIE, OWL?!
W-WHAT?
ME FUCKIN' FLANNIE, YOU FUCKIN' DRONGO!
I'M SORRY...
PARDON?

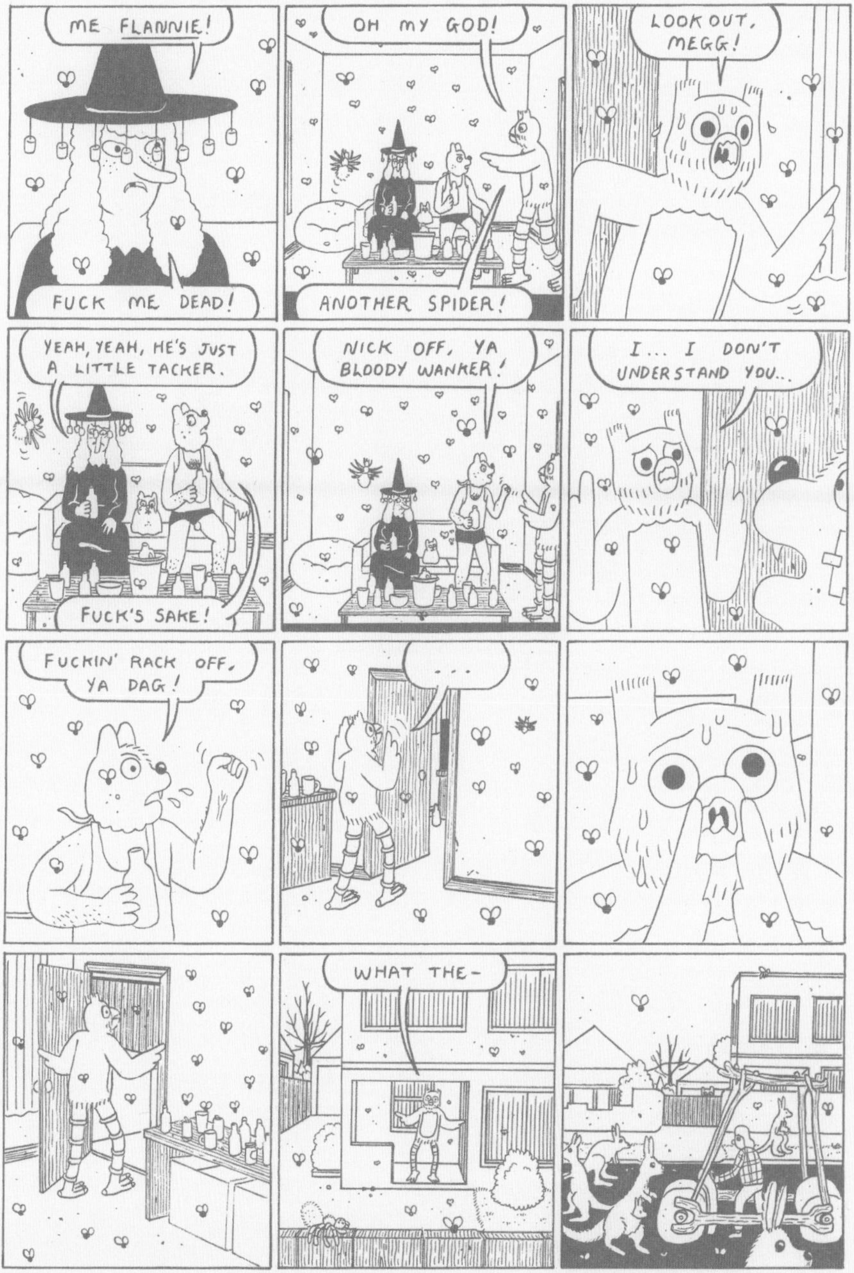
ME FLANNIE!
FUCK ME DEAD!
OH MY GOD!
ANOTHER SPIDER!
LOOK OUT, MEGG!
YEAH, YEAH, HE'S JUST A LITTLE TACKER.
FUCK'S SAKE!
NICK OFF, YA BLOODY WANKER!
I... I DON'T UNDERSTAND YOU...
FUCKIN' RACK OFF, YA DAG!
...
WHAT THE-

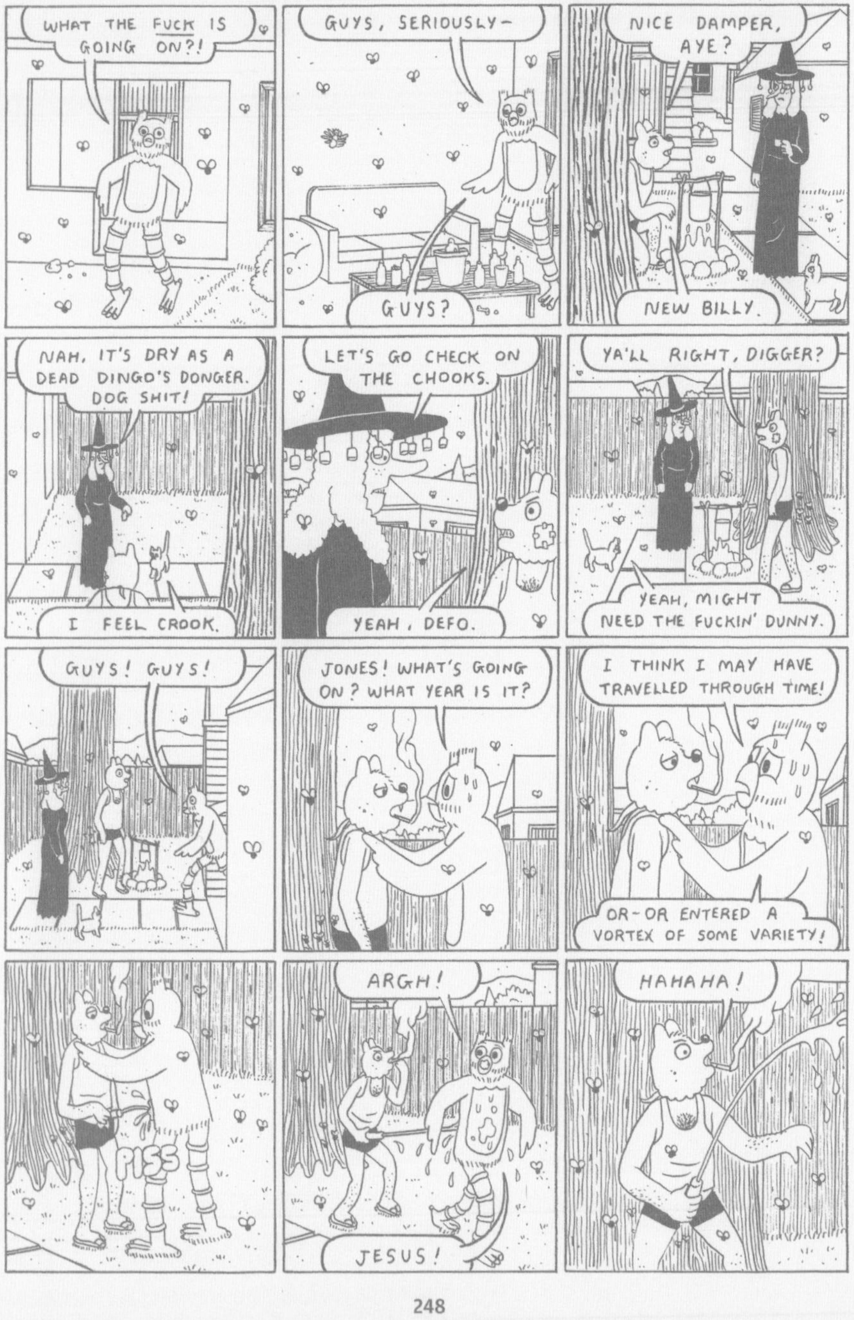
WHAT THE FUCK IS GOING ON?!
GUYS, SERIOUSLY-
GUYS?
NICE DAMPER, AYE?
NEW BILLY.
NAH, IT'S DRY AS A DEAD DINGO'S DONGER. DOG SHIT!
I FEEL CROOK.
LET'S GO CHECK ON THE CHOOKS.
YEAH, DEFO.
YA'LL RIGHT, DIGGER?
YEAH, MIGHT NEED THE FUCKIN' DUNNY.
GUYS! GUYS!
JONES! WHAT'S GOING ON? WHAT YEAR IS IT?
I THINK I MAY HAVE TRAVELLED THROUGH TIME!
OR-OR ENTERED A VORTEX OF SOME VARIETY!
PISS
ARGH!
JESUS!
HAHAHA!

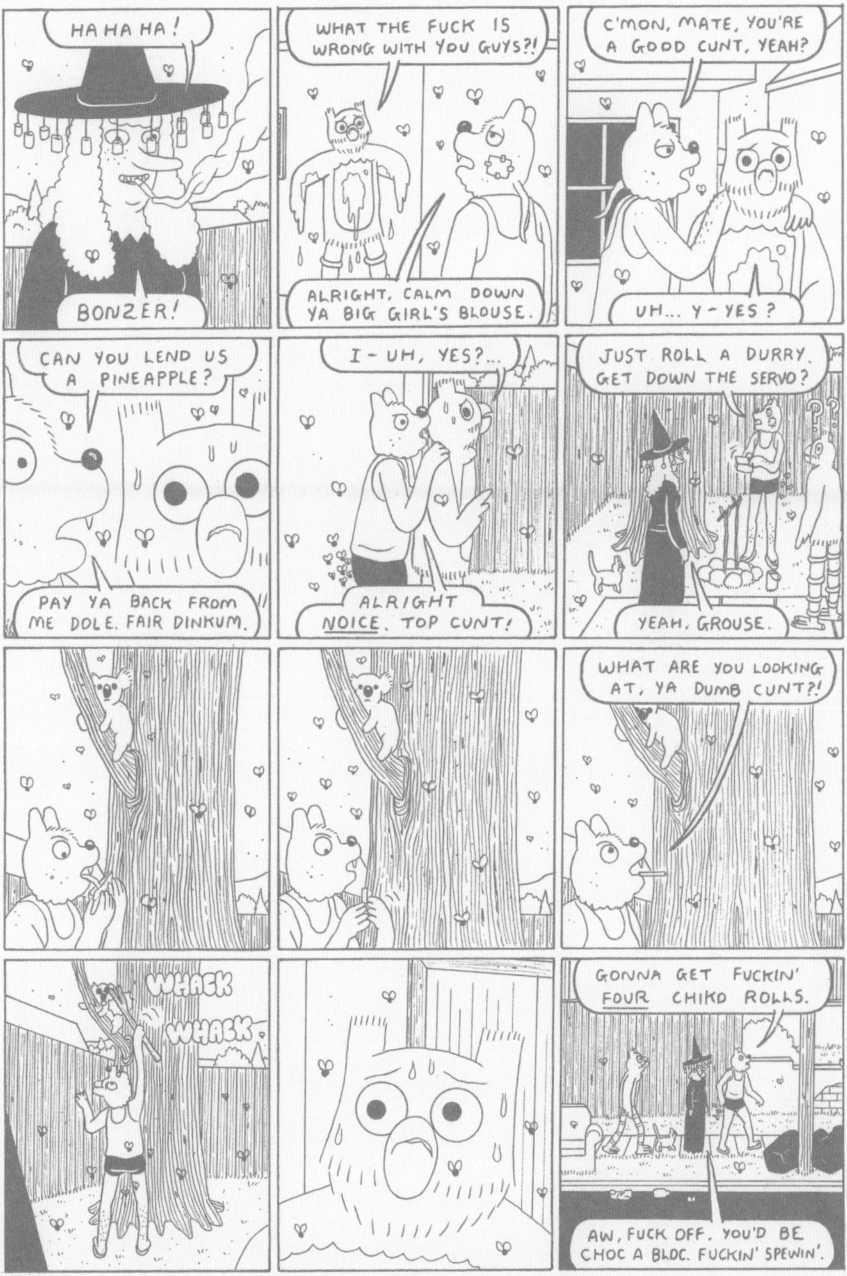
HA HA HA!
BONZER!
WHAT THE FUCK IS WRONG WITH YOU GUYS?!
ALRIGHT, CALM DOWN YA BIG GIRL'S BLOUSE.
C'MON, MATE, YOU'RE A GOOD CUNT, YEAH?
UH... Y-YES?
CAN YOU LEND US A PINEAPPLE?
PAY YA BACK FROM ME DOLE. FAIR DINKUM.
I-UH, YES?...
ALRIGHT NOICE. TOP CUNT!
JUST ROLL A DURRY. GET DOWN THE SERVO?
YEAH, GROUSE.
WHAT ARE YOU LOOKING AT, YA DUMB CUNT?!
WHACK
WHACK
GONNA GET FUCKIN' FOUR CHIKO ROLLS.
AW, FUCK OFF. YOU'D BE CHOC A BLOC. FUCKIN' SPEWIN'.

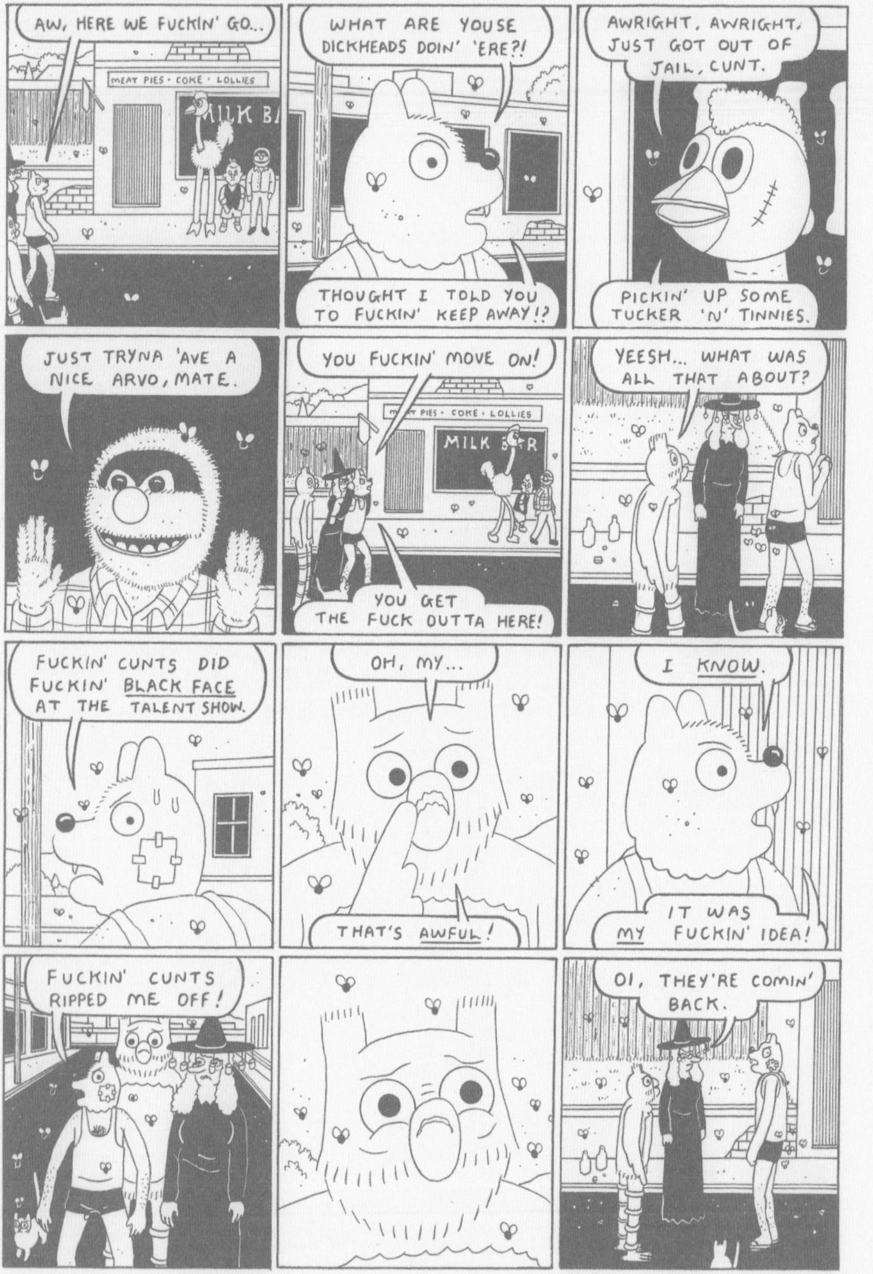

AW, HERE WE FUCKIN' GO...
MEAT PIES • COKE • LOLLIES
MILK BA
WHAT ARE YOUSE DICKHEADS DOIN' 'ERE?!
THOUGHT I TOLD YOU TO FUCKIN' KEEP AWAY!?
AWRIGHT, AWRIGHT. JUST GOT OUT OF JAIL, CUNT.
PICKIN' UP SOME TUCKER 'N' TINNIES.
JUST TRYNA 'AVE A NICE ARVO, MATE.
YOU FUCKIN' MOVE ON!
YOU GET THE FUCK OUTTA HERE!
YEESH... WHAT WAS ALL THAT ABOUT?
FUCKIN' CUNTS DID FUCKIN' BLACK FACE AT THE TALENT SHOW.
OH, MY...
THAT'S AWFUL!
I KNOW.
IT WAS MY FUCKIN' IDEA!
FUCKIN' CUNTS RIPPED ME OFF!
OI, THEY'RE COMIN' BACK.

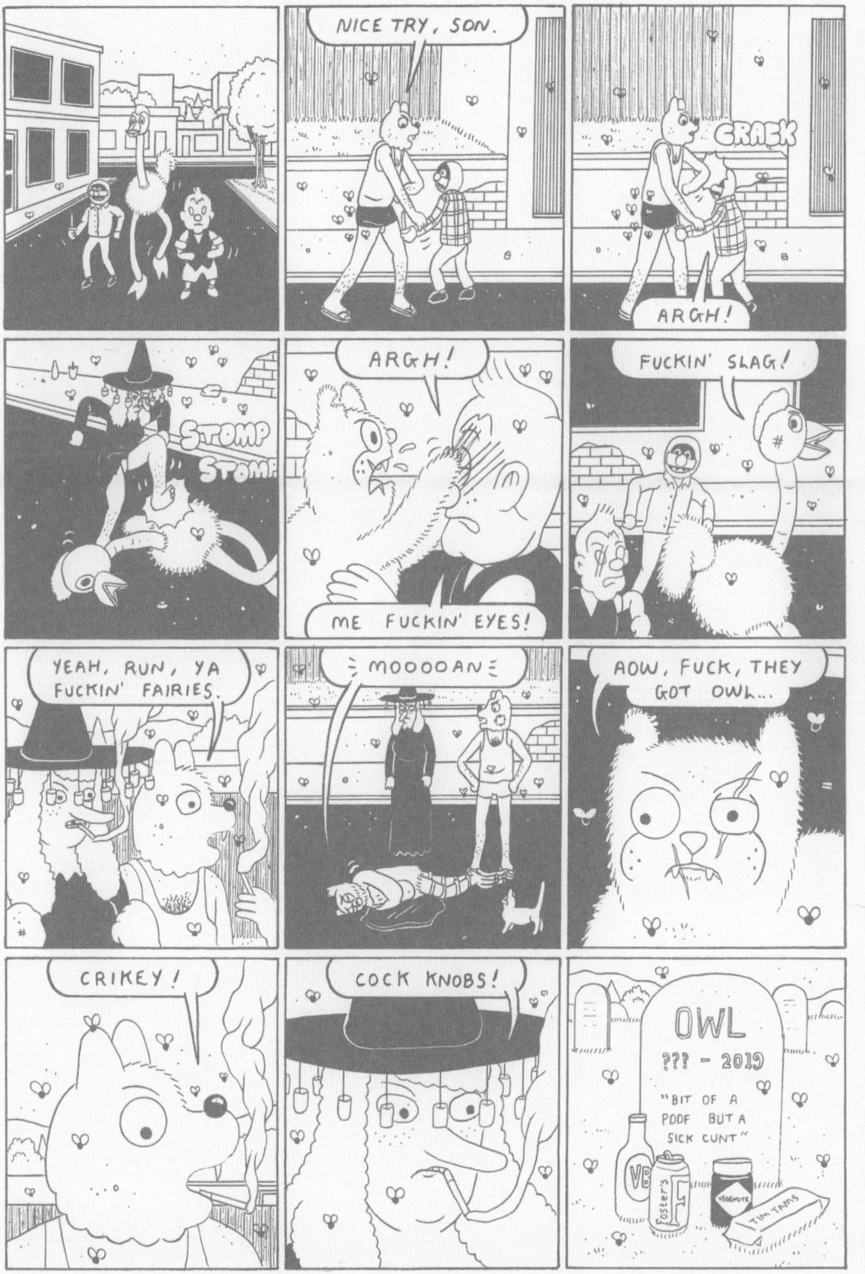
NICE TRY, SON.
CRACK
ARGH!
STOMP
STOMP
ARGH!
ME FUCKIN' EYES!
FUCKIN' SLAG!
YEAH, RUN, YA FUCKIN' FAIRIES.
MOOOOAN
AOW, FUCK, THEY GOT OWL...
CRIKEY!
COCK KNOBS!
OWL
??? - 2019
"BIT OF A PODF BUT A SICK CUNT"
VB
Foster's
VEGEMITE
TIM TAMS

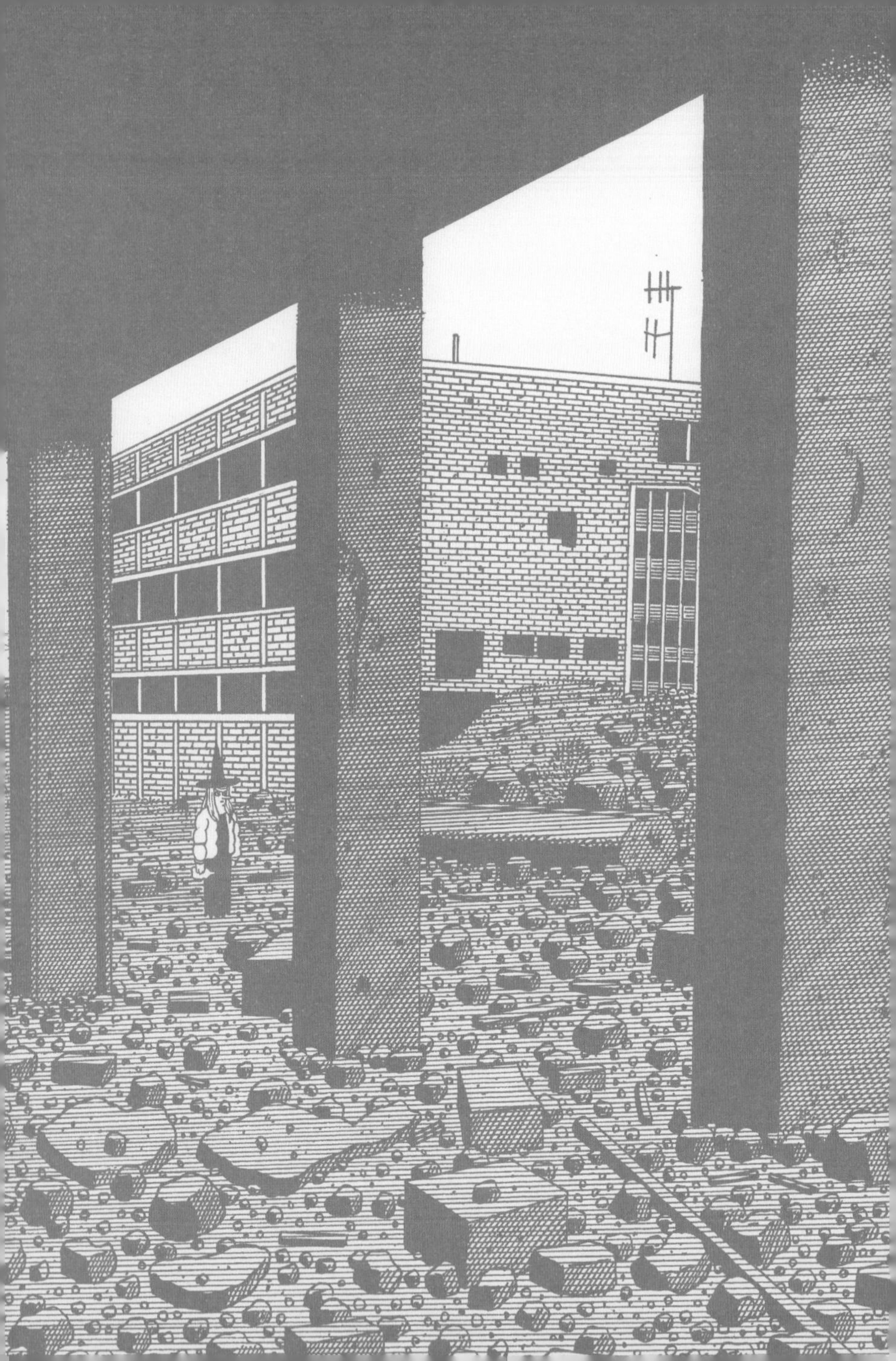

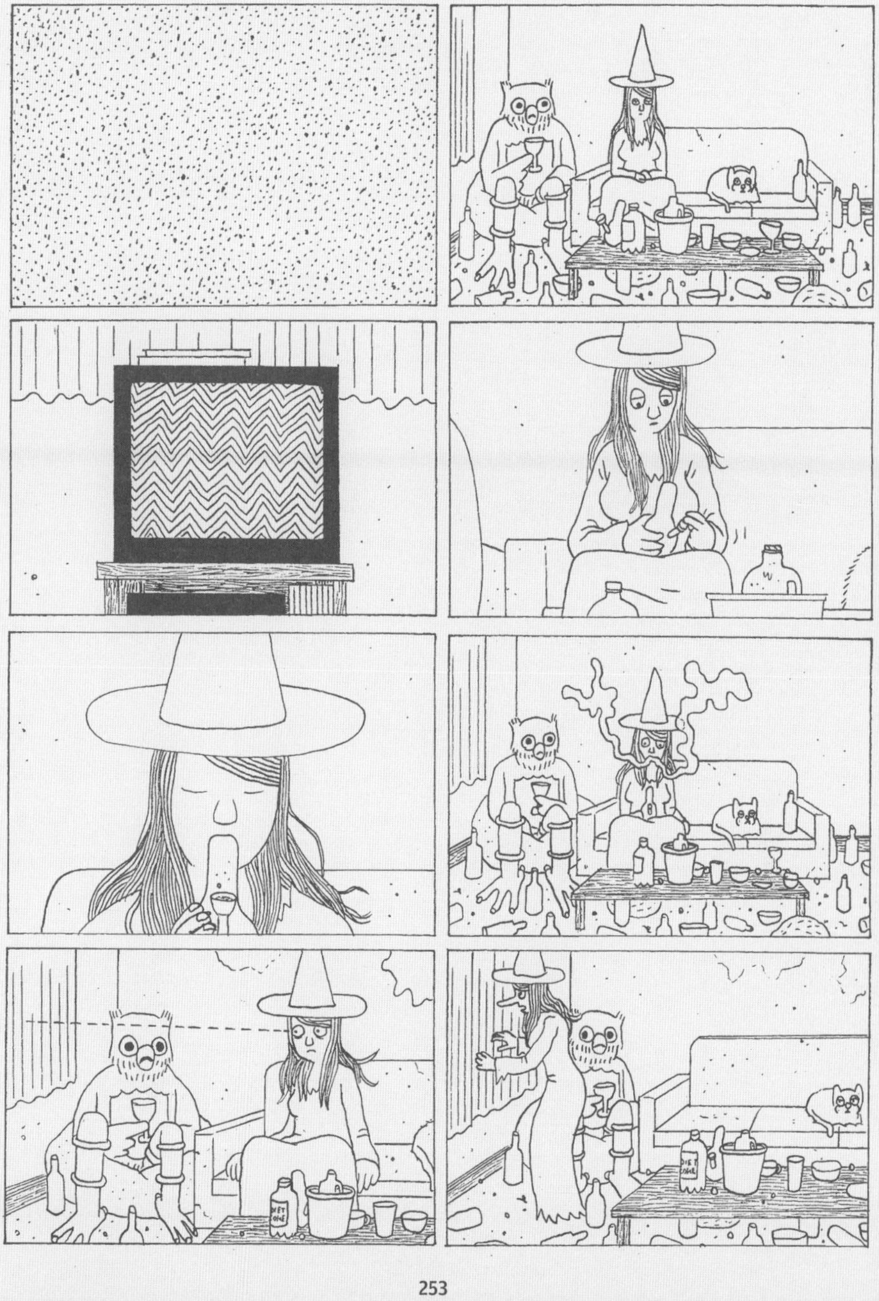

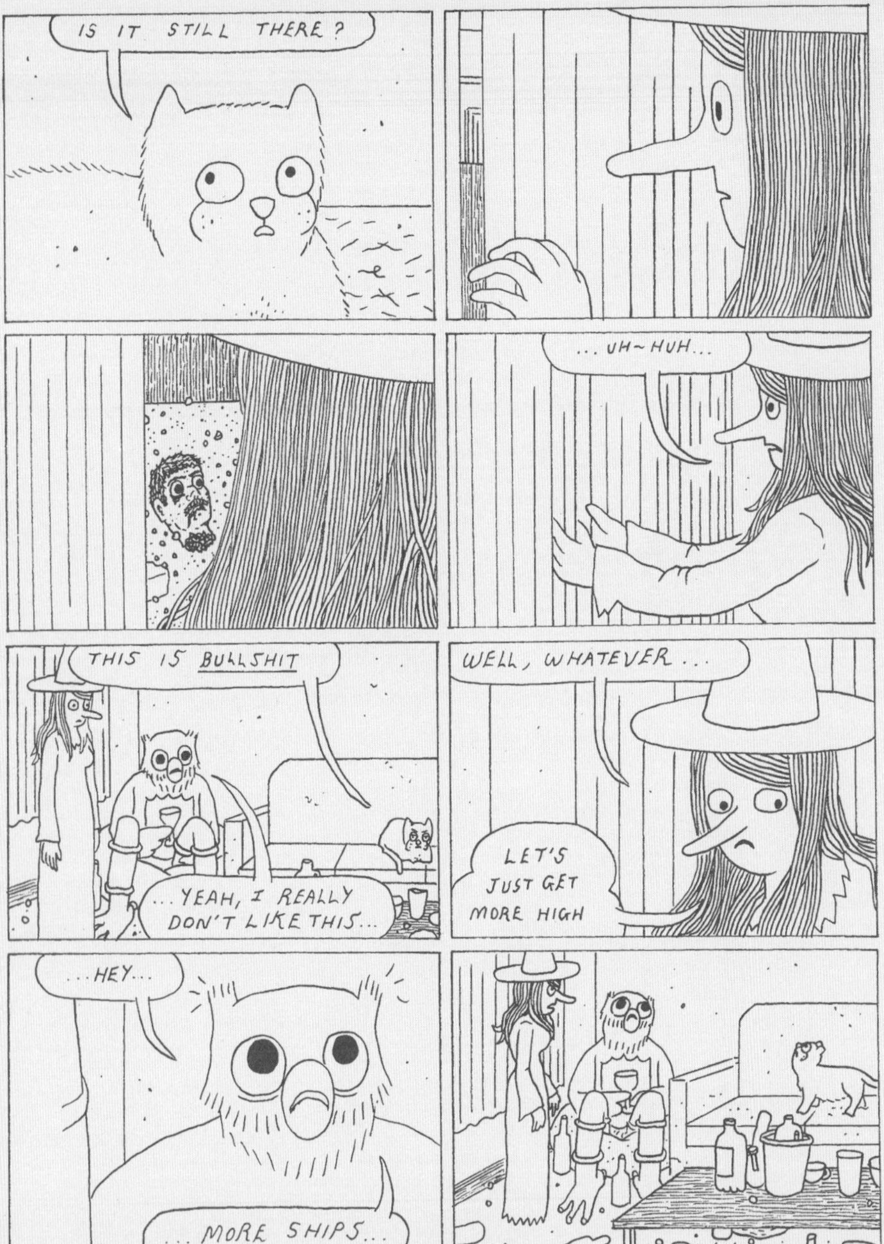
IS IT STILL THERE?
...UH~HUH...
THIS IS BULLSHIT
...YEAH, I REALLY DON'T LIKE THIS...
WELL, WHATEVER...
LET'S JUST GET MORE HIGH
...HEY...
...MORE SHIPS...

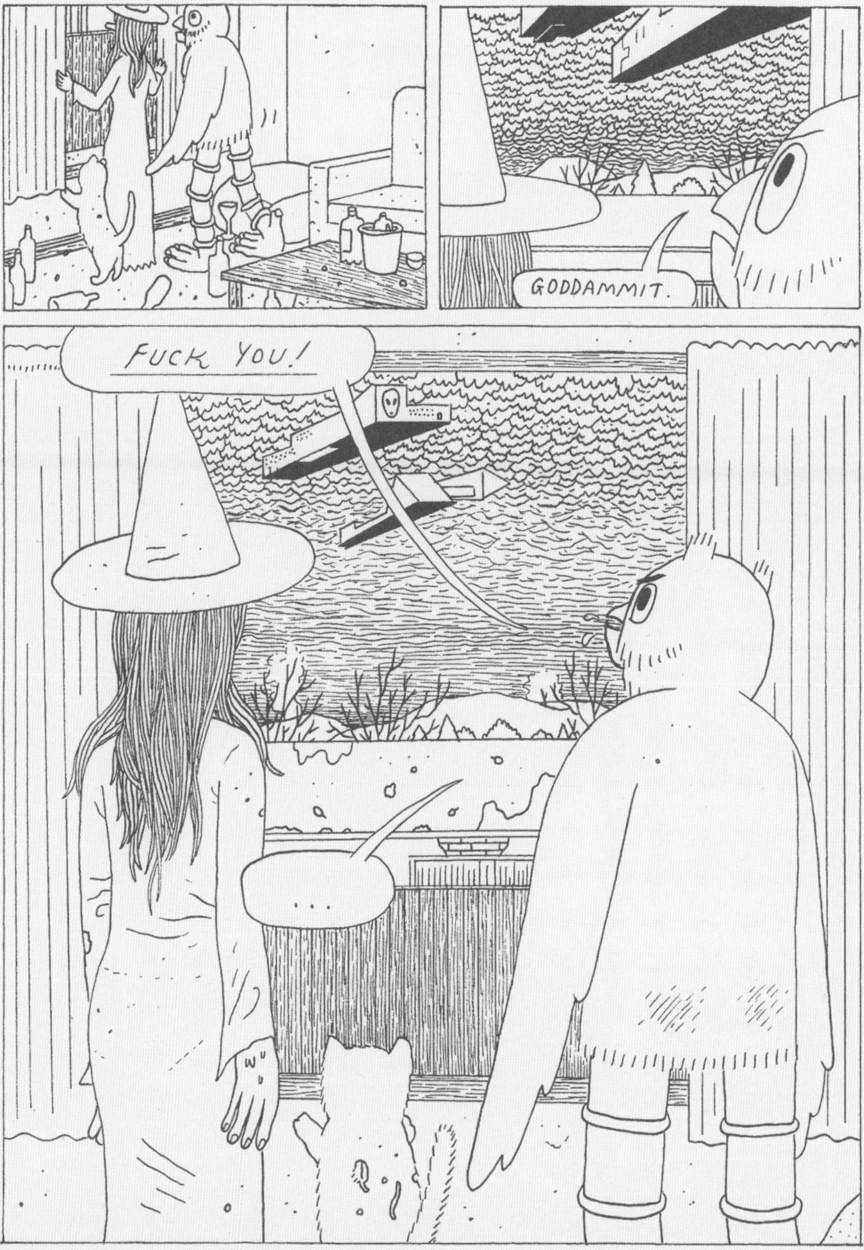
GODDAMMIT.
FUCK YOU!
...

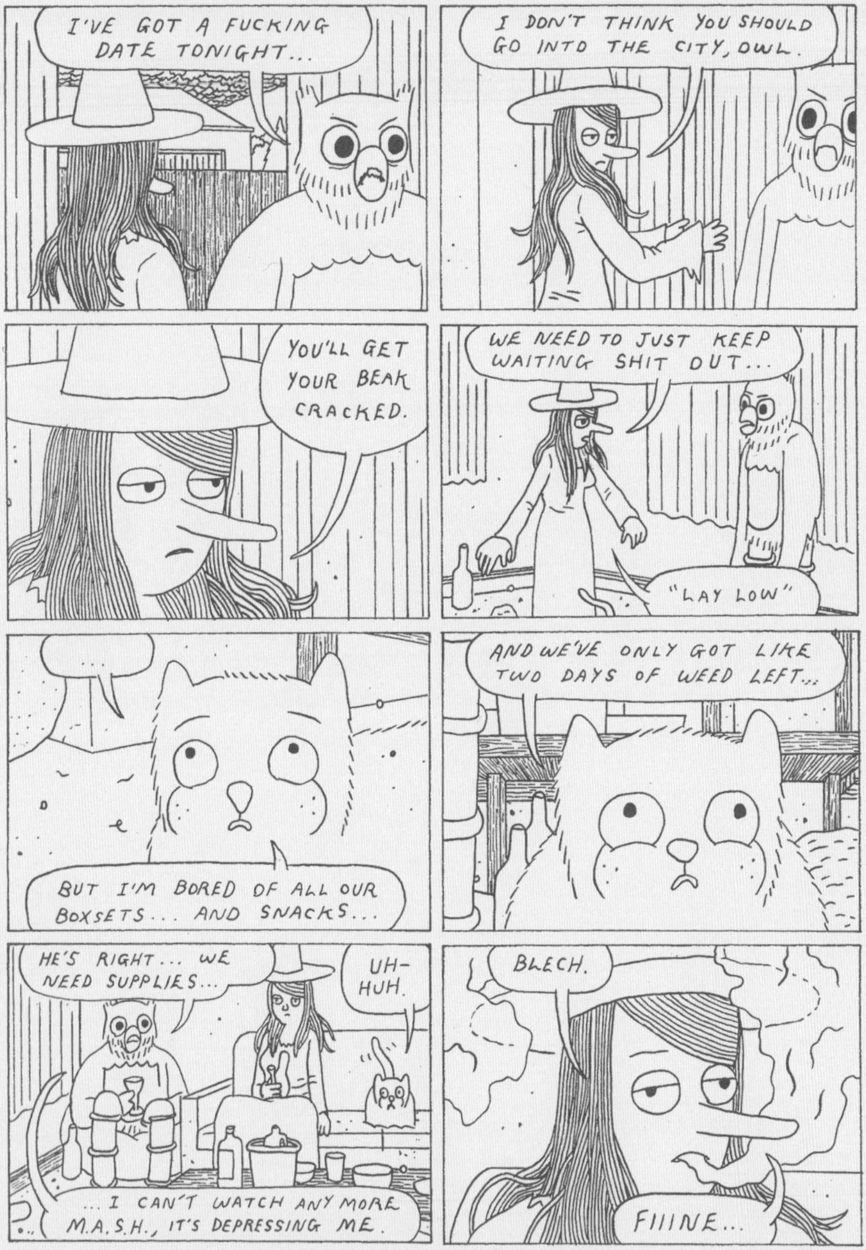
I'VE GOT A FUCKING DATE TONIGHT...
I DON'T THINK YOU SHOULD GO INTO THE CITY, OWL.
YOU'LL GET YOUR BEAK CRACKED.
WE NEED TO JUST KEEP WAITING SHIT OUT...
"LAY LOW"
...
BUT I'M BORED OF ALL OUR BOXSETS... AND SNACKS...
AND WE'VE ONLY GOT LIKE TWO DAYS OF WEED LEFT...
HE'S RIGHT... WE NEED SUPPLIES...
UH-HUH.
...I CAN'T WATCH ANY MORE M.A.S.H., IT'S DEPRESSING ME.
BLECH.
FIIINE...

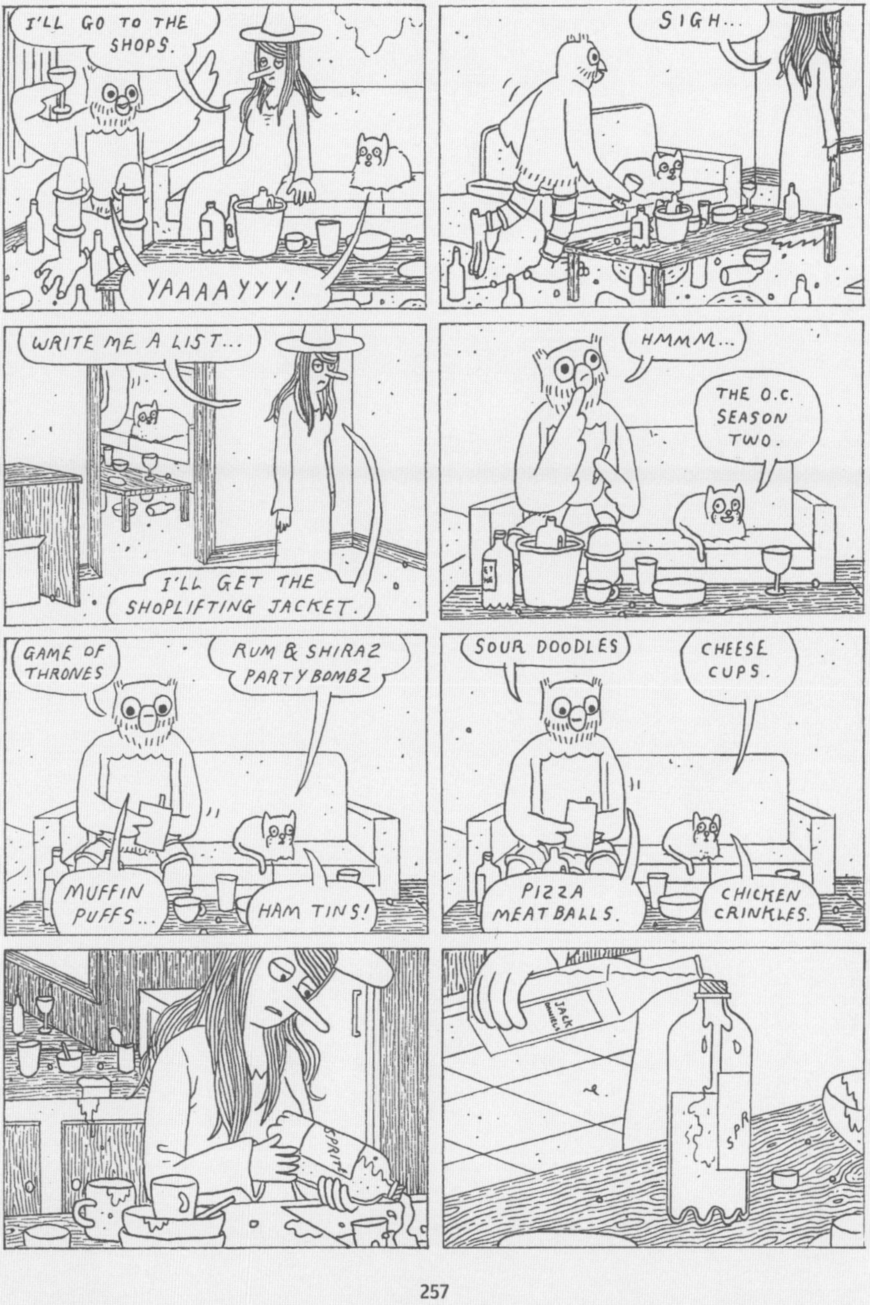
I'LL GO TO THE SHOPS.
YAAAAYYY!
SIGH...
WRITE ME A LIST...
I'LL GET THE SHOPLIFTING JACKET.
HMMM...
THE O.C. SEASON TWO.
GAME OF THRONES
RUM & SHIRAZ PARTY BOMBZ
MUFFIN PUFFS...
HAM TINS!
SOUR DOODLES
CHEESE CUPS.
PIZZA MEATBALLS.
CHICKEN CRINKLES.
JACK DANIELS
SPR

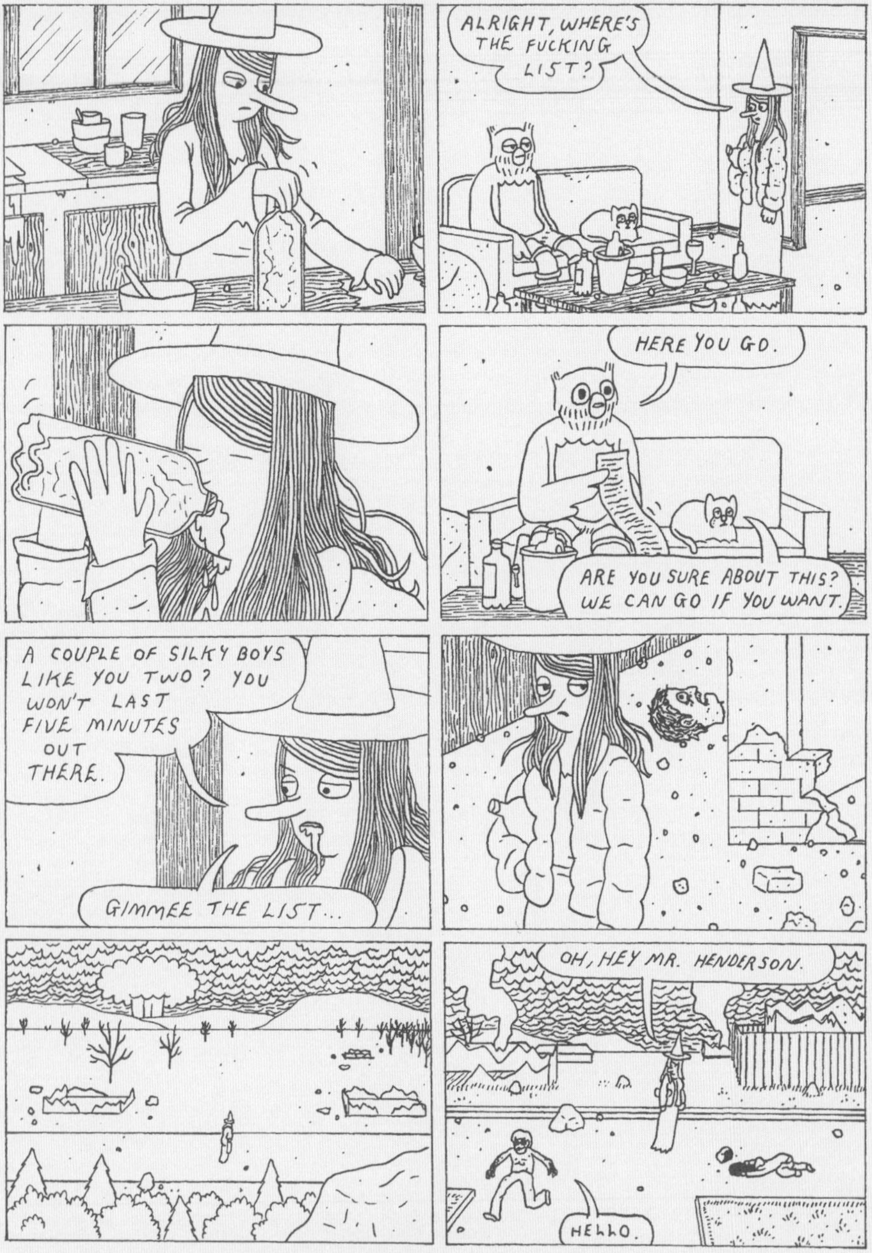
ALRIGHT, WHERE'S THE FUCKING LIST?
HERE YOU GO.
ARE YOU SURE ABOUT THIS? WE CAN GO IF YOU WANT.
A COUPLE OF SILKY BOYS LIKE YOU TWO? YOU WON'T LAST FIVE MINUTES OUT THERE.
GIMMEE THE LIST...
OH, HEY MR. HENDERSON.
HELLO.

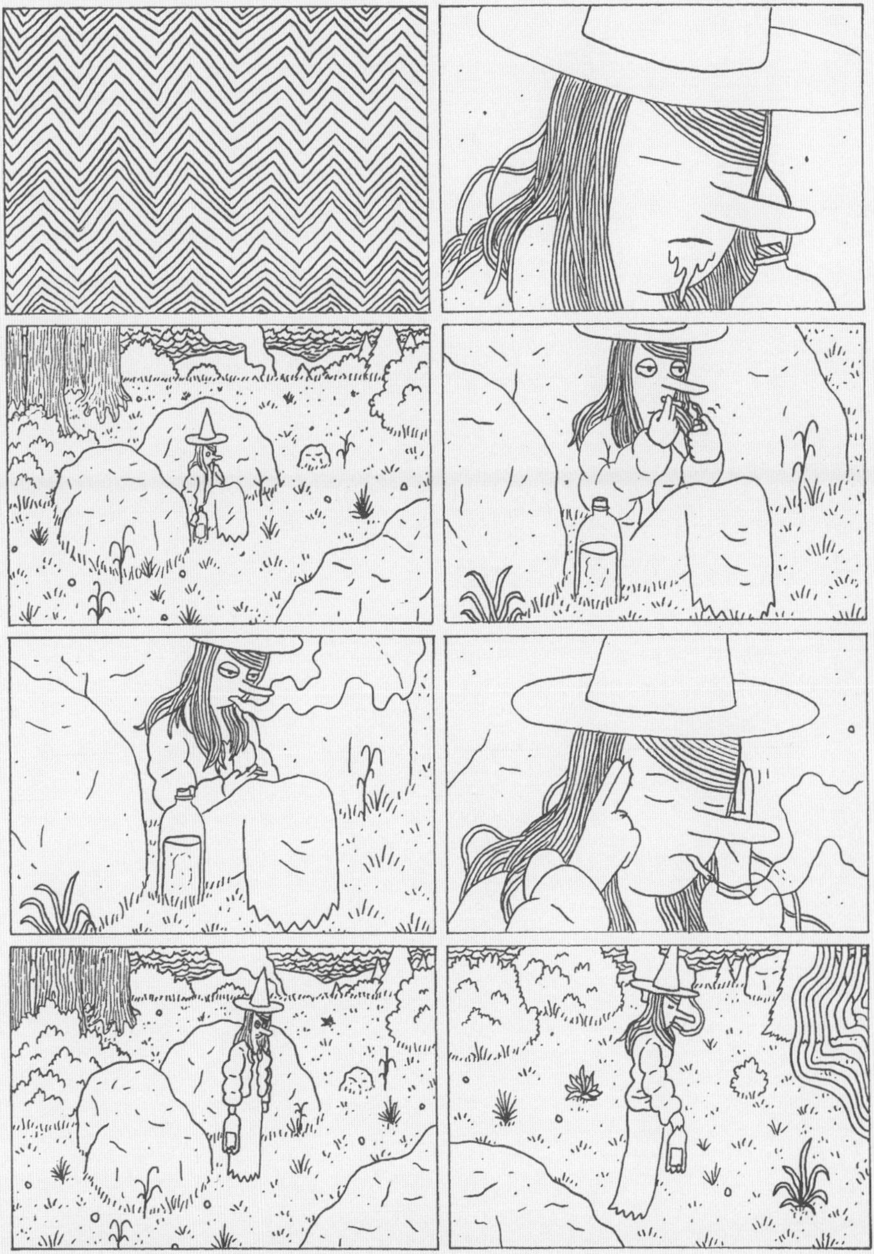

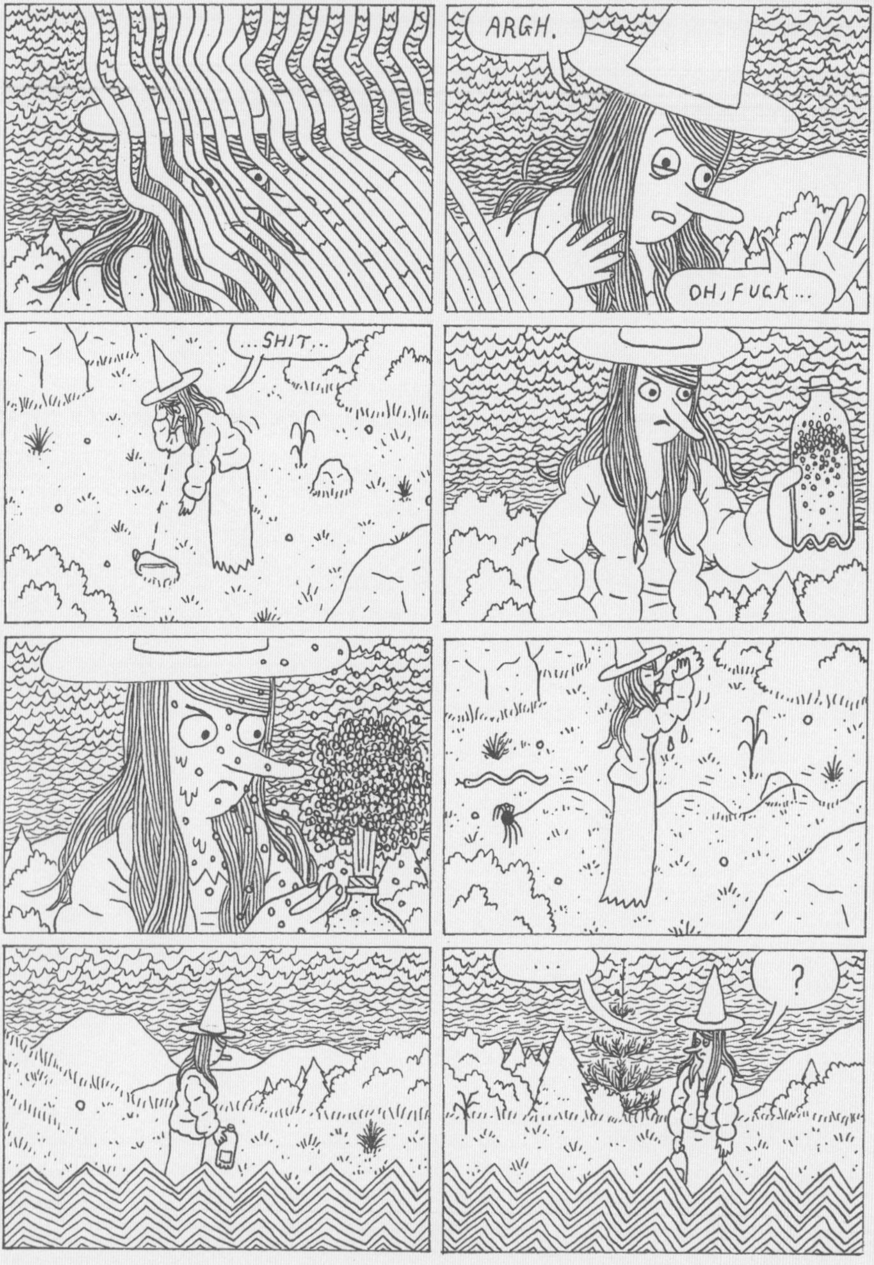
ARGH.
OH, FUCK...
...SHIT...
...
?

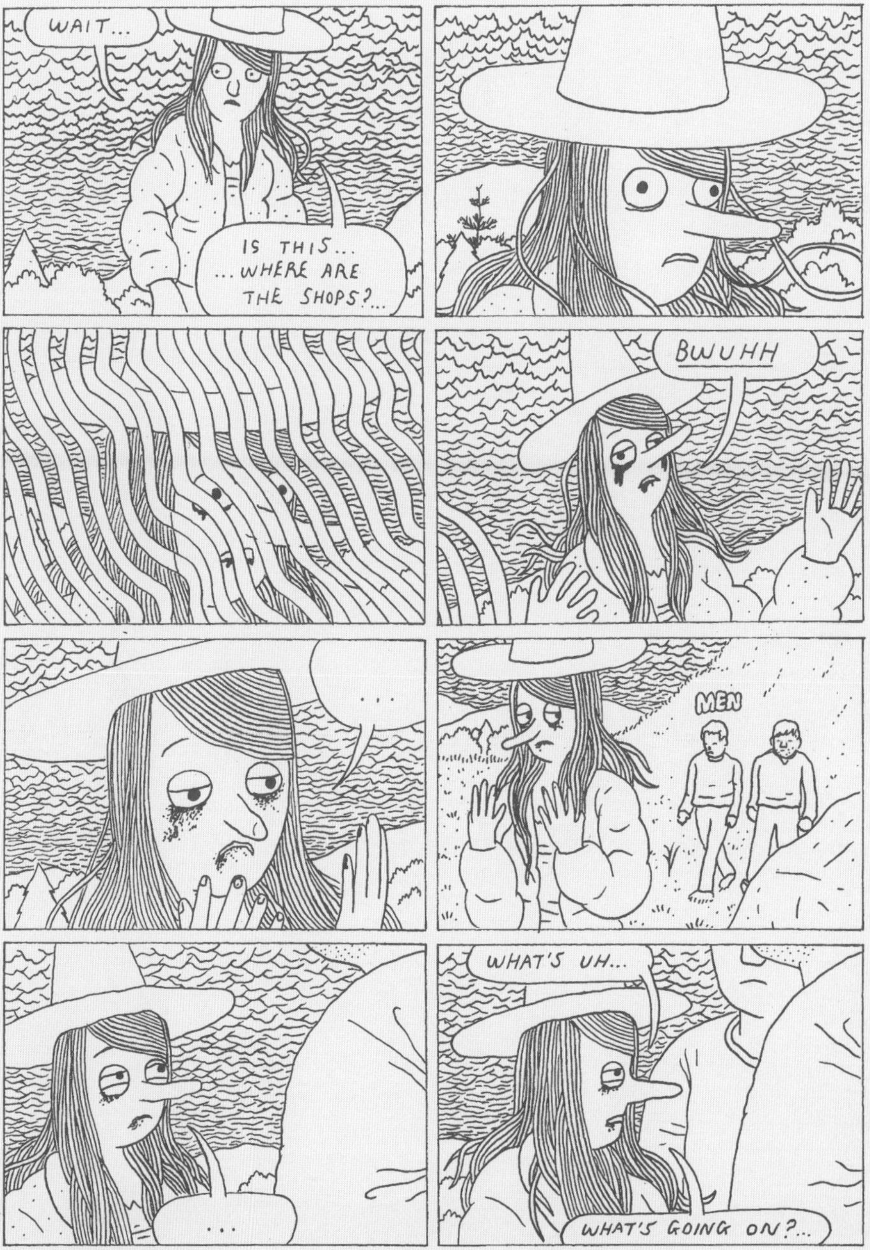
WAIT...
IS THIS...
...WHERE ARE THE SHOPS?...
BWUHH
...
MEN
...
WHAT'S UH...
WHAT'S GOING ON?...

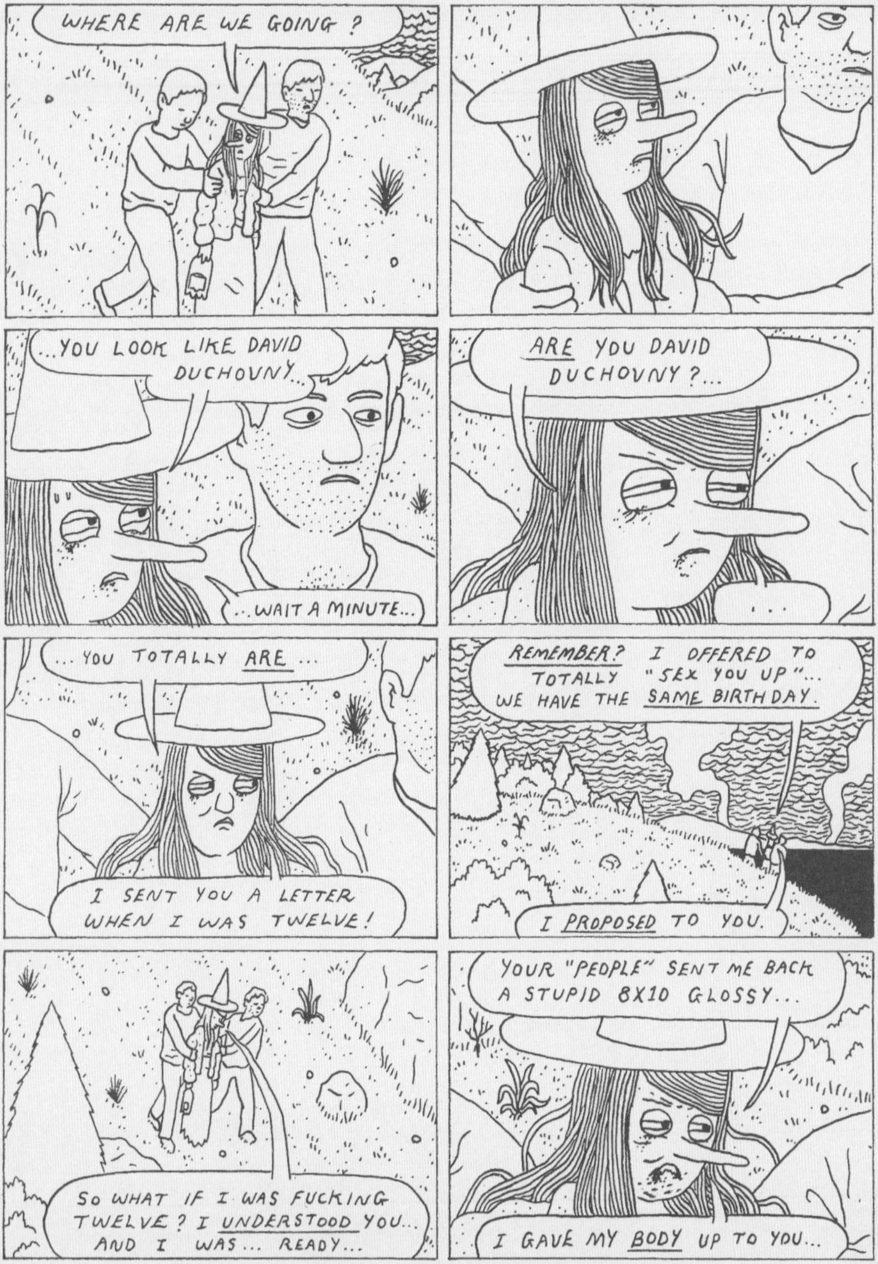
WHERE ARE WE GOING ?
...YOU LOOK LIKE DAVID DUCHOVNY...
...WAIT A MINUTE...
ARE YOU DAVID DUCHOVNY?...
...YOU TOTALLY ARE ...
I SENT YOU A LETTER WHEN I WAS TWELVE!
REMEMBER? I OFFERED TO TOTALLY "SEX YOU UP"... WE HAVE THE SAME BIRTHDAY.
I PROPOSED TO YOU.
SO WHAT IF I WAS FUCKING TWELVE? I UNDERSTOOD YOU... AND I WAS... READY...
YOUR "PEOPLE" SENT ME BACK A STUPID 8X10 GLOSSY...
I GAVE MY BODY UP TO YOU...

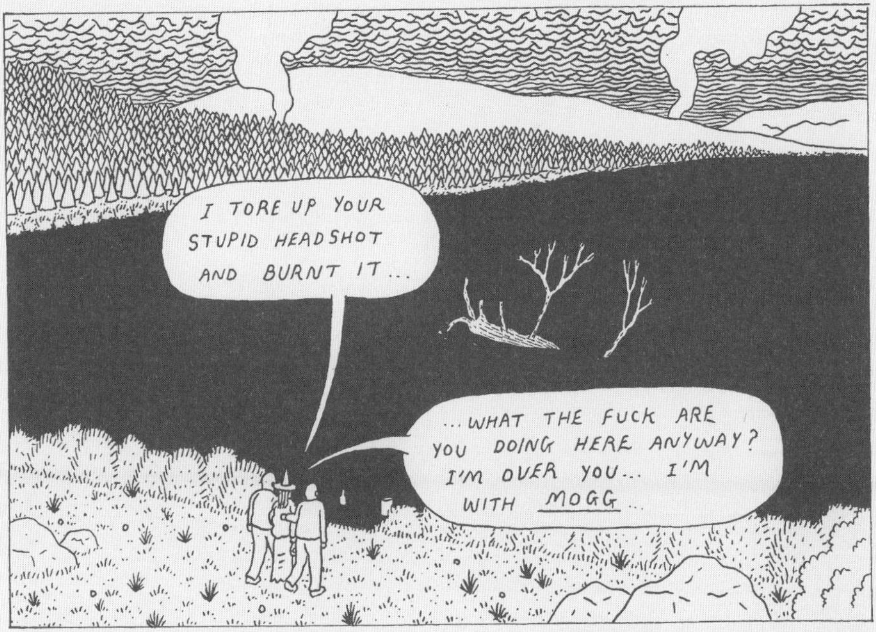
I TORE UP YOUR STUPID HEADSHOT AND BURNT IT...
...WHAT THE FUCK ARE YOU DOING HERE ANYWAY? I'M OVER YOU... I'M WITH MOGG...

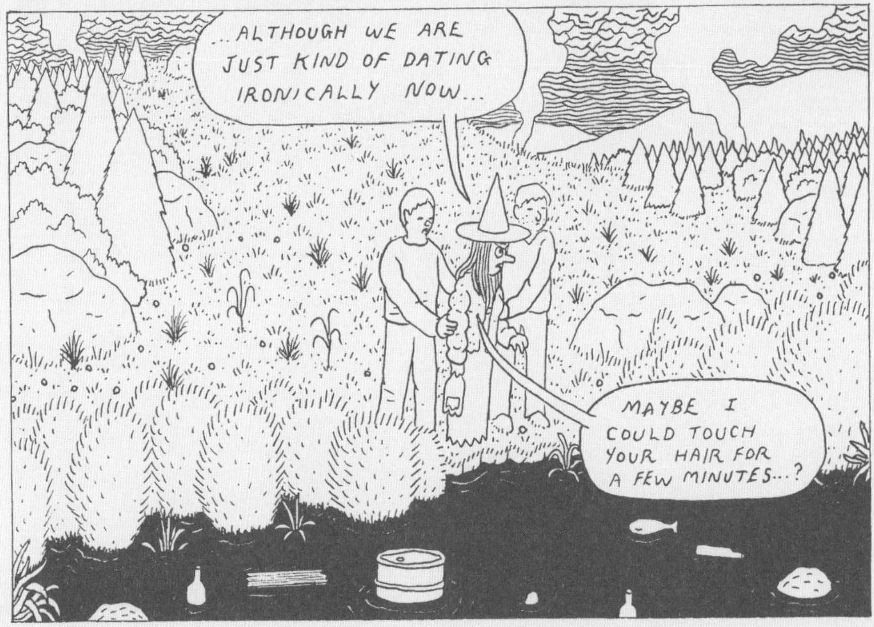
...ALTHOUGH WE ARE JUST KIND OF DATING IRONICALLY NOW...
MAYBE I COULD TOUCH YOUR HAIR FOR A FEW MINUTES...?

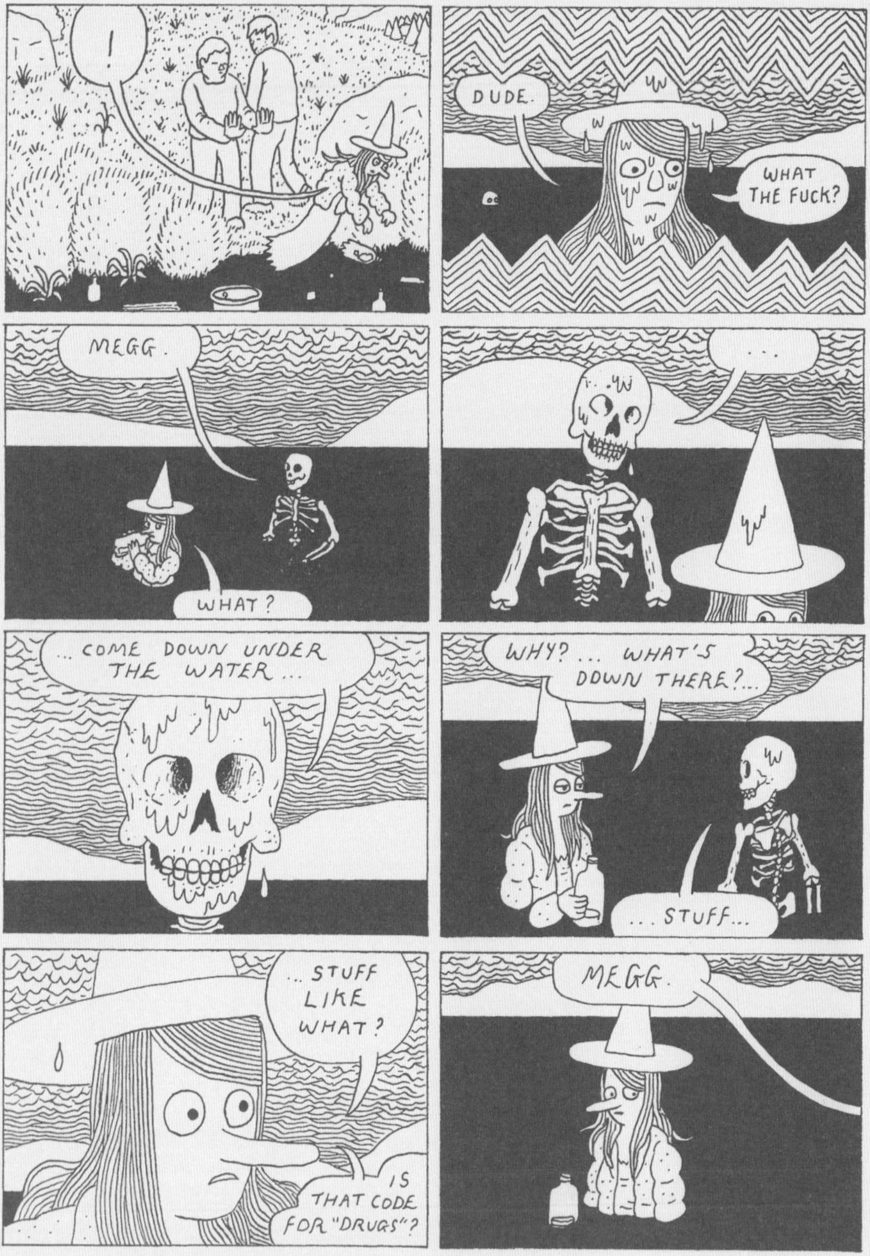
!
DUDE.
WHAT THE FUCK?
MEGG.
WHAT?
...
... COME DOWN UNDER THE WATER ...
WHY? ... WHAT'S DOWN THERE?...
... STUFF...
... STUFF LIKE WHAT?
IS THAT CODE FOR "DRUGS"?
MEGG.

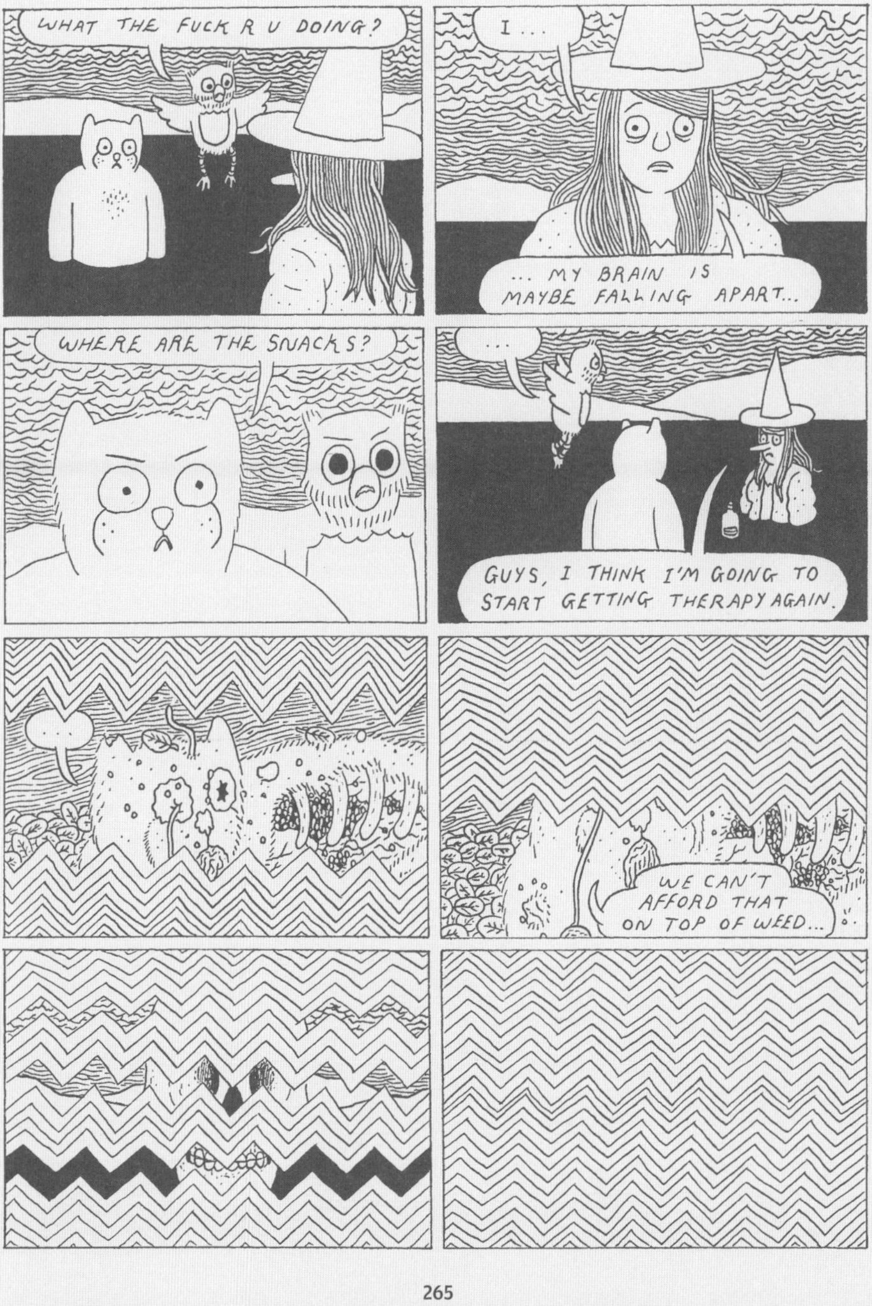
WHAT THE FUCK R U DOING?
I...
... MY BRAIN IS MAYBE FALLING APART...
WHERE ARE THE SNACKS?
...
GUYS, I THINK I'M GOING TO START GETTING THERAPY AGAIN.
...
WE CAN'T AFFORD THAT ON TOP OF WEED...

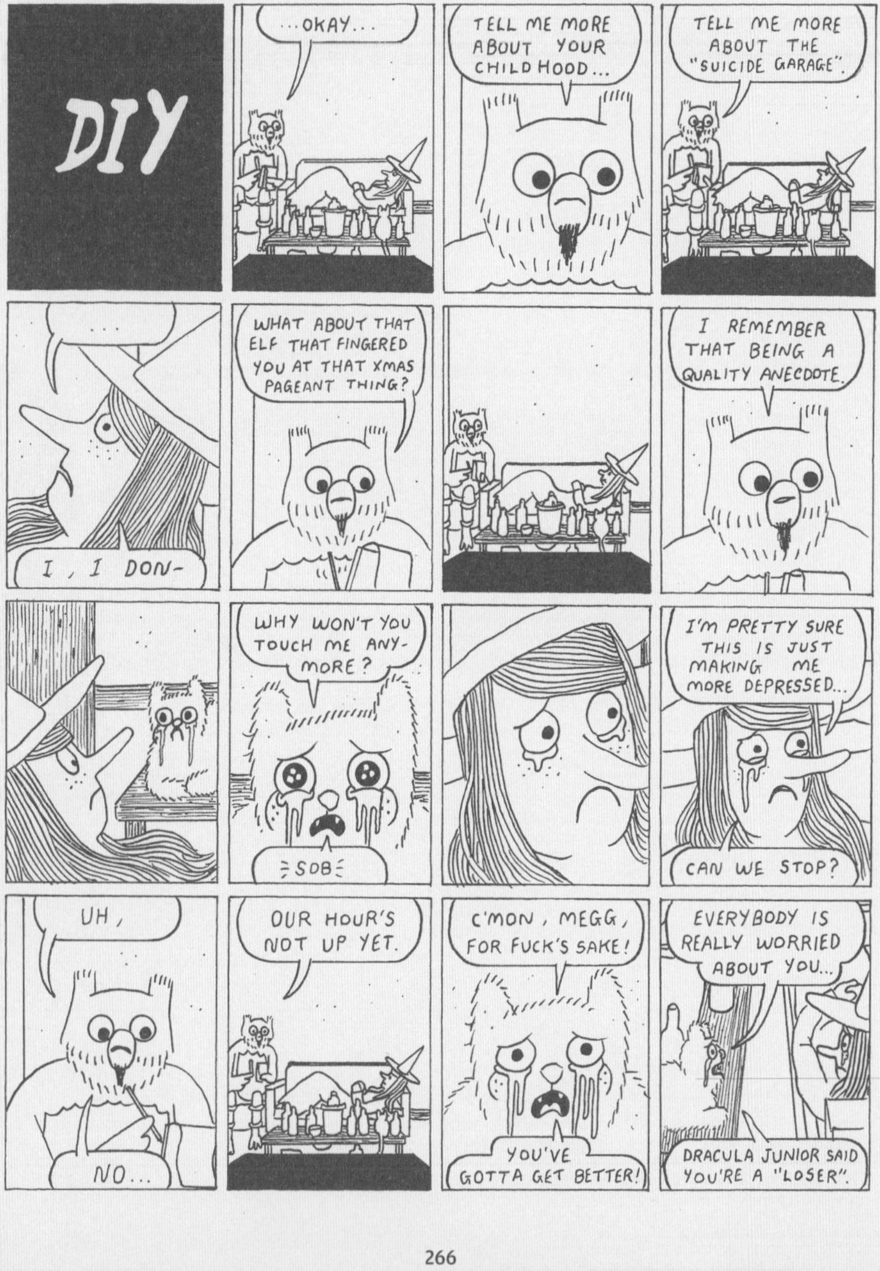
DIY
...OKAY...
TELL ME MORE ABOUT YOUR CHILDHOOD...
TELL ME MORE ABOUT THE "SUICIDE GARAGE".
...
I, I DON-
WHAT ABOUT THAT ELF THAT FINGERED YOU AT THAT XMAS PAGEANT THING?
I REMEMBER THAT BEING A QUALITY ANECDOTE.
WHY WON'T YOU TOUCH ME ANYMORE?
SOB
I'M PRETTY SURE THIS IS JUST MAKING ME MORE DEPRESSED...
CAN WE STOP?
UH,
NO...
OUR HOUR'S NOT UP YET.
C'MON, MEGG, FOR FUCK'S SAKE!
YOU'VE GOTTA GET BETTER!
EVERYBODY IS REALLY WORRIED ABOUT YOU...
DRACULA JUNIOR SAID YOU'RE A "LOSER".

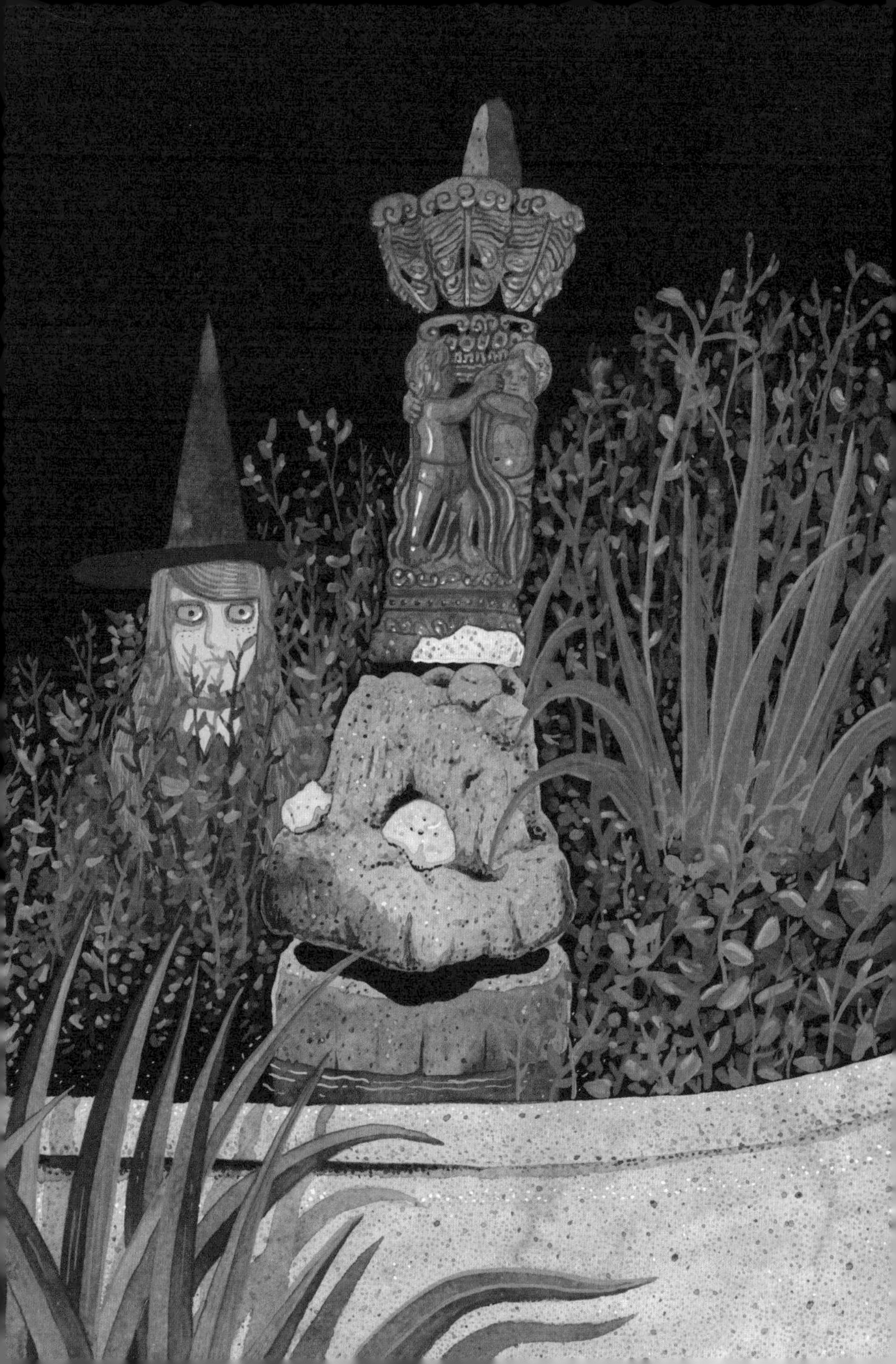

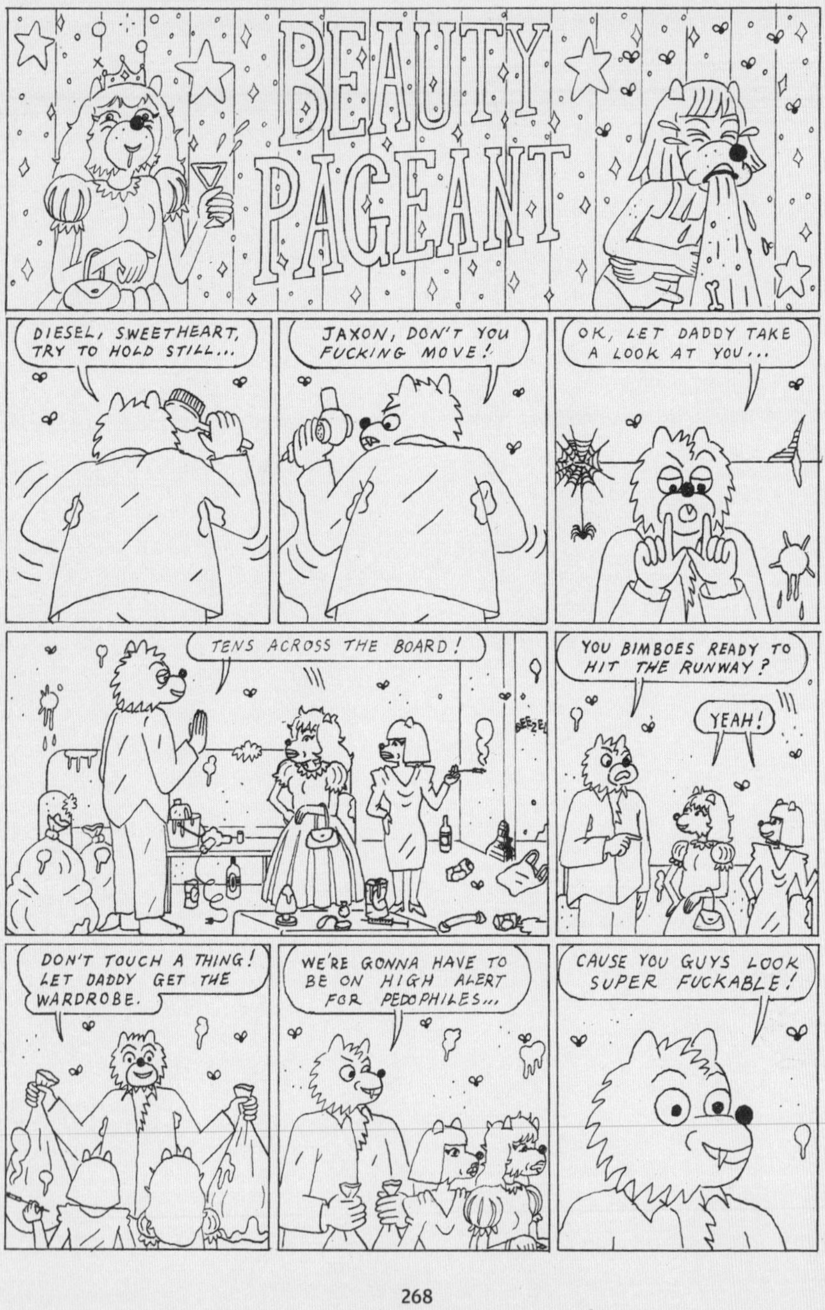
BEAUTY PAGEANT
DIESEL, SWEETHEART, TRY TO HOLD STILL...
JAXON, DON'T YOU FUCKING MOVE!
OK, LET DADDY TAKE A LOOK AT YOU...
TENS ACROSS THE BOARD!
YOU BIMBOES READY TO HIT THE RUNWAY?
YEAH!
DON'T TOUCH A THING! LET DADDY GET THE WARDROBE.
WE'RE GONNA HAVE TO BE ON HIGH ALERT FOR PEDOPHILES...
CAUSE YOU GUYS LOOK SUPER FUCKABLE!

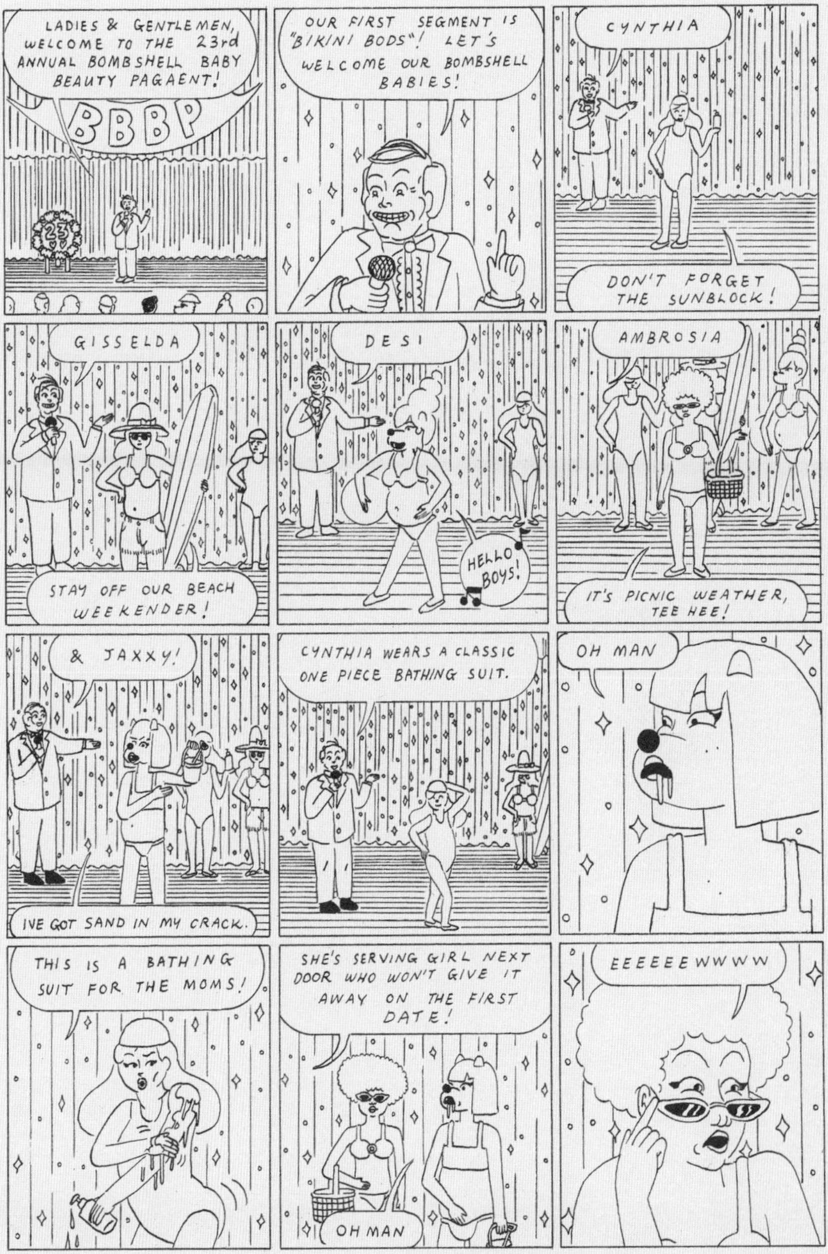
LADIES & GENTLEMEN, WELCOME TO THE 23rd ANNUAL BOMBSHELL BABY BEAUTY PAGAENT!
BBBP
23
OUR FIRST SEGMENT IS "BIKINI BODS"! LET'S WELCOME OUR BOMBSHELL BABIES!
CYNTHIA
DON'T FORGET THE SUNBLOCK!
GISSELDA
STAY OFF OUR BEACH WEEKENDER!
DESI
HELLO BOYS!
AMBROSIA
IT'S PICNIC WEATHER, TEE HEE!
& JAXXY!
IVE GOT SAND IN MY CRACK.
CYNTHIA WEARS A CLASSIC ONE PIECE BATHING SUIT.
OH MAN
THIS IS A BATHING SUIT FOR THE MOMS!
SHE'S SERVING GIRL NEXT DOOR WHO WON'T GIVE IT AWAY ON THE FIRST DATE!
OH MAN
EEEEEEWWWW

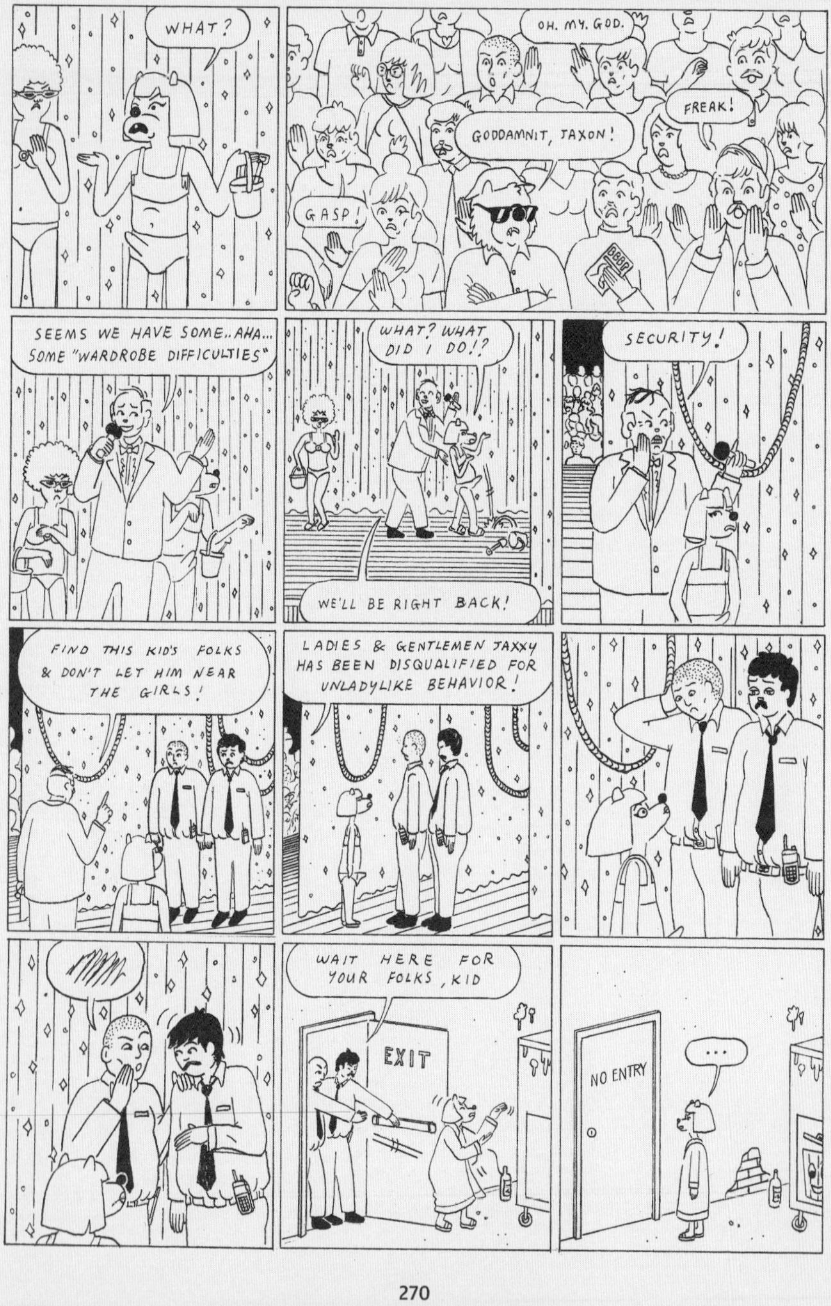
WHAT?
OH. MY. GOD.
FREAK!
GODDAMNIT, JAXON!
GASP!
SEEMS WE HAVE SOME..AHA... SOME "WARDROBE DIFFICULTIES"
WHAT? WHAT DID I DO!?
WE'LL BE RIGHT BACK!
SECURITY!
FIND THIS KID'S FOLKS & DON'T LET HIM NEAR THE GIRLS!
LADIES & GENTLEMEN JAXXY HAS BEEN DISQUALIFIED FOR UNLADYLIKE BEHAVIOR!
WAIT HERE FOR YOUR FOLKS, KID
EXIT
...
NO ENTRY

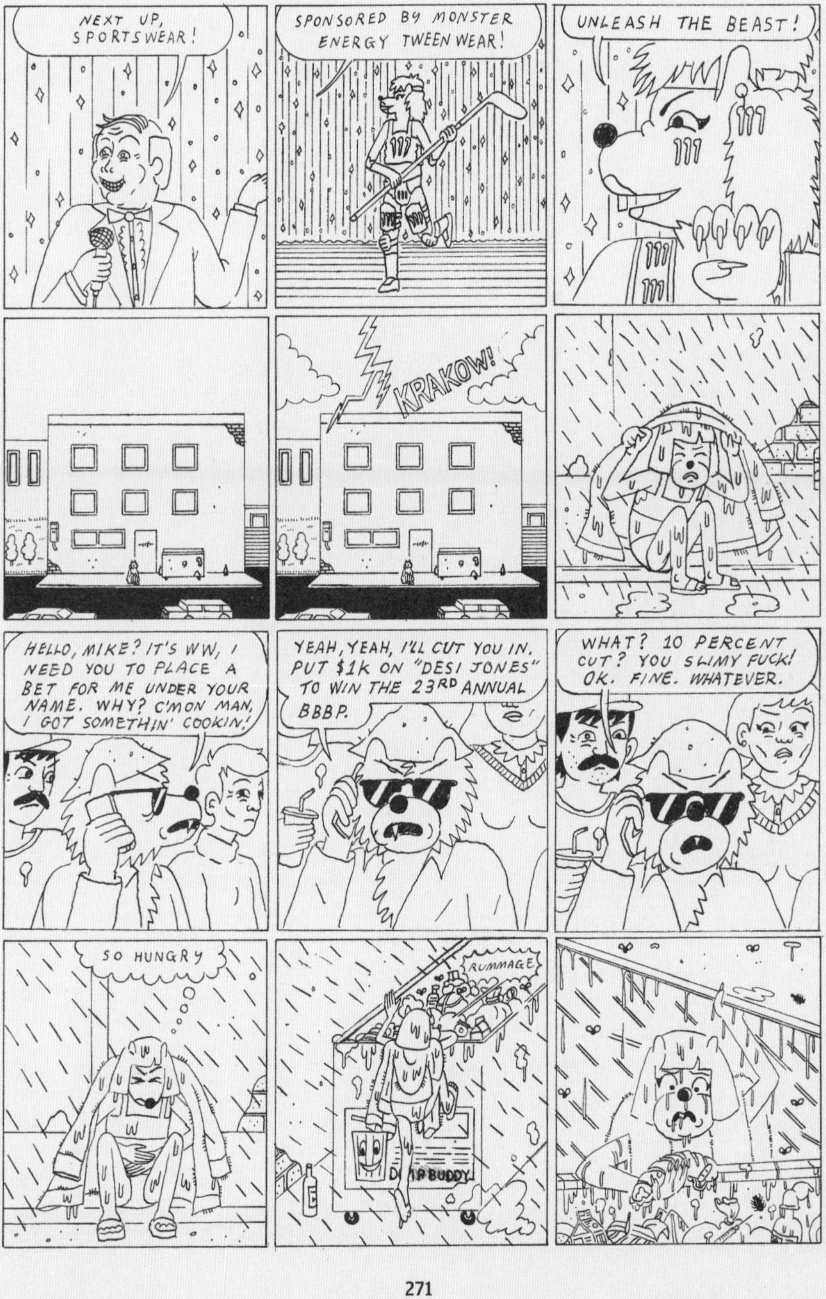
NEXT UP, SPORTSWEAR!
SPONSORED BY MONSTER ENERGY TWEEN WEAR!
UNLEASH THE BEAST!
KRAKOW!
HELLO, MIKE? IT'S WW, I NEED YOU TO PLACE A BET FOR ME UNDER YOUR NAME. WHY? C'MON MAN, I GOT SOMETHIN' COOKIN'!
YEAH, YEAH, I'LL CUT YOU IN. PUT $1K ON "DESI JONES" TO WIN THE 23RD ANNUAL BBBP.
WHAT? 10 PERCENT CUT? YOU SLIMY FUCK! OK. FINE. WHATEVER.
SO HUNGRY
RUMMAGE

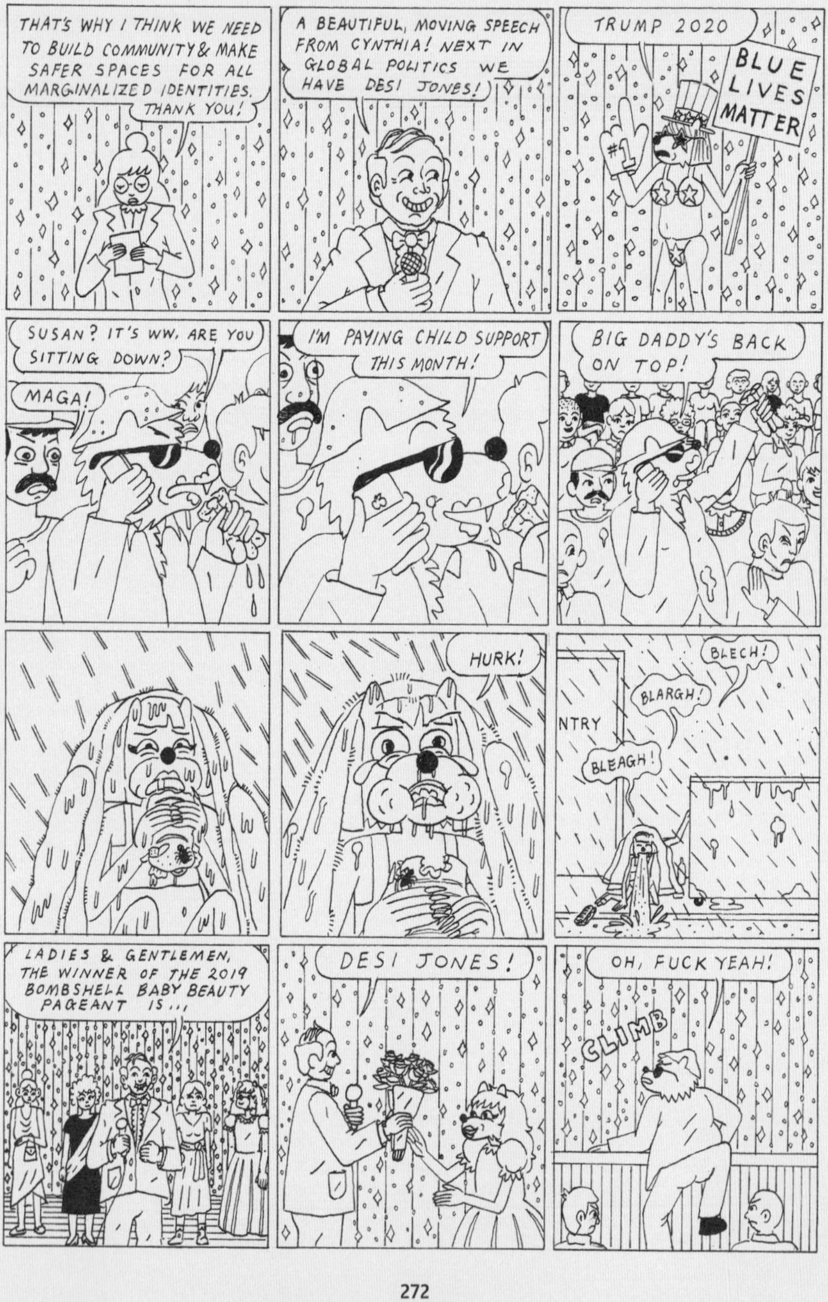
THAT'S WHY I THINK WE NEED TO BUILD COMMUNITY & MAKE SAFER SPACES FOR ALL MARGINALIZED IDENTITIES. THANK YOU!
A BEAUTIFUL, MOVING SPEECH FROM CYNTHIA! NEXT IN GLOBAL POLITICS WE HAVE DESI JONES!
TRUMP 2020
#1
BLUE LIVES MATTER
SUSAN? IT'S WW. ARE YOU SITTING DOWN?
MAGA!
I'M PAYING CHILD SUPPORT THIS MONTH!
BIG DADDY'S BACK ON TOP!
HURK!
BLECH!
BLARGH!
NTRY
BLEAGH!
LADIES & GENTLEMEN, THE WINNER OF THE 2019 BOMBSHELL BABY BEAUTY PAGEANT IS...
DESI JONES!
OH, FUCK YEAH!
CLIMB

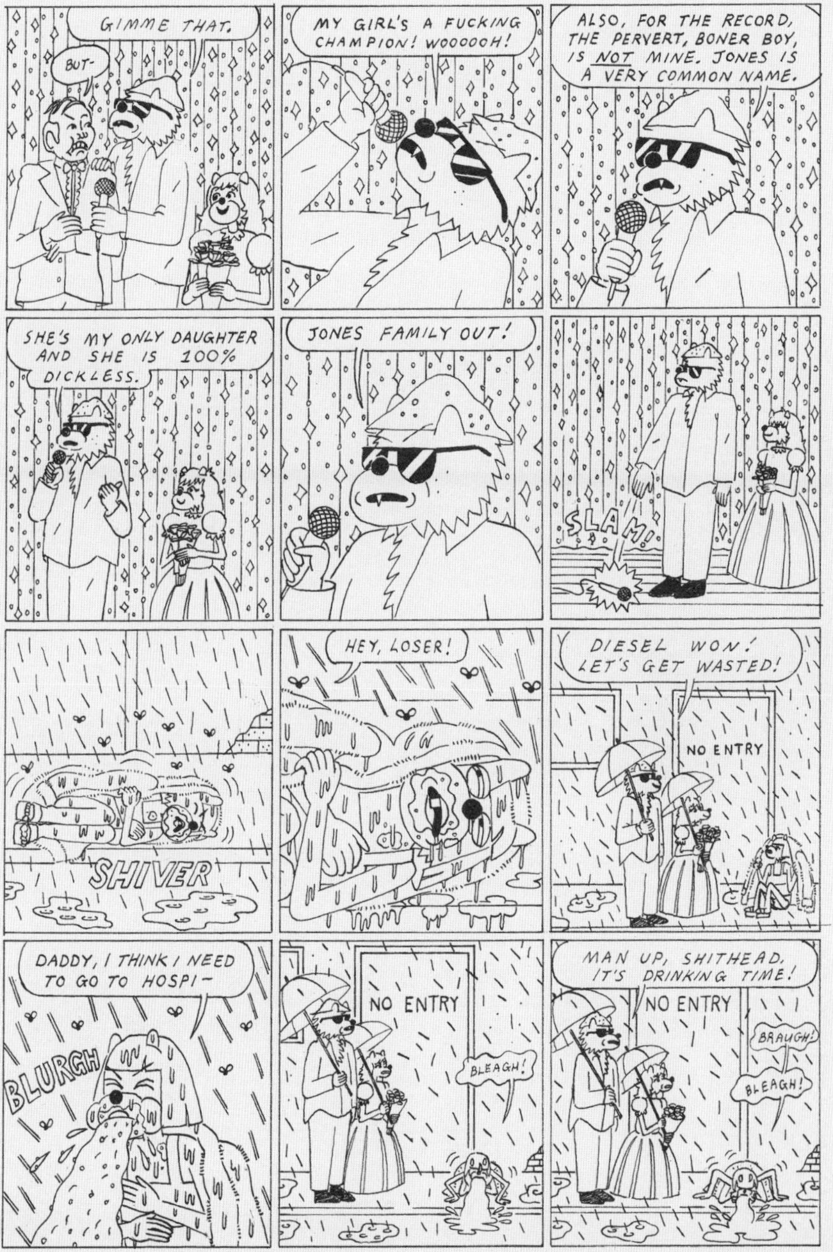
GIMME THAT.
BUT-
MY GIRL'S A FUCKING CHAMPION! WOOOOOH!
ALSO, FOR THE RECORD, THE PERVERT, BONER BOY, IS NOT MINE. JONES IS A VERY COMMON NAME.
SHE'S MY ONLY DAUGHTER AND SHE IS 100% DICKLESS.
JONES FAMILY OUT!
SLAM!
SHIVER
HEY, LOSER!
DIESEL WON! LET'S GET WASTED!
NO ENTRY
DADDY, I THINK I NEED TO GO TO HOSPI-
BLURGH
NO ENTRY
BLEAGH!
MAN UP, SHITHEAD. IT'S DRINKING TIME!
NO ENTRY
BRAUGH!
BLEAGH!

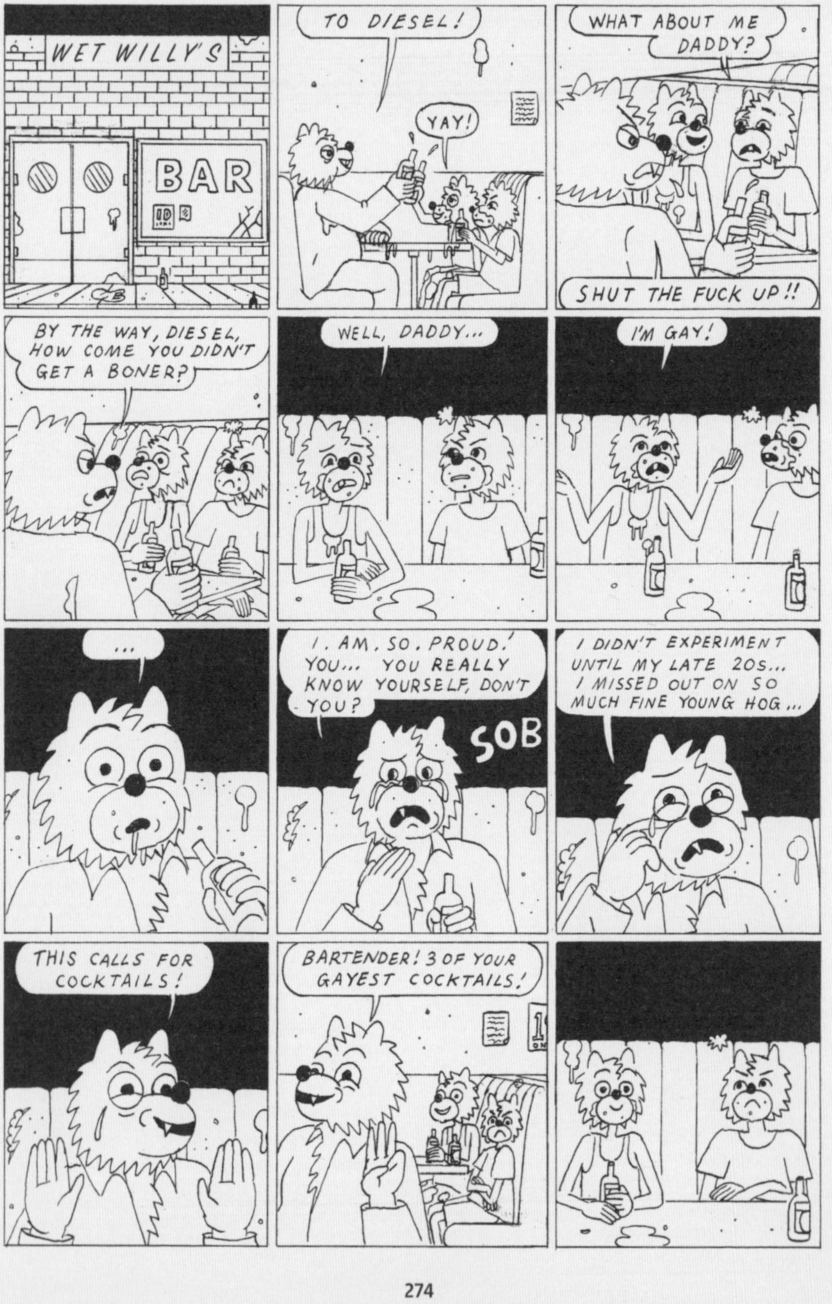
WET WILLY'S
BAR
TO DIESEL!
YAY!
WHAT ABOUT ME DADDY?
SHUT THE FUCK UP!!
BY THE WAY, DIESEL, HOW COME YOU DIDN'T GET A BONER?
WELL, DADDY...
I'M GAY!
...
I. AM. SO. PROUD. YOU... YOU REALLY KNOW YOURSELF, DON'T YOU?
SOB
I DIDN'T EXPERIMENT UNTIL MY LATE 20S... I MISSED OUT ON SO MUCH FINE YOUNG HOG...
THIS CALLS FOR COCKTAILS!
BARTENDER! 3 OF YOUR GAYEST COCKTAILS!

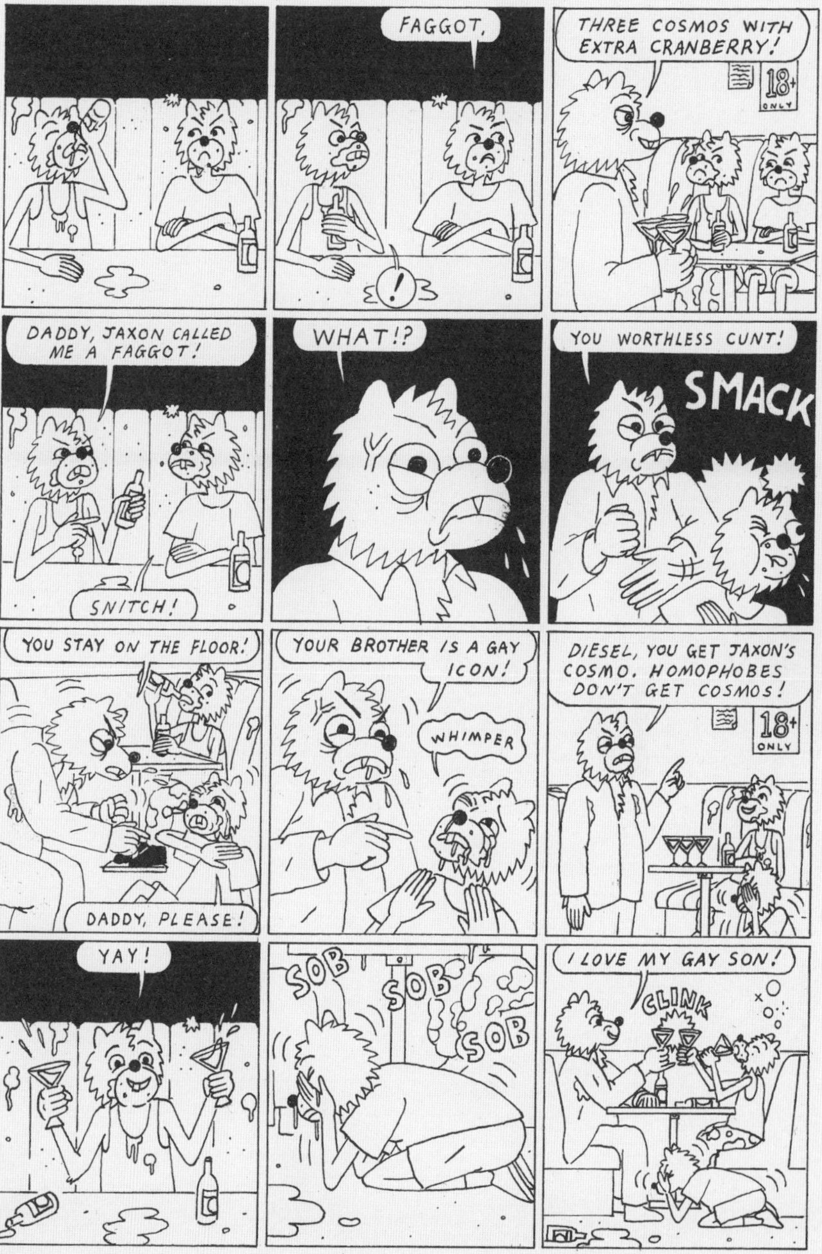
FAGGOT.
THREE COSMOS WITH EXTRA CRANBERRY!
18+ ONLY
DADDY, JAXON CALLED ME A FAGGOT!
SNITCH!
WHAT!?
YOU WORTHLESS CUNT!
SMACK
YOU STAY ON THE FLOOR!
DADDY, PLEASE!
YOUR BROTHER IS A GAY ICON!
WHIMPER
DIESEL, YOU GET JAXON'S COSMO. HOMOPHOBES DON'T GET COSMOS!
18+ ONLY
YAY!
SOB
SOB
SOB
I LOVE MY GAY SON!
CLINK

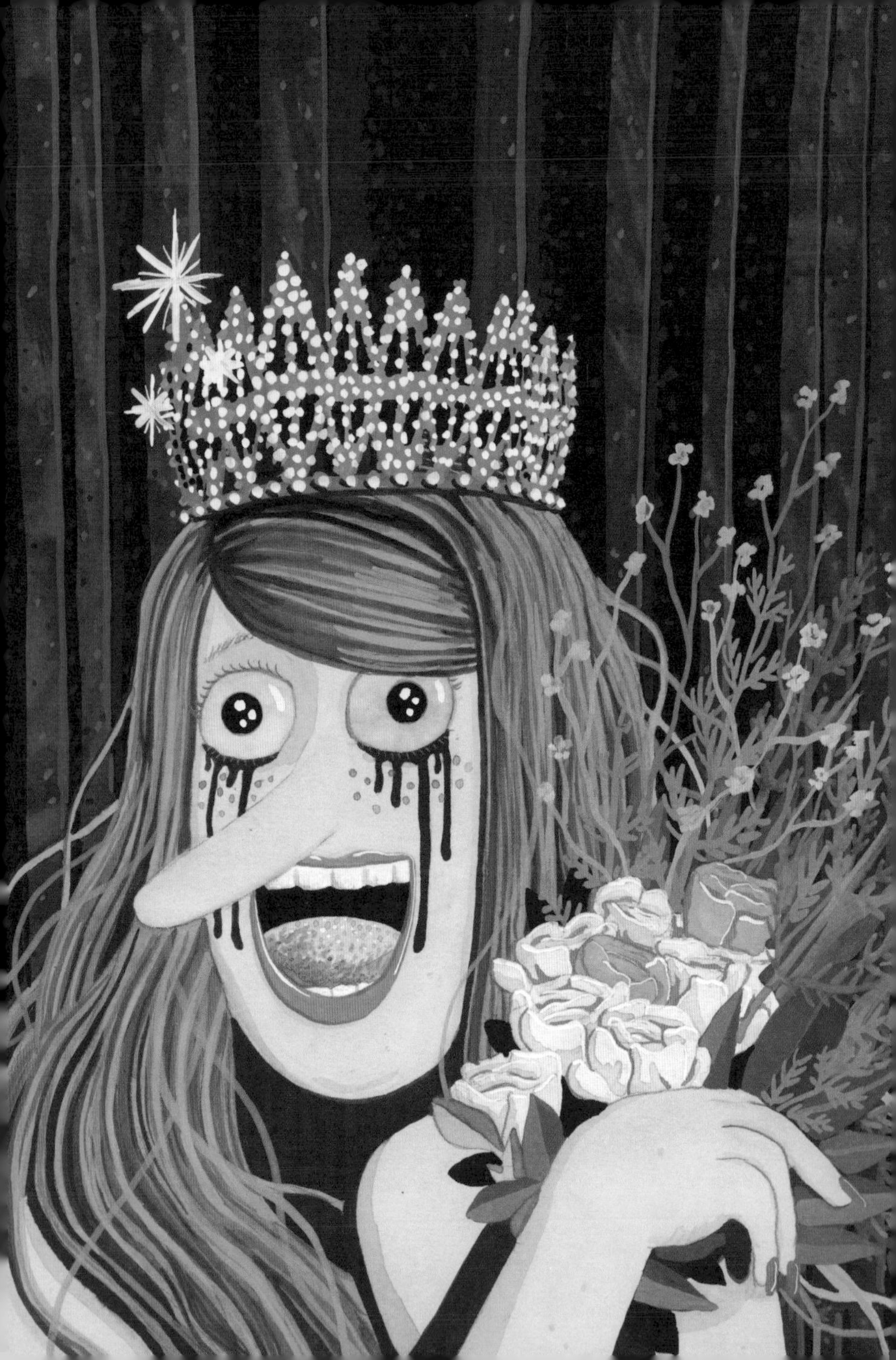

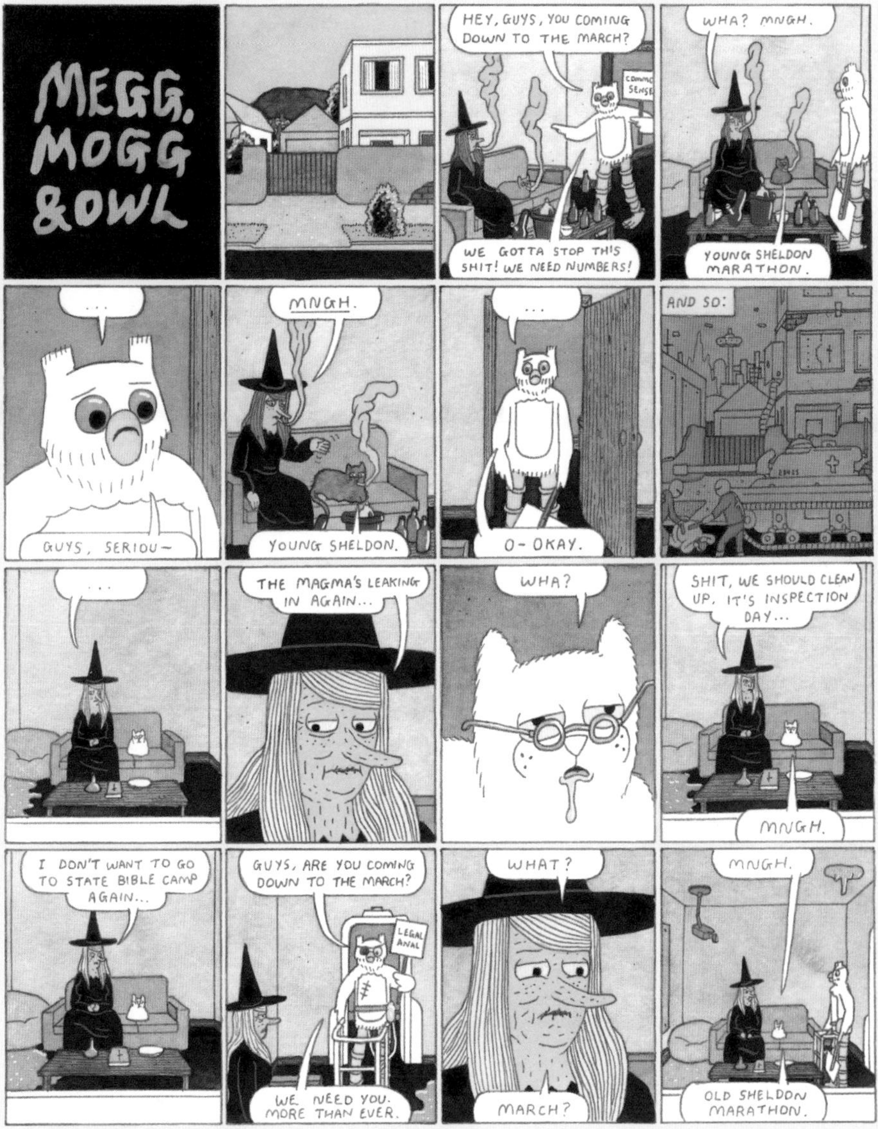
MEGG, MOGG & OWL
HEY, GUYS, YOU COMING DOWN TO THE MARCH?
WE GOTTA STOP THIS SHIT! WE NEED NUMBERS!
WHA? MNGH.
YOUNG SHELDON MARATHON.
...
GUYS, SERIOU—
MNGH.
YOUNG SHELDON.
...
O-OKAY.
AND SO:
...
THE MAGMA'S LEAKING IN AGAIN...
WHA?
SHIT, WE SHOULD CLEAN UP, IT'S INSPECTION DAY...
MNGH.
I DON'T WANT TO GO TO STATE BIBLE CAMP AGAIN...
GUYS, ARE YOU COMING DOWN TO THE MARCH?
LEGAL ANAL
WE NEED YOU. MORE THAN EVER.
WHAT?
MARCH?
MNGH.
OLD SHELDON MARATHON.

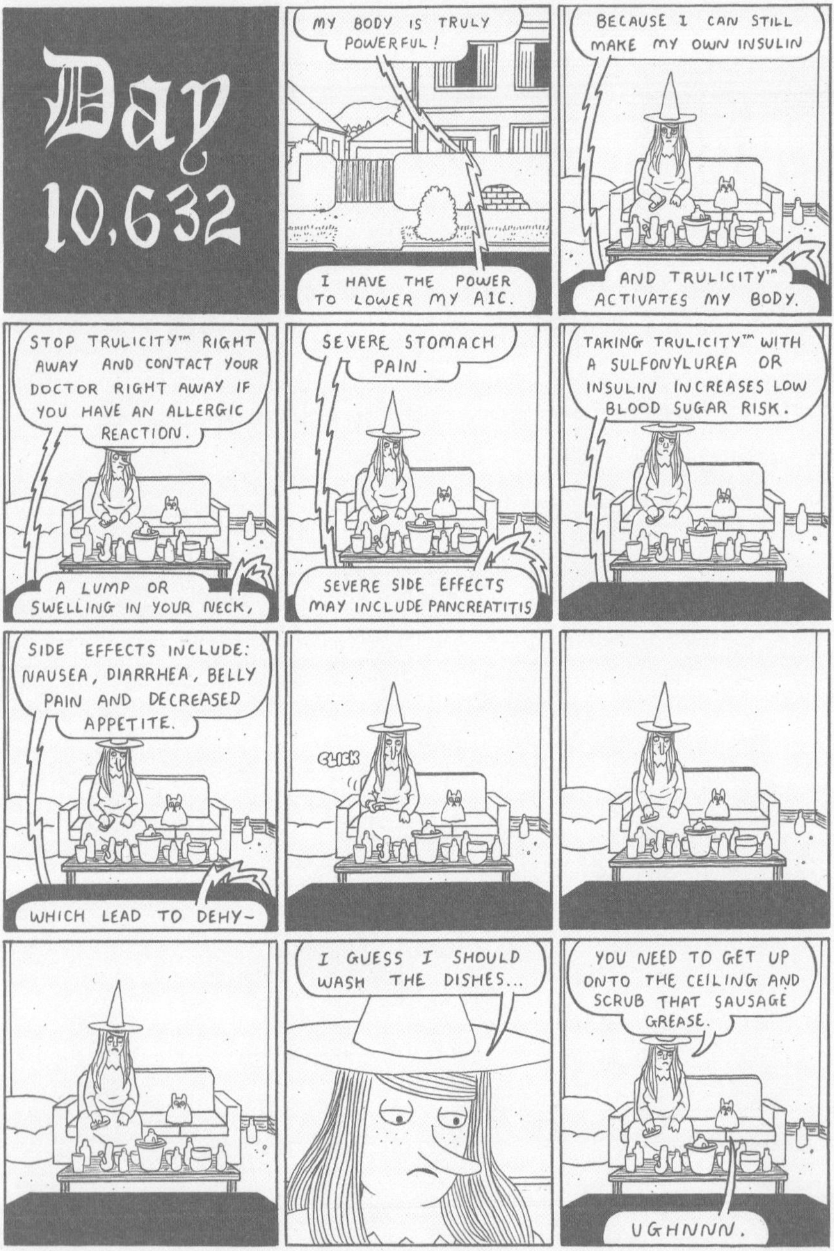
Day 10,632
MY BODY IS TRULY POWERFUL!
I HAVE THE POWER TO LOWER MY A1C.
BECAUSE I CAN STILL MAKE MY OWN INSULIN
AND TRULICITY™ ACTIVATES MY BODY.
STOP TRULICITY™ RIGHT AWAY AND CONTACT YOUR DOCTOR RIGHT AWAY IF YOU HAVE AN ALLERGIC REACTION.
A LUMP OR SWELLING IN YOUR NECK,
SEVERE STOMACH PAIN.
SEVERE SIDE EFFECTS MAY INCLUDE PANCREATITIS
TAKING TRULICITY™ WITH A SULFONYLUREA OR INSULIN INCREASES LOW BLOOD SUGAR RISK.
SIDE EFFECTS INCLUDE: NAUSEA, DIARRHEA, BELLY PAIN AND DECREASED APPETITE.
WHICH LEAD TO DEHY-
CLICK
I GUESS I SHOULD WASH THE DISHES...
YOU NEED TO GET UP ONTO THE CEILING AND SCRUB THAT SAUSAGE GREASE.
UGHNNN.

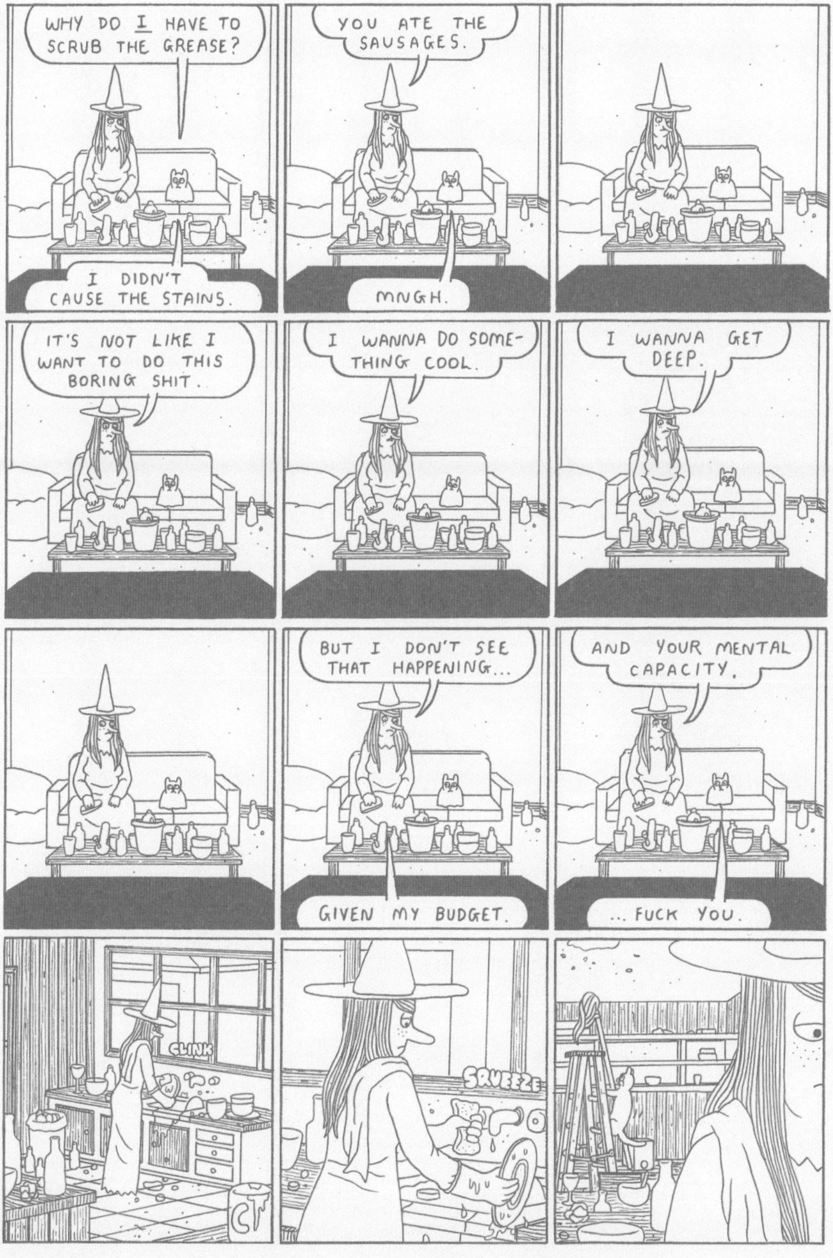
WHY DO I HAVE TO SCRUB THE GREASE?
I DIDN'T CAUSE THE STAINS.
YOU ATE THE SAUSAGES.
MNGH.
IT'S NOT LIKE I WANT TO DO THIS BORING SHIT.
I WANNA DO SOME-THING COOL.
I WANNA GET DEEP.
BUT I DON'T SEE THAT HAPPENING...
GIVEN MY BUDGET.
AND YOUR MENTAL CAPACITY.
... FUCK YOU.
CLINK
SQUEEZE

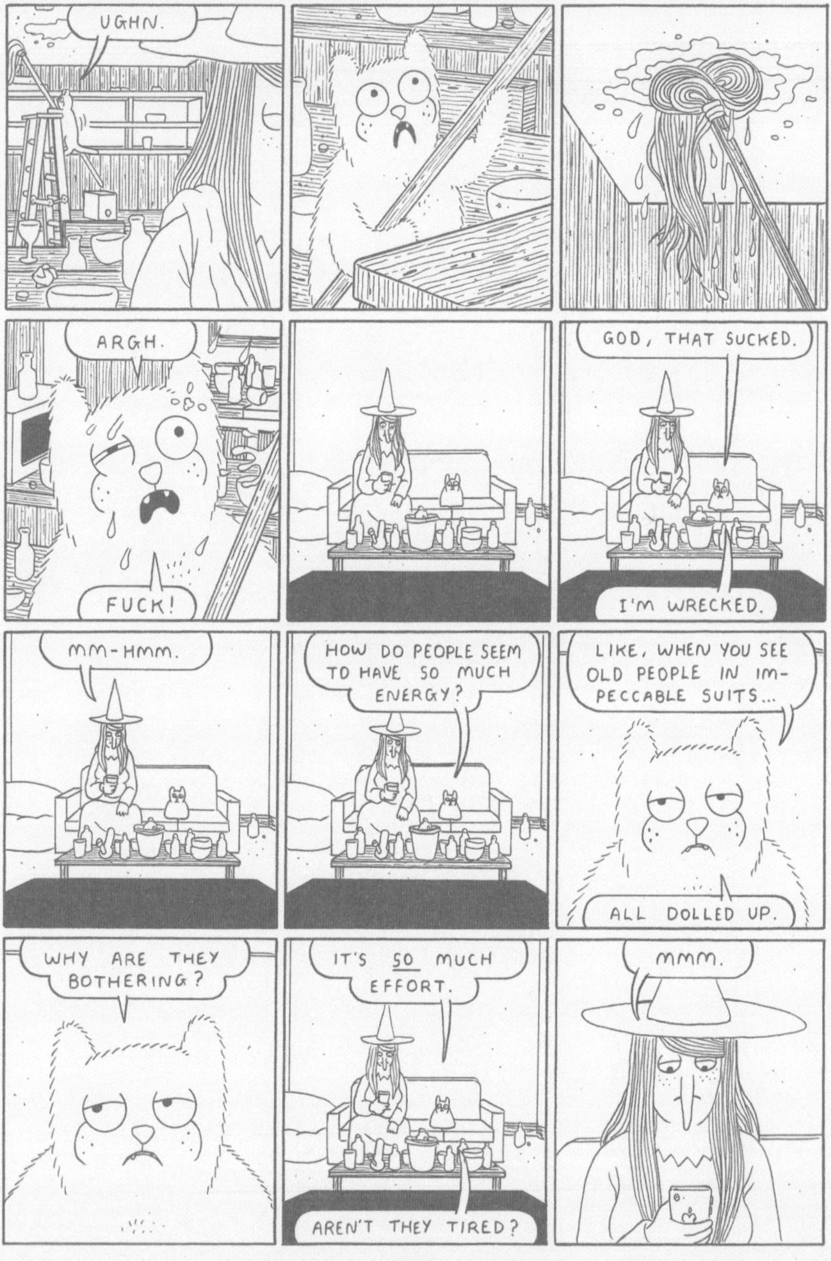
UGHN.
ARGH.
FUCK!
GOD, THAT SUCKED.
I'M WRECKED.
MM-HMM.
HOW DO PEOPLE SEEM TO HAVE SO MUCH ENERGY?
LIKE, WHEN YOU SEE OLD PEOPLE IN IMPECCABLE SUITS...
ALL DOLLED UP.
WHY ARE THEY BOTHERING?
IT'S SO MUCH EFFORT.
AREN'T THEY TIRED?
MMM.

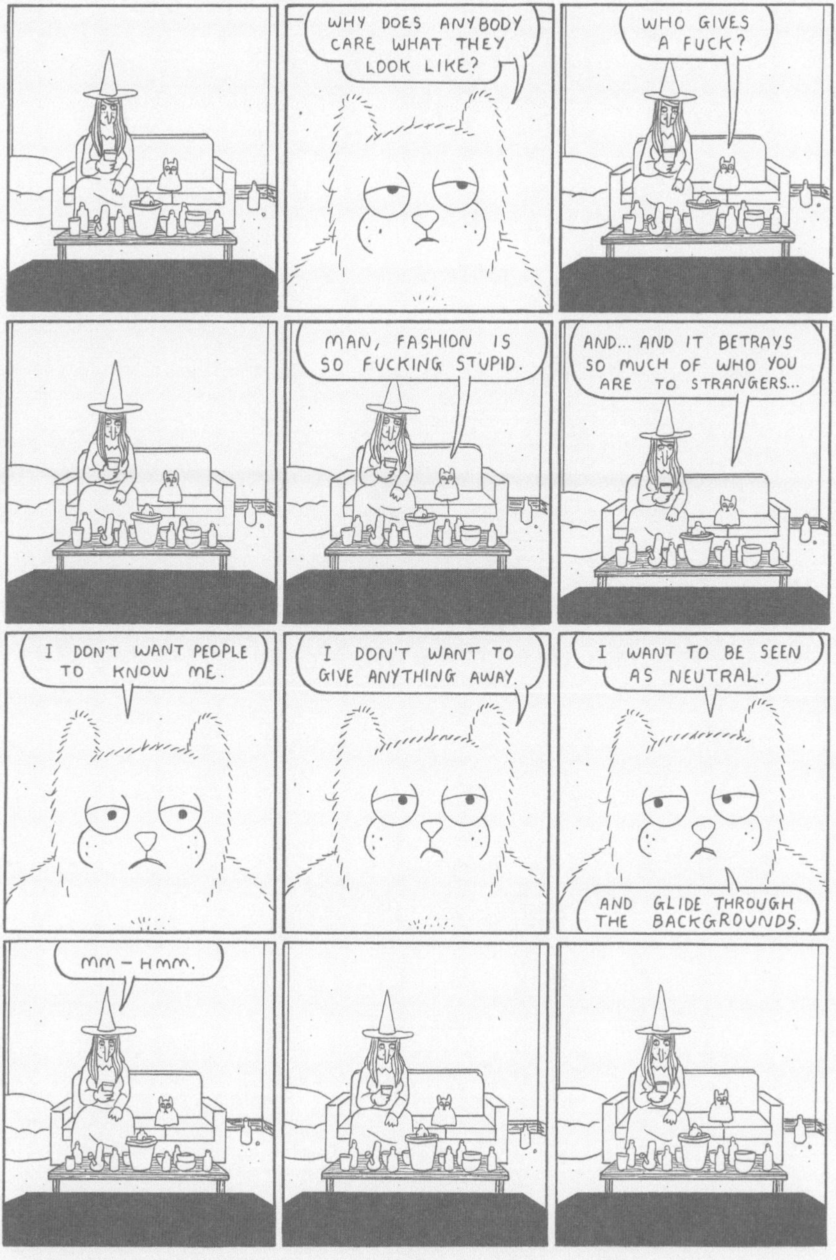
WHY DOES ANYBODY CARE WHAT THEY LOOK LIKE?
WHO GIVES A FUCK?
MAN, FASHION IS SO FUCKING STUPID.
AND... AND IT BETRAYS SO MUCH OF WHO YOU ARE TO STRANGERS...
I DON'T WANT PEOPLE TO KNOW ME.
I DON'T WANT TO GIVE ANYTHING AWAY.
I WANT TO BE SEEN AS NEUTRAL.
AND GLIDE THROUGH THE BACKGROUNDS.
MM-HMM.

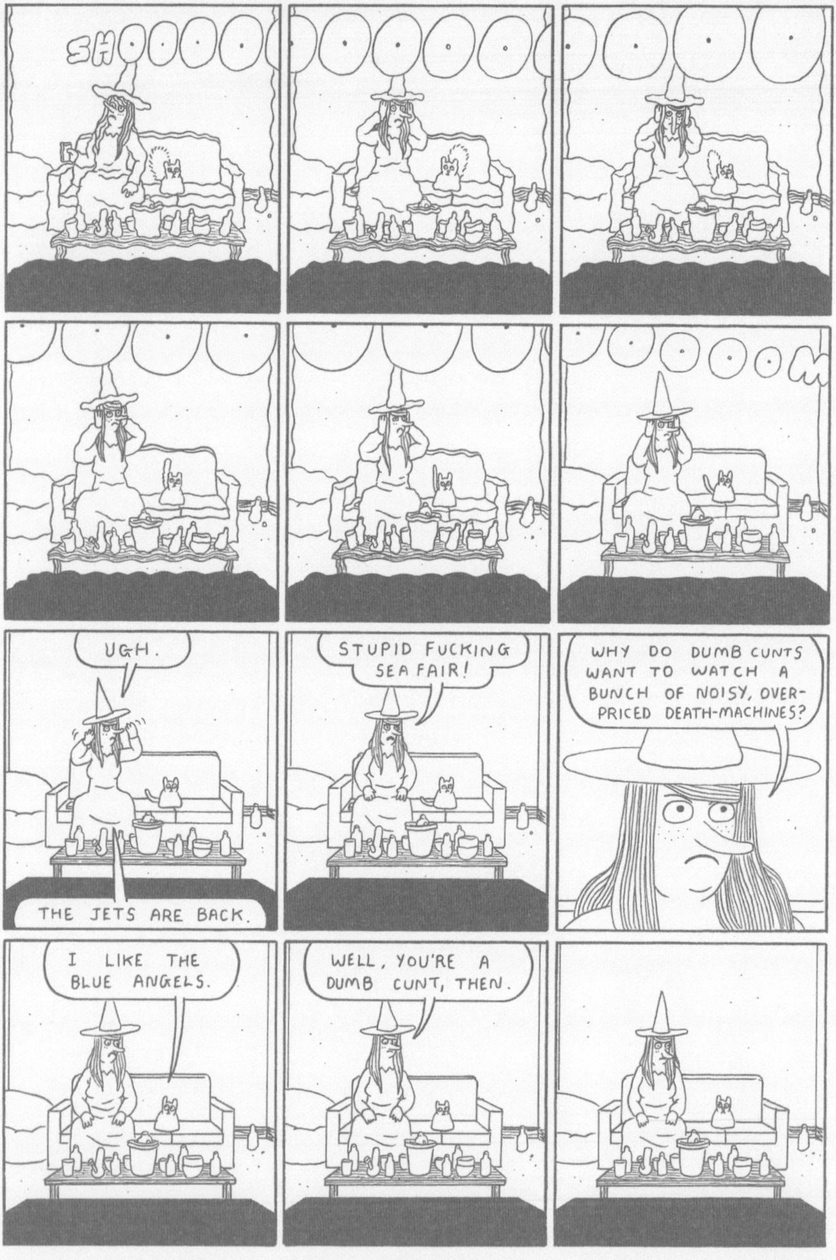
SHOOOOOOOOOOOOOOOOOOOOOOOOM
UGH.
THE JETS ARE BACK.
STUPID FUCKING SEA FAIR!
WHY DO DUMB CUNTS WANT TO WATCH A BUNCH OF NOISY, OVER-PRICED DEATH-MACHINES?
I LIKE THE BLUE ANGELS.
WELL, YOU'RE A DUMB CUNT, THEN.

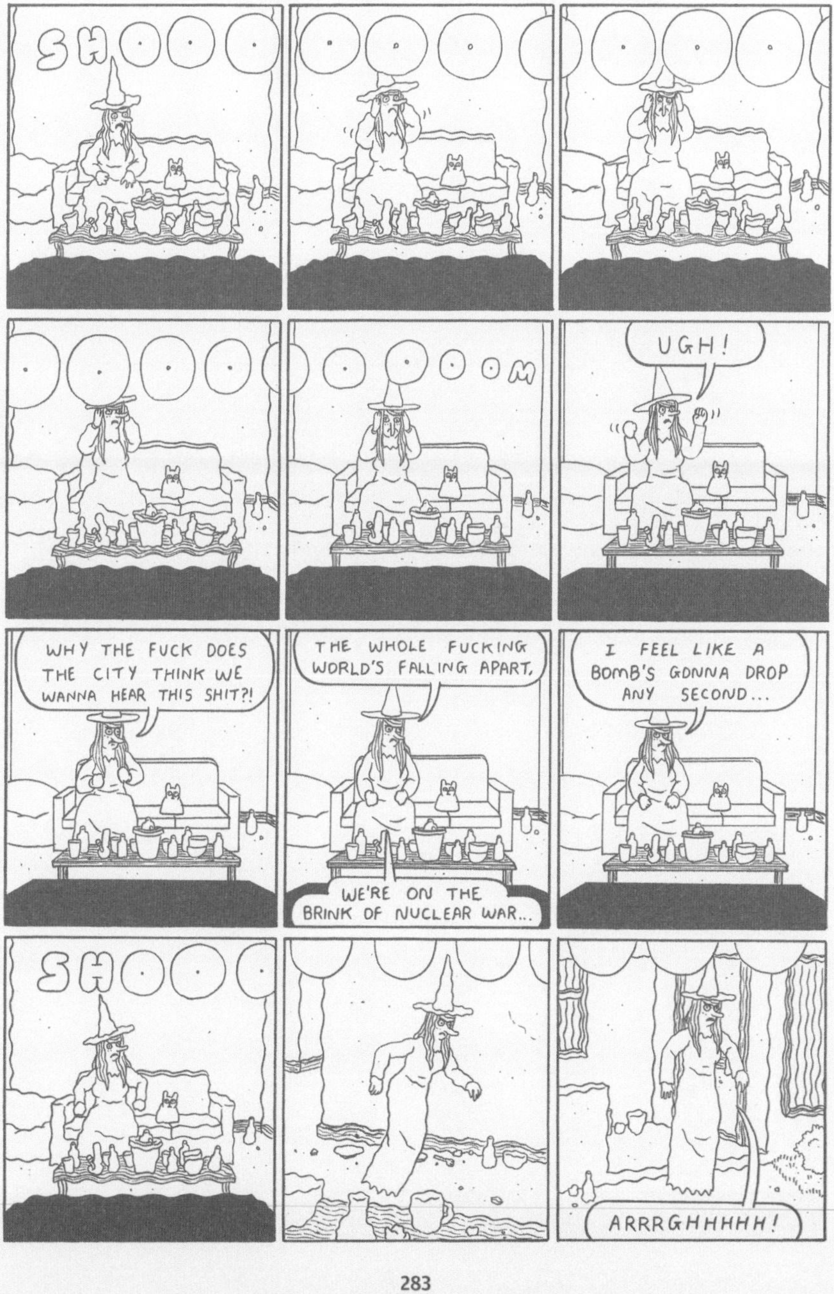
SHOOOOOOOOOOOOOOOOOM
UGH!
WHY THE FUCK DOES THE CITY THINK WE WANNA HEAR THIS SHIT?!
THE WHOLE FUCKING WORLD'S FALLING APART,
WE'RE ON THE BRINK OF NUCLEAR WAR...
I FEEL LIKE A BOMB'S GONNA DROP ANY SECOND...
SHOO
ARRRGHHHHH!

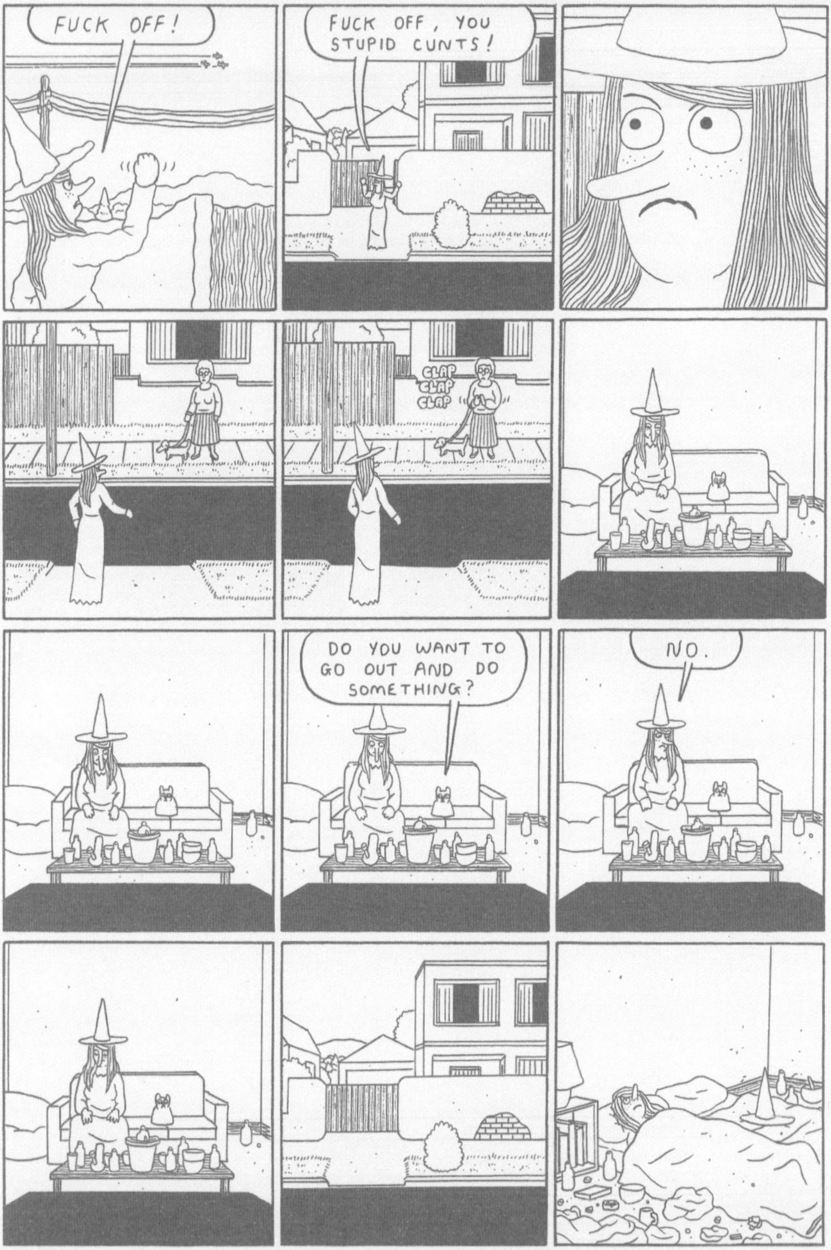
FUCK OFF!
FUCK OFF, YOU STUPID CUNTS!
CLAP CLAP CLAP
DO YOU WANT TO GO OUT AND DO SOMETHING?
NO.

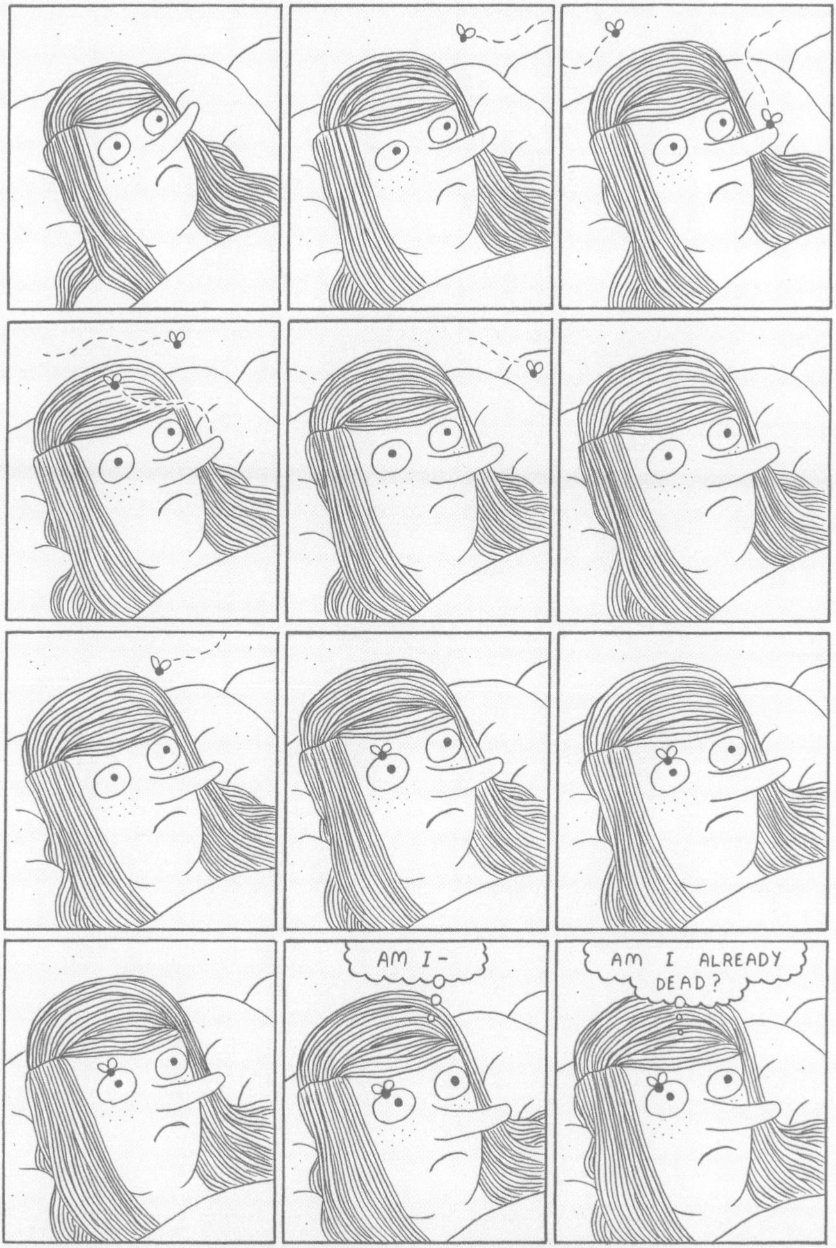
AM I-
AM I ALREADY DEAD?

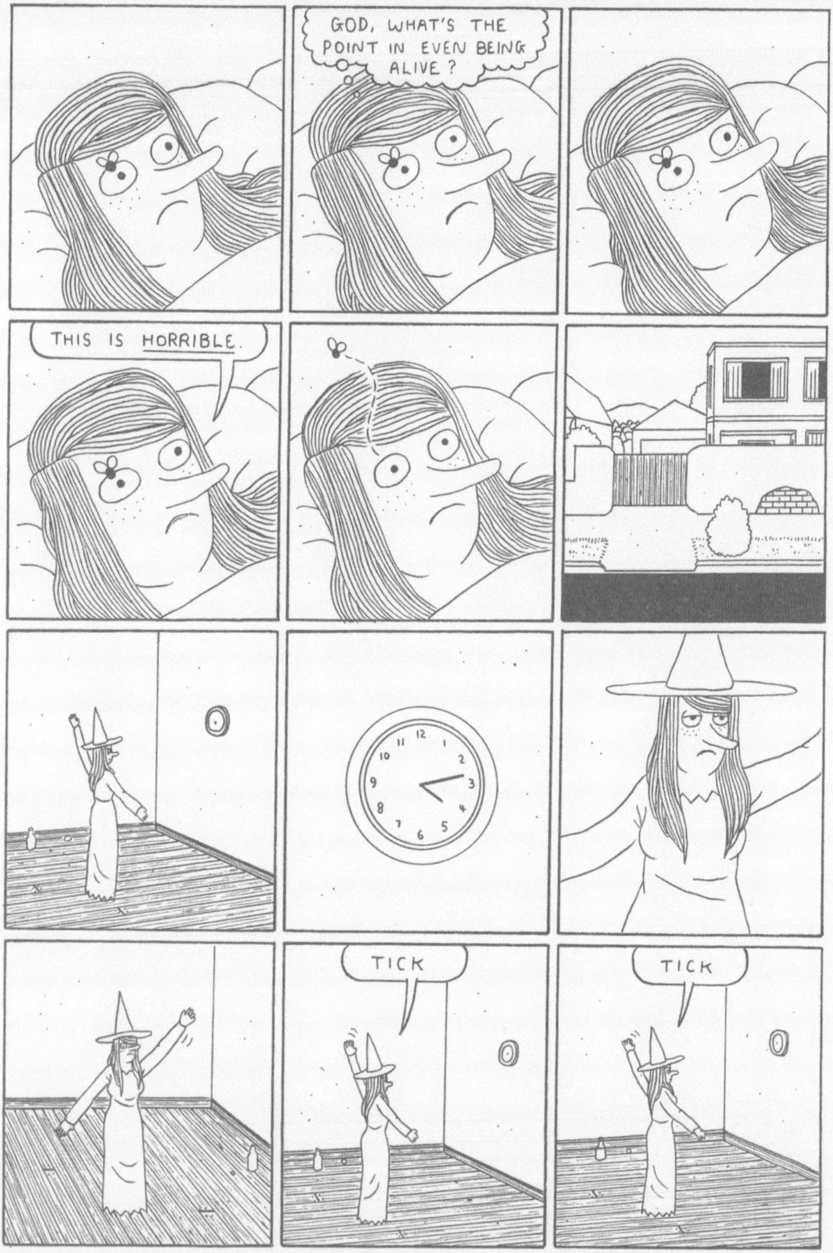
GOD, WHAT'S THE POINT IN EVEN BEING ALIVE?
THIS IS HORRIBLE.
TICK
TICK

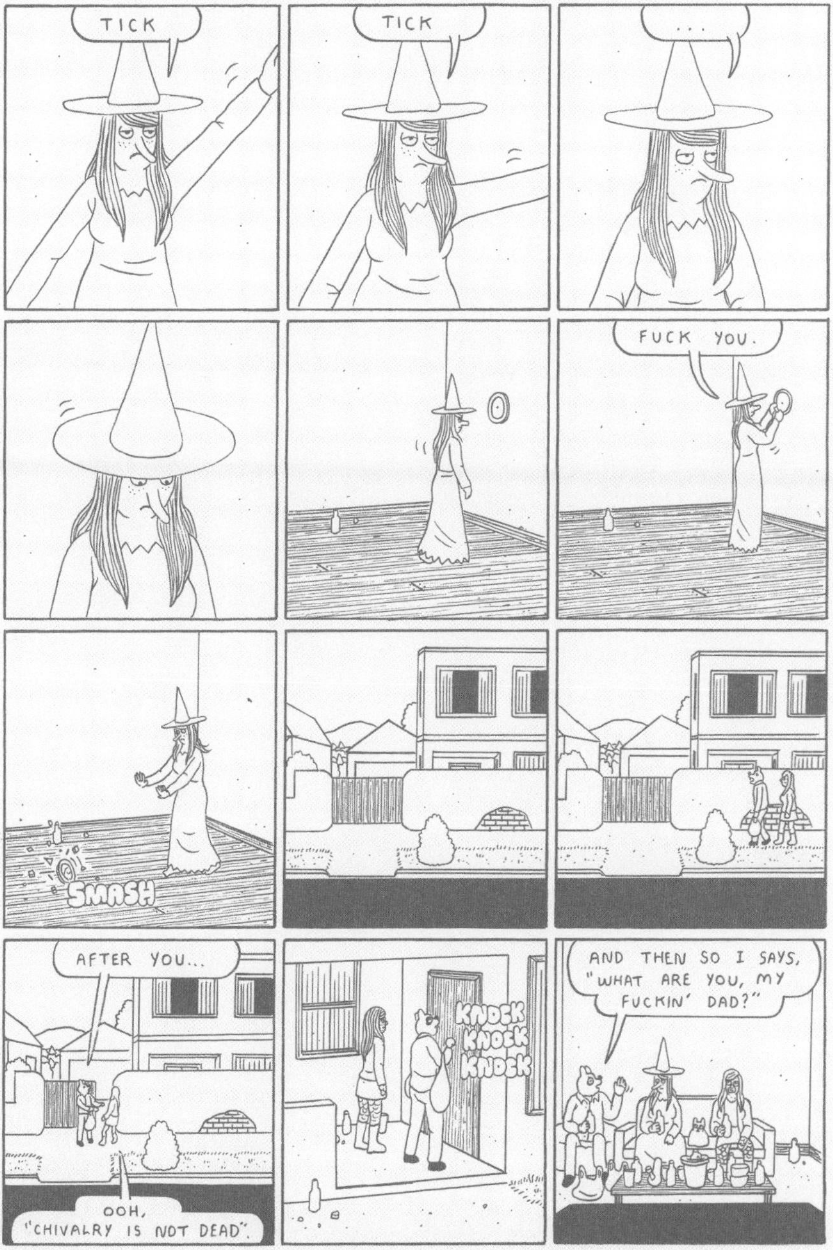
TICK
TICK
. . .
FUCK YOU.
SMASH
AFTER YOU...
OOH, "CHIVALRY IS NOT DEAD".
KNOCK KNOCK KNOCK
AND THEN SO I SAYS, "WHAT ARE YOU, MY FUCKIN' DAD?"

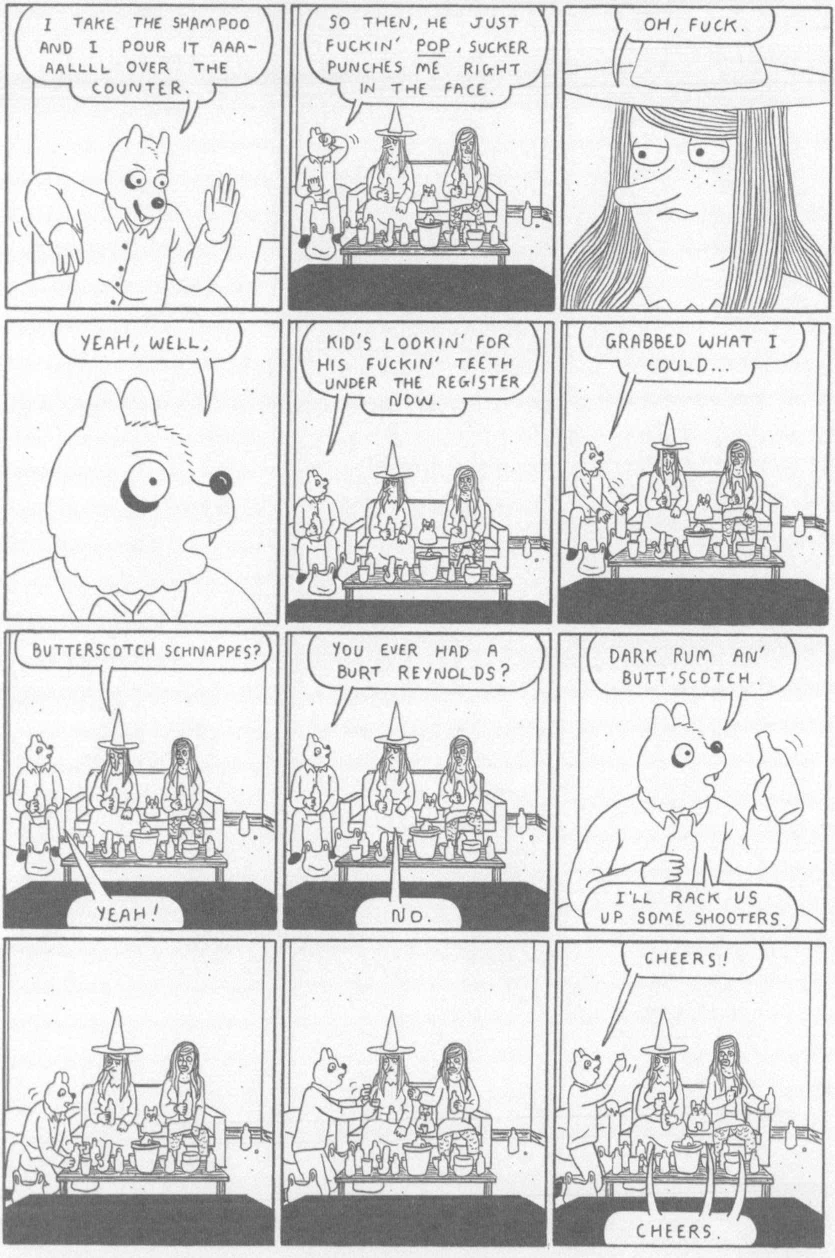
I TAKE THE SHAMPOO AND I POUR IT AAA-AALLLL OVER THE COUNTER.
SO THEN, HE JUST FUCKIN' POP, SUCKER PUNCHES ME RIGHT IN THE FACE.
OH, FUCK.
YEAH, WELL,
KID'S LOOKIN' FOR HIS FUCKIN' TEETH UNDER THE REGISTER NOW.
GRABBED WHAT I COULD...
BUTTERSCOTCH SCHNAPPES?
YEAH!
YOU EVER HAD A BURT REYNOLDS?
NO.
DARK RUM AN' BUTT'SCOTCH.
I'LL RACK US UP SOME SHOOTERS.
CHEERS!
CHEERS.

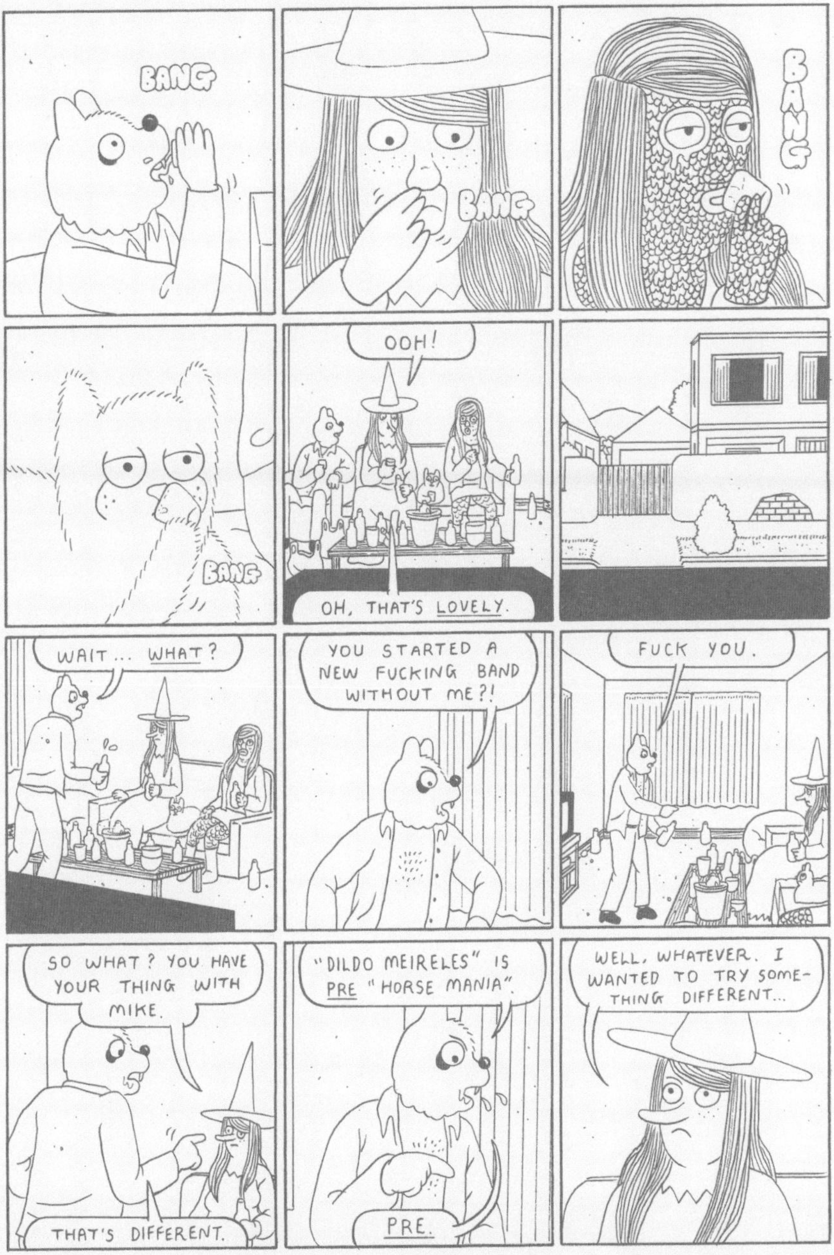
BANG
BANG
BANG
BANG
OOH!
OH, THAT'S LOVELY.
WAIT... WHAT?
YOU STARTED A NEW FUCKING BAND WITHOUT ME?!
FUCK YOU.
SO WHAT? YOU HAVE YOUR THING WITH MIKE.
THAT'S DIFFERENT.
"DILDO MEIRELES" IS PRE "HORSE MANIA".
PRE.
WELL, WHATEVER. I WANTED TO TRY SOME-THING DIFFERENT...

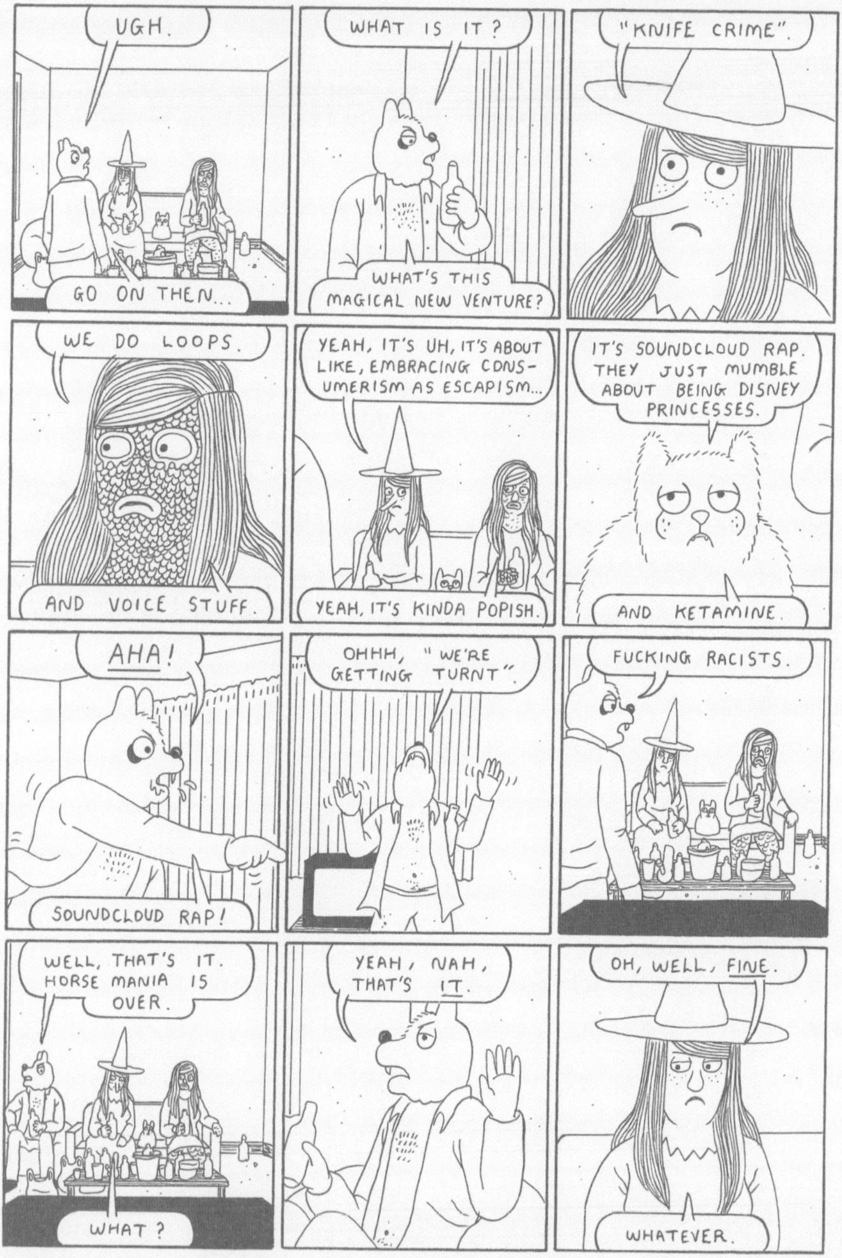
UGH.
GO ON THEN...
WHAT IS IT?
WHAT'S THIS MAGICAL NEW VENTURE?
"KNIFE CRIME".
WE DO LOOPS.
AND VOICE STUFF.
YEAH, IT'S UH, IT'S ABOUT LIKE, EMBRACING CONSUMERISM AS ESCAPISM...
YEAH, IT'S KINDA POPISH.
IT'S SOUNDCLOUD RAP. THEY JUST MUMBLE ABOUT BEING DISNEY PRINCESSES.
AND KETAMINE.
AHA!
SOUNDCLOUD RAP!
OHHH, "WE'RE GETTING TURNT".
FUCKING RACISTS.
WELL, THAT'S IT. HORSE MANIA IS OVER.
WHAT?
YEAH, NAH, THAT'S IT.
OH, WELL, FINE.
WHATEVER.

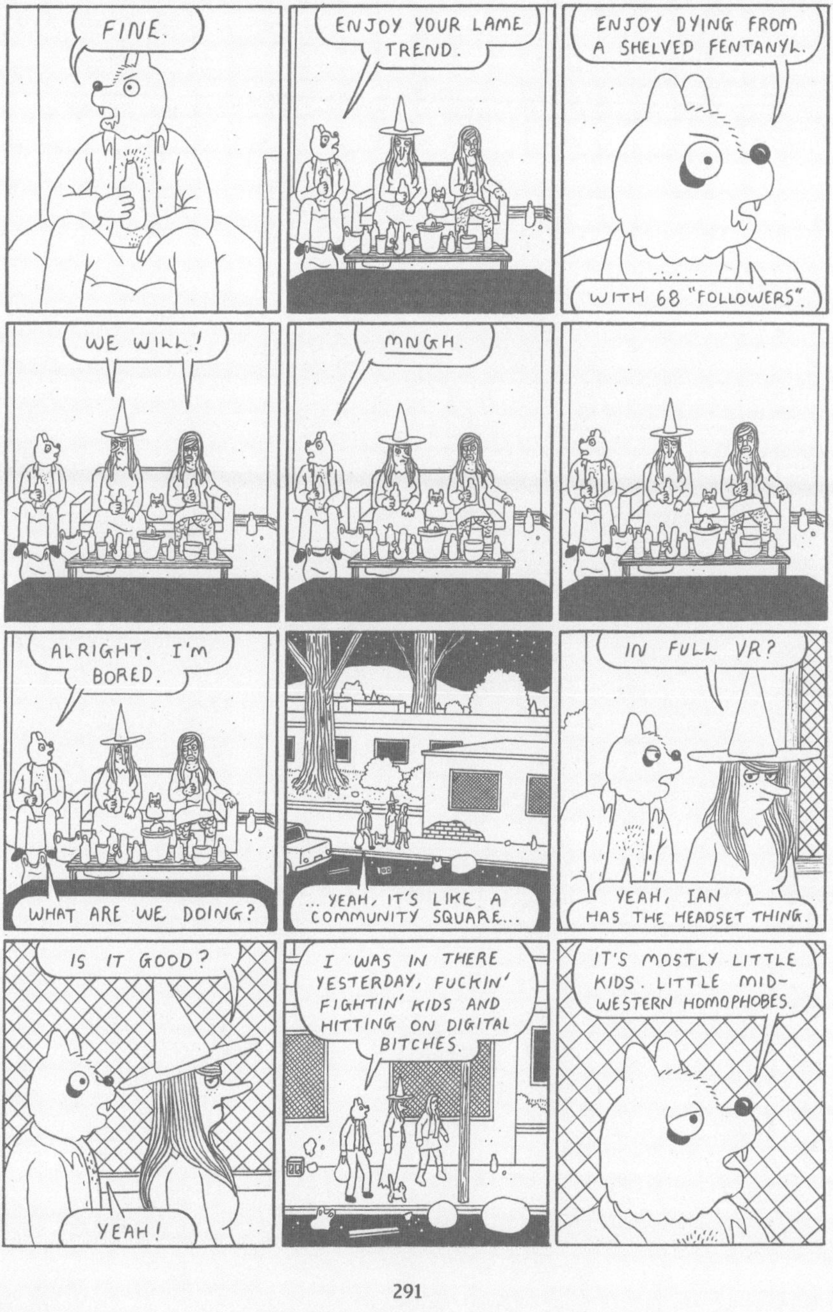
FINE.
ENJOY YOUR LAME TREND.
ENJOY DYING FROM A SHELVED FENTANYL.
WITH 68 "FOLLOWERS".
WE WILL!
MNGH.
ALRIGHT. I'M BORED.
WHAT ARE WE DOING?
... YEAH, IT'S LIKE A COMMUNITY SQUARE...
IN FULL VR?
YEAH, IAN HAS THE HEADSET THING.
IS IT GOOD?
YEAH!
I WAS IN THERE YESTERDAY, FUCKIN' FIGHTIN' KIDS AND HITTING ON DIGITAL BITCHES.
IT'S MOSTLY LITTLE KIDS. LITTLE MID-WESTERN HOMOPHOBES.

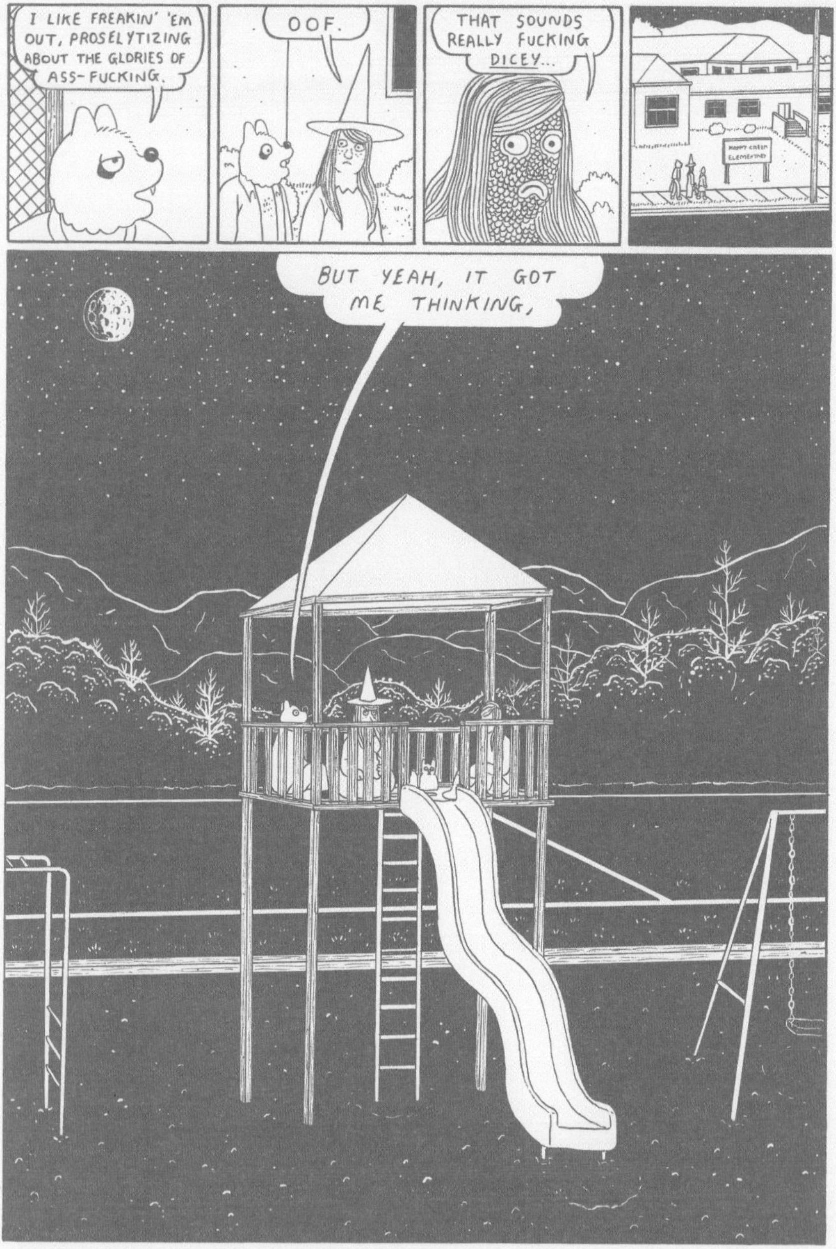
I LIKE FREAKIN' 'EM OUT, PROSELYTIZING ABOUT THE GLORIES OF ASS-FUCKING.
OOF.
THAT SOUNDS REALLY FUCKING DICEY...
BUT YEAH, IT GOT ME THINKING,

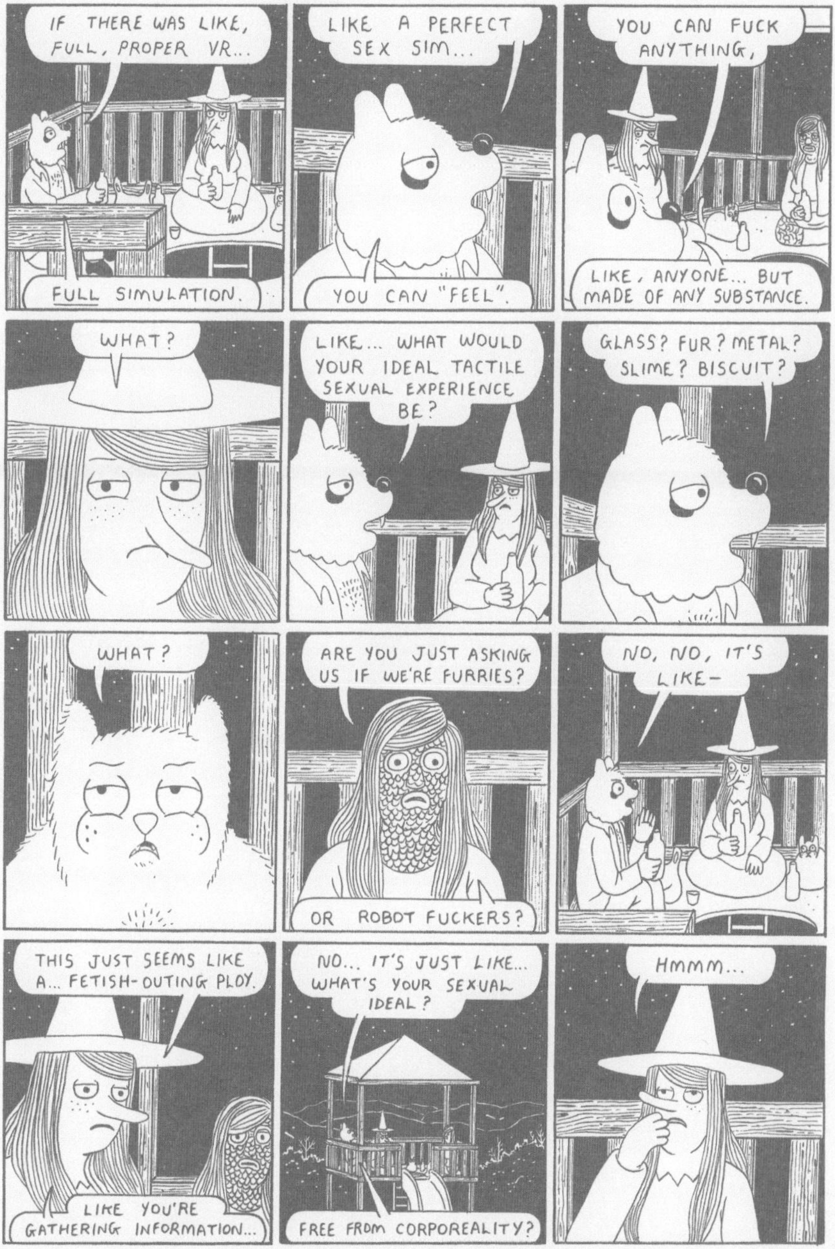
IF THERE WAS LIKE, FULL, PROPER VR...
FULL SIMULATION.
LIKE A PERFECT SEX SIM...
YOU CAN "FEEL".
YOU CAN FUCK ANYTHING,
LIKE, ANYONE... BUT MADE OF ANY SUBSTANCE.
WHAT?
LIKE... WHAT WOULD YOUR IDEAL TACTILE SEXUAL EXPERIENCE BE?
GLASS? FUR? METAL? SLIME? BISCUIT?
WHAT?
ARE YOU JUST ASKING US IF WE'RE FURRIES?
OR ROBOT FUCKERS?
NO, NO, IT'S LIKE-
THIS JUST SEEMS LIKE A... FETISH-OUTING PLOY.
LIKE YOU'RE GATHERING INFORMATION...
NO... IT'S JUST LIKE... WHAT'S YOUR SEXUAL IDEAL?
FREE FROM CORPOREALITY?
HMMM...

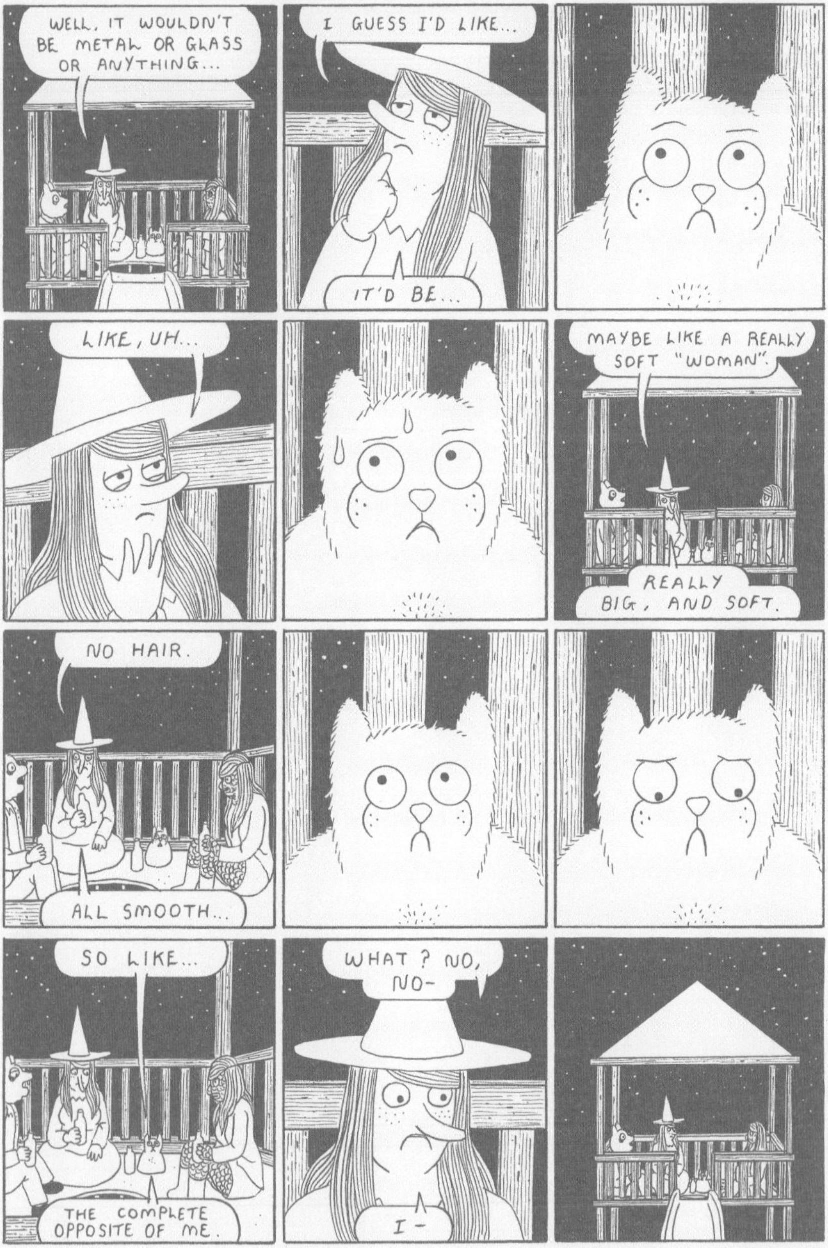

WELL, IT WOULDN'T BE METAL OR GLASS OR ANYTHING...
I GUESS I'D LIKE...
IT'D BE...
LIKE, UH...
MAYBE LIKE A REALLY SOFT "WOMAN".
REALLY BIG, AND SOFT.
NO HAIR.
ALL SMOOTH...
SO LIKE...
THE COMPLETE OPPOSITE OF ME.
WHAT? NO, NO-
I-

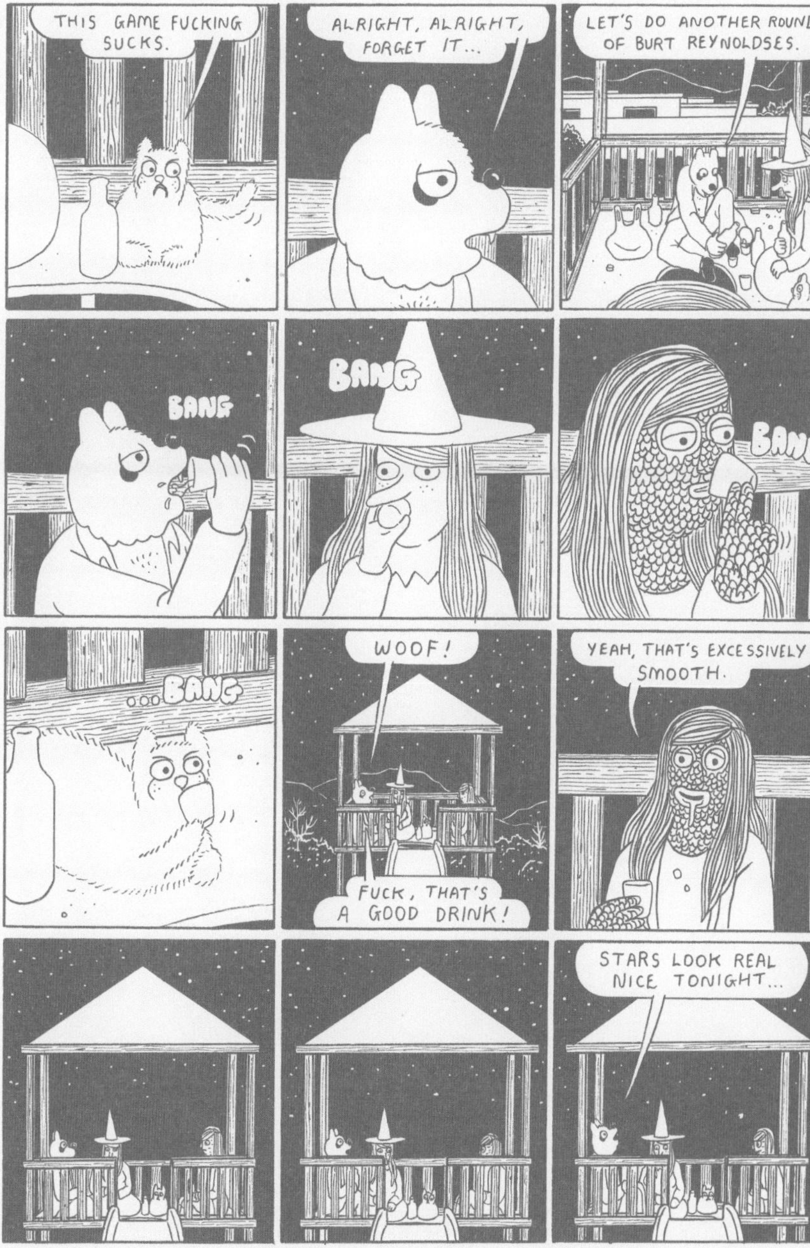
THIS GAME FUCKING SUCKS.
ALRIGHT, ALRIGHT, FORGET IT...
LET'S DO ANOTHER ROUND OF BURT REYNOLDSES.
BANG
BANG
BANG
...BANG
WOOF!
FUCK, THAT'S A GOOD DRINK!
YEAH, THAT'S EXCESSIVELY SMOOTH.
STARS LOOK REAL NICE TONIGHT...

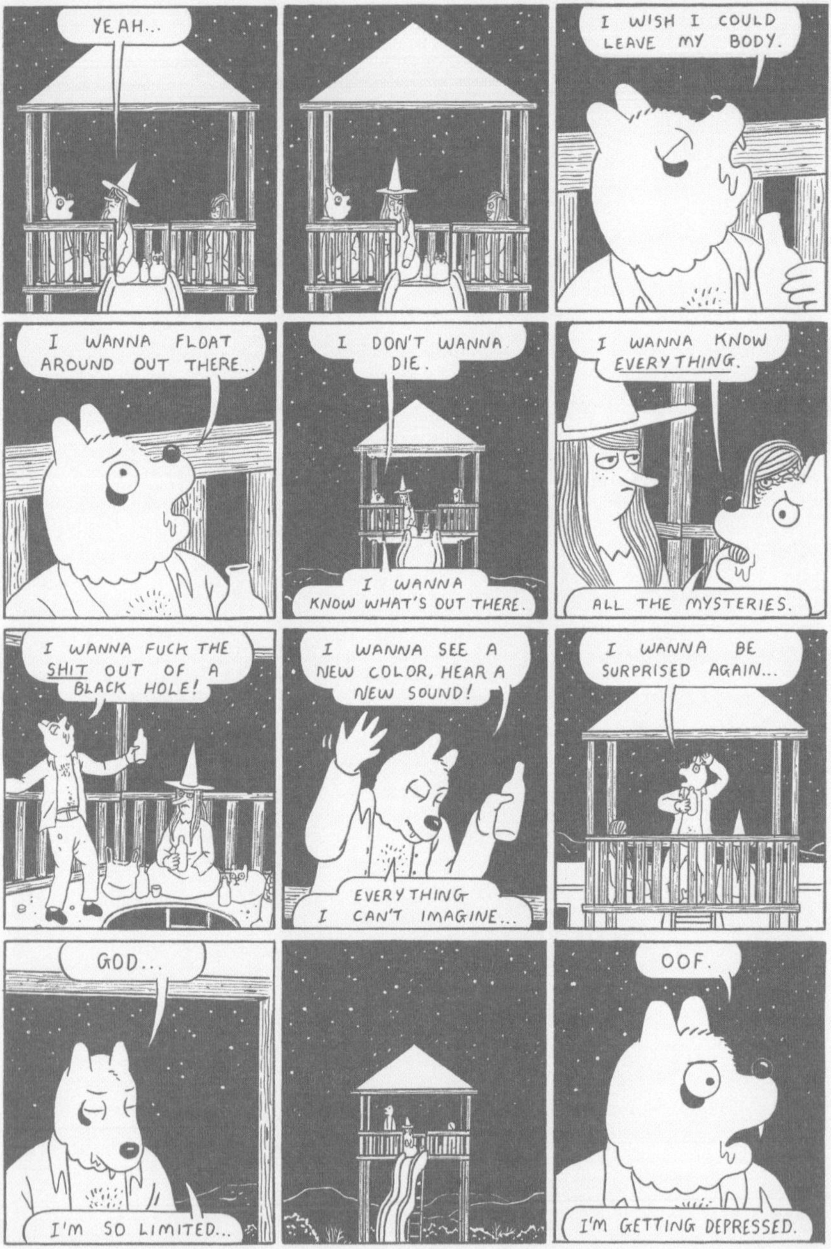
YEAH...
I WISH I COULD LEAVE MY BODY.
I WANNA FLOAT AROUND OUT THERE...
I DON'T WANNA DIE.
I WANNA KNOW WHAT'S OUT THERE.
I WANNA KNOW EVERYTHING.
ALL THE MYSTERIES.
I WANNA FUCK THE SHIT OUT OF A BLACK HOLE!
I WANNA SEE A NEW COLOR, HEAR A NEW SOUND!
EVERYTHING I CAN'T IMAGINE...
I WANNA BE SURPRISED AGAIN...
GOD...
I'M SO LIMITED...
OOF.
I'M GETTING DEPRESSED.

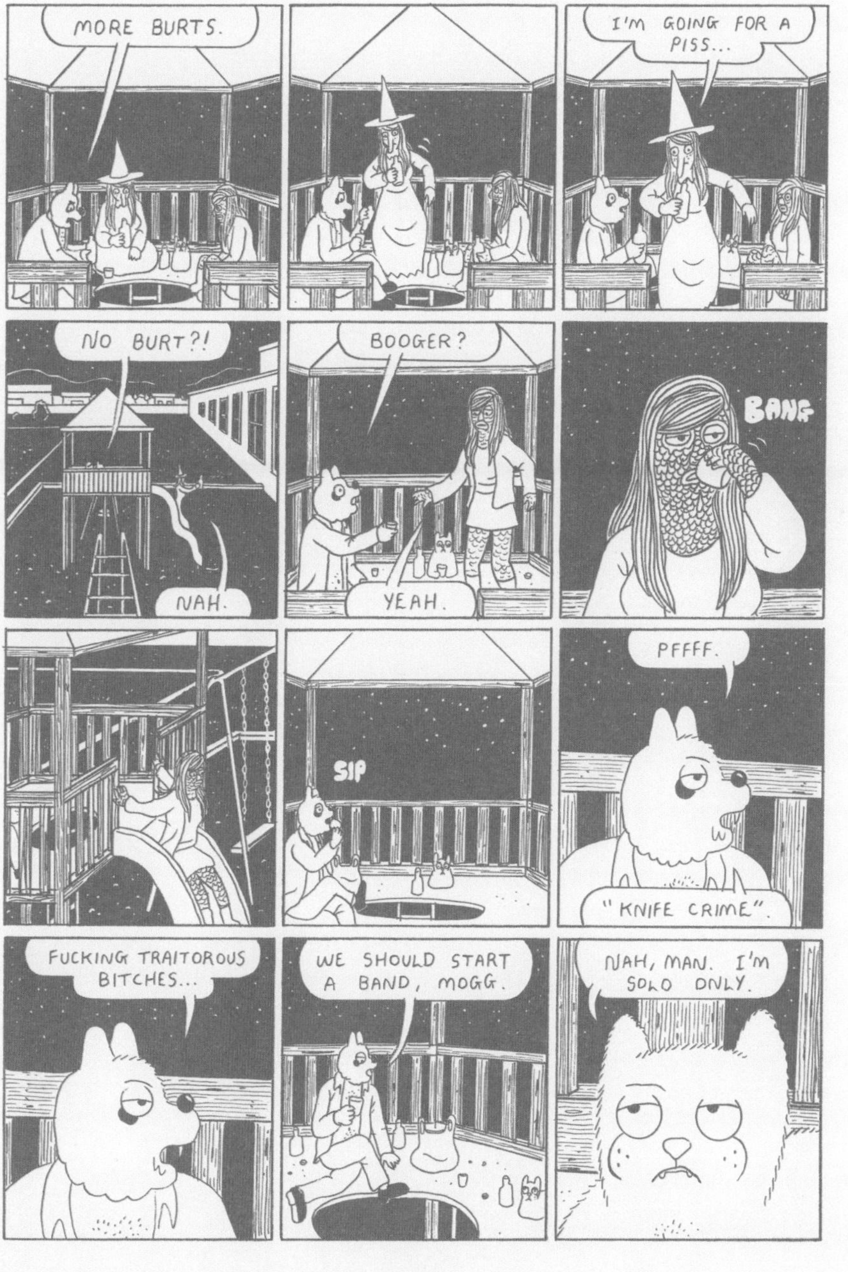
MORE BURTS.
I'M GOING FOR A PISS...
NO BURT?!
NAH.
BOOGER?
YEAH.
BANG
SIP
PFFFF.
"KNIFE CRIME".
FUCKING TRAITOROUS BITCHES...
WE SHOULD START A BAND, MOGG.
NAH, MAN. I'M SOLO ONLY.

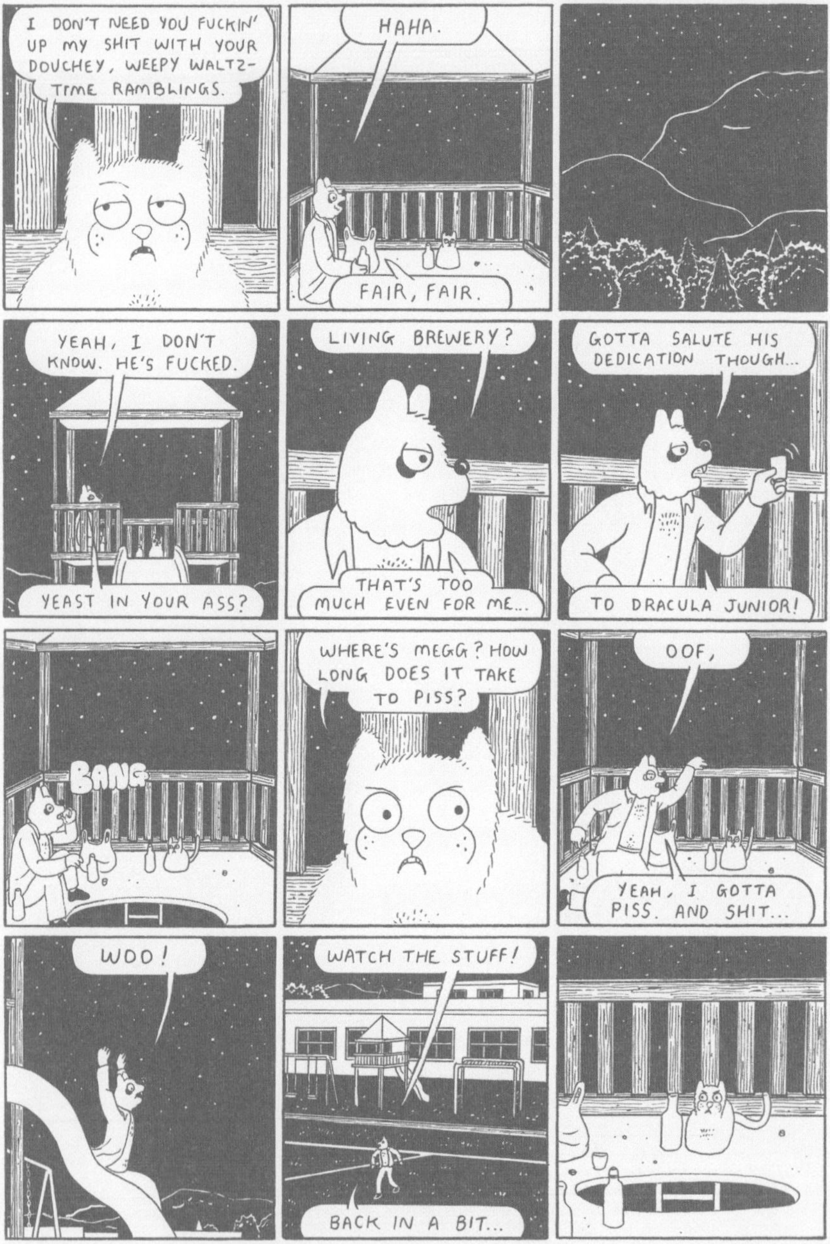

I DON'T NEED YOU FUCKIN' UP MY SHIT WITH YOUR DOUCHEY, WEEPY WALTZ-TIME RAMBLINGS.
HAHA.
FAIR, FAIR.
YEAH, I DON'T KNOW. HE'S FUCKED.
YEAST IN YOUR ASS?
LIVING BREWERY?
THAT'S TOO MUCH EVEN FOR ME...
GOTTA SALUTE HIS DEDICATION THOUGH...
TO DRACULA JUNIOR!
BANG
WHERE'S MEGG? HOW LONG DOES IT TAKE TO PISS?
OOF,
YEAH, I GOTTA PISS. AND SHIT...
WOO!
WATCH THE STUFF!
BACK IN A BIT...

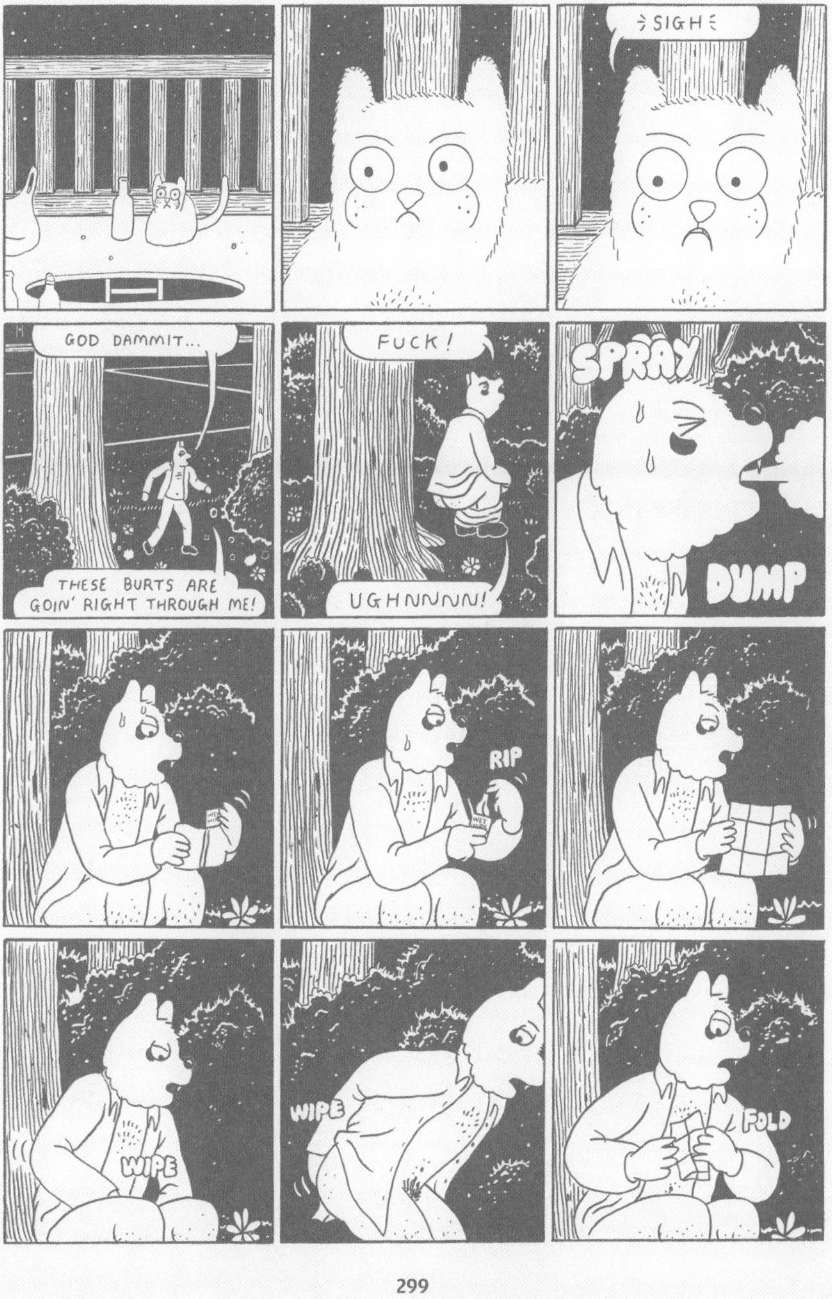
SIGH
GOD DAMMIT...
THESE BURTS ARE GOIN' RIGHT THROUGH ME!
FUCK!
UGHNNNN!
SPRAY
DUMP
RIP
WIPE
WIPE
FOLD

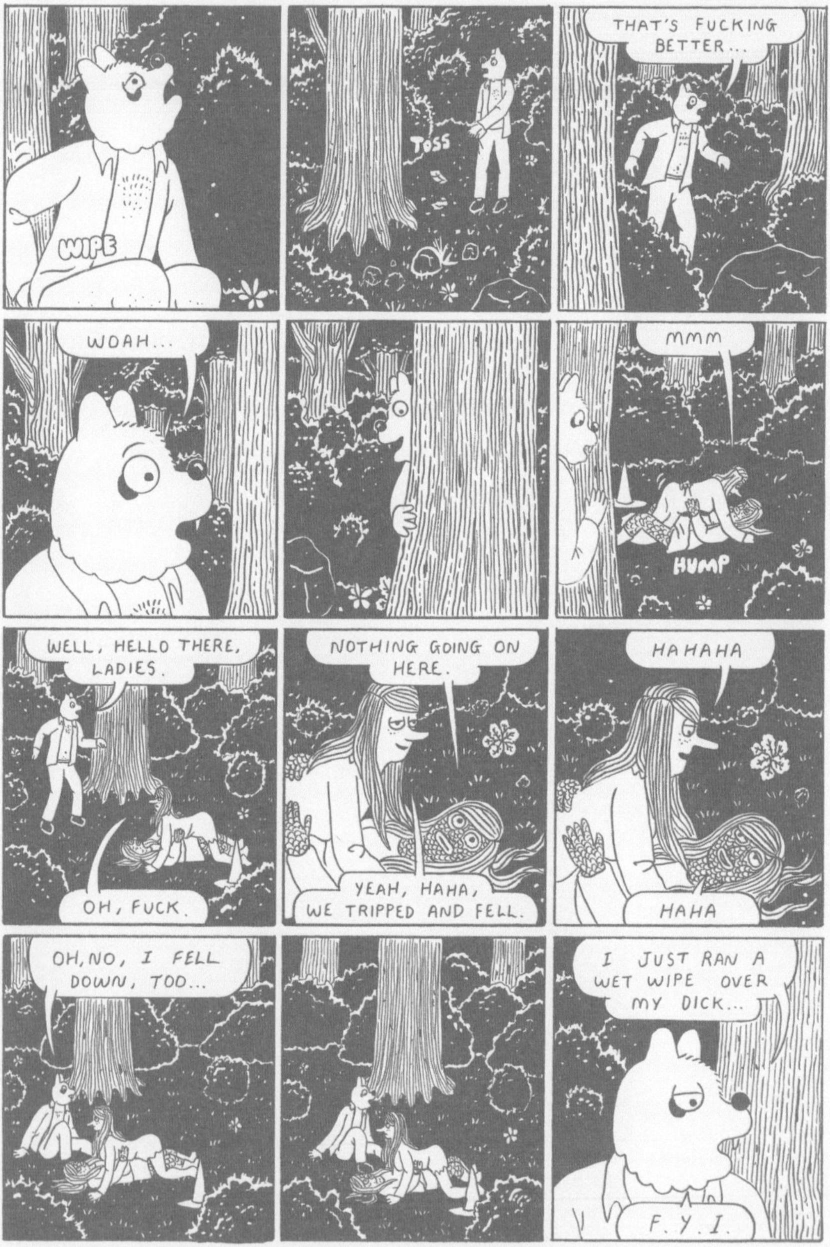
WIPE
TOSS
THAT'S FUCKING BETTER...
WOAH...
MMM
HUMP
WELL, HELLO THERE, LADIES.
OH, FUCK.
NOTHING GOING ON HERE.
YEAH, HAHA, WE TRIPPED AND FELL.
HAHAHA
HAHA
OH, NO, I FELL DOWN, TOO...
I JUST RAN A WET WIPE OVER MY DICK...
F. Y. I.

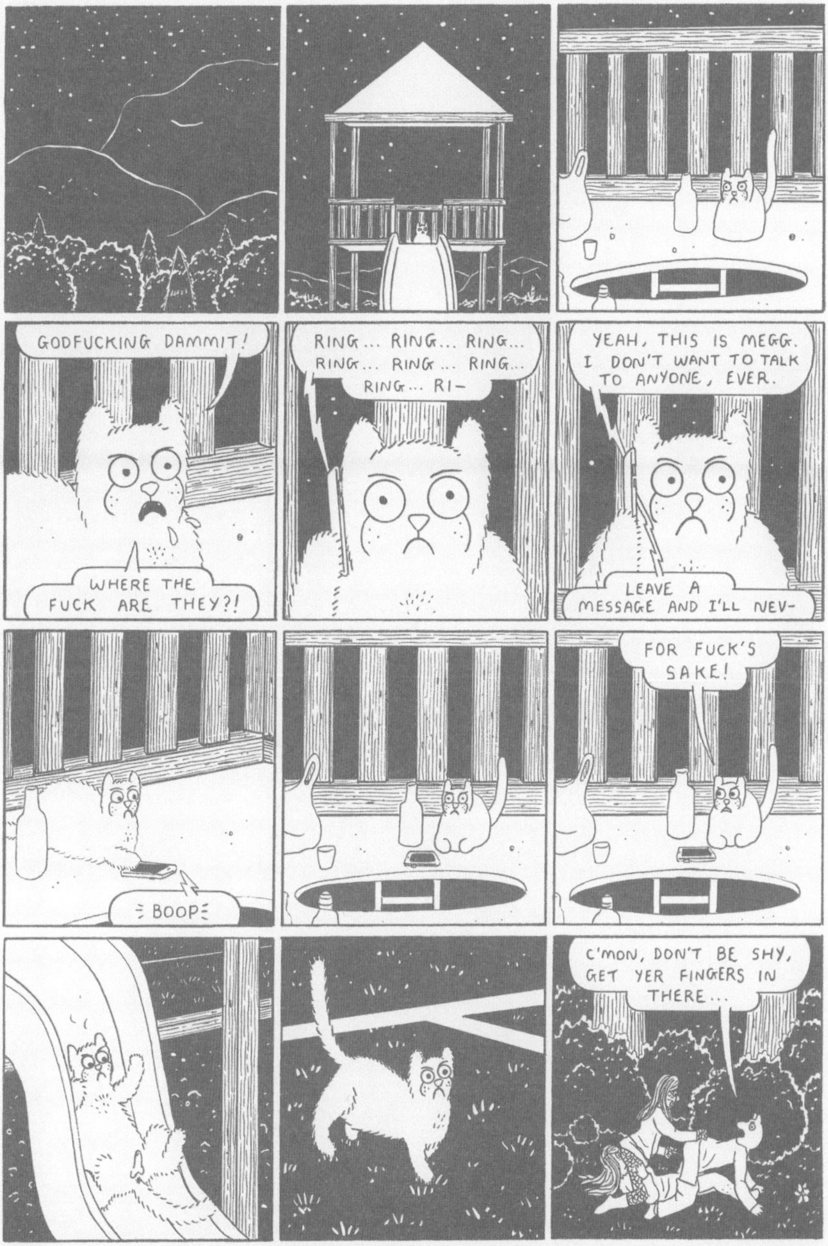
GODFUCKING DAMMIT!
WHERE THE FUCK ARE THEY?!
RING... RING... RING... RING... RING... RING... RING... RI-
YEAH, THIS IS MEGG. I DON'T WANT TO TALK TO ANYONE, EVER.
LEAVE A MESSAGE AND I'LL NEV-
BOOP
FOR FUCK'S SAKE!
C'MON, DON'T BE SHY, GET YER FINGERS IN THERE...

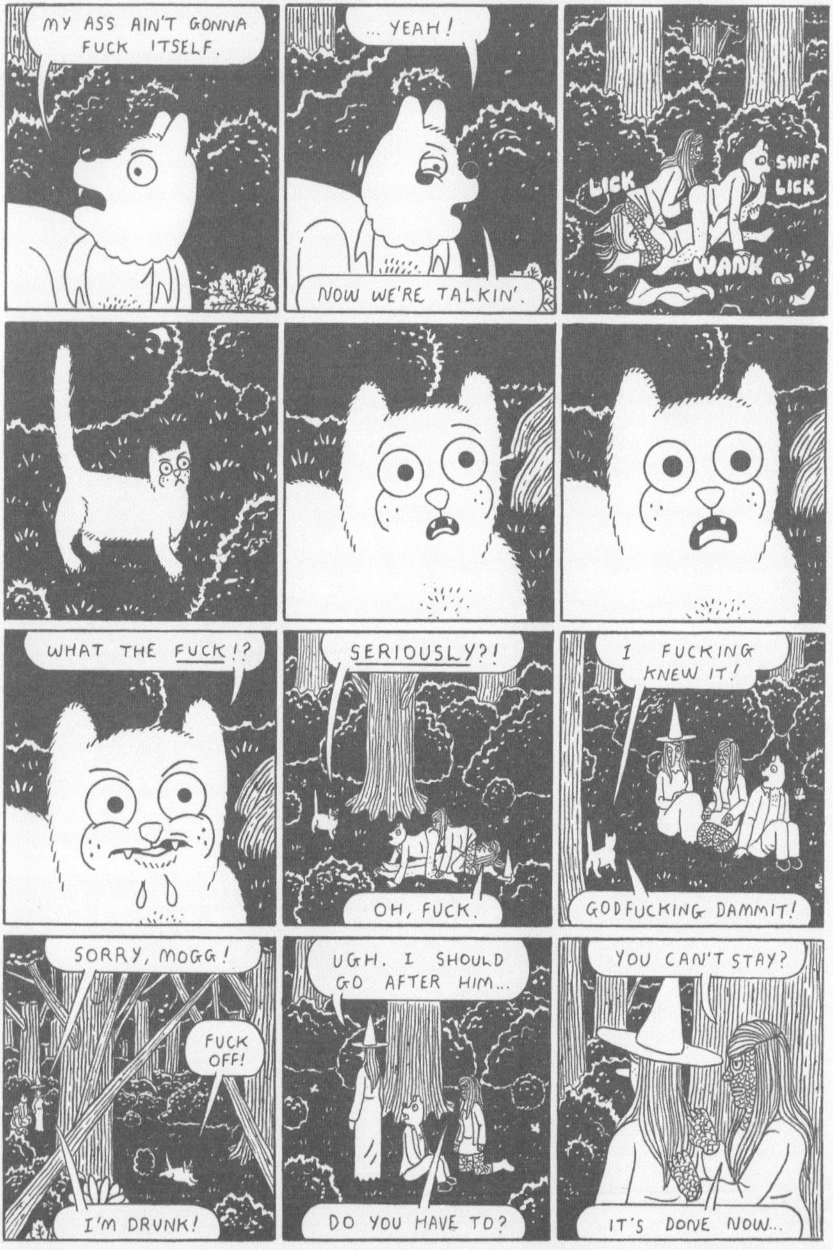

MY ASS AIN'T GONNA FUCK ITSELF.
... YEAH!
NOW WE'RE TALKIN'.
LICK
SNIFF
LICK
WANK
WHAT THE FUCK!?
SERIOUSLY?!
OH, FUCK.
I FUCKING KNEW IT!
GODFUCKING DAMMIT!
SORRY, MOGG!
FUCK OFF!
I'M DRUNK!
UGH. I SHOULD GO AFTER HIM...
DO YOU HAVE TO?
YOU CAN'T STAY?
IT'S DONE NOW...

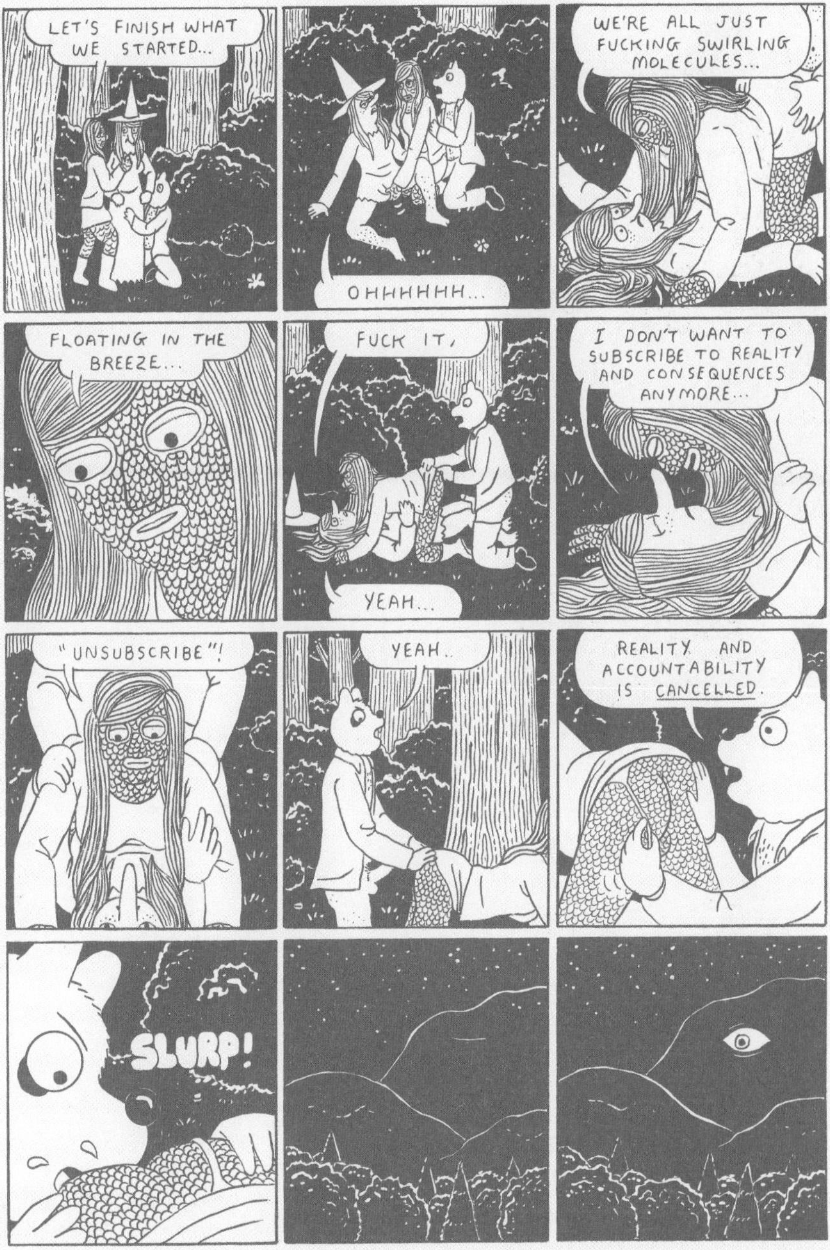
LET'S FINISH WHAT WE STARTED...
OHHHHHH...
WE'RE ALL JUST FUCKING SWIRLING MOLECULES...
FLOATING IN THE BREEZE...
FUCK IT,
YEAH...
I DON'T WANT TO SUBSCRIBE TO REALITY AND CONSEQUENCES ANYMORE...
"UNSUBSCRIBE"!
YEAH..
REALITY AND ACCOUNTABILITY IS CANCELLED.
SLURP!

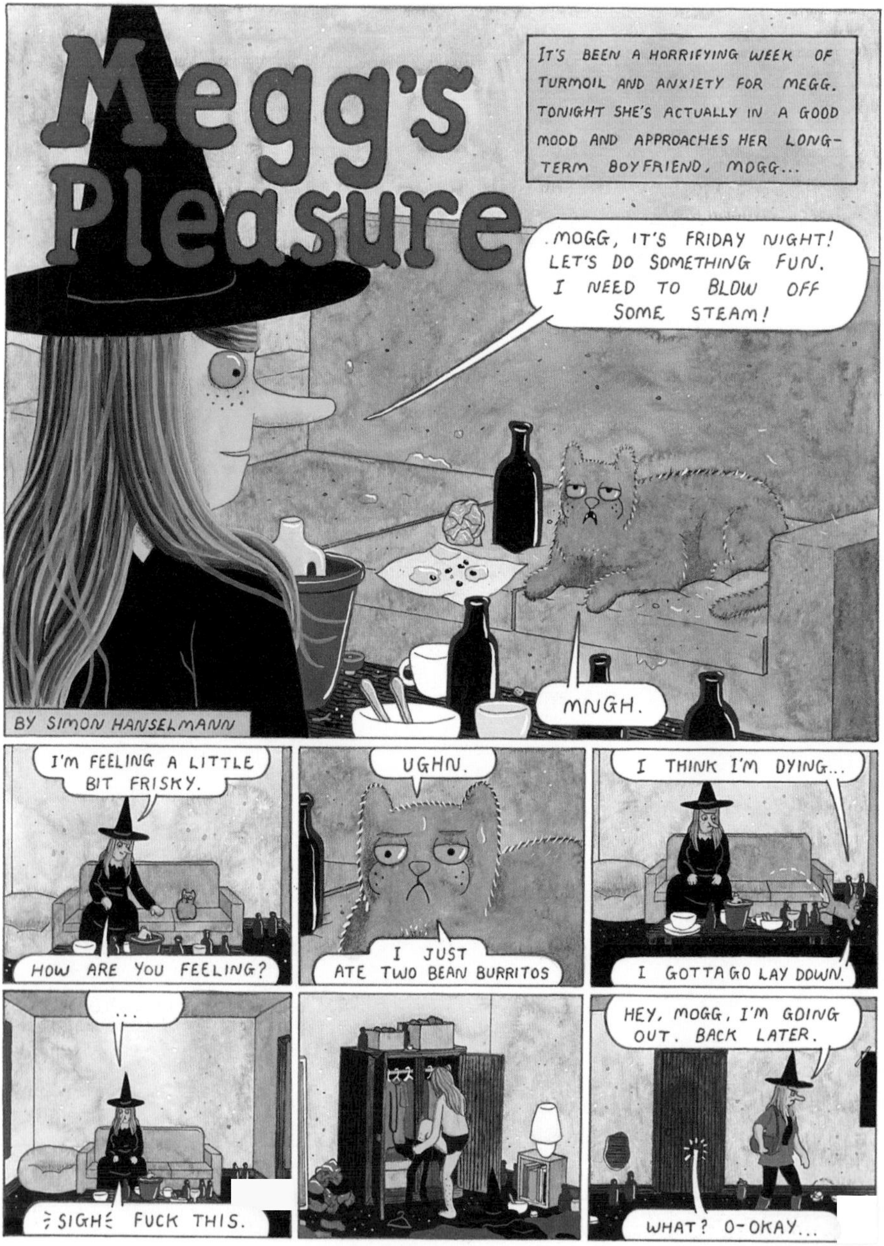
Megg's Pleasure
IT'S BEEN A HORRIFYING WEEK OF TURMOIL AND ANXIETY FOR MEGG. TONIGHT SHE'S ACTUALLY IN A GOOD MOOD AND APPROACHES HER LONG-TERM BOYFRIEND, MOGG...
MOGG, IT'S FRIDAY NIGHT! LET'S DO SOMETHING FUN. I NEED TO BLOW OFF SOME STEAM!
MNGH.
BY SIMON HANSELMANN
I'M FEELING A LITTLE BIT FRISKY.
HOW ARE YOU FEELING?
UGHN.
I JUST ATE TWO BEAN BURRITOS
I THINK I'M DYING...
I GOTTA GO LAY DOWN.
...
SIGH FUCK THIS.
HEY, MOGG, I'M GOING OUT. BACK LATER.
WHAT? O-OKAY...

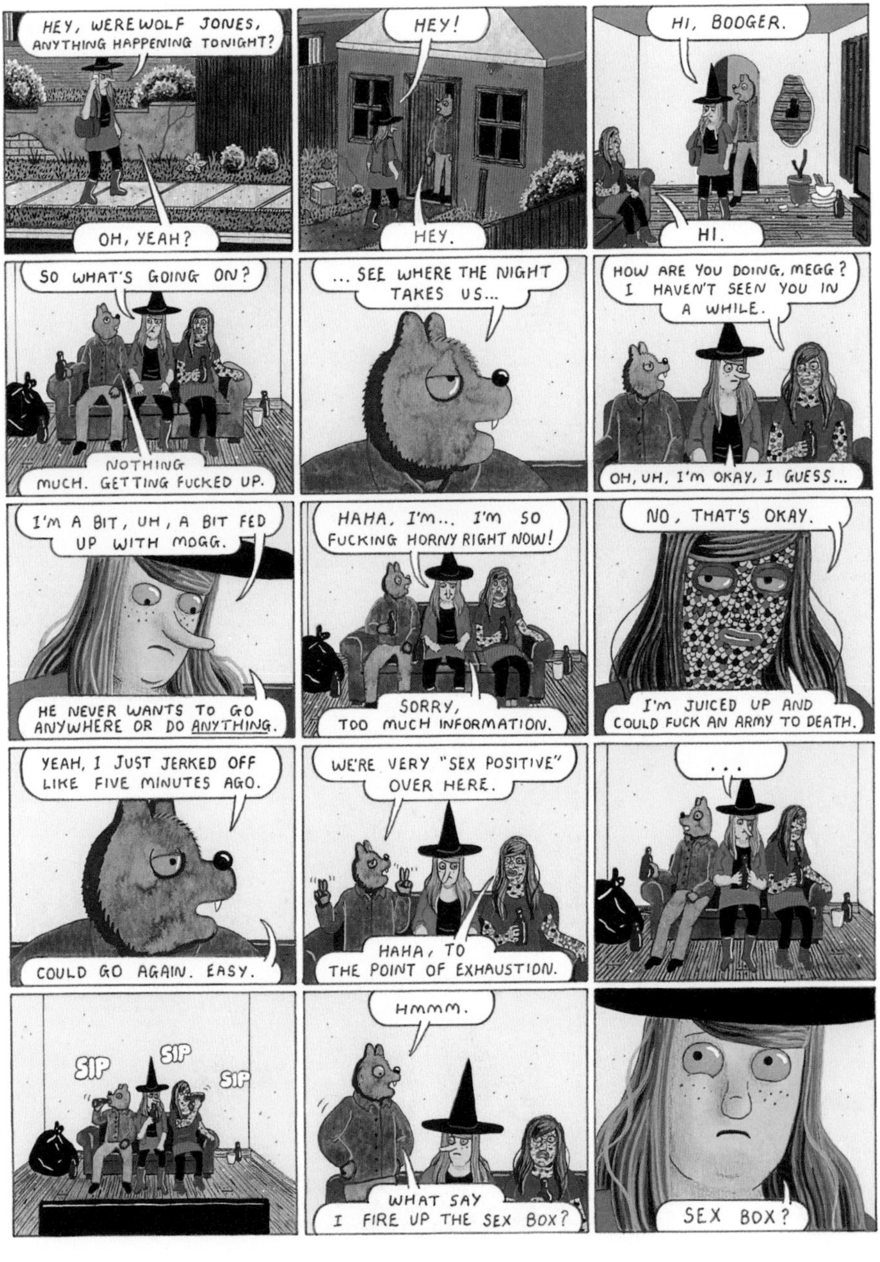
HEY, WEREWOLF JONES, ANYTHING HAPPENING TONIGHT?
OH, YEAH?
HEY!
HEY.
HI, BOOGER.
HI.
SO WHAT'S GOING ON?
NOTHING MUCH. GETTING FUCKED UP.
... SEE WHERE THE NIGHT TAKES US...
HOW ARE YOU DOING, MEGG? I HAVEN'T SEEN YOU IN A WHILE.
OH, UH, I'M OKAY, I GUESS...
I'M A BIT, UH, A BIT FED UP WITH MOGG.
HE NEVER WANTS TO GO ANYWHERE OR DO ANYTHING.
HAHA, I'M... I'M SO FUCKING HORNY RIGHT NOW!
SORRY, TOO MUCH INFORMATION.
NO, THAT'S OKAY.
I'M JUICED UP AND COULD FUCK AN ARMY TO DEATH.
YEAH, I JUST JERKED OFF LIKE FIVE MINUTES AGO.
COULD GO AGAIN. EASY.
WE'RE VERY "SEX POSITIVE" OVER HERE.
HAHA, TO THE POINT OF EXHAUSTION.
. . .
SIP
SIP
SIP
HMMM.
WHAT SAY I FIRE UP THE SEX BOX?
SEX BOX?

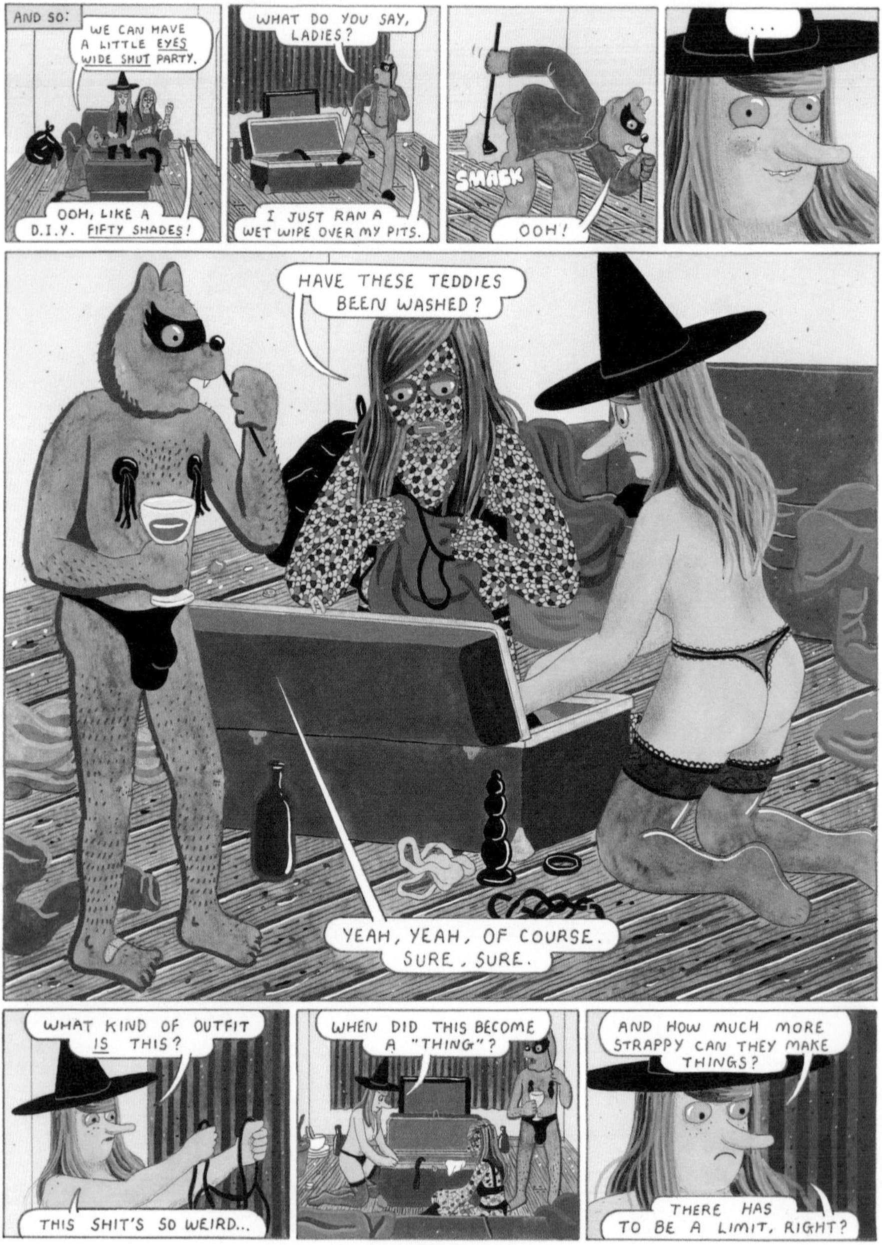
AND SO:
WE CAN HAVE A LITTLE EYES WIDE SHUT PARTY.
OOH, LIKE A D.I.Y. FIFTY SHADES!
WHAT DO YOU SAY, LADIES?
I JUST RAN A WET WIPE OVER MY PITS.
SMACK
OOH!
...
HAVE THESE TEDDIES BEEN WASHED?
YEAH, YEAH, OF COURSE. SURE, SURE.
WHAT KIND OF OUTFIT IS THIS?
THIS SHIT'S SO WEIRD...
WHEN DID THIS BECOME A "THING"?
AND HOW MUCH MORE STRAPPY CAN THEY MAKE THINGS?
THERE HAS TO BE A LIMIT, RIGHT?

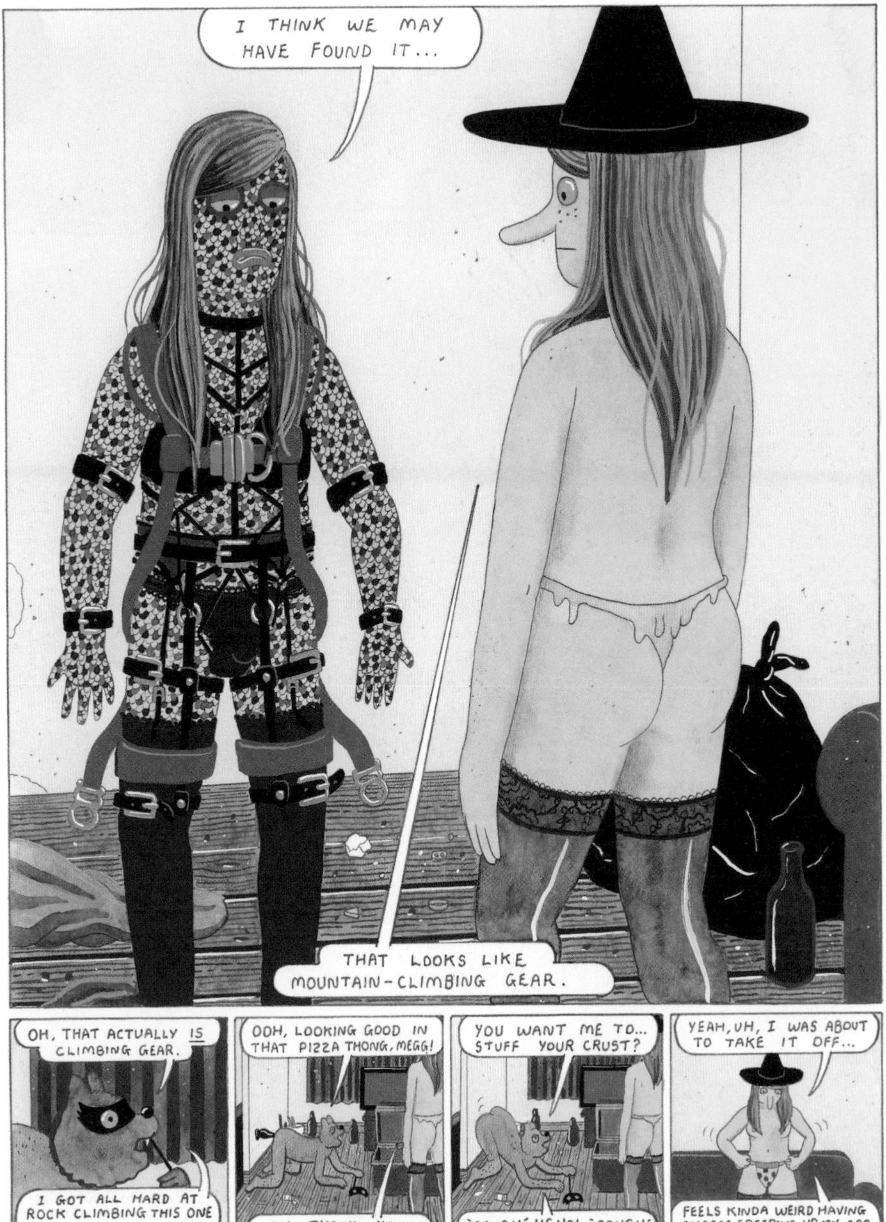
I THINK WE MAY HAVE FOUND IT...
THAT LOOKS LIKE MOUNTAIN-CLIMBING GEAR.
OH, THAT ACTUALLY IS CLIMBING GEAR.
I GOT ALL HARD AT ROCK CLIMBING THIS ONE TIME. SO I STOLE THAT.
OOH, LOOKING GOOD IN THAT PIZZA THONG, MEGG!
OH, THANK YOU...
YOU WANT ME TO... STUFF YOUR CRUST?
COUGH UGHN COUGH
YEAH, UH, I WAS ABOUT TO TAKE IT OFF...
FEELS KINDA WEIRD HAVING CHEESE CREEPING UP MY ASS.

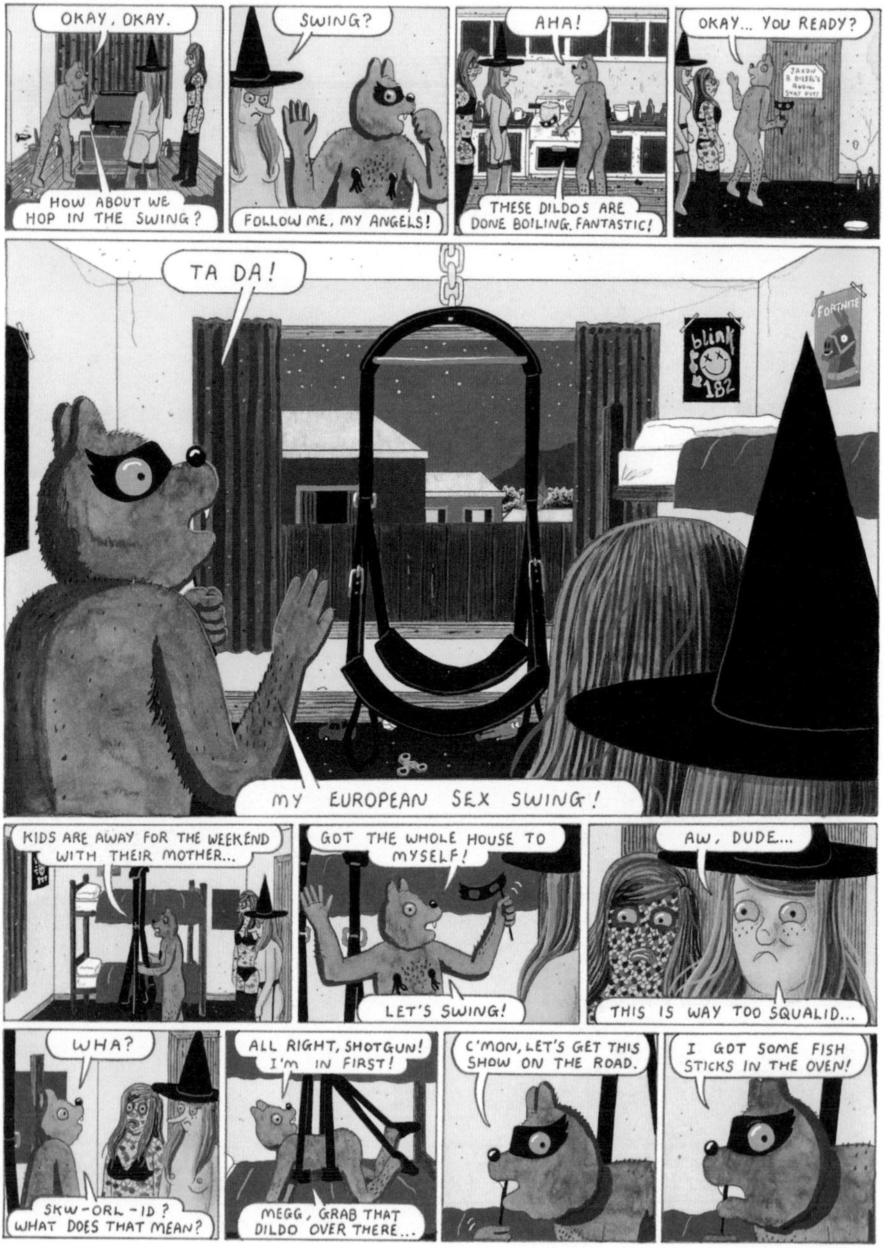
OKAY, OKAY.
HOW ABOUT WE HOP IN THE SWING?
SWING?
FOLLOW ME, MY ANGELS!
AHA!
THESE DILDOS ARE DONE BOILING. FANTASTIC!
OKAY... YOU READY?
JAXON B DIESEL'S ROOM. STAY OUT!
TA DA!
blink 182
FORTNITE
MY EUROPEAN SEX SWING!
KIDS ARE AWAY FOR THE WEEKEND WITH THEIR MOTHER...
GOT THE WHOLE HOUSE TO MYSELF!
LET'S SWING!
AW, DUDE...
THIS IS WAY TOO SQUALID...
WHA?
SKW-ORL-ID? WHAT DOES THAT MEAN?
ALL RIGHT, SHOTGUN! I'M IN FIRST!
MEGG, GRAB THAT DILDO OVER THERE...
C'MON, LET'S GET THIS SHOW ON THE ROAD.
I GOT SOME FISH STICKS IN THE OVEN!

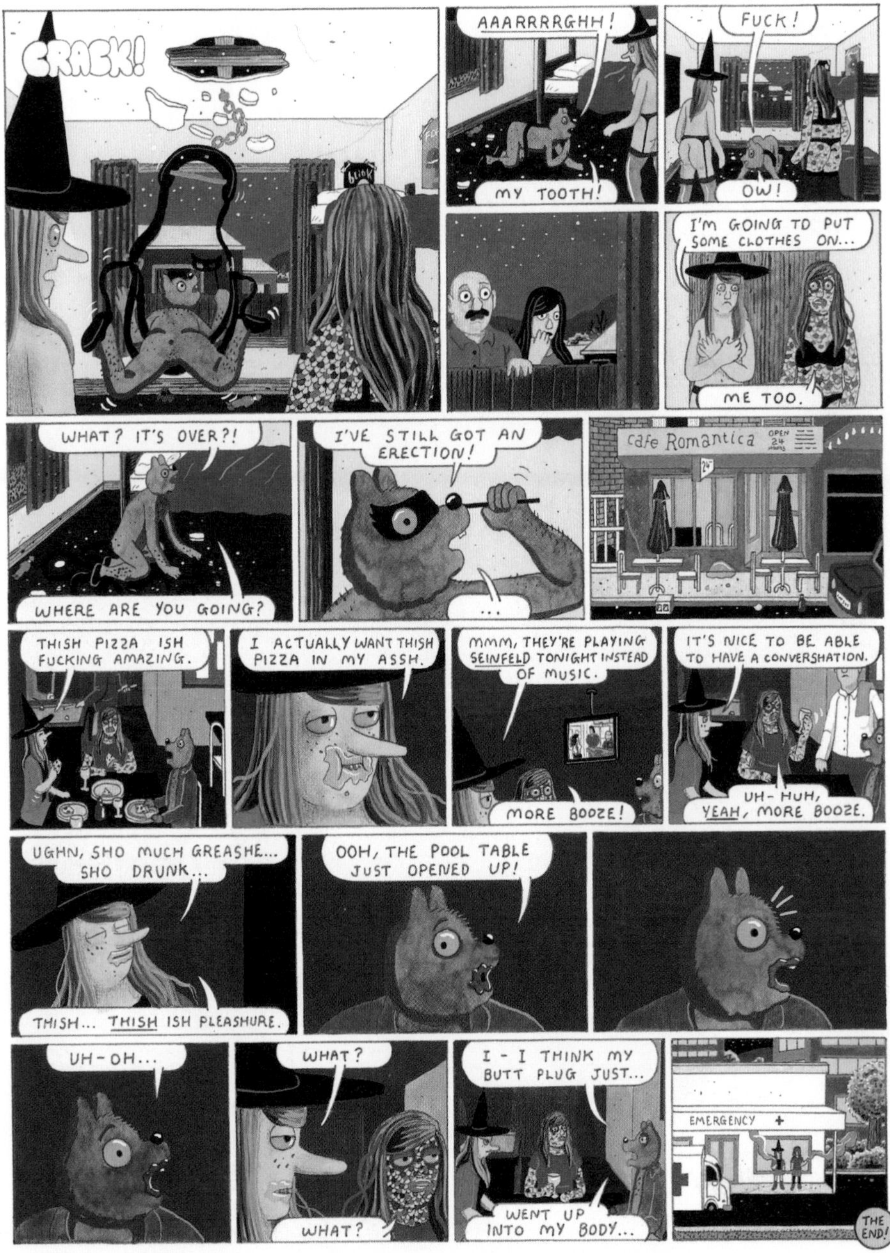
CRACK!
AAARRRRGHH!
MY TOOTH!
FUCK!
OW!
I'M GOING TO PUT SOME CLOTHES ON...
ME TOO.
WHAT? IT'S OVER?!
WHERE ARE YOU GOING?
I'VE STILL GOT AN ERECTION!
...
Cafe Romantica
OPEN 24 HOURS
THISH PIZZA ISH FUCKING AMAZING.
I ACTUALLY WANT THISH PIZZA IN MY ASSH.
MMM, THEY'RE PLAYING SEINFELD TONIGHT INSTEAD OF MUSIC.
MORE BOOZE!
IT'S NICE TO BE ABLE TO HAVE A CONVERSHATION.
UH-HUH, YEAH, MORE BOOZE.
UGHN, SHO MUCH GREASHE... SHO DRUNK...
THISH... THISH ISH PLEASHURE.
OOH, THE POOL TABLE JUST OPENED UP!
UH-OH...
WHAT?
WHAT?
I-I THINK MY BUTT PLUG JUST...
WENT UP INTO MY BODY...
EMERGENCY
THE END!

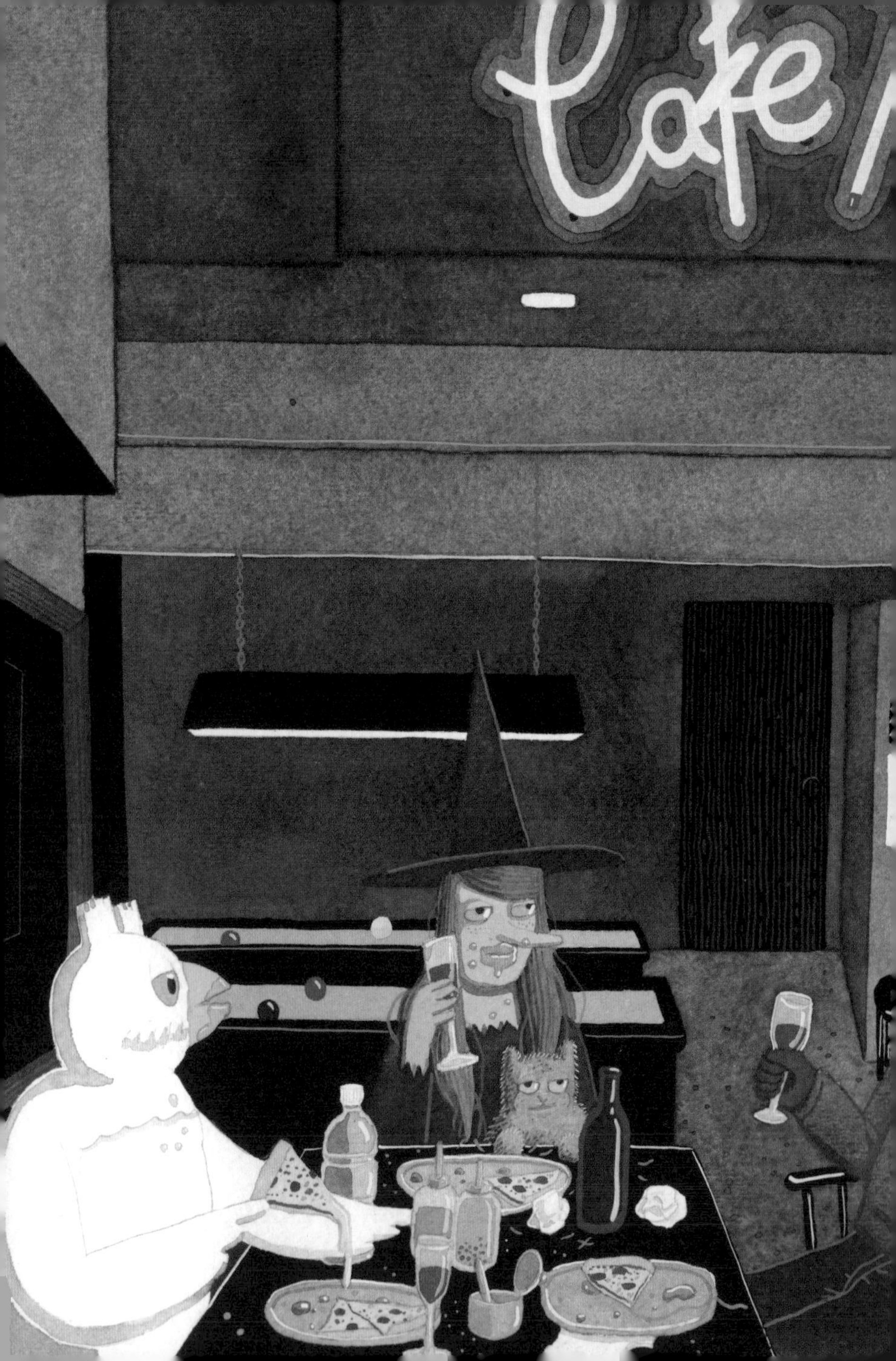
Cafe

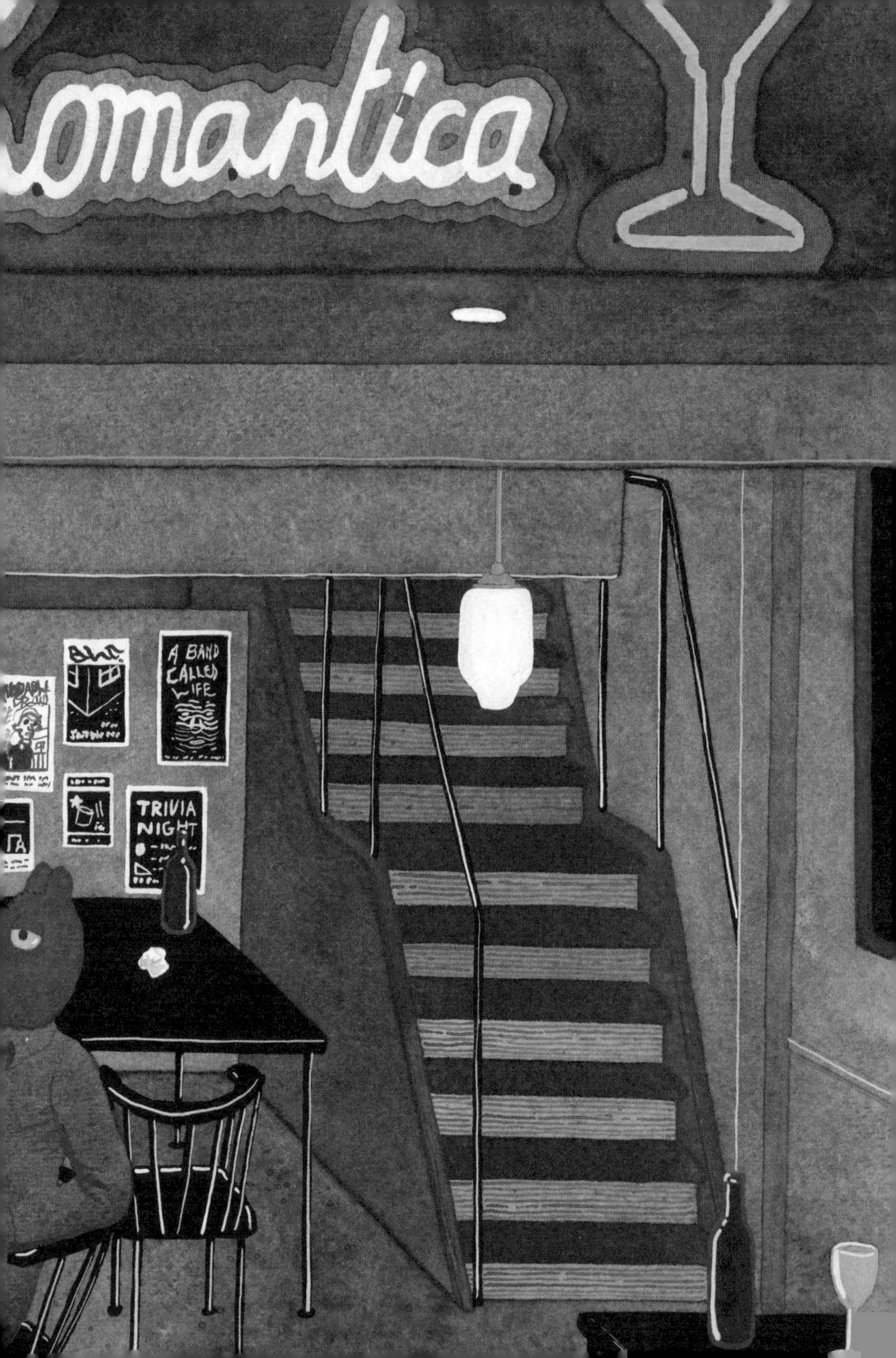
omantica
A BAND CALLED LIFE
TRIVIA NIGHT

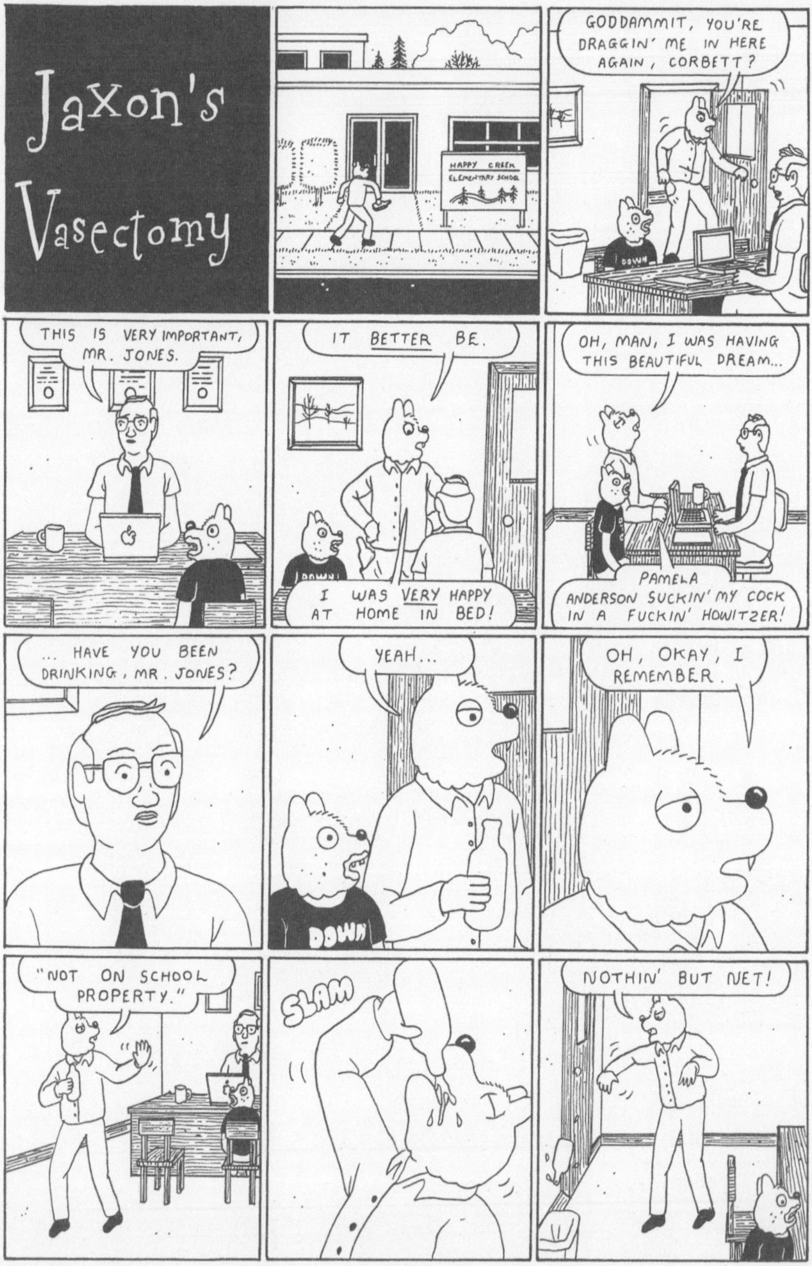
Jaxon's Vasectomy
HAPPY CREEK ELEMENTARY SCHOOL
GODDAMMIT, YOU'RE DRAGGIN' ME IN HERE AGAIN, CORBETT?
DOWN
THIS IS VERY IMPORTANT, MR. JONES.
IT BETTER BE.
I WAS VERY HAPPY AT HOME IN BED!
OH, MAN, I WAS HAVING THIS BEAUTIFUL DREAM...
PAMELA ANDERSON SUCKIN' MY COCK IN A FUCKIN' HOWITZER!
... HAVE YOU BEEN DRINKING, MR. JONES?
YEAH...
OH, OKAY, I REMEMBER.
"NOT ON SCHOOL PROPERTY."
SLAM
NOTHIN' BUT NET!

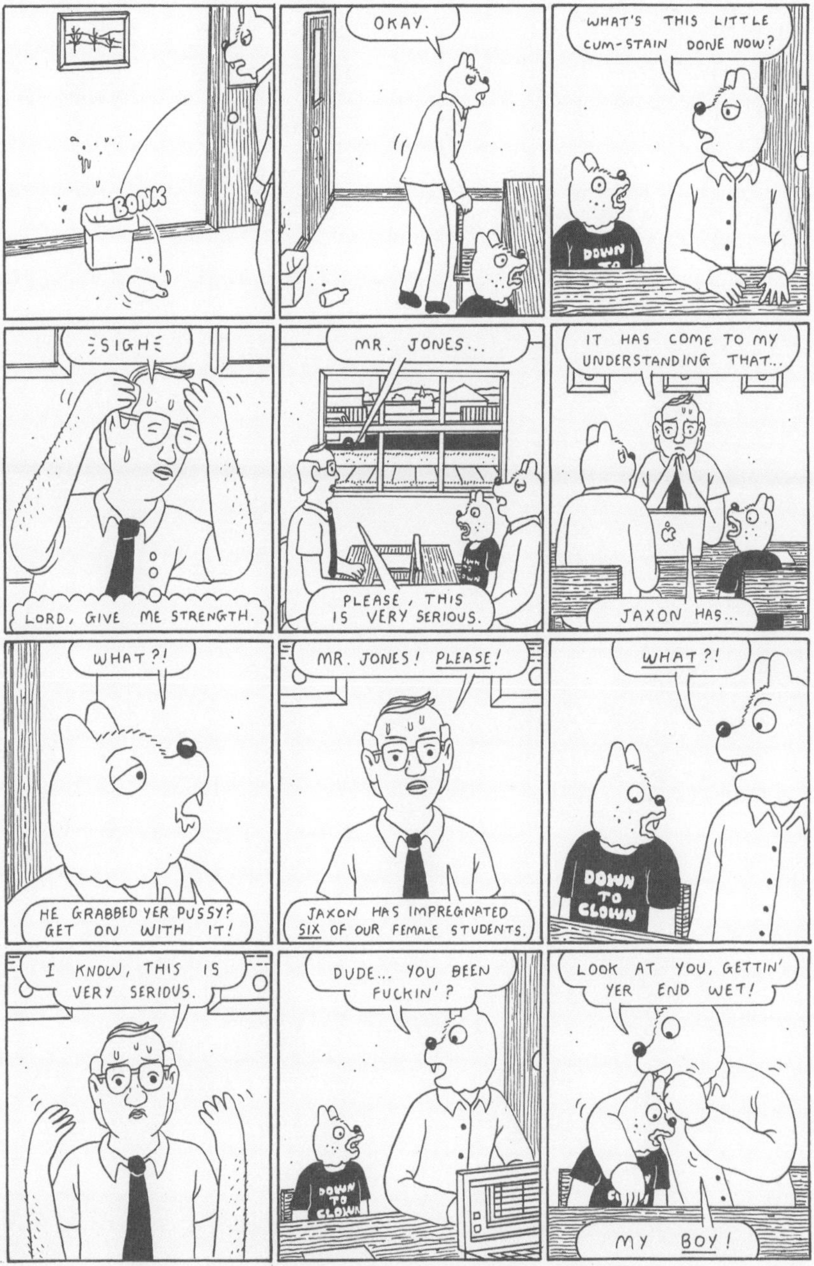
BONK
OKAY.
WHAT'S THIS LITTLE CUM-STAIN DONE NOW?
DOWN TO
SIGH
LORD, GIVE ME STRENGTH.
MR. JONES...
PLEASE, THIS IS VERY SERIOUS.
IT HAS COME TO MY UNDERSTANDING THAT...
JAXON HAS...
WHAT?!
HE GRABBED YER PUSSY? GET ON WITH IT!
MR. JONES! PLEASE!
JAXON HAS IMPREGNATED SIX OF OUR FEMALE STUDENTS.
WHAT?!
DOWN TO CLOWN
I KNOW, THIS IS VERY SERIOUS.
DUDE... YOU BEEN FUCKIN'?
DOWN TO CLOWN
LOOK AT YOU, GETTIN' YER END WET!
MY BOY!

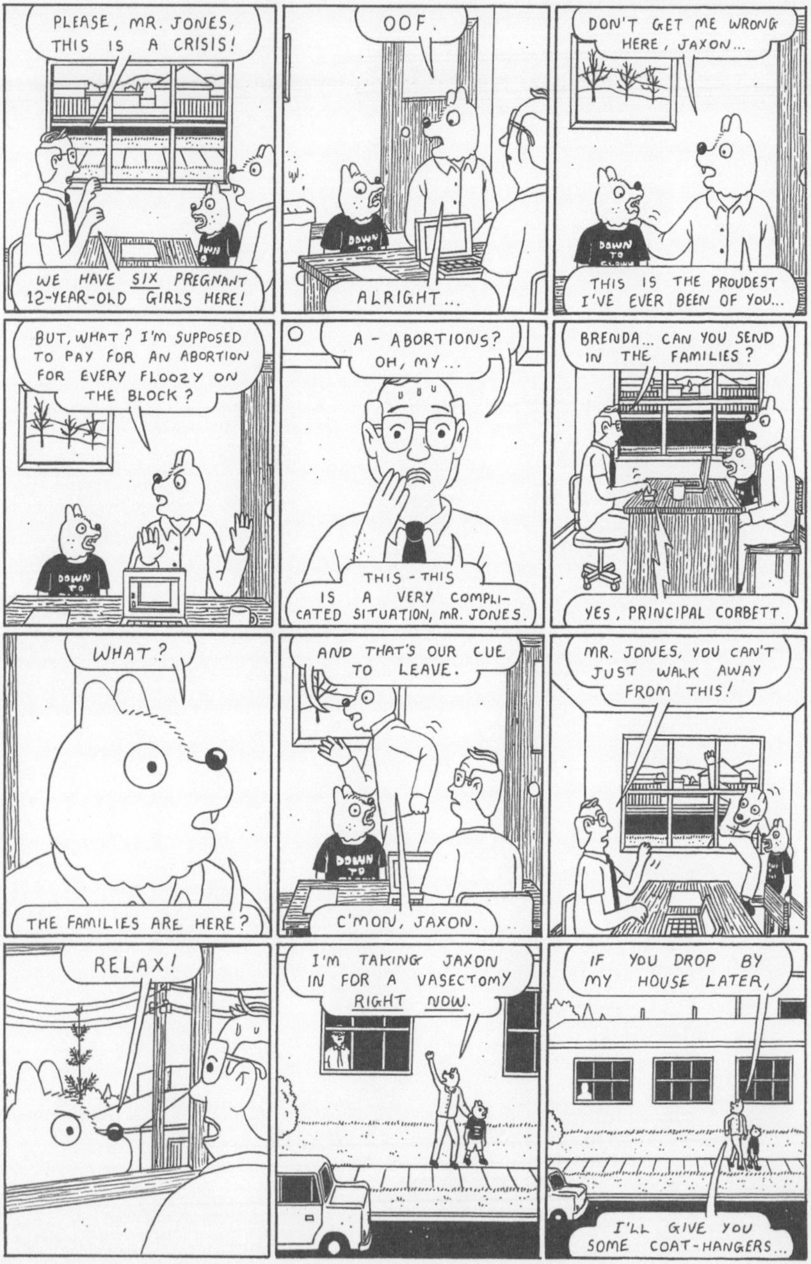
PLEASE, MR. JONES, THIS IS A CRISIS!
WE HAVE SIX PREGNANT 12-YEAR-OLD GIRLS HERE!
OOF.
ALRIGHT...
DON'T GET ME WRONG HERE, JAXON...
THIS IS THE PROUDEST I'VE EVER BEEN OF YOU...
BUT, WHAT? I'M SUPPOSED TO PAY FOR AN ABORTION FOR EVERY FLOOZY ON THE BLOCK?
DOWN TO
A - ABORTIONS? OH, MY...
THIS - THIS IS A VERY COMPLICATED SITUATION, MR. JONES.
BRENDA... CAN YOU SEND IN THE FAMILIES?
YES, PRINCIPAL CORBETT.
WHAT?
THE FAMILIES ARE HERE?
AND THAT'S OUR CUE TO LEAVE.
DOWN TO
C'MON, JAXON.
MR. JONES, YOU CAN'T JUST WALK AWAY FROM THIS!
RELAX!
I'M TAKING JAXON IN FOR A VASECTOMY RIGHT NOW.
IF YOU DROP BY MY HOUSE LATER,
I'LL GIVE YOU SOME COAT-HANGERS...

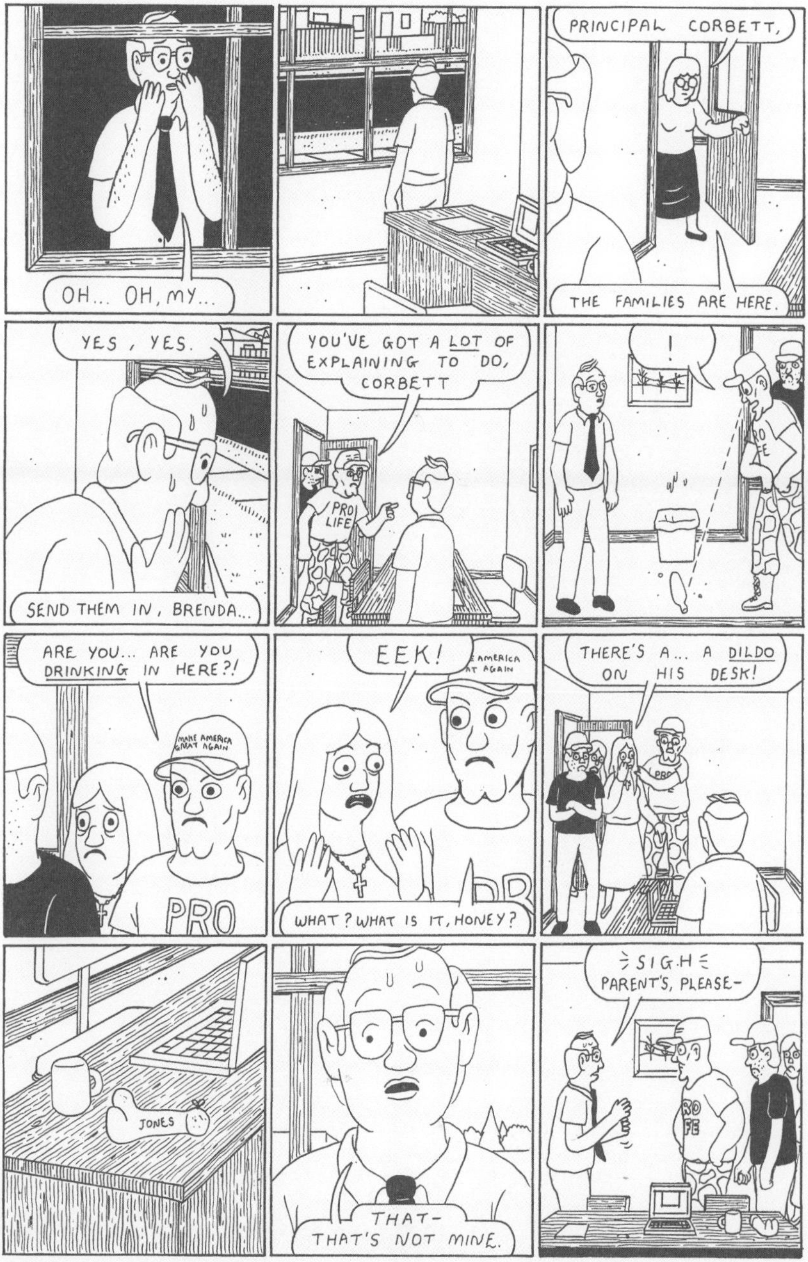
OH... OH, MY...
PRINCIPAL CORBETT,
THE FAMILIES ARE HERE.
YES, YES.
SEND THEM IN, BRENDA...
YOU'VE GOT A LOT OF EXPLAINING TO DO, CORBETT
PRO LIFE
!
ARE YOU... ARE YOU DRINKING IN HERE?!
MAKE AMERICA GREAT AGAIN
PRO
EEK!
WHAT? WHAT IS IT, HONEY?
THERE'S A... A DILDO ON HIS DESK!
JONES
THAT- THAT'S NOT MINE.
SIGH
PARENT'S, PLEASE-

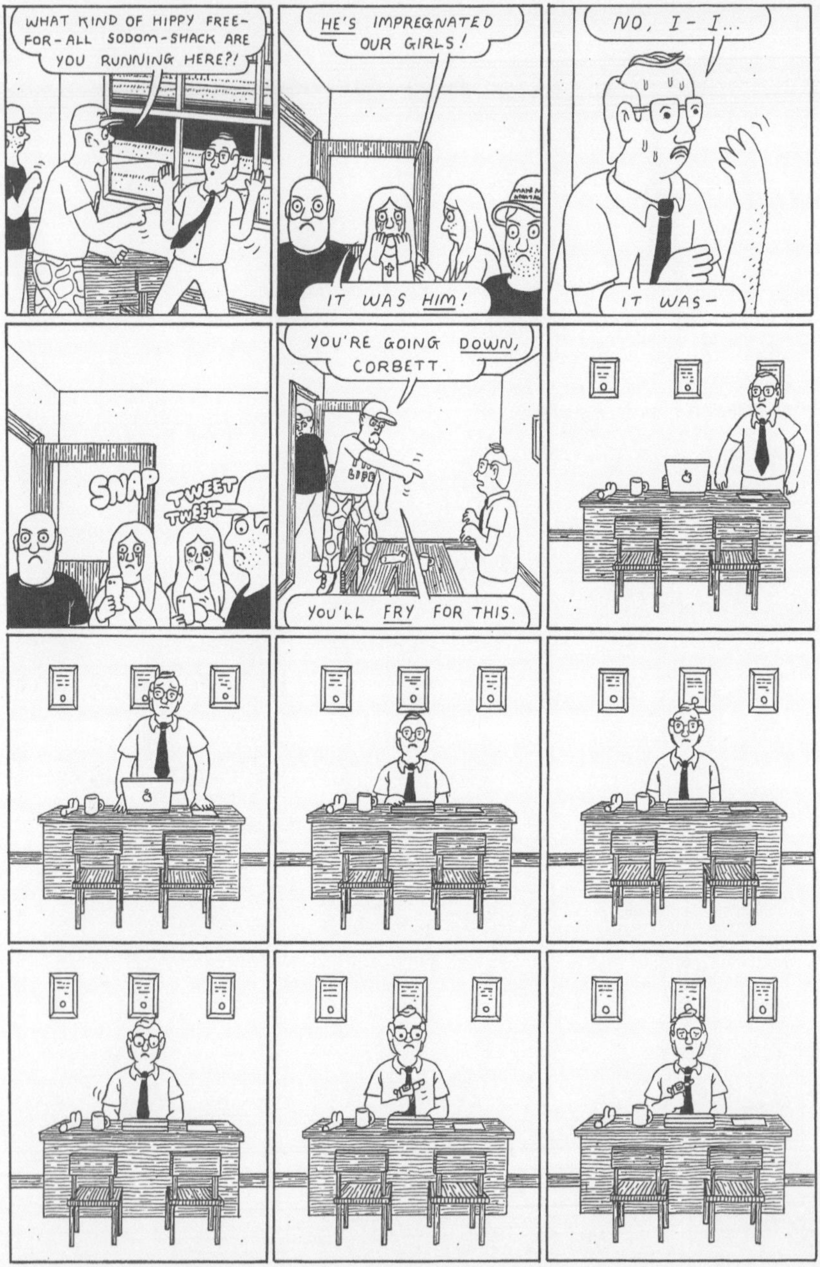
WHAT KIND OF HIPPY FREE-FOR-ALL SODOM-SHACK ARE YOU RUNNING HERE?!
HE'S IMPREGNATED OUR GIRLS!
IT WAS HIM!
NO, I- I...
IT WAS-
SNAP
TWEET TWEET
YOU'RE GOING DOWN, CORBETT.
YOU'LL FRY FOR THIS.

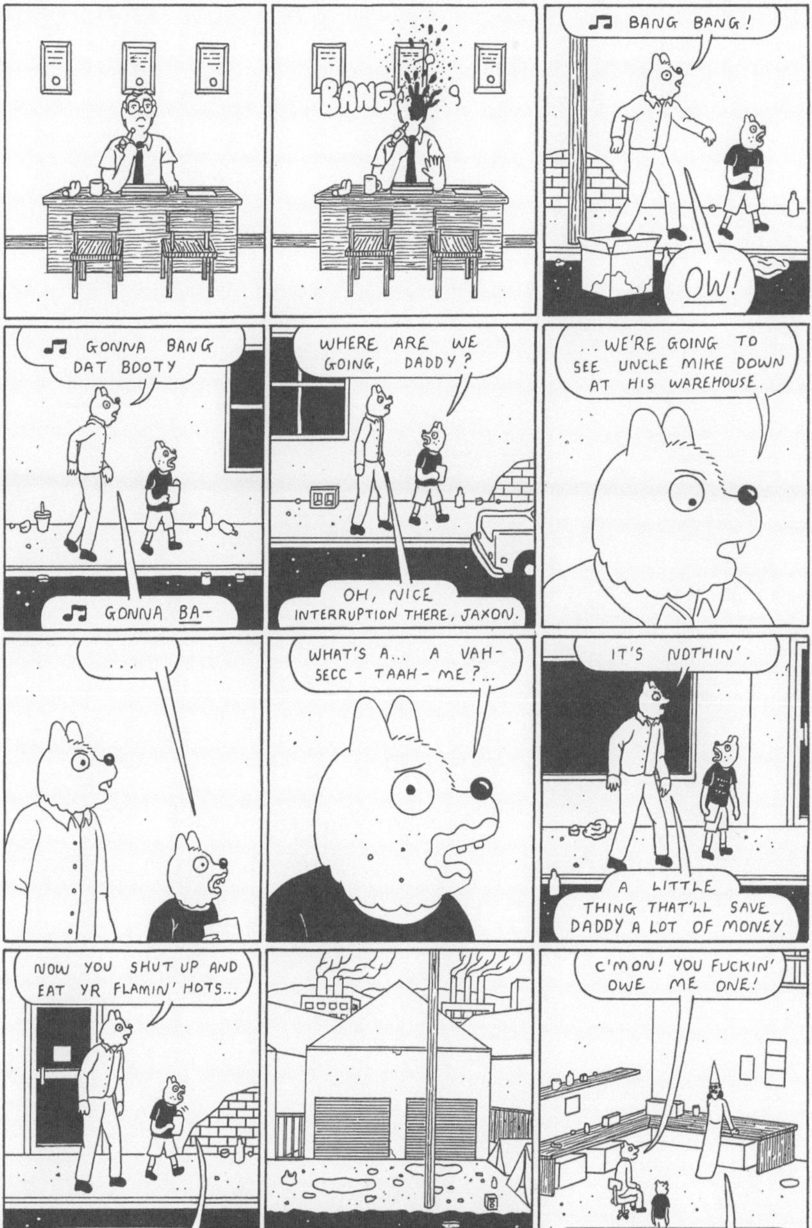
BANG
♫ BANG BANG!
OW!
♫ GONNA BANG DAT BOOTY
♫ GONNA BA-
WHERE ARE WE GOING, DADDY?
OH, NICE INTERRUPTION THERE, JAXON.
...WE'RE GOING TO SEE UNCLE MIKE DOWN AT HIS WAREHOUSE.
...
WHAT'S A... A VAH-SECC-TAAH-ME?...
IT'S NOTHIN'.
A LITTLE THING THAT'LL SAVE DADDY A LOT OF MONEY.
NOW YOU SHUT UP AND EAT YR FLAMIN' HOTS...
O-OKAY...
C'MON! YOU FUCKIN' OWE ME ONE!
WHAT? OH, FUCK YOU.

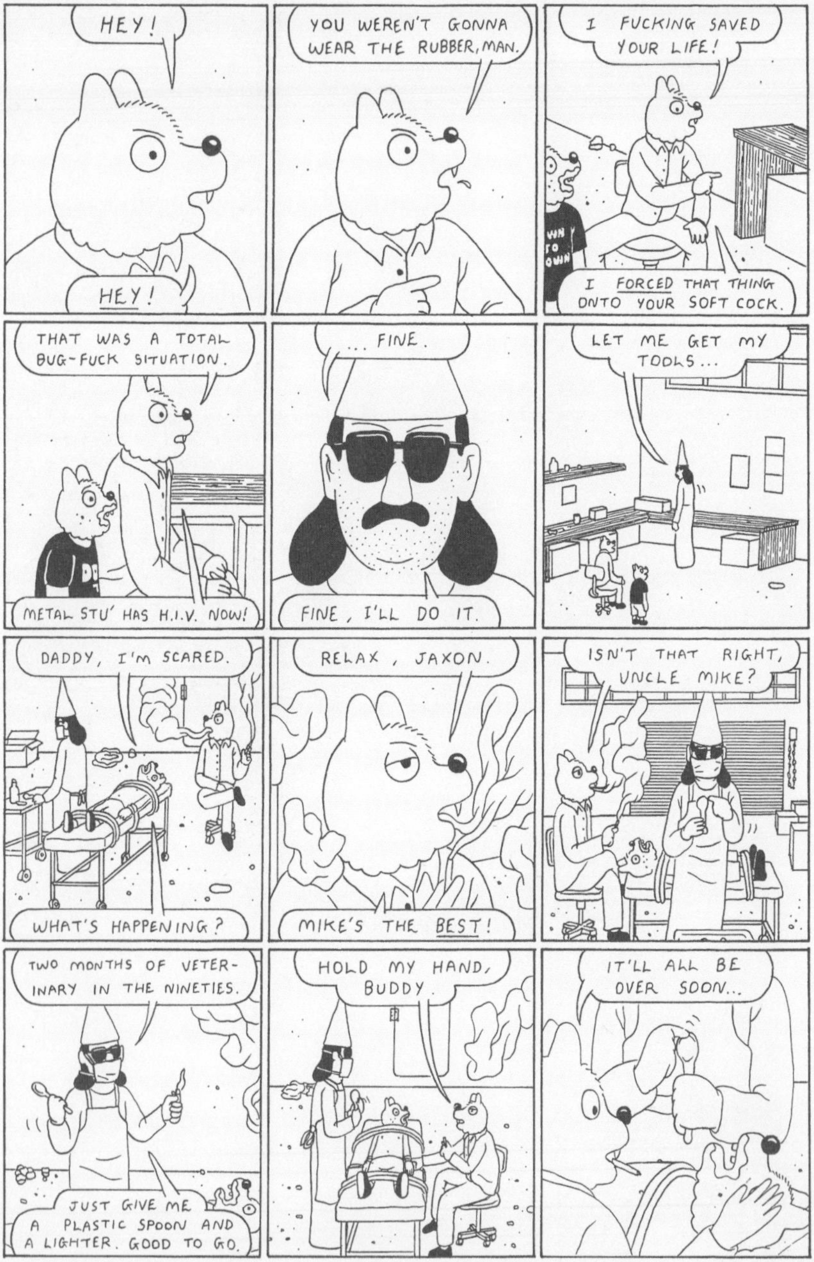
HEY!
HEY!
YOU WEREN'T GONNA WEAR THE RUBBER, MAN.
I FUCKING SAVED YOUR LIFE!
I FORCED THAT THING ONTO YOUR SOFT COCK.
THAT WAS A TOTAL BUG-FUCK SITUATION.
METAL STU' HAS H.I.V. NOW!
... FINE.
FINE, I'LL DO IT.
LET ME GET MY TOOLS...
DADDY, I'M SCARED.
WHAT'S HAPPENING?
RELAX, JAXON.
MIKE'S THE BEST!
ISN'T THAT RIGHT, UNCLE MIKE?
TWO MONTHS OF VETER-INARY IN THE NINETIES.
JUST GIVE ME A PLASTIC SPOON AND A LIGHTER. GOOD TO GO.
HOLD MY HAND, BUDDY.
IT'LL ALL BE OVER SOON...

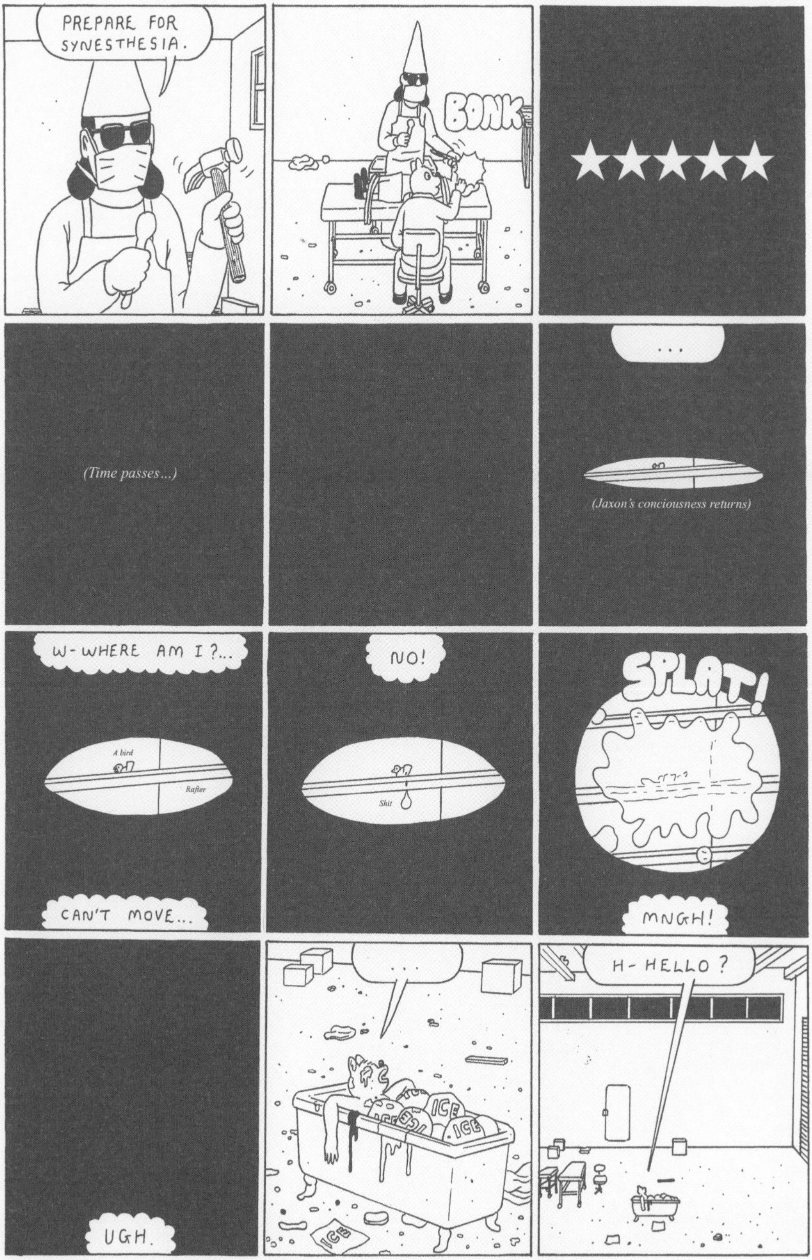
PREPARE FOR SYNESTHESIA.
BONK
(Time passes...)
...
(Jaxon's conciousness returns)
W-WHERE AM I?...
A bird
Rafter
CAN'T MOVE...
NO!
Shit
SPLAT!
MNGH!
UGH.
...
ICE
H-HELLO?

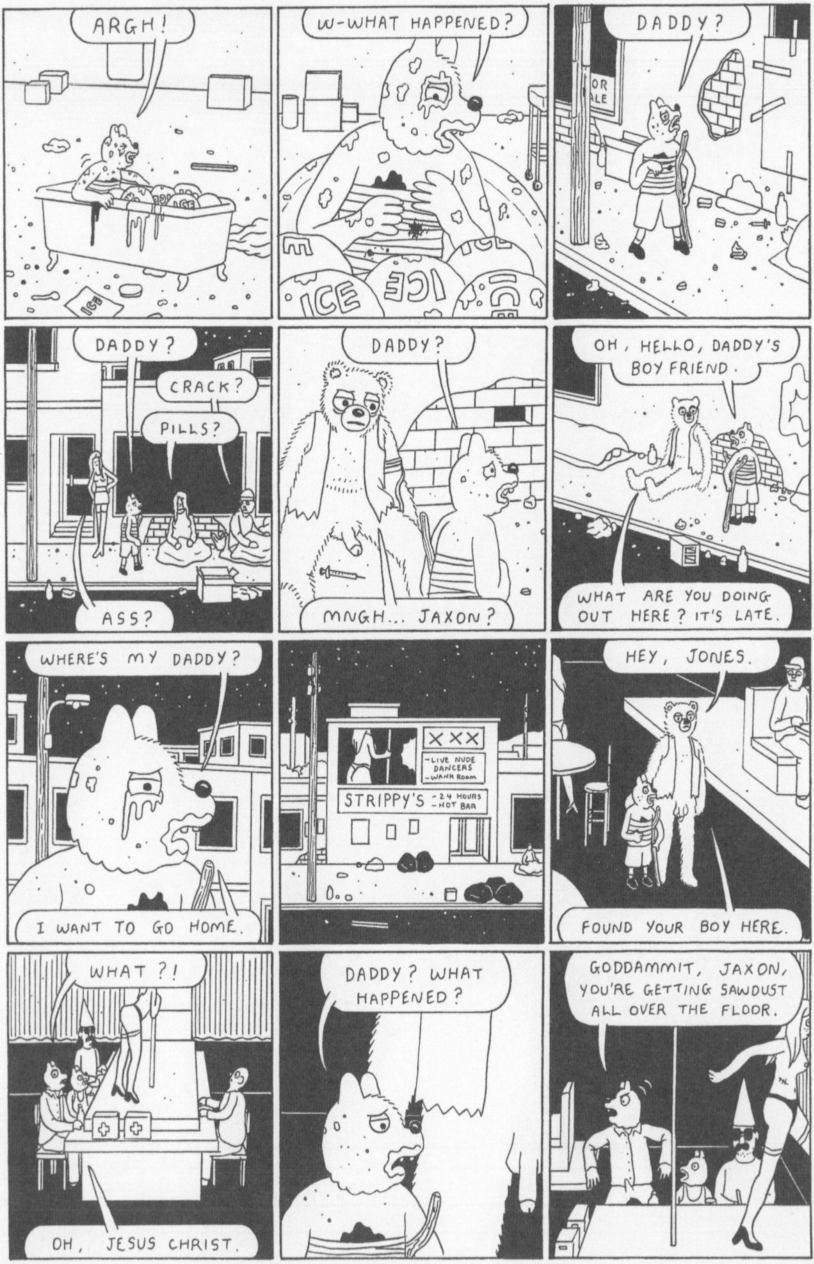
ARGH!
W-WHAT HAPPENED?
ICE
ICE
DADDY?
DADDY?
CRACK?
PILLS?
ASS?
DADDY?
MNGH... JAXON?
OH, HELLO, DADDY'S BOY FRIEND.
WHAT ARE YOU DOING OUT HERE? IT'S LATE.
WHERE'S MY DADDY?
I WANT TO GO HOME.
XXX
-LIVE NUDE DANCERS
-WANK ROOM
STRIPPY'S
-24 HOURS
-HOT BAR
HEY, JONES.
FOUND YOUR BOY HERE.
WHAT?!
OH, JESUS CHRIST.
DADDY? WHAT HAPPENED?
GODDAMMIT, JAXON, YOU'RE GETTING SAWDUST ALL OVER THE FLOOR.

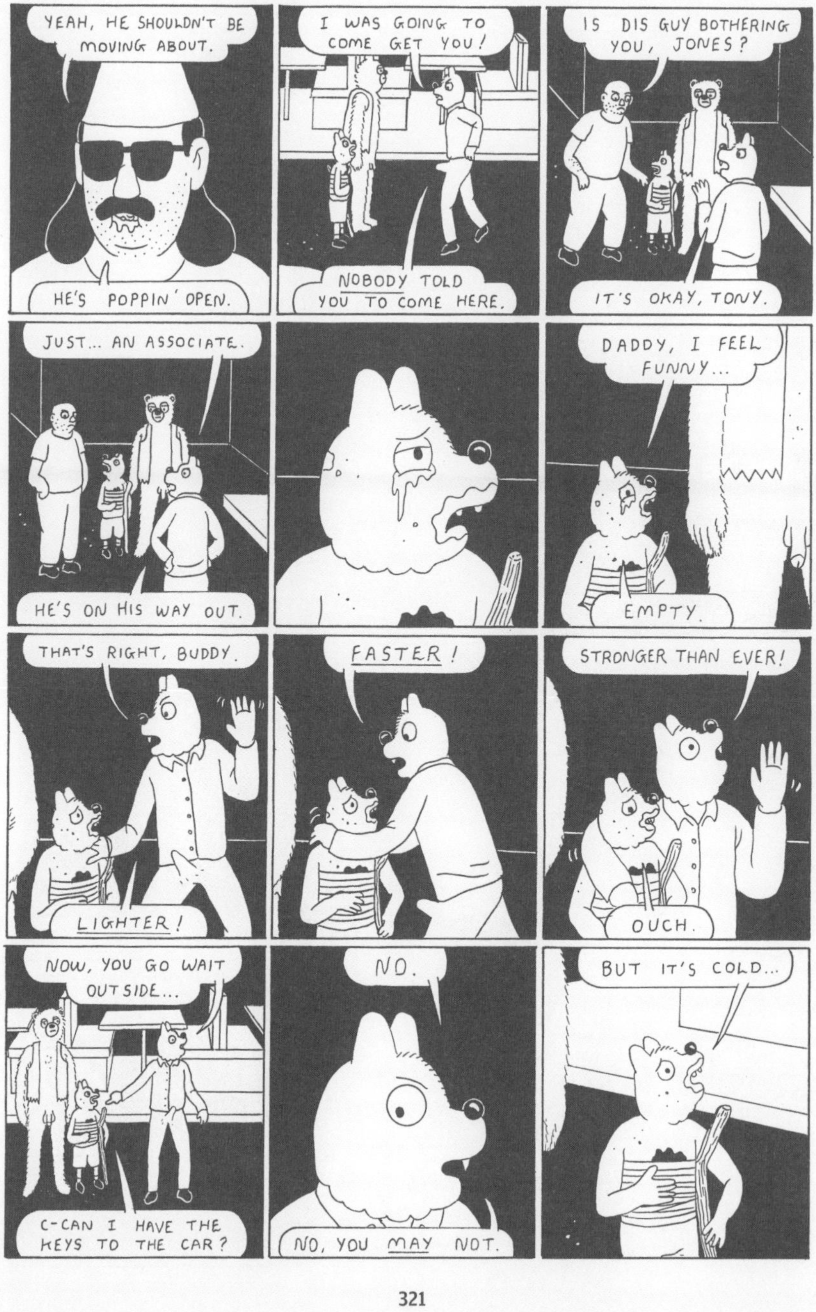
YEAH, HE SHOULDN'T BE MOVING ABOUT.
HE'S POPPIN' OPEN.
I WAS GOING TO COME GET YOU!
NOBODY TOLD YOU TO COME HERE.
IS DIS GUY BOTHERING YOU, JONES?
IT'S OKAY, TONY.
JUST... AN ASSOCIATE.
HE'S ON HIS WAY OUT.
DADDY, I FEEL FUNNY...
EMPTY.
THAT'S RIGHT, BUDDY.
LIGHTER!
FASTER!
STRONGER THAN EVER!
OUCH.
NOW, YOU GO WAIT OUTSIDE...
C-CAN I HAVE THE KEYS TO THE CAR?
NO.
NO, YOU MAY NOT.
BUT IT'S COLD...

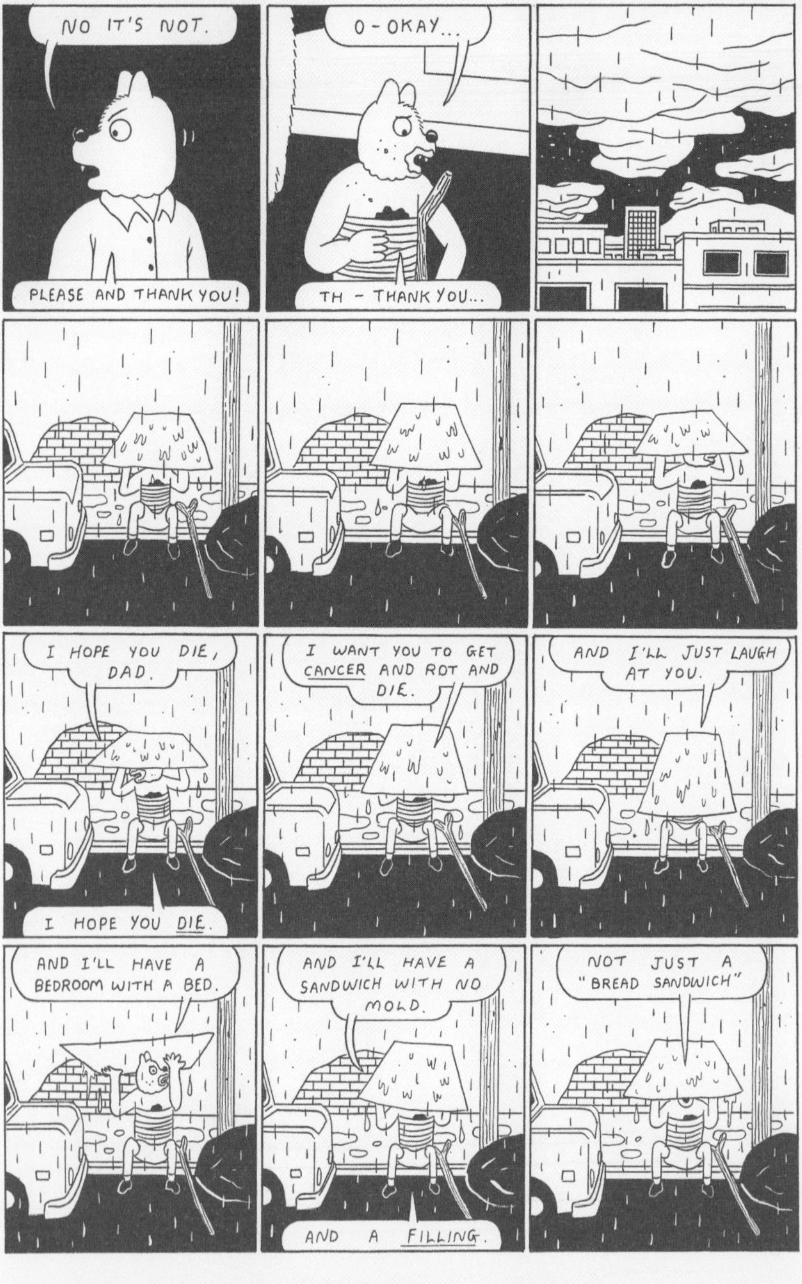
NO IT'S NOT.
PLEASE AND THANK YOU!
O-OKAY...
TH-THANK YOU...
I HOPE YOU DIE, DAD.
I HOPE YOU DIE.
I WANT YOU TO GET CANCER AND ROT AND DIE.
AND I'LL JUST LAUGH AT YOU.
AND I'LL HAVE A BEDROOM WITH A BED.
AND I'LL HAVE A SANDWICH WITH NO MOLD.
AND A FILLING.
NOT JUST A "BREAD SANDWICH"

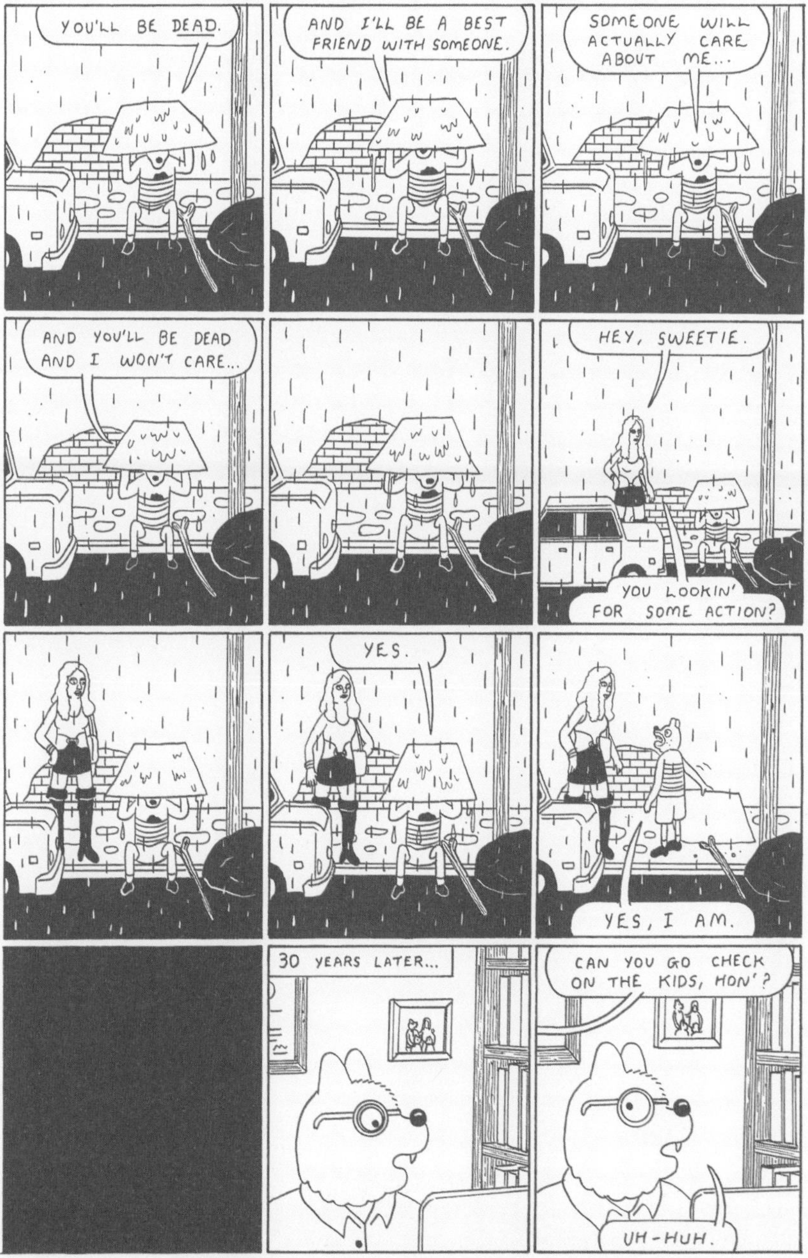
YOU'LL BE DEAD.
AND I'LL BE A BEST FRIEND WITH SOMEONE.
SOMEONE WILL ACTUALLY CARE ABOUT ME...
AND YOU'LL BE DEAD AND I WON'T CARE...
HEY, SWEETIE.
YOU LOOKIN' FOR SOME ACTION?
YES.
YES, I AM.
30 YEARS LATER...
CAN YOU GO CHECK ON THE KIDS, HON'?
UH-HUH.

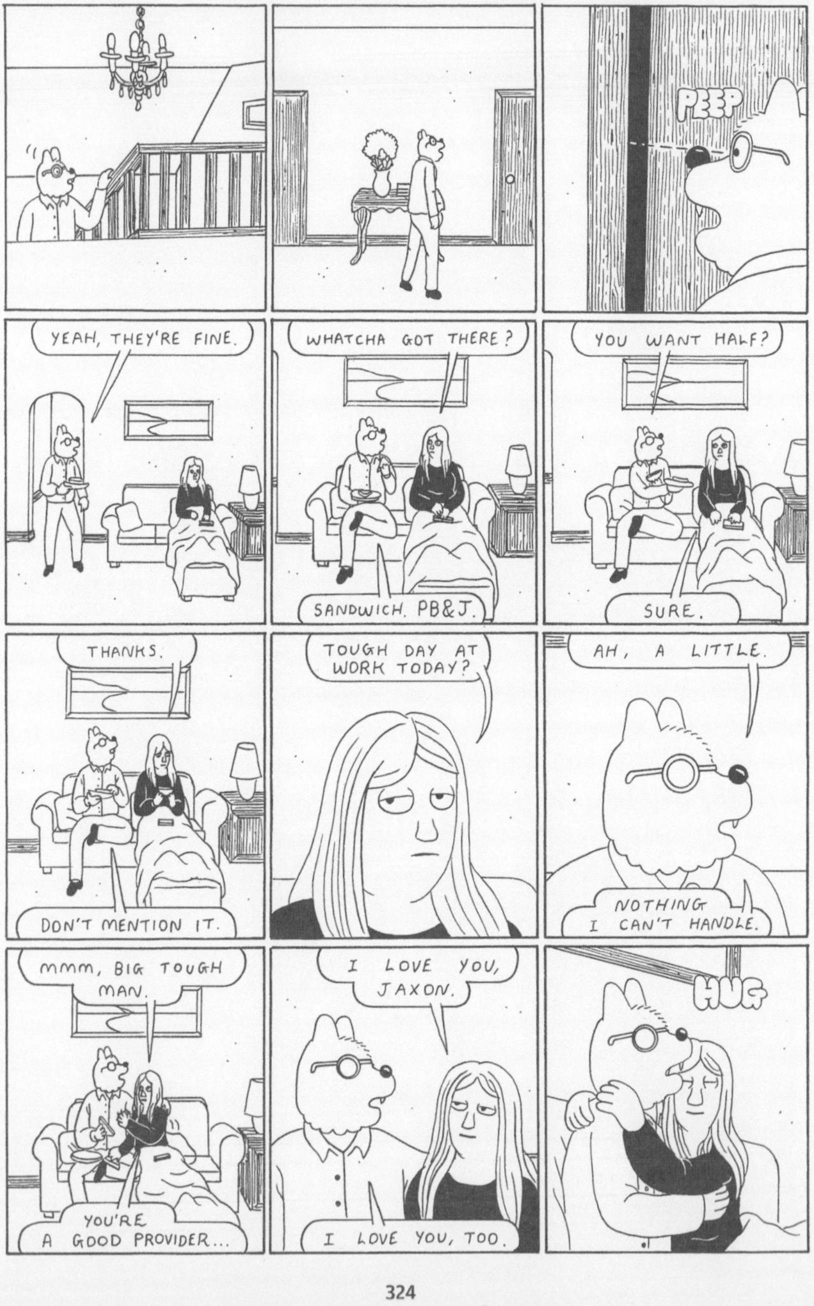
PEEP
YEAH, THEY'RE FINE.
WHATCHA GOT THERE?
SANDWICH. PB&J.
YOU WANT HALF?
SURE.
THANKS.
DON'T MENTION IT.
TOUGH DAY AT WORK TODAY?
AH, A LITTLE.
NOTHING I CAN'T HANDLE.
MMM, BIG TOUGH MAN.
YOU'RE A GOOD PROVIDER...
I LOVE YOU, JAXON.
I LOVE YOU, TOO.
HUG

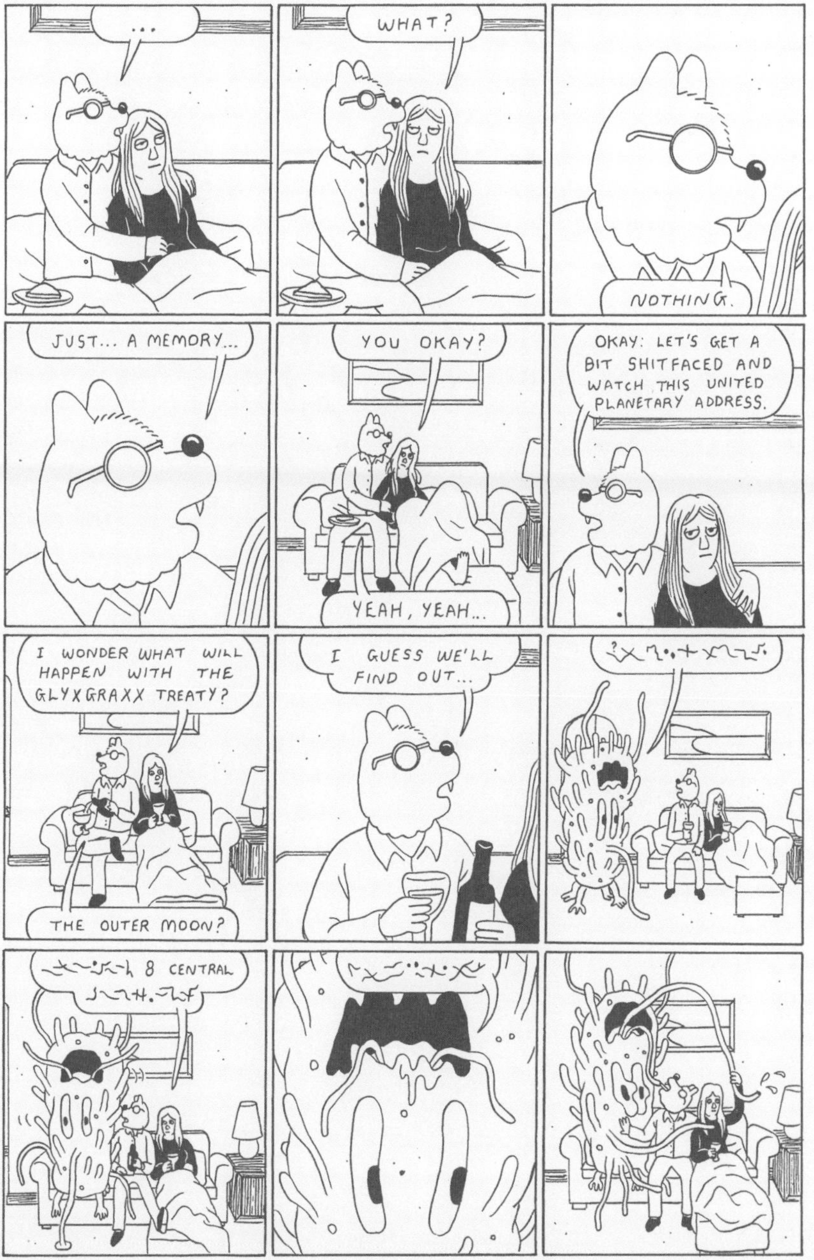
...
WHAT?
NOTHING.
JUST... A MEMORY...
YOU OKAY?
YEAH, YEAH...
OKAY: LET'S GET A BIT SHITFACED AND WATCH THIS UNITED PLANETARY ADDRESS.
I WONDER WHAT WILL HAPPEN WITH THE GLYXGRAXX TREATY?
THE OUTER MOON?
I GUESS WE'LL FIND OUT...
8 CENTRAL

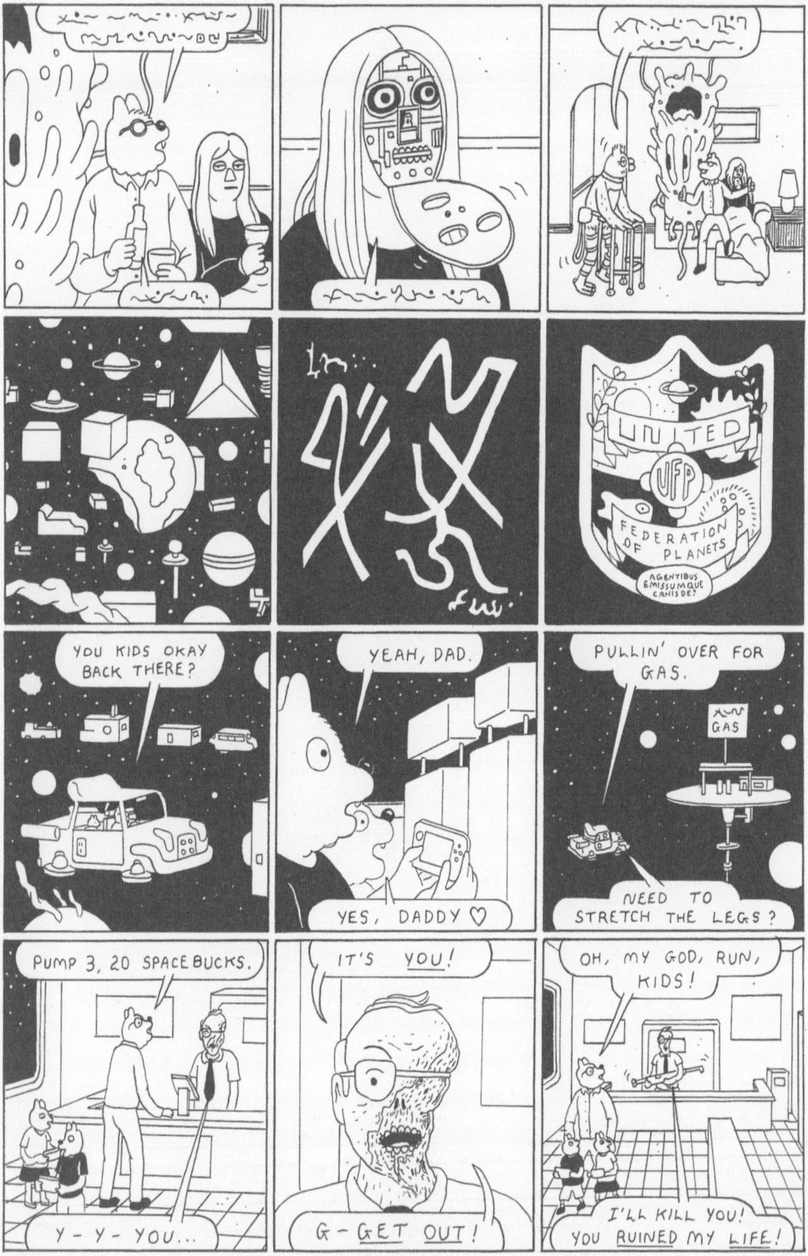
UNITED
UFP
FEDERATION OF PLANETS
AGENTIBUS EMISSUMQUE CANIS DEI?
YOU KIDS OKAY BACK THERE?
YEAH, DAD.
YES, DADDY ♡
PULLIN' OVER FOR GAS.
GAS
NEED TO STRETCH THE LEGS?
PUMP 3, 20 SPACEBUCKS.
Y-Y-YOU...
IT'S YOU!
G-GET OUT!
OH, MY GOD, RUN, KIDS!
I'LL KILL YOU! YOU RUINED MY LIFE!

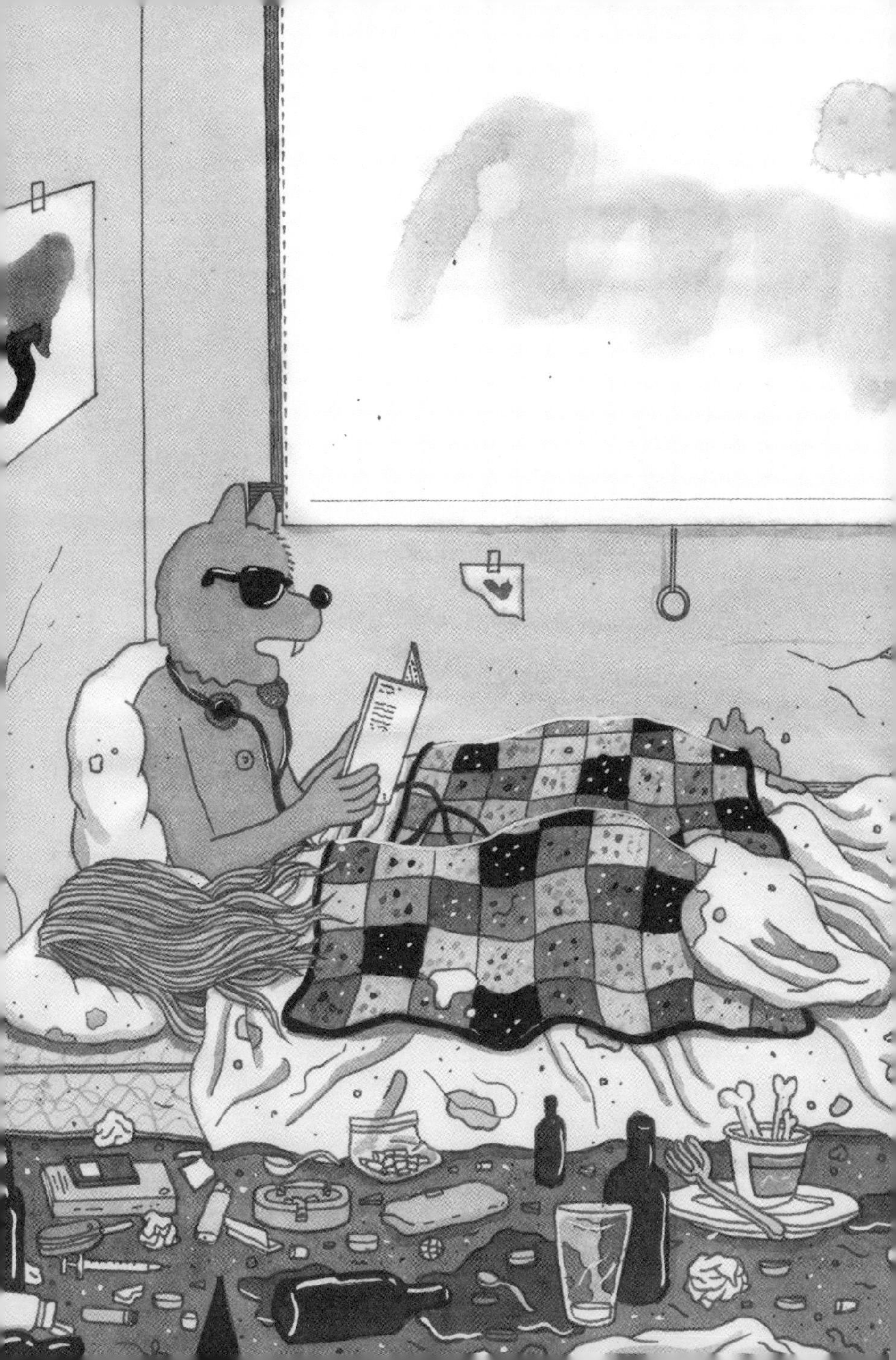

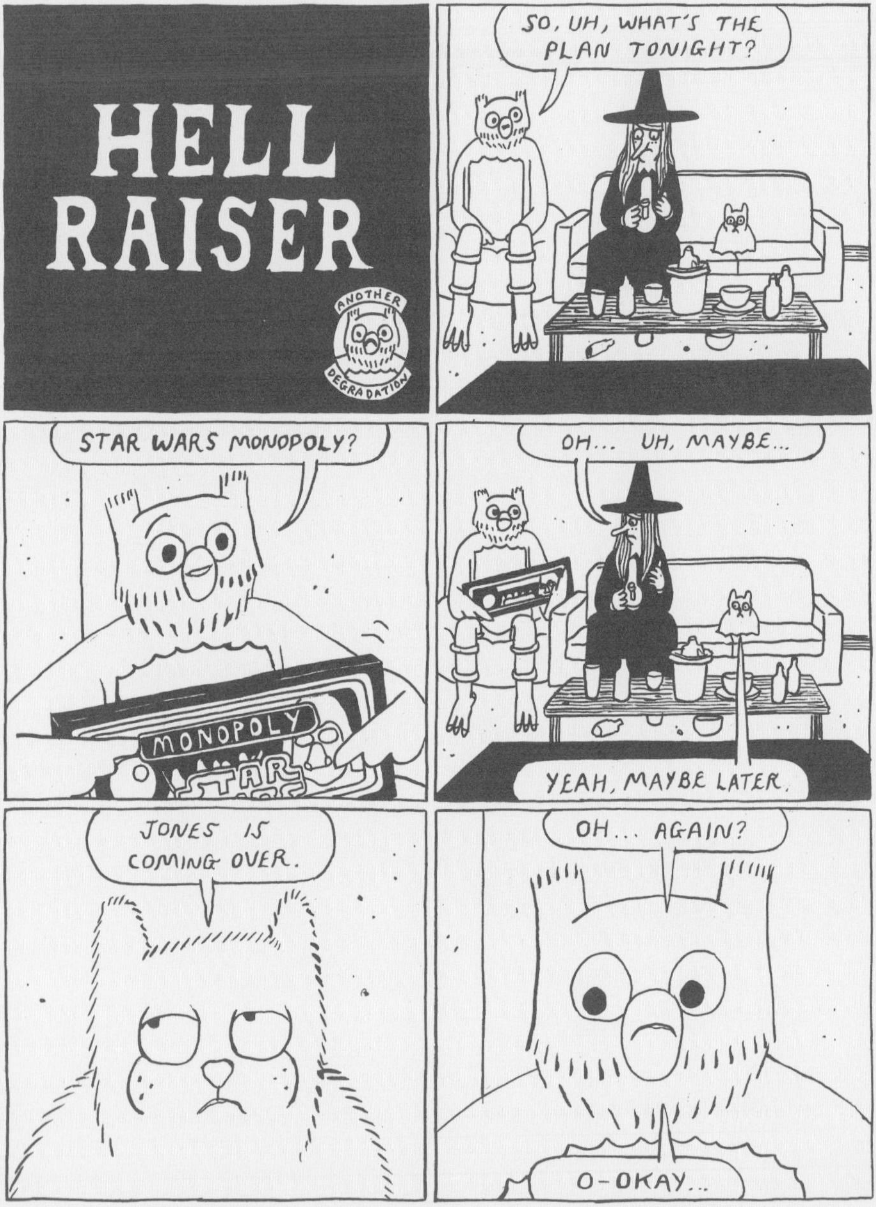
HELL RAISER
ANOTHER DEGRADATION
SO, UH, WHAT'S THE PLAN TONIGHT?
STAR WARS MONOPOLY?
MONOPOLY
OH... UH, MAYBE...
YEAH, MAYBE LATER.
JONES IS COMING OVER.
OH... AGAIN?
O-OKAY...

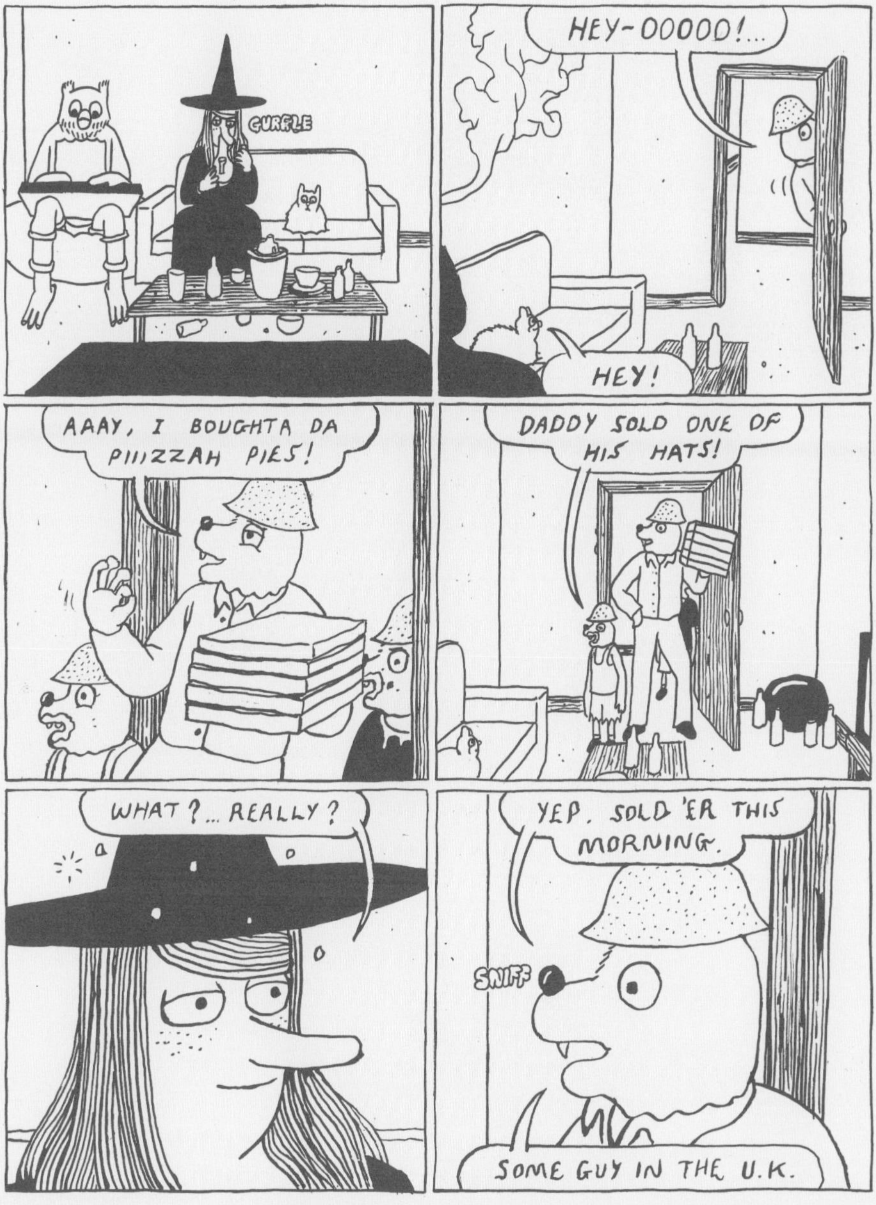
GURGLE
HEY-OOOOD!...
HEY!
AAAY, I BOUGHTA DA PIIIZZAH PIES!
DADDY SOLD ONE OF HIS HATS!
WHAT?... REALLY?
YEP. SOLD 'ER THIS MORNING.
SNIFF
SOME GUY IN THE U.K.

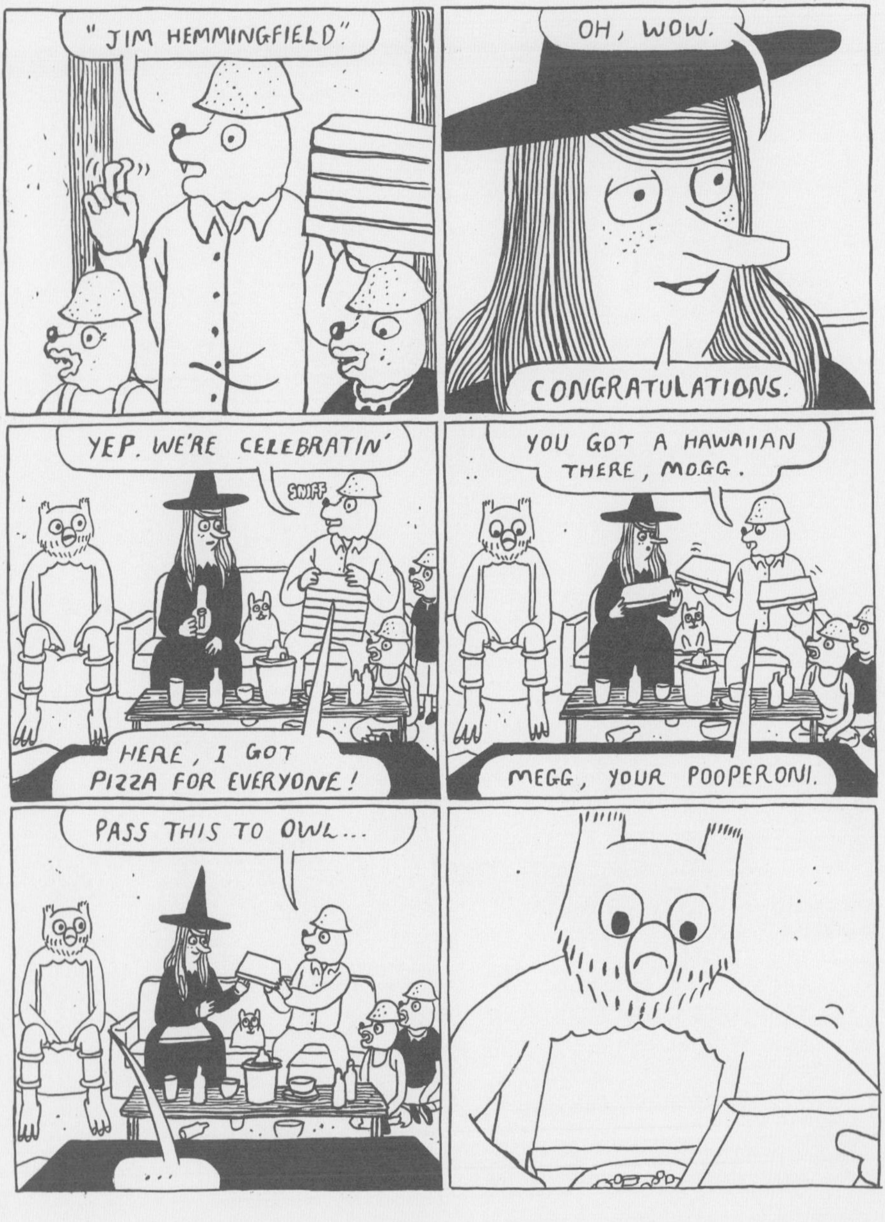
"JIM HEMMINGFIELD."
OH, WOW.
CONGRATULATIONS.
YEP. WE'RE CELEBRATIN'
SNIFF
HERE, I GOT PIZZA FOR EVERYONE!
YOU GOT A HAWAIIAN THERE, MOGG.
MEGG, YOUR POOPERONI.
PASS THIS TO OWL...
...

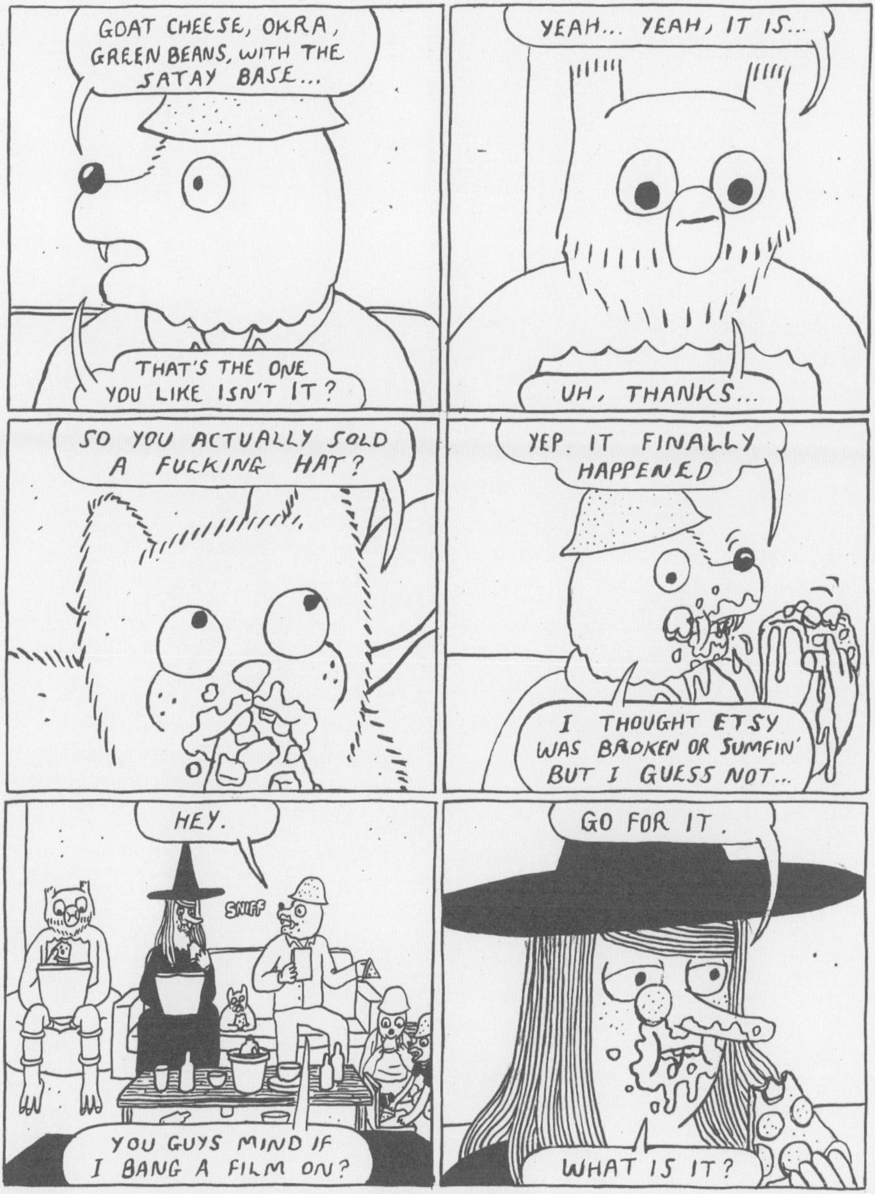
GOAT CHEESE, OKRA, GREEN BEANS, WITH THE SATAY BASE...
THAT'S THE ONE YOU LIKE ISN'T IT?
YEAH... YEAH, IT IS...
UH, THANKS...
SO YOU ACTUALLY SOLD A FUCKING HAT?
YEP. IT FINALLY HAPPENED
I THOUGHT ETSY WAS BROKEN OR SUMFIN' BUT I GUESS NOT...
HEY.
SNIFF
YOU GUYS MIND IF I BANG A FILM ON?
GO FOR IT.
WHAT IS IT?

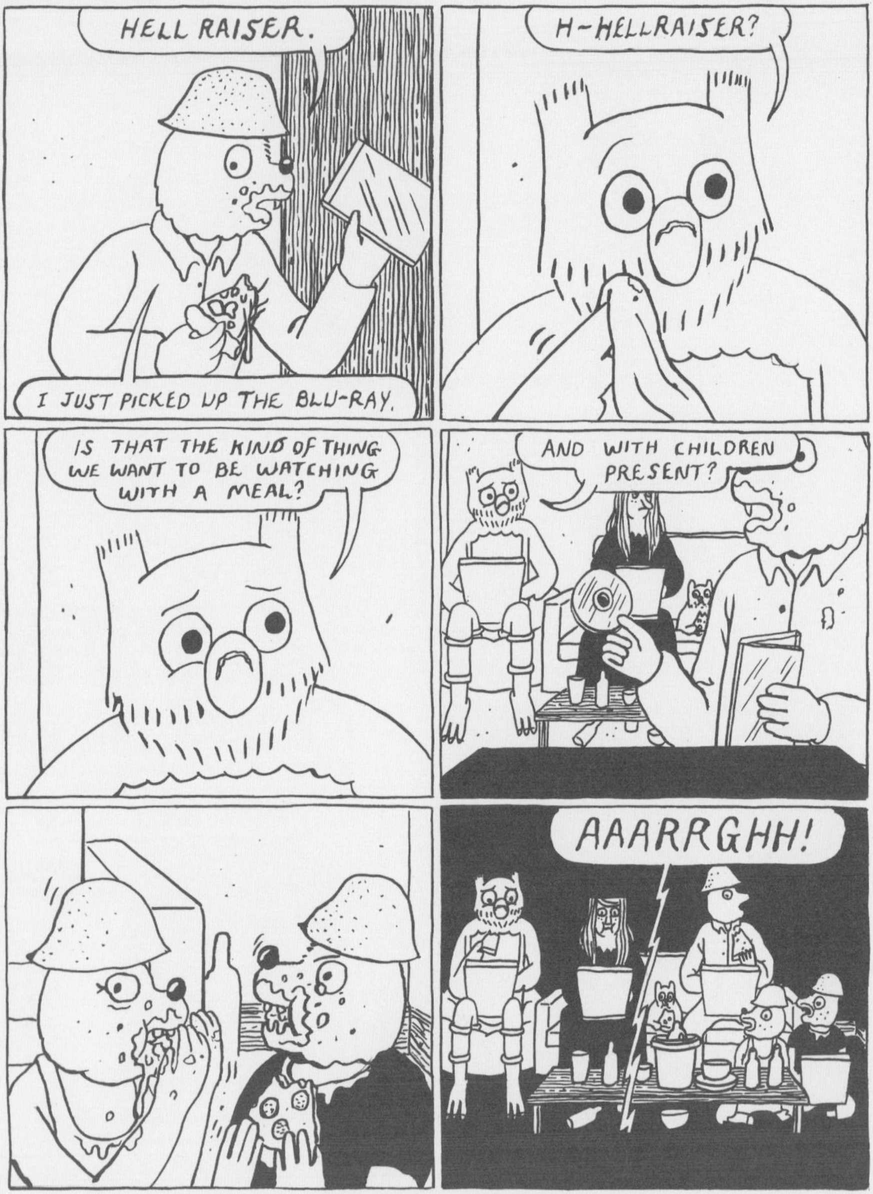
HELL RAISER.
I JUST PICKED UP THE BLU-RAY.
H-HELLRAISER?
IS THAT THE KIND OF THING WE WANT TO BE WATCHING WITH A MEAL?
AND WITH CHILDREN PRESENT?
AAARRGHH!

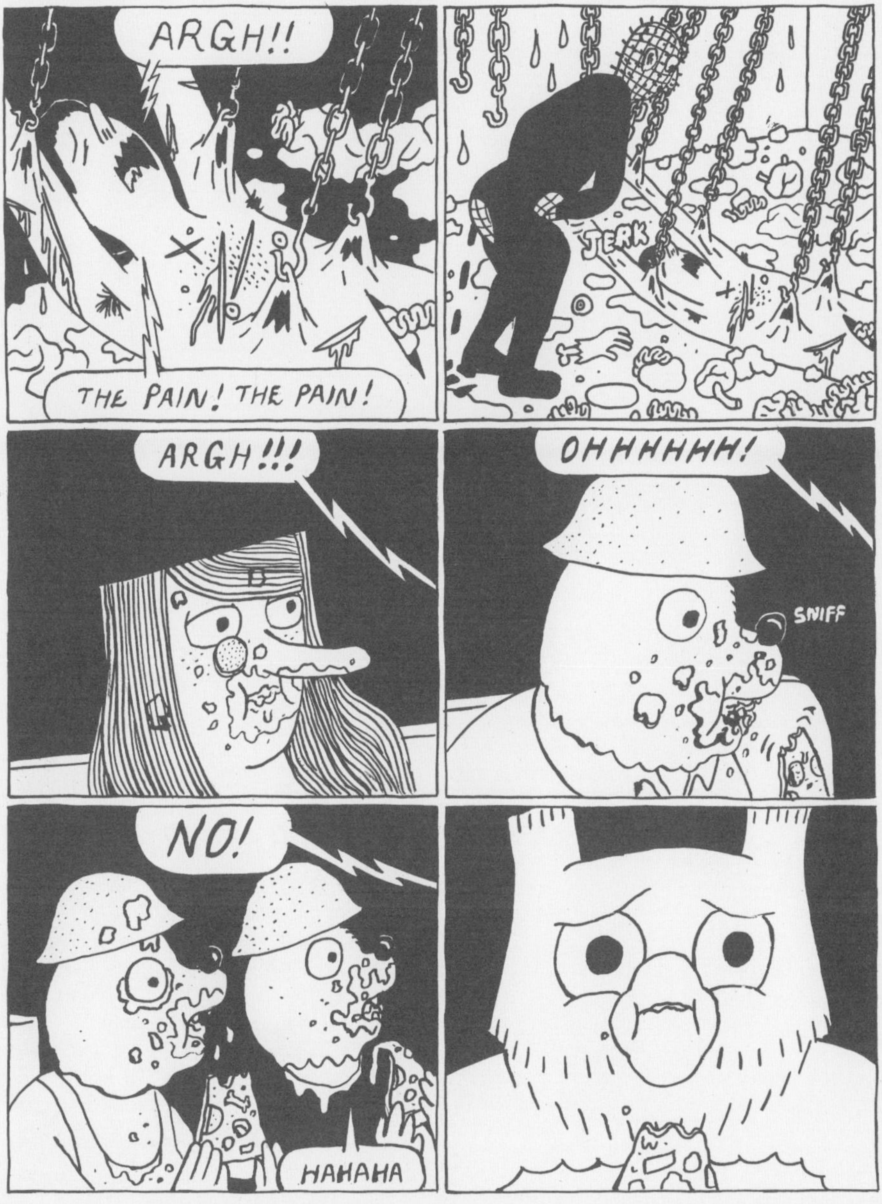
ARGH!!
THE PAIN! THE PAIN!
JERK
ARGH!!!
OHHHHHH!
SNIFF
NO!
HAHAHA

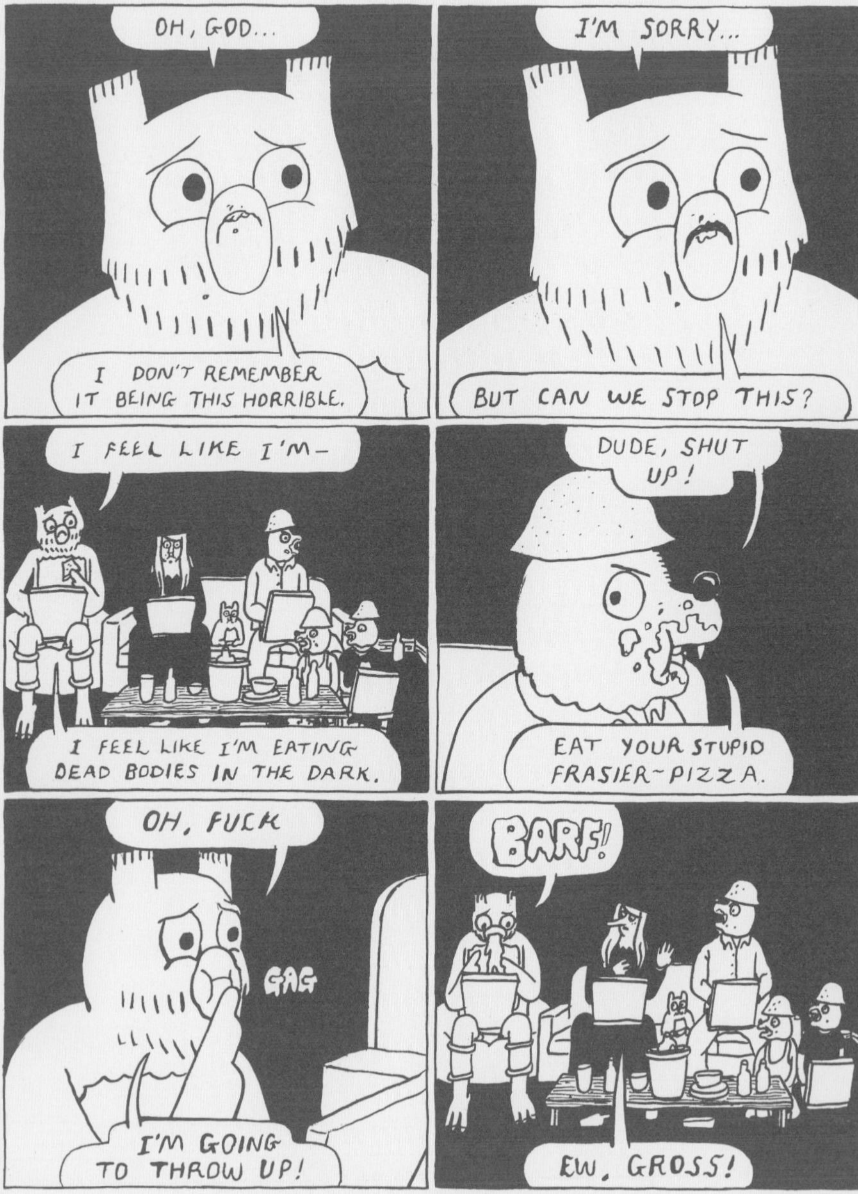
OH, GOD...
I DON'T REMEMBER IT BEING THIS HORRIBLE.
I'M SORRY...
BUT CAN WE STOP THIS?
I FEEL LIKE I'M–
I FEEL LIKE I'M EATING DEAD BODIES IN THE DARK.
DUDE, SHUT UP!
EAT YOUR STUPID FRASIER~PIZZA.
OH, FUCK
GAG
I'M GOING TO THROW UP!
BARF!
EW, GROSS!

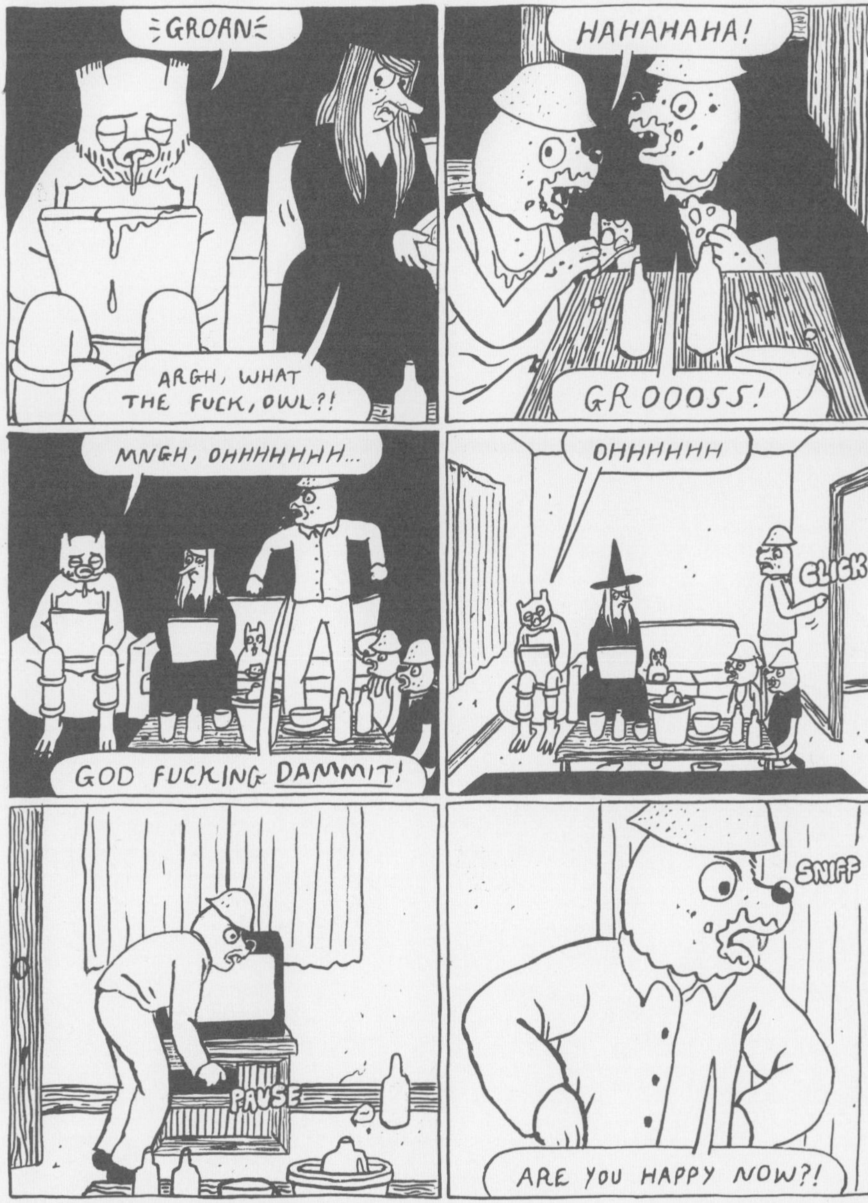
GROAN
ARGH, WHAT THE FUCK, OWL?!
HAHAHAHA!
GROOOSS!
MNGH, OHHHHHHH...
GOD FUCKING DAMMIT!
OHHHHHH
CLICK
PAUSE
SNIFF
ARE YOU HAPPY NOW?!

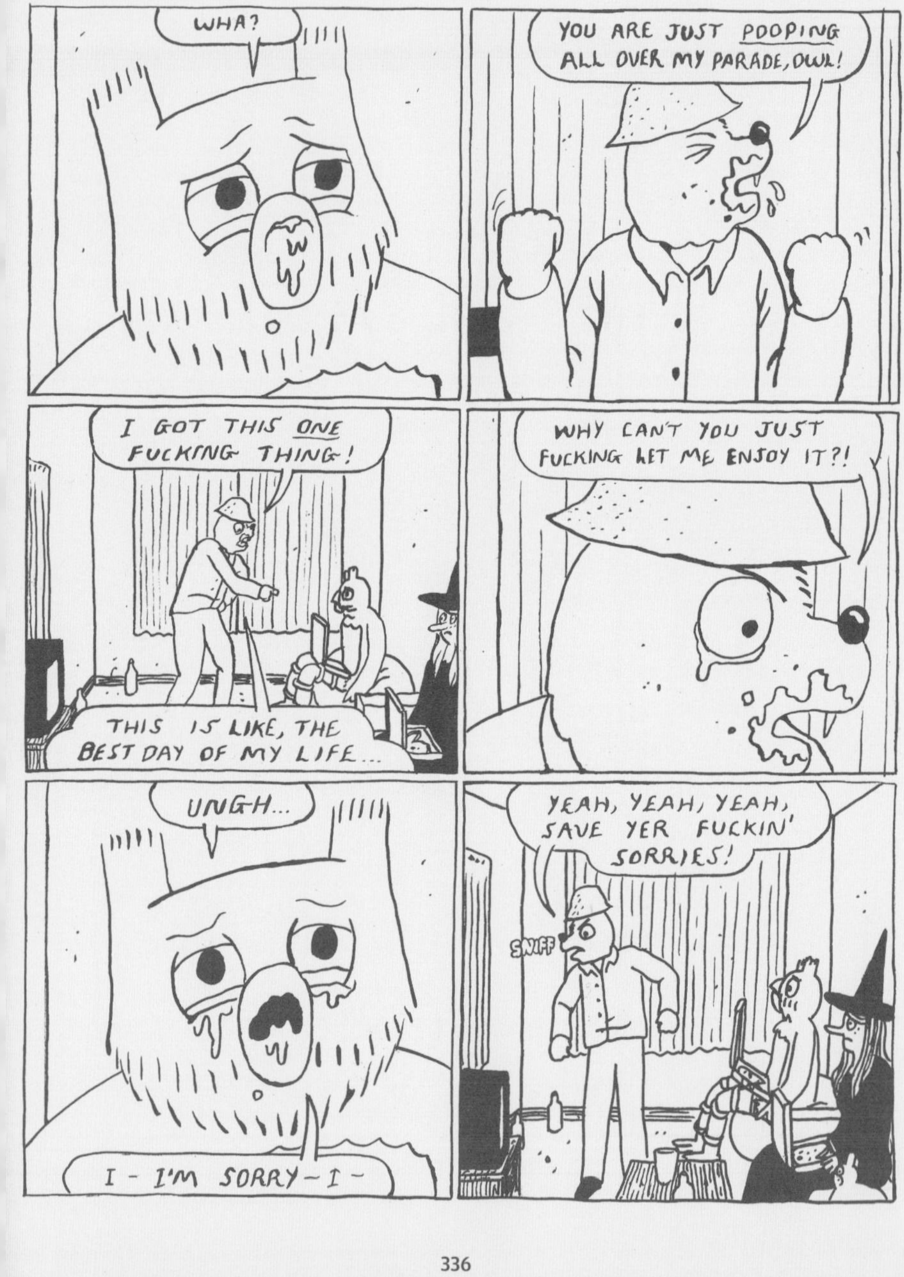
WHA?
YOU ARE JUST POOPING ALL OVER MY PARADE, OWL!
I GOT THIS ONE FUCKING THING!
THIS IS LIKE, THE BEST DAY OF MY LIFE...
WHY CAN'T YOU JUST FUCKING LET ME ENJOY IT?!
UNGH...
I - I'M SORRY - I -
YEAH, YEAH, YEAH, SAVE YER FUCKIN' SORRIES!
SNIFF

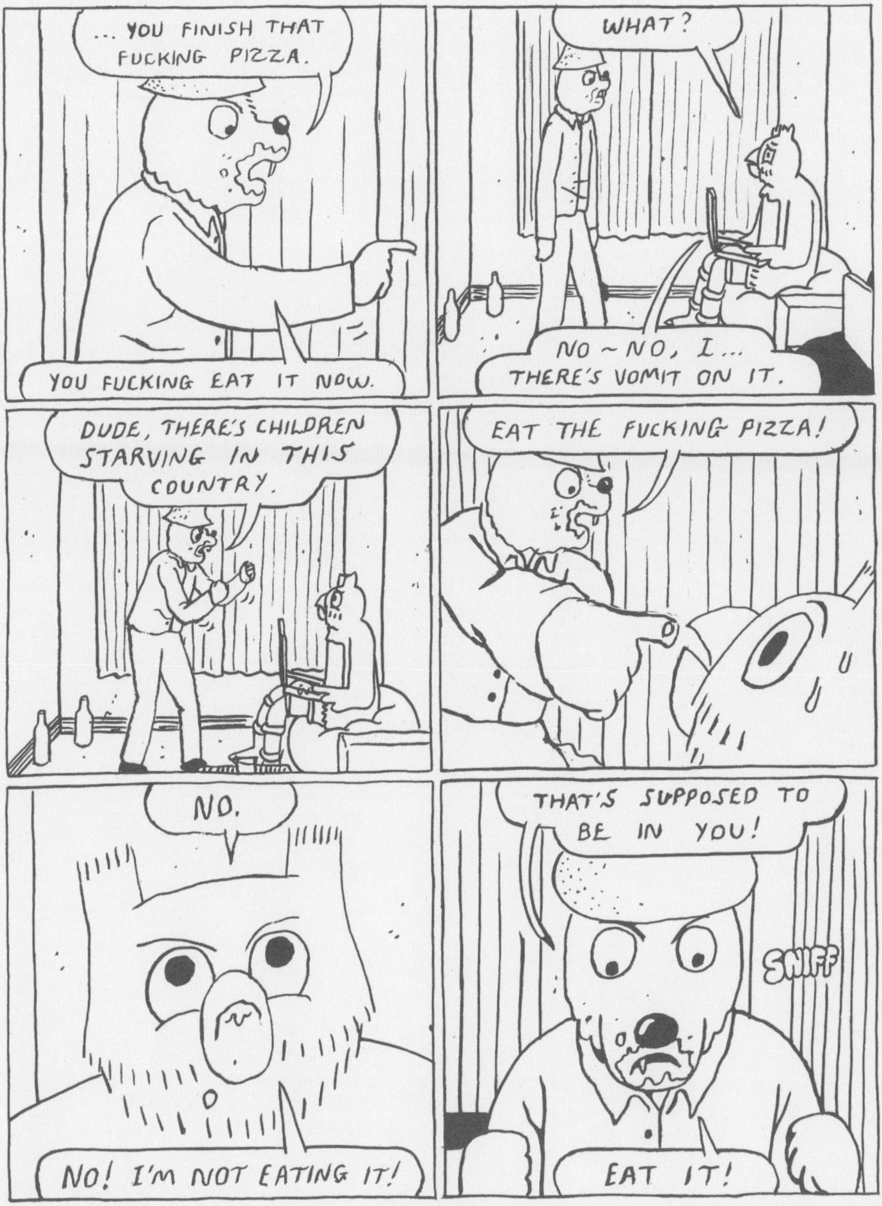
... YOU FINISH THAT FUCKING PIZZA.
YOU FUCKING EAT IT NOW.
WHAT?
NO ~ NO, I... THERE'S VOMIT ON IT.
DUDE, THERE'S CHILDREN STARVING IN THIS COUNTRY.
EAT THE FUCKING PIZZA!
NO.
NO! I'M NOT EATING IT!
THAT'S SUPPOSED TO BE IN YOU!
SNIFF
EAT IT!

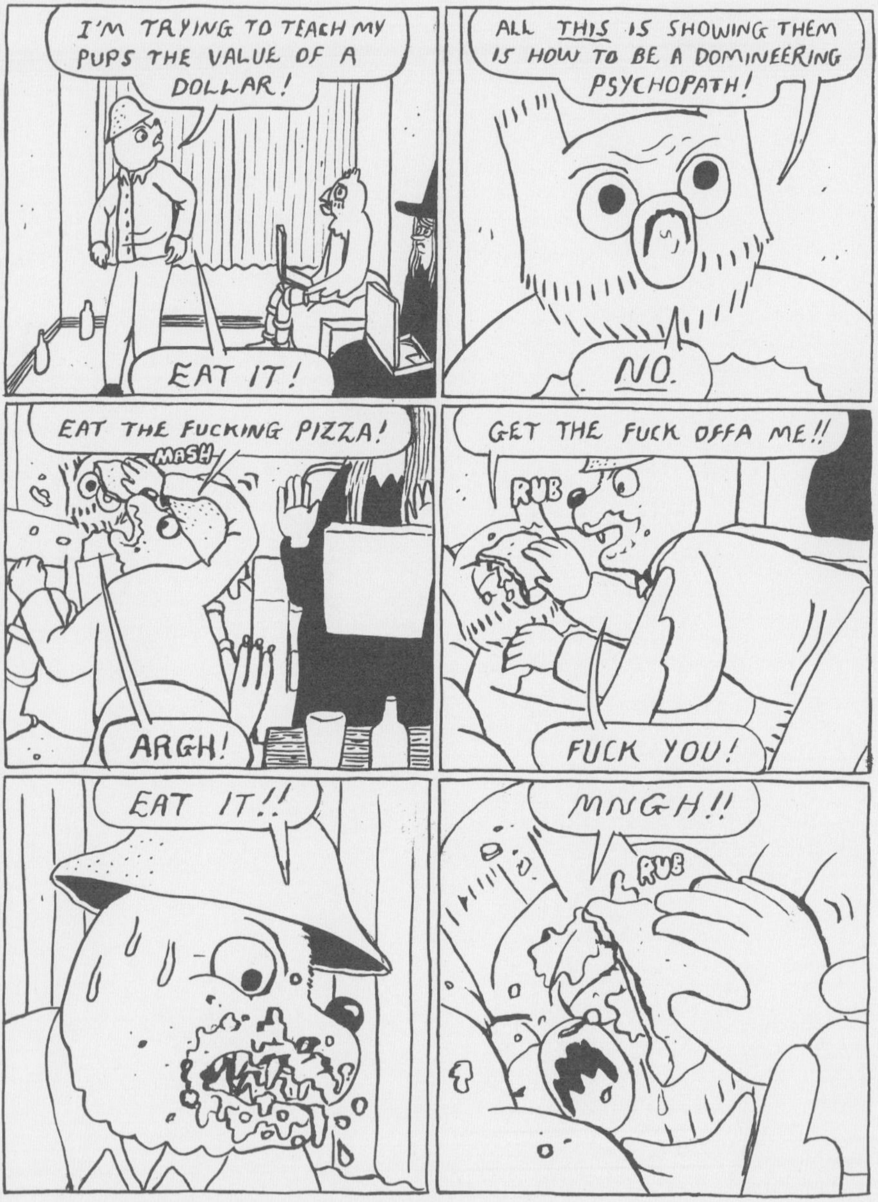
I'M TRYING TO TEACH MY PUPS THE VALUE OF A DOLLAR!
EAT IT!
ALL THIS IS SHOWING THEM IS HOW TO BE A DOMINEERING PSYCHOPATH!
NO.
EAT THE FUCKING PIZZA!
MASH
ARGH!
GET THE FUCK OFFA ME!!
RUB
FUCK YOU!
EAT IT!!
MNGH!!
RUB

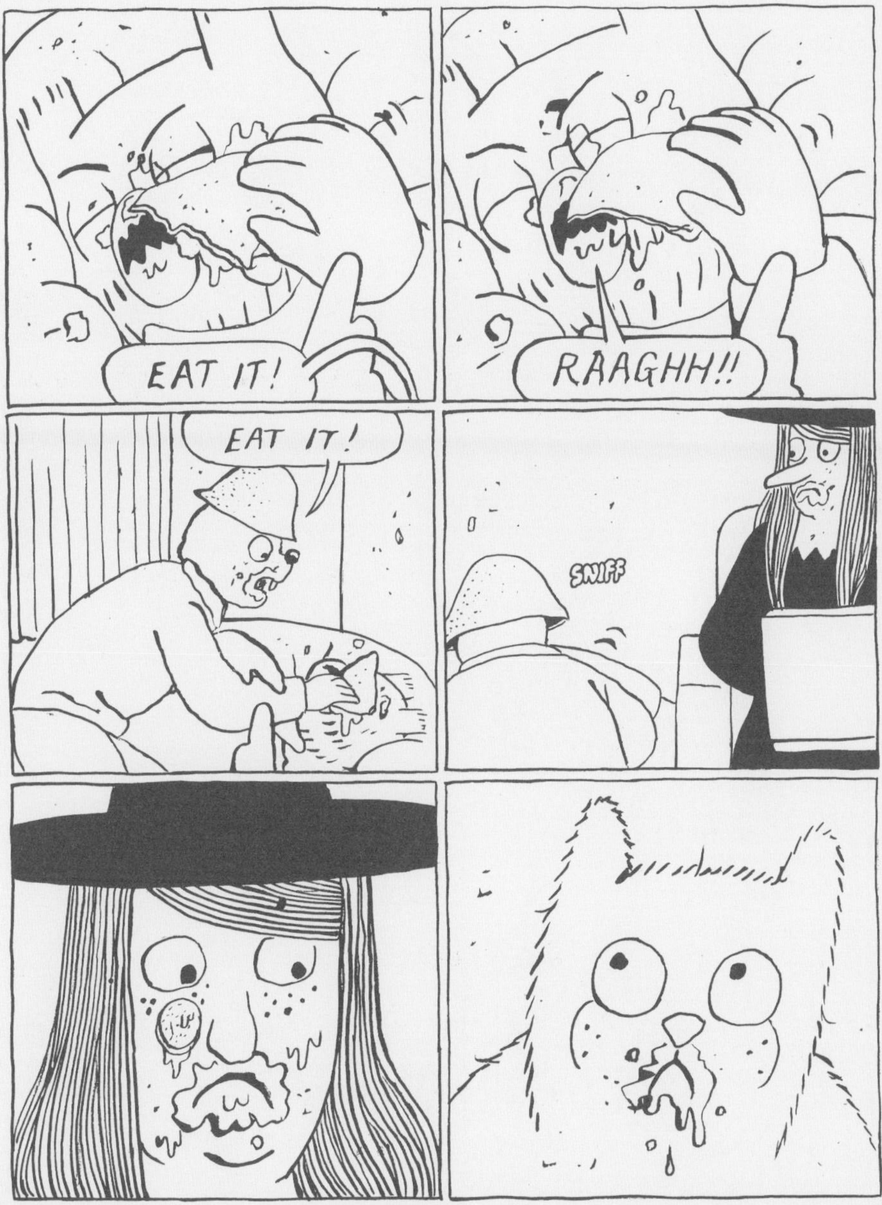
EAT IT!
RAAGHH!!
EAT IT!
SNIFF

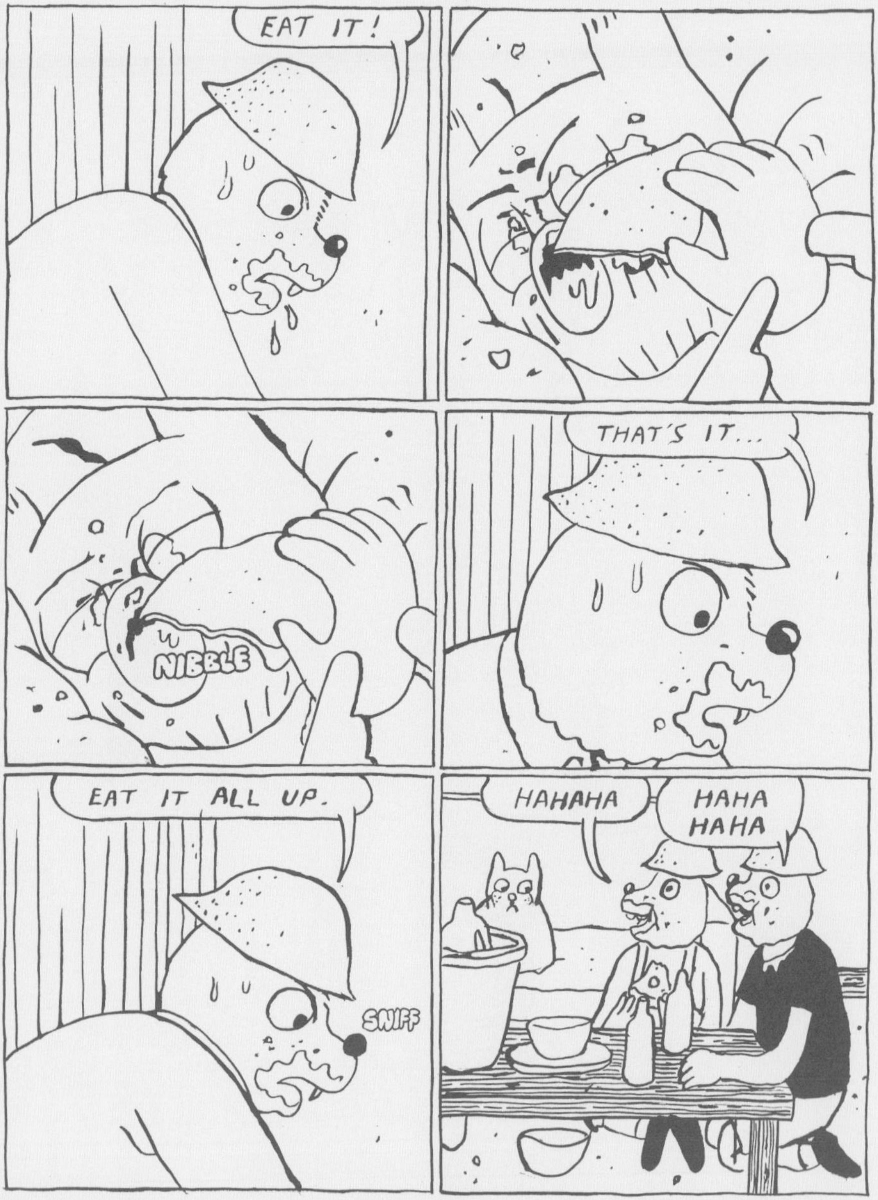
EAT IT!
NIBBLE
THAT'S IT...
EAT IT ALL UP.
SNIFF
HAHAHA
HAHA HAHA

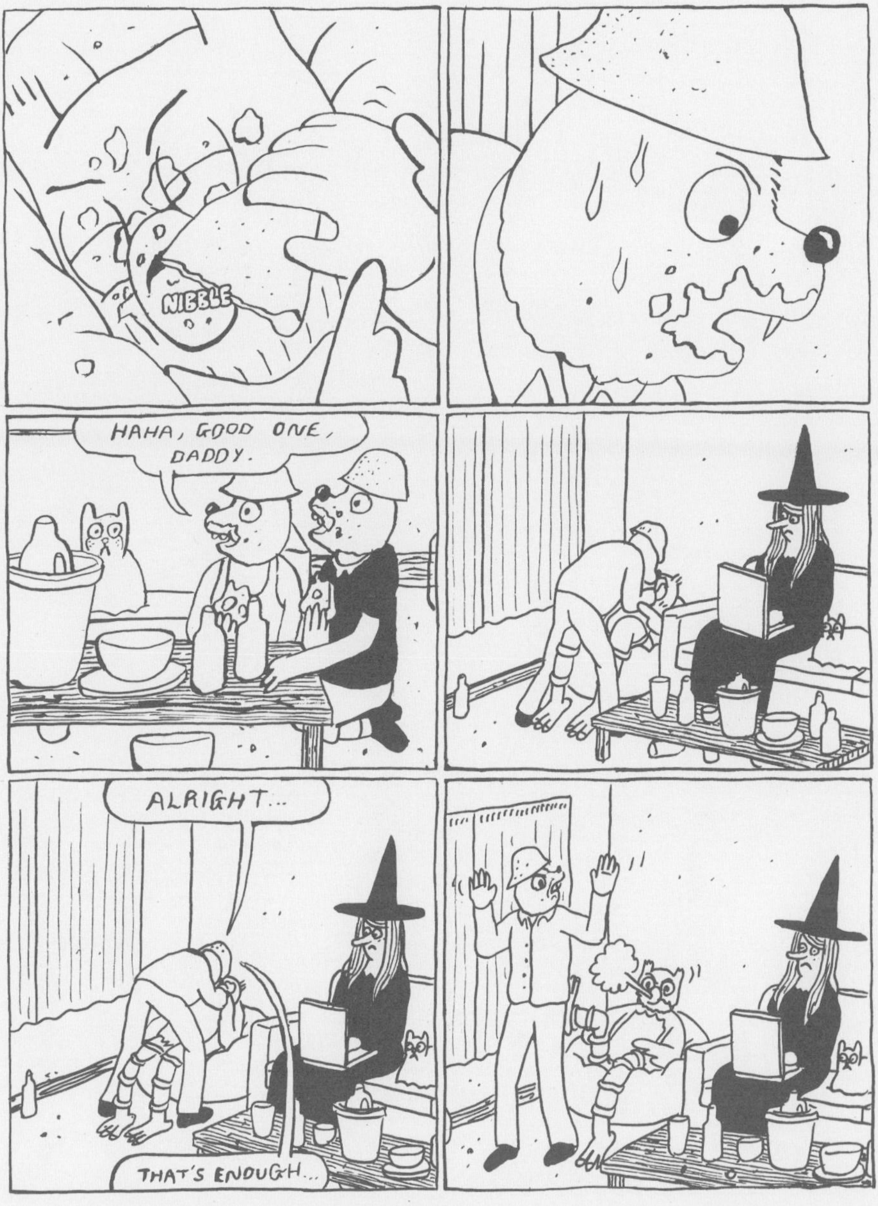
NIBBLE
HAHA, GOOD ONE, DADDY.
ALRIGHT...
THAT'S ENOUGH...

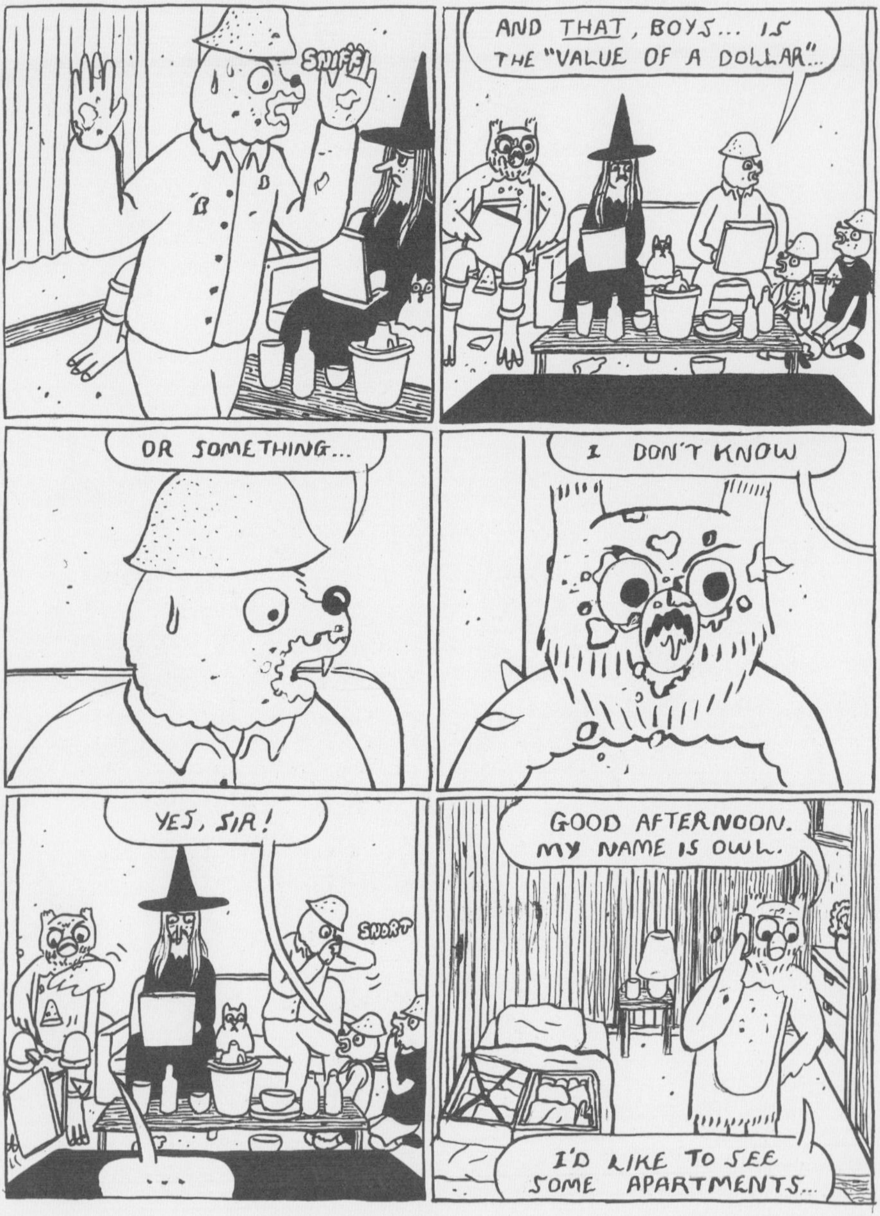
SNIFF
AND THAT, BOYS... IS THE "VALUE OF A DOLLAR"...
OR SOMETHING...
I DON'T KNOW
YES, SIR!
SNORT
...
GOOD AFTERNOON. MY NAME IS OWL.
I'D LIKE TO SEE SOME APARTMENTS...

MISSING
HAVE YOU SEEN OUR FRIEND OWL?

LAST SEEN DECEMBER 31ˢᵗ '14
WEARING: NOTHING
ARTICULATE, SENSITIVE SOUL

555-165-4202 | 555-165-4202 | 555-165-4202 | 555-165-4202 | 555-165-4202 | 555-165-4202 | 555-165-4202 | 555-165-4202 | 555-165-4202 | 555-165-4202 | 555-165-4202 | 555-165-4202 | 555-165-4202

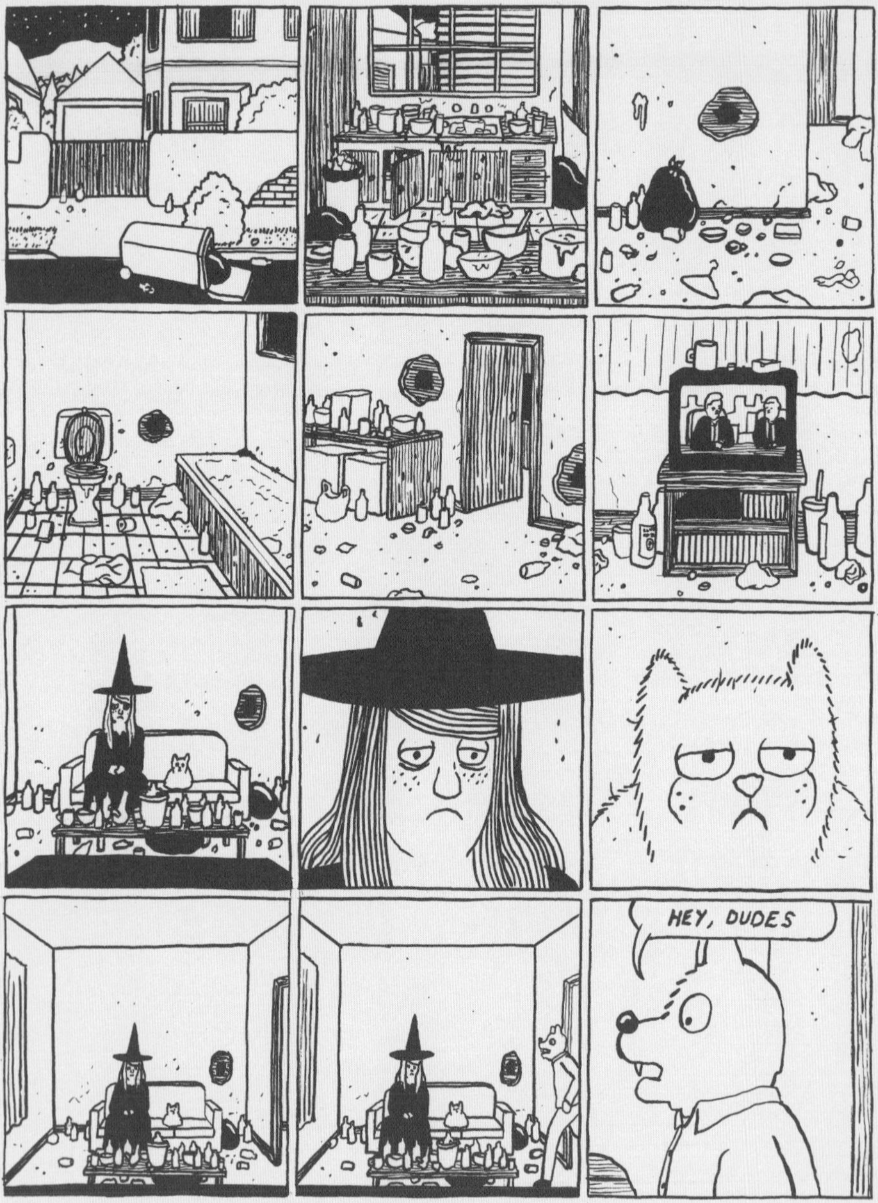
HEY, DUDES

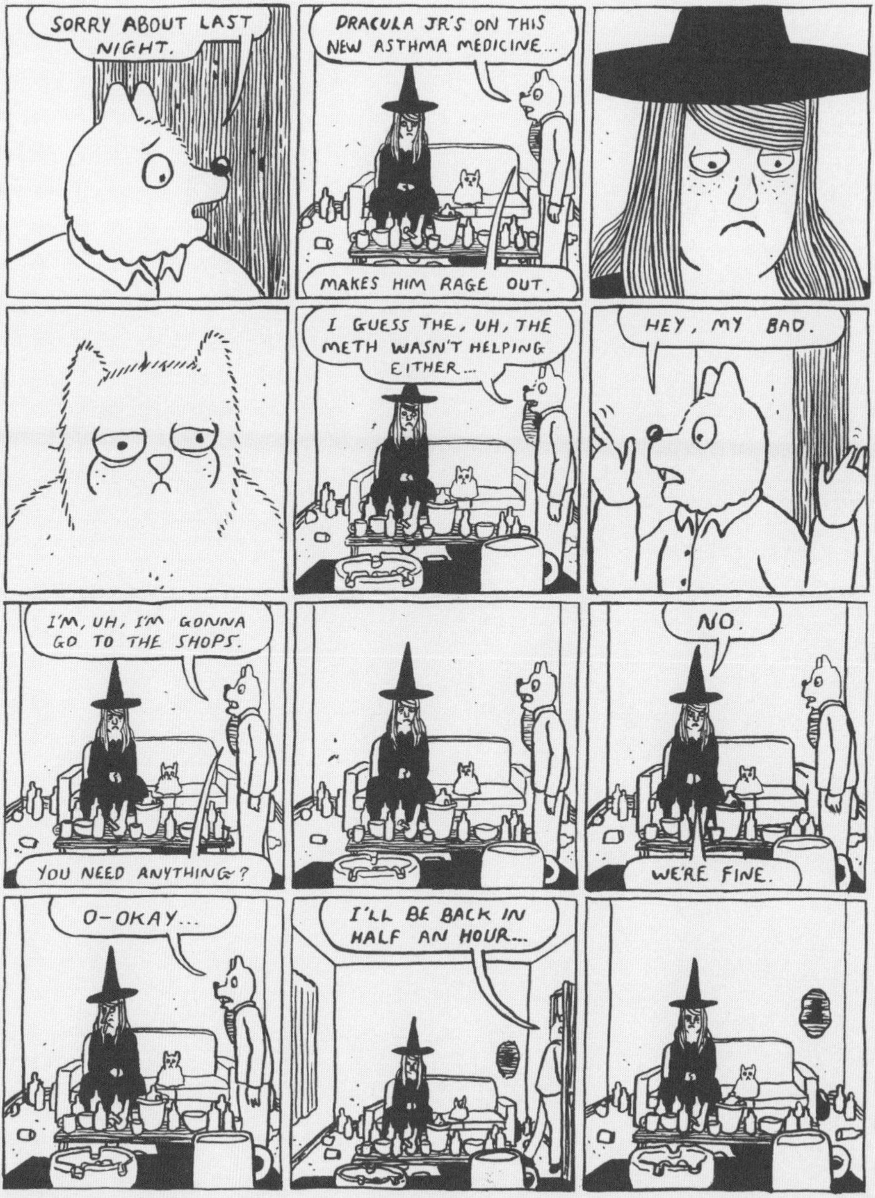
SORRY ABOUT LAST NIGHT.
DRACULA JR'S ON THIS NEW ASTHMA MEDICINE...
MAKES HIM RAGE OUT.
I GUESS THE, UH, THE METH WASN'T HELPING EITHER...
HEY, MY BAD.
I'M, UH, I'M GONNA GO TO THE SHOPS.
YOU NEED ANYTHING?
NO.
WE'RE FINE.
O-OKAY...
I'LL BE BACK IN HALF AN HOUR...

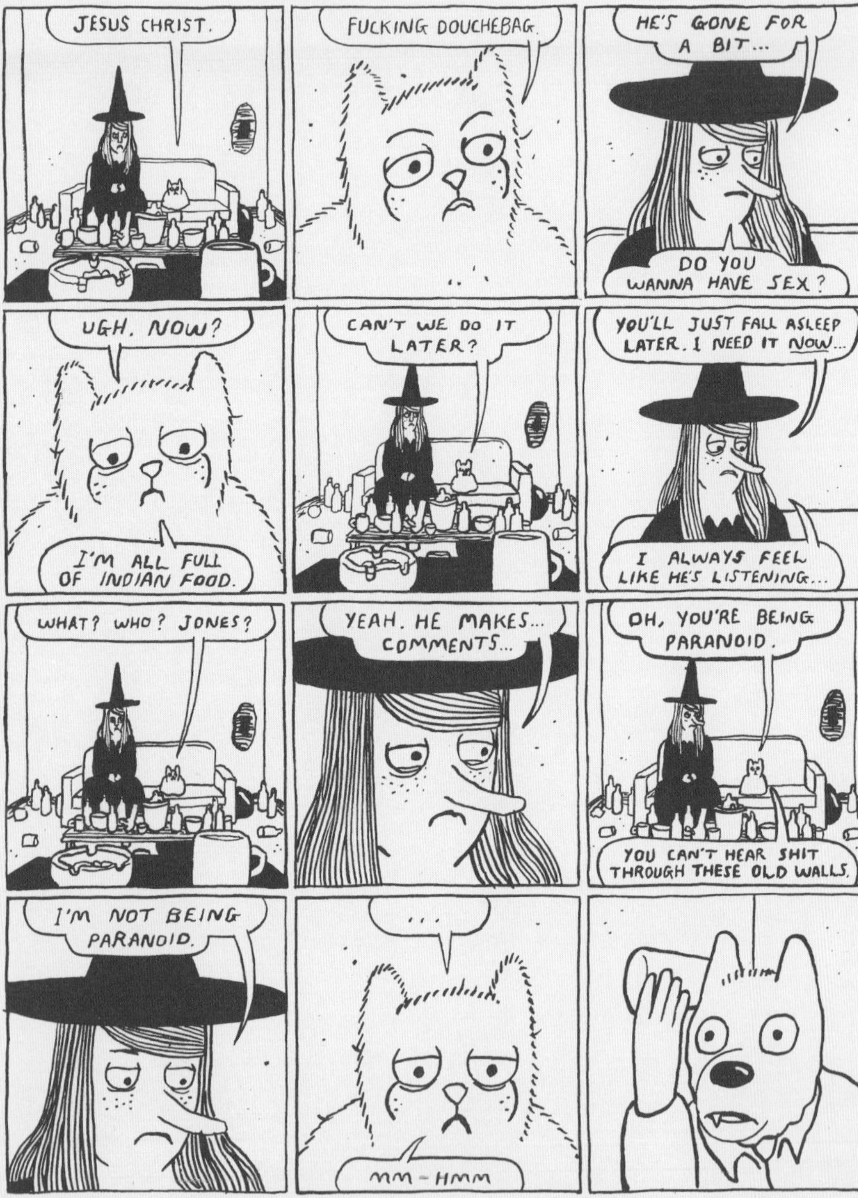

JESUS CHRIST.
FUCKING DOUCHEBAG.
HE'S GONE FOR A BIT...
DO YOU WANNA HAVE SEX?
UGH. NOW?
I'M ALL FULL OF INDIAN FOOD.
CAN'T WE DO IT LATER?
YOU'LL JUST FALL ASLEEP LATER. I NEED IT NOW...
I ALWAYS FEEL LIKE HE'S LISTENING...
WHAT? WHO? JONES?
YEAH. HE MAKES... COMMENTS...
OH, YOU'RE BEING PARANOID.
YOU CAN'T HEAR SHIT THROUGH THESE OLD WALLS.
I'M NOT BEING PARANOID.
...
MM-HMM

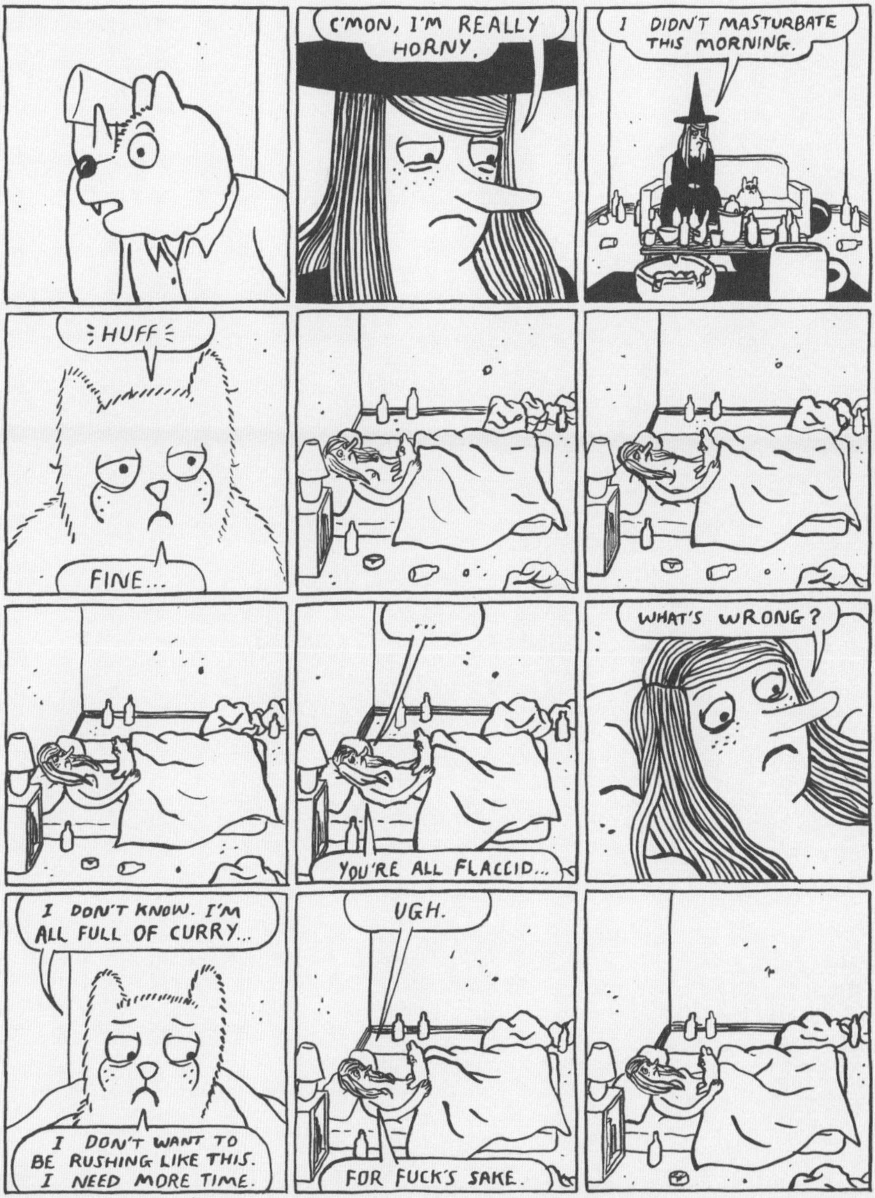
C'MON, I'M REALLY HORNY.
I DIDN'T MASTURBATE THIS MORNING.
HUFF
FINE...
WHAT'S WRONG?
...
YOU'RE ALL FLACCID...
I DON'T KNOW. I'M ALL FULL OF CURRY...
I DON'T WANT TO BE RUSHING LIKE THIS. I NEED MORE TIME.
UGH.
FOR FUCK'S SAKE.

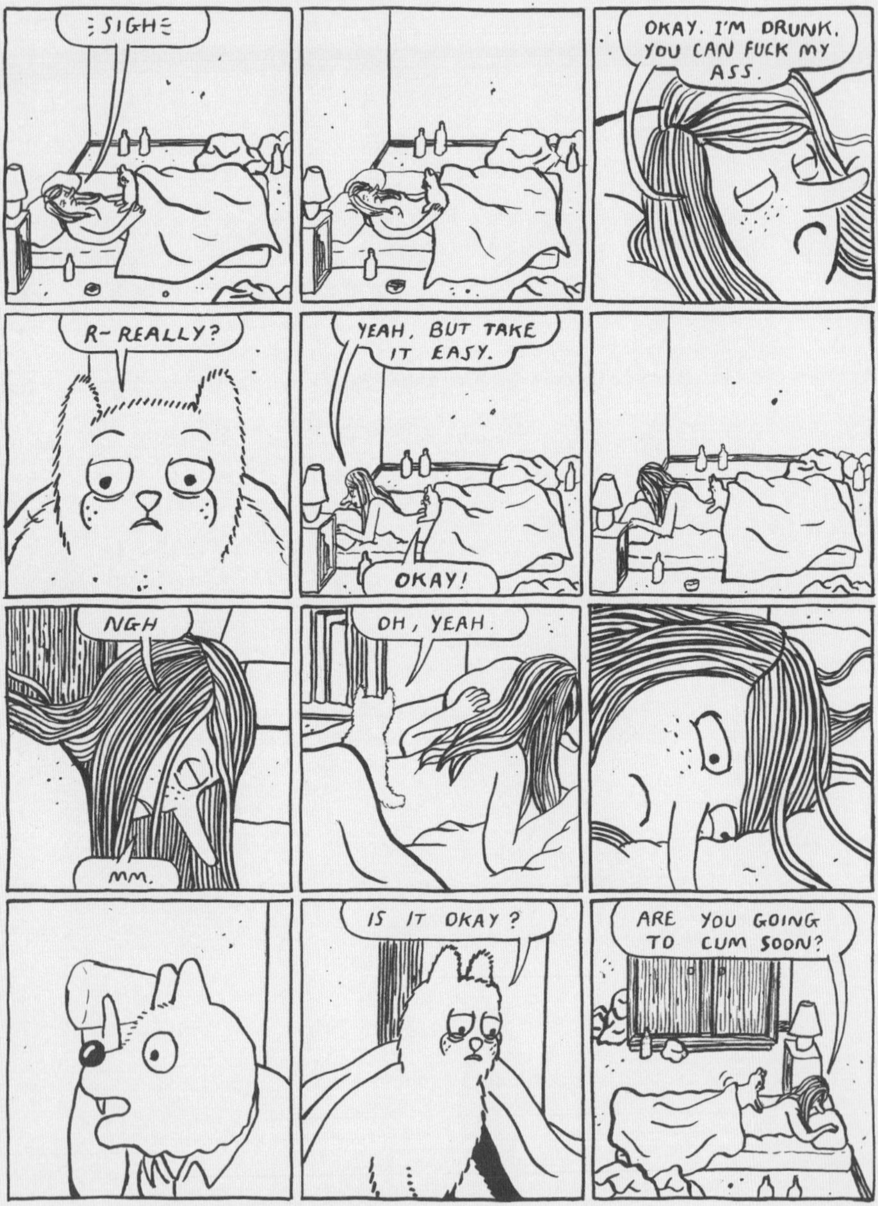
SIGH
OKAY. I'M DRUNK. YOU CAN FUCK MY ASS.
R-REALLY?
YEAH, BUT TAKE IT EASY.
OKAY!
NGH
MM.
OH, YEAH.
IS IT OKAY?
ARE YOU GOING TO CUM SOON?

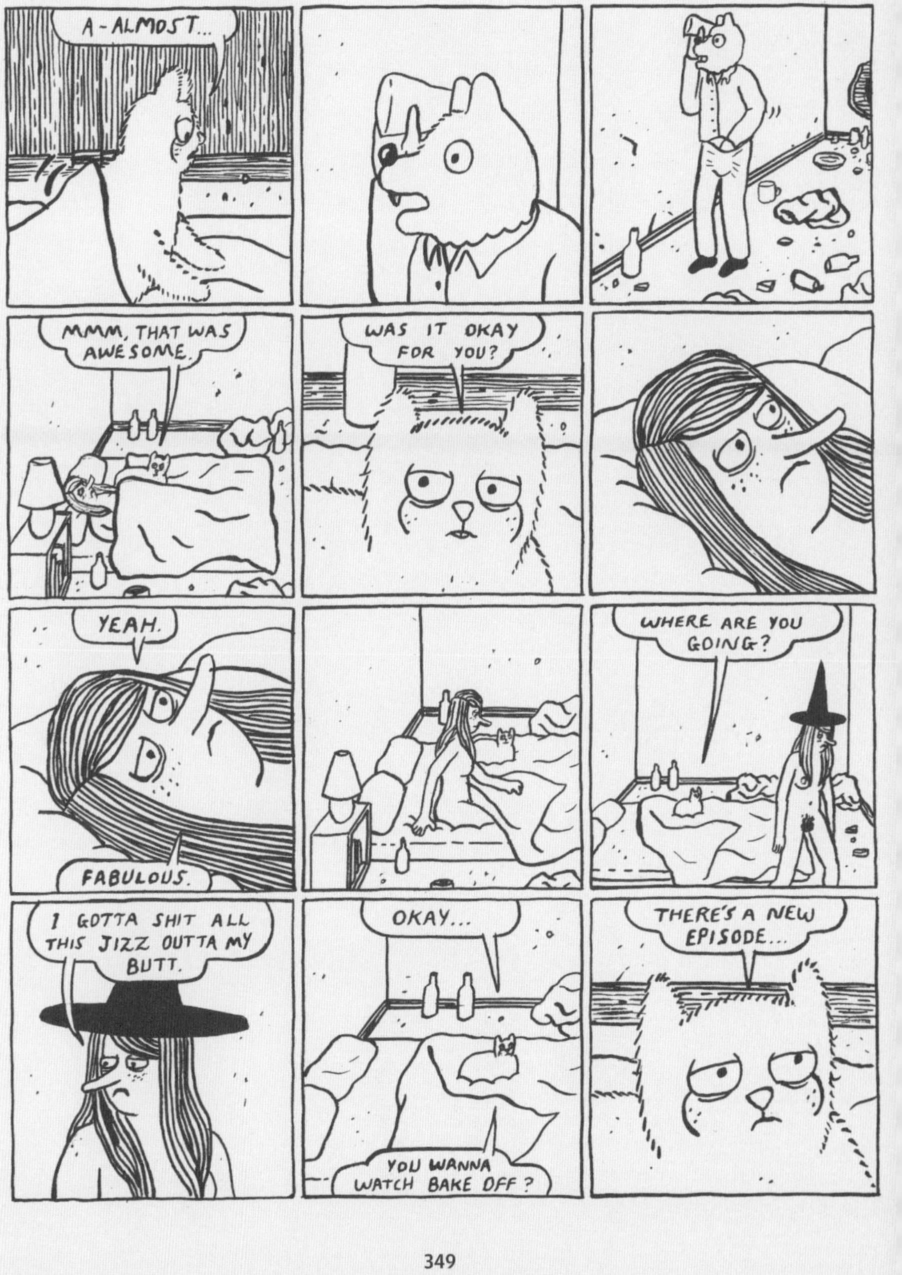
A-ALMOST...
MMM, THAT WAS AWESOME.
WAS IT OKAY FOR YOU?
YEAH.
FABULOUS.
WHERE ARE YOU GOING?
I GOTTA SHIT ALL THIS JIZZ OUTTA MY BUTT.
OKAY...
YOU WANNA WATCH BAKE OFF?
THERE'S A NEW EPISODE...

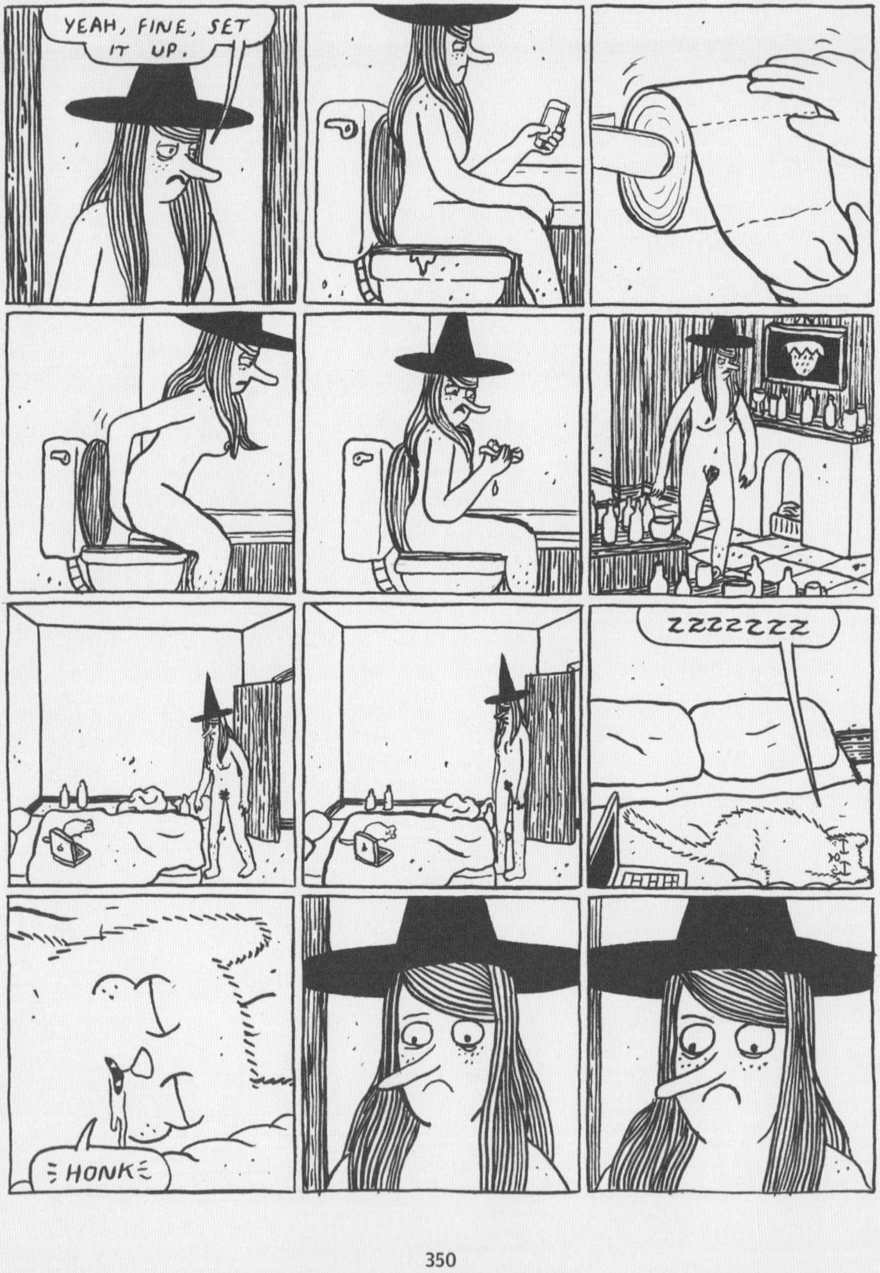
YEAH, FINE, SET IT UP.
ZZZZZZZ
HONK

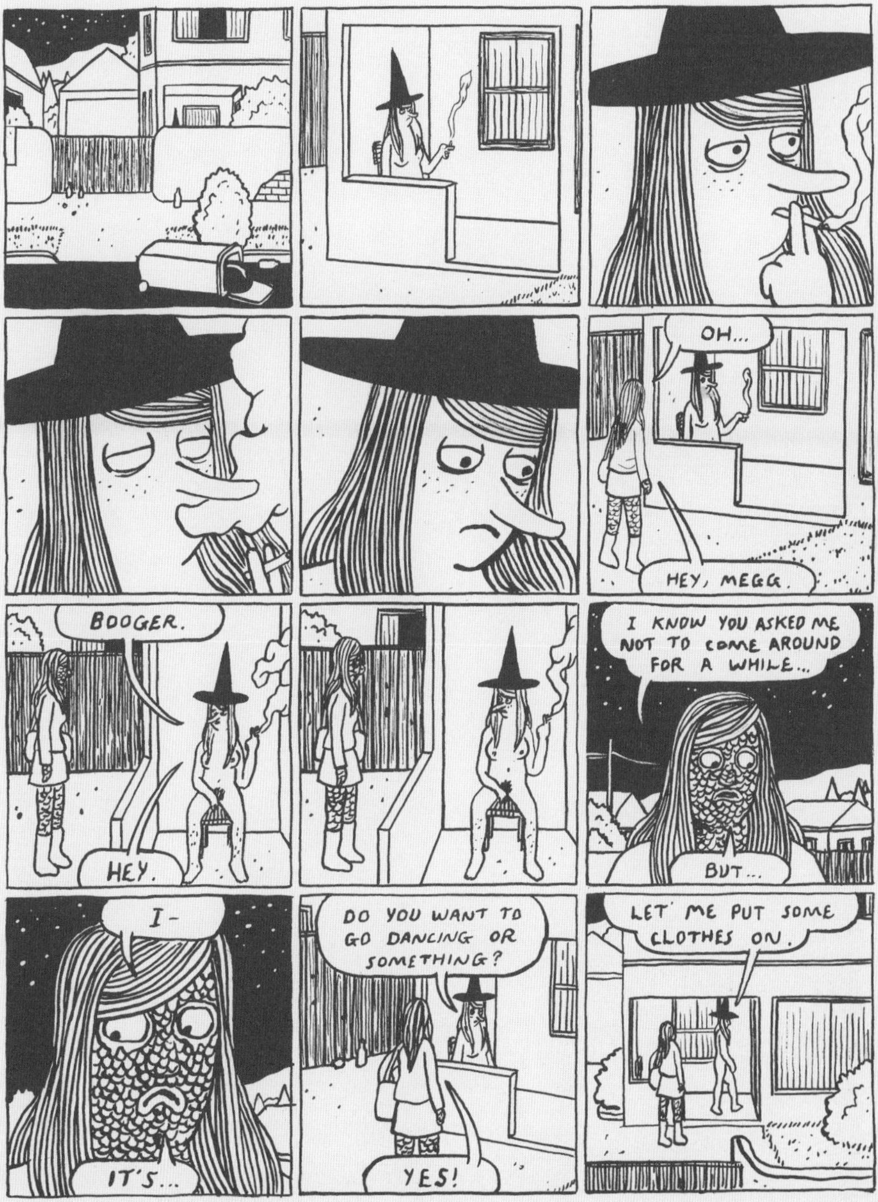
OH...
HEY, MEGG.
BOOGER.
HEY.
I KNOW YOU ASKED ME NOT TO COME AROUND FOR A WHILE...
BUT...
I-
IT'S...
DO YOU WANT TO GO DANCING OR SOMETHING?
YES!
LET ME PUT SOME CLOTHES ON.

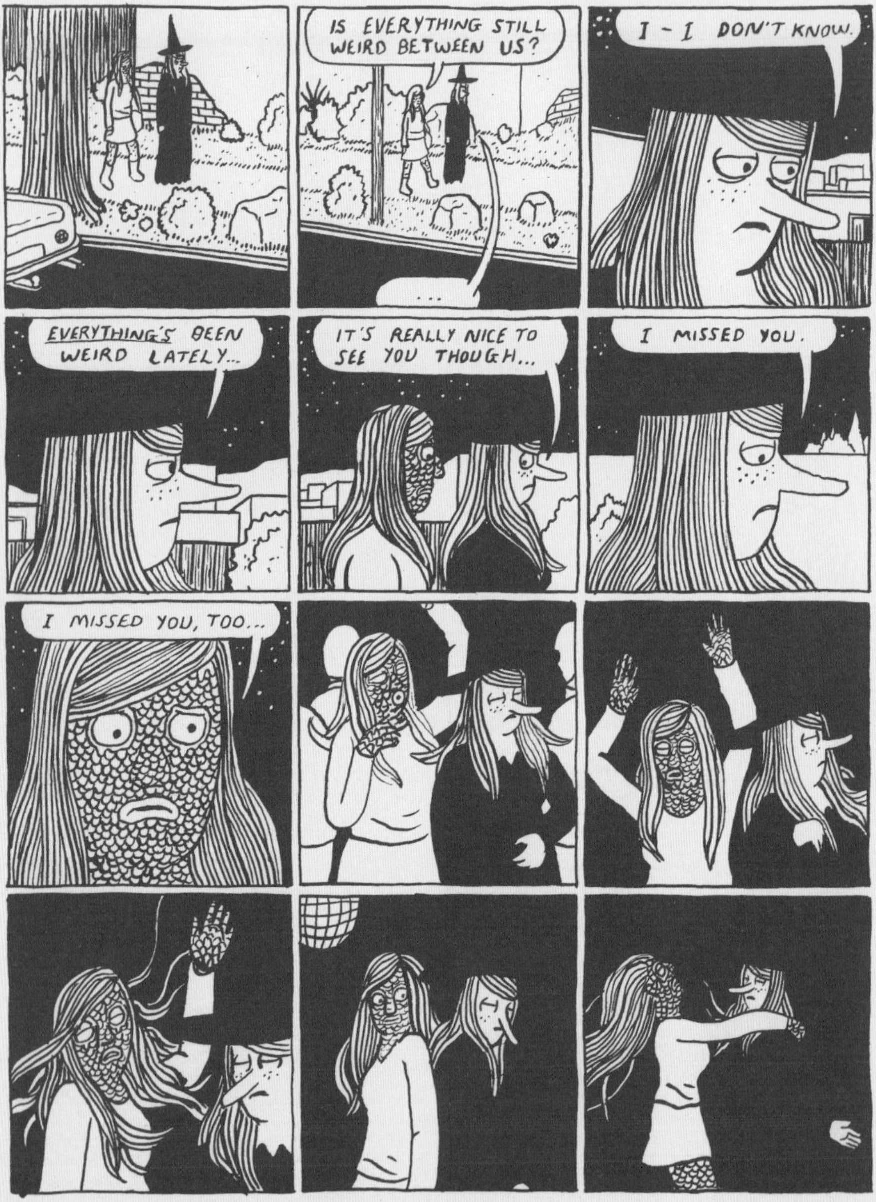
IS EVERYTHING STILL WEIRD BETWEEN US?
...
I - I DON'T KNOW.
EVERYTHING'S BEEN WEIRD LATELY...
IT'S REALLY NICE TO SEE YOU THOUGH...
I MISSED YOU.
I MISSED YOU, TOO...

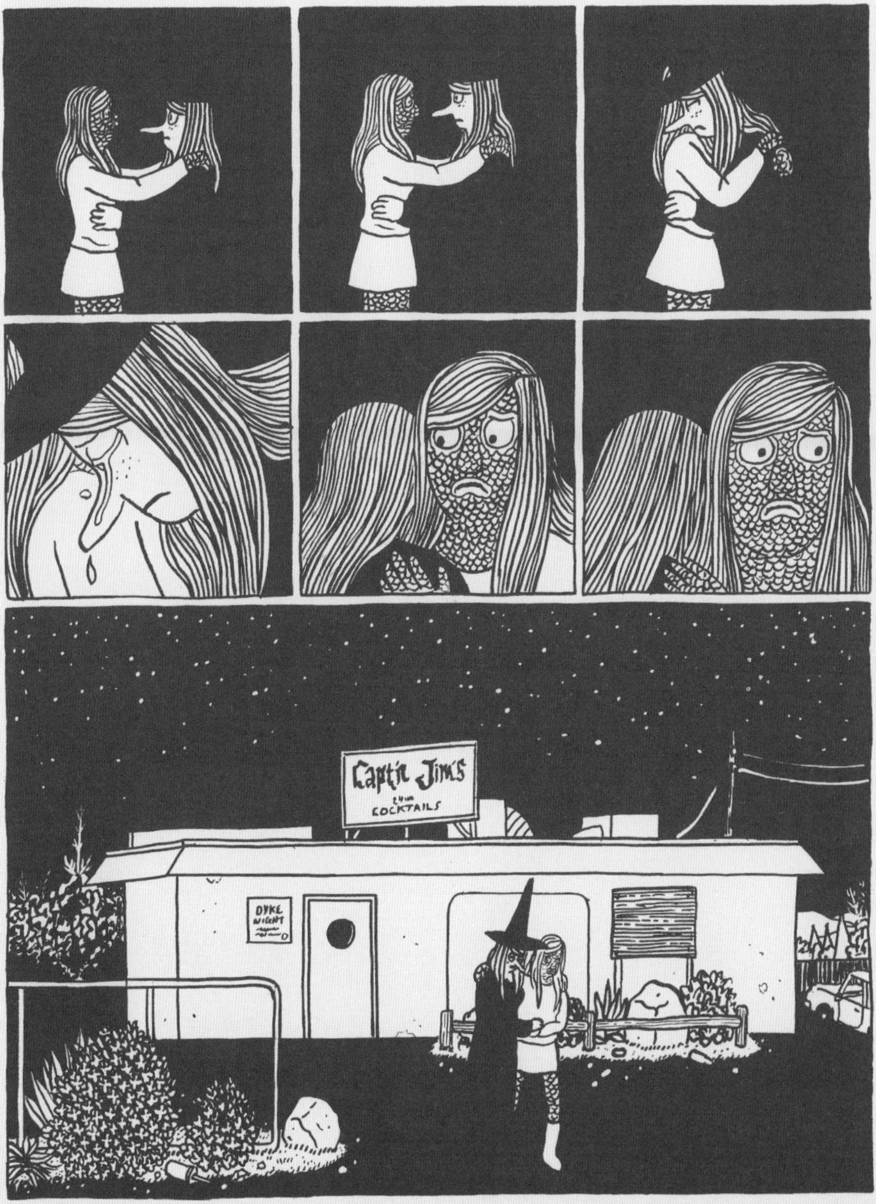
Captn Jim's
COCKTAILS
DYKE NIGHT

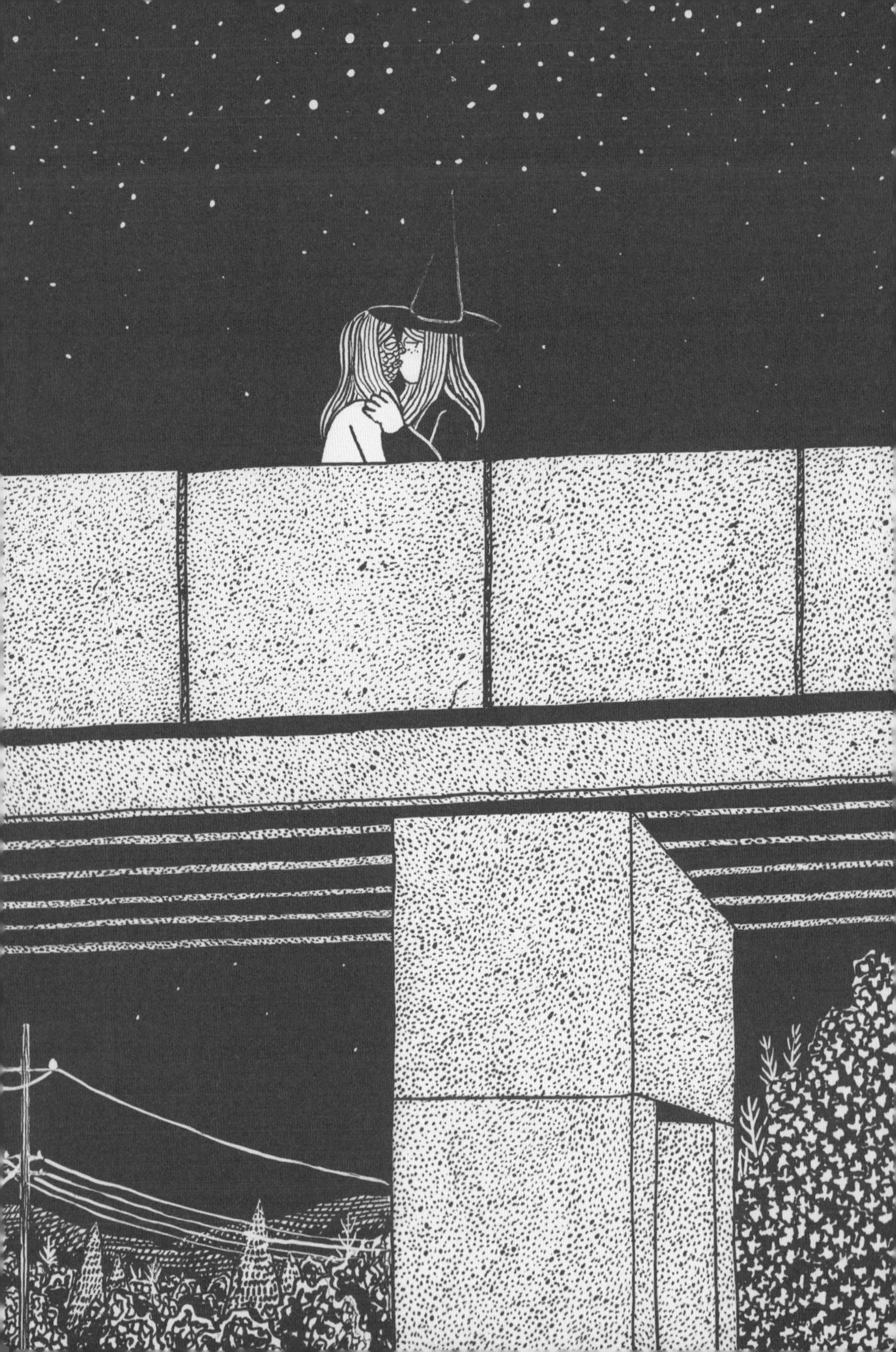

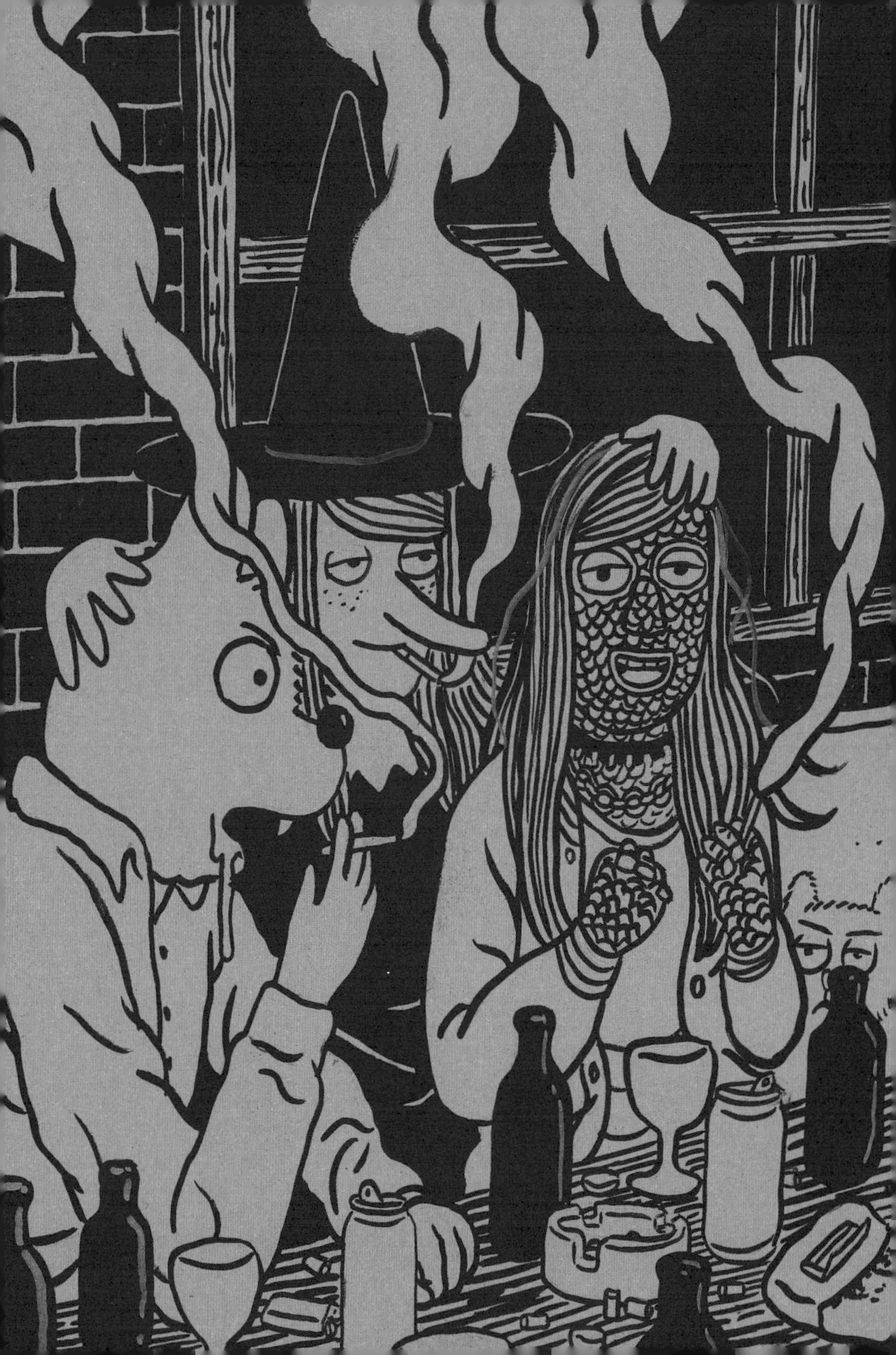

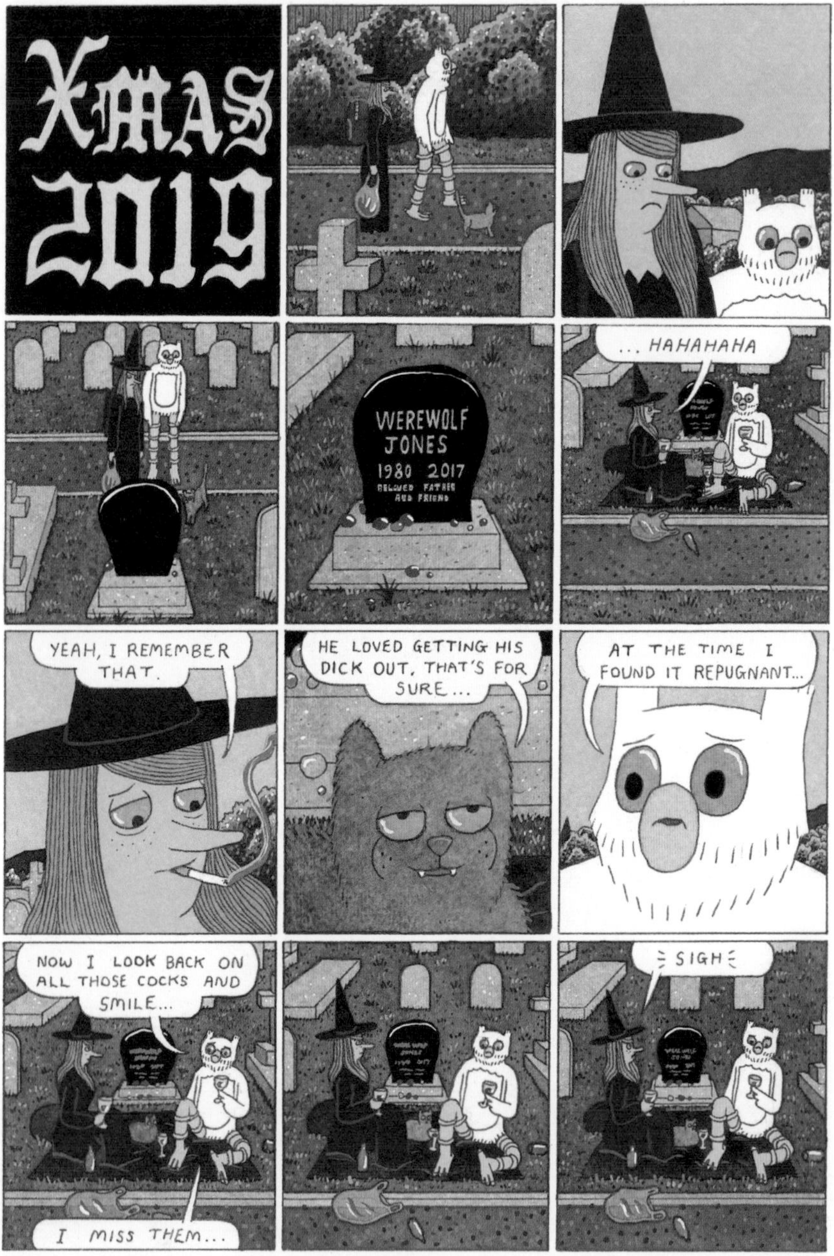
XMAS 2019
WEREWOLF JONES 1980 2017 BELOVED FATHER AND FRIEND
... HAHAHAHA
YEAH, I REMEMBER THAT.
HE LOVED GETTING HIS DICK OUT, THAT'S FOR SURE...
AT THE TIME I FOUND IT REPUGNANT...
NOW I LOOK BACK ON ALL THOSE COCKS AND SMILE...
I MISS THEM...
SIGH

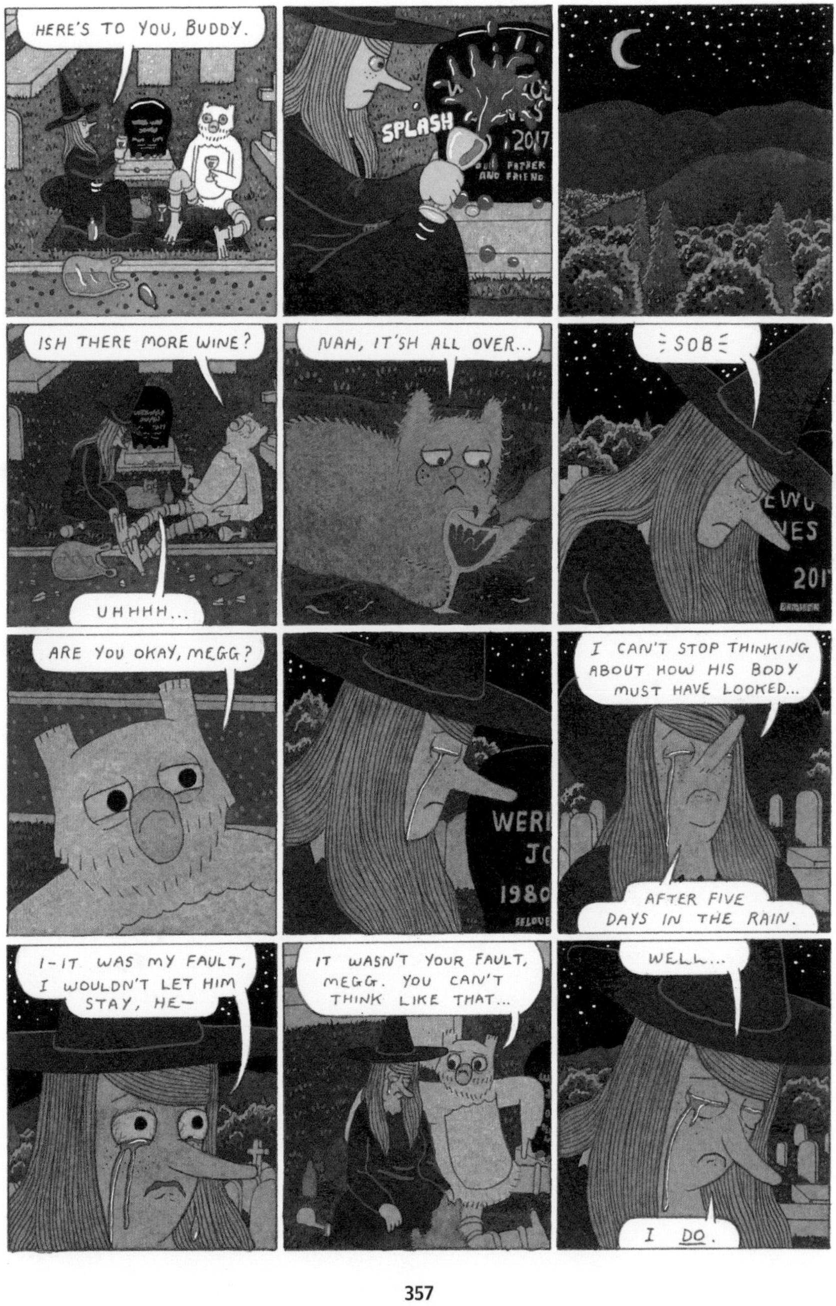
HERE'S TO YOU, BUDDY.
SPLASH
ISH THERE MORE WINE?
UHHHH...
NAH, IT'SH ALL OVER...
SOB
ARE YOU OKAY, MEGG?
I CAN'T STOP THINKING ABOUT HOW HIS BODY MUST HAVE LOOKED...
AFTER FIVE DAYS IN THE RAIN.
I-IT WAS MY FAULT, I WOULDN'T LET HIM STAY, HE—
IT WASN'T YOUR FAULT, MEGG. YOU CAN'T THINK LIKE THAT...
WELL...
I DO.

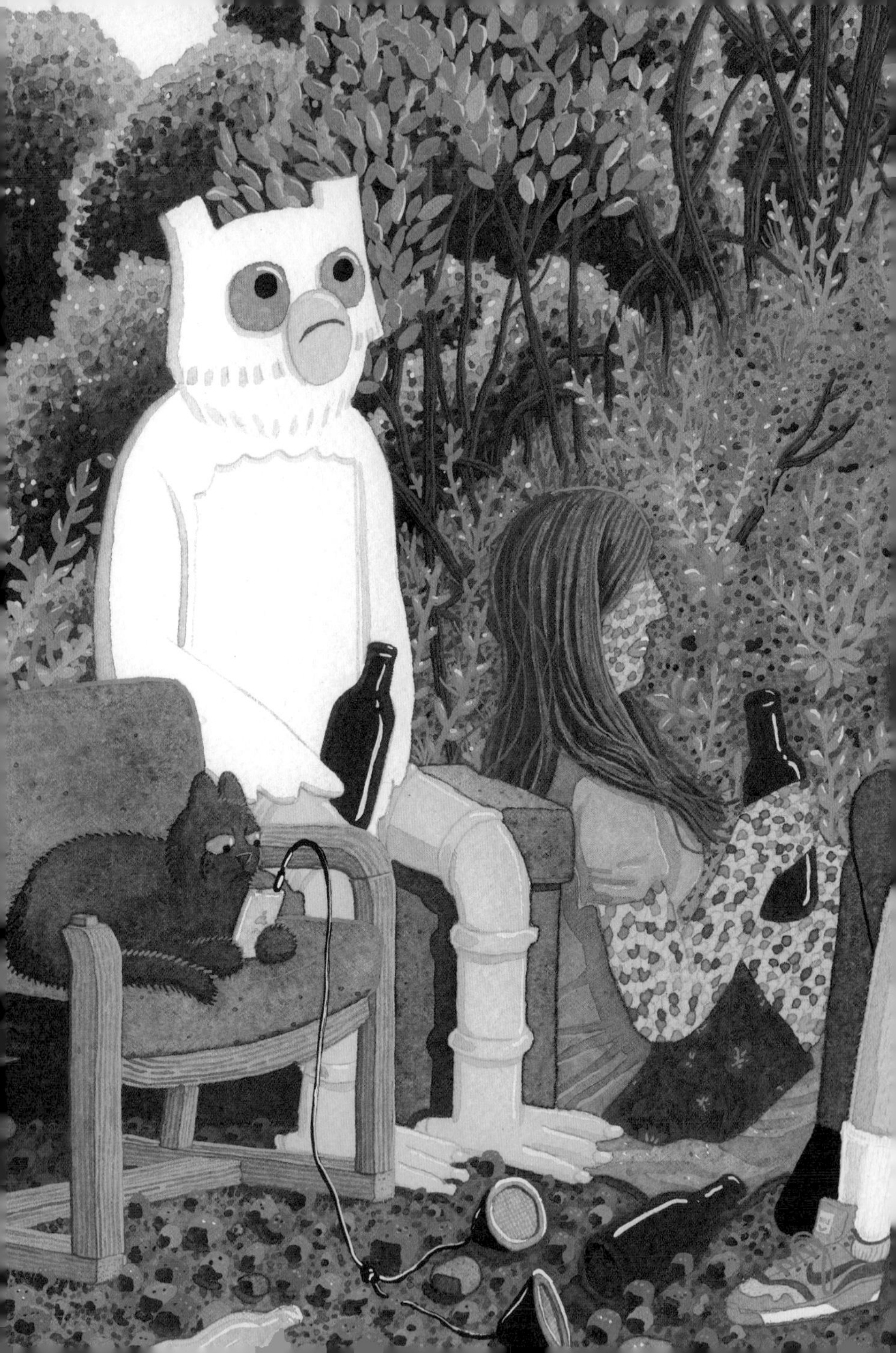

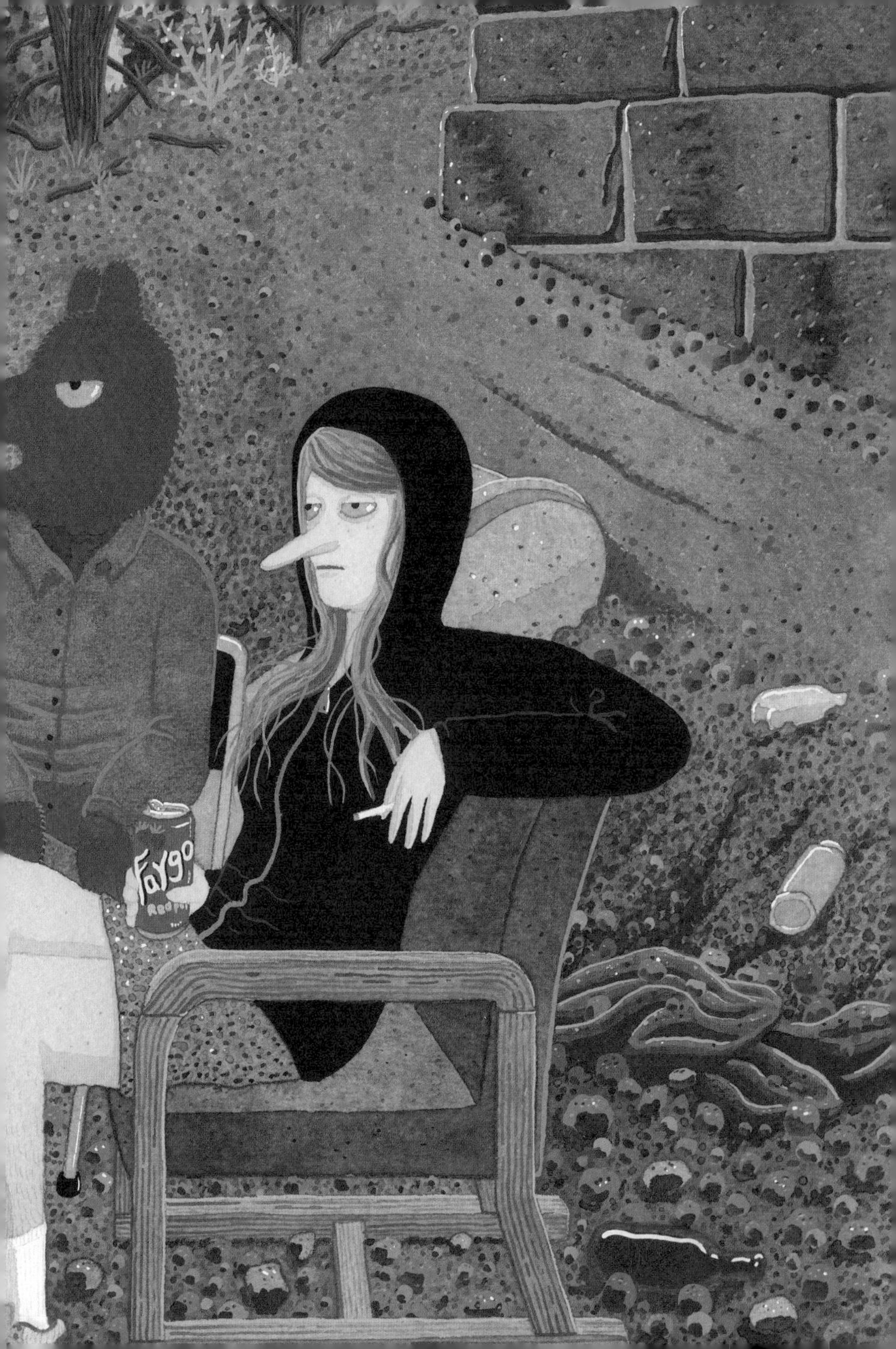
Faygo

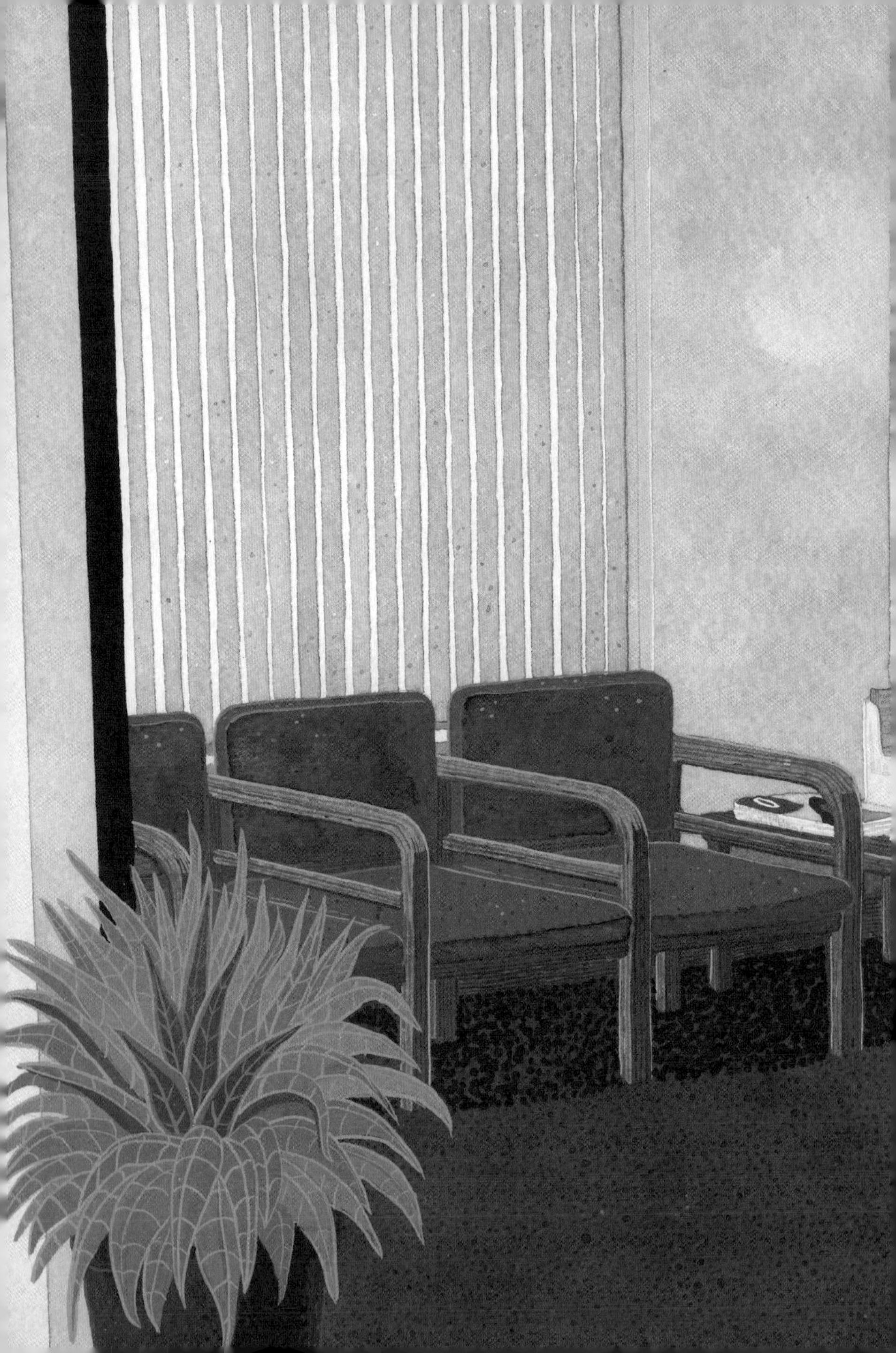

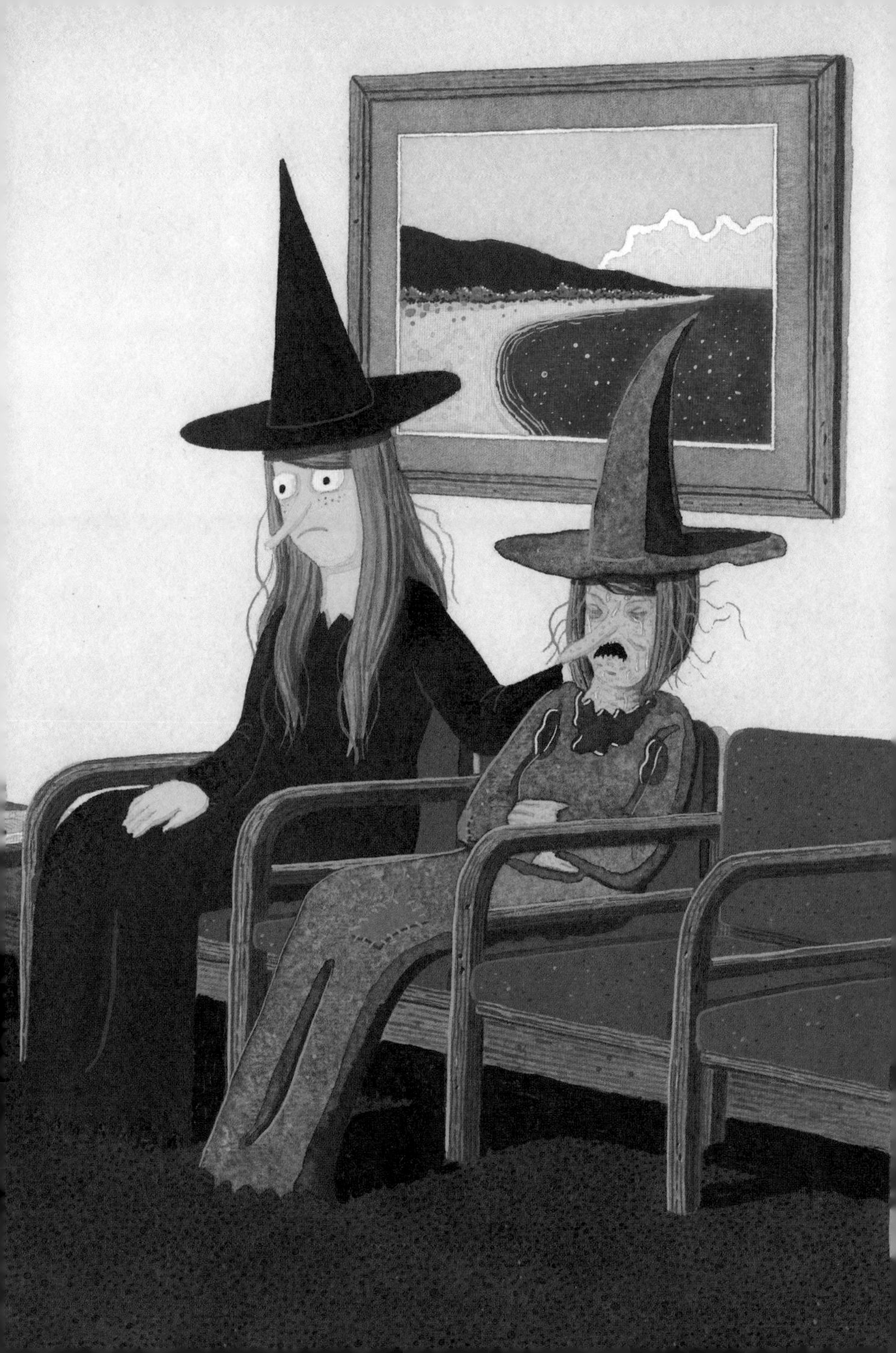

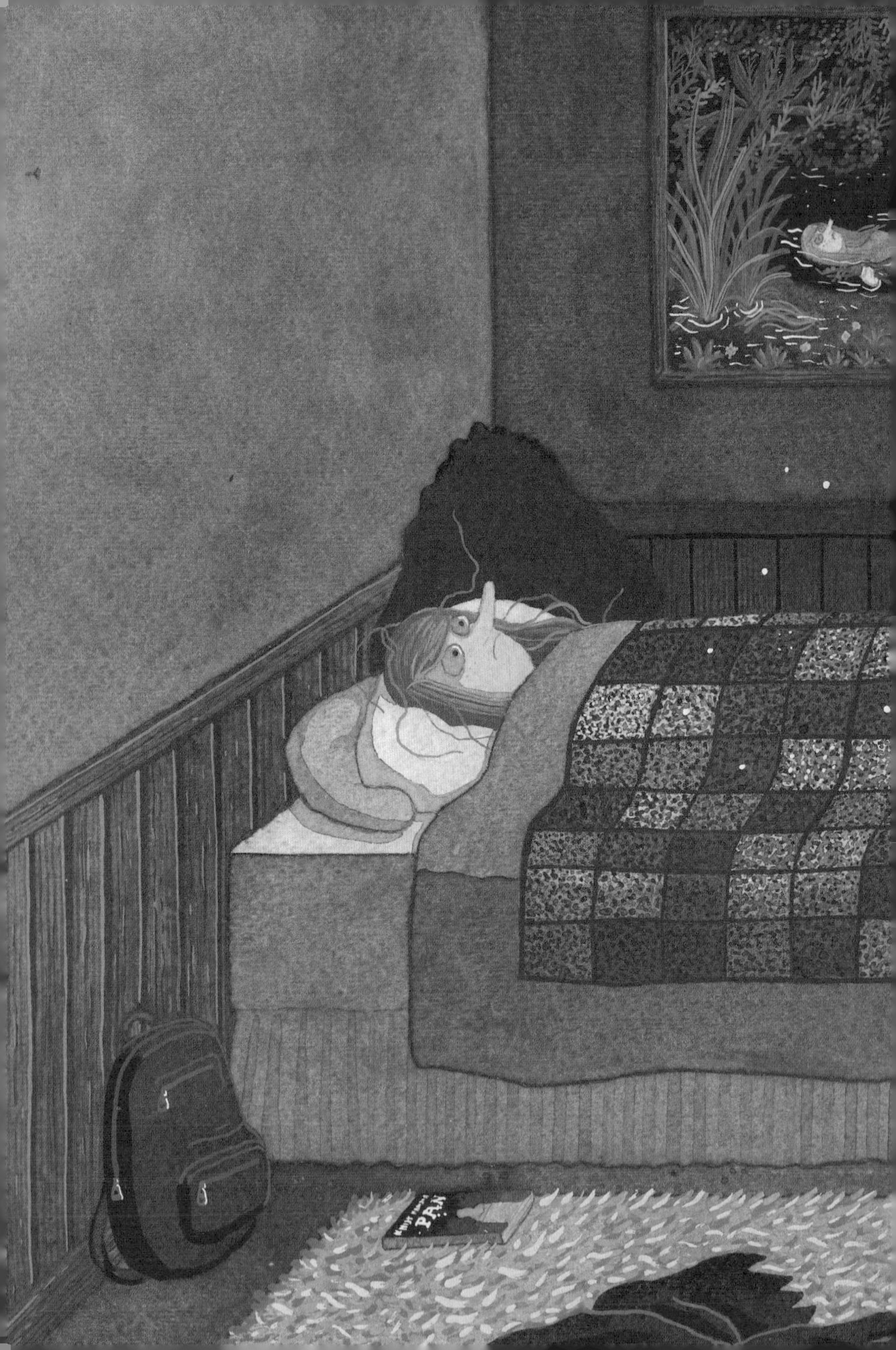
PAN